# A·N·N·U·A·L  E·D·I·T·I·O·N·S

# Multicultural Education
## 06/07

*Thirteenth Edition*

**EDITOR**

**Fred Schultz**

*University of Akron (Retired)*

Fred Schultz, former professor of education at the University of Akron, attended Indiana University to earn a B.S. in social education in 1962, an M.S. in the history and philosophy of education in 1966, and a Ph.D. in the history and philosophy of education and American studies in 1969. His B.A. in Spanish was conferred by the University of Akron in May 1985. He is actively involved in researching the development and history of American education with a primary focus on the history of ideas and social philosophy of education. He also likes to study languages.

 **Contemporary Learning Series**

2460 Kerper Blvd., Dubuque, IA 52001

Visit us on the Internet
*http://www.mhcls.com*

# Credits

1. **The Social Contexts of Multicultural Education**
   Unit photo—© PunchStock/Creatas
2. **Teacher Education in Multicultural Perspectives**
   Unit photo—© Getty Images/David Buffington
3. **Multicultural Education as an Academic Discipline**
   Unit photo—© CORBIS/Royalty Free
4. **Identity and Personal Development: A Multicultural Focus**
   Unit photo—© Getty Images/Vicky Kasala
5. **Curriculum and Instruction in a Multicultural Perspective**
   Unit photo—© image 100 Ltd
6. **Special Topics in Multicultural Education**
   Unit photo—© Getty Images/SW Productions
7. **For Vision and Voice: A Call to Conscience**
   Unit photo—© PunchStock/Creatas

Q
370.117
M 9L1
2006/07

# Copyright

Cataloging in Publication Data
Main entry under title: Annual Editions: Multicultural Education. 2006/2007.
1. Multicultural Education—Periodicals. I. Schultz, Fred, *comp.* II. Title: Multicultural Education.
ISBN 0–07–354586–4      658'.05      ISSN 1092–924X

Thirteenth Edition

Cover image © Image 100 and Creatas/PunchStock
Printed in the United States of America    1234567890QPDQPD98765    Printed on Recycled Paper

# Editors/Advisory Board

Members of the Advisory Board are instrumental in the final selection of articles for each edition of ANNUAL EDITIONS. Their review of articles for content, level, currentness, and appropriateness provides critical direction to the editor and staff. We think that you will find their careful consideration well reflected in this volume.

# Preface

In publishing ANNUAL EDITIONS we recognize the enormous role played by the magazines, newspapers, and journals of the public press in providing current, first-rate educational information in a broad spectrum of interest areas. Many of these articles are appropriate for students, researchers, and professionals seeking accurate, current material to help bridge the gap between principles and theories and the real world. These articles, however, become more useful for study when those of lasting value are carefully collected, organized, indexed, and reproduced in a low-cost format, which provides easy and permanent access when the material is needed. That is the role played by ANNUAL EDITIONS.

We can hope that this new century will be a gentler and more humane century than the past one. We have much in common as human beings and as the heirs of great civilizations; we must cherish and value those cultural values and heritages that make us unique and diverse. An education for transformative intellectual and social development should focus on those things that emancipate and liberate us from cultural stereotypes. All voices should be included in the dialogue regarding how to achieve such educational goals. How we best help our students to develop their voices and to be heard is a major question for all concerned teachers.

The concept of multicultural education evolved and took shape in the United States out of the social travail that wrenched the nation in the late 1960s, through the 1970s and 1980s, and into the present. The linkages between diverse and coexisting ethnic, racial, and socioeconomic heritages have been explored. There has been enthusiastic support for the idea of a volume in this series exclusively devoted to multicultural education. Having been teaching and studying multicultural education for 33 years, it is a pleasure to serve as editor of *Annual Editions: Multicultural Education 06/07*.

The critical literature on gender, race, and culture in educational studies increases our knowledge base regarding the multicultural mosaic that so richly adorns North American cultures. When the first courses in multicultural education were developed in the 1960s, the United States was in the midst of urban and other social crises, and there were no textbooks available. Educators who taught in this area had to draw heavily from academic literatures in anthropology, sociology, social psychology, social history, sociolinguistics, and psychiatry. Today, there are textbooks available in the area, but there is also a need for a regularly, annually published volume that offers samples from the recent journal literature in which the knowledge bases for multicultural education are developed. This volume is intended to address that need.

The National Council for the Accreditation of Teacher Education (NCATE) in the United States has in place national standards requiring that accredited teacher education programs offer course content in multicultural education. A global conception of the subject is usually recommended, in which prospective teachers are encouraged to develop empathetic cultural sensitivity to the demographic changes and cultural diversity that continues to develop in the public schools as a result of dramatic demographic shifts in the population.

In this volume we first explore the social contexts for the development of multicultural education. Its role in teacher education is then briefly defined in the essays in unit 2. In unit 3, the nature of multicultural education as an academic discipline is discussed, and several issues related to this topic are explored. The readings in unit 4 look at multicultural education from the perspective of people in the process of developing their own unique personal identities, in the context of their interactions with their own as well as others' cultural heritages and personal life experiences. The readings in unit 5 focus on curriculum and instruction in multicultural perspective. Unit 6 addresses special topics relevant to development of multicultural insight, and the essays in unit 7 explore alternative visions for multicultural education and the need for a critically conscious quest for emancipatory educational futures for all people of all cultural heritages.

This year I would like to acknowledge the very helpful contributions of the advisory board members. Their assistance in finding useful sources is appreciated. I would also like to acknowledge Dr. Stephen H. Aby, research librarian at the University of Akron, whose assistance is greatly valued.

This volume will be useful in courses in multicultural education at the undergraduate and graduate levels. It will add considerable substance to the sociocultural foundations of education, educational policy studies and leadership, as well as to coursework in other areas of preservice and inservice teacher education programs. We hope you enjoy this volume, and we would like you to help us improve future editions. Please complete and return the form at the back of the book. We look forward to hearing from you.

Fred Schultz
*Editor*

# Contents

# UNIT 1
# The Social Contexts of Multicultural Education

The concepts in bold italics are developed in the article. For further expansion, please refer to the Topic Guide and the Index.

# UNIT 2
## Teacher Education in Multicultural Perspectives

**Unit Overview**                                            24

The concepts in bold italics are developed in the article. For further expansion, please refer to the Topic Guide and the Index.

# UNIT 3
# Multicultural Education as an Academic Discipline

The concepts in bold italics are developed in the article. For further expansion, please refer to the Topic Guide and the Index.

# UNIT 4
# Identity and Personal Development: A Multicultural Focus

# UNIT 5
# Curriculum and Instruction in a Multicultural Perspective

The concepts in bold italics are developed in the article. For further expansion, please refer to the Topic Guide and the Index.

# UNIT 6
## Special Topics in Multicultural Education

The concepts in bold italics are developed in the article. For further expansion, please refer to the Topic Guide and the Index.

The concepts in bold italics are developed in the article. For further expansion, please refer to the Topic Guide and the Index.

# UNIT 7
# For Vision and Voice: A Call to Conscience

The concepts in bold italics are developed in the article. For further expansion, please refer to the Topic Guide and the Index.

# Topic Guide

This topic guide suggests how the selections in this book relate to the subjects covered in your course. You may want to use the topics listed on these pages to search the Web more easily.

On the following pages a number of Web sites have been gathered specifically for this book. They are arranged to reflect the units of this *Annual Edition*. You can link to these sites by going to the student online support site at *http://www.mhcls.com/online/*.

**ALL THE ARTICLES THAT RELATE TO EACH TOPIC ARE LISTED BELOW THE BOLD-FACED TERM.**

# Internet References

The following internet sites have been carefully researched and selected to support the articles found in this reader. The easiest way to access these selected sites is to go to our student online support site at *http://www.mhcls.com/online/*.

# AE: Multicultural Education 06/07

The following sites were available at the time of publication. Visit our Web site—we update our student online support site regularly to reflect any changes.

## General Sources

### Administration for Children and Families
*http://www.acf.dhhs.gov*

This site provides information on federally funded programs that promote the economic and social well-being of families, children, and communities.

### Children's Defense Fund (CDF)
*http://www.childrensdefense.org*

At this site of the CDF, an organization that seeks to ensure that every child is treated fairly, there are reports and resources regarding current issues facing today's youth, along with national statistics on various subjects.

### Educational Resources Information Center
*http://www.eric.ed.gov*

This invaluable site provides links to all ERIC sites: clearinghouses, support components, and publishers of ERIC materials. You can search the ERIC database, find out what is new, and ask questions about ERIC.

### Education Week on the Web
*http://www.edweek.org*

At this *Education Week* home page, you will be able to open archives, read special reports, keep up on current events, look at job opportunities, and access a variety of articles of relevance in multicultural education.

### Global SchoolNet Foundation
*http://www.gsn.org*

Access this site for multicultural education information. The site includes news for teachers, students, and parents, as well as chat rooms, links to educational resources, programs, and contests and competitions.

### National Education Association
*http://www.nea.org*

Something about virtually every education-related topic can be accessed at or through this site of the 2.3-million-strong National Education Association.

### National MultiCultural Institute (NMCI)
*http://www.nmci.org*

NMCI is one of the major organizations in the field of diversity training. At this Web site, NMCI offers conference data, resource materials, diversity training and consulting service information, and links to other related sites.

### Phi Delta Kappa
*http://www.pdkintl.org/home.shtml*

This important organization publishes articles about all facets of education. By clicking on the links at this site, for example, you can check out the journal's online archive.

## UNIT 1: The Social Contexts of Multicultural Education

### American Psychological Association
*http://www.apa.org/topics/homepage.html*

By exploring the APA's "Resources for the Public," you will be able to find links to an abundance of articles and other resources that are useful in understanding the factors that are involved in the development of prejudice.

### Association for Moral Education
*http://www.amenetwork.org/*

AME is dedicated to fostering communication, cooperation, training, curriculum development, and research that links moral theory with educational practices. From here it is possible to connect to several sites on ethics, character building, and moral development.

### Center for Innovation in Education
*http://www.center.edu*

This is the home page of the Center for Innovation in Education, self-described as a "not-for-profit, non-partisan research organization" focusing on K–12 education reform strategies. Click on its links for information and varying perspectives on numerous reform initiatives.

### International Project: Multicultural Pavilion
*http://curry.edschool.virginia.edu/curry/centers/multicultural/papers.html*

Here is a forum for sharing stories and resources and for learning from the stories and resources of others, in the form of articles on the Internet that cover many of the racial, gender, and multicultural issues that arise in the field of multicultural education.

### National Black Child Development Institute
*http://www.nbcdi.org*

Resources for improving the quality of life for African American children through public education programs are provided at this site.

## UNIT 2: Teacher Education in Multicultural Perspectives

### Awesome Library for Teachers
*http://www.awesomelibrary.org/teacher.html*

Open this page for links and access to teacher information on many topics of concern to multicultural educators.

# www.mhcls.com/online/

**Education World**

*http://www.education-world.com*

Education World provides a database of literally thousands of sites that can be searched by grade level, plus education news, lesson plans, and professional-development resources.

**Teacher Talk Forum**

*http://education.indiana.edu/cas/tt/tthmpg.html*

Visit this site for access to a variety of articles discussing life in the classroom. Clicking on the various links will lead you to electronic lesson plans covering a variety of topic areas from Indiana University's Center for Adolescent Studies.

## UNIT 3: Multicultural Education as an Academic Discipline

**Goals 2000: A Progress Report**

*http://www.ed.gov/pubs/goals/progrpt/index.html*

Open this site to survey a progress report by the U.S. Department of Education on the Goals 2000 reform initiative. It provides a sense of the goals that educators are reaching for as they look toward the future.

**Teachers Helping Teachers**

*http://www.pacificnet.net/~mandel/*

This site provides basic teaching tips, new teaching methodology ideas, and forums for teachers to share their experiences. Download software and participate in chat sessions. It features educational resources on the Web, with new ones added each week.

## UNIT 4: Identity and Personal Development: A Multicultural Focus

**Ethics Updates/Lawrence Hinman**

*http://ethics.acusd.edu*

This site provides both simple concept definition and complex analysis of ethics, original treatises, and sophisticated search engine capability. Subject matter covers the gamut, from ethical theory to applied ethical venues. There are many opportunities for user input.

**Kathy Schrock's Guide for Educators**

*http://school.discovery.com/schrockguide/*

This classified list of Web sites is useful for enhancing curriculum and professional growth of teachers.

**Let 100 Flowers Bloom/Kristen Nicholson-Nelson**

*http://teacher.scholastic.com/professional/assessment/100flowers.htm*

Open this page for Kristen Nicholson-Nelson's discussion of ways in which teachers can help to develop children's multiple intelligences. She provides a useful bibliography and resources.

**The National Academy for Child Development**

*http://www.nacd.org*

This international organization is dedicated to helping children and adults reach their full potential. This page presents links to various programs, research, and resources.

## UNIT 5: Curriculum and Instruction in a Multicultural Perspective

**American Indian Science and Engineering Society**

*http://www.aises.org*

This is the AISES "Multicultural Educational Reform Programs" site. It provides a framework for learning about science, mathematics, and technology by which minority students and their teachers can make meaningful cultural connections to teaching and learning. It also provides Web links.

**Child Welfare League of America**

*http://www.cwla.org*

The CWLA is the United States' oldest and largest organization devoted entirely to the well-being of vulnerable children and their families. This site provides links to information about issues related to the process of becoming multicultural.

**STANDARDS: An International Journal of Multicultural Studies**

*http://www.colorado.edu/journals/standards/*

This fascinating site provides access to a seemingly infinite number of international archives.

## UNIT 6: Special Topics in Multicultural Education

**American Scientist**

*http://www.amsci.org/amsci/amsci.html*

Investigate this site to access a variety of articles and to explore issues and concepts related to race and gender.

**American Studies Web**

*http://lumen.georgetown.edu/projects/asw/*

This site provides links to a wealth of resources on the Internet related to American studies, from gender studies to race and ethnicity. It is of great help when doing research in demography and population studies.

**CYFERNet: National Network for Family Resiliency Program & Directory**

*http://www.agnr.umd.edu/nnfr/home.html*

This page will lead you to a number of resource areas of interest for learning about resiliency: General Family Resiliency, Violence Prevention, and Resiliency Topics for Young Children are a few.

**National Institute on the Education of At-Risk Students**

*http://www.ed.gov/offices/OERI/At-Risk/*

The At-Risk Institute supports research and development activities designed to improve the education of students at risk of educational failure due to limited English proficiency, race, geographic location, or economic disadvantage.

**U.S. Department of Education**

*http://www.ed.gov/pubs/TeachersGuide/*

Explore this government site for examination of institutional aspects of multicultural education. National goals, projects, grants, and other educational programs are listed here as well as many links to teacher services and resources.

## UNIT 7: For Vision and Voice: A Call to Conscience

### Classroom Connect
*http://www.classroom.net*
This is a major Web site for K–12 teachers and education students, with links to schools, teachers, and resources online. It includes discussion of the use of technology in the classroom.

### EdWeb/Andy Carvin
*http://edwebproject.org*
The purpose of EdWeb is to explore educational reform and information technology. Access educational resources world-wide, learn about trends in education policy, and examine success stories of computers in the classroom.

### Online Internet Institute
*http://www.oii.org*
A collaborative project among Internet-using educators, proponents of systemic reform, content-area experts, and teachers who desire professional growth, this site provides help for integrating the Web with individual teaching styles.

We highly recommend that you review our Web site for expanded information and our other product lines. We are continually updating and adding links to our Web site in order to offer you the most usable and useful information that will support and expand the value of your Annual Editions. You can reach us at: *http://www.mhcls.com/annualeditions/*.

# UNIT 1

# The Social Contexts of Multicultural Education

## Unit Selections

1. **Challenging Assumptions About the Achievement Gap**, Al Ramirez and Dick Carpenter
2. **A Wider Lens on the Black-White Achievement Gap**, Richard Rothstein
3. **The Biology of Risk Taking**, Lisa F. Price
4. **Metaphors of Hope**, Mimi Brodsky Chenfeld
5. **Where Are We Now?**, Gary Orfield and Erica Frankenberg
6. **Five Things You Should Know About Poverty Around the World**, Habitat World
7. **Five Things You Should Know About Poverty in the United States**, Habitat World

## Key Points to Consider

- Should the federal government institute a national standard of accountability for public schooling?

- What facets of the history of the human struggle for civil rights should be taught to students?

- Should affirmative action be discontinued? Why or why not?

- Why has there been a recent increased level of racial segregation in the United States? What does this mean for public education?

- What impact do changing racial configurations in population have on education?

## Student Website

www.mhcls.com/online

## Internet References

Further information regarding these websites may be found in this book's preface or online.

**American Psychological Association**
*http://www.apa.org/topics/homepage.html*

**Association for Moral Education**
*http://www.amenetwork.org/*

**Center for Innovation in Education**
*http://www.center.edu*

**International Project: Multicultural Pavilion**
*http://curry.edschool.virginia.edu/curry/centers/multicultural/papers.html*

**National Black Child Development Institute**
*http://www.nbcdi.org*

The social contexts of multicultural populations are so complex and interrelated (usually, but not always) that they are very difficult to describe adequately. Nonetheless, this is the situation in many urban areas of the United States and some rural areas of the nation. The same may be said for Canada, and there are some other nations that share this experience. Culture is the most powerful social influence on human life. As we become more culturally diverse as societies, we experience unique social phenomena that can affect how we define ourselves as national social orders.

Multicultural national communities face special challenges in daily life. Such societies also have unique opportunities to develop truly great culturally pluralistic national civilizations in which the aesthetic, artistic, literary, and moral standards of each cultural group can contribute to the creation of new standards. Groups can learn from one another, they can benefit from their respective strengths and achievements, and they can help one another to transcend problems and injustices of the past. We ought, therefore, to see the multicultural national fabric that is our social reality as a circumstance of promise, hope, and pride.

In examining the social context of multicultural education, we need to help teachers and education students to sense the promise, the great social opportunity, which our multicultural social reality presents. We have the task of empowering students with a constructive sense of social consciousness and a will to transcend the social barriers to safety, success, and personal happiness that confront, in one form or another, almost one-third of them. It is essential that we invest in all the children and young adults of multicultural nations, in order that great social promise and hope may be brought to fulfillment in the future.

We can ask ourselves certain very important questions as we work with children and young adults in our schools. Are they safe? Are they hungry? Are they afraid? Are they angry? Do they have a sense of angst; are they filled with self-doubt and uncertainty as to their prospects in life? For far too many children and adolescents from all socioeconomic groups, social classes, and cultural groups the answers to these questions are "yes." Far greater numbers of children from low-income minority cultural groups answer "yes" to at least some of these questions than do children from higher socioeconomic families.

Having done this, educators and civic leaders should consider a few questions. What are the purposes of schooling? Are schools limited to their acknowledged mission of intellectual development? Or, are schools also capable of advancing—as did classical Greek and Roman educators—education in honor, character, courage, resourcefulness, civic responsibility, and social service? This latter concept of the mission of schooling is still the brightest hope for the full achievement of our great promise as a multicultural society in an interdependent community of nations.

What are the obstacles to achieving this end? Each child must be able to advance intellectually in school as far as may be possible. We need to help children develop a sense of honor, self-respect, and pride in their own cultural heritage, which will lead them in their adult years to want to serve, help, and heal the suffering of others. We need intellectually curious and competent graduates who are knowledgeable about their own ethnic heritages and committed to social justice for all persons, in their own nation as well as in the community of nations.

The problems we face in achieving such an intellectual and social end are significant. Developing multicultural curriculum materials for schools and integrating them into the course content and activities can help to sensitize all students to the inherent worth of all persons. All youth deserve the opportunity to learn about his/her own cultural heritages.

North American nations have qualitative issues to face in the area of intercultural relations. Our problems differ because of very different national experiences and very different school systems. Around the world, other nations have to wrestle with providing adequate opportunity for minority populations while maintaining high intellectual standards. The articles in this unit attempt to discuss all of these concerns, and they attempt to address the thoughtful concerns of those who have studied the rhetoric of debate over multiculturalism in school curricula.

There have been dramatic demographic changes in the characteristics of the world's population and in the interdependence of the world's nations in a global economy. We must reconsider how we develop human talent in our schools, for young people are the ones who will be the most basic resource in the future. Some unit essays give important background on the history of the civil rights movement in the United States as well as on the origins of many racial and cultural stereotypes that have inhibited the efforts of educators to help young people become more accepting of cultural diversity.

The unit essays are relevant to courses in cultural foundations of education, educational policy studies, multicultural education, social studies education, and curriculum theory and construction.

# Challenging Assumptions About the Achievement Gap

The national dialogue about the achievement gap can help policy makers and educators find ways to better serve minority students. However, school policy and practice must be founded not on perceptions of group stereotypes, Mr. Ramirez and Mr. Carpenter argue, but on knowledge about each student's needs and strengths.

AL RAMIREZ AND
DICK CARPENTER

HERE IN Colorado, snow is particularly significant. It affects our economy through winter recreation and tourism, reduces the danger of forest fires , and provides water for most residents. And while to the casual observer the snow all looks the same, Coloradans know differently. We evaluate each snowfall not only by its quantity but also by its quality, that is, how wet it is. Sometimes the moisture content of the snow is low, which sets off a rush of snowboarders and skiers to the mountains but supplies little water to the arid landscape. Other times the moisture content is high, which contributes greatly to the state's water supply. Thus differences within the general category of snow are critical to our state's health and future.

Similarly, "within-group" differences are important to recognize when we look at student achievement, particularly as it relates to race or ethnicity. Since the *Brown v. Board of Education* decision more than 50 years ago, much attention has been paid to significant "between-group" differences. This focus resulted in policies and practices designed to reduce such disparities. Yet, until quite recently, educational researchers, policy makers, and practitioners have paid far less attention to within-group differences that are probably as important as those between groups and could, in fact, help us figure out how to narrow the differences between groups.

Take, for example, Latinos, who now constitute the largest minority group in the U.S. and who are certainly well represented in the public schools.[1] As a group, Latino students share many similar characteristics that set them apart from other groups. On average, Latino students tend to be poorer, attend more segregated schools, and live in urban areas. Latino students also account for the largest number of students served in programs of English-language acquisition. While these characteristics typify the group of students we call Latinos, it would be a mistake to assume that all Latino students have similar needs or require the same type of education.[2]

Yet current policies and educational practices directed toward Latino students are built on such assumptions and have had the unintended consequence of hurting the students' futures, educational and otherwise. Among these overgeneralized policies and practices are presuming that all students with Spanish surnames need English-language-acquisition classes; creating a policy of defacto segregation by assigning Latino students only to schools with English as a Second Language (ESL) programs; and presuming Latino students are potential dropouts rather than college-bound students.

When policy makers and education professionals remain oblivious to these false assumptions, misinterpretations occur, and stereotypical thinking prevails. Indeed, our investigation of the achievement gap underscores the relative insignificance of race and ethnicity, compared to other factors that most affect student learning. Furthermore, we have found that the "achievement gap" between Latino and white students may be a "phantom gap" derived from the practice of lumping all nonwhite students into a single comparison group. In short, the importance of within-group differences eclipses the importance of between-group differences.

## ACHIEVEMENT GAP RESEARCH

Research on the academic achievement gap between majority and minority students is sometimes misapplied by policy makers and practitioners, and this in turn can lead to ineffective and even counterproductive programs for students.[3] Media coverage further exacerbates this misunderstanding about the lagging academic performance of minority groups, for it oversimplifies complex data in order to fit the conventions of news reporting and to manufacture catchy headlines. Moreover, policy discussions and debates about the achievement gap have missed the mark by casting the problem as a "minority group" phenomenon, without considering the dynamic interplay of variables that affect the learning of any individual child.

Of the achievement gap research that does consider factors in addition to race or ethnicity, much of it involves such home-based variables as socioeconomic status, home language, and parent involvement or such school-based variables as school segregation and teacher quality. However, the findings are far from conclusive.

Beginning with home-based variables, much of the research indicates that the income level of a student's family is highly correlated with academic success in school, a phenomenon that is indeed true for Latino students.[4] Moreover, in some studies the effect of socioeconomic status often overwhelms the relationship between race or ethnicity and academic achievement, since minority groups tend to be overrepresented among the poor. Yet not all researchers agree about the impact of socioeconomic status on student learning, and some cite other factors as having more influence.[5]

Regarding home language, the research remains mixed and crammed with cross-cutting issues. Some researchers believe that a student's language background is central to success in school, particularly when it is related to the level of parents' education.[6] For example, the U.S. Department of Education reported that, in 1999, the percentage of Latino parents with a high school or higher education was 49% for those who spoke mostly Spanish at home and 83% for those who spoke mostly English at home. Other researchers find that maintaining Spanish as the home language enhances academic achievement when combined with other factors.[7] Still others contend that language background accounts for little in explaining student achievement.[8]

In contrast to the mixed findings on the role of language, there is general agreement among researchers on the importance of parent involvement, particularly for black and Latino students.[9] While parent involvement takes many forms, numerous researchers have concluded that the most significant type is assisting children with schoolwork at home.[10] Parent involvement also plays an important role in students' course-taking patterns. For example, James Valadez illustrates how Latino parents influence their children's enrollment in algebra and advanced mathematics courses.[11]

Turning to school-based variables, some researchers conclude that school segregation significantly affects the academic achievement of minority students. Gary Roberts describes a spiraling relationship in which student achievement and segregation interact in a negatively correlated fashion.[12] John Ogbu writes of a "cultural ecological" model in which minority students perceive ongoing patterns of discrimination and prejudice when comparing their experiences to those of their majority peers, which then inhibits academic achievement.[13] Other authors have identified what they call an "oppositional culture," which is most prevalent in schools with smaller percentages of minority students.[14] In such situations, minority student engagement, participation, and achievement all suffer, and any achievement gap is exacerbated.

Finally, although teacher quality has enjoyed attention in the literature of the achievement gap, researchers differ regarding its significance. For example, Harold Wenglinsky, Jonah Rockoff, and Peter Denner and his colleagues all find a strong relationship between teacher quality, defined in terms of training or experience, and student learning.[15] Yet Theodore Eisenberg indicates that advanced subject-matter knowledge on the part of teachers does not translate into higher levels of student learning.[16] Considering the emphasis given to this factor in the No Child Left Behind Act and the importance this law attaches to closing the achievement gap, teacher quality is a particularly salient variable.

## WHAT WE STUDIED

Based on our experiences in schools and our review of the educational research on the achievement gap, we hypothesized that academic achievement for Latino students would be based on factors similar to those that affect all students. Furthermore, we hypothesized that within-group differences in the Latino student population would be much larger than the differences between white students and Latino students. In order to test these suppositions, we examined data in the National Educational Longitudinal Study (NELS:88).

NELS:88 is a comprehensive study authorized by the U.S. Congress and conducted by the National Center for Education Statistics. It is a series of cohort studies of American students that began in 1988 with eighth-grade students who were followed into high school, postsecondary education, and the work force. Follow-up studies were done in 1990, 1992, 1994, and 2000. NELS:88 uses both questionnaire data and test data for each student. In addition, NELS:88 involves questionnaires for the school principal, for two teachers, and for parents.

The sample for our study was drawn from the 12th-grade follow-up study. To determine both within-and between-group differences, we calculated effects for whites, blacks, and Latinos. Thus our sample included data on 15,618 students: 2,170 Latinos, 1,660 blacks, and 11,788 whites. We chose to look at mathematics as the measure of student achievement. While including other subjects would provide a more complete picture of achievement, idiosyncrasies of the database required that we limit our achievement measure to mathematics only.

The NELS:88 database contains many hundreds of possible variables to draw upon and combine in examining factors that could be important to student achievement. Thus it was necessary for us to identify factors that, based on other research, have been shown to influence student learning generally. Our review led us to investigate the relationship between mathematics achievement and the following variables:

- socioeconomic status,
- language other than English regularly spoken at home,
- participation at any time in an ESL program,
- time spent on homework,
- class size,
- number of minority students in the class,
- number of units of algebra taken,
- number of undergraduate courses taken by the teacher in the subject he or she teaches most frequently,
- number of graduate courses taken by the teacher in the subject he or she teaches most frequently,
- family composition (i.e., two parents in the home),
- level of parent involvement, and
- urbanicity (i.e., urban, suburban, or rural).

## FINDINGS AND RECOMMENDATIONS

Our analysis discovered that the "achievement gap" really consists of "multiple gaps" that exist both between and within groups. Socioeconomic status and participation in ESL were the most significant factors for all groups of students. For the most part, white and Latino student achievement were mirror images of each other, and each was affected similarly by each of the factors we examined. But this was not the case for black students in the sample. For example, Latino and white student achievement reflected similar differences based on urbanicity, but the same did not hold true for black students. Latino students who spoke English at home, who had never been enrolled in an ESL class, who came from intact families, and who spent more time on homework demonstrated higher levels of academic achievement than Latino students who did not share these characteristics. These relationships were similar for white students.

Turning to between-group differences, none of the variables we considered revealed a statistically significant gap between whites and Latinos. Socioeconomic background, experience in an ESL class, units of algebra, and level of parent involvement had a similar impact on the achievement of both white and Latino students. How-

ever, hours of homework were not a good predictor of student achievement for Latino students, while this variable was a good predictor for both black students and white students. Finally, while the differences we found between white students and Latino students were not significant, the differences between black students and white students and between black students and Latino students were significant.

While these findings are important, a caveat is worth bearing in mind. They do not indicate a simple, straight-line relationship, in which increases or decreases in one variable affect student achievement in direct proportion. Nevertheless, our findings do clearly indicate that family income, the number of parents in the home, the number of algebra units taken, the level of parent involvement, and the level of English-language skills are significant predictors of academic achievement for Latino students. Moreover, the differences on these factors among Latinos are greater than those between Latinos and whites. And many of the same factors exert a similar effect on achievement for white students.

Our research also indicates that the achievement gap is not monolithic. Instead, it is a richly textured, complex, and nuanced framework. Our findings underscore the need to disaggregate student data into many combinations of subsets in order to understand the dynamic relationships that exist within and between groups. The practice of lumping together data from all students of color—and even data from divisions within a single group—is a mistake that is bound to produce poor policy choices and poor educational practices.

Data-driven decision making is gaining popularity with educators and policy leaders. This methodology holds much promise to help us better understand the needs of students, to evaluate the effectiveness of our education programs, and to inform parents and key stakeholders about our schools. However, we must remain wary of the allure of numbers and conscious of the destructiveness of flawed research. We must be careful about jumping to conclusions simply because we find a number that implies a difference between groups of students. We must always investigate the underlying factors that contribute to the average score for any group of students. As our research demonstrates, taking action based on limited data and analysis is professionally irresponsible. We have an ethical obligation to be thorough in our understanding of the phenomena we study in our schools.

Finally, what is evident from our investigation is that both school-based factors and home-based factors are important to the success of every child, regardless of racial or ethnic differences. School policy and practice must be founded not on perceptions of group stereotypes, but rather on knowledge about each student's needs and strengths. Thus the voices of parents, teachers, and students must be included when practitioners and policy makers seek to design better ways to serve students. The national dialogue about the achievement gap has the potential to help policy makers and educators find ways to better serve Latino and other minority students. But if we are to create such constructive policies, research and practice must be based on thoughtful reflection about what we know rather than what we assume.

## References

1. Gill Griffin, "Color Change: African-Americans and Latinos Reassess Their Relationships in Wake of Changing Demographics," *San Diego Union-Tribune*, 23 February 2003, pp. 1-2.

2. Hersholt C. Waxman, Shwu-yong L. Huang, and Yolanda N. Padron, "Motivation and Learning Environment Differences Between Resilient and Nonresilient Latino Middle School Students," *Hispanic Journal of Behavioral Sciences*, vol. 19, 1997, pp. 137-56.

3. Fenwick W. English, "On the Intractability of the Achievement Gap in Urban Schools and the Discursive Practice of Continuing Racial Discrimination," *Education and Urban Society*, vol. 34, 2002, pp. 298-311; and Alejandro Portes and Rubén G. Rumbaut, *Immigrant America: A Portrait* (Berkeley: University of California Press, 1990).

4. Sampson L. Blair and Marilou C. Legazpi, "Racial/Ethnic Difference in High School Students' Academic Performance: Understanding the Interweave of Social Class and Ethnicity in the Family Context," *Journal of Comparative Family Studies*, vol. 30, 1999, pp. 539-55; and Alejandro Portes and Dag McLeod, "Educational Progress of Children of Immigrants: The Roles of Class, Ethnicity, and School Context," *Sociology of Education*, vol. 69, 1996, pp. 255-75.

5. Sharon Anne O'Conner and Kathleen Miranda, "The Linkages Among Family Structure, Self-Concept, Effort, and Performance on Mathematics Achievement of American High School Students by Race," *American Secondary Education*, vol. 31, 2002, pp. 72-95; and Sammis B. White, "Socioeconomic Status and Achievement Revisited," *Urban Education*, vol. 28, 1993, pp. 328-43.

6. Tracey Derwing et al., "Some Factors That Affect the Success of ESL High School Students," *Canadian Modern Language Review*, vol. 55, 1999, pp. 532-47.

7. David P. Dolson, "The Effects of Spanish Home Language Use on the Scholastic Performance of Hispanic Pupils," *Journal of Multilingual and Multicultural Development*, vol. 6, 1985, pp. 135-55; and Ana Celia Zentella, "Latino Youth at Home, in Their Communities, and in School: The Language Link," *Education and Urban Society*, vol. 30, 1997, pp. 122-30.

8. David Adams et al., "Predicting the Academic Achievement of Puerto Rican and Mexican-American Ninth-Grade Students," *Urban Review*, vol. 26, 1994, pp. 1-14; and Raymond Buriel et al., "The Relationship of Language Brokering to Academic Performance, Biculturalism, and Self-Efficacy Among Latino Adolescents," *Hispanic Journal of Behavioral Sciences*, vol. 20, 1998, pp. 283-96.

9. William Jeynes, "A Meta-analysis: The Effects of Parental Involvement on Minority Children's Academic Achievement," *Education and Urban Society*, vol. 35, 2003, pp. 202-18.

10. Charles V. Izzo et al., "A Longitudinal Assessment of Teacher Perceptions of Parent Involvement in Children's Education and School Performance," *American Journal of Community Psychology*, vol. 27, 1999, pp. 817-39.

11. James R. Valadez, "The Influence of Social Capital on Mathematics Course Selection by Latino High School Students," *Hispanic Journal of Behavioral Sciences*, vol. 24, 2002, pp. 319-39.

12. Gary J. Roberts, "The Effect of Achievement on Student Friendships in Desegregated Schools," *Equity and Choice*, vol. 5, 1989, pp. 31-36; Russell W. Rumberger and J. Douglas Willms, "The Impact of Racial and Ethnic Segregation on the Achievement Gap in California High Schools," *Educational Evaluation and Policy Analysis*, vol. 14, 1992, pp. 377-96; and Richard R. Valencia, "Inequalities and the Schooling of Minority Students in Texas: Historical and Contemporary Conditions," *Hispanic Journal of Behavioral Sciences*, vol. 22, 2000, pp. 445-59.

13. John U. Ogbu, *Minority Education and Caste: The American System in Cross-Cultural Perspective* (New York: Academic Press, 1978).

14. Jeremy D. Finn and Kristin E. Voelkl, "School Characteristics Related to Student Engagement," *Journal of Negro Education*, vol. 62, 1993, pp. 249-68; and Tomas D. Rodriguez, "Oppositional Culture and Academic Performance Among Children of Immigrants in the U.S.," *Race, Ethnicity, and Education*, vol. 5, 2002, pp. 199-216.

15. Harold Wenglinsky, "How Schools Matter: The Link Between Teacher Classroom Practices and Student Academic Performance," *Education Policy Analysis Archives*, vol. 10, 2002, available at http://epaa.asu.edu/epaa/v10n12; Jonah Rockoff, "The Impact of Individual Teachers on Student Achievement: Evidence from Panel Data," abstract available at http://econwpa.wustl.edu/eprints/pe/papers/0304/0304002.abs; and Peter R. Denner et al., "Connecting Performance to Student Achievement: A Generalization and Validity Study of the Renaissance Teacher Work Samples Assessment," paper presented at the annual meeting of the Association of Teacher Educators, Jacksonville, Fla., 2003.

16. Theodore A. Eisenberg, "Begle Revisited: Teacher Knowledge and Student Achievement in Algebra," *Journal for Research in Mathematics Education*, vol. 8, 1997, pp. 216-22.

---

*AL RAMIREZ is an associate professor in the Department of Educational Leadership & Policy Studies, University of Denver. DICK CARPENTER is an assistant professor in the Department of Leadership, Research, and Foundations, University of Colorado, Colorado Springs.*

---

# A Wider Lens On the Black-White Achievement Gap

The gap in academic achievement between white, middle-class students and their minority and lower class counterparts is widely recognized as one of the most significant challenges facing our schools. Mr. Rothstein argues that efforts to close the achievement gap that focus solely on school policies, while ignoring the social-class characteristics that influence student learning, will fail.

## RICHARD ROTHSTEIN

*T*HE 50TH ANNIVERSARY of the Supreme Court's school desegregation order in *Brown v. Board of Education* has intensified public awareness of the persistent gap in academic achievement between black students and white students. The black-white gap is made up partly of the difference between the achievement of all lower-class students and that of middle-class students, but there is an additional gap between black students and white students—even when the blacks and whites come from families with similar incomes.

The American public and its political leaders, along with professional educators, have frequently vowed to close these gaps. Americans believe in the ideal of equal opportunity, and they also believe that the best way to ensure that opportunity is to enable all children, regardless of their parents' stations, to leave school with skills that position them to compete fairly and productively in the nation's democratic governance and occupational structure. The fact that children's skills can so clearly be predicted by their race and family economic status is a direct challenge to our democratic ideals.

Policy makers almost universally conclude that these existing and persistent achievement gaps must be the result of wrongly designed school policies—either expectations that are too low, teachers who are insufficiently qualified, curricula that are badly designed, classes that are too large, school climates that are too undisciplined, leadership that is too unfocused, or a combination of these factors.

Americans have come to the conclusion that the achievement gap is the fault of "failing schools" because common sense seems to dictate that it could not be otherwise. After all, how much money a family has or the color of a child's skin should not influence how well that child learns to read. If teachers know how to teach reading—or math or any other subject—and if schools emphasize the importance of these tasks and permit no distractions, children should be able to learn these subjects, whatever their family income or skin color.

This commonsense perspective, however, is misleading and dangerous. It ignores how social-class characteristics in a stratified society such as ours may actually influence learning in school. It confuses social class, a concept that Americans have historically been loath to consider, with two of its characteristics: income and, in the U.S., race. For it is true that low income and skin color themselves don't influence academic achievement, but the collection of characteristics that define social-class differences inevitably influences that achievement.

### SOCIAL CLASS AND ITS IMPACT ON LEARNING

Distinctly different child-rearing patterns are one mechanism through which class differences affect the academic performance of children. For example, parents of different social classes often have different ways of disciplining their children, different ways of communicating expectations, and even different ways of reading to their children. These differences do not express themselves constantly or in the case of every family; rather, they influence the average tendencies of families from different social classes.

That there would be personality and child-rearing differences, on average, between families in different social classes makes sense when you think about it. If upper-middle-class parents have jobs in which they are expected to collaborate with fellow employees, create new solutions to problems, or wonder how to improve their contributions, they are more likely to talk to their children in ways that differ from those of lower-class parents whose own jobs simply require them to follow instructions without question. Children who are reared by parents who are professionals will, on average, have more inquisitive attitudes toward the material presented by their teachers than will children who are reared by working-class parents. As a result, no matter how competent the teacher, the academic achievement of lower-class children will, on average, almost inevitably be less than that of middle-class children. The probability of such reduced achievement increases as the characteristics of lower-social-class families accumulate.

Many social and economic manifestations of social class also have important implications for learning. Health differences are among them. On average, lower-class children have poorer vision than middle-class children partly because of prenatal conditions and partly because of how their eyes are trained as infants. They have poorer oral hygiene, more lead poisoning, more asthma, poorer nutrition, less adequate pediatric care, more exposure to smoke, and a host of other problems. Each of these well-documented social-class differences is likely to have a palpable effect on academic achievement, and the combined influence of all of these differences is probably huge.

The growing unaffordability of adequate housing for low-income families is another social-class characteristic that has a demonstrable effect on average achievement. Children whose families have difficulty finding stable housing are more likely to be mobile, and student mobility is an important cause of low student achievement. Urban rents have risen faster than working-class incomes. Even families in which parents' employment is stable are more likely to move when they fall behind in rent payments. In some schools in minority neighborhoods, this need to move has boosted mobility rates to more than 100% for every seat in the school, more than two children were enrolled at some time during the year.[1] It is hard to imagine how teachers, no matter how well trained, could be as effective for children who move in and out of their classrooms as they can be for children whose attendance is regular.

Differences in wealth between parents of different social classes are also likely to be important determinants of student achievement, but these differences are usually overlooked because most analysts focus only on annual income to indicate disadvantage. This practice makes it hard to understand, for example, why black students, on average, score lower than white students who family incomes are the same. It is easier to understand this pattern when we recognize that children can have similar family

*incomes* but be ranked differently in the social-class structure, even in economic terms. Black families with low income in any particular year are likely to have been poor for longer than white families with similar income in that year. White families are also likely to own far more assets that support their children's achievement than are black families at the same level of current income.

I use the term "lower class" here to describe the families of children whose achievement will, on average, be predictably lower than the achievement of middle-class children. American sociologists were once comfortable with this term, but it has fallen out of fashion. Instead, we tend to use such euphemisms as "disadvantaged" students, "at-risk" students, "inner-city" students, or students of "low socioeconomic status." None of these terms, however, can capture the central characteristic of lower-class families: a collection of occupational, psychological, personality, health, and economic traits that interact predicting performance—not only in schools but in other institutions as well—that, on average, differs from the performance of families from higher social classes.

Much of the difference between the average performance of black children and that of white children can probably be traced to differences in their social-class characteristics. But there are also cultural characteristics that are likely to contribute a bit to the black-white achievement gap. These cultural characteristics may have identifiable origins in social and economic conditions—for example, black students may value education less than white students because a discriminatory labor market has not historically rewarded black workers for their education—but values can persist independently and outlast the economic circumstances that give rise to them.

Some lower-class children do achieve at high levels, and many observers have falsely concluded from this that therefore all lower-class children should be able to succeed with appropriate instruction. One of the bars to our understanding of the achievement gap is that most Americans, even well-educated ones, are not expert in discussions of statistical distributions. The achievement gap is a phenomenon of averages, a difference between the average achievement level of lower-class children and the average achievement level of middle-class children. In human affairs, every average characteristic is a composite of many widely disparate characteristics.

For example, we know that lead poisoning has a demonstrable impact on young children's I.Q. scores. Children with high exposure to lead —from fumes or from ingesting paint or dust—have I.Q. scores that, on average, are several points lower than those of children who are not so exposed. But this does not mean that every child with lead poisoning has lower I.Q. Some children with high lead levels in their blood have higher I.Q. scores than typical children with no lead exposure. When researchers say that lead poisoning seems to affect academic performance, they do not mean that every lead-exposed child performs less well. But the high performance of a few lead-exposed children does not disprove the conclusion that lead exposure is likely to harm academic achievement.

This kind of reasoning applies to each of the social-class characteristics that I discuss here, as well as to the many others that, for lack of space or my own ignorance, I do not discuss. In each case, class differences in social or economic circumstances probably cause differences in the average academic performance of children from different social classes, but, in each case, some children with lower class characteristics perform better than typical middle-class children.

## SCHOOL REFORMS ALONE ARE NOT ENOUGH

The influence of social class characteristics is probably so powerful that schools cannot overcome it, no matter how well trained their teachers and no matter how well designed their instructional programs and climates. But saying that a social class achievement gap should be expected is not to make a logical statement. The fact that social-class differences are associated with, and probably cause, a big gap in academic performance does not mean that, in theory, excellent schools could not offset these differences. Indeed, today's policy makers and educators make many claims that higher standards, better teachers, more accountability, better discipline, or other effective practices can close the achievement gap.

The most prominent of these claims has been made by the Heritage Foundation (conservative) and the Education Trust (more liberal), by economists and statisticians who claim to have shown that better teachers do in fact close the gap, by prominent educators; and by social critics. Many (though not all) of instructional practices promoted by these commentators are well designed, and these practices probably do succeed in delivering a better education to some lower-class children. But a careful examination of each claim that a particular school or practice has closed the race or social-class achievement gap shows that the claim is unfounded.

In some cases, a claim may fail because it reflects a statistical fluke—a school successful for only one year, in only one subject, or in only one grade—or because it reports success only on tests of the most basic skills. In other cases, a claim may fail because the successful schools identified have selective student bodies. Remember that the achievement gap is a phenomenon of averages—it compares the average achievement of lower-and middle-class students. In both social classes, some students perform well above or below the average performance of their social-class peers. If schools can select (or attract) a disproportionate share of lower-class students whose performance is above average for their social class, those schools can appear to be quite successful. Many such schools are excellent and should be commended. But their successes provide no evidence that their instructional approaches would close the achievement gap for students who are average for their social-class groups.

## LIMITATIONS OF THE CURRENT TESTING REGIME

Whether efforts to close the social-class achievement gap involve in-school reforms or socioeconomic reforms, it is difficult to know precisely how much any intervention will narrow the gap. We can't estimate the effect of various policies partly because we don't really know how big the achievement gap is overall or how big it is in particular schools or school systems.

This lack of knowledge about the size of the gap or the merits of any particular intervention might surprise many readers because so much attention is devoted these days to standardized test scores. It has been widely reported that, on average, if white students score at around the 50th percentile on a standardized math or reading test, black students typically score around the 23rd percentile. (In more technical statistical terms, black students score, on average, between 0.5 and 1.0 standard deviations below white students.)

But contrary to conventional belief, this may not be a good measure of the gap. Because of the high stakes attached to standardized tests in recent years, schools and teachers are under enormous pressure to raise students' test scores. The more pressure there has been, the less reliable these scores have become. In part, the tests themselves don't really measure the gap in the achievement of high standards because high standards (such as the production of good writing and the development of research skills and analysis) are expensive to test, and public officials are reluctant to spend the money. Instead, schools have tended to use inexpensive standardized tests that mostly, though not entirely, assess more basic skills. Gaps that show up on tests of basic skills may be quite different from the gaps that would show up on tests of higher standards of learning. And it is not the case that students acquire a hierarchy of skills sequentially. Thus truly narrowing the achievement gap would not require children to learn "the basics" first. Lower-class children cannot produce typical middle-class academic achievement unless they learn basic and more advanced skills simultaneously, with each reinforcing the other. This is, in fact, how middle-class children who come to school ready to learn acquire both basic and advanced skills.

The high stakes recently attached to standardized tests have given teachers incentives to revise the priorities of their instruction, especially for lower-class children, so that they devote greater time to drill on basic skills and less time to other, equally important (but untested) learning areas in which achievement gaps also appear. In a drive to raise test scores in math and reading, the curriculum has moved away not only from more advanced mathematical and literary skills, but also from social studies, literature, art, music, physical education, and other important subjects that are not tested for the purpose of judging school quality. We don't know how large the race or social-class achievement gaps are in these subjects, but there is no reason to believe that gaps in one domain are the same as the gaps in others or that the relationships between gaps in different domains will remain consistent at different ages and on different tests.

For example, educational researchers normally expect that gaps in reading be greater than gaps in math, probably because social-class differences in parental support play a bigger role for reading then for math. Parents typically read to their very young children, and middle-class parents do so more and in more intellectually stimulating ways, but few parents do math problems with their young children. Yet, on at least one test of entering kindergartners, race and social-class gaps in math exceed those in reading.

## THE IMPORTANCE OF NONCOGNITIVE SKILLS

We also don't know the extent of the social-class gaps in noncognitive skills—such character traits as perseverance, self-confidence, self-discipline, punctuality, the ability to communicate, social responsibility, and the ability to work with others and resolve conflicts. These are important goals of public education. In some respects, they may be more important than academic outcomes.

Employers, for example, consistently report that workers have more serious shortcomings in these noncognitive areas than in academic areas. Econometric studies show that noncognitive skills are a stronger predictor of future earnings than are test stores. In public opinion surveys, Americans consistently say they want schools to produce good citizens and socially responsible adults first and high academic proficiency second. Yet we do a poor job—actually, no job at all—of assessing whether schools are generating such noncognitive outcomes. And so we also do a poor job of assessing whether schools are successfully narrowing the social-class gap in these traits or whether social and economic reform here, too, would be necessary to narrow these gaps.

There is some evidence that the noncognitive social class gaps should be a cause for concern. For very young children, measures of antisocial behavior mirror the gaps in academic test scores. Children of lower social classes exhibit more antisocial behavior than children of higher social classes, both in early childhood and in adolescence. It would be reasonable to expect that the same social and, economic inequalities that seem likely to produce gaps in academic test scores also produce differences in noncognitive traits.

---

**When minority students with lower test scores than white students are admitted to colleges, the lower-scoring minority students may exhibit more leadership, devote more serious attention to their studies, and go on to make greater community contributions.**

In some areas, however, it seems that noncognitive gaps may be smaller than cognitive ones. In particular, analyses of some affirmative action programs in higher education find that, when minority students with lower test scores than white students are admitted to colleges, the lower-scoring minority students may exhibit more leadership, devote more serious attention to their studies, and go on to make greater community contributions. This evidence reinforces the importance of measuring noncognitive student characteristics, something that few elementary or secondary schools attempt. Until we begin to measure these traits, we will have no insight into the extent of the noncognitive gaps between lower-and middle-class children.

## MOVING FORWARD

Three tracks should be pursued vigorously and simultaneously if we are to make significant progress in narrowing the achievement gap. The first track is school improvement efforts that raise the quality of instruction in elementary and secondary schools. The second track is expanding the definition of schooling to include crucial out-of school hours in which families and communities now are the sole influences. This means implementing comprehensive early childhood, after-school, and summer programs. And the third track is social and economic policies that will enable children to attend school more equally ready to learn. These policies include health services for lower-class children and their families, stable housing for working families with children, and the narrowing of growing income inequalities in American society.

Many of the reforms in curriculum and school organization that are promoted by critics of education have merit and should be intensified. Repairing and upgrading the scandalously decrepit school facilities that serve some lower-class children, raising salaries to permit the recruitment of more qualified teachers for lower-class children, reducing class sizes for lower-class children (particularly in the early grades), insisting on higher academic standards that emphasize creativity and reasoning as well as basic skills, holding schools accountable for fairly measured performance, having a well-focused and disciplined school climate, doing more to encourage lower-class children to intensify their own ambitions—all of these policies and others can play a role in narrowing the achievement gap. These reforms are extensively covered in a wide range of books, articles, and public discussions of education so I do not dwell on them here. Instead, my focus is the greater importance of reforming social and economic institutions if we truly want children to emerge from school with equal preparation.

Readers should not misinterpret this emphasis as implying that better schools are not important or that school improvement will not make a contribution to narrowing the achievement gap. Better school practices can no doubt narrow the gap. However, school reform is not enough.

In seeking to close the achievement gap for low-income and minority students, policy makers focus inordinate attention on the improvement of instruction because they apparently believe that social-class differences are immutable and that only schools can improve the destinies of lower-class children. This is a peculiarly American belief—that schools can be virtually the only instrument of social reform—but it is not based on evidence about the relative effectiveness of economic, social, and educational improvement efforts.

While many social-class characteristics are impervious to short-term change, many can easily be affected by public policies that narrow the social and economic gaps between lower-and middle-class children. These polices can probably have a more powerful impact on student achievement (and, in some cases, at less cost) than an exclusive focus on-school reform. But we cannot say so for sure, because social scientists and educators have devoted no effort to studying the relative costs and benefits of nonschool and school reforms. For example, established an optometric clinic in a school to improve the vision of low-income children could have a bigger impact on their test scores than spending the same money on instructional improvement.[2] Greater proportions of low-income than middle-class children are distracted by the discomfort of untreated dental cavities, and dental clinics can likewise be provided at costs comparable to what schools typically spend on less effective reforms. We can't be certain if this is the case, however, because there have been no experiments to test the relative benefits of these alternative strategies. Of course, proposals to improve all facets of the health of lower-class children, not just their vision and oral health, should be evaluated for their academic impacts.

A full array of health services will be costly, but that cost cannot be avoided if we are truly to embrace the goal of raising the achievement of lower-class children. Some of these costs are not new, of course, and some can be recouped by school clinics by means of reimbursements from other under utilized government programs, such as Medicaid.

Other social reforms—for example, an increase in the number of Section 8 housing vouchers to increase the access of lower-class families to stable housing—also could have a significant educational impact.

Incomes have become more unequally distributed in the United States in the last generation, and this inequality contributes to the academic achievement gap. Proposals for a higher minimum wage or increases in earning income tax credits, which are designed to help offset some of this inequality, should be considered education policies as well as economic ones, for they would be likely to result in higher adademic performance from children whose families are more secure.

Although conventional opinion is that "failing" schools contribute mightily to the achievement gap, the evidence indicates that schools already do a great deal to combat it. Most of the social class difference in average academic potential exists by the time children are 3 years old. This difference is exacerbated over the years that children spend in school, but during these years, the growth in the gap occurs mostly in the after-school hours and during the summertime, when children are not actually in classrooms.[3]

So in addition to school improvement and broader reforms to narrow the social and economic inequalities that produce gaps in student achievement, investments should be made to expand the definition of schooling to cover those crucial out-of-school hours. Because the gap is already huge at 3 years old, the most important focus of this investment should probably be early childhood programs. The quality of these programs is an important as the existence of the programs themselves. To narrow the gap, early childhood care, beginning with infants and toddlers, should be provided by adults who can offer the kind of intellectual environment that is typically experienced by middleclass infants and toddlers. This goal probably requires professional caregivers and low child/adult ratios.

Providing after-school and summer experiences to lower-class children that are similar to those middle-class children take for granted would be likely to play an essential part in narrowing the achievement gap. But these experiences should not be restricted only to remedial programs in which lower-class children get added drill in math and reading. Certainly, remedial instruction should be part of an adequate after-school and summer program—but only apart. The advantage that middle-class children gain after school and in the summer probably comes mostly from the self-confidence they acquire and the awareness they develop of the world outside their homes and immediate communities and from organized athletics, dance, drama, museum visits, recreational reading, and other activities that develop their inquisitiveness, creativity, self-discipline, and organizational skills. After-school and summer programs can be expected to have a chance of narrowing the achievement gap only by attempting to duplicate such experiences.

For nearly half a century, the association of social and economic disadvantage with a student achievement gap has been well known to economists, sociologists, and educators. However, most have avoided the obvious implications of this understanding: raising the achievement of lower-class children requires the amelioration of the social and economic conditions of their lives, not just school reform. Perhaps we are now ready to reconsider this needlessly neglected opportunity.

---

1. David Kerbow, "Patterns of Urban Student Mobility and Local School Reform," *Journal of Education for Students Placed at Risk,* vol. 12, 1996, pp. 147-69; and James Bruno and JoAnn Isken, "Inter- and Intraschool Site Student Transiency: Practical and Theoretical Implications for Instructional Continuity at Inner-City

Schools," *Journal of Research and Development in Education*, vol. 29, 1996, pp. 239-52.

2. Paul Harris, "Learning-Related Visual Problems in Baltimore City: A Long-Term Program," *Journal of Optometric Vision Development*, vol. 33, 2002, pp. 75-115; and Marge Christensen Gould and Herman Gould, O.D., "A Clear Vision for Equity and Opportunity," *Phi Delta Kapan*, December 2003, pp, 324-29.

3. See Meredith Phillips, "Understanding Ethnic Differences in Academic Achievement: Empirical Lessons from National Data," in David W. Grissmer and J. Michael Ross, eds., *Analytic Issues in the Assessment of Student Achievement* (Washington, D,C.: U.S. Department of Education, NCES 2000-050, 2000), pp. 103-32, available at http://nces.ed.gov/pubs2000/2000osoa.pdf; Richard L. Allington and Anne McGill Franzen, "The Impact of Summer Setback on the Reading Achievement Gap," *Phi Delta Kappan*, September 2003, pp. 68-75; and Doris Entwisle and Karl L. Alexander, "Summer Setback: Race, Poverty, School Composition, and Mathematics Achievement in the First Two Years of School," *American Sociological Review*, February 1992, pp. 72-84.

Richard Rothstein is a research associate with the Economic Policy Institute, Wasington, D.C., and a visiting lecturer at Teachers College, Columbia University, New York City. This chapter is adapted from the introduction to his new book, Class and Schools: Using Social, Economic, and Educational Reform to Close the Black-White Achievement Gap (*Economic Policy Institute/Teachers College, 2004*). © 2004, Economic Policy Institute/Teachers College. Copies may be ordered at www.epinet.org.

# The Biology of Risk Taking

*For help in guiding adolescents into healthy adulthood, educators can look to new findings in the fields of neuroscience and developmental psychology.*

**Lisa F. Price**

*I celebrate myself,*

*And what I assume you shall assume,*

*For every atom belonging to me as good belongs to you.*

— Walt Whitman, *Leaves of Grass*

Adolescence is a time of excitement, growth, and change. Whitman's words capture the enthusiasm and passion with which teenagers approach the world. Sometimes adolescents direct this passion toward a positive goal, such as a creative essay, an art project, after-school sports, or a healthy romance. At other times, they divert their passions to problematic activities, such as drug experimentation, reckless driving, shoplifting, fights, or school truancy.

Why do adolescents take risks? Why are teens so passionate? Are adolescents just young adults, or are they fundamentally different? Advances in developmental psychology and neuroscience have provided us with some answers. We now understand that adolescent turmoil, which we used to view as an expression of raging hormones, is actually the result of a complex interplay of body chemistry, brain development, and cognitive growth (Buchanan, Eccles, & Becker, 1992). Moreover, the changes that teenagers experience occur in the context of multiple systems—such as individual relationships, family, school, and community—that support and influence change.

Educators are in a pivotal position to promote healthy adolescent growth. Understanding the biological changes that adolescents undergo and

the behaviors that result can provide the foundation for realistic expectations and effective interventions.

## The Impact of Puberty

The hormonal changes of adolescence are often considered synonymous with puberty. The word *puberty* comes from the Latin term *pubertas*, meaning "age of maturity." As implied by the word's etymology, the changes of puberty have long been understood to usher in adulthood; in many cultures, puberty and the capacity to conceive continue to mark entry into adulthood. In contrast, puberty in modern Western culture has become a multistep entry process into a much longer period of adolescence (King, 2002).

Hormonal changes of adolescence include adrenarche, gonadarche, and menarche (Dahl, 2004; King, 2002). Adrenarche refers to the increased production of adrenal hormones and occurs as early as age 6-8. These hormones influence skeletal growth, hair production, and skin changes. Gonadarche refers to the pulsatile production of a cascade of hormones and contributes to driving the growth spurt and genital, breast, and pubic hair development. Menarche refers to the beginning of girls' menses, which generally occurs late in girls' pubertal development.

### The Stages and Ages of Puberty

The clinician J. M. Tanner developed a system for classifying male and female pubertal growth into five stages (Tanner I-V). In the 1960s, he identified a trend of progressively earlier

age at menarche across cultures (1968). Since then, investigators have identified similar trends of earlier arrival of other markers of puberty, such as breast and pubic hair development (Herman-Giddens et al., 1997). These trends have diverged across race in the United States, with proportionately more African American girls experiencing earlier-onset puberty than white girls. The implications of these trends have ranged from debates over the threshold for premature puberty to investigations into factors that contribute to earlier-onset puberty (Kaplowitz & Oberfield, 1999).

Boys who enter puberty at an earlier age experience certain advantages, including higher self-esteem, greater popularity, and some advances in cognitive capabilities (King, 2002). These same boys may also be more likely to engage in risk-taking behavior, possibly because they often socialize with older boys (Steinberg & Morris, 2001). Girls, on the other hand, often have more problems associated with earlier entry into puberty, including lower self-esteem and elevated risk for anxiety, depression, and eating disorders. These girls are also more likely to engage in risk-taking behaviors, including earlier sexual intercourse.

### Don't Blame It On Hormones

In the past, hormones were believed to be in a state of great flux, which presumably caused adolescents to be dramatic, erratic, intense, and risk-prone. Evidence suggests, however, that only minimal association exists between adolescent hormone levels and emotional/behavioral problems (Buchanan et al., 1992; King, 2002). Youth with higher levels of hormones do not appear to be at higher risk for emotional or behavioral problems (Dahl, 2004).

**Adolescence is a time of excitement, growth, and change.**

Today, adolescent specialists view emotional intensity and sensation-seeking as normative behaviors of adolescence that are more broadly linked to pubertal maturation than to hormone levels. Pubertal stage rather than chronological age is linked to romantic and sexual pursuits, increased appetite, changes in sleep patterns, and risk for emotional disorders in girls. One group of investigators studying teen smoking and substance use found that increased age had no correlation with increased sensation-seeking or risky behavior (Martin et al., 2002). Instead, they determined that pubertal maturation was correlated with sensation-seeking in boys and girls, which, in turn, led to a greater likelihood of cigarette smoking and substance use.

Pubertal stage was clearly linked to difficulties that Derek began experiencing in school. He had been a solid student in 6th grade who scored in the average range and generally turned his homework in on time. He socialized with a group of same-age friends and was teased occasionally because he was skinnier and shorter than his peers. By 7th grade, however, he had begun his growth spurt. He was now a few inches taller and had developed facial hair. Although he appeared more confident, he also seemed more aggressive and was involved in several fights at school. He began to spend part of his time with a few 8th grade boys who were suspected of writing graffiti on a school wall.

A teacher who had a good relationship with Derek took him aside and spoke with him about the change in his behavior from 6th to 7th grade. Derek was able to talk about his own surprise at the changes, his wish for more respect, and his ambivalence about entering high school—he was worried about what teachers would

expect of him. Derek and the teacher agreed to talk periodically, and the teacher arranged for Derek to meet with the school counselor.

## The Adolescent Brain

Neuroscientists used to believe that by the time they reached puberty, youth had undergone the crucial transformations in brain development and circuitry. Data obtained through available technology supported this view, identifying similar brain structures in children and adults. The adolescent brain seemed entirely comparable to the adult brain.

This view of adolescent brain development has undergone a radical shift during the last decade, with the identification of ongoing brain changes throughout adolescence, such as synaptic pruning and myelination. People have the mature capacity to consistently control behavior in both low-stress and high-stress environments only after these neurobiological developments are complete. This maturation does not take place until the early 20s.

Synaptic pruning refers to the elimination of connections between neurons in the brain's cortex, or gray matter. In the 1990s, researchers determined that during adolescence, up to 30,000 synapses are eliminated each second (Bourgeois & Rakic, 1993; Rakic, Bourgeois, & Goldman-Rakic, 1994). The removal of these redundant synaptic links increases the computational ability of brain circuits, which, in turn, enhances a function intricately connected to risk taking: the capacity to regulate and rapidly stop activity. Myelination, which refers to the wrapping of glial cell membranes around the axon of neurons, results in increased speed of signal transmission along the axon (Luna & Sweeney, 2004). This facilitates more rapid and integrated communication among diverse brain regions.

Synaptic pruning and myelination, along with other neurobiological changes, facilitate enhanced cognitive capacity as well as behavioral control, also known as *executive function*. Executive function is the ability to interact in a self-directed, appropriate, organized, and purpose-

ful manner. The prefrontal cortex plays a vital role in guiding executive function, which is also influenced by such areas of the brain as the hippocampus (which coordinates memory), the amygdala (which coordinates emotional processing), and the ventral striatum (which coordinates reward-processing). The prefrontal cortex is less mature, however, in young adolescents than in adults.

Given these three factors—an inability to completely regulate and refrain from certain activities, an absence of fully integrated communication among the various regions of the brain, and a less developed prefrontal cortex—it is not surprising that adolescents biologically do not have the same capacities as adults to inhibit their impulses in a timely manner.

## Biology and Thrill-Seeking

By their mid-teens, adolescents appear to have achieved many decision-making abilities seen in adults (Steinberg & Cauffman, 1996). In fact, studies have found that teens can identify the same degree of danger in risky activities that adults can—driving while intoxicated, for example (Cauffman, Steinberg, & Woolard, 2002). However, certain methodological flaws in studies of adolescents may have prevented investigators from accurately assessing adolescent risk taking (Steinberg, 2004). These flaws include evaluating teens individually rather than in the context of a group, within which most risk-taking behavior occurs; asking teens to evaluate theoretical situations, which may not sufficiently represent the challenges of actual situations; and evaluating teens in settings that reduce the influence of emotion or induce anxiety rather than generate the exhilaration associated with risk taking.

One result of these flaws may be that measures of adolescents' cognitive abilities—particularly their evaluation of risk—do not adequately reflect their actual cognitive and emotional processes in real time. Consequently, teens *appear* to have the cognitive capacities of adults yet continue to engage in more risky behaviors.

The emotional lives of adolescents also appear to shift during these years. Adolescents seek more intense emotional experiences than children and adults do. They appear to need higher degrees of stimulation to obtain the same experience of pleasure (Steinberg, 2004). Developments in an area of the brain called the limbic system may explain this shift in pursuit and experience of pleasure (Spear, 2000).

> **Teenagers generally thrive in reasonable, supportive environments that have a predictable, enforced structure.**

Ongoing cognitive development and emotional shifts result in a biologically based drive for thrill-seeking, which may account for adolescents' continued risk taking despite knowledge of the accompanying hazards. Some interventions attempt to reduce the potential for risky behavior through external means—laws and rules, for example—rather than placing sole emphasis on the practice of educating teens in risk assessment (Steinberg, 2004). Others have considered teens' ability to reason well in "cool" circumstances but their failure to do so when in "hot" situations that arouse the emotions. Providing adolescents with sufficient scaffolding, or a good balance of support and autonomy, may be particularly important (Dahl, 2004).

This kind of scaffolding would be especially effective with a student like Shauna. Shauna raised the concerns of school faculty soon after she started 9th grade. Her attendance, class participation, and assignment completion were erratic. She had also run away from home during the summer and received a warning for shoplifting. The school counselor learned that Shauna's parents had separated over the summer and that her mother was struggling to set limits in the absence of Shauna's father. The school counselor, several teachers, and the vice principal decided to meet with both of Shauna's parents.

Although tension between the parents was evident, both parents agreed that Shauna should come home immediately after school instead of going to the mall, which she had recently started to do. Both parents also felt strongly that she needed to regularly attend school and complete assignments. The parents arranged to meet with Shauna together to discuss their shared expectations for her. The parents and teachers agreed to stay in contact with one another regarding Shauna's attendance and homework. The group also decided that a home-based reward system might encourage Shauna's success at school. The reward system would involve outings to the mall and to friends' homes, with incrementally less adult supervision and more autonomy as she continued to succeed.

## The Role of Educators

These new findings suggest some beneficial approaches that educators might follow to guide adolescents into healthy adulthood.

- *Ensure that schools provide adolescents with vital support.* School bonding provides a protective influence for youth. The mentorship of a teacher can make the difference in a teen's course.
- *Keep a long view.* Researchers have found that the benefits of successful interventions may disappear for a few years in adolescence to reappear in later adolescence (Masten, 2004). Other teens are late bloomers whose troubled earlier years are followed by success.
- *Prioritize your concern.* The junior who has never been a problem and gets into trouble once is at a different level of risk than the 7th grader who has a long history of worrisome behaviors, such as fights, school truancy, mental illness, exposure to trauma, loss of important adult figures, or absence of stable supports. Act early for adolescents with long histories of risk taking.
- *Remember that puberty is not the same for all teens.* Some adolescents enter puberty earlier than others, giving them a perceived social advantage as well as possible disadvantages. There may be a biological drive to risk taking in teens, which is expressed by individual teens at different ages.
- *Remember that teens are not adults.* Having the scientific evidence to support the view that teens are not adults can be helpful to educators working with families, adolescents, or other professionals who may have unrealistic expectations for adolescents.
- *Take advantage of adolescent passion.* Direct adolescents' enthusiasm toward productive ends. A teen's passion can become a bridge to learning about such topics as music theory, history, politics, race relations, or marketing.
- *Reduce risk with firm structure.* Although teenagers dislike rules, they generally thrive in reasonable, supportive environments that have a predictable, enforced structure. For example, an authoritative stance in parenting—which reflects firmness coupled with caring—has repeatedly been found to be the most effective parenting strategy. Continue to maintain school rules and expectations, even when an adolescent continues to break the rules.
- *Collaborate to solve problems.* Working with risk-taking adolescents can be demanding, taxing, and worrisome. Talk regularly with colleagues for support. Contact appropriate consultants when your concern grows. Teens who see teachers collaborate with other adults benefit from these healthy models of problem solving.

It's important for educators to keep in mind that up to 80 percent of adolescents have few or no major problems during this period (Dahl, 2004). Remembering that most adolescents do well can encourage the positive outlook that educators need to effectively work with youth during this exciting and challenging time in their lives.

# References

Bourgeois, J-P., & Rakic, P. (1993). Changes of synaptic density in the primary visual cortex of the macaque monkey from fetal to adult stage. *Journal of Neuroscience, 13,* 2801–2820.

Buchanan, C. M., Eccles, J. S., & Becker, J. B. (1992). Are adolescents the victims of raging hormones? *Psychological Bulletin, 111,* 62–107.

Cauffman, E., Steinberg, L., & Woolard, J. (2002, April 13). *Age differences in capacities underlying competence to stand trial.* Presentation at the Biennial Meeting of the Society for Research for Adolescence, New Orleans, Louisiana.

Dahl, R. E. (2004). Adolescent brain development: A period of vulnerabilities and opportunities. *Annals of the New York Academy of Science, 1021,* 1–22.

Herman-Giddens, M. E., Slora, E. J., Wasserman, R. C., Bourdony, C.J., Bhapkar, M. V., Koch, G. G., et al. (1997). Secondary sexual characteristics and menses in young girls seen in office practice. *Pediatrics, 99,* 505–512.

Kaplowitz, P. B., & Oberfield, S. E. (1999). Reexamination of the age limit for defining when puberty is precocious in girls in the United States. *Pediatrics, 104,* 936–941.

King, R. A. (2002). Adolescence. In M. Lewis (Ed.), *Child and adolescent psychiatry* (pp. 332–342). Philadelphia: Lippincott Williams & Wilkins.

Luna, B., & Sweeney, J. A. (2004). The emergence of collaborative brain function: fMRI studies of the development of response inhibition. *Annals of the New York Academy of Science, 1021,* 296–309.

Martin, C. A., Kelly, T. H., Rayens, M. K., Brogli, B. R., Brenzel, A., Smith, W. J., et al. (2002). Sensation seeking, puberty, and nicotine, alcohol, and marijuana use in adolescence. *Journal of the American Academy of Child and Adolescent Psychiatry, 41,* 1495–1502.

Masten, A. S. (2004). Regulatory processes, risk, and resilience in adolescent development. *Annals of the New York Academy of Science, 1021,* 310–319.

Rakic, P., Bourgeois, J-P., & Goldman-Rakic, P. S. (1994). Synaptic development of the cerebral cortex. *Progress in Brain Research, 102,* 227–243.

Spear, P. (2000). The adolescent brain and age-related behavioral manifestations. *Neuroscience and Biobehavioral Reviews, 24,* 417–463.

Steinberg, L. (2004). Risk taking in adolescence: What changes, and why? *Annals of the New York Academy of Science, 1021,* 51–58.

Steinberg, L., & Cauffman, E. (1996). Maturity of judgment in adolescence. *Law and Human Behavior, 20,* 249–272.

Steinberg, L., & Morris, A. S. (2001). Adolescent development. *Annual Review of Psychology, 52,* 83–110.

Tanner, J. M. (1968). Early maturation in man. *Scientific American, 218,* 21–27.

---

**Lisa F. Price**, *M.D., is the Assistant Director of the School Psychiatry Program in the Department of Psychiatry at Massachusetts General Hospital, 55 Fruit St., YAW 6900, Boston, MA 02114. She is also an Instructor in Psychiatry at Harvard Medical School.*

---

# METAPHORS OF HOPE

## Refusing to be disheartened by all the negative press surrounding education today, Ms. Chenfeld travels the country and encounters one inspiring educator after another. She tells four of their stories here.

MIMI BRODSKY CHENFELD

ON the Big Island of Hawaii, there's a forest of lava-crusted hills and bare corpses of trees called Devastation Trail. Old volcanic eruptions burnt the Ohia trees and left this once-lush terrain barren and ashen.

Walking on the wooden paths through the devastation, one could easily miss the tiny flowers remarkably pushing through the charred earth. The markers that identify these flowers read: Thimbleberry, Swordfern, Creeping Dayflower, and Nutgrass. While others aimed their cameras at the stark, mysterious lava hills, I focused on the flowers. In the midst of such a desolate scene, these perky "signs of life" seemed to be symbols of courage and persistence.

Reading daily the bleak headlines and articles that stress the stress by focusing on bullying, violence, gangs and cliques, and numerous random acts of unkindness and hostility in our seemingly devastated educational landscape, one could easily sink into despair. However, as a stubborn optimist, I always search for markers of thimbleberry, swordfern, creeping dayflower, and nutgrass—metaphors of hope!

When Mr. T (also known as Tom Tenerovich) was moved upstairs after years of teaching kindergarten classes, he observed that second-graders were more vocal, more argumentative, more opinionated! A voracious reader of books about education, he was familiar with many theories and pro-

grams. *But reading about ideas is different from doing.*

One idea that intrigued Mr. T was that of Town Meeting. He and his students discussed building a structure that would enable all voices to be heard, problems to be solved, and good listening habits to be formed.[1]

The class added mayor and assistant mayor to the list of jobs on their classroom helpers board. During the year, every student would be assigned to these jobs for a one-week term of office.

The Town Meeting works this way: each week, the mayor and assistant mayor, along with Tom, write an agenda for two, 30- to 40-minute Town Meetings. Any student can submit a proposal for discussion, but it has to be written and include name, date, and the issue to be discussed. Some of the issues concerning the students have included changing seats, playground rules, classmates being hurtful, picking team members, and activities for "Fun Fridays."

At the Town Meeting, the class discusses the topic and votes to resolve the issue. "Even if they disagree, it's so sweet to hear how they disagree," Tom reports. "They're really beginning to listen to each other." He continues,

It's amazing the way it works out. None of the kids are bossy when they become mayor. Even our most timid children became good mayors. Believe it or not, one of my most high-maintenance tough kids

was the best mayor! He took charge in a fair way—he knew what to do—he behaved appropriately.

Even I became an agenda issue! One of the kids reminded me that I hadn't done something I promised. That was important to the children, and I had to remedy it.

Committees formed from discussions: academic committees, playground committees (to see that no students were left out of games or weren't chosen for teams), and classroom improvement committees. Tom was thrilled to see how the twice-weekly Town Meetings honoring the feelings and agendas of the students carried over into the everyday life of the group. "This really is democracy in action! Points of view are freely expressed. All opinions are valued and respected. You can see and feel the increase of courtesy and kindness."

The school mascot is a bobcat. Tom and his second-graders added the idea of Bobcat Purrs to their Town Meeting. Like "warm fuzzies," pats on the back, recognition of positive acts, observations of improvements, Bobcat Purrs were "built into our meetings," Tom explains, "and became part of our culture. Children wrote up a 'purr,' decorated it, and handed it to the mayor, who read it and presented it. No one was ever left out. We promised *not* to just recognize our best friends. Children looked for what their classmates were doing well. They were very specific."

One student, who had experienced alienation, low self-image, and loneliness in earlier years and whose posture defined his feelings, received a Bobcat Purr during a Town Meeting that stated how proudly he was standing. He was standing up straight! The boy beamed!

Another student who had difficulty finishing her work received a Bobcat Purr from a classmate honoring her for finishing *all* of her work. Everyone rejoiced.

When children live in a climate that accentuates the positive, their eagle eyes catch the flickering light of flames that are almost burnt out.

*The picture I want to snap for my Album of Hope is of a proud second-grader standing up straight with the mayor, assistant mayor, his teacher, and all of his classmates honoring him with a Bobcat Purr during the Town Meeting.*[2]

## SWORDFERN: CATHY

Cathy Arment and her first-graders are not involved in the building of structures like Town Meetings. With their teacher, this group of students from diverse cultures, races, and religions works hard and plays hard together. Cathy described a memorable scene in a telephone message: "I was reading the children Jonathan London's *Froggy's First Kiss*—you know, for Valentine week. Mim, I looked up from the story to see the children sitting in clusters, their arms around each other, their eyes wide as I turned the pages, so totally involved. I almost began to weep at the sight of their beauty."

> *Here we have students with Ethiopian, Mexican, Appalachian, Southeast Asian, and African American backgrounds. How did such a diverse group of children learn to love one another?*

Here we have students with Ethiopian, Mexican, Appalachian, Southeast Asian, and African American backgrounds—children who are newcomers, some from dysfunctional homes, some from foster homes, some with hardship home lives, some at risk. How did such a

diverse group of children learn to love one another?

Cathy and I talked at length. With all the realities of alienation, anxiety, insecurity, and mean-spiritedness that these students face, *how is such a warm and loving environment created?* What is the strategy? What are the techniques? Cathy thought long and hard about these questions. She realized that she did not have a preconceived plan for helping her students build positive classroom relationships. She hadn't adopted a program specifically aimed at such outcomes. Nowhere in her plan book were consciously chosen activities based on proven behavior management theories. *She just did what she did because of who she was and what she believed.* Reviewing her ideas, she said:

> All I can think of is that from day one, we are together. We verbalize feelings—good and bad. We're not afraid to share. From our first moment together, we talked about respecting everyone. Some of my children have heavy accents. They are "different." Many of them have been made fun of. We talk about how hurtful it is to be teased, to put people down and to be put down. We begin to listen to each other. To care about each other. *My children never, ever tease!* And—I'm a human being, too—I share with them. They'll ask me, "Teacher, what did YOU read? What did YOU do over the weekend? Did YOU have a fun holiday?" When a child has a low day, we all try to cheer that child. Sometimes I have a gray day. The kids will go out of their way to brighten me. They know we stick together, that I care for them very deeply. They know that we are all safe in our room.

When the children wrote and illustrated their "I Have A Dream" papers inspired by Dr. Martin Luther King, Jr.'s famous speech, many of them expressed the warm feelings they experienced in the classroom and wrote dreams like these: "I have a dream to be with my family and to give love to

everybody and to care about everybody" (Abigail). "I have a dream that people would be nice to other people and, if people are hurt, other people could help them just like other people help me" (Carissa).

The Israeli-Yemenite dancer Margolith Ovid once said, "The greatest technique in the universe is the technique in the human heart."

*The picture I would snap for my Album of Hope is of Cathy's kids, arms around each other, sitting in clusters, listening to* Froggy's First Kiss.[3]

## CREEPING DAYFLOWER: MS. GIBSON

Before the new school year even begins, Dee Gibson sends warm *Welcome to the Family* cards to her future students! These fortunate first-graders know—from everything said and done, from words and actions, activities and discussions, planning and projects—that their class is a second family in which each and every family member is important and connected to everyone else. This is not a theme or a curriculum item or a subject area—*it's the way it is* in Ms. Gibson's class. Because she is passionate, articulate, and committed to creating, with her children and families, a safe, encouraging, caring community that really is a second family (and for some children over the years, a first family!), the experiences of her students are very special. They help one another. They cooperate. They plan and talk together. They are totally involved in the life they share together in this home away from home.

> *We can't take the environment for granted. We are the architects of the culture of the school, of the program.*

When the children were asked such questions as "What is it like being in this kind of class family? What do you do? How do you feel?" the responses were honest and forthcoming:

> We're all together. We get in pods.
> We work together. If two kids are

having an argument, the whole class stops till we work it out. We really feel like everyone cares about each other.—*Jay*

* * *

We're like teamwork. We help each other with work and to pick up. Everyone here sticks together —*Lauri*

* * *

All the kids are friends. Arguing doesn't really happen much— everyone cooperates.—*Ryan*

* * *

Our teacher treats people fair. The other kids act very kind together. She teaches us how to work together.—*Barrett*

* * *

We don't really get in fights!—*Nikki*

* * *

Everybody is nice to each other, and they act like a family.
Ms. Gibson is like one of the family.—*Danielle*

The language in this class is the language of respect, acceptance, courtesy, responsibility, and cooperation. It's not limited to a week's celebration of a theme! It's the vocabulary of a close-knit family. That's an everyday reality.

*The picture I want to take for my Album of Hope is of the children holding up their summer "Welcome to the Family" cards. A sequel to that picture is of children discovering that the welcome cards were not a gimmick! They were the real thing.*[4]

## NUTGRASS: ANNE AND CLAUDETTE

Partners in Educating All Children Equally (PEACE), Anne Price and Claudette Cole travel to schools, programs, and conferences, spreading very simple messages—especially to administrators who too often don't attend workshops that are aimed directly at the heart. Anne and Claudette remind those directors, managers, principals, and superinten-

dents that their influence in the creation of positive, life-affirming school climates is immeasurable. They *really can* make the difference between the life and death of an entire program or school.

Claudette and Anne discuss ways of helping teachers to develop positive relationships with their students and to motivate the students to develop caring and respectful relationships with one another. What are some suggestions for doing so? Usually, without hesitation, most of the administrators offer such actions as recognizing students, paying attention to them, appreciating their talents and efforts, encouraging them to cooperate with and be considerate of one another, and inviting students to share ideas and input so that they are directly involved in the success of the school.

Claudette and Anne gently turn these ideas around, directing them to the administrators. "Just as we advocate developmentally appropriate practices for teaching children, so we have to apply those ideas to our staff." Anne explains their simple, direct approach: "It's our responsibility to pay attention to the needs of staff so they can meet the children's needs."

What are some of the greatest trouble spots in the dynamics of any school or program? Absenteeism, turnover, bullying, discipline problems, low morale, lack of trust, miscommunication—to name just a few. It's so obvious to Anne and Claudette that these problems, often reflecting a disconnected and resentful staff, carry over to the students and poison the atmosphere. (Think lava!)

Think of ways to inspire and create a healthy workplace for all who spend time there. Claudette asks, "Does the staff feel appreciated? Respected? Do they feel they have ownership of and an investment in the success of the program? Are their efforts and contributions valued? Do we keep all avenues of communication open? Do we trust enough to be honest with each other without fear of reprisal?"

Anne reminds participants in her workshops that we can't take the environment for granted. *We are the architects of the culture of the school, of the program.* "You'll see the difference in an environment where children, staff, fami-

lies, and communities are nurtured and respected. Ideas flow freely, teamwork flourishes, staff feels open and trusting with each other and with the administration—now, will the turnover be as great? The absenteeism? The low morale?" She challenges her groups to talk honestly about these vital components that make for a healthy, positive school culture.

"And," she warns, "you can't give it if it's not in you to give. That's why we constantly have to think about our commitments, beliefs, and goals. How we feel about those deeper questions will generate our behavior."

Claudette and Anne inspire those who lead to look deeply into their own hearts and souls and honestly find whether their beliefs, actions, and words are in harmony. Their decisions will shape the culture of their schools, affecting children, staff, families, and neighbors.

*The image for my Album of Hope is a group of administrators exchanging ideas and experiences, sharing feelings, and being energized by the process and promise of making a real difference in the lives of those they guide.*[5]

These are just four examples of courageous, confident, hopeful educators who, like our four brave little flowers, insist on growing through hardened and lava-crusted times! I must tell you, I have gathered hundreds and hundreds of examples of educators throughout the land who inspire and nurture caring, compassionate communities of learners.

All of them give themselves wholly to this "holy" process. Their words aren't slogans. Their promises are not bulletin-board displays or mottos. Their commitments are demonstrated every day by how they meet and greet, listen and talk, share and care in their numerous interactions with children and adults.

They know that nothing is to be taken for granted. Tom's Town Meeting is not guaranteed to succeed. A teacher who does not teach in the "key of life," who doesn't listen to or respect the students, who is rigid and devoid of joy and humor, can follow the recipe for a Town Meeting to the last syllable, but it will yield nothing that will teach the children, *through doing*, the art of building positive classroom relationships.

> *I have gathered hundreds and hundreds of examples of educators throughout the land who inspire and nurture caring, compassionate communities of learners.*

Cathy didn't adopt a specific program. She and her children *are* the program, and their mutuality, kindness, and concern for one another are expressed in everything they do. There is no place for bullying in the safe place of Cathy's classroom. She teaches by heart!

Unless one believes it deeply and demonstrates that belief in everything he or she does (from the smallest acts to the largest), even a stellar concept like *family* will be another act of betrayal. Dee Gibson truly believes in establishing a second family with her children. This is not a once-a-month, set-aside time slot; it's the air they breathe and everything they do. Children are acutely alert to hypocrisy. They know when their teachers speak empty words. Lip service is disservice! They learn those lessons well.

Anne and Claudette, in their workshops, invite administrators to examine their own beliefs, motivations, and actions. Joanne Rooney, in her excellent article "Principals Who Care: A Personal Reflection," wrote:

> Good principals model care. Their words and behavior explicitly show that caring is not optional. Nothing can substitute for this leadership. Phoniness doesn't cut it. No principal can ask any teacher, student, or parent to travel down the uncertain path of caring if the principal will not lead the way.[6]

The way through these often grim times is through dedication and commitment, courage, persistence and fierce optimism. Just as Swordfern, Nutgrass, Creeping Dayflower, and Thimbleberry push their bright colors through seemingly solid lava, countless teachers and administrators shine their lights—brightening the sacred spaces they influence, dotting the charred landscape with blossoms of hope.

## Notes

1. Tom was inspired by A. S. Neill, *Summerhill School* (New York: St. Martin's Griffin, 1992).
2. Tom Tenerovich and his second-graders enjoyed their Town Meetings at the Royal Palm Beach Elementary School, Royal Palm Beach, Fla. Tom currently teaches second grade at Equestrian Trails Elementary school in Wellington, Fla.
3. Cathy Arment and her loving first-graders listened to *Froggy's First Kiss* at the Etna Road School, Whitehall-Yearling Public Schools, Whitehall, Ohio, where she was voted Teacher of the Year 2004.
4. Dee Gibson and her family of first-graders thrive in the Walden School, Deerfield Public Schools, Deerfield, Ill. Dee was featured in my guest editorial, "Welcome to the Family," *Early Childhood Education Journal*, Summer 2003, pp. 201–2.
5. Anne Price and Claudette Cole are PEACEmakers in Cleveland, Ohio. You can contact Anne and Claudette at www.peaceeducation.com.
6. Joanne Rooney, "Principals Who Care: A Personal Reflection," *Educational Leadership*, March 2003, p. 77.

---

**MIMI BRODSKY CHENFELD** *began teaching in 1956. She works and plays with people of all ages and grade levels throughout the country. Among her books are* Teaching in the Key of Life *(National Association for the Education of Young Children, 1993),* Teaching by Heart *(Redleaf Press, 2001), and* Creative Experiences for Young Children, *3rd ed. (Heinemann, 2002). She lives in Columbus, Ohio. She dedicates this article to the memory of Pauline Gough, whose life's work, brightening the way for educators and children, is a stellar example of metaphors of hope.*

---

From *Phi Delta Kappan*, December 2004, pp. 271-275. Copyright © 2004 by Phi Delta Kappan. Reprinted by permission of the publisher and author. Mimi Brodsky Chenfield, teacher/author, has also published TEACHING IN THE KEY OF LIFE (NAEYC), TEACHER BY HEART (Redleaf), and CREATIVE EXPERIENCES FOR YOUNG CHILDREN (Heinemann).

# Where Are We Now?

"The problem of the 21st century will be the problem of the color line.... By any standard of measurement or evaluation the problem has not been solved in the 20th century and thus becomes part of the legacy and burden of the next century."

*—Historian John Hope Franklin, echoing the words of*
*W.E.B. DuBois at a different century's turn*

## BY GARY ORFIELD AND ERICA FRANKENBERG

School desegregation, celebrated as a historic accomplishment, is being abandoned in practice as much of urban America turns back to segregated neighborhood schools. The abandonment is driven, in part, by Supreme Court decisions ending desegregation orders.

Some say that this demonstrates that desegregation failed and that we are worse off than before the famous court decision whose 50th anniversary we are celebrating.

Others assume—perhaps because of the little discussion of desegregation in educational policy debates—that we have done all that can be done.

Still, an overwhelming majority of Americans favor desegregated schools. Likewise, almost all parents want their children to be prepared to get along with children of all backgrounds in a society that is on pace to become half non-white within their lifetimes.

According to a recent Gallup Poll, increasing majorities of Americans believe that integration has improved the quality of education for both Blacks and Whites. This does not mean that most Americans do not also prefer neighborhood schools—they do—but it makes clear that most people would like integrated schools if they didn't have to do anything in order to get them.

The truth about the desegregation story is that we did accomplish a great deal—when we were serious about it.

When all branches of government worked together for a few years in the 1960s, the South went from almost total racial separation to become the region with the nation's most integrated schools. In fact, most parents whose children went to integrated schools and most students who now attend them see it as a very positive experience that tends to have lasting impacts on their lives.

But we, the people, haven't put any real effort into desegregation in several decades. Perhaps because we have failed to demand continued diligence in creating an integrated society, our executive and legislative leaders have forgotten the promise of *Brown*—while the courts have been moving backward.

## WHY SHOULD WE CARE?

School desegregation originally began to ensure the constitutional rights for Black—and later Latino—students under the Fourteenth Amendment. Fifty years later, we have additional reasons to continue *Brown's* worthy pursuit.

First, racial segregation is strongly linked to segregation by class: Nearly 90% of intensely segregated schools for Blacks and Latinos are also schools in which at least half of the student body is economically disadvantaged.

These schools are traditionally associated with fewer resources, fewer advanced course offerings, more inexperienced teachers and lower average test scores. At the same time, despite the unequal resources that are traditionally associated with high poverty and minority schools, students in these schools are being subjected to increasingly rigorous testing that can have serious stakes attached for student promotion and graduation.

Second, decades of social science research has found that racially diverse classrooms improve student experiences: enhanced learning, higher academic achievement for minorities, higher educational and occupational aspirations, increased civic engagement, a greater desire to live, work, and go to school in multiracial settings, and positive, increased social interaction among members of different racial and ethnic backgrounds. Significantly, these benefits affect both white and minority students.

## Segregation Today

**At the dawn of the 21st century, education for Blacks is more segregated than it was in 1968.**

**Black students are the most likely racial group to attend what researchers call "apartheid schools,"—schools that are virtually all non-white and where poverty, limited resources, social strife and health problems abound. One-sixth of America's black students attend these schools.**

**Whites are the most segregated group in the nation's public schools. Only 14% of white students attend multiracial schools (where three or more racial groups are present).**

**Latino students are the most segregated minority group in U.S. schools. They are segregated by race and poverty; immigrant Latinos also are at risk of experiencing linguistic segregation.**

**Asian American students are the most integrated group in the nation's public schools. Three-fourths of Asian Americans attend multiracial schools.**

**Racial segregation in schools is strongly linked to segregation by class. Nearly 90% of intensely segregated, black and Latino schools are also schools where at least half of the student body is economically disadvantaged.**

**Residential segregation impacts schools. With the decrease in busing to achieve school integration and the overwhelming return to neighborhood schools, where we live matters.**

**Today's segregated schools are still unequal. Segregated schools have higher concentrations of poverty, much lower test scores, less experienced teachers and fewer advanced placement courses.**

**Students in integrated schools perform better on tests, possess elevated aspirations for educational and occupational attainment, and lead more integrated lives**

Supreme Court decisions of the 1990s have made it easier for urban school districts to be released from decades-old desegregation plans.

In some areas, very high levels of integration remain. In others, particularly our large central city districts that educate one-quarter of black and Latino students, high levels of isolation by race and poverty exist. In many large suburban districts, rapid racial change and spreading segregation are occurring.

We have learned a great deal about how to design policies to encourage racial diversity, such as coordinating efforts to tackle residential and school desegregation.

As our country grows increasingly multiracial and this diversity expands into our suburban areas, we must think carefully about not replicating policies of resegregation that have produced the overwhelmingly minority and poor inner-city school systems.

The growth of the charter school movement, which neglected segregation issues and has unfortunately contributed to resegregation, especially for black students, is an example of how essential it is to incorporate equity provisions into any new education reform, particularly when residential segregation remains so high.

We must ensure that where desegregated schools exist, segregation within the school does not minimize interracial exposure. To that end, teachers must be trained in techniques to create positive environments that maximize the benefits of racial diversity. And students must rise up and help us cross our nation's long-standing racial and ethnic divide.

Finally, we—young and old, rich, poor and working class— all of us, across racial and ethnic lines, must remember the words of the Rev. Dr. Martin Luther King:

Desegregation simply removes … legal and social prohibitions. Integration is creative, and is therefore more profound and far-reaching. Integration is the positive acceptance of desegregation and the welcomed participation of Negroes into the total range of human activities.

His solution, as ours should be, is not to abandon desegregation, but to deepen it.

## THE POWER TO CHANGE

Today our public schools are more segregated than they were in 1970, before the Supreme Court ordered busing and other measures to achieve desegregation.

*Gary Orfield is a professor of education and social policy at the Harvard Graduate School of Education and co-director of the Civil Rights Project at Harvard University. Erica Frankenberg is a doctoral student at the Harvard Graduate School of Education.*

# Five Things You Should Know About Poverty Around the World

## 1 Geography matters.

Geography may have more to do with whether you live in poverty than almost anything else. Shift your world view: Think of a globe divided into north and south and consider these statistics:

- The southern hemisphere has the dubious distinction of being home to the majority of the world's one-room shelters.
- Two-thirds of the estimated 35 million housing units needed annually to shelter families moving to urban areas and to replace "life-threatening" housing would need to be built in the Asia/Pacific region.
- Africa fares no better, as it is home to the largest percentage of people in the world living under the $1 per day poverty line.

*—United Nations; United Nations Human Settlements Programme; World Bank*

## 2 Half the world's population lives on less than $2 a day.

With global population topping 6 billion today, one out of every two people scrapes out daily survival on a mere $2. One out of every six lives on $1 a day. But experts indicate that poverty is more than a lack of income. Rather, it is the result of insecurity, inequality, poor health and illiteracy. Its effects are worsened by the increasing gap in most societies between the richest and the poorest.

*—United Nations Population Report: State of the World's Population 2002*

## 3 Poor health makes people poor and being poor makes people sick.

A wage earner's illness can push families over the edge into poverty. In fact, the "newly poor" cite illness most frequently as the cause of their slide into poverty's grasp. For families who are already poor, illness can push them even farther into destitution. Worse, the poor are more often sick than people who are not poor. Continued exposure to diseases, unsafe working conditions, substandard housing and a lack of access to adequate health care degrade the health of the poor.

*—United Nations Population Report: State of the World's Population 2002*

## 4 Gender matters.

One out of every four developing countries has a constitution or national law that prevents women from owning land or taking mortgages in their own name. Women especially lack rights in Africa, western Asia and Latin America. And even though women comprise more than half the world's population, they hold only about 1 percent of the world's wealth.

*—United Nations Human Settlements Programme; Women in Human Settlements Development Programme*

## 5 Lacking clean water and adequate sanitation exacerbates poverty.

Some 2.4 billion people lack adequate sanitation; 1.1 billion have no clean water. This lack of access increases health risks, leading to the death of more than 2.2 million people—many of them children—from water- and sanitation-related diseases annually.

*—United Nations Human Settlements Programme; United Nations Children's Fund*

*Taking Measure* Tools and Information to Help Your Advocacy Efforts

# Five Things You Should Know About Poverty in the United States

## 1 A minimum-wage, full-time job does not guarantee a decent, affordable place to live.

Nowhere in the United States can a minimum-wage worker afford a two-bedroom apartment at Fair Market Rent, based on the generally accepted affordability standard of paying no more than 30 percent of income for housing. To afford FMR on a two-bedroom housing unit, one would have to earn between $8.72 per hour in West Virginia and $21.14 per hour in Massachusetts.

*—National Housing Conference,*
*National Low Income Housing Coalition*

## 2 In 2001, one in seven Americans had critical housing needs.

This includes 14.4 million Americans who paid more than half their income for housing and/or lived in physically substandard housing. Working families with critical housing needs are found in both cities and suburbs. And while the highest percentage of housing needs is found in the Northeast and West, the most rapidly growing segment of housing need is in the Midwest.

*—National Housing Conference*

## 3 A child is born into poverty every 46 seconds.

With one out of every six American children (11.6 million) living below the poverty line in 2000, more children live in poverty today than did 20 or 30 years ago. The pro-

portion of poor children in working families is at a record high, and the majority of poor children are white, even though the proportion of black and Hispanic children is far higher.

*—Children's Defense Fund, U.S. Census Bureau*

## 4 Poverty housing is not limited to inner cities.

Poverty remains a problem in rural America, with all but 11 of the 200 poorest counties in the United States being "non-metropolitan." Nearly 2 million rural homes are moderately or severely inadequate, with structural problems, leaky roofs, faulty wiring and no indoor plumbing. Health-threatening substandard housing afflicts millions of rural families, particularly along the U.S./Mexico border, on Native American reservations and in regions such as the Mississippi Delta and Appalachia.

*—Housing Assistance Council*

## 5 Race and/or ethnicity matters.

Minorities continue to experience higher poverty rates than whites. While less than 8 percent of whites live in poverty, nearly 25 percent of American Indians and Alaska Natives, nearly 23 percent of African-Americans, more than 21 percent of Hispanics and more than 10 percent of Asians and Pacific Islanders spend their lives in poverty.

*—Poverty USA; U.S. Census Bureau*

# UNIT 2
# Teacher Education in Multicultural Perspectives

## Unit Selections

## Key Points to Consider

- Why is multicultural education so frequently seen as an isolated and segregated part of teacher education programs?

- What are the reasons for so much resistance to coursework in the area of multicultural education in teacher education programs?

- What can we learn about teaching styles and methods from case studies of teachers from cultures other than our own?

- Is the concept of social justice a topic suitable for a multicultural classroom? Explain.

- What seem to be the major points of disagreement about the role of multicultural education in teacher education programs?

- What attitudes need to change regarding multicultural education? Explain.

## Student Website
www.mhcls.com/online

## Internet References
Further information regarding these websites may be found in this book's preface or online.

**Awesome Library for Teachers**
   *http://www.awesomelibrary.org/teacher.html*
**Education World**
   *http://www.education-world.com*
**Teacher Talk Forum**
   *http://education.indiana.edu/cas/tt/tthmpg.html*

At a time when the minority student body at the elementary and secondary school levels is beginning to approach 50 percent of the school population, fewer students from cultural minorities are choosing teaching as a career. This social reality within teacher education programs in the United States only underscores the need for multicultural education, as well as for coursework in specific cultural studies areas in the education of American teachers.

Multicultural educational programming of some sort is now an established part of teacher education programs, but debate continues as to how it can be integrated effectively into these programs. The National Council for the Accreditation of Teacher Education (NCATE) has established a multicultural standard for the accreditation of programs for teacher education in the United States. Many educators involved in teaching courses in multicultural education have wondered why such coursework is so often a segregated area of teacher education curricula. And many who are involved in multicultural teacher education believe that all teacher educators should become knowledgeable in this area. Teaching preservice teachers to respect cultural diversity can enhance their ability to respect individual students' diversity in learning styles and beliefs. Prospective teachers need to be sensitized to the reality of cultural diversity and to the need to learn about the values and beliefs of their students.

There is still much misunderstanding within the teacher education establishment as to what multicultural education is. This will continue as long as many of its opponents consider it a political rather than an intellectual or educational concept. If all children and young adults are to receive their educational experiences in schools that nourish and respect their respective heritages as people, all teachers must learn those intellectual and affective skills that can empower them to study and to learn about diverse cultures throughout their careers. Multicultural education course content in teacher education programs is about both cultural diversity and individual students from differing cultural heritages.

Teachers will have to consider how each student's development is shaped by the powerful force of those values prevailing in his or her home and neighborhood. In a civilization rapidly becoming more culturally pluralistic, resistance to overwhelmingly Eurocentric domination of social studies and language arts curricula in the schools will continue. About 5 billion of the projected 6 billion people on Earth are people with a non-Eurocentric conception of the world. Scholars in the social sciences, humanities, and teacher education in North America, who study minority-majority relations in the schools, now realize that the very terms "minority" and "majority" are changing when we speak of the demographic realities of the cultural configurations existent in most major urban and suburban educational systems. This is also true when we consider minority-majority relations in vast isolated rural or wilderness areas where those of western or northern European descent can be found to be "minorities" in the midst of concentrations of indigenous peoples. Many teachers will teach students whose values and views of the world are very different from their own, hence the relevance of teachers learning how to learn about human cultures and belief systems in order that they can study the lives and heritages of their students in the schools.

Many teachers of European ethnic heritage are having difficulty understanding the importance of the fact that North American society is becoming more culturally pluralistic. From a multicultural perspective, one of the many things course content seeks to achieve is to help all prospective teachers realize the importance of becoming lifelong learners. The knowledge base of multicultural education is further informed by the history of the struggle for civil rights in North American societies. Multicultural educational programming in teacher education programs seeks to alter how prospective teachers perceive society as a whole, not just its current minority members. We must take a broad view of multicultural education. Culturally pluralistic themes need to be apparent throughout teacher education programs and integrated into the knowledge bases of teacher education. Broadly conceived, multicultural education seeks to help members of all ethnic, cultural backgrounds to appreciate one another's shared human concerns and interrelationships; it should not be conceived as simply the study of minority cultural groups. Teachers need to be prepared in such a manner that they learn genuine respect for cultural as well as personal diversity.

Teachers should be prepared to take a global perspective of the world and to think critically about the issues confronting them, their students, and society as a whole (seen as part of an interdependent community of nations). Multicultural education should not be politicized. It should be a way of seeing the world as enriched by cultural and personal diversity. Preservice teachers should learn from case studies that exemplify and report on the differing cultural traditions in child rearing, entry into adulthood (rites of passage), and varying cultural styles of child-adult interaction in school settings.

The essays in this unit explore why it is important not to see multicultural education as just a political concept, but rather as an area of critical inquiry from which we can all learn alternative diverse styles of teaching appropriate to the learning styles and cultural backgrounds of students. The articles stress the importance of teachers being able to learn differing ways, share in social interaction in classroom settings, and to see the impact of race, gender, and social class on their ideas about themselves as teachers, how they perceive other teachers, and how they perceive their students.

This unit's articles are relevant to courses that focus on introduction to the cultural foundations of education, educational policy studies, history and philosophy of education, and curriculum theory and construction, as well as methods courses in all areas of teacher education programs.

# *Learning To Teach in Urban Settings*

Valerie Duarte and Thomas Reed

Teacher education programs throughout the United States are grappling with how to raise the achievement levels of children in diverse communities. The fact that urban schools show a downward trend in achievement levels among their student populations speaks to the gravity of the situation and brings to the forefront the need for more culturally responsive teachers in urban settings.

The challenge confronting urban schools results from a number of issues. Urban settings are historically more economically disadvantaged than suburban districts and therefore do not have the ability to offer competitive compensation packages to teachers. Urban schools also serve a student population that is characterized largely by poverty, and that is overwhelmingly minority (many non-English speaking). One of every three school-age children is from a minority background (National Center for Education Statistics [NCES], 2000), yet most are taught by white classroom teachers (National Education Association, 1997). The incongruity that exists between the student population and the curriculum being taught also speaks clearly to the need for more culturally responsive teachers (Gay, 2002). Furthermore, urban schools often experience a large turnover in their teaching staff from year to year, and so are unable to attract and retain highly qualified personnel (Oakes, Franke, Quartz, & Rogers, 2002). As a result, many urban classrooms are staffed with teachers who are new to the teaching field. Although these teachers' commitment to working with minority groups in urban settings may be strong, they often lack knowledge and understanding of the students' varied cultures (Gay, 2002; Sleeter, 2001).

Teacher candidates tend to view multicultural teaching primarily as planning "special events" outside of the everyday curriculum. For example, they might celebrate Black History Month in February by studying famous black Americans. Such a narrow view tends to distort children's understanding of culture as something separate and distinct from everyday life, reinforcing the notion that culture occurs outside of the classroom.

Teacher candidates need an understanding of urban cultures, as well as the pedagogy and skills that will help them implement a meaningful curriculum for urban students

> Teacher candidates need an understanding of urban cultures, as well as the pedagogy and skills that will help them implement a meaningful curriculum for urban students.

(Gay, 2002). They need to be more cognizant of the fact that a commitment to teach in urban settings goes beyond knowledge about the curriculum and how children learn and touches a much deeper issue—that of how to connect the curriculum to children's everyday lives. Teacher candidates need to make the classroom and the curriculum more congruent and more meaningful for children (Villegas & Lucas, 2002). A culturally responsive teacher uses the children's cultures and background experiences as instructional vehicles to make learning more effective. Research illustrates that connecting curriculum to culture can lead to improved academic achievement among diverse populations (Gay, 2002). Teachers cannot be expected to be culturally responsive in the classroom, however, if they are not adequately prepared with the necessary knowledge, skills, and dispositions.

Most universities require teacher candidates to take at least one course on multiculturalism (Artiles & McClafferty, 1998), sometimes at the beginning of the teacher education program. However, these courses may offer no more than a general awareness of the differences among cultures. It is difficult to determine accurately the impact of these courses, since studies regarding teacher candidates' particular beliefs and attitudes remain inconclusive (Sleeter, 2001). Nevertheless, it is clear that individual beliefs and attitudes are more likely to undergo change following in-depth investigation, dialogue, and continued support throughout the teacher education program. (Villegas & Lucas, 2002).

## Pre/Post Questionnaire

**Preparing Preservice Teachers for Diverse Communities**

Directions: Please address each of the questions below and answer as completely as you can.

1. Describe, in detail, the students, classroom, school, and neighborhood where the major segment of the student population would be considered part of a minority group.
2. How do you think children's cultural backgrounds affect achievement?
3. How would you modify instruction to meet the academic needs of children from diverse backgrounds?
4. How do you think students' physical and emotional needs affect achievement?
5. How would you address these physical and emotional needs in the classroom?
6. If you were offered a position to teach in an urban school, tell why you would or would not accept the offer.
7. Describe the learning experiences that you have had here at USCS that you feel prepared you for teaching in an urban setting.

*Figure 1*

## PURPOSE AND DESCRIPTION OF THE STUDY

In light of these challenges, the authors designed a project to address the need for more culturally responsive teachers. The teacher candidates in our program had limited background experiences in urban settings, making clear the need for a curriculum that provided a broader and more comprehensive view of what it means to teach in urban schools. In addition, candidates needed restructured field experiences, to help them decide whether or not they felt capable of meeting the challenge of teaching urban children.

Twenty early childhood education majors (18 female, 2 male; 19 white, 1 African American) enrolled in a 3-hour clinical experience conducted in a public school setting. During the fall semester, students completed an initial survey (see Figure 1) designed to reflect their attitudes, beliefs, and values towards teaching in urban settings. Upon their return in the spring semester, students were asked to volunteer for assignment in a rural school (control group) or an urban school (experimental group).

During the course of the spring semester, the students assigned at the urban school participated in two workshops given by a diversity expert in a school setting. Participants viewed, responded to, and reflected on two videos that were designed to raise social consciousness, and they read and reflected on two books covering diversity. Students assigned at the rural school received no additional training and support. At the conclusion of the semester, students in both groups revisited the initial survey.

The experimental group was assigned to an elementary school that is predominantly African American (98 percent). The school was selected for participation after researchers received a modest grant from the state department of education for developing partnerships. Funds from the grant were used to buy books, provide the diversity speaker with a stipend, and give classroom teachers a small stipend for their participation. Many of the teachers at this school had taught there for a number of years, and therefore were experienced with the norms of the culture in this community. A strong commitment to education was evident in the large number of after-school activities and parent activities that were held at the school.

A diversity expert from a neighboring school district was asked to conduct two workshops at the school site. Since our preservice teachers were mostly white middle-class candidates, we hoped the workshops would help them become more knowledgeable regarding the impact of culture on learning, while providing them with opportunities for discussion and reflection.

The two books selected for use with the experimental group were *And Don't Call Me a Racist!* (Mazel, 1998) and *White Teacher* (Paley, 2000), both chosen for their contributions to understanding diverse issues in and out of the public school arena. Teacher candidates were asked to respond to a series of questions based on each of these books.

Two selections also were made from the video series *Teaching Children Tolerance*. Teacher candidates were asked to view and respond to "A Time for Justice" (Guggenheim, 1992) and "Starting Small" (McGovern, 1997). Again, candidates were asked to respond to a series of questions based on each of these videos.

## FINDINGS

### Initial Survey

Students' responses to the initial questionnaire indicated that our teacher candidates held stereotypical attitudes and beliefs regarding minority children and minority neighborhoods. Typically, they described a minority neighborhood as being low-income, and populated by people of color and people who spoke a language different from theirs. They described the children as underachievers, having behavior and learning problems, and living in homes where the parents did not care about their learning. Schools were described as old and dirty with boring classrooms, insufficient resources, and ineffective learning programs. They believed that what was being taught in the school may not be reinforced in the home. The 20 candidates' opinions mostly dovetailed, and tended to support other research findings regarding white preservice students' attitudes (Sleeter, 2001).

Almost all of the students agreed that the home played a significant role in children's learning, as it is the foundation for creating the strong positive belief system needed for achievement. Many students reported that language was another important aspect to consider. However, they offered few specifics regarding how to modify instruction to meet the urban children's needs.

When asked about the effect of children's physical and emotional needs on learning, most of the students agreed that these areas were important, but again gave no specific suggestions as to how to address these needs. The general consensus was that children's most basic needs could be met by giving hugs, offering snacks, and being loving. Most of the comments were teacher-centered and addressed a need for teachers to become more involved in those interpersonal activities with children that broaden communication. Beyond that, however, they showed little evidence of having strategies in mind that would improve instruction.

When asked about making a commitment to teaching in an urban school, about half of the respondents said they would accept a position; they reasoned that teachers can make a difference in the quality of schools and in the lives of children, and what better place to be than where they are needed. Others appeared more interested in receiving a salary and stated that teaching in an urban setting was better than not teaching at all. Some respondents said they would decline the opportunity to teach in an urban setting, citing their opinion, that the children there are poorly behaved.

When asked to identify experiences from our program that may have prepared them for teaching in an urban setting, the teacher candidates were ambivalent. Some mentioned previous practicum experiences, a course in children's literature, and language classes. At least three candidates believed that this part of their education was lacking and reported having had no learning experiences that helped prepare them for teaching diverse populations.

## Responses to the Assigned Books

*White Teacher.* This book chronicles Vivian Paley's experiences as a white teacher in a predominantly black school. Teacher candidates were asked to read a selected chapter in the book and make a connection to their past experiences. Classroom management surfaced as a primary concern. Many students wrote of Paley's frustration regarding a perceived inability to be an effective classroom disciplinarian. The teacher candidates discussed, at some length, how children tend to carry "baggage" from home that makes it difficult to teach them and effectively manage classroom behavior. Teacher candidates also recognized that their lack of understanding of cultural terms and ethnic words and phrases contributed to the challenge of teaching.

*And Don't Call Me a Racist!* Teacher candidates were asked to read and respond to this book, which contains quotes (some historical) from famous and influential people regarding race. Students discussed what in the book made them angry, surprised, and proud. The comments varied widely, but many students were surprised about how often African Americans felt compelled to hide their color to get along in a white world. Many said they were impressed with the resilience, perseverance, and fortitude that African Americans exhibited in advancing the movement for racial equality.

Much of the rhetoric in this text—comments about selling slaves, blacks being inferior to whites, blacks being unable to think for themselves, the United States as a racist nation—angered the candidates. Several ideas in the readings made the candidates uncomfortable, chiefly: 1) being white affords you privileges unobtainable to minorities, 2) reverse discrimination is a way to make up for past atrocities, 3) the educated black person as a social monstrosity, and 4) some African Americans appear to suffer from a constant burden that never seems to go away. Several aspects made the candidates proud, beginning with the realization of all the gains regarding integration and equal opportunities that exist because of the civil rights movement, and that with a renewed emphasis on diversity, racism has a chance to be reduced further. Others thought that resisting old traditional viewpoints on an individual basis helped to reduce racism as a whole. However, what seemed to be most significant were the mentions of inspiring African Americans, such as Frederick Douglass, Oprah Winfrey, Colin Powell, Martin Luther King, Jr., and Maya Angelou.

## Responses to the Videos

*A Time for Justice.* The students watched this video chronicling the civil rights movement, and were asked to respond to a questionnaire about the video and discuss it in a group. Several aspects of the video disturbed the candidates, including the images of white police officers going unpunished after beating civil rights protesters, the killing of white men who advocated for civil rights, churches being bombed, children needing the escort of the National Guard to enter public schools, and separate public facilities and restaurants for white and blacks. One candidate remarked, "I didn't know it was that bad."

Students also were asked to indicate how watching this video gave them hope. Many of the respondents were impressed by the dedication and commitment from those involved in the civil rights movement. The bus boycotts and sit-ins also impressed upon the students the importance of following through on a commitment.

Finally, students responded to questions about what they envisioned their role to be in eradicating discrimination. Candidates responded that guiding children to appreciate others and accept differences was paramount. They also mentioned the importance of teaching history and awareness of the civil rights movement as part of the curriculum, establishing a just and fair classroom, and using multicultural reading materials. The teacher as a role model seemed to be at the forefront of the students' ideas as the primary way to reduce discriminatory behavior and actions among school children.

*Starting Small.* The teacher candidates also viewed *Starting Small,* which shows a number of kindergarten settings around the United States where teachers are engaged in instruction focused on gaining understanding of one another's cultural differences, as well as appreciating how people are alike. Candidates responded to another questionnaire. Their discussion centered around the activities that were presented in the video and how these activities would enhance curriculum. The candidates found the video offered valuable information specific to activities that could be done in early childhood classrooms to incorporate the students' cultural backgrounds. Most of the students believed that teaching tolerance and a respect for diversity should be the foundation of the curriculum. They added that one way to accomplish this goal would be to bring speakers from the community into the classroom to discuss their cultures, and by having the children share artifacts from their home cultures that are connected to curriculum areas (e.g., a quilt from a Native American group showing mathematical patterns).

## ENDING SURVEY

At the end of the spring semester, all 20 participants responded to the same questionnaire that they had been given in the fall. Their responses indicate that most had broadened their definition of what constituted an urban setting where the segment of student population was minority. Now, they recognized that all parents want the best for their children and that the circumstances of being at a low socioeconomic level do not necessarily indicate that children have poor ability or that schools are dysfunctional. At least one student indicated that some teachers have a preconceived notion regarding the achievement level of minority students that may negatively affect a teacher's expectations regarding achievement.

### Control Group

When asked about the impact of culture on achievement, students from the control group seemed to confuse cultural background for socioeconomic status and they continued to believe that culture and academic success were connected; in other words, they seemed to consider that children from a lower socioeconomic base are not as likely to reach the same achievement levels as children from higher socioeconomic groups. Those from, a lower socioeconomic base are not likely to have the same knowledge foundation to build on; a lack of valuable home learning experiences and learning materials for children to use before coming to school would therefore have a negative impact on the child's ability to perform in school.

When asked about how they would meet the academic needs of children from diverse backgrounds, the control group stated that many activities should be created to address these differences, but gave no specific ideas for instructional strategies. In addition, the control group appeared more aware that trying home circumstances make it difficult for children to achieve in school, and that children might seek fulfillment through less acceptable means. The control group recognized the need for teachers to maintain a positive attitude and be approachable, and stated that teachers should be helpful and not penalize students. They suggested that lesson plans should facilitate

children's growth and development, and that seeking a one-to-one relationship with a needy child and seeking assistance from school personnel were positive steps to take.

When asked whether they would accept a position to teach in an urban school, most of the participants responded "Yes," citing that all children need someone to care for them, that they wanted to make a difference, and that it's an opportunity to have a positive impact in the lives of children. One respondent said, "Yes, I am a teacher." We viewed these responses as altruistic, stemming from the idea that a teacher is a professional who has a duty to perform. However, two respondents replied "no"; one stated, "No, [I wouldn't accept the position] unless it was the only one offered."

The control group participants believed that previous practicum programs gave them the opportunity to learn about diversity. Both settings were primarily in schools populated by African American children.

### Experimental Group

Students in the experimental groups also appeared to have a much broader sense of what constituted teaching in an urban setting where the segment of the student population was minority. The respondents overwhelmingly noted that a child's background can affect achievement, and that minority children often have fewer learning experiences and less formally educated parents to help them at home. When asked about strategies needed to modify instruction, the experimental group offered clearly defined ideas, including: utilizing real-life scenarios that would make learning experiences more meaningful; presenting materials to accommodate different learning styles; utilizing multicultural and diverse literature to focus on issues supporting the minority experience; knowing more about the children and designing instruction to facilitate learning that includes their cultural background; modifying and adjusting instruction as needed; and providing one-on-one instruction and involving parents as classroom assistants, as well as keeping them informed about what is going on in the classroom. One respondent pointed out that "doing what benefits everyone" is key to any successful instructional strategy.

Most of the students agreed that children suffering from emotional distress because of their home circumstances will find it difficult to concentrate and focus on the task at hand while at school—they will be easily distracted, and may distract others as well. Teachers need to remember that when children come to school worried about family problems, their motivation to learn will be impaired. One respondent indicated that if teachers were aware of Maslow's hierarchy of needs and designed instruction to facilitate emotional development, students would be more likely to perform better.

The experimental group stated that teachers need to include activities focused on enhancing and building self-esteem among children, allowing time for talking about problems, and using play as a means to respond to problems. They mentioned safety as an important issue and stressed that children should feel safe coming to school and living in the community. They also stressed the importance of working with families by identifying community resources. Many of the suggestions centered on stressing to the family the need to seek help in solving a problem before the child is enrolled in school.

When asked about making a commitment to teach in an urban school, the experimental group reported overwhelmingly that this was what they wanted to do. This group showed a clear change in perception, expressing confidence in themselves with such comments as, "Yes, I have what it takes" and "Yes, because I expect to be the best," while the control group's support for acceptance of a position was the result of feeling it to be their responsibility as a teacher. Some respondents continued to be unsure, stating that they needed more experience, or that they felt as though they were not up to the challenge of teaching in an urban school.

The respondents credited previous methods and practicum experiences with providing them opportunities to learn about diversity issues. Even more so, they gave overwhelming credit to the workshops, mentors, and diverse activities provided through this project as a very significant part of their overall experience, and as the key to their growing confidence and desire to teach in urban settings.

## DISCUSSION

In this project, the authors sought information that would serve as a guide in preparing a stronger undergraduate program for teaching in urban settings. We recognized that a well-designed teacher education program is vital for increasing the number of culturally responsive teachers in schools, and it is our goal to ensure the readiness of teacher candidates as effectively as we can. We also recognize that due to candidates' limited experiences, we need to restructure field experiences to include opportunities for candidates to grow in the strategies needed to be successful in urban settings.

At the same time, we wanted candidates to examine their own beliefs and attitudes regarding teaching in diverse settings, and to be able to refine these same beliefs. We hoped that they would identify strategies that could be incorporated into their teaching styles and enhance their ability to teach in urban settings. Ultimately, we hoped to increase the percentage of participants who would feel comfortable accepting a teaching position in an urban setting.

We believe the experimental group very clearly found themselves to be better informed due to the opportunities built into the project. Research states that merely placing promising candidates in urban settings is not enough to ensure their success, or that their confidence and skills will grow. They also need opportunities to openly discuss their beliefs and actions with expert teachers in the classroom. The experimental group stated that they had learned more about how to deal with the community and cultural norms of the school population, citing specific ways in which children's needs should be met (e.g., providing food, keeping children safe). Their responses demonstrated a child-centered approach, whereas responses from the control group focused on teacher-centered actions (i.e., don't penalize, be positive, remember that teachers are there to be helpful).

The experimental group showed a change in perception about themselves as opposed to the control group, whose purpose was mainly the result of feeling that this was their responsibility as a teacher. The experimental group demonstrated a more sensitive disposition to the needs of children in urban settings and the project helped them make the choice to seek a position in an urban community.

## References

Artiles, A., & McClafferty, K. (1998). Learning to teach culturally diverse learners: Charting change in preservice teachers' thinking about effective teaching. *The Elementary School Journal, 98*(3), 189-211.

Gay, G. (2002). Preparing for culturally responsive teaching. *Journal of Teacher Education, 53*(2), 106-117.

Guggenheim, C. (1992). *A time for justice. America's civil rights movement* [video]. Montgomery, AL: Teaching Children Tolerance.

Mazel, E. (Ed.). (1998). *And don't call me a racist!* Lexington, MA: Argonaut Press.

McGovern, M. (1997). *Starting small. Teaching tolerance: A project of the Southern Poverty Law Center* [video]. Montgomery, AL: Teaching Children Tolerance.

National Center for Education Statistics. (2000). *Digest of educational statistics.* Washington, DC: Government Printing Office.

National Education Association. (1997). The status of American public school teachers, 1995-96. Washington, DC: Author.

Oakes, J., Franke, M., Quartz, K., & Rogers, J. (2002). Research for high-quality urban teaching: Defining it, developing it, assessing it. *Journal of Teacher Education, 53*(3), 228-235.

Paley, V. (2000). *White teacher* (3rd ed.). Cambridge, MA: Harvard University Press.

Sleeter, C. (2001). Preparing teachers for culturally diverse schools: Research and the overwhelming presence of whiteness. *Journal of Teacher Education, 52*(2), 94-106.

Villegas, A. M., & Lucas, T. (2002). Preparing culturally responsive teachers: Rethinking the curriculum. *Journal of Teacher Education, 53*(1), 20-33.

*Valerie Duarte* and *Thomas Reed* are Associate Professors, School of Education, University of South Carolina Spartanburg.

# Caught in a Bind:
## Student Teaching in a Climate of State Reform

**Janet Ferguson & Beverly Brink**

Student teaching may require student teachers to address the demands of two masters that often have very different expectations and philosophies. They are caught in a bind of being expected to implement methods advocated in university coursework while also being expected to fit into the classroom to which they are assigned. This bind is further complicated by the tensions inherent in school reform efforts. As schools try to meet the needs of every child, they have adopted all manner of innovations, very often competing with each other. For instance, multi-age classrooms can be instituted in districts that also prescribe leveled readers and ability grouping of children for instruction, ultimately defeating the purpose of multi-age classroom configurations. University expectations to implement literature-based assignments within a highly complex classroom such as a multi-age classroom can be further complicated by myriad demands on the student teacher.

In keeping with national trends, the State of Washington has mandated state standards, benchmarks, and high stakes testing at the fourth, seventh, and tenth grade levels. Test results are publicly reported by grade level, school, and district. Beginning in 2008, students unable to achieve mastery on the state mandated test will be denied a high school diploma. As a result, many schools carefully craft the curriculum to align with state standards and to ensure that students pass the state standards test. Schools serving large numbers of poor students, students whose first language is not English, and minority students who traditionally do not perform well on standardized tests are under particular pressure to raise test scores to expected levels.

Within this environment, we offer a social constructivist program of preservice teacher education on a branch campus of the state land grant university. Our program allows students to earn a Master's in Teaching (MIT) degree and K-8 certification. Our constructivist approach, in contrast to approaches based on teachers transmitting knowledge, requires preservice students to be active par-

ticipants in the formation of their own intellectual development and to evaluate their performance in terms of its effects on children, school, and society. The social nature of learning is strongly emphasized. Conversely, some educators believe that children who are at risk for school failure need structured, skill and drill types of reading and writing activities and offer direct instruction based on workbooks, basal readers, phonics drills, penmanship exercises, and writing experiences that focus on form rather than function (Allington & McGill-Franzen,1989). Student teachers whose coursework emphasizes social constructivism may suffer great anxiety in student teaching and may be judged ill prepared by mentor teachers and administrators who subscribe to such approaches.

State educational reform with its emphasis on standards, testing, and increased accountability has also exacerbated the dilemma of teacher educators. We also may be caught in a bind of competing beliefs when designing coursework. For example, literacy courses include a component to familiarize preservice students with the standards, benchmarks, evaluation procedures, and the lexicon of reform used by the state. Of more concern, however, is the diminished view of the teacher as curriculum maker who adapts to meet the strengths, needs, and interests of a particular group of children. New teachers will not be hired, we are told, for their ability to be creative, innovative, attuned to the needs of children or knowledgeable about how children learn but for their willingness to implement a curriculum designed by committees that align well with what will be tested in fourth, seventh and tenth grade. In the words of one principal, "Our teachers are not independent contractors."

This study took place at a suburban K-6 school that serves a large percentage of children considered at risk for school failure due to their poverty status. Following a Qualitative case Study design (Stake, 1995), our purpose was to describe a challenging student teaching context and investigate the outcomes for the student teachers.

## Literacy Coursework

In keeping with social constructivist philosophy, the literacy coursework in our MIT program is designed to prepare preservice teachers to implement a literacy program that has meaning making at its core. Reading and writing are viewed as mutually supportive interactive processes that are most successfully undertaken within the context of authentic communication. The program embraces a transactional model where learners are viewed as having rich prior knowledge and background and bring an innate ability and inclination to construct their own knowledge (Weaver, 1994). Student teachers operating out of the social constructivist view try to create rich environmental contexts and situations from which students can learn.

Our literacy course is blocked with a Social Context course to emphasize the social nature of learning. An emphasis on Bronfenbrenner's theory (1979) of the ecological nature of human development helps our MIT students understand the many layers of social influence on children.

## Supervision of Student Teachers

In supervising student teachers, we strive to be consistent with our constructivist goals by allowing student teachers to construct their own knowledge about learning and teaching, by adopting the role of supervisor-as-collaborator in creating knowledge about teaching and learning; by using a variety of data sources; and by taking a holistic approach over a series of lessons unfolding in an instructional cycle (Curley, 1999). We observe and conference with each student teacher weekly, and our weekly group seminars often include the mentor teachers.

## Placement Site

This K-6 elementary school is located in a rural/suburban area with a high percentage of working class families. It offers unique opportunities for studying student teachers' integration of literacy theory and practice in the field experience. There are a large percentage of children who have a high probability of educational failure due to their poverty status. It is a Title I school that has several block-grant programs including a breakfast program, summer reading program, after school program, weekly volunteer reading tutors, and a homework room which assists students with social and educational support from the staff and the community. The pressures of state mandated standards testing are strongly felt by teachers and administrators. Literacy instruction generally follows a transmission model directed by the teacher. Most students are expected to learn the same things at the same time. It is quite likely that the state mandated standards testing has increased teachers' emphasis on individual accountability and "doing one's own work."

## Participants and Data Collection

Two student teachers, Helen and Betty, who live near the school were placed there and volunteered to participate in the research project, which did not require any extra work of them. Their mentor teachers were Toni and Darlene, veteran teacher leaders in the school.

The student teachers' supervisor's observation and conference field notes from the supervision sessions were maintained throughout the school year (Wolcott, 1995). These notes tracked student teachers' areas of professional focus and goals, implementation actions, interactions with children and mentor teacher, and plans for moving forward (Curley, 1999). The student teachers kept dialogue journals as a method of promoting and assessing their reflectivity (Bolin, 1988). The literacy professor made field notes of direct observation of the student teachers and of participant observation with the principal, student teachers, mentor teachers, and children. Interviews of student teachers and interviews of mentor teachers were conducted during the fall semester and at the end of student teaching. Interviews were partially transcribed. Documents such as coursework assignments, lesson plans, school policies and program descriptions were also collected. Data were prepared and analyzed according to established qualitative methods (Erickson, 1986; Wolcott, 1995; Yin, 1994).

## Data Analysis and Findings

### Helen

Helen was placed in a fourth grade classroom with mentor teacher, Toni, who had sixteen years of teaching experience. Helen described Toni's instructional style as "teacher-oriented" where directions were clear and expectations for quality work were high. She described the mentor teacher's strengths as "structured, organized, and caring". Children were expected to comply with her rules. Work was to be completed individually with minimal movement and conversation. Her rationale for this instructional stance was that the state standards test demands "independent thinking."

In this classroom, five children were being medicated for Attention Deficit Disorder; one child was labeled Mildly Mentally Retarded and reading levels reportedly ranged from first to sixth grade. Pullout programs were intended to support the learning of children who were deemed behind grade level expectations. There was a reliance on textbooks, worksheets, kits, and the Accelerated Reader program. Candy was readily given out as a reward for compliant behavior and work that met the teacher's standards. Due to her "training as a special education teacher", Toni had systems to track students' misbehaviors and delinquent assignments. This documentation was utilized in briefing the principal and parents on students' progress, or lack thereof.

Helen was often left in charge of the classroom as Toni met regularly with the principal regarding a child labeled Behaviorally Disordered. Helen often expressed concern about this, fearful of the amount of responsibility she was given and both the legal and the ethical consequences of "messing up" due to her inexperience.

Initially Toni assumed that Helen would teach in much the same way that Toni taught. In the beginning, Helen complained to her university supervisor about the "mismatch" of teaching styles and whether she could "fit in." She was eager to please Toni and concerned about being able to "cover the material" in the same way that Toni did. On September 28, Helen wrote,

> I have been thinking about the type of classroom that I am working in and the type of classroom that I would like to have. The classroom that I am placed in is more direct instruction and independent working. I feel that it is important to have some direct instruction. Some things need to be taught step by step but most often the teacher needs to guide the children's learning and let them explore their thinking and work in groups or with partners on fun, exploratory, active projects.

However, as the fall semester progressed, Toni became more willing to allow Helen to use her own teaching style and methods. On November 14, Helen wrote,

> I enjoy having time to run the classroom by myself. This gives me opportunities to reinforce my own skills, practice monitoring, handle problematic situations, and implement some of the ways that I would have children participate. I feel more comfortable to do things and handle situations the way I would in my own classroom. I don't have to always be worrying that I will be contradicting what Toni would say or do.

Toni was also very supportive and frequently complimented Helen publicly. She found many ways of calling attention to Helen's competence with the student teaching supervisor, other university visitors to the campus, the principal, and other teachers. She would often say, "I'm so lucky to have Helen (in my classroom)."

### Betty

Betty was placed in a K-2 classroom of 54 students with Darlene. This class was taught by two teachers, only one of whom was involved in mentoring her. Betty described Darlene's strengths as "the ability to think ahead, flexibility, spontaneity and enthusiasm, and classroom management techniques." Of the 54 children enrolled in the class, one was labeled Behaviorally Disordered and two were labeled Developmentally Delayed. Betty also noted "many children from dysfunctional family environments" that include drug abuse and jailed parents. There

seemed to be a loss of empathy for the situations of many children and an almost 'punishing' attitude toward them.

Betty initially described the classroom as "teacher directed" but "somewhat chaotic" as the 54 children were flexibly grouped and regrouped throughout the two adjoining classrooms. Generally an effort was made to group older children with younger children so the older ones could "model" behaviors for the younger children. For the first months of student teaching, Betty had difficulty learning the many names and the complicated routines and schedules of this classroom. The frequent use of phonics worksheets was a real problem for her. Although a definite management system was in place, Betty observed, "teaching was often interrupted" by the need to redirect children to appropriate behaviors and routines. A token economy of stickers accumulated toward a reward from the "goodie box" was utilized.

Although the mentor teacher subscribed mainly to skills-based teaching herself, she indicated she was entirely open to Betty trying out methods of her choice. Following Darlene's practice, Betty was required to have the first grade students complete a phonics worksheet every day. Initially she had a difficult time managing the classroom. The children who were bored and/or unable to complete the worksheets independently often misbehaved. In her November 30 journal, Betty wrote,

> I had my first chance to teach phonics but I don't think it went too well. The ones closest to the math calendar wall kept turning around to play with the wall objects. Others toward the back of the circle were playing with each other or turning around to watch the second graders do math.

With help from her supervisor, Betty found ways to link the concepts and skills of the individual worksheets with the children's prior knowledge and to extend the learning with creative activities. She invited children to work cooperatively in pairs and later in groups of four for certain lessons, incorporating constructivist principles into traditional approaches.

Initially hesitant and self-conscious, Betty's confidence soared with the success of her phonics lessons and with the praise and support from Darlene. As Betty utilized manipulatives and continued to build on children's prior knowledge, she had more success with teaching. This further built her confidence and she began to express herself more naturally. As the semester progressed, she gained more and more confidence in her ability to dramatize, sing, dance and incorporate games into her instruction. Classroom management problems decreased as children became more cooperative, attentive and engaged. Betty wrote in her journal on February 21,

> My phonics lesson was fun. I taught the consonant blend "th" and had students make a thumbprint and then make an animal out of their prints. Then they wrote words with the "th" blend in it or

a sentence using those words. Wish I would have had them guess the word "thumb" on their wall chart before the thumbprint activity.

Finally on March 14, Betty wrote,

Phonics was with a workbook page Darlene wanted me to use. I tried to make it interesting but hard to do. I asked for lots of help so they remained engaged.

### Collaborative Project

Both Betty and Helen grasped the social nature of learning and were thus committed to having children work cooperatively on projects. Helen wrote in her journal on October 10,

I feel that it is important that children are able to work with other children, share their reasoning, and help each other problem solve. I think that children should always be able to ask others for help when they have a question.

Given their commitment to collaboration, it was not surprising that Betty and Helen decided to work together on their required action research project and to include the children in their collaboration. The action research project is a College of Education requirement for obtaining a master's degree. It is undertaken during the spring semester and culminates with a formal defense before a faculty committee.

Part of the school's improvement plan focused on improving writing achievement. Both Toni and Darlene had worked with Helen and Betty in planning for writing instruction that would satisfy writing goals and individual student portfolio requirements. These included narrative writing for both first graders and fourth graders. In discussing writing instruction with the student teachers, the mentor teachers expressed frustration with the lack of ability, background, and previous instructions for these two groups of children. According to both Darlene and Toni, the children seemed to make little progress on writing tasks and appeared unmotivated to complete assignments.

Helen and Betty's collaborative action research project had fourth grade students acting as tutors for first and second grade students in creating a piece of narrative writing. Students met with each other for a half-hour one or two days a week for a period of 14 weeks. Each session focused on a particular step of the narrative writing process; brainstorming, creating a graphic organizer, drafting, revision, editing, publishing, and sharing. Prior to joint sessions, fourth grade students received a mini-lesson on the day's writing focus for their tutees as well as their own stories. Through analysis of surveys, their own and students' reflective journals, writing artifacts, and teacher interviews, Betty and Helen concluded that the project did enhance the academic skills and motivation for writing for both groups. From Helen's journal: "I noticed today that my kids were all working away on

their stories. No one asked the page limit." Off-task behavior was minimal and children were frequently "utterly engaged" in their writing together. A severely disabled fourth grader who had been unable to produce a coherent piece of writing all year, later composed a book about her cat. Both Toni and Darlene made accommodations in their class schedules so that the second graders and the fourth graders could work together and offered frequent verbal support for the project to Betty and Helen. Toni indicated to Helen that she "might" use this technique in the future.

### Summary of Findings

- When student teachers were placed in classrooms in which there was great disparity in the philosophy and methods advocated by the teacher preparation program and the mentor teacher, threatening and stressful situations arose.

- When the mentor teacher was supportive and willing to allow the student teacher to develop her own teaching style and repertoire of techniques, as Toni and Darlene were, students, mentor teacher, and student teacher are all likely to benefit.

- With guidance, student teachers accepted responsibility for children's learning rather than resorting to blaming their poverty status for their failure.

- Given a collaborative style of supervision, student teachers found ways to implement instructional strategies learned in their literacy coursework and continued to embrace constructivism within a transmission-oriented curriculum.

- Within this complex student teaching environment, student teachers successfully completed student teaching amid lavish praise from their mentor teachers and the principal, the student teaching supervisor, and university faculty who heard the successful defense of their collaborative action research project. The district hired both Betty and Helen as full time teachers for the following year.

## Discussion

Student teacher placements in schools where prevailing beliefs and instructional strategies differ substantially from the teacher preparation coursework are common. On the one hand, student teachers may be ill prepared to implement the expected curriculum and teaching methods of the school; while on the other, the university supervisor and methods instructors have expectations for student teaching experiences they may be unable to meet. Since the university supervisor and the mentor teacher are powerful gate keepers, this further complicates the situation for the student teacher.

Some universities, mindful of the difficulties of this situation, choose to ignore it and continue to hope for better matches between placements and teacher preparation programs in the future. Others grapple with the realities of philosophical mismatches.

In our experience, the bind can be alleviated when methods instructors are aware of the contexts in which student teachers operate. Acquainting preservice teachers with state mandated standards, benchmarks, testing procedures, and the reform lexicon is helpful as is the inclusion of "test taking literacy." Student teachers want us to address directly how constructivist principles of literacy instruction can be incorporated into a transmission-oriented curriculum by providing ideas and strategies for blending the two worlds. For example, skills often taught by direct instruction can be taught in the context of self-selected reading and read alouds through modeling and demonstration by the teacher.

The university supervisor can further assist student teachers to connect theory to practice by having them reflect on the gray areas—i.e., how to build a lesson around a mandated, skills-based worksheet or textbook excerpt. The required material becomes one tool to achieve broader learning goals that are couched within constructivist principles. The student teaching supervisor is in a unique position to mediate the differences in teaching philosophies and techniques with the student teacher by finding such "soft spots or gray areas." Rather than sending our students out into the school and simply hoping for the best, (with the expectation that many of them will simply "hit the wall" shortly, if not immediately), we have found that if we discuss the clashes openly in class, equip students with constructivist principles, require inquiry through action research, and supervise the student teaching process to encourage a theory to practice connection, we can improve their chances of success.

The role of the mentor teacher is also significant, here. Mentor teachers, by and large, want the student teacher to fit into their routines and perspectives (Koerner, 1992). For many student teachers, this is a difficult task. Ideally, the mentor teacher provides a low degree of direction for the student teacher while offering a high level of support (Ferguson & Peck, 1996) as Toni and Darlene did. Low direction allows the student teacher to try out ideas and experiment with methods and techniques that make sense to her. Mentor teachers create a high level of support when they encourage, praise, and provide positive feedback to the student teacher for experimentation and risk-taking. Unfortunately, this ideal of a high support, low direction student teaching environment, is rare.

We are encouraged to continue to supervise, and thus, mediate such engagement. We saw student teachers take a critical, yet sympathetic, view toward what they saw and did themselves. They recognized the disparities and found ways to treat children differently. We saw them taking the required textbooks and workbooks and utilizing them in creative ways. In fact, they were successfully negotiating the "swamp land" between theory learned at the university and practices required in some public schools by making up their own minds about who the children were, what influences they had to contend with, and what strategies worked best in their individual settings. By offering alternative perspectives such as Bronfenbrenner's ecological model (1994) of who children are and under what circumstances they are required to develop, student teachers seemed more likely to consider alternatives to transmission methods. We find that we are inspired to recommit to a philosophy of constructivism in preparing student teachers for the realities of teaching in the 21st Century.

# References

Allington, R. & McGill-Franzen. A. (1989). School response to reading failure: Chapter 1 and special education students in grades 2, 4 & 8. *Elementary School Journal, 89,* 529-542.

Bolin, F. S. (1988). Helping student teachers think about teaching. *Journal of Teacher Education, 39*(2), 48-55.

Bronfenbrenner, U. (1979). *The ecology of human development.* Cambridge, MA: Harvard University Press.

Curley, J. L. (1999). *Preparing student teachers for diverse classrooms: A case study of constructivist supervision.* Unpublished doctoral dissertation. Eugene, OR: University of Oregon.

Erickson, F. (1986). Qualitative research on teaching. In M. Wittrock (Ed.), *Handbook of research on teaching* (pp. 119-161). New York: Macmillan.

Ferguson, J. L. & Peck, C. A., (1996). *Toward a competence orientation to student teacher supervision: An action research report.* Unpublished manuscript, Washington State University, Vancouver.

Koerner, M. ( 1992). The cooperating teacher: An ambivalent participant in student teaching. *Journal of Teacher Education, 43.* 46-56.

Stake, R. E. (1995). *The art of case study research.* Thousand Oaks, CA: Sage.

Weaver, C. (1994). *Reading process and practice.* Portsmouth, NH: Heinemann.

Wolcott, H. (1994). *Transforming qualitative data: Description, analysis, and interpretation.* Thousand Oaks, CA: Sage.

Yin, R. K., (1994). *Case Study Research: Design and methods* Applied Social Research Methods Series, Vol. 5. Beverly Hills, CA: Sage.

*Janet Ferguson is an assistant professor of education at East Stroudsburg University, East Stroudsburg, Pennsylvania. Beverly Brink is an assistant professor of education at Washington State University, Vancouver, Washington.*

From *Teacher Education Quarterly,* Fall 2004, pp. 55-64. Copyright © 2004 by Caddo Gap Press. Reprinted by permission.

# Exploring the Perspectives of Teacher Educators of Color:

## What Do They Bring to Teacher Education?[1]

**A. Lin Goodwin**
*Teachers College, Columbia University*

Much has been written about the paucity of teachers of color[2] in the profession (Cochran-Smith, 2004; Dilworth & Brown, 2001; Gordon, 2000). The majority of teachers in the U.S. are White, female, monolingual, and middle class (Goodwin, 1997; Rong & Preissle, 1997; Zimpher & Ashburn, 1992); only 13% of teachers identify as persons of color (Dilworth & Brown, 2001). The concern about the limited presence of teachers of color is typically related to the increasing numbers of children of color in U.S. schools (Hodgkinson, 2001) and continuing evidence that their levels of achievement fall far below that achieved by their White peers (Gay, 2000; Goodwin, 2002; Villegas & Lucas, 2002). There is general agreement that children of color—and indeed all children—benefit from interaction with teachers who represent the diversity that is increasingly characterizing the U.S. population and who bring a culturally diverse mindset into the classroom and the curriculum (Dilworth & Brown, 2001).

There is also agreement that, despite numerous efforts to recruit teachers of color, the proportion of teachers of color is not likely to achieve parity with that of students of color and that the profession cannot rely on teachers of color solely to support the development of children of color (Gay, 2000). Thus, there has been a great deal of attention paid in the past twenty years to preparing White teachers to work with children of color in culturally responsive ways.

Most teachers continue to receive their preparation from teacher education programs in schools and colleges of education. This begs the question—who are these teachers in preparation studying with? Who are they learning from? Demographic data reveal that the percentage of teacher educators of color is equally as dismal as the percentage of teachers of color. The teacher education professoriate is dominated by European American men and women, specifically, 88% are White and 81 % of these are between 45 and 60 years old (Ladson-Billings, 2001). This means that most teacher educa-

tors are quite distant from their own P-12 classroom experience and teacher preparation (if they had these experiences to begin with), and are not likely to have first-hand knowledge of teaching children of color, especially in urban and central city schools. What we have then is a national phenomenon whereby a majority White, and monolingual, teaching force is being taught by a majority White, and "culturally encapsulated" (Melnick & Zeichner, 1997, p. 23) teacher education force, even while the nation's classrooms become more black and brown, immigrant and non-English speaking.

This study explored the perspectives of a group of teacher educators of color in an effort to capture their perceptions of teaching and teacher education. The driving purpose behind the study was to find out what teacher educators of color bring to their work and to the teaching profession—what are their experiences, goals, intentions, passions, challenges and hopes—and how do they see themselves in relation to their White peers? Seven teacher educators were interviewed with each interview running about an hour. Respondents were either invited to participate in the study or identified through a nomination process, using three criteria: each had to be (1) a person of color, with (2) prior experience as a teacher educator in a variety of capacities who expressed (3) willingness to participate in the study.

Each was asked three questions: (1) Describe your perspective as a teacher educator of color; (2) Describe at least two significant experiences which have shaped your perspective as a teacher educator of color; and (3) Describe the ways in which your perspective as a teacher educator of color influences your work. Data were sorted according to the research questions and then examined for major themes, using a constant comparative method (Strauss & Corbin, 1998).

Together, the group represented the four major visible racial/ethnic groups (Carter & Goodwin, 1994) in this country, specifically Latina (2: Columbian; Mexican American), African American (2), Asian American (2: Japanese; Chinese American), and

Native American (1). The sample was also all female although gender was not a criterion for selection. All the respondents have had prior teaching experience either in the elementary (5) or secondary (2) grades, and described serving as teacher educators in a variety of capacities including as cooperating or mentoring teachers (4), supervisors of preservice (4) and/or inservice teachers (3), and as college- or graduate-level instructors (3). One respondent had been the director of a teacher education program.

While years of experience in the education field ranged from 27 to five and a half years, seven of the five were very experienced with more than fifteen years in the profession. At the time of the study, all seven respondents were working in colleges or graduate schools of education—five as professors, one as an instructor. The one respondent not actively teaching was engaged in teacher education research, but had most recently been a teacher educator and spoke of herself in that capacity[3]. All seven women defined teacher education as their primary responsibility or priority.

To gain a sense of the level of diversity of the setting within which each respondent worked, respondents were asked to identify other faculty of color colleagues as well as to provide the percentage of students of color at their institutions. One respondent spoke programmatically and indicated there were no other faculty of color in her program. The rest of the respondents talked in institutional terms with other teacher educators of color ranging in number from two to twelve (when instructors were included) or two to six (professorial rank only). All the respondents indicated that they were one of a small number of faculty, which is in keeping with a predominantly White and male teacher education professoriate (Fuller, 1992; Irvine, 1992; Ladson-Billings, 2001).

In terms of students, respondents either based their response on their particular program (e.g., secondary social studies, early childhood/elementary) or on the general *preservice* student teacher population at their institution. Individual program percentages reported were much higher and ranged from 20 to 28 percent preservice students of color (one exception was the bilingual certification program which was reported to have 75% students of color). In contrast, institutional percentages of preservice students of color were reported to be much lower, ranging from less than one percent to five percent of the student body. Thus, institutional figures were more reflective of national trends that show students of color entering teacher education at very low rates (Cochran-Smith, 2004; Dilworth & Brown, 2001; Fuller, 1992; Gordon, 2000).

## Findings

### Perspectives of Teacher Educators of Color

The discussion of findings that follows is organized according to the three interview questions. Question one—*Describe your perspective as a teacher educator of color*—asked respondents to offer their perspectives in terms of (a) what schools of education should emphasize in their preparation of teachers, (b) the skills and knowledge they feel teachers should possess, (c) the skills and knowledge they feel teacher educators should pos-

sess, (d) the kinds of field experiences to which they feel student teachers should be exposed, (e) how they feel their perspectives compare to the views of their European-American colleagues, and (f) how/if they feel their perspectives are acknowledged or supported by their colleagues and/or institution. In sorting through the responses to question 1, it appeared that respondents did not really differentiate between probes (a) and (b) and so the responses to these two components of the question were collapsed.

*What should schools of education emphasize in their preparation of teachers, and what skills and knowledge should teachers possess?* Respondents identified a wide range of skills and knowledge including a strong grounding in teaching methods, informed decision-making, conflict resolution skills, ability to integrate or connect subject matter, flexibility, problem solving, the capacity for continuous professional development and growth, ability to work collaboratively, knowledge of trends in the field or profession, communication skills, curiosity, knowledge of student development or how children "feel, respond and learn," and leadership skills. None of these skills or kinds of knowledge was mentioned by more than two respondents. Thus, it appeared that respondents did not necessarily agree on the essential skills and knowledge for teachers, even while those they did outline most teacher educators would not argue against.

However, there were two points of convergence where respondents demonstrated a high level of agreement. First, all the respondents agreed that it is important for schools of education to ensure that teachers acquire deep subject matter knowledge. Knowledge of content and the structure of the disciplines were uniformly considered important by all the respondents. Second, respondents all were in agreement that teachers should be aware of the cultural dimensions of practice and the implications of diversity for instruction. Everyone in the sample agreed that teachers should have knowledge of culturally diverse groups. This knowledge was defined as *specific* knowledge about the lives and ways of groups labeled as "different" in this country, *political-historical* knowledge, and *community* knowledge.

First, respondents spoke generally of "cultural knowledge," "sensitivity to 'others'… awareness of stereotypes," "knowledge of different people, different ethnic groups, knowledge of diversity," but punctuated these general principles with specific emphases such as "understanding children of color and the circumstances they are in," acquiring "knowledge of students' development, cultures, languages, and access to resources," and "having a real sense of the history of the culture, [being] well-versed in the literature that has emerged from that community."

Second, respondents defined cultural knowledge as political knowledge and intimated a relationship between cultural understanding and positive social change for children in their use of terms such as "social responsibility," "social action," "advocacy" and "urgency" in their descriptions. Their responses emphasized the institutionalized nature of oppression and "the moral dimension of education." This translates into teachers "finding ways of addressing the issues of discrimination and its consequences," and "understanding policies that affect schooling as we know it at different historical junctures" and "how the structures of schooling promote inequality."

Finally, three of the group tied cultural understanding to the community, both in terms of creating community and relating to children through knowledge of the communities to which they belong. In the words of one respondent, teachers need to simultaneously "build community in the classroom…[and make a] commitment to working with the community long term." According to this teacher educator, "home-school relationships give [teachers] the opportunity to understand the nature or character of the problems [teachers] are faced with." Another respondent emphasized knowing "how to talk to parents," while a third underscored knowledge of "where children are or what each is about."

Respondents clearly did not define culture as merely a source of content, or as a quality simply to be celebrated, but expressed concern with the long history of differential and unequal schooling experiences as well as inadequate access to resources endured by children of color and poverty (cf. Carter & Goodwin, 1994). These teacher educators emphasized how important it is for teachers to "make things more culturally relevant when children are different (culturally) from themselves," but also pointed out that:

> Something explicit must be said/done about cultural difference so that teachers do not get reinforcement for the idea that 'everyone's the same after all'. They are (the same) and they aren't, and teachers need to understand this in a profound way.

*What skills and knowledge should teacher educators possess?* In most cases, respondents began by stating that teacher educators should possess skills and qualities similar to those they consider necessary for teachers. However, in each case, respondents also added additional skills and knowledge they deemed specifically pertinent for teacher educators, namely teaching knowledge, knowledge of diverse contexts, and political knowledge. Knowledge of teaching was mentioned by six of the seven respondents: "strong knowledge base on teaching, curriculum development," "ability to demonstrate a range of teaching skills," "proficiency with teaching," etc. Respondents seemed to agree that "teaching experience would be nice" or that "teaching experience is important."

Respondents also specified that teacher educators should have experience in particular settings, such as "teaching experience in varied school settings (i.e., monocultural, multicultural, high SES, low SES)," or experiences with "inner city or something that is culturally different, something where there are potential inequities." One teacher educator expressed a strong sentiment that teacher educators "should have to teach in an urban school"

Last, respondents stressed that teacher educators should "have a broader understanding of the social/political context of our society and how schooling has been inequitable." The notion of having a political or moral stance was evident in the responses of five of the seven teacher educators. This means understanding that "teaching is a value-laden and moral activity" and that teacher educators need to be able to "talk about

different subject matter such as race, racism, values, etc.," and should be "politically and socially involved in issues related to diverse populations." The words of one member of the group were especially pointed:

> Teacher educators should possess a moral commitment to justice and equity. Once that underlines our work, then we can make our advisement, curriculum approaches and content, selection of resources, and evaluation strategies be student-centered and socially responsible.

*What kinds of field experiences should student teachers be exposed to?* Respondents were of several minds when it came to field experiences. However, they all agreed that students should be exposed to as wide a variety of settings as possible. Nonetheless, definitions of "variety" differed. One respondent was very explicit:

> Students should have at least one field experience in each of the following:
> (1) a school setting with at least 50% students of color
> (2) a school setting that is facing many challenges (i.e., economic, political, racial and/or organizational)
> (2) a school setting that is in the process of school improvement.

Others spoke more generally of "a variety of classrooms" or "variety is key." However, no matter how respondents defined "variety," they each indicated in some way that it is important for student teachers to gain experience with diverse populations. For example, one respondent advocated "several experiences in a variety of contexts with students of mixed ethnic and racial groups," while another stated,

> My own bias over the years has been to expose all students to public schools, preferably those that teach something useful about the real world of education. Today that means having at least some cultural diversity, including racial and ethnic diversity in urban areas.

Another respondent felt that field experiences should be those that demonstrate "a commitment to multiculturalism." Two other respondents emphasized involvement with the students' community outside of school; thus student teachers would be engaged in "community service, working with students in non-academic circumstances" which would allow them to "get a different take on the conditions, the difficulties with which families must deal." Thus, the range of responses offered not withstanding, six of the seven respondents articulated the importance of diverse field placement settings.

*How do your perspectives regarding all the above compare to the views of your European American colleagues?* This question drew a unanimous response. Respondents uniformly expressed differences of perspective or priority when they compared themselves to their European American counterparts. Invariably, these differences stemmed from the way these teacher educators of color define priorities given the unique cultural lens through which each views the world. As one respondent said:

I find that culturally I have been influenced by a vision of teaching that calls for paying attention to the whole person and I have found that to be or not to be the case with teachers from all groups. Maybe it is a philosophical perspective about the all-encompassing nature of teaching, as a moral act and not a technical profession.

Questions or issues of culture and race were identified as prominent departure points. Respondents felt their European American colleagues "pay lip service to it (diversity);" and their commitments to diversity are "on the surface," "it's PC to say something like that." According to respondents, for European American faculty, because "it's an issue of PC… they are going to go along to some extent," yet "when they pick a school or experience, it has nothing to do with race, poverty, they don't apply what they say they believe in." Respondents also stated that their position "as a member of an oppressed group in society" meant that they were "generally more interested in 'difference' than my European American colleagues" and understood the importance of not "los[ing] sight of micro-social issues." Being able to look at society through different eyes also meant being "more willing to see the relevance of discriminatory practices than they (European American colleagues) are, to see the hierarchies that may follow." Overall, these teacher educators of color mistrusted "how hard they (European American colleagues) work to get at [diversity issues]," and perceived that "as long as it's (diversity issues) superficial and they don't have to do anything, it's okay."

Respondents also spoke at length about several shared experiences: they defined themselves as constantly "beating the drum" in support of issues of culture and diversity in the face of a perceived reluctance on the part of White colleagues to work in urban schools; they spoke of European American colleagues' "narrow focus" which cannot adequately prepare student teachers for the real world of teaching; and they expressed concern about teacher education curricula centered on "the Western canon approach." There was sometimes a touch of sadness in respondents' answers when they described what they perceive to be a lack of caring on the part of their European American colleagues: "One of the things I think is missing is compassion; if they [European American colleagues] don't have it, they can't teach it." Respondents saw this lack of caring as specific to communities of color.

One respondent commented that she has "had a hard time convincing my colleagues that inner city teachers deserve access to resources," while another noted that "the most important distinction" in her 25 years of experience between teacher educators of color and those who are European American "has been [the] distinction of commitment to making a change in the community. I see a passion (in European American teacher educators) for producing students who can read and write but I don't see commitment to community transformation."

Because this study is based on perception and self report, there might be the temptation to minimize the power of the feelings articulated by these seven teacher educators of color, to accuse them of being too "sensitive" or "radical" or of misinterpreting the context in which they each work. Yet, it is

important to acknowledge that perceptions of reality are expressions of how reality is defined and experienced. What then becomes clear from these responses is that these respondents feel their differences keenly and do not see their practice and commitments as aligned with those of their White colleagues.

The lack of philosophical or professional congruence respondents seemed to feel with their White colleagues was not reflected in the level of support they perceived to be available. Their answers to the question, *Are your perspectives acknowledged and supported by your colleagues and/or institution?* were not uniform. Four of the group either felt that their views were consistent with institutional philosophy and they were therefore "ideologically supported" or that they felt themselves to be personally respected. Two respondents expressed varying levels of support from some to none, while the remaining respondent expressed a complete absence of support to the extent that she believes her views have "cost me greatly." Thus, the majority of respondents believed themselves to be supported by their colleagues and/or institution, which is curious given the isolation and conflict they expressed in response to the previous question. One explanation may be that there may be support for their views in theory, but that there is a gap between theory and practice so that in their daily' work they are engaged in forwarding an agenda that appears to have few takers.

### Significant Shaping Experiences

The second question asked respondents to *Describe at least two significant experiences which have shaped your perspective as a teacher educator of color.* Respondents were invited to choose any experiences from any period in their lives. Since each story was unique and space does not allow the recounting of all fourteen, analysis took the form of trying to identify themes that seemed to characterize the stories. Three themes emerged. The first theme seemed to be embedded in childhood experiences of "otherness." Four of the seven respondents recalled specific moments during their formative years when they felt the pain of being different. One respondent remembered being called racial names by children who spat on her and threw gravel at her. When she went to her teacher for solace and informed her that she had been called racial names, her teacher responded by saying, "That's okay, that's what you are." The other respondents talked more generally of feeling "conspicuous as a school child" or "experiencing isolation…being a student of color."

A second theme was the impact of teaching experiences when four respondents were made acutely aware of the deficit or negative views fellow teachers had of children of color. One teacher educator remembered how a White teacher commented on how "Ray-ray's hair smelled funny" because of the "hair grease he was using." The respondent (who, like "Ray-ray," is African American) said she thought to herself that if she hadn't been there to intervene and explain, the teacher would have assumed that something was wrong with Ray-ray or that he wasn't clean. She concluded her story by saying, "It dawned on me how little White folks know about other folks, how inattentive they are and how willing they are to think there's something wrong with you." Another respondent recalled a poignant tale involving one of her students:

> I was twenty-five and taught in East Harlem. I was asked to place a student in a class for speech-impaired and slow learners. I gave him the required tests in his native language. He was not speech impaired, nor a slow learner. I explained that I could not sign the recommendation. I was asked to resign. I brought up [my] training and certification as a translator and interpreter and threatened to bring in lawyers in defense of the child. I also spoke to the parents, got him a scholarship at a local parochial school. His parents took him out of school. Then I resigned, but in my resignation I made sure the child's ability to benefit from schooling was not going to be harmed by this school. When this child got to fifth grade he went on to one of the selective middle schools and then to Bronx Science (a highly selective school in New York city). He graduated from Cornell and is now a biologist with a drug company. This is the child I carry in my mind when I think what a teacher needs to know and be able to do.

Yet another respondent spoke emotionally of an entire teaching career spent with children of color and a majority of White teaching colleagues and being confronted with "the blatant ignorance as well as the almost perverse pleasure that seemed to be taken in [the failures of] children in these areas that was so egregious, so offensive, so appalling."

The consequence of memories characterized by the two themes described above seemed to be that respondents felt compelled to become advocates for children of color. Members of the group spoke of feeling that "something has to be done, people can't do this to children," that their colleagues needed to be made aware of their own "insensitivity, stereotypes and ethnocentric ideas" and of "not wanting my students of color to experience that (isolation)." These memories strengthened respondents' resolve to fight for children.

The third theme could be termed "awakenings." Five respondents were "awakened" to the culturally grounded nature of teaching as a result of their own experiences as students or faculty in higher education. One respondent talked about finally working at an institution where the student body is diverse and she is "part of a faculty of color" which has made her feel "unusually supported." Quite the opposite is true for another respondent who was teaching predominantly White students at a predominantly White institution. She characterized her students as "isolated and parochial" and realized that "things haven't changed much since I went through (teacher preparation)." As a result, she has had "very disturbing thoughts about who's going into teaching." Still another respondent recalled being introduced to sociolinguistics and ethnography, which enabled her to think about her teaching in a whole new light. She said she realized "I could have been much more powerful in the beginning (of her teaching career)" if she had then what she possesses now, the tools necessary to come to know different communities in deeper, more meaningful ways.

In each case, the stories appear as sign posts on each respondent's journey toward a pedagogy that meets the needs of a diverse population of students whether P-12 or post-secondary. As persons who do not fit the cultural mainstream, their own experiences as children have given them firsthand knowledge of what it feels like to be defined as "other." As teachers, they were able to then look at schooling practices through culturally sensitized eyes and recognize inequitable practices and injustice. As adults they are now able to confront racism, discrimination and inequality because they are equipped with tools, knowledge and strategies that were not available to them as children; as adults and professionals they have found their critical voice. It seems safe to say that given their childhood experiences, these respondents are uniquely positioned to empathize with students of color because they have been where these students now are. They may also be better able to discern hidden potential in children of color simply because they themselves had much potential as learners, talents that may have escaped the eyes of mainstream educators. These stories are the foundation of culturally grounded and culturally responsive practice.

### The Influence of Perspective

Finally, respondents were asked to *Describe the ways in which your perspective as a teacher educator of color influences your work.* In answering this question, respondents were guided to think in terms of teaching, advisement and supervision. They were also asked if they felt their practices differ when working with students of color as opposed to White students.

*Teaching.* Six of the seven respondents were able to articulate ways in which their teaching is influenced by their perspectives as persons of color. As one teacher educator said, "being a person of color influences everything that I do." Respondents shared that they "select readings differently from faculty not of color" and "try to include studies or articles about issues of difference—race, gender, linguistic difference" or "texts or articles that are written by authors of color and/or represent the perspectives of people of color." They also consider the settings where student teachers will work and "choose materials that will help [them] work in different environments and not feel scared." The idea of seeing with different or "racialized eyes" (Goodwin, 2001) was mentioned again; respondents expressed the belief that they "tend to see some blatant inequities that other people just miss" and in their classes they "tend to focus more on trying to get students to see exceptions to the rule... to ask hard question . . . raise controversial issues." The one respondent who did not specify ways in which her culture and race influence her teaching works in bilingual education and stated that everything she does is grounded in who she is racially and culturally and in the central role she feels culture plays in schooling.

*Advisement.* When it came to advisement, respondents were less likely to talk in terms of what they do as faculty of color and more likely to talk in terms of how students of color perceive them. Therefore, it seemed appropriate to collapse the responses to this question with their comments regarding how they work with students of color versus European American students. Five of the group felt that students of color seek them out and feel more comfortable speaking with them, particularly about non-school related concerns. In turn, respondents reported that they felt "unable to not work with them" even when these students were not their "official advisees." Four of the teacher educators reported making sure that they held students of color to high standards or the same standards as all other students, "because I feel and know that an excellent education is the key to survival for many people of color in this country." This also meant making sure "that students are getting the proper advisement" for program completion and being "very directive" with students of color who are "in trouble." Two of the respondents talked about relating to students of color through a common home language, while another talked about taking cultural factors into account. For this respondent, "cultural factors" was defined very broadly to include any student who might not fit into the mainstream (one example she offered was a student coming from a rural area to her very urban institution). Thus, she felt compelled to reach out to any student who was "feeling a sense of not belonging." Finally, two respondents discussed "not falling into stereotypes" and taking care not to make assumptions about students. Thus, all the respondents felt that they did indeed work differently with students of color, not in preferential ways, but in ways that rendered advisement more personal and culturally responsive.

*Supervision.* This aspect of the question netted the fewest responses because three of the seven were not supervising at the time. However, of the four that were supervising, one stated that she is assigned more students of color to supervise. Two others described challenging students' "normative views" and helping students to "focus on what the possibilities are rather than the problems" in student teaching classrooms. Finally, the teacher educator who works in bilingual education indicated again that all her work is embedded in a cultural context and so it was hard for her to separate how she might behave otherwise.

# Discussion

One goal of this study was to identify what teacher educators of color bring to their work and to the teaching profession and to explore how they see themselves in relation to their White peers. The data indicate that one strong theme that exemplified the responses of all members of the group—their experiences, goals, perceptions—was diversity. Respondents clearly placed *issues of diversity at the center of their teaching* practice as well as their thinking about all facets of teacher preparation including advisement, curriculum, supervision, and student teaching. For these teacher educators of color, it was patently evident that diversity is *integral* to teacher education, fueled apparently by their deep concern for "the demographic imperative" which demands "that the educational community must take action in order to alter the disparities deeply embedded in the American educational system" (Cochran-Smith, 2004, p. 4). This concern for equity was obvious in these teacher educators' definitions of diversity. For them it is more than surface knowledge of customs and holidays, more than a topic to be addressed in a course or workshop; it includes intimate, substantive and

specific knowledge about "other," socio-political knowledge that forces institutionalized racism and structural, systemic inequality to the surface, and community knowledge that sees children as embedded in rich contexts and members of whole, strongly identified groups.

While none of the respondents called themselves *culturally responsive or relevant pedagogues,* implicit in their narratives were the characteristics of culturally responsive pedagogy:

> Culturally relevant teachers foster classroom social relations…that extend beyond the classroom. (Ladson-Billings, 1992, p. 113)

> Effective teachers of minority students…acknowledge the state of oppression in which their students exist but insist that the students overcome these negative situations and present them with academically challenging tasks on a regular basis. (First & Crichlow, 1989, cited in Ladson-Billings, 1992, p. 112)

> …culturally responsive teachers…contextualize teaching by giving attention to the immediate needs and cultural experiences of their students. (Irvine, 1992; p. 83)

> In reconceptualizing the curriculum, teacher educators must critically analyze the content to ensure that it reflects the diverse perspectives of the country's multicultural population. The multiple voices of students and communities must be incorporated. (Gollnick, 1992, p. 70)

> Culturally responsive teaching makes academic success a non-negotiable mandate for all students and an accessible goal. (Gay, 2000, p. 34)

Their deep understanding of diversity seemed to be grounded in their own histories as people of color and to be informed by their own confrontation with racism, inequity and oppression. The power of authentic or firsthand experiences as "other" in this country seemed to undergird respondents' conception of *teaching as work that is inherently moral and political.* As witnesses to the devastating consequences of racism, low expectations and deficit assumptions of children of color, respondents placed much emphasis on ensuring that diverse learners have access not just to educational opportunity, but to true caring from those who would teach them.

In centering their practice and their philosophies on diversity, respondents positioned themselves as *strongly committed to public, urban schools* and to the children who occupy these schools. They seemed primarily interested in working in those settings too often viewed as problematic by mainstream teacher educators and most often not seen as viable employment options by European American novice teachers. What seemed to define these teacher educators of color was their sense of advocacy for students and children of color exemplified by their willingness to go against the normative grain. They appeared to hold themselves to a standard of commitment that they feel is lacking in the academy. Underlying respondents' answers was *a sense of isolation and separation from their European Amer-*

*ican colleagues.* Said one respondent of her European American colleagues,

> I see regard, respect, and a humanisitic kind of understanding, but I don't see a commitment to the populations (of color) we work with, a passion that I feel.

Another respondent talked about her White colleagues not feeling the same sense of urgency as she:

> We really need help in our schools. I feel public education is in grave danger. I don't think my White counterparts are as concerned. If something is wrong (in public schools), people can just up and leave, they have the means. They don't have to worry that their children won't have friends to play with.

For her it seemed to come down to an issue of invisible White privilege (Mcintosh, 1989) where European American counterparts weren't often aware of—indeed did not need to be aware of—the direness of the situation for children of color in public schools. The stakes are high for these children because they often have no option but to depend on public, urban schools to give them the passport they need to participate fully in all levels of American society and "develop the skills and dispositions of deliberative citizenship" (Cochran-Smith, 2004, p. 22).

## Conclusion

Why might the views, intentions, knowledge, and experiences of teacher educators of color be important, particularly in terms of teacher education curricula and the preparation of a predominantly White teaching force for an increasingly diverse student population? Why should the teacher education profession worry about the limited number of teacher educators of color?

First, this study indicates that teacher educators of color have a great deal to offer in terms of *thinking and acting* in culturally responsive ways, and bring habits of mind that embrace a social justice agenda. This is not to say that all teacher educators of color are naturally culturally responsive or social justice oriented, or that European American faculty are not. Yet, an examination of the state of teacher education indicates that there has been little change in teacher education practices despite dramatic social changes (Cochran-Smith, 2004; Gay, 2000; Ladson-Billings, 2001; Melnick & Zeichner, 1997) and that programs have failed to be "a force for freeing students of their parochialism" (Zimpher & Ashburn, 1992, p. 44; also: Cochran-Smith, 2004; Ladson-Billings, 2001). Instead, "the culture of teacher education has shown itself to be highly resistant to new ways of conceiving knowledge...and issues of race, class, culture, gender, and ecology will continue to be marginalized while the teacher education curriculum is located in Eurocentric and, androcentric knowledges and practices" (McWilliam cited in Ladson-Billings, 2001, p. 5).

Second, the ways in which these teacher educators of color define multiculturalism and cultural diversity stands in stark contrast to the manner in which teacher' education programs define and practice multicultural curriculum. The majority of

teacher education programs continue to isolate multicultural teacher education in single courses (Cochran-Smith, 2004: Larkin, 1995; Melnick & Zeichner, 1997) and adopt an "easy rhetoric of cultural pluralism" that fails to recognize that "cultural differences are inextricably tied to racial segregation, economic depression, and political powerlessness" (Larkin, 1995, p. 2, 3). As a consequence, "multicultural education is very often reduced to folksongs and folktales, food fairs, holiday celebrations, and information about famous people" (Sleeter, 1995, p. 23) by White teachers who "greatly minimize the extent and impact of racial...discrimination, viewing it as isolated incidents that hurt a person's feelings" (Sleeter, 1995, p.19-20). As Sleeter (1995) points out, "most White teachers simply do not know very much about non-White groups" (p. 22), and "most teacher educators have not had the transformative learning experiences necessary to interrupt the conservative assumptions underlying teacher education programs" (Cochran-Smith 2004, p. 13).

Thus, White teachers and teacher educators are missing "cultural frames of reference" (Cochran-Smith, 2003, p. 4) that give them the insight or inside knowledge to authentically enact culturally responsive practices. In comparison, by firmly centering their practice in diversity and social justice, the teacher educators of color in this study underscore that multicultural education cannot be an add-on in teacher education. Rather, their responses indicate that they believe that multicultural education must be woven throughout teacher education as "a comprehensive approach to the teaching role which informs and guides all aspects of classroom practice" (Larkin, 1995, p. 11).

This study reveals that respondents' identification with children of color—and lived experiences as people of color—provides them a unique and genuine perspective on the teacher education enterprise. This perspective guides the work that they do with students of color (as well as other students) so that questions of culture and cultural issues become moral imperatives rather than interesting asides. They also see such learners not as "other people's children" (Delpit, 1995) but as reflections of themselves and intimately understand the profound impact inequity and a lack of care can have, not just on academic achievement, but on a person's spirit, identity and sense of efficacy. One teacher educator in this study put it well:

> You either decide to honor someone's ability to express her love, knowledge, grief and joy or you don't. When one tampers with another's ability to communicate those four emotions, the consequences are psychological, cognitive, emotional, intellectual. When we allow assessments in ways that do not take that into account, I feel that our assessment of children is immoral, illegal, irrelevant, and invalid.

Teacher educators of color possess an empathic understanding of the lives of children of color, which results in a strong desire to engage in social action and redress inequities. Thus, while they subscribe to the skills and knowledge typically considered important for teacher education programs to impart and implicitly agree with the standards set by the profession, they come at this professional knowledge base from a different vantage point. Their perspective places teacher preparation within a socio-historical context that acknowledges that children of color and poverty have been (and continue to be) unequally served and underscores the urgency of ensuring ready and open access to learning for all. They are a valuable resource that can be, indeed must be, tapped if teacher education is truly to become "part of larger movements for social change and [can] demonstrate to others that social justice itself is a valid outcome and an essential purpose of multicultural teacher preparation" (Cochran-Smith, 2003, p. 9).

## Notes

1. My deep thanks go to the seven teacher educators who participated in this study and spoke with such candor and passion about their experiences.

2. I acknowledge that the term "of color" is contested and political. I use it in this piece to describe those people who identify themselves as Black or African American, Asian/ Asian American or Pacific Islander, Latinan/o or Hispanic, and American Indian or Native American.

3. Currently, all seven respondents continue as teacher educators of preservice teachers (6) and inservice teachers (1).

## References

Carter, R. T. & Goodwin, A. L. (1994). Racial identity and education. In L. Darling Hammond (Ed.), *Review of Research in Education,* Vol. 20 (pp. 291-336). Washington, DC: American Educational Research Association.

Cochran-Smith, M. (2003). Standing at the crossroads: Multicultural teacher education at the beginning of the 21st century. *Multicultural Perspectives, 5*(3), 3-11.

Cochran-Smith, M. (2004). *Walking the road: Race, diversity and social justice in teacher education.* New York: Teachers College Press.

Delpit, L. (1995). *Other people's children: Cultural conflict in the classroom.* New York: The New Press.

Dilworth, M. E. & Brown, C. E. (2001). Consider the difference: Teaching and learning in culturally rich schools. In V. Richardson (Ed.), *Handbook of research on teaching* (4th ed.) (pp. 643-667). Washington DC: American Educational Research Association.

Fuller, M. L. (1992). Teacher education programs and increasing minority school populations: An educational mismatch? In C. A. Grant (Ed.), *Research and multicultural education* (pp. 184-202). Bristol, PA: The Falmer Press.

Gay, G. (2000). Culturally responsive teaching: Theory, research and practice. New York: Teachers College Press.

Gollnick, D. M. (1992). Understanding the dynamics of race, class and gender. In M. E. Dilworth (Ed.), *Diversity in teacher education: New expectations* (pp. 63-78). San Francisco, CA: Jossey-Bass.

Goodwin, A. L. (1997). Historical and contemporary perspectives on multicultural teacher education: Past lessons, new directions. In J. E. King, E. R. Hollins & W. Hayman (Eds.), *Preparing teachers for cultural diversity* (pp. 5-22). New York: Teachers College Press.

Goodwin, A. L. (2001). Seeing with different eyes: Re-examining teacher expectations through racial lenses. In S. H. King and L. Castenell (Eds.), *Racism and racial inequality: Implications for teacher education* (pp. 69-76). Washington, DC: American Association of Colleges for Teacher Education.

Goodwin, A. L. (2002). The social/political construction of low teacher expectations for children of color: Re-examining the achievement gap. *Journal of Thought, 37*(4), 83-103.

Gordon, J. A. (2000). *The color of teaching.* New York: Routledge/ Falmer.

Hodgkinson, H. (2001). Educational demographics: What teachers should know. *Educational Leadership, 58*(4), 6-11.

Irvine, J. J. (1992). Making teacher education culturally responsive. In M. E. Dilworth (Ed.), *Diversity in teacher education: New expectations* (pp. 79-92). San Francisco, CA: Jossey-Bass.

Ladson-Billings, G. (1992). Culturally relevant teaching: The key to making multicultural education work. In C. A. Grant (Ed.), *Research and multicultural education* (pp. 106-121). Bristol, PA: The Falmer Press.

Ladson-Billings, G. (2001). *Crossing over to Canaan: The journey of new teachers in diverse classrooms.* San Francisco, CA: Jossey-Bass.

Larkin, J. M. (1995). Curriculum themes and issues in multicultural teacher education programs. In J. M. Larkin & C. E. Sleeter (Eds.), *Developing multicultural teacher education curricula* (pp. 1-16). Albany, NY: State University of New York Press.

McIntosh, P. (1989). White privilege: Unpacking the invisible knapsack. *Peace and Freedom, 49*(4), 10-12.

Melnick, S. L. & Zeichner, K. M. (1997). Enhancing the capacity of teacher education institutions to address diversity issues. In J. E. King, E. R. Hollins & W. C. Hayman (Eds.), *Preparing teachers for cultural diversity* (pp. 23-39). New York: Teachers College Press.

Rong, X. L. & Preissle, J. (1997). The continuing decline in Asian American teachers. *American Educational Research Journal, 34*(2), 267-296.

Sleeter, C. E. (1995). White preservice students and multicultural education coursework. In J. M. Larkin & C. E. Sleeter (Eds.), *Developing multicultural teacher education curricula* (pp.17-30). Albany, NY: State University of New York Press.

Strauss, A. & Corbin, J. (1998). *Basics of qualitative research: Techniques and procedures for developing grounded theory.* Thousand Oaks, CA: Sage.

Villegas, A. M. & Lucas, T. (2002). Preparing culturally responsive teachers: Rethinking the curriculum. *Journal of Teacher Education, 53*(1),20-32.

Zimpher, N. & Ashburn, E. (1992). Countering parochialism in teacher candidates. In M. E. Dilworth (Ed.), *Diversity in teacher education: New expectations* (pp. 40-62). San Francisco, CA: Jossey-Bass.

*A. Lin Goodwin is an associate professor of education at Teachers College, Columbia University, New York City, New York. E-mail goodwin@tc.columbia.edu*

From *Issues in Teacher Education,* Fall 2004, pp. 7-24. Copyright © 2004 by Caddo Gap Press. Reprinted by permission.

# Autobiography of a Teacher:
## A Journey toward Critical Multiculturalism

Sarah J. Ramsey, *Lock Haven University of Pennsylvania*

## Abstract

Many of us do not realize the prejudices we learn by living our lives. However, though reflection we can understand who we are, why we are that way, and how we can change. As a teacher I naively believed that I had transcended prejudicial thinking and acting. Yet, through much reflection during my doctoral program, I came to understand myself from a new perspective. By revisiting my white privilege, being the other, and my place as an educator, I unfold the invisible construction of myself. This both personal and cultural autobiography challenges others to look behind the invisible veil of their own social construction of self so that new understandings are possible.

## Introduction

In his 1992 book on race in America, Studs Turkel told the story of a cab driver who, in times of stress and exhaustion, reverted to racist thoughts and feelings. The cab driver said, "No matter how much education you may have had, the prejudices you were taught come out. These sinister forces are buried deep inside you" (p. 6). Many of us do not realize the prejudices that we were taught just by living our lives. But through reflection, realization is possible, and it is through reflection that we can change. As a former public school teacher I naively believed that I had transcended prejudicial thinking and acting. However, through much reflection during my doctoral program, I struggled to make visible the historical transparencies of race and privilege that I had been looking through. I was tearing away the veil of ignorance.

My story has two beginnings that are chronologically forty years apart. In the fall of 2002 I enrolled in a course entitled "Diversity and Equity." At the time, my cultural identity allowed me to assume that I would be learning about the other; however, I soon realized that I would be forced to critically examine my own identity. For me this examination took place in the form of autobiography.

As Susan Edgerton (1991) described, autobiography aids in the understanding of self. My autobiography tells the story of the places I have been and describes the language, routines, habits, perception, thoughts, attitudes, and unconscious actions that have shaped and changed my understandings about multiculturalism. "Understanding 'place' in this way suggests the process known as 'making the familiar strange' (Green, 1973) . . . critically examining the clichés by which one has learned to live—clichés expressed not only through language but also via routines, habits, and modes of perception as well" (Edgerton, 1991, p. 78-79). Further, there is a connection between our constructions of self and our constructions of other (Edgerton, 1991) and that by discussing those constructions we can only grow in our understanding of the multicultural world in which we live.

As Steinberg and Kincheloe (2001) acknowledged, there is little agreement among scholars in defining multiculturalism. Therefore, in order to set a context for me to discuss multiculturalism, I will use the five positions delineated by Steinberg and Kincheloe: (a) conservative, (b) liberal, (c) pluralist, (d) left-essentialist, and (e) critical. *Conservative multiculturalism* encourages assimilation to Western middle class standards based on a traditional patriarchal culture, and "promotes the western canon as a universally civilizing influence" (p. 3). By focusing on the sameness of individuals from diverse backgrounds *liberal multiculturalism* supports assimilation as proposed by conservative multiculturalism. Further, liberal multiculturalism maintains the separation between politics and education. *Pluralist multiculturalism* has a greater focus on race, class and gender differences and supports education about various cultures and ethnicities. This position "has become the mainstream articulation of multiculturalism". *Left-essentialist multiculturalism* upholds the notion that the categories of race, class, and gender are based on a set of static fundamental values and only authentic members of the group have authority to represent themselves or the group regarding their oppression and related issues. *Critical multiculturalism* focuses on issues of power and domination; identifies sources of race, class and gender inequities; and analyzes privileges all with the goal of social justice. To this end, marginalized groups are encouraged and assisted in resisting their oppression. Using these positions I present my own complicated, very personal, and at times painful journey.

## The Beginning

### A Place of White Privilege

Now I come to the second beginning. I lived in the same small Midwestern town for the first 23 years of my life. I did in essence leave when I went away to college; but returned during the summers. I lead a fairly privileged life. I had two parents. Dad worked; Mom stayed at home and took care of the children. My father's income provided the resources to fulfill the majority of my desires, from the latest fashions to a car. In addition, his status in the community and in the state provided a network of influential people. Education was valued and my parents supported my involvement in extra curricular activities ranging from sports to music. I never questioned my status. Rothenberg (2000) described my feelings about my privileged status quite well; it was "not privilege at all, just the way things were, the way they were supposed to be" (p. 73).

I was exposed to very little diversity during my common school education. I went to school with American Indians but was practically oblivious to them having different experiences from mine. I often visited my mother's hometown where there is a large African American population, but saw the *coloreds,* as my relatives called them, as people that "traded" at my family's store, but not as people with whom I would have social interactions. As an undergraduate student, I encountered a great diversity of people. I had my first conversation with an African American person, and became good friends with some students from Mexico. I became interested in other religions and cultures immediately and was fascinated by all the people who were different.

## Academically Othered

While in college, I realized that I might not have been as privileged as I believed. Ironically, I was underprivileged with respect to my education. My entire common education was in a small rural school. Just as Yeo (2001) discussed, smaller rural schools "are unable to provide a broad range of courses, thereby severely disadvantaging their students" (p. 515). This was definitely true in my situation. There was no college preparatory track in my high school, and I had chosen to attend an academically rigorous university. The lack of advanced math courses available in high school made me deficient for college level mathematics. Further, my senior English class consisted of "listening" to Romeo and Juliet and writing one library research paper. Needless to say; the required English composition courses were a struggle for me. There was no foreign language requirement for graduation, so I did not take a foreign language. This made foreign language at the collegiate level an impossibility. I struggled through my entire undergraduate education and constantly felt inferior in regard to my academic ability. This was my first experience with feeling othered.

## A Place in Education

Although I had a Bachelor's degree in computer information systems, I did not like the world of computer programming. One year after graduation, I moved to a large metropolitan area to pursue a career in retail management. After working in retail for several years, I decided that I was really meant to be a teacher. Although I had considered this career as an undergraduate, I had not taken it seriously until several careers later. So, I went back to school and got a Masters degree along with elementary certification. This began my experiences with children from diverse backgrounds. I did all of my field experiences including student teaching in the same school district, which had a predominantly African American population. In addition, many of the students lived in poverty. As I mentioned previously, my initial awareness began with a conscious recognition that others were different from me, but as a teacher I recognized that I was different from others. I became the minority.

### Racially Othered

After receiving my degree in elementary education, I interviewed for a teaching position in this same district where I did my field experience. However, I did not get the job. When I asked the principal why, he very candidly told me that he had to hire a black teacher. I felt that it was unfair that someone should have an upper hand just because of skin color, and I complained of reverse discrimination. I was angry that someone had an advantage over me. Ironically, I failed to acknowledge that I constantly had the upper hand because I was white and my privilege had always gotten me what I wanted. I was again the other. Eventually, I began to understand that this district along with many others was concerned with its teaching staff reflecting the diversity of the student population.

### Enacting Pluralist Multiculturalism

As fate would have it, I ended up teaching for that very principal. A teaching position at his school opened not too long before school started and I was offered the position. I accepted and spent my entire public school teaching career at this school. The children in my classroom came from a multitude of cultural backgrounds and often times the students had just moved to the United States and did not speak English. Each year presented a variety of challenges.

Becoming a teacher was a critical point in the development of my multicultural awareness. The lack of diversity in my own background made me unaware of the complexities of living each day in a room of culturally, racially, and socioeconomically different people. Many would say that I was naive, but I believe that my naivete provided the foundation necessary for me to enter this context with little experience that would support stereotypical views of the people I would encounter. I believed that I had an unbiased perspective, looking for the potential in each student. I used every resource available to complement what I did in the classroom. My expectation for each student was to learn no matter his race, socioeconomic status or past academic and behavioral history. In spite of this seemingly enlightened perspective, I was enacting a curriculum that reflected my Eurocentric notion of pluralist multiculturalism. I was guilty of the "tacos and egg rolls" curriculum that Rothenberg (2000) described. I felt it was important for my students to be "exposed" to other cultures, and that exposure consisted of doing units on pueblo Indians and participating in a contest to communicate to Japanese students what a day was like in an America school. If the culture I chose as a focus overlapped with the culture represented by students in my class, it was purely accidental. However, the few white students in my class were privileged through my enactment of traditional white curriculum, curriculum as institutionalized text (Pinar, Reynolds, Slattery, & Taubman, 2000). I reflected Rothenberg's ignorance with respect to presenting a Eurocentric worldview. She described it this way, "Since it had never occurred to me that it was impossible to place any other experience, history, or culture at the center of my focus, I could not identify the perspective from which I taught. For me it was not a perspective, it was 'reality'" (2000, p. 111).

### Racial Conflict

I enjoyed working with my students very much; it was the teachers that presented most of my challenges. Although the student population was majority African American, the teaching staff was predominantly Caucasian. This created a great deal of friction among many of the faculty and staff because we questioned the others' qualifications to teach our students. The black teachers believed that the white teachers did not know how to teach black children. And the white teachers believed that these middle class black teachers had no more connection to the black children in the school than did the white teachers. The white teachers believed that what made the African American students in our school different in terms of academics was their families' financial situations and their uncertain living conditions. These disagreements were often manifested in behavior such as faculty refusing to attend a holiday party because it was at a particular person's home.

Even with all this racial tension, I never felt scared around another person just based on skin color until I became a victim of crime. While living in the city, I had two very disturbing experiences. First, three African American males, who looked to be in their late teens or early twenties, tried to steal my car. I came out of a store to find them in my car attempting to drive away in reverse. They could not get the car into drive, so they abandoned it. Second, two African American adolescents were hanging around me in the parking lot of a grocery store while I put groceries into my car. I was not concerned; I thought they worked at the store and were waiting for me to finish so they could take the cart back into the store. I had my purse over my shoulder and when I turned to face them, in a flash my purse was gone. One of the boys had pulled my purse hard enough to break the strap and was running down the street with it.

These two experiences left me feeling violated and fearful of this particular group. My perception of African American young men had been interrupted by these experiences and I had entered Anzaldúa's (1999) la facultad.[1] My fear was compounded by the fact that this particular group was targeted and stereotyped by the media. To come to terms with my feelings, I made a commitment to learn more about this group that I now feared. I took a course in African American studies, which focused on adolescents. It was a very enlightening experience not only because I was the only white in the class, but also because I began to develop a new understanding of African Americans.

### Evolution to Critical Multiculturalism

In 1996, I moved back to my home state to continue my work in education. I took a position as a university-based professional developer where I worked with both preservice and inservice teachers. In this position, I visited many classrooms in the state. Because I visited mostly suburban and rural schools, the sea of white faces that I saw in the classrooms overwhelmed me. Although this sea of white reflected my own educational experiences, it seemed very foreign to me. These classrooms seemed boring; there was no variety. In addition, I saw that many of the teachers in these schools came with a similar set of assumptions regarding multiculturalism that I had as a teacher. This prompted my commitment to put multicultural issues at the core of my own education as well as my teaching.

The courses I took as part of my doctoral work were the most influential in expanding my consciousness of multiculturalism. I would say that almost every course I took had a component that connected to multicultural issues. A major idea that I gained from a course entitled The American College Student comes from a simplistic phrase that is sometimes considered cliché, but has taken on significant meaning for me: "Behind every face is a story." It is important for me to encourage others to be conscious of the effect their comments, actions, and words can have. I expect of myself as well as others consideration of all possibilities and to never assume that you know what a person is like just from his or her appearance.

I now teach elementary education majors and consciously use my history and understandings to inform my pedagogy. I have come to take a critical stance when working with preservice teachers by challenging them to look behind their veils to examine their own social constructions of self so that new understandings of curriculum are possible. Multiculturalism is an issue that students need to acknowledge and discuss, particularly in an environment such as teacher education where the majority student is a white female coming into teaching having not interrogated her own cultural identity. To borrow from Frances Rains (2001), I feel that it is my duty as a teacher educator to help my students ''unlearn the stereotypes and misinformation that might otherwise become the wobbly foundation'' (p. 528) for their understanding of others. Further, I hold the same goal as Rothenberg (2000), who said, "For me, the goal of helping students see the world through many different people's eyes continues to be a primary and laudable aim for undergraduate education" (p. 157). Finally, I strive for my students to be critical, to be conscious" of the way the power dynamics of race, class, gender and other social dynamics have operated to help produce one's identity and consciousness" (Steinberg & Kincheloe, 2001, p. 26).

## The End?

I would like to close with this quote from Gloria Anzaldúa (1999), "Knowledge makes me more aware, it makes me more conscious. 'Knowing' is painful because after 'it' happens I can't stay in the same place and be comfortable. I am no longer the same person I was before" (p. 70). Through this autobiography, I have become a different person. It is uncomfortable to acknowledge what I have done and how I have felt, but I have grown through the experience. This autobiography does not end here, it is only the beginning of my life-long journey toward living my life and teaching from a perspective that has at the forefront my new maxim; behind every face is a story.

## Note

1. For a detailed discussion of this concept see Chapter 3 of *Borderlands LaFrontera: The New Mestiza* by Gloria Anzaldúa.

## References

Anzaldúa, G. (1999). *Borderlands la frontera: The new mestiza.* San Francisco: Aunt Lute Books.

Edgerton, S. H. (1991). Particularities of 'otherness': Autobiography, Maya Angelou, and me. In J. Kincheloe, & W. F. Pinar (Eds.), *Curriculum as social psychoanalysis: 'The significance of place* (pp. 77-97). Albany, NY: State University of New York Press.

Pinar, W., Reynolds, W., Slattery, P., & Taubman, P. (2000). *Understanding curriculum: An introduction to the study of historical and contemporary curriculum discourses.* New York: Peter Lang.

Rains, F. V. (2001). No, I didn't make it rain last night or rethinking what and how we teach about First Americans. In S. R. Steinberg (Ed.), *Multi/intercultural conversations: A reader* (pp. 511-526). New York: Peter Lang.

Steinberg, S. R., & Kincheloe, J. L. (2001). Setting the context for critical multi/interculturalism: The power blocs of class elitism, white supremacy, and patriarchy. In S. R. Steinberg (Ed), *Multi/intercultural conversations: A reader* (pp. 3-30). New York: Peter Lang.

Rothenberg, P. (2000). *Invisible privilege: A memoir about race, class, & gender.* Lawrence, KS: University Press of Kansas.

Turkel, S. (1992). *Race: How blacks and whites think and feel about the American obsession.* New York: The New Press.

Yeo, F. (2001). Thoughts on rural education: Reconstructing the invisible and the myths of country schooling. In S. R. Steinberg (Ed.), *Multi/intercultural conversations: A reader* (pp. 511-526). New York: Peter Lang.

## About the Author

*Sarah J. Ramsey is an Assistant Professor of Elementary Teacher Education at Lock Haven University of Pennsylvania. Correspondence should be directed to Sarah J. Ramsey, Ph.D., Lock Haven University, Lock Haven, PA 17745.*

# AN INVESTIGATION Of STUDENTS' PERCEPTIONS OF MULTICULTURAL EDUCATION EXPERIENCES IN A SCHOOL Of EDUCATION

Ambika Bhargava, Lisa D Hawley, Chaunda L Scott, Mary Stein, Adelaid Phelps

## Introduction

Changing demographics and the need for professionals to understand perspectives and beliefs of others has led many to reflect on the extent to which diversity issues are integrated into undergraduate and graduate programs (Heuberger, Gerber, & Anderson, 1999). This is particularly true as teachers and helping professionals are considered catalysts of change. However, educators need specific knowledge, skills and attitudes to influence the world in which they live. Banks (2001) stated that it is only when teachers are empowered that they have the ability to influence their personal, social, political and economic worlds.

The past twenty years of educational research include studies that describes the importance of muliticultural education. However, Smith (1998) discussed not only an absence of multicultural education as a content knowledge base in teacher education programs, but also indicated the lack of a knowledge base among instructors and professors who teach such courses. Although Smith (1998) advocated *culturally responsive pedagogy* as a moral and ethical responsibility in the preparation of teachers, the integration of multicultural perspectives has been difficult to achieve.

Both the standards for the National Accreditation of Teacher Education (NCATE) and the Council for Accreditation of Counseling and Related Education Programming (CACREP) require multicultural training as integral in the training of teachers and school counselors. Yet,

there is a lack in the literature regarding the overall effectiveness of this training across schools of education and human services.

Nieto (2000) asserted that one must become a multicultural person before one can become a multicultural teacher—this involves a transformational re-education. First, she said, individuals must learn more about people and events about which they know little. This knowledge could come from literature, cultural activities, appropriate and accurate media outlets, or other sources. Second, individuals need to successfully traverse the process of confronting individual racism and bias that are often so deeply rooted as to be unconscious. The dissonance that often occurs in cultural training experiences requires a high level of expertise by professors in teacher and counselor training institutions.

## Assessment of Efforts

Assessment of teacher education programs and efforts in infusing multicultural education reveal that we have a long way to go. Vacarr (2001) argued that while college campuses have focused on training teachers for working in diverse environments and transforming the curriculum to embody multiculturalism, a gap exists between conceptual understandings and the ability to respond to classroom challenges involving differences. Globetti, Globetti, Brown, and Smith's (1993) instrument measuring university students' multicultural awareness and sensitivity found that although students were aware of various subcultures on campus, they

lacked sensitivity in terms of responding to differences.

Moreover, White students exhibited a lack of sensitivity toward African-Americans and were reluctant to interact with different racial minority groups. Rumill, Harshorn, and Gordon (1994) sought to determine the effect that stereotypes had on how university students rated students who were from different racial, ethnic, or religious groups than their own. They found that White college students judged their black peers' credentials on the basis of skin color. These results were attributed, in part, to the lack of knowledge and experiences many white college students have with people of different colors and cultures.

Rudney, Marxen, and Risku (1996) found that students overwhelmingly agreed on the importance of multicultural education in their role as teacher. However, their survey of preservice teachers' field placement experiences in an urban setting revealed that, "graduates were most likely to speak in generalities regarding the importance of meeting the needs of diverse student populations and least likely to provide examples of appropriate theory-based professional action" (p. 35). Thus it appears that there is a gap between conceptual understanding and the ability to translate this understanding to practice.

In 1982, the National Council for the Accreditation of Teacher Education (NCATE) included multicultural education among its criteria for the accreditation of teacher preparation programs. Similarly, the Council for

Accreditation for Counselor Education and Related Programming (2001) requires each counselor preparation program to infuse issues of diversity and advocacy throughout the training. With this impetus, many colleges and universities included multicultural education for preservice teachers as a mandate towards fulfilling the multicultural education requirement.

## Teacher Preparation & Multicultural Education

Given that most prospective teachers and school counselors are White, middle-class females with limited or no experiences with minorities (Zimpher & Ashburn, 1989), it is critical that teacher/counselor preparation programs include mechanisms for prospective professionals in these fields to not only learn about diversity, but to experience their practice in diverse settings. Even with the integration of multicultural education coursework and field experiences designed specifically to help students become culturally responsive professionals, it is unrealistic to expect that all students will complete a program having the knowledge, skills, and attitudes that represent the desired goals (Jordan, 1995).

A lack of cultural awareness and a lack of specific instruction in culturally relevant pedagogy have created classroom environments that fail to facilitate the success of culturally diverse students. Research consistently indicates that teacher perceptions of students based on race, class, and gender influence their expectations for student behavior and academic performance (Gollnick & Chinn, 1998; Sadker & Sadker, 1994; Sleeter & Grant, 1992).

All things being equal, individual teachers make a significant difference in the learning experience of students. Therefore, creating equitable education must begin with individual teachers. Knowledge of diversity, skills for effectively working with diverse populations, and transforming attitudes toward cultural diversity are all goals for the preservice teacher/counselor prepared in multicultural education (Banks 1997; Bennett, 1995; Gay, 1993; Nieto, 2000).

As a result of these and other research findings, many institutions of higher education have implemented a variety of programs to help remedy the situation

and have made ongoing efforts to increase student awareness of, and sensitivity to, cultural differences. This has led to an infusion of courses, programs, and curriculum related to multicultural education and issues of diversity. In education and counseling programs, an understanding of multiculturalism and diversity is often viewed as being critical to the preparation and development of teachers and counselors.

The purpose of this article is to discuss a pilot-study describing education, counseling, and human resource development students' knowledge, attitudes, and experiences regarding their experiences with multicultural education at a large, suburban institution of higher education.

## Method

The primary source of data was a 21-question survey that focused on students' knowledge, attitudes and experiences regarding multicultural education. Seventeen of these survey questions were rated on a Likert scale, and the last four were open-ended questions. The open-ended questions include (1) describe how you are a change agent, (2) provide suggestions for School of Education and Human Services, (3) provide three words describing your experiences, and (4) any feedback you would like to provide.

Multicultural training was described to the students as a focus on students' ability to work effectively with various cultural identities. The cultural identities were described as race, religion, ethnic origin, country of origin, gender, socio-economic status, sexual orientation, disability as well as understand the complex issues of power, oppression and prejudice. Responses to the closed ended questions consisted of a Likert scale and included the following categories: Not Applicable, Limited Experience, Some Experience, Considerable Experience, Thorough Experience and Extensive Integration of Experience.

### Participants

The participants in this study consisted of graduate and undergraduate students completing their last semester of course work in the School of Education and Human Services. One hundred students

completed the online survey. The survey also included demographic information and degree information. Students could complete the survey in the University's Educational Resources Laboratory or at home. The participants included 87% female; 62% between the ages of 20-29 years; 25% in counseling, 34% in curriculum and instruction, 17% in human development and child studies, 17% in human resource development, and 7% in reading.

### Reliability and Validity

Due to the exploratory nature of the study, results lack generalizability to other schools of education and human services. The survey construction was developed to explore student perceptions and was not created with the purpose of internal consistency. The data was triangulated to increase the validity and reliability of the study using Likert scale questions, open-ended questions and the literature. The percentage of participants is also high for an exploratory study with 100 students completing the survey.

### Data Analysis

Each close-ended question was divided into percentages based on the frequency of response. The four open-ended questions were analyzed using qualitative methods from a grounded theoretical approach. Each open-ended response was imported into NUD*IST to assist in content analysis. The open-ended responses were read and re-read to develop understanding of the meaning of the data.

The data was then coded into tentative categories based on common ideas, recurring words/phrases, and similar themes creating a coding scheme. Three of the four questions include themes relevant to the overall qualitative responses. The fourth question, "any feedback you would like to provide," did not elicit enough response to complete a content analysis. Identified themes from each of the three open questions were identified. Some surprises were also identified in the data.

## Results

### Open-Ended Question Data

Several themes emerged from three of the four open questions. The first open question referred to examples of ways one acts as an agent of change in a diverse society. Four themes emerged from the participant's response including professional role, personal beliefs, professional development and advocates. Each theme is followed by an example from the questionnaire.

*Role:* To act as a change agent in one's professional role.

"I will help all students feel included when I become a teacher."

*Personal beliefs:* One's values and beliefs are a framework for a change agent.

"Treat everyone as equals and always be open-minded."

*Professional development:* Active involvement in continued learning on diversity.

"I read about and try to educate myself on counseling diverse populations."

*Advocates:* Response includes an action related to advocacy.

"Educate others, speak up against stereotypes and racism, continue to learn about other cultures and values."

Respondents also provided suggestions for the School of Education and Human Services to improve training regarding diversity. Themes emerged referring to curriculum and training in the School of Education and Human Services including the use of guest speakers, specific curriculum issues, field experiences and the make-up of the academic community.

*Diverse speakers:* Increase the number of speakers on diverse topics and from a variety of differing cultural experiences.

"Have more guest speakers come in of different races."

*Curriculum Issues:* Suggestions and feedback directly related to curriculum experiences.

"More information regarding how to implement what we have been exposed too."

*Field experiences:* The importance of experiences in diverse settings.

"Provide more opportunities for OU students to experience settings in which integration is needed."

*Role of Professors/Student Body:* Suggestions related to the role of professors and the student body in diversity training.

"Address them head on. Avoid treating the topic as if it was taboo just because someone may be offended just by discussing the issue."

The third open question focused on students describing in three words their experience of diversity experiences in the School of Education and Human Services. Themes emerged based on similarity of responses.

*Comprehensive:* The presentation of diversity was in-depth and ubiquitous.

"Broad." "Comprehensive." "Extensive."

*Affirming Statements:* Students described their diversity instruction as positive.

"Beneficial." "Engaging." "Positive."

*Increased awareness:* Students described an increase in understanding of diversity issues.

"Enlightening." "Informative." "Educational."

*Lacks exposure:* Students described little exposure to diversity issues.

"Limited." "Scarce." "Inadequate."

*Dissatisfied:* Students identify criticisms regarding their experience with diversity issues in the School of Education and Human Services.

"Not in-depth." "Not reality." "Uninformed."

The open questions provide a glimpse of student reactions to diversity training. A couple of general themes, which are consistent with the data, involve the need for students to interact with other cultures on a regular basis through classroom and faculty composition, classroom curriculum, and field experiences. Secondly, students also describe a lack in the ability to move from knowledge acquisition to application. Throughout the data students described being firm in awareness of the importance of diversity and being competent in knowledge of diversity issues, yet, less confident in

their ability to apply this knowledge in a work setting.

## Closed-Ended Question Data

The Likert scale results revealed some positive and some negative trends. Responses to the closed ended questions of the Likert scale included the following categories: Not Applicable, Limited Experience, Some Experience, Considerable Experience, Thorough Experience, and Extensive Integration of Experience.

High scores on category 3, 4 and 5 were considered positive, implying that the students had positive multicultural learning experiences and exposure. Ratings of 1 and 2 were considered negative, implying that the students had negative multicultural learning experiences and exposure. In retrospect, the categories "considerable and thorough" may have been difficult to distinguish. Therefore, for purposes of analysis categories 3 and 4 were chunked together truncating the scores to eliminate the extreme.

The positive trends indicated that:

- Sixty-six percent (66%) of the students surveyed believed that there was considerable or thorough incorporation of literature and research related to diversity.
- Fifty eight to sixty four percent (58-64%) of the students believed that there was considerable or thorough discussion on culture, race, gender and socioeconomic status.
- Fifty-one percent (51%) also believed that there was considerable or thorough discussion on special needs.
- Sixty-seven percent (67%) felt included in class discussions.
- Fifty nine percent (59%) indicated that there was considerable or thorough preparation to plan and implement a multicultural curriculum.
- Fifty-six percent (56%) believed they had considerable or thorough preparation to respond to the unique needs of families as cultural units.
- A large majority (47% considerable or thorough and 43% extensive) indicated that they believe that all students can learn and are entitled to equitable learning opportunities.

The negative trends indicated:

- Only thirty-one percent (31%) believed that there was considerable or thorough discussion on sexual orientation.

- Only forty-two percent (42%) of the students surveyed believed that there was considerable or thorough discussion on white privilege.
- Fifty-one percent (51%) believed that they had considerable or thorough opportunities to participate in varied cultural experiences, but only forty-seven percent (47%) engaged in the cultural experience provided.

## Discussion

Effective teachers and counselors are critical in creating schools that provide quality education for all our children. It is also important to ensure that a teacher education curriculum is neither 'race-blind' nor 'culture-blind' (Smith, 1998. p.17). Schools of Education and Human Services have a responsibility to prepare students to be culturally responsive and respond to the educational needs of a diverse student population. Thus the student's educational experiences must include both knowledge acquisition of issues of diversity and strategies for effectively working with minority students as well as with their families.

Smith (1998, p. 17) identified the importance of teacher education programs not giving undue attention to the 'literature of failure' and paying greater attention to the 'literature of success' regarding minority children. Similarly, a large majority of participants in this particular study indicated that they believed that all students can learn and are entitled to equitable learning opportunities. Throughout the results, students identified important belief systems related to diversity and education.

Specifically, students discussed the value of equitable treatment in the classroom. The data is more ambiguous in demarking the contribution of their educational experiences to creating their belief systems. However, students did indicate they understood the strong value the School of Education and Human Services places on diversity.

One concern the data indicated is the lack of effective educational experiences in specific applications related to students' work settings. This is a key concern for institutions of higher education who are attempting to prepare helping professionals to work effectively in the field.

The lack of specific tools for the work environment could be indicative of a lack of research in the practical knowledge, ineffective teaching at the higher education level and the lack of access to cultural informants. While there is an abundance of research discussing the importance of diversity, there is much less describing concrete tools such as curriculum applications, dealing with classroom cultural conflicts and creating culturally appropriated assessment tools.

The survey results indicated that although students felt they had opportunities to participate in varied cultural experiences, few engaged in the cultural experience provided. Research has indicated that a significant portion of students' acquisition of knowledge about others comes through experience and interactions with people who are different (Kang & Dutton, 1997). Therefore, the importance of integrating cultural informants and experts in both practical and theoretical activities would both expose students to cultural specific knowledge and engage the students in a more meaningful way.

Kang and Dutton (1997) found a significant portion of students' acquisition of knowledge about others comes through experience and interactions with people who are different. The students in this research study indicated the importance of, and also the lack of, diverse speakers and field experiences in their educational experiences. Therefore, the effort of academic communities to facilitate interaction with diverse populations is vital to increasing students' exposure and knowledge base.

Another concern the data indicated was the lack of training when working with issues related to sexual orientation. This is an interesting parallel process, considering many school districts struggle with how to "handle" sexual orientation and gender identity. Miller, Miller and Schroth (1997) studied practicing teachers and their perceptions of their multicultural training. The researchers found that teachers observed faculty demonstrating more bias toward sexual orientation than to any other culture.

Another study focusing on teacher educators' and student teachers' attitudes found preservice teachers' to be culturally sensitive for all subgroups except sexual orientation (Taylor, 2001). The lack of exposure to issues of sexual

orientation is a concern and necessitates further research of faculty knowledge base, preservice instructional material and K-12 instruction.

Less than fifty percent of the students felt that there was adequate discussion on white privilege. This data raises a concern about the need for more discussions and teaching platforms on the topic of white privilege, especially in predominately White academic communities. However, it is because this issue is not considered a problem that we need to critically examine it. Implied in discussions of race is the issue of 'white privilege.' It is imperative that we examine our cultural assumptions and examine how we treat others.

By examining the life experiences that have shaped the perspectives of individuals already committed to multicultural education, we may begin to understand the motivation that inspires them to commit to a multicultural perspective. This increased understanding may then inform teacher preparation for multicultural education and the equitable education of all students. It is crucial that all teachers and faculty today develop a new perception of their roles and systematically address inequalities in order to improve educational outcomes for all students (Darling-Hammond, 1995, Scott, 2000).

Based on their study of university students' multicultural awareness levels, Globetti et. al. (1993) suggested that the content of multicultural courses should involve students in experiential learning using methods such as role-playing, values clarification, and brainstorming. It has also been advocated that engaging preservice teachers in an exploration of their own cultures can help structure multicultural courses with a personal infusion of cultural history. Instructional strategies should be constructed to relate life experiences with cultural diversity (McCall, 1995; Morales, 2000). In addition, curriculum that engages preservice teachers and counselors in activities relevant to a variety of cultures provides an opportunity to gain insight regarding the communities in which they teach.

Further study is needed to actually observe teachers and school counselors interacting with diverse populations in classrooms and clinical settings to see examples of appropriate transfer of theoretical knowledge in action. Lawrence (1997) suggested that unlike studies using mainly a Likert scale, those based on narrative and experience offer the possibility of discovering more textured nuances. This does not ensure, however, that knowledge is carried into the school setting. The only way to discover the impact such learning has on classroom practice is to follow the preservice teacher into the classroom.

This current study offers us a glimpse of student perceptions of their multicultural training experiences. Based on the research, it appears that students understand the value of working with others with a pluralistic point of view. As teacher and counselor trainers, we need to continue to develop methods to move students from general understandings to engaging in specific culturally appropriate skills and applications in the educational field. If anything, this is an indictment that we are moving from a conceptual stage of diversity and multicultural training to direct service applications.

## References

Banks, J.A. (1997). Multicultural education; Characteristics and goals. In J.A. Banks & C.A. McGee Banks, (Eds.). *Multicultural education: Issues and perspectives* (3rd ed.). Boston: Allyn & Bacon.

Banks, J.A. (2001). *Cultural diversity and education: Foundations, curriculum and teaching.* Needam Heights, MA: Allyn & Bacon.

Bennett, C.I. (1995). *Comprehensive multicultural education: Theory and practice* (3rd ed.). Boston: Allyn & Bacon

Council for Accreditation of Counseling and Related Education Programs (2001). *Standards for the accreditation of counseling and related education programs.* Alexandria, VA: Author.

Darling-Hammond, L. (1997, February). School contexts and learning: What is needed to give every child the right to learn. Paper presented at the Cross-Cultural Roundtable, Teachers College, Columbia University, New York.

Gay, G. (1993). Building cultural bridges: A bold proposal for teacher education. *Education and Urban Society, 25* (3), 285–289.

Globetti, E. C., Globetti, G., Brown, C. L., & Smith, R. E. (1993). Social interaction and multiculturalism. *NASPA Journal, 30* (3), 209–218.

Gollnick, D.M., & Chinn, P.C. (1998). *Multicultural education in a pluralistic society* (5th ed.). Upper Saddle River, NJ: Prentice-Hall.

Heuberger, B., Gerber, D., & Anderson, R. (1999). Strength through cultural diversity: Developing and teaching diverse courses. *College Teaching, 47*(3), 107–113.

Jordan, M. R. (1995). Reflections on the challenges, possibilities, and perplexities of preparing preservice teachers for culturally diverse classrooms. *Journal of Teacher Education, 46* (5), 369–374.

Kang, H. & Dutton, B. (1997). Becoming multicultural: Focusing on the process. *Multicultural Education, 4* (4), 19–22.

Lawrence: S. M. (1997). Beyond race awareness: White racial identity and multicultural teaching. *Journal of Teacher Education, 48* (2), 108–117.

McCall, Ava. (1995). Constructing conceptions of multicultural teaching: Preservice teachers' life experiences and teacher education. *Journal of Teacher Education, 46* (5), 340–350.

Miller, S., Miller K.L. & Schroth, G. (1997). Teacher perceptions of multicultural training in preservice programs. *Journal of Instructional Psychology, 24* (4), 222–232.

Morales, Rosario (2000). Effects of teacher preparation experiences and students' perceptions related to developmentally and culturally appropriate practices. *Action in Teacher Education, 22* (2), 67–75.

National Council for Accreditation of Teacher Education. (1982). *Standards for the accreditation of teacher education.* Washington, DC: Author

Nieto, S. (2000). *Affirming diversity: The sociopolitical context of multicultural education* (3rd ed.). New York: Longman.

Rudney, Gwen L., Marxen, Carol E., & Risku, Michael T. (1996). Preservice Teachers' Growth in Multicultural Understanding: Assessing the Assessment. This study examined the effectiveness of a human relations component within the teacher education program at the University of Minnesota, Morris.

Rumill, P. D., Harshorn, C. S., & Gordon, S. E. (1994). Diversity and multiculturalism on campus: Enhancing awareness or perpetuating stereotypes? *College Student Affairs Journal, 13* (2), 36–42.

Sadker, M., & Sadker, D. (1994). *Failing at fairness: How our schools cheat girls.* New York: Scribners.

Scott, C.L. (2000). Effectively teaching adult basic education courses in multicultural classrooms. Ninth Annual African American Adult Education Research Pre-Conference Proceedings (pp. 1–9). 2001 Adult Education Research Conference. Michigan State University, East Lansing, MI.

Taylor, P.A. (2001). Good news and bad news: A comparison of teacher educators' and preservice teachers' beliefs about diversity issues. *ED 454216.*

Sleeter, C.E., & Grant, C.A. (1992). *Making choices for multicultural education: five approaches to race, class, and gender* (2nd ed.). Columbus, OH: Merrill/Macmillan.

Smith, G. P. (1998). *Common sense about uncommon knowledge: The knowledge bases for diversity.* Washington, DC: American Association of Colleges for Teacher Education.

Vacarr, B. (2001). Moving beyond polite correctness: Practicing mindfulness in the diverse classroom. *Harvard Educational Review, 71* (2), 285–295.

Zimpher, N. L., & Ashburn, E. A. (1989). The RATE project: A profile of teacher education students. *Journal of Teacher Education, 40* (6), 27–31.

*Ambika Bhargava, Lisa D. Hawley, Chaunda L. Scott, Mary Stein, & Adelaide Phelps are assistant professors in the Department of Human Development and Child Studies of the School of Education and Human Services at Oakland University, Rochester, Michigan.*

# Culturally Relevant Teaching

## One Teacher's Journey Through Theory and Practice

By James C. Jupp

### TEACHERS AS BORDER CROSSERS

My experience in education, like the experience of many teachers, is one of crossing cultural borders in schools. As many other Anglo teachers from the middle class have found, the majority of my teaching experience has been one in which I was the only white person in the classroom—first in Mérida, Yucatán, México, where for five years I taught English as a foreign language to secretaries and government clerks, then in South Texas for another five years as a teacher in "one-hundred percent free- and reduced-lunch" rural communities, and finally in downtown Austin, Texas, for the last three years as an urban teacher for "minority" and "low socioeconomic status" children. My particular rite of passage was discovering that my cultural frame was irrelevant and understanding that I needed to learn immediately what was relevant—not to myself, but to my students and the communities in which I worked.

After teaching English as a foreign language in Mérida to adults, my first job teaching children was in Los Fresnos, Texas, a small town about 10 miles from Brownsville and the Mexican border. With an emergency certificate in hand, I struggled to teach as I was taught, through cultural transmission or "banking education" (Freire, 1998b [1970]) that places the teacher as knower and provider of knowledge. Fortunately for me, my assistant principal and mentor took an interest and provided me with bilingual materials, ideas, and encouragement during my first three years in the classroom as we drank coffee many times at a variety of Mexican cafés, fast food joints, and diners. In the end, I became a career teacher because my mentor looked out for me and made sure that I learned one important lesson: I had to begin with the children's culture—in my particular case, Mexican immigrant and Mexican-American cultures—and build toward academic knowledge from there.

I went through a similar learning curve when I began teaching at Fulmore Middle School in downtown Austin. Assuming new-teacher status, I found myself struggling

again with re-imagining the classroom for urban Mexican immigrants, Mexican-American, and African-American sixth graders who presented different needs, sets of interests, and family situations than I had experienced in South Texas. And again, I found a mentor in the department head, who met with me almost daily and helped me design alternative structures for urban classrooms. These allowed for structured choice that provided a balance between open assignments, which degenerated into chaos, and teacher-directed lessons, which were boring for everyone involved including me.

Even after teaching Mexican, Mexican-American, and African-American students for the last 12 years, I am still left scrounging for materials that work and developing lessons day-to-day in an ongoing attempt to leverage the children's home cultures into the sphere of academics valued by mainstream culture, and I still continue the search for materials and delivery methods that make for culturally relevant teaching. Culturally relevant teaching—a term I borrow from Gloria Ladson-Billings's work—is an area of theory/practice that attempts to integrate students' cultural backgrounds into the classroom with the goal of promoting academic achievement (1994, 1995).

I write this for educators who—like myself—find themselves crossing cultural borders and who could benefit from an understanding of one teacher's journey into culturally relevant teaching. In order to help teachers negotiate cultural borders, I provide a theoretical frame based on reflexivity, discuss documenting competence and its limits, and provide two units I have developed in which I apply the frame. More specifically: In the first section, I provide a theoretical frame based on reflexivity that discusses notions of synthesis, dialogue, and caring as ways of co-constructing the classroom with children and community. In the second section, I analyze the tendency toward documenting competence of culturally relevant teaching and discuss its limits. In the third section, I frame culturally relevant teaching, from my Anglo middle-class point of view, as existential struggle and transformation in developing competency in my own encounters with Mexican immigrant, Mexican-American, and African-American students.

## CULTURALLY RELEVANT TEACHING AND THREE REFLEXIVE TURNS: SYNTHESIS, DIALOGUE, AND CARING

In bringing reflexivity into the area of culturally relevant teaching, I take a theoretical direction from philosophy and especially ethnography (De Stigter, 1998; Emerson et al., 1995; Foley, 2002), which I use to subordinate several concepts related to theory/practice in culturally relevant teaching. Reflexivity, in its broadest anthropological sense, refers to self-awareness, understanding of the position of teacher or researcher, co-creation of social spaces researched, and awareness of the implications of production and consumption of knowledge as power-laden (Foley, 2002). Douglas Foley's "Critical Ethnography: The Reflexive Turn" provides a useful typology of reflexivity from which I focus on one particular type as a useful construct for culturally relevant teaching: autoethnographic reflexivity.

Autoethnographic reflexivity, when applied to classroom experiences, refers to a teacher-student and student-teacher way of knowing based on interaction and dialogue that serves to transform both sides of the relationship. The use of autoethnographic reflexivity repositions the teacher in important ways:

> First, being a dialogic knower or witness to a cultural scene positions the ethnographer [teacher] as a much less imperial authoritative knower. Second, it obligates the researcher [teacher] to embrace her/his personal indebtedness and responsibility toward other individuals. (Foley, 2002, 475)

It is this autoethnographic reflexivity, though already implicit in much of the literature about culturally relevant teaching, that I want to make explicit as necessary for teachers who enact culturally relevant teaching, especially for white middle-class teachers crossing cultural borders who find themselves teaching children of color. It is autoethnographic reflexivity in the teacher-student and student-teacher relationship that I use to draw together three distinct "reflexive turns" concerning the co-creation of the classroom spaces among teacher, students, and community. These three reflexive turns are: (1) the synthesis of child and curriculum with community, (2) Freirian transformational dialogue, and (3) feminist theories of caring.

### Synthesis

The first reflexive turn in culturally relevant teaching requires an understanding of learning and thinking as synthesis. In the first synthesis, culturally relevant teaching focuses on the synthesis of children's cultural experiences and interests with the classroom curriculum. Rather than holding the children's cultural experiences and interests to one side and the classroom curriculum to another, learning and thinking—if they transcend abstract trickery or meaningless memorization—integrate the students' cultural experiences and interests with the classroom curriculum (Dewey, 1990 [1902]; Dewey, 1997 [1916]; Ladson-Billings, 1995; Moll, 1992). John Dewey's The Child and the Curriculum (1990 [1902]) provides a description of this first necessary synthesis of teacher and student, which favors neither child-centered nor teacher-centered instruction. Taking the cultural experiences and interests of the child as "self-explanatory or self-contained is inevitably to result in indulgence and spoiling" (1990 [1902], 193). Subject matter curriculum provides a map that gives "the benefits of the results of others' explorations without the waste of energy and loss of time involved in wanderings" (199). Thinking and learning, it follows, require the synthesis of child and subject matter. In the second synthesis, I argue that teachers and students go one step further—the synthesis required in thinking and learning is one of child, curriculum, and the community, which is "a resource of enormous importance" (Moll, 1992, 21) that includes but is not limited to children, teachers, parents, administrators, and other community members.

Of particular importance for culturally relevant teaching is the problem that arises when children's cultural experiences and interests conflict severely with academic school culture in terms of social class, ethnicity, or language. More often than not, the school's culture represents the dominant social class, ethnicity, and language, while the students' experiences—especially in the case of students labeled low socioeconomic status, at-risk, minority, or limited English proficiency—represent those from dominated groups that are systematically "denied access to high status positions within the institutional structure of society" (Cummins, 1986, 22).

Culturally relevant teaching—in its most general sense—draws on and reinvigorates this notion of thinking and learning as synthesis of child, curriculum, and community for children coming from marginalized and dominated social groups. The mission of the teacher in culturally relevant teaching becomes one of creating conditions in which the cultural experiences and interests of children from dominated cultures become synthesized with the curriculum and community in order to "provide a way for students to maintain their cultural integrity while succeeding academically" (Ladson-Billings, 1995, 476). Given that learning and thinking never take place in an apolitical vacuum (Apple, 1979) and that notions of universal psychology and childhood are outdated, the first reflexive turn in culturally relevant teaching requires the teacher, through materials and delivery strategies, to engage in the endless struggle of synthesizing child, curriculum, and community.

## Dialogue

The second reflexive turn required in culturally relevant teaching is dialogue. Dialogue represents a way of knowing that co-creates intersubjectivity and common understandings (Freire, 1998a [1969]; Freire, 1998b [1970]; Collins, 1990). This dialogue can be used to overcome differences between dominant and dominated groups "as a means for the transformation of both" (Freire, 1998b [1970], 163). Dialogue as a way of knowing hopes that listening, conversing, and living together provide a method of overcoming differences between dominant and dominated social groups in the formation of solidarity:

> there will be in the living *with* the oppressed, knowing oneself to be one of them—only with a different perception of reality—that one will understand the ways of being and behaving of the oppressed that reflect diverse forms of the structure of domination. (1998b, 56-57)

This living *with* and its resultant critical thinking, when applied to classroom theory/practice, allows for the ongoing synthesis of child, curriculum, and community required in the first section.

With the use of dialogue for synthesis, teaching becomes culturally relevant through a collaborative effort that stresses interaction of dominant and dominated cultures as an additive process for both groups (Cummins, 1986). Through this process of adding one another's cultural experiences, students from the dominated culture critically manipulate norms of the dominant culture—such as academic language and achievement—for the ends of social change without losing ties with their communities, while teachers from the dominant group might take on a cultural frame of reference that—through an imaginative leap—echoes and supports in significant ways that of the dominated group. Lisa Delpit describes such a critical manipulation of the dominant culture's codes of power in relation to teaching African-American students, which insists on the dominant culture's "skills within the context of critical and creative thinking" (1986, 384). Delpit's emphasis on the critical examination and manipulation of dominant cultures moves toward grounding theory about culturally relevant teaching within specific learning communities, their needs, and their practices rather than using a programmatic or "universal" set of ideas assumed to be best practice for all children.

## Caring

The third reflexive turn required in culturally relevant teaching is the feminist notion of caring. Here I use the word caring specifically to refer to feminist work most associated with Nell Noddings (1984). The ethic of care represents another way of knowing (Collins, 1990; Goldstein, 1998; Ladson-Billings, 1992; Noddings, 1984) that co-creates common understandings of reality. The caring relationship "involves stepping out of one's own personal frame of reference and into another's" (Noddings in Goldstein, 1998, 247). This intermingling of frames of reference requires that "the one caring meets the cared for with engrossment…with full attention and with receptivity to his perspective and situation" (Goldstein, 2002, 12). This notion of engrossment leads to displacement, which is "when the one-caring is feeling with the cared-for, fully receiving him, his motives—his motives become her motives" (Goldstein, 2002, 13).

Caring relationships in the classroom "encourage students to work within a collective structure" (Ladson-Billings, 1994, 60) that focuses on developing a community or family feel:

> Patricia Hillard [a teacher in Ladson-Billings's study] defines her relationship with the students as that of an extended family. Each year the school year begins with the shaping of an 'undefined contract.'…the students form 'extended family groups' within the classroom and even make up names for the families. (Ladson-Billings, 1994, 62)

Furthermore, teachers engaging in culturally relevant teaching cultivate "relationships beyond the boundaries of the classroom" (Ladson-Billings, 1994, 64) that move toward church, recreation, and home.

## DOCUMENTING COMPETENCY AND ITS LIMITS

While the theory behind culturally relevant teaching—synthesis of children and curriculum with community, intersubjectivity and common understanding through dialogue, and feminist understandings of caring—form a backdrop on which culturally relevant teaching takes place, many studies related to culturally relevant teaching have turned to documenting specific examples of competency. The challenge of culturally relevant teaching, it seems, lies not in discussing the theoretical ideal but rather in enacting those ideas with a classroom full of students (for studies that document approaches to or versions of what I broadly term culturally relevant teaching, see Fairbanks, 1998a; Fairbanks, 1998b; Henry, 1996; Ladson-Billings, 1994; Ladson-Billings, 1995; Moll, 1992; Moll & González, 1994; Nee-Benham, 1997; Scheurich, 1998; Robinson, 1998).

### Documenting Competency

Rather than provide a review of the literature—which is beyond the scope of this article—let me describe representative studies of culturally relevant teaching that demonstrate the area's tendency toward "documenting competency" (Moll, 1992). The literature, in a general sense, divides along the following categories, for which I provide an example of each: working with language minority students, accommodating cultural differences in the classroom, bringing students' lives into the classroom, and providing profiles of culturally relevant teachers. While these categories overlap one another (for instance, studies that focus on cultural differences will also provide a study of teachers, or those that focus on language minority students might also attempt to bring students' lives into the classroom), I provide categories for studies and apply them based on a representative emphasis of the studies I discuss.

*Working with language minority students.* Luis Moll's "Bilingual Classroom Studies and Community Analysis: Some Recent Trends" focuses on connecting children's "funds of knowledge" at home to bilingual classrooms in schools so as to avoid a deficit view of bilingual children that accompanies basic skills instruction (1992). Children's funds of knowledge refers to "the sociocultural dynamics of the children's households, especially on how these households function as part of a wider, changing economy, and how they distribute resources of all types through the creation of strategic social ties and networks" (Moll, 1992, 21). The study then presents a teacher who, informed by the researchers' ethnographic field notes concerning the community's funds of knowledge, creates a dual language-learning curriculum. This curriculum is based on construction work—a topic taken from the homes of the children—which includes studying the architecture of different cultures, constructing a model of a dwelling, bringing in a speaker from the community, and researching a topic related to construction work. The purpose of tapping into bilingual children's funds of knowledge is to support language acquisition in the first and second languages and to create spaces for advanced academic work with language minority students. While students' funds of knowledge are important in all culturally relevant teaching, Moll reminds us that they are especially important in working with students whose home language is not English.

*Accommodating cultural difference in the classroom.* Annette Henry's "Literacy, Black Self-Representation, and Cultural Practice in an Elementary Classroom: Implications for Teaching Children of African-Caribbean Heritage" (1996) emphasizes accommodating African-Caribbean children's culture in the classroom. Using a both/and pedagogy for teaching dominant cultural codes through the children's African-Caribbean cultural lens, the teachers in the study used "orature—which includes rap, sermons, humor, proverbs, and so forth" (123), the ring shout with "torsos swaying, feet tapping, hands clapping … singing and chanting in call-and-response" (123), and Jamaican dialect along with standard English to include and represent African-Caribbean children's cultures in the classroom. The point of accommodating the children's culture, according to Henry, is to "foster Black students' membership in North American society with a sense of self-identity as people of African descent" (129).

*Bringing students' lives into the classroom.* In Colleen Fairbanks's article "Imagining Neighborhoods: Social Worlds of Urban Adolescents," the author uses the class-

room as a space for dialogue between teachers and students in order to "open the classroom to students' lived experiences and the possibility for negotiated classroom interactions" (1998b, 135). Fairbanks provides a variety of writing formats such as journal entries, formal assignments, and projects that "were embedded within other classroom activities which dealt with overall themes of study and arose from discussion of readings" (136). Students' writing explored their understandings of neighborhood, social, and personal questions; the meaning of political agency; and lived experiences "describing their lives in their own and others' language" (153) as a way of co-creating the classroom in order to "create lovely things—together" (155).

*Providing profiles.* Ladson-Billings's *Dreamkeepers* (1994) provides extensive profiles of teachers who enact culturally relevant teaching. From her profiles of teacher-Dreamkeepers, she finds that culturally relevant teaching represents a complex of beliefs, attitudes, and behaviors internalized by experienced teachers. The teachers in the study, for example, often live in the communities where they teach and are visible members of that community, hold the teaching profession in high esteem, show self-esteem through their physical dress and polished mannerisms, believe teaching is an art that allows all children to learn when it is practiced successfully, and see students as community members with valuable knowledge to offer in the classroom. Additionally, these teachers work to develop relationships with their students, see students in classrooms as co-constructors of knowledge rather than as recipients of time-honored canons, focus on critical thinking in relation to materials presented, ensure that students develop necessary academic skills for continued schooling, and create a standard for excellence while respecting students' differences. Most interestingly, practitioners of culturally relevant teaching use an eclectic mix of methods tailored to their specific children that range from child-centered to teacher-centered.

## Limits

From a discussion recorded in "Introducing the M-CLASS" —the introduction to *Inside City Schools*—Walter Wood raises the central question that confronts those who personally wish to enact teaching that is culturally relevant:

> How do we bridge what we are talking about as good practices and the realities of my classroom—the lack of furniture, the lack of materials, and sometimes the discipline we have to put up with?…Sometimes I think that we intellectualize, and then we go back to the real world and get away from it very quickly. (Warshauer Freedman, 1999, 17)

What is often missing in the victory stories inherent in documenting competency of culturally relevant teaching are the personal struggles and transformations necessary to become the type of teacher who succeeds in crossing borders reflexively—providing the necessary synthesis, making spaces for dialogue with students and community, or taking the risks involved in caring. Most of the victory stories concerning culturally relevant teaching, which often describe the attitudes, practices, and ways of knowing of veteran teachers, pretend these teachers come into being fully made—like Athena being born fully formed from Zeus's head.

As a teacher who forged routines, methods, and materials, I speak from experience when I say that, even with all the studies that document culturally relevant teaching, the micro-mechanics of enacting it always come down to the lives of the students in the room; the teacher's willingness to experiment; knowledge and respect for the parents and children of the community; the development and availability of culturally relevant materials; and the teacher's ability to forge relationships with students, competent teachers in the school, and community members. In the schools in rural and urban minority, at-risk, limited English proficiency, and low socioeconomic status communities that I worked in for the last eight years after teaching in Mexico for five years, many teachers I knew didn't experience these victory narratives so interesting to university researchers. In contrast, many either figured out a way to manage in a sort of nonfunctioning purgatory, or they simply left the profession—sometimes burned out after having finally gained competence. Others, like myself, struggled and transformed themselves while developing the particular classroom structures that allowed for culturally relevant teaching to take place. None of the teachers I know—even the very best ones I've met—could characterize their experience within the frame of the victory story.

## MY JOURNEY: STRUGGLE AND TRANSFORMATION

### Synthesis, Dialogue, and Caring Experienced

Rather than me teaching my expert knowledge, the students and community taught me in those difficult years—first in South Texas and then in inner-city Austin—that I had to change in order to connect with students who saw me as a "new teacher" in the community who (probably like many of the new teachers they had seen over the last years) would leave immediately for a more comfortable position teaching in the suburbs. I had to continually wonder, probe, ask myself: "What do the students know and want to learn about? What types of activities will they participate in? What types of authority, academic or disciplinary, will they accept from me?" And, after a few hopeless days of constantly questioning my own competence and purposes, I occasionally made discoveries of materials and strategies that worked, and suddenly, the students were working and learning—*synthesizing* academic material and their cultural experiences.

After a particularly upsetting incident when I separated two girls who were fighting in the stairwell, I discovered that one of the girls—who was supposed to be inside my second period class—had been bitten on the cheek. I put my arms around her while she cried, "She bit me...that fucking bitch bit me." I then told another student to get the nurse and went back into the classroom. There, a boy said, "Sir, you don't look too good." I responded to the whole class, "Do you think I don't care what happens to you?" For the rest of the class, we discussed ourselves, what had happened, and gangs in the school. I learned a lot from making myself available for *dialogue*.

When I first arrived in Austin, I taught bilingual fourth grade in a position that was later closed. But for roughly the first six weeks of school, I had an adorable group of 15 kids. After the second day of school, when I was walking the kids out to the entrance for pick-up, I felt a little hand wrap around mine. Amalia, who was a soft-spoken under-aged girl, turned to me and hugged me before she got in the car with her mother. Her mother and I waved at each other, and I felt a tenderness for her that I didn't have the privilege of experiencing again until I recently became a father. She and the other members of that group taught me that *caring* makes the institution of school a different place.

### Two Units I've Developed Along the Way

So what does my teaching look like when it is based on long-term learning from students who have different backgrounds from mine? What does it look like when I apply my ideas in the classroom? To answer that question, I offer a few units I've developed over the years that fit into culturally relevant teaching. The part played by synthesis, dialogue, and caring, though not always explicit in each unit, comes to the surface here and there throughout while I focus on the struggles and the will to transform that make the classroom a source of pride and accomplishment for myself, a place where we—teachers, students, community—overcome difficulty.

*1. Children's Language, Culture, and Community: South Texas Legends (three weeks).*

I started working on this unit my first year as a public school teacher. After I made friends with the assistant principal based on shared interests in Hispanic-American literature, he became my mentor. During my first year in the classroom teaching sixth grade children, he watched as I struggled through lesson planning, trying to teach traditionally without much luck. After several conversations, he gave me a bilingual resource that I have since found of inestimable value in teaching Mexican immigrants and Mexican-American students: *Stories That Must Not Die* (Sauvageau, 1989). Just as the students were tiring of my reliance on authoritative teaching and discipline, through the friendship and conversations with my mentor I took the first steps in developing this unit, which I taught in different ways over the next eight years. Here I'll provide a collage of the ways I approached this unit.

I usually started the unit using teacher-led discussions concerning Mexican and Mexican-American legends and folklore: *La Llorona* or the Sobbing Woman, *La Lechuza* or the Jealous Barn Owl, *los curanderos* or faith-healers, *mal de ojo* or the evil eye, and *remedios caseros* or home remedies. After having the students respond to these broad topics in small groups, they shared their understandings as a whole group.

- A *lechuza* is an evil lady who can change into an owl. Once one came and landed on our house, and my Dad got the shotgun and shot at it. They say that the *lechuza* means death for someone in the family.

- *Mal de ojo* is when someone gives a compliment, like to a baby. Then they have to touch him or that's bad, *mal de ojo*, like envy. But it's a lot of other things too…

- *La Llorona* … she's the lady that killed her kids and drowned herself in the river. She walks along the river looking for her dead children…

After activating what the children know, we read round robin, in pairs, and silently, doing three-sentence summaries of what was read and identifying the characters from the discussion of our readings. Every section of reading is followed by telling stories that the children know, and telling stories is often followed by more reading in fluid movements following the mood of the group. If the stories that the kids exchange are engaging, we'll story swap the whole class period. If there aren't a bunch of storytellers in class, we'll read more from the book. During this sharing of legends, student experts emerge in each class, and on occasion, I've pulled them from class so they can share stories with other classes during the day. Since the materials I use are often bilingual, the Spanish-speaking children often request to read the legends in their home language, or they ask me to do it for them. Usually toward the beginning of the unit, I invite one of the expert storytellers' parents to join us—because the child gets the stories from the parents. On several occasions, the parents' visits turn into a listening treat in which the class hears legend after legend for an entire class period.

As the unit progresses, I expand the notion of legends, moving from culturally specific South Texas legends to a general definition of legends. I also accept urban legends and neighborhood scary stories so that all students, even those few without a Mexican-American background, can participate. I contribute by sharing legends from books that I've read or from the Internet—freely sharing during the sessions—and children bring in legends from books and the Internet also. One standard homework assignment that I have given in the past is for students to find an example of a legend either in the library or on the Internet that they could share with the group. This differs from story swapping in that it requires students to move toward written legends that are presented in a more literary form. Children then summarize on a note card the written legend they found and present it to the class.

In order to provide an incentive for active listening, I monitor students as they listen to others' presentations of legends and provide them with a listening grade, or I have the students summarize each of the legends presented using the same three-sentence format described above. I use web sites such as "The Moon Lit Road" (Dominey, 2002), link them to my Internet site, and have the children read from or listen to legends on the site in the computer lab for several days, filling out "Evidence of Reading" forms that require a variety of reading skills including sequencing events, summarizing, inferring, and predicting.

After engaging the students in their home culture and language for several weeks in the ways mentioned above, I assign a culminating project. One of the projects that I did several years ago required the students to become ethnographers and tape-record stories from the community. This ethnography project required students to find an elder in the community—a parent, grandparent, aunt, uncle, or elderly family friend—and interview them about the community, the "old days," and legends they know. One interesting scary story, narrated by the student's grandmother, follows.

> My mother always told me to stay away from the [irrigation] canals when we played, but of course we didn't. We thought that the parents were always worried about silliness….we always went to the canals to play. In the summer, we went swimming and we had all types of games that we would play along them—like water games and ball games, you know, child's play. But the parents would always get mad when they found out, because they knew that sometimes children drowned in the canal.

> Well…we kept playing, and one time we met a new kid—a kid we had never seen at school. Anyways, we asked him his name, and he said it was Enrique. Enrique liked to swim in the canal, but he also played all types of games like *busca-busca* [hide and seek]….We played together for a long time every day, maybe a month. Then one day we walked down Enrique's street, and he told us where he lived. He went inside.

> After that we didn't see Enrique for a long time…when we went by his house, an old lady said we should stop playing games with her. "Enrique died a long time ago," she cried. When we asked some of the other neighbors about the old lady and Enrique, they said that Enrique had drowned in the canal….we had played with him every day for a month.

*2. Bringing Lives into the Classroom: The Reflective Essay*

I had always been a better teacher of literature than of writing—as language arts teachers often prove themselves to be more interested in one side or the other of the reading-writing split. And working in South Texas didn't always help—we were forced to do at least two TAAS (Texas state standardized tests) essays per six weeks on prompts assigned by the department head. While I'm embarrassed to admit that I taught prescribed writing for five years in a row, at the same time I reserve a space of pride that 93 percent of the students in our 100 percent low socioeconomic status school passed state standards on the conventions of writing in the standard academic essay. But at best, I feel ambivalent of this type of "success"—the formal testing type—knowing that a lot was lost using prescriptive methods to respond to prompts.

When I came to Austin and began working in a "majority minority," "inner-city" middle school with approximately "75% of the students on free and reduced lunch," I found a new department head who challenged the prescriptive way that I was teaching the state essay. He argued, ceaselessly, that I needed to let students choose their topics while manipulating the modes of discourse on the TAAS test. Using topic generation and narrowing, student examples of successful TAAS essays, and newspaper articles as models, I took the plunge rather successfully into the world of choice—of course, with the coaching and feedback of my new mentor. The persuasive letters, I found, began to be about problems in the school or housing projects, and we later delivered them to the indicated recipients. Children revised and edited the drafts, making suggestions of where to expand or delete, where to add dialogue, and where to fix sentence errors, and they word-processed and printed out two copies of their papers: the first for grading and the second to be stapled together in class packets for independent reading later. The packets of student essays became a favorite read during independent reading time.

But it was not until I discovered Linda Rief's "life graphs" and "neighborhood maps" (1992) that students began making choices that showed depth of reflection and voice despite lacking mechanics. What developed out of the life graphs and neighborhood maps turned into a recurring assignment of writing reflective and personal essays after using extensive pre-writing scenarios.

I begin this unit by sharing a humorous personal essay that I wrote called "The Perfect Family" (Jupp, 1999) as a model of the type of writing that the assignment required. Then we read several short essays from Gary Soto's *The Effects of Knut Hamsun on a Fresno Boy: Recollections and Personal Essays* (2001), including "Like Mexicans," to reinforce more serious reflection to contrast with my humorous publication. After the students read models of personal reflective writing, I had them construct life graphs. In making life graphs, the students plot positive and negative numbers on the y-axis and only positive numbers on the x-axis. The numbers on the y-axis are used to chart life experiences as excellent (+5) to terrible (-5). The x-axis is used to represent age at the time of the experience.

While making the life graph—which is colored, illustrated, and used to choose a meaningful life event about which to write, children begin dialoguing with me and their peers about their lives while they chart events on the graph. The life graphs generate community talk and caring for one another that is later translated into writing, so life graphs allow for rehearsal of what will be in the personal reflections. After the life graphs are done, students who want to share the events they are going to write about do so.

After determining the criteria for grading the essay as a learning community (neatness, organization, mechanics, sentence errors) and posting them on butcher paper in the room, students start drafting. At the end of each day of drafting, students share what they are writing, and the class evaluates whether they are meeting the established grading criteria. Finally, when students finish their drafts, revising and editing take place. Here is an example of sixth grade work that despite its problems in mechanics shows promise as a reflective personal essay:

> It's been 10 years since I haven't seen my dad. Its being hard since that day. My mom has to work two shifs all day for she could dress me and buy what we need.
>
> It all began with this one night Sunday in the year of 1993. My dad was got by the police. It was horrible cops all over the house all I said was look mom all the colorfull lights. My sister the oldest was crying, also my mom. At that time she was twelve or thirteen she knew what was going on.

And a few pages later, the author writes the reflection:

> When I was growing up I had to lie to my friends they always ask me for him and I said he is working in California. I know that was a lie but I still had to say it because I was emberrest of my own dad. I still don't know where he is, or well, I know he's in jail but I don't know if he's alive or if he's dead. I hope he's not dead because that will hurt me. I don't know him very well I don't even have a picture of him....I always say that I don't have a dad because I've never had the love of a dad. Well, I had to realize that it all has to be true because I'm living it.

The final days of the unit, students spent two entire periods reading their work to the class community and admiring a variety of essay types—tragic, comic, and dramatic. Reading about personal reflections allows the class members to get to know each other better. Friendships develop, and so does caring talk.

## CRITIQUING REFLEXIVITY: LEGITIMACY, CYNICISM, AND HOPE

In his essay "Nueva España: Orfandad y Legitimidad" (1979), Octavio Paz argues that the Catholic co-optation of indigenous symbols like the Virgin of Guadalupe as Virgin Mary or the interpretation of Quetzalcoatl as St. Thomas represent attempts at legitimizing pre-Hispanic Mexican culture. Because the Catholic God could want an indigenous goddess as Virgin Saint, or because St. Thomas and Quetzalcoatl are the same person coming from the same civilizational tradition, Catholic rule in the colonies, through legitimizing these indigenous symbols, becomes "inclusive" of indigenous cultures as part of the colonial regime.

I find this struggle for legitimization of "the other" in the Spanish Colonial Period analogous to concepts of border crossing, reflexivity, and their extension in the classroom: culturally relevant teaching, including my own experiments. Border crossing, reflexivity, and culturally relevant teaching represent a movement toward legitimization of the cultural other in American cultural life in the same way that the Spanish colonial society legitimized the indigenous other. After all, we still live in the historical remnants of the colonizer-colonized relationship, and schools are important sites of social reproduction in a U.S. regime based on merit, consumerism, work, and self-reliance (Apple, 1979). Through the lenses of the colonizer-colonized relationship, social reproduction, and regime, we see the tricky game we play when we attempt to legitimate cultural others in our schools, our lessons, and our children's minds: To whose benefit is the legitimization of the other found in culturally relevant teaching?

There are several interpretations of the legitimization of the cultural other inherent in border crossing, reflexivity, and culturally relevant teaching. On one side, radical skeptics argue that the move toward legitimization of the other is but symbolic, that there is, in fact, no difference between the regime before and after its new legitimate culture(s). The powers that be have merely repositioned themselves around different idols in making power legitimate for a different type of oppression. On the other side, the liberal practitioner argues that this reorganization and repositioning of power around new idols of the cultural other make for change, betterment, and progress. Perhaps, in this view, the synthesis, dialogue, and caring that accompanied this shift of cultural idols *actually changed* schools for the better, allowing for more inclusion and making the society a better place.

I argue that in this dangerously conservative political climate, we need to see radical skeptics and liberals as complementary. While liberals can learn from radical skeptics concerning the traps of legitimization and the difficulty of working the colonized-colonizer relationship in a critical way, radical skeptics need to set foot in a school and see how children respond in concrete class-room circumstances to the liberal pedagogy represented in culturally relevant teaching. Even though the liberal pedagogy that legitimizes cultural difference is limited in its possibility, what are the alternatives in real classrooms of our dominant institutions at present? What can be accomplished in the institution of school as it exists in the present? How do we respond in practice to the demands we face in our classrooms? I argue that culturally relevant teaching, which *de facto* is a part of legitimizing the cultural other, represents an important concrete plan that requires more attention in public education. Culturally relevant teaching, like the kind I discuss and explore, represents the best stance for white teachers working with children of color within a dominant social order.

## References

Apple, M. W. (1979). On analyzing hegemony. *Journal of Curriculum Theorizing* 1(1): 10-27.

Collins, P. H. (1990). Chapter 10: Toward an Afrocentric feminist epistemology. *Black feminist thought: Knowledge, consciousness, and the politics of empowerment* (201-220). New York: Routledge.

Cummins, J. (1986). Empowering minority students: A framework for intervention. *Harvard Educational Review* 56(1): 18-36.

Delpit, L. (1986). Skills and other dilemmas of a progressive Black educator. *Harvard Educational Review* 56(4): 379-385.

De Stigter, T. (1998). Good deeds: An ethnographer's reflections on usefulness. In C. Fleischer and D. Schaafsma (Eds.), *Literacy and democracy* (28-52). Urbana, IL: National Council of Teachers of English.

Dewey, J. (1990 [1902]). *The child and the curriculum* (179-209). Chicago: University of Chicago Press.

Dewey, J. (1997 [1916]). *Democracy and education*. New York: The Free Press.

Dominey, C. (2002). Online at www.themoonlitroad.com.

Emerson, R. M.; Fretz, R. I.; and Shaw, L. L. (1995). *Writing ethnographic fieldnotes*. Chicago: University of Chicago Press.

Fairbanks, C. (1998a). Nourishing conversations: Urban adolescents, literacy, and democratic society. *Journal of Language and Reading* 30(2): 187-203.

Fairbanks, C. (1998b). Imagining neighborhoods: Social worlds of urban adolescents. In C. Fleischer and D. Schaafsma (Eds.), *Literacy and democracy* (136-156). Urbana, IL: National Council of Teachers of English.

Foley, D. (2002). Critical ethnography: The reflexive turn. *Qualitative Studies in Education* 15(5): 469-490.

Freire, P. (1998a [1969]). *La educación como práctica de la libertad* (47th ed.). México, D.F.: Siglo Vientiuno Editores.

Freire, P. (1998b [1970]). *Pedagogía del oprimido* (51st ed.). México, D.F.: Siglo Vientiuno Editores.

Goldstein, L. (1998). More than gentle smiles and warm hugs: Applying the ethic of care to early childhood education. *Journal of Research in Early Childhood Education* 12(2): 244-261.

Goldstein, L. (2002). *Reclaiming caring in teaching and teacher education*. New York: Peter Lang.

Henry, A. (1996). Literacy, Black self-representation, and cultural practice in an elementary classroom: Implications for teaching children of African-Caribbean heritage. *Qualitative Studies in Education* 9(2): 119-134.

Jupp. J. (1999). The perfect family. *Mesquite Review* 13: 37-38.

Ladson-Billings, G. (1994). *The dreamkeepers: Successful teachers of African American children*. San Francisco: Jossey-Bass.

Ladson-Billings, G. (1995). Toward a theory of culturally relevant pedagogy. *American Educational Research Journal* 32(3): 465-491.

Moll, L. C. (1992). Bilingual classroom studies and community analysis: Some recent trends. *Educational Researcher* 21(2): 20-24.

Moll, L. C. and González, N. (1994). Lessons from research with language minority children. *Journal of Reading Behavior* 26(4): 439-455.

Nee-Benham, M. K. P. A. (1997). The story of an African-American teacher scholar: A woman's narrative. *International Journal of Qualitative Studies in Education* 10(1): 63-83.

Noddings, N. (1984). Caring: *A feminine approach to ethics and education*. Berkeley: University of California Press.

Paz, O. (1979). Nueva españa: Ofandad y legitimidad. *El ogro filantrópico* (38-52). Mexico, D.F.: Cuadernos Joaquin Mortiz.

Rief, L. (1992). *Seeking diversity*. Portsmouth, NH: Heinemann.

Robinson, J. (1998). Literacy and lived lives: Reflections on the responsibilities of teachers. In C. Fleischer and D. Schaaf- sma (Eds.), *Literacy and democracy* (1-27). Urbana, IL: National Council of Teachers of English.

Sauvageau, J. (1989). *Stories that must not die.* Los Angeles: Pan American Publishing Company, Inc.

Scheurich, J. (1998). Highly successful and loving, public preK-5 schools populated mainly by low SES children of color: Core beliefs and cultural characteristics. *Urban Education* 33(4): 451-491.

Soto, G. (2001). *The effects of Knut Hamsun on a Fresno boy: Recollections and personal essays.* New York: Persea Books.

Warshauer Freedman, S. (1999). Introducing the M-CLASS. In S. Warshauer Freedman et al. (Ed.), *Inside city schools: Investigating literacy in multicultural classrooms.* New York: Teachers College Press.

*James C. Jupp* is a teacher at Fulmore Middle School in Austin, Texas, and a doctoral student at the University of Texas. He reviews young adult books about Latin America and the Latino experience for *Multi-Cultural Review* and is working on his first novel.

# UNIT 3

# Multicultural Education as an Academic Discipline

## Unit Selections

## Key Points to Consider

- What should be some minimal standards of practice in the field of multicultural education?

- What should be the qualifications for persons who wish to become specialists in multicultural education?

- It has been argued that all American students should learn the multicultural reality of our nation. Why is this true? How can it be accomplished?

- Is a "melting pot" approach to multicultural education outdated? How can multicultural education be applied to the classroom?

- What issues are raised by total infusion models of multicultural education in teacher education programs?

- What should all American students know about racism and prejudice by the time they graduate from high school?

- How do we help people learn to accept cultural diversity? What can teachers do to foster acceptance of cultural differences?

## Student Website

www.mhcls.com/online

## Internet References

Further information regarding these websites may be found in this book's preface or online.

**Goals 2000: A Progress Report**
*http://www.ed.gov/pubs/goals/progrpt/index.html*

**Teachers Helping Teachers**
*http://www.pacificnet.net/~mandel/*

**"M**ulticultural education" emerged as an area of scholarship out of the social upheavals of the 1960s and the concern of many in the scholarly community that there was a critical need for research-based knowledge of the cultural contexts of education. Much of our early knowledge base came from critically important research in anthropology and sociology (as well as psychiatric studies of the impact of prejudice and victimization on targeted racial and cultural minorities), from the 1920s to our present time. These studies examined intercultural relations in all sorts of urban, suburban, small town, and rural settings in the United States. They used ethnographic field inquiry methods developed by anthropologists and later used by some sociologists and educators. The earliest of these studies, from the 1920s through the 1950s, focused on such concerns as child-rearing practices, rites of passage into adulthood, perceptions of other cultural groups, and the social stratification systems of communities and neighborhoods. Studies of how victimized and involuntarily segregated racial and cultural groups responded to being "targeted" for discriminatory treatment documented the intercultural state of affairs in American society in the 1930s and 1940s.

As the civil rights movement of the 1950s in the United States continued to grow in momentum throughout the 1960s, continued anthropological and sociological inquiry about the education of minority cultural youth continued to develop. Out of the urban and other social crises of the 1960s emerged a belief among those educators concerned about questions of racial and cultural justice that there was a serious need for an area of educational studies, which would specifically focus on the study of intercultural relations in the schools from a "multi-" cultural perspective. It would challenge the by-then-traditional Eurocentric melting pot visions of how one became "American." The problem with the Eurocentric "melting pot" was that it was a very exclusionary pot; not everyone was welcome to jump into it. The philosophy of a culturally pluralist democracy in which all cultural heritages would be treasured and none rejected became attractive to those who witnessed the arbitrary and cruel effects of racial and cultural prejudice in schools, as well as in other areas of life in "mainstream" society.

The belief that all teachers should respect the cultural heritages of their students and that all students have the right to know their cultural heritages and to develop pride in them began to spread among socially concerned educators. The studies that had been conducted on intercultural relations among teachers and students by the early 1970s clearly demonstrated the need for an academic discipline that would focus on building knowledge bases about our multicultural social reality as well as on how to teach about other cultural heritages and to improve the quality of instruction in multicultural school settings. Many of us realize today that all young Americans need to know about the American experience from a multicultural perspective that rejects and transcends the old Anglo- and Eurocentric presuppositions of melting pot theories of assimilation into American social life.

As part of the movement for civil rights, persons from non-English-speaking backgrounds also sought to guarantee that their children would be given the opportunity to grow up both bilingual and bicultural. By the time the U.S. Supreme Court handed down its decision in *Lau v. Nichols* in 1974, there were dozens of cases in the federal court system concerning the causes of bilingual education and English as a second language.

The academic leadership of the nation's cultural minorities and many other concerned scholars has forged a competent community dedicated to the task of setting standards of practice for multicultural education as an academic discipline. There is spirited dialogue going on in the field as to what these standards of practice should be as well as about what academic qualifications people ought to have to conduct multicultural education. James Banks, professor of multicultural education at the University of Washington, and others are concerned about the future survival and development of multicultural education as an academic discipline that must also maintain its focus on classroom practice as well as on defensible theoretical constructs.

Multicultural education must develop an ongoing cadre of competent scholarly leaders to direct the further development of the field as well as to ensure that attempts to merely infuse multicultural content into existing teacher education course content does not dilute the academic quality of multicultural education or the standards of practice in the field. Multicultural education is an interdiscipline that draws its knowledge base from anthropology, sociology, social history, and even psychiatry. Focused, adequately prepared specialists in this new interdiscipline are necessary on school faculties if it is to maintain its academic integrity.

The essays in this unit reflect concerns regarding academic standards and goals for multicultural education, as the field continues to develop and to enter a new period in its history. The authors of these essays raise important qualitative issues that must be addressed as the time approaches when a majority of Americans will be from "minority" cultural heritages and when traditional conceptions of minority and majority relations in the United States will have little meaning.

This unit's essays are relevant to courses in curriculum theory and construction, educational policy studies, history and philosophy of education, cultural foundations of education, and multicultural education.

# Whose World Is This?

Jayne R. Beilke

*Whose world is this?*
*The world is yours, the world is yours*
*It's mine, it's mine, it's mine*
*Whose world is this?*
*Nas (1994)*

## Introduction

As defined by critical theorists, critical multicultural education requires the development of a critical consciousness (*conscientization*). The elements of critical consciousness include dialogue, problem-posing, and the exploration of generative themes such as race, class, and gender. The formation of a partnership between university students and a community nonprofit, youth-serving agency, can be a powerful catalyst in the development of critical multicultural consciousness.

This article describes an on-going partnership between university secondary education majors in a multicultural education class and the local Boys and Girls Club. It draws upon student reflective journals to illustrate the process of developing critical multicultural consciousness and the potential for praxis (change).

## Muncie Boys and Girls Club

The Muncie Boys and Girls Club is located in Industry, one of Muncie's two historically Black neighborhoods. Industry neighborhood was the site of the Ball Brothers glass factories that produced canning jars during the Progressive Era. In 1886, the discovery of natural gas deposits drew the industrialist Ball Brothers from New York to Muncie and ushered in glass manufacturing throughout east-central Indiana.

Shortly after the turn of the 20th century, the natural gas deposits were exhausted due to the lack of conservation (Lynd and Lynd, 1929). Manufacturing firms relocated, but a town of 20,000 inhabitants had been established, due in large part to streams of southern blacks and Appalachian whites who had been drawn to Muncie by the prospect of jobs.

Travelling from Ball State University to the Club, one passes Munsyana Homes, Muncie's oldest housing projects, which were built in 1941. Munsyana Homes are two-story drab lime-green and beige rectangular cinder block buildings that occupy several city blocks. Despite the outward appearance of order and containment, the Homes are the scene of heavy drug trafficking and related crime. Nearby is a liquor store whose owner once won the city's "Outstanding Business of the Year" award. Abandoned convenience stores, a thriving blood plasma center, small businesses, storefront churches and the abandoned relics of the glass factories all mix together in Industry.

The Muncie Boys and Girls Club is housed in a brick building built in 1951. The original windows were removed long ago to prevent theft and vandalism. There is no visible tagging (graffiti) anywhere on the Club facility, which is a sign that neighborhood gangs recognize it as neutral space. It has a large gymnasium, a recreation room filled with pool tables, an arts and crafts room, a small kitchen, a lounge with a television set and sofas, and an education room. It serves 170 inner city children and youth each day ranging from 5 to 17 years of age. Representative of the city's persistent residential segregation, most of the African American members of the Club live in the black neighborhoods while poor whites live in Shedtown.

University students who grew up and live in Muncie call the Southside "the low end." Although the majority of the Club's clients are African American, an increasing number identify themselves as "other" or biracial. The common denominator, however, is not race, but social class. The Club's members represent families of lower socioeconomic status who populate the city's working class. At the elementary school next door, the entire student body qualifies for the federal free or reduced lunch program.

A membership to the Boys and Girls Club costs one dollar a month, but "scholarships" are readily available for children who cannot afford it. The purpose of the membership fee is to encourage commitment—a sense of belonging—rather than to provide monetary support for the Club, which is supported by the United Way and private donations. Club staff members are all too aware that children join gangs for just that reason—to belong. During its busiest period, after school until 6:00 pm, the Club can be a chaotic place, as evidenced by one student's first impression:

*Amy\*: In a way the Club looked worse than I had imagined. Children were screaming and shouting for no reason. I tried talking to the kids and asking them their names and what they did there. Two of the four kids I talked to just blew me off. The other two kind of talked to me, but in a very loud, obnoxious manner to the point where I couldn't understand them very well. I was stunned by the constant noise and opening and slamming of doors.*

The Boys and Girls Club is an example of non-formal education (NFE), defined (after Philip Coombs) as "any organized, systematic educational activity outside the framework of the formal [school] system designed to provide selective types of learning to particular sub-groups in the population, adults as well as children" (Paulston & LeRoy, 1982, 336-7). NFE is perhaps most closely associated with literacy programs in countries such as Nicaragua (Arnove, 1986) and Brazil and Guinea-Bissau (Freire, 1978).

The national Boys and Girls Club curriculum consists of the following program areas: athletics, education, gang and drug prevention, good citizenship, and survival skills (e.g. cooking). Local chapters are allowed to customize the curriculum to fit their needs.

## Towards Critical Multicultural Consciousness through Community Engagement

Planned activities can last anywhere from 20 minutes to an hour. Participation in recreation is held out as a reward for completing homework. Although they do not typically hold teaching licensure, staff members function as a combination of teacher, social worker, and mentor. They are united by their commitment to working with underserved youth and are more often than not familiar with the territory. They know, for example, that mobility plays a large role in the lives of children from lower socioeconomic families. Such families may move frequently in an attempt to avoid the rent collector, Child Protective Services, or an abusive spouse. For many children, the Club provides a stable environment for a few hours a week.

## University Teaching Majors

While talking with a resident of the Whiteley neighborhood, she referred to the university as "out there." Puzzled, I said, "You speak of it as though it were another world." She responded emphatically, "it *is* another world!" Located a scant two miles northwest of the Club, the university is named for the aforementioned Ball Brothers who, in 1918, purchased a failing normal school and infused it with capital. Ball State University is now a comprehensive university with a student population of 18,500.

Although teaching majors no longer dominate the university, they remain integral to its institutional mission.

The majority of education majors come from rural communities within a 90-mile radius of the university. They are often first generation college students who graduated from high schools with homogenous white, middleclass populations. For many of them, the sheer size of the university itself is an eye-opening experience.

Secondary education (junior high, middle school, high school) majors who are preparing to be junior high, middle school, and high school teachers are required to take one course in multicultural education. Informal profiles constructed by the students at the beginning of the course reveal that they identify themselves as middleclass, Christian, and small town (sometimes rural). Consistent with their belief that whiteness is normative, these students do not identify themselves racially; while African American and Asian students always do so.

Most of the students prefer country and Christian contemporary music. A few white and black students also listen to rap music and gospel. When asked what they would change about public education if they had the power, they initially have no suggestions. It has, after all, worked for them—they are part of the 30 per cent of high school students who attend postsecondary institutions.

## Critical Multicultural Education

The conceptual framework of critical theory is derived from the works of Paolo Freire, Henry Giroux, Peter McLaren, and others. Brazilian educator Paolo Freire contributed the concept of *conscientization*, or "the process in which [people] achieve a deepening awareness both of the sociocultural reality that shapes their lives and of their capacity to transform that reality" (Freire, 1985, footnote 2, p. 93). In order to achieve that reality, one must first locate—or perceive clearly (objectively)—his/her place (role) in that reality. In the process of interrogating one's sociopolitical reality, one becomes progressively more critical of it. One also begins to recognize his/her role as a change agent.

According to Freire, then, this agency allows people not only to critically name the world, but also to *change* it (Freire, 1982). Critical theorists believe that we inhabit "a world rife with contradictions and asymmetries of power and privilege" (McLaren, 1994, 175). This world is both constructed by and acted upon by its inhabitants, who are bound by class, race, and gender interests. It follows that the world they create is then necessarily racist, classist, and gendered.

The critical educator employs a dialectical approach. That is, s/he recognizes that the problems of society are part of the interconnectedness between society and the individual. In other words, the critical educator blames neither the "victim" nor the system, but sees clearly his/her role as creator, actor, and acted upon, within the larger society. The critical educator searches for the larger social, economic, and political implications of seemingly isolated phenomena (McLaren, 1994). For example, the public school curriculum ostensibly prepares students for meaningful work, citizenship, and socialization. But in a larger sense it also plays a powerful role in social reproduction, or the perpetuation of the class system.

One of the most insidious forms of social reproduction—and a frequent target of critical theorists—is tracking. Beginning in elementary school, students are "sorted" on the basis of test scores. By the time they reach high school, they are tracked into a constellation of vocational education, tech prep, or college preparatory courses. Although this is done in the name of efficiency, critical theorists would argue that it acts to maintain a working class and to produce a relatively small leadership class.

Building upon critical theory, Peter McLaren has defined critical multiculturalism as a perspective from which "representations of race, class and gender are understood as the result of large social struggles over signs and meanings" (McLaren, 2000, 221). "Power signs" are words that evoke strong images such as "Black," "poor," "welfare mothers," and "homeless." People who fall into these categories are viewed monolithically. They also serve as reference points upon which social and school policies are predicated. Persons so signified are objectified and marginalized by the dominant society. An example of this marginalization is the racializing of standardized test scores in an attempt to link ethnicity to intelligence.

According to McLaren, the application of critical theory to multiculturalism invokes this central question: "How do we develop an understanding of difference that avoids an essentializing of Otherness?" (McLaren, 1994, 286). Multicultural education courses often denigrate "the Other" as someone who needs to be acted upon—to be assimilated into the dominant society (Delpit, 1995). This is apt to occur in multicultural education courses with a service learning component where critical theory is not well integrated into the field placement and reinforced dialogically (Rosenberger, 2001). In her research on service learning, Marilynne Boyle-Baise has identified three paradigms—charity, civic education, and community building—each with its own goals and outcomes (Boyle-Baise, 2002).

It is not surprising that research reveals that pre-service teachers are most likely to belong to the first category. After all, they often cite the desire "to make a difference" as one of their reasons for choosing education as a profession. In its most benign form, the charity impulse translates into "good deeds." At its worst, it perpetuates whiteness, middle class status and Christianity as normative. Rather than "making a difference," critical theory requires students to think differently about their world.

## Critical Pedagogy

The first task of developing a critical multicultural perspective is to see oneself more objectively by "unpacking" power, privilege, and racial identity. Community engagement can be a powerful pedagogical force in that process.

But in order to develop a critical consciousness, critical theory must be inextricably integrated with the community agency field experience. Course materials and class discussions must reinforce and explicate the phenomena encountered in the field. In order for students to deconstruct their world, faculty must make conscious pedagogical choices.

I chose the following books as texts: Jonathan Kozol's *Savage Inequalities*, Alex Kotlowitz' *There Are No Children Here*, and Gregory H. Williams' *Life on the Color Line*. The sophomores in my university class still use high school, rather than the university, as a reference point. Kozol's portraits of under-resourced schools with their powerful imagery of sewage flowing into classrooms and football fields without goalposts are a jarring contrast to the schools attended by my students. Students often mistake the wealthy schools described by Kozol as private—rather than public—schools.

Kotlowitz' book is a documentary of two boys (Pharaoh and Lafeyette) growing up in the Henry Horner housing projects in Chicago. Although it is less than four hours away from Muncie, most of my students have never been to Chicago. This book introduces them to the world of the urban poor. Pharaoh, in particular, is a sympathetic character whose sweetness stands in stark contrast to his life in the projects. But along with chronicling drive-by shootings and the death of Lafeyette's best friend, the book celebrates the resilience of the boys (who belong to the Boys Club[1]) and their mother, LaJoe.

In his memoir of growing up as an impoverished light-skinned black in Muncie during the 1950s, Williams' book describes the city's racial divisiveness. Williams and his brother were brought to Muncie from Virginia, where his father passed for white until personal and economic misfortune left him penniless. Williams attended the elementary school next to the Club and played basketball at the Club. A story of poverty as much as racism, it underscores the persistence of residential and economic segregation in Muncie. In addition to the books, the course materials include other relevant print materials and videos about race, class, oppression and power.

According to Freire, the elements of critical pedagogy include dialogue, problem-posing, and generative themes. Dialogical communication allows for liberation by providing "individual and collective possibilities for reflection and action" (McLaren, 1994, 307). It calls for a balance to be struck between the more or less empowered parties. By communicating in an authentic way—*truly* relating—students are able to participate in the decisions made in the class.

Dialogical communication can produce honest, authentic debate among students over issues such as bilingual education, affirmative action, and welfare policies. Beyond the classroom, a key element of dialogue is accomplished through reflective journals. Each week, students reflect on a topic related to the required readings. The Club allows for the application of theory to practice.

Through e-mail, the classroom dialogue can be extended and problems posed.

Problem-posing education allows students and teachers to investigate universal or, after Freire, "generative" themes. Power signs and representations prevent us from seeing clearly. By problemitizing the world, however, students are given a critical lens through which to view the world—a lens unblurred by class, race, or gender constructs. Community engagement creates the opportunity in which problemitizing can occur. For example:

*Rachel: They asked us to design a mural for the new Keystone Club room, so we thought we would have a go at it. We were supposed to come up with something that would represent teenaged kids, and that would give the room some life. After an hour of brainstorming we had come up with a good idea. We had planned to do squares of bright color on the wall with black silhouettes of kids doing different things such as playing games, watching TV, hanging out with friends, and so on. But when we told the director, she said, "but what if the kids think these are all black kids, and there is some kind of meaning behind this?" We had not thought of that at all, and truthfully I was a little embarrassed. So we made a few adjustments, with the help of one of the Keystone Kids, and the end result came out pretty cool.*

Like many non-profit agencies in 2002, the Club struggled financially. Both corporate and individual donations declined as the lingering result of the attack on the World Trade Towers and the economic recession (Lewis, 2002). In the wake of 9/11, people sent donations to New York City rather than to local agencies. Potentially more devastating, the economic recession accounted for shortfalls for virtually all non-profit organizations from animal shelters to soup kitchens.

*Rachel: When we got to the Club, once again the money was not there for them to go out and buy the paints needed.*
*Luckily, Ms Hampton [education director] remembered that they had some paints they were going to use a few years ago to paint a rainbow on the wall of the art room. So we rummaged around and found those. Thankfully the paints were all in good enough shape that they were still usable.*
*Now that I think about it, I realize how much money the organizations I was involved with my whole life had. I cannot remember a time that we did not get something because the money was not there. Anytime that I need something I just go out and buy it but after visiting the Boys and Girls club last Saturday I realized that they do not have that option.*

A prime generative theme addressed by critical multicultural education is that of racial identity. In order to deconstruct race, a certain de-centering of one's identity must first occur. Several developmental theories of racial identity, which view race as a social and psychologically constructed process, have been advanced. Janet Helms (1990) defines racial identity as "a sense of group or collective identity based on one's perception that he or she shares common racial heritage with a particular racial group" (p. 3). Understanding the sociocultural construct of race is crucial to developing a critical perspective.

As discussed earlier in this article, white students rarely see themselves in terms of racial identity. While they are quick to point out that they are middleclass, they do not identify themselves as white. For that reason, it is important to first define one's white cultural identity before moving on to a nonracist white identity. The ability to see oneself as the Other is an example of disintegration, where one begins to experience dissonance about one's racial identity:

*Amy: Last week a perfect display of who the "other" was occurred. Directly quoting a child as I walked into the Club, he said, "shit, you are the whitest person I ever seen, you about as white as this piece of wood." If you might have guessed the piece of wood was a very light beige/flesh color. I hesitated and didn't know how to respond so I didn't say much. The whole point of integrating this quote into my journal is because I strongly believe it defines me as being the "other" at the Club.*

*Liz: The Club definitely influenced my view on being Hispanic. For a long time I was embarrassed by it, and later on I didn't even think about being Hispanic either way because I was with white people all of the time. The kids at the club helped remind me that I do look different, and they helped me see how beneficial my appearance and being a minority will be.*

In Peggy McIntosh' (1989) brief but classic article "White Privilege: Unpacking the Invisible Knapsack," she lists unearned assets which can be found in a metaphorical knapsack of privilege. Examples range from the assurance that "I can if I wish arrange to be in the company of people of my race most of the time" to "I can choose blemish cover or bandages in 'flesh' color and have them more or less match my skin." University students generally interpret the word "privilege" as a trapping of the upper class. By interrogating the meaning of privilege (i.e., something that is taken for granted) students find examples of privilege writ small:

*Destiny: One thing that stuck in my head was when this little girl asked me what I had in my mouth. I said it was a retainer and she said, "oh, did you ever have braces?" I told her yes and she said, "My dentist told me and my momma I needed braces but she say she can't afford them." That made me really think about how some of these kids are deprived of certain things.*

By deconstructing class privilege, students not only begin to see themselves more clearly, but can also recognize strengths and resilience in Club members. By the age of 8, Jerry was already the primary caregiver for his younger sisters, while his mother worked. He often bullied some of the smaller Club members as well as my university students.

But Jerry's complexity became evident over the course of the semester. When a new, white child showed up at the Club, Jerry became his protector. In return, the child's grateful parents asked Jerry to accompany them on a trip to Washington DC the following summer. While on the trip, the Club's loudspeaker squawked out the message that Jerry had called to "tell everyone hello."

Spending time with Jerry allowed my students to recognize his belligerence as a form of resistance to victimization (Allport, 1954). During a tutoring session, he threatened to "knock those glasses right off your face" if my student wouldn't provide him with the correct answers. Gently refusing to do so, the student noticed that Jerry had tears in his eyes as he patiently continued to help him with his composition. Other students also began to "see" him more clearly:

*Richard: It was quite a surprise to get to the Boys and Girls Club and find that their Fall Festival was scheduled that day. Enter Jerry. He's black and I think he's in junior high. Jerry asked me if the kids were playing, and I said they didn't have tickets. He proceeded to cover for those kids. He had a dozen or so tickets, and he used them paying for other kids to play musical chairs.*

*Jerry was my interesting event at the Festival. I didn't get the opportunity to talk with him much, but I can see something in him. I see a person who's being like a big brother to some of the kids. I see someone willing to do things for others. I see someone who may very well turn out to be a community-oriented person, serving his home (wherever that may be in the future).*

## Under Construction: Pedagogy to Praxis

The process of conscientization is not developmental; one does not take orderly, discrete steps from problem-posing or dialogue to praxis. Rather, it is a holistic process in which all elements are interconnected and occur as integrated parts of the whole. Critical pedagogy through community engagement can effectively foster dialogue and problem-solving but praxis is more difficult to achieve.

Freire defines praxis as being "reflection and action upon the world in order to transform it" (Freire, 1982, 36). The goal of praxis is liberatory—the achievement of a more just and equitable world for all inhabitants. One of its prerequisites is the evidence of humanization of the Other through the formation of authentic relationships. In a university multicultural education course bounded by time constraints and frequency of student contact, it is difficult to achieve the kind of cognitive dissonance that produces praxis. Nevertheless, like privilege, praxis writ small does occur through the establishment of authentic relationships:

*Mike: I am starting to get more comfortable because I have been getting to know the kids better, and vice versa. I have learned that just helping a kid do math problems or look up words can be rather cold and impersonal. It is still satisfying to help them do these things, but sometimes it seems like a one way experience. When it's over, the satisfaction seems to fade quickly unless I have made a personal connection with the kid. In the future, I am going to try to think of each interaction with kids (or anyone else for that matter) as a shared experience and consciously look for ways to develop relationships.*

To "consciously look for ways" signals the intentionality that Freire says is necessary for action. In Mike's case, the passive act of tutoring a student by using drill sheets and vocabulary practice is in itself not satisfactory. By creating an authentic relationship, both parties can learn something from each other and precipitate action:

*Jason: My most enduring image of the Boys/Girls Club was witnessing, through the different ages of the children, a cruel assembly line of poverty, oppression, and ignorance turning innocent, happy and hopeful children into delinquent, angry and hopeless children. I remember a young little boy, innocently and comfortably grabbing my hand, holding it with a smile, as he led me to find him a basketball. As well, I remember a boy, only a few years older than the former one, who angrily threw a basketball down and walked off court cursing over something so trivial he probably forgot it by the end of the day. If I had the power, I would end the process of tracking students in schools.*

To summarize, I advance the following definition of critical multicultural consciousness through engagement: *Critical multicultural consciousness through community engagement is predicated on the formation of a mutually beneficial partnership between educational entities (formal or nonformal) for the purpose of conscientization. The process is guided by critical pedagogy (including dialogue, problem-posing, and generative themes) and the hopeful possibility of praxis (social action).* Within these wide boundaries, critical multicultural consciousness affords pre-service teachers the opportunity to interrogate and deconstruct their world-view.

As a process, critical multicultural consciousness is neither paradigmatic nor developmental. It does, however, require a certain redefinition of authority, a coherent integration between theory and practice so that each informs the other, a commitment to the formation of authentic relationships, and recognition of transformation writ small.

## Conclusion: Beyond the Scholarship of Engagement

With the publication of *Scholarship Reconsidered*, Ernest L. Boyer challenged the traditional role of faculty as being removed from their communities. He recommended a reconnection between scholarship and community that would ultimately provide "service" for the common good. In the calls for service that emanated in reaction to the "Me Decade" of the 1980s (notably, Putnam, 1995), Boyer's book was a clarion call to university faculty to reconnect with communities and engage through the scholarship of discovery, integration, application, integration, and teaching (Boyer, 1990).

According to Boyer's paradigm, the scholarship of discovery focuses on research or the production of knowledge. The scholarship of integration is an endorsement of generalization rather than specialization. The scholarship of application speaks directly to service: i.e., using knowledge for the "common good." And the scholarship of teaching urges faculty to find creative ways to transmit knowledge to students. Boyer's paradigm of the scholarship of engagement, however, raises troubling questions about the role of faculty, the constituency of "community," and the meaning of "the common good" itself. University faculty provide solutions with little input from stakeholders. In fact, university faculty stand apart from both community agents and students.

When Boyer speaks of community, he is referring to a community of scholars rather than endorsing an equitable, mutually beneficial, partnership between community agencies and universities. When advocating a team approach to problem solving, he is referring to a team of scholars working together.

This is no less true in regards to the scholarship of teaching, where faculty are urged to be creative and inspired, but retain their hierarchical role in the academy. But in order to support community engagement in a critical sense—and to approach critical consciousness—the authority role of faculty must be redefined. At the very least, the scholarship of teaching must become more facilitative than didactic.

Boyer envisions the scholarship of engagement as providing the solutions to environmental, educational, political, social, and "other" problems: "Other problems" are defined as those that "require more carefully crafted study and, indeed, solutions that rely not only on new knowledge, but on integration, too" (Boyer, 1990, 77). But Boyer's idea of the common good is hegemonic. Social problems are not problemitized, and solutions are perceived as corrections to aberrations of the status quo. Essentially, Boyer sees the world as one that is acted upon by elites.

Collaborations between educational institutions and community agencies have become ubiquitous over the last decade. The literature related to community service learning and multicultural education is steadily growing. Within that larger discourse, critical theory has much to offer theorists and practitioners.

Grounded in critical theory, critical multicultural consciousness mandates no less, however, than a reconceptualization of the scholarship of engagement. It challenges scholars to go beyond Boyer's emphasis on the intellect to include Freire's emphasis on the heart (humanism). The addition of a critical component to the scholarship of engagement will not only allow scholars, practitioners, and

students to problemitize the field of community service learning itself, but, in the spirit of Freire, to change it.

## Notes

1. The Boys Club became the Boys and Girls Club in 1990.
   * pseudonyms are used unless permission has been given.

## References

Allport, G. W. (1954). *The nature of prejudice.* Reading, MA: Addison-Wesley.

Arnove, R. F. (1986). *Education and revolution in Nicaragua.* New York: Praeger Publishers.

Boyer, E. L. (1990). *Scholarship reconsidered: Priorities of the professoriate.* Washington, DC: Carnegie Foundation for the Advancement of Teaching.

Boyle-Baise, M. (2002). *Multicultural service learning: Educating teachers in diverse communities.* New York: Teachers College Press.

Delpit, L. (1995). Education in a multicultural society. In *Other people's children: Cultural conflict in the classroom.* New York: The New Press.

Freire, P. (1982). *Pedagogy of the oppressed.* New York: Continnum (original work published 1970).

Freire, P. (1978). *Pedagogy in process: The letters to Guinea-Bissau.* New York: Seabury Press.

Freire, P. (1985). *The politics of education.* New York: Bergin & Garvey.

Helms, J., (ed.). (1990). *Black and white racial identity: Theory, research, and practice.* Westport, CT: Greenwood.

Kotlowitz, A. (1991). *There are no children here: The story of two boys growing up in the other America.* New York: Anchor Books.

Kozol, J. (1991). *Savage inequalities: Children in America's schools.* New York: Harper Perennial.

Lewis, N. (2002). Charitable giving slides. *Chronicle of Philanthropy: 27.*

Lynd, R. S. and H. M. (1929). *Middletown: A study in modern American culture.* New York: Harcourt Brace & Company.

MacIntosh, P. (1989). White privilege: Unpacking the invisible knapsack. *Peace and Freedom* July/August: 10-12.

McLaren, Peter. (2000). White terror and oppositional agency: Towards a critical multiculturalism. In Duarte, E. M. & S. Smith, eds. *Foundational perspectives in multicultural education* (213-240). New York: Longman.

McLaren, P. (1994). *Life in schools: An introduction to critical pedagogy in the foundations of education.* 2nd ed. White Plains, NY: Longman.

Nas (Nasir Jones). (1994). The world is yours. *Illmatic.* Sony Music Entertainment, Inc. Manufactured by Columbia Records. New York. Executive producers Faith N. & M. C. Serch.

Paulston, R. G. & LeRoy, G. (1982). Nonformal education and change from below. In Altbach, P. G., R. F. Arnove, & G. P. Kelly, eds. *Comparative education.* New York: MacMillan.

Putnam, R. D. 1995. Bowling alone. *Journal of Democracy 9:* 65-78.

Rosenberger, C. (2000). Beyond empathy: Developing critical consciousness through service learning. In O'Grady, C. R., (ed.), *Integrating service learning and multicultural education in colleges and universities* (23-43). Mahwah, NJ: Lawrence Erlbaum Associates.

Williams, G. H. (1995). *Life on the color line: the true story of a White boy who discovered he was Black.* New York: Dutton (Penguin Group USA).

*Jayne R. Beilke is an associate professor in the Department of Educational Studies of Teachers College at Ball State University, Muncie, Indiana.*

# Expanding Appreciation for "Others" among European-American Pre-Teacher Populations

By Carolyn Slemens Ward

## History

During the four and one-half years that I have taught social foundations and multicultural education for aspiring teachers and special education teachers at the Western Illinois University-Quad Cities campus, the class has evolved from being a hodge-podge of required content that maintained little student accountability and provided questionable attitude-changing experiences to a class where a significant majority of students express positive expansion in knowledge, understanding, tolerance, and appreciation of cultural diversity as evidenced by survey results. The improvement of the class followed much soul searching, sleepless nights, risk taking, failures, tenacity, continuous reading, and research.

The Western Illinois University-Quad Cities campus is located in an urban area with surrounding suburbs, and many of the students travel long distances from small town and rural communities. Although the urban area is ethnically diverse, the teacher education program is comprised of a predominantly European-American student population. My classes usually include one African-American at the most, perhaps two or three Mexican-Americans, with the remaining students of European-American background.

I find that when first entering the multicultural education classroom, many Quad City students who are already overloaded, working part-time, parenting, and who may exhibit poor time-management skills, view the sixteen-week, three-hour course as just another hoop to jump through in order to obtain a teaching certificate. By the end of the course, anonymous survey results along with student comments indicate that a significant majority of students' understandings and attitudes regarding ethnic and cultural diversity issues have expanded and improved.

## Objectives

Our nation's teachers play a key role in alleviating or exacerbating educational inequality across our nation. Oftentimes this educational inequality is based on ethnicity, class, and gender as well as additional cultural factors. It is essential that teacher education programs include courses that address multicultural issues with the goal of developing true respect for those who are different than one's self.

At the start of my social foundations and multicultural education class, students are informed that some may discover that teaching is not for them. A teacher fulfills too important a role in a child's life to not be an encourager, a respecter of all students, an empowering agent, a cultural mediator, and a holder of high expectations for every student in his/her classroom. Teachers may be masters of their subject areas while at the same time do irreparable harm to some of their students through ignorance of various cultural backgrounds or an outright disrespect for those who are different from themselves.

In order to gain respect for all others, pre-service teachers. need to first understand what culture is; research their own cultural backgrounds and how individual cultural backgrounds influence the way one judges others; realize why we need multicultural education in our schools through an examination of the educational, economic, political, and social inequities in our society; and be exposed to the true history of the United States—warts and all. How has this country historically treated and presently treat people from various cultural and ethnic groups? What does this say about the present as well as past macro-culture of this nation? What are the elements that comprise our macro-culture?

With the aforementioned background, issues of racism, classism, sexism, homophobia, ableism, and misunderstanding of language minority students are more easily understood. Upon successful completion of the course, the student is able to:

- Demonstrate an understanding of multicultural education and the role of culture in the educational process.

- Develop a greater appreciation and understanding of individual differences represented in the social foundations and multicultural education classroom and how individual perspectives have been influenced by various cultural backgrounds.

- Describe (based on valid and reliable research) current demographic, economic, social, cultural, and political trends impacting U.S. society and schooling.

- Identify the impact of historical, contemporary, and future issues of diversity in the educational process based on valid and reliable research, i.e., race, ethnicity, social class, gender, sexual orientation, ability, and language.

- Improve the ability to think logically, critically, and in an integrated manner in terms of analyzing the need for educational reform in order to meet the needs of a diverse learning community.

- Formulate plausible curriculum and delivery strategies to address the diverse needs of students.

- Demonstrate a realization regarding the efficacy of teachers in making a positive difference in individual lives as well as in an inequitable society—a social reconstructionist approach to multicultural education. (Sleeter & Grant, 1999)

## Specific Activities

One focus of the course is a required eight-week journalizing field experience of tutoring/mentoring those who are at risk of failing academically, socially, and/or emotionally. Students are involved with several Title I schools in the area as well as agencies/organizations such as the Boys and Girls Club, the Martin Luther King, Jr. Community Center, and additional after school programs for children and adults. Students are encouraged to widen their life experiences by working with others who are significantly different from themselves whether it be in terms of social class, ethnicity, ability, etc.

Another course requirement is to attend a school board meeting and write a brief summary. Students are provided information about school boards and are encouraged to notice if the board truly represents the diversity found in the school-community. Many times, attending these meetings proves to be revealing regarding community power structures and the role of the school-community concerning important school district decisions.

Finally, pedagogical methods are introduced and discussed through empowering and cooperative group projects that address multicultural issues under the following topics:

- Human relations approaches to teaching,
- Student empowering strategies,
- Critical thinking strategies,
- Cooperative learning strategies,
- Classroom management strategies concerning diverse student populations, and
- Multicultural education curricula for K–12 classrooms.

Students develop peer evaluation criteria for the group presentations and then evaluate each presentation accordingly, while the presentations are also evaluated by the instructor on pre-established criteria.

Instructional methods and materials for the course are varied with a high level of student-accountability through multiple and varied assessments along with ongoing dialogue in the classroom as well as through a WebCT3 site that includes a stu-

dent dialogue box with optional anonymity. For example, one assignment is to report about a relevant current event while another is to create a personal cultural collage to share with other class members.

There are also a variety of experiential exercises such as small cooperative group illustrations of children growing up in various socio-economic classes and then surmising what the life-chances for these children are in our society (Ward, 2002). Finally, several guest speakers sharing their various cultural experiences in the U.S. add reality, interest, and excitement to the course.

An additional objective for the course is to develop a sense of community within the multicultural education classroom. I find myself more of a facilitator than an instructor at times—facilitating discussions and reactions to several powerful video presentations concerning racism, learning disabilities, and sexual orientation as well as other topics. A touch of humor as well as patience and not taking oneself too seriously always help here. The small group projects that research and demonstrate various teaching methods for multicultural education also aid in developing this sense of community, as I ensure that project groups are as culturally and ethnically diverse as possible.

Many students find that working in culturally diverse groups in presenting research projects is empowering and is the highlight of the course; others cite the eight-week journalizing field experience of tutoring/mentoring students who are at risk of failing academically, socially, and/or emotionally as the most enlightening course experience; while others mention the many discussions concerning various cultural issues as the most meaningful. The variety and multiplicity of learning activities, assignments, and assessments are essential for college/university classrooms comprising students who demonstrate a variety of learning styles and multiple intelligences, even though the classes may *appear* to be rather homogenous. Because of the variety, almost all students excel with several assignments, activities, and assessments.

Along with the variety of assignments and assessments, students are provided with clear assignment criteria in order to lessen confusion and promote equal treatment that is expected from students. This does not mean that I am not available to provide extra help for individual students—serving as coach at times. Additionally, because the four tests administered throughout the semester are in essay for-

mat, students are encouraged to retake tests in order to improve their scores. The objective is for students to learn and reflect upon the presented material—not to "catch" students failing.

## Supporting Data

While attempting to determine whether or not student access to an anonymous dialogue box through a WebCT3 site was a positive factor in expanding knowledge, understanding, and boundaries of tolerance and appreciation of various cultural issues, I found that over a period of two semesters teaching two multicultural education classes per semester, the smaller classes which had no access to the anonymous dialogue box rated their knowledge, understanding, and expanding boundaries of tolerance and appreciation of cultural issues somewhat higher than the larger classes which *had* access to the anonymous dialogue box. The more intense sense of community within the smaller classes as well as increased time for instructor conversations with individual students may have given the edge to smaller class size over having anonymous dialogue access. The statements that were rated at the end of the semester from 0, low, to 5, high, for each category on the anonymous survey were:

1. "I feel that I have increased my *understanding and knowledge* about the following: racism, gender, class, sexual orientation, ability, bilingual education, U.S. culture." With n=86, the mean percent for the highest rating of 5 was as follows for each category: racism 63%, gender 48%, class 50%, sexual orientation 51%, ability 53%, bilingual education 75%, and U.S. culture 57%. (One to three students in each of the four classes selected a 0-2 rating for some categories.)
2. "I feel that my boundaries of *tolerance and appreciation* have been expanded regarding individuals coming from the following (different from mine) backgrounds." The mean percent for the highest rating of 5 was as follows for each category: race/ethnicity 78%, gender 61%, class 67%, sexual orientation 69%, ability 65%, language 72%. (One to two students in each of the four classes selected a 0-2 rating for some categories.)

The higher mean percent rating for the categories of bilingual education and language may have been influenced by the fact that this topic was the last addressed in the semester, or it may have been that class members actually had little knowledge and appreciation concerning limited English proficient (LEP) students and methods to address their needs.

Student comments were positive as written on student evaluation forms, especially for the most recent two years. Positive comments include:

"What I liked best about this course was the respect that was established between *all* people."

"I very much appreciated the community aspect of the class. I enjoyed coming to each session and seeing other points of view."

"I really enjoyed this class, even though it forced me to realize I'm not as open minded as I thought".

"What I liked best about this class is that it opened my eyes to the prejudice within myself and engrained in our society."

Comments such as these encourage me to continue taking risks and to continuously learn and improve myself as a multicultural educator and role model in order to make a positive difference in the world of education and, thus, in our society.

## References

Sleeter, C. & Grant, C. (1999). *Making choices for multicultural education: Five approaches to race, class, and gender* (3rd ed.). Upper. Saddle River, NJ: Merrill/Prentice Hall..

Ward, C. (2002). Preparing K-12 teachers to teach for social justice: An experiential exercise with a focus on inequality and life-chances based on socio-economic status, *Multicultural Education, 9*:4, 22-24.

---

**Carolyn Siemens Ward** is an associate professor in the department of Educational and Interdisciplinary Studies at Western Illinois University-Quad Cities, Moline, Illinois.

---

From *Multicultural Education*, Winter 2003, pp. 46-48. Copyright © 2003 by Caddo Gap Press. Reprinted by permission.

# Dewey, Freire,

## and a pedagogy for the oppressor

### by Rick A. Breault

Cultural diversity and democracy will, to a degree, always be in conflict with each other. A democracy challenges diverse groups within a society because it implies equality, common goals, and cooperation. Diversity, on the other hand, pushes a democracy to its limits of trust and forces it to honor its rhetoric by demanding an equal political and economic voice while supporting separate cultural identities. Because of what Wood (1988) described as "democracy's essentially fluid character" (p. 166), nations like the United States will always struggle to find a balance between acceptance of the social order and the democratic empowerment which implies the freedom to remake society.

## Oppression
### in a Democratic Society

Despite the tension between these elements of society, there is another aspect of society that at once makes a relatively successful coexistence possible and hinders the progress of modern democracy. Oppression is not the sole property of third world dictatorships nor did it end with the Civil Rights Act. While oppression can bring a sort of stability to a society, the stability is illusive and stifling. For a well-integrated multicultural democracy to be possible, the grip of oppression must be broken. It will

not be broken easily and unless the goals of multiculturalism and democracy are seen as one and the same, may not be broken at all.

In their traditional role of helping disseminate the cultural myths that make up the American dream, schools have nurtured the oppression of those who might wake us from that dream. Oppression is not a term the general public usually associates with the American experience and, relatively speaking, the United States is a land of freedom. However, when a nation sets a higher standard of freedom for the world it must also live by a stricter definition of oppression.

Paulo Freire (1970) defined an oppressive situation as any "in which 'A' objectively exploits 'B' or *hinders his pursuit of self-affirmation as a responsible person*" [emphasis added] (p. 40). According to that definition, even the freest of societies must revise its list of oppressed peoples to include all those who are kept from reaching their potential by the attitudes or institutions of another group. For meaningful change to occur, members of the dominant group need to recognize their institutions and attitudes as oppressive and learn to see themselves as potential oppressors rather than as beneficiaries of a preexisting, inevitable system. Schools, as perpetuators of the

democratic way of life, have an obligation to stimulate the self-examination needed to bring about that recognition.

## An Oppressor's View
## of the World

In order to be comfortable in the world they have created, oppressors learn to see the oppressed in a variety of ways, depending on the level of comfort their moral character will allow. The most entrenched position along this continuum belongs to those who view the oppressed as a pathology in an otherwise healthy society. They see society's role as one of "adjusting these 'incompetent and lazy folks'" to the dominant culture (Freire, 1970, p. 60). The adherents of that position will not easily accept the "oppressor" label nor be convinced that their position is unjust. They often believe that what is strange or foreign is morally or intellectually inferior and assume superior intelligence for themselves (Dewey, 1916.)

Other oppressors view the rest of society with less condescending eyes. This group views the oppressed not as individuals but as a class of people that is a byproduct of a generally successful social structure. These oppressors might be aware of their relative position in society and that the resulting oppression is unjust, but they do not see themselves as actively maintaining oppression or as having any power to change the situation. Oppression is something that began in the past and, given time, will be exorcised through existing democratic and capitalist mechanisms.

At the opposite end of the continuum is a group whose perspective is characterized by "pious, sentimental, and individualistic gestures" (Freire, 1970, p. 35). This well-meaning group's status as former oppressors leads them to believe that only they can create a just society in behalf of the oppressed peoples. "They talk about the people, but they do not trust them… " (p. 46). Sympathy or pity, however, will not bring about genuine multicultural understanding and participation in society (Dewey, 1956). Finally, there is a group that, by definition, are among the oppressors but who are on a fence. They feel compassion and concern for the inequity around them and know that change is needed. Yet, they struggle with the implications of a diverse society and sometimes resent what is seen as a burden of guilt put upon them.

## A Pervasive Dualism

Each of these perspectives is rooted in soil common to most oppressive cultures—the tendency towards dichotomous thinking. Whether referring to gender, race, or economics, the seemingly unassailable wall is the belief that diversity and unity are not compatible (Ladson-Billings, 1990). Still, as Dewey (1916) explained, unless we avoid all sorts of dualistic thinking, we will never achieve a "full and flexible social interaction and intercourse" (p. 323).

The tendency towards dualism in American society can be seen clearly in its schools. Dichotomous thinking has led to the belief that one cannot develop both intellect and emotion without slighting one. What results is a curriculum that does not value emotional, intuitive types of learning as highly as rational/technical

studies (Belenky, et al., 1986). The same need for stability and sameness that comforts the oppressors has led schools to assist in a cultural invasion that imposes one world view and convinces the invaded of their intrinsic inferiority (Freire, 1970). More subtly, the curriculum tends to maintain the status quo by conveying the false notion that consensus has been reached on most issues, that most questions can be settled by applying rational criteria, and that American democracy has reached a level of sophistication that precludes a need for intensive cultural self-examination (Beyer, 1988; Freire, 1970).

Critics of oppressive societies, too, exhibit the same either/or thinking. Ladson-Billings (1990), for example, maintains that while much of non-Western thought believes in a unity of opposites, Western thought seems incapable of reconciling diversity and unity. That in itself is a dualistic generalization. Another dualism embraced by many multicultural reformers is their unwillingness to grant legitimacy to the fears and doubts of the dominant culture. From an oppressors' perspective, any restriction on their current way of life is a threat to their own rights. That perception cannot simply be ignored or legislated away. If we are willing to point out oppression, racism, or insensitivity, we must also discuss openly the fear and resentment that perpetuates injustice— even if those views are offensive to us and to human dignity. To be culturally competent is to hear and try to understand the voices of all concerned. Only when oppressors reach their own conclusion that their views dehumanize others and themselves will attitudinal change begin.

## The Inadequacy of Current Efforts

In overcoming the conflict between the oppressed and their oppressors, Freire claims that only the oppressed can break the cycle of oppression. Other multicultural ap-

proaches assume a similar, if only slightly more active role for the dominant group. The assumption being that the attitudes of oppressors will change if the teacher presents positive images of the culture and contributions of various ethnic groups.

In both cases, we see the oppressed trying to bring about change through the same tactics for which they criticize the oppressors—imposition, slogans, myths, and images. If those tactics made no long term change in the spirit of the oppressed people, there is no reason to believe that they will be any more effective on the oppressors (Anderson, 1992; Dewey, 1938). We do not have to settle for dutiful toleration of other cultures. We can cultivate, in most students, a sincere embrace of diversity—if we patiently allow a change in attitudes to come, by choice, from within.

## A Change in Mind and Heart

Healthy, white, upper-class students are seldom considered at-risk. Yet, when we discuss the need for multicultural awareness, they are the *culturally-impaired*. They come from a social class that is at-risk to maintain the status quo. Yet, we have not considered dealing with their "disability" with the same sensitivity that we handle other disabilities. To do so requires a pedagogy that gradually leads towards a more inclusive world view without leading to self-defensive resentment.

From the earlier look at the mind of the oppressor several traits typical of oppressor groups can be summarized:

1. The extent to which they support the existing oppressive social system varies.

2. They often feel intellectually or morally superior to the oppressed groups.

3. Oppression is often viewed as an abstract rather than a human condition.

4. Oppressors sometimes feel powerless to change the system they helped create.

5. They believe that the existing system can correct oppressive conditions.

6. Many do not trust the oppressed groups to bring social change themselves.

7. They fear a loss of control of their own rights.

8. They tend to think dualistically in relation to cultural diversity.

9. They have a strong need for social stability and maintenance of the status quo.

Although most of those traits have been addressed in one way or another in the school curricula, any effort that does not take into consideration the interaction between traits is inadequate. Consider programs in which students volunteer time to help inner city children read or to "fix up" the rundown neighborhoods of the poor. Those programs might create social conscience or awareness, but they might also reinforce the notion that oppressed people are generally unable to help themselves.

Contradictory messages are also sent when some classic literature is replaced with ethnically diverse works or special weeks or months in which we recognize the culture of diverse groups are inserted into the school calendar. From a dichotomous perspective, any insertion of multi-ethnic curricula takes away from the "real" contributions of great people who happened to be white males. Also, when special recognition weeks are put into the year as a sort of "honorable mention" and emphasize quaint, colorful customs and a list of famous *name-a-group*-Americans, members of the dominant group who already feel intellectually superior to other groups will have their opinions reinforced.

Special events, public service, and a multi-ethnic curriculum should not be abandoned. Instead, what is needed is a holistic approach that introduces the key issues and elements of a diverse society with more attention to the attitudes and experiences of the target audience. To do so requires curricular freedom to identify a few common themes running through each of the traits and then to design general classroom considerations based on those themes.

## a Three Prong Approach

Some of the traits of the dominant class in a democratic society come about by default. The children of that class are not allowed to develop and learn within a democratic environment, so they are not prepared to allow others to do so. Their class position allows them to enjoy the privileges of a democracy but they are educated in a hierarchical system of authority and correct answers and are often raised in homes where money and power are the primary sources of freedom and authority.

When these young people enter the larger society they bring with them the only conception of democracy they know—those with the most "right" answers or the most wealth deserve the greatest voice in the government. To nurture a deeper appreciation and grasp of democracy, the school can create an environment in which students are empowered in a truly democratic sense.

What does it mean to be democratically empowered? According to George Wood (1988), a person who is empowered:

- believes in the individual's right and responsibility to participate publicly;
- has a sense of political efficacy—knowing that one's contribution is important;
- comes to value the principles of democratic life—equality, community and liberty;
- knows that worthwhile alternative social arrangements to the status quo exist; and
- gains the requisite intellectual skills to participate in public debate (p. 176).

In a world that is often very undemocratic, the classroom ought to be a democratic oasis (Dewey, 1916; Freire, 1970; Wood, 1988). In this oasis, students fully participate in decision-making and democracy becomes more a mode of living and working than an understanding of a political system. Each individual is given the opportunity to "escape from the limitations of the social group into which he/she was born" and to develop distinctive capacities, yet, a social return is demanded from all (Dewey, 1916, p. 20). Here students learn the connection between classroom, local, and national social problems (Beyer, 1988).

The teacher who wishes to democratically empower students provides opportunities to identify problems that interest them and then leads them to see their connection to the larger society. From there, the teacher and students work as co-investigators in order to respond to the problem. This cycle of challenge and response is necessary for students to begin seeing the world as "a reality in process, in transformation" (Freire, 1970, p. 71). Most importantly, they will see themselves as the transformers—as having a sense of political efficacy.

Throughout this process, students will begin to see themselves and their roles in society differently. And, it is hoped, they will begin to see others differently. Since democracy relies on trust in the ability and inclusion of diverse groups, the curriculum must also counteract the dichotomous ways of thinking that sabotage attempts at integrating the society.

One way of doing so is to help students become convergent thinkers. Instead of seeing a situation as a competition between conflicting options, students would see the potential for the merging, compromise, or interplay of ideas. Although democracy does not imply intellectual relativism, we do want the students to take the culture and beliefs of other groups seriously.

Helping children to understand the connectedness of their own ideas and of those in the larger society is also necessary to combat dualistic thinking. The classroom is the ideal place to show by example that autonomy and interconnection are not mutually exclusive. In a school that lacks racial or ethnic diversity, the emphasis can be on diversity of gender, social class, religion, political perspective or geography.

The traditional subject-centered classroom also nurtures dichotomous thinking and inhibits empowerment and convergent thinking. A school setting where choice is minimized and where the student is subservient to subject matter is contrary to democratic living and thinking. The same is true where memorization takes precedence over thinking or where the need for a quick, correct answer is more important than the exploration of alternative perspectives (Belenky, et al., 1986; Dewey, 1916, 1938, 1956; Freire, 1970). Such an approach encourages dichotomous thinking and sends the message that democracy is something you practice only after you leave school.

Progressivist/constructivist education may be the best route out of dualistic treatment of subject matter. This type of education relies on the use of real-life problems as a context for learning other subject matter. It is cooperative and reflective—always evaluating facts with experience and vice versa. Education, in this case, is not simply preparation for the future, but a means to learn about and change the present and to live together more effectively.

Progressivism emphasizes the social responsibility inherent in education. Belenky and her colleagues (1986) believe that "If one can discover the experiential logic behind... ideas... the owners of the ideas cease to be strangers" (p. 115). Freire (1970) claims that without love, trust, and faith, no genuine educational dialogue can exist. Dewey (1916), too, reminds us that no true social group can exist as long as "in-dividuals use one another to get desired results without reference to their emotional and intellectual disposition or without their consent" (p. 5). When students engage in joint activity and real communication with each other and the teacher they grow to see the moral implications in democratic living.

## Some Common Themes

Individual and social morality run throughout each of the three prongs of this plan—democratic empowerment, convergent thinking and progressive/constructivist pedagogy. The compromise and healthy diversity required by a democracy, the variety of perspectives needed to think convergently, and progressive pedagogy can all benefit from a group-oriented approach to classroom dynamics. Therefore, to prepare students for more integrated, socially conscious democratic living, cooperation must also be present in every aspect of the curriculum.

To work toward the common goals of the society, students must learn to refer their own use of abilities and talents to that of others (Dewey, 1916). Until one recognizes that a democracy is strengthened by integrating the diverse perspectives of its citizens, there will be little commitment to cultural diversity. Most of our country's history is a history of the assimilation and inclusion of new cultures and traditions. If the curriculum were organized according to the ways in which new Americans built what is the modern United States, students might develop a more positive view of diversity (Wong, 1992).

The social studies are especially important in the nurturing of multicultural relations. History organized around conflict reinforces the differences between peoples and the idea that only force can reconcile opposing opinions. Thematic integration of social studies, the arts, literature, and the sciences can help minimize dichotomous thinking by connecting the accomplishments of individuals to the development of the nation and emphasizing points of connection.

Real-life problems and personal relations are holistic and students react according to what they have experienced and felt about members of diverse cultures. Seldom do they try to recall what they learned about the contributions of people of color before responding in love or in hatred. Whatever attempts the schools make to improve multicultural understanding should be as close as possible to the experiences of real life.

Members of the dominant class are often isolated from real world contacts with members of the oppressed groups. They may even perceive themselves as being the oppressed ones in school or at home. A curriculum that is participatory and experiential allows students to witness democracy in action, to practice taking different perspectives (Angell & Avery, 1992) and to be encouraged to develop, and recognize in others, the range of intelligences that are seldom rewarded in school (Gardner, 1983). In the process they may also witness the effects of oppression and be encouraged to help bring about change.

According to Dewey (1938), every experience somehow changes the person who has had the experience and, therefore, the quality of subsequent experiences. If experiences are provided in which diversity is seen to have a positive influence, the effect that experience has on the students is more likely to influence future experiences positively. However, all knowledge—constructed, experienced or received—has little value unless it is reflected upon and internalized in some meaningful way.

Oppressors themselves are often oppressed and silenced by their narrow perceptions (Freire, 1970; Belenky, et al., 1986) but seldom recognize that self-oppression. Belief that a well-integrated multicultural democracy is possible implies a certain trust that most students can come to that same belief on their own, if provided with the right balance of new experiences and reflection. When we rely on sermons and imposition as a quick fix, we give the appearance of having little faith in the merits of multiculturalism or democracy to do the convincing.

Just as the society is asked to assimilate new cultures without stripping them of their heritage, so should educators allow former oppressors to assimilate new ways of thinking by reconciling new information in light of existing perceptions and previous experiences and without minimizing or feeling guilty about their own heritage.

## Some Underlying
## Assumptions

This proposal, like most curricula, rests on a few basic assumptions. First, in order for well-insulated, white middle-class students to learn to live in a diverse society, there must be some trust in what Dewey (1916) called *plasticity*—the ability to retain from previous experiences something which will assist in adapting to new situations.

We already believe that the endless lists of facts and figures that we give students will be meaningful when needed in the future. Is it any less realistic to believe along with Dewey (1956) that, "… we may produce in schools a… type of society we should like to realize, and by forming minds in accord with it gradually modify the larger and more recalcitrant features of adult society" (p. 317).

Dewey's ideas also suggest another assumption—that children are more open-minded toward and prepared for diversity than adults. He urges that, "With respect to sympathetic curiosity, unbiased responsiveness, and openness of mind, we may say that the adult should be growing in childlikeness" (1916, p. 50). Elementary students seem to have more of a capacity and interest

in people different from themselves and in different points of view yet have sufficient cognitive development to make a diversity of viewpoints accessible (Angell & Avery, 1992; Dewey, 1956). Young children have little problem cooperating and enjoying each others' presence because they have a shared culture—childhood—and shared goals, such as play. A diverse democracy need not be too terribly different.

As we muddle through the rhetoric about diversity, all parties sometimes lose sight of the common goals of democracy. Our dualistic tendencies push us into selfish territorialism rather than keeping sight of the collective good and of those things which lie beyond our direct interests. A society is democratic in so far as it "makes provision for participation in its good for all its members on equal terms and… secures flexible readjustment of its institutions through interaction of the different forms of associated life" (Dewey, 1916, p. 99).

Such a society is made up of citizens who have a personal interest in social relationships and exhibit a disposition toward bringing about social change without introducing disorder (Dewey, 1916). They see themselves as a transformative part of a forward moving society (Freire, 1970). For this vision of multicultural democracy to take hold and to prepare the dominant group in society for a role different than they play now, we have no choice but to view the school as an agent of social reconstruction.

To simply reproduce the past is to reproduce the oppression to which it gave birth. Students can be shown a more progressive model of democracy, one in which the future is better than the past. For generations, oppressors have asked schools to help create a society in which they can feel comfortable. Now it is time for

the schools to help the oppressors build a society in which all citizens can be comfortable.

## References

Anderson, J. (1992). Intercultural competencies. *Kappa Delta Pi Record* 29 (1), 15.

Angell, A. V. & Avery, P. G. (1992). Examining global issues in the elementary classroom. *The Social Studies* 83 (May/June), 113–117.

Belenky, M. F., Clinchy, B. M., Goldberger, N. R., & Tarule, J. M. (1986). *Women's ways of knowing: The development of self, voice, and mind.* New York: Basic Books.

Beyer, L. E. (1988). Schooling for the culture of democracy. In L. E. Beyer & M. W. Apple (Eds.), *The Curriculum: Problems, Politics, and Possibilities* (pp. 219–238). Albany, NY: State University of New York Press.

Dewey, J. (1916). *Democracy and education.* New York: Macmillan.

Dewey, J. (1963). *Experience and education.* New York: Collier Books. (Original work published 1938).

Dewey, J. (1956). *The child and the curriculum/The school and society.* (combined edition with introduction by Leonard Carmichael). Chicago: University of Chicago Press.

Freire, P. (1970). *Pedagogy of the oppressed.* (M. Bergman Ramos, Trans.). New York: Continuum.

Gardner, H. (1983). *Frames of mind: A theory of multiple intelligences.* New York: Basic Books.

Ladson-Billings, G. (1990). The multicultural mission: Unity and diversity. *Social Education* 56 (5), 308–310.

Wong, F. F. (1992). Diversity and discontent. *AAHE Bulletin* 45 (2), 3–5.

Wood, G. H. (1998). Democracy and the curriculum. In L. E. Beyer & M. W. Apple, (Eds.), *The Curriculum: Problems, Politics, and Possibilities* (166–187). Albany, NY: State University of New York Press.

—*Rick A. Breault is an associate professor of education in the Department of Curriculum and Instruction at Illinois State University, Normal, Illinois.*

From *Multicultural Education*, Spring 2003, pp. 2-6. © 2003 by Caddo Gap Press. Reprinted by permission.

# Knowledge Construction Awareness

*Recent research in CSCL (Computer Supported Collaborative Learning) and CSCW (Computer Supported Cooperative Work) has provided insights into how various forms of awareness information should be computer supported to enable collaboration in distributed environments. Researchers are investigating how technology through awareness can support effectively the interactions among people. This paper presents a new kind of awareness, Knowledge Construction Awareness (KCA) and the design of a software tool that allows us to capture information about group work and evaluate how this kind of awareness affects the collaborative work process in computer-mediated interactions. The authors present an exploratory study of ten groups that used their software tool.*

**Cèsar A. Collazos, Luis A. Guerrero, & Josè A. Pino**
Universidad de Chile

Researchers in the educational systems area attempt to provide technological support for cooperative and collaborative learning advocated by educational theories (1). Researchers in groupware and computer supported cooperative work (CSCW) are investigating how technology can effectively support the interactions among people. One of the elements for increasing communication opportunities is *awareness* (2).

In Computer Supported Collaborative Learning (CSCL), awareness can be used for enhancing collaborative opportunities. The awareness usually provided in physical collaborative learning environments allows learners to implicitly maintain information about the others' interactions with common problem areas and corresponding tasks. If two learners are co-located they cannot help see, hear and perhaps even feel the presence and actions of the other. In distributed collaborative learning environments, where collaboratively oriented activities are mediated by various forms of information and communication technologies (ICT), these abilities are greatly reduced. The actions of the others can take place in deafening silence and their actions can almost be invisible. As a result, collaboratively oriented activities such as negotiation of meaning, creation of joint understanding, and division of labor and responsibility require meta-communicative actions for maintaining certain cognitive and collective effects on the distributed collaboration (3).

This paper is first and foremost a theoretical contribution to the different kinds of awareness. Second, it presents a set of indicators and an exploratory experiment with a software tool designed to gather information that permits us to estimate the quality of the cooperation process. Section 2 presents some of the recent literature in the area of awareness. In section 3 we present our proposed *knowledge construction awareness (KCA)* with its main characteristics. Then we will describe the cooperation indicators as well as a method that allow us to evaluate some key points identified in the collaborative learning phases. Section 5 describes the tool (software) we used. Section 6 describes the experimental design. In section 7, results are presented. Section 8 includes conclusions and a proposal for future work.

## Literature Review

### Awareness in CSCW

In CSCW, according to Malone, a collaboration process is led by five processes: co-presence, awareness, communication, collaboration, and coordination (4). Co-presence gives the feeling that the user is in a shared workspace with someone at the same time. Awareness is a state where users recognize each other's activities on the premise of co-presence, for example, "what are they doing together?", "where are they working?". In the communication process, people share information. Then in collaboration, a user works on the specific task with other users and accomplishes the task and common goals. A coordination process is needed to resolve the conflict towards effective collaboration. Awareness, in particular, is

## Table 1: Types of CSCW Awareness

| Awareness | Description |
|---|---|
| Organizational | People maintain awareness of an association of people, their reason for being together and their shared knowledge (6). |
| Task | It involves understanding the purpose of a task, the specific goals and requirements of the group in pursuing the task, and how the task on hand fits into a larger plan. (6). |
| Situation | It refers to the state of knowledge that an individual requires to operate or maintain a complex and dynamic system (6). |
| Informal | The general sense of who is around and what they are up to—the kind of things that people know when they work together in the same office (6). |
| Social | Information that a person maintains about others in a social or conversational context (6). |
| Group structural | It involves knowledge about roles, responsibilities, and status of a person (6). |
| Community | It proposes a notion of facilitating encounters and knowledge sharing among people having shared interests and experiences in museums, conferences, etc. (7). |
| Multi synchronous | Basically, multi-synchronous applications are characterized by their abilities to support divergence. The main goal of this kind of awareness is to make people aware of parallel streams of activities (8). |

one of the most interesting elements to achieve cooperation and to increase communication opportunities (5).

Researchers on CSCW have already proposed the following tools to promote awareness, that are implemented using multi-media technologies to bond physically distributed environments.

1. To give information on the surroundings of the target user, e.g., Portholes (2). Portholes is basically a system for maintaining image information which is both generated and consumed at a number of sites connected via Internet.
2. To provide common or public spaces where users can meet, e.g., Video Window. Video Window facilitates informal communication through the inclusion of video images in remote sites.
3. To simulate informal communication opportunities in the real world using computers, e.g., VENUS (5). VENUS provides interest awareness, so that co-workers can obtain communication opportunities triggered by natural activities among workspaces.

Table 1 presents a summary of different kinds of CSCW awareness.

### Awareness in CSCL

In CSCL, awareness is also very important for effective collaborative learning and it plays a part in how the learning environment creates collaboration opportunities naturally and efficiently. Goldman (9) identifies three types of student interaction: social, task, and conceptual. For each kind of interaction there is a corresponding type of awareness; in addition Gutwin *et al.* (10) add another type of awareness called *workspace awareness*. *Social awareness* is the knowledge that students have about the social con-

nections within the group. *Task awareness* is the information about how the task will be completed. *Concept awareness* is the awareness of how a particular activity or piece of knowledge fits into the student's existing knowledge. *Workspace awareness* is the up-to-the-minute knowledge about other student interactions with the shared workspace, such as where other students are working, what they are doing, and what they have already done in the workspace. Yamagami & Seki have proposed a kind of knowledge awareness that gives feedback to the cooperative activities with an increased emphasis on sharing know-how of an organization (11). Ogata & Yano have proposed another kind of knowledge awareness, assuming it is the information enhancing collaboration opportunities in a shared knowledge space and making possible to shift from a personal learning environment to a collaborative one (12). However, these theoretical constructs have not provided any kind of knowledge acquisition awareness.

The questions in Table 2, organized according into the categories described above, are examples of what students should consider during the collaborative activity in order to be aware of what is happening in the group as they work in their task. These questions are based on (10).

## Knowledge Construction Awareness

Through awareness, the participants build shared understanding about the objects of collaboration and the objectives of the tasks. If people are aware of the activities of the others and about the impacts that occur in the knowledge that is generated through collaboration, they will have information that helps in the synchronization of their work.

## Table 2: Questions Students Should Consider During Collaborative Activities.

| Awareness | Questions |
|---|---|
| Social | What should I expect from other members of this group? |
| | How will I interact with this group? |
| | What role will I take in this group? |
| | What roles will the other members of the group assume? |
| Task | What do I know about this topic and the structure of the task? |
| | What do others know about this topic and task? |
| | What steps must we take to complete the task? |
| | How will the outcome be evaluated? |
| | What tools/materials are needed to complete the task? |
| Concept | How does this task fit into what I already know about the concept? |
| | What else do I need to find out about this topic? |
| | Do I need to revise any of my current ideas in light of this new information? |
| | Can I create a hypothesis from my current knowledge to predict the task outcome? |
| Workspace | What are the other members of the group doing to complete the task? |
| | What are they? |
| | What are they doing? |
| | What have they already done? |
| | What will they do next? |
| | How can I help other students to complete the project? |

The goal of *knowledge construction awareness* (KCA) is to promote meta-cognitive skills. In order to achieve that goal, it is necessary to wonder how one may become aware of one's own knowledge. It is a self-control and self-monitoring of the learning process. The questions in Table 3 are examples of what students should consider during the collaborative activity in order to be aware of the knowledge construction. Some of the questions have been included by Goldman and Gutwin in their typology of student interaction: social, task, conceptual and workspace respectively (see Table 2).

Such questions can make a diagnosis of the problematic-situation changing the knowledge of the problem among members of the group. This is explained by an appropriation process (13). Appropriation is the socially oriented version of Piaget's biologically originated concept of assimilation (14). Appropriation is mutual: each partner gives meaning to the other's actions according to her own conceptual framework (15). Some studies reported that humans modify the meaning of their actions retrospectively according to the actions of others that follow it (16).

KCA is important because it may promote meta-cognitive skills, helping to make strategic decisions and acquiring a better model of learning. If a student is aware of her own knowledge construction she can make explicit strategic decisions. These strategic decisions enter into the meta-cognitive zone when they are made explicit and communicated to the student in order to enable her to reason about past or future actions. Such reasoning is precisely required by the negotiation involved when the learners search to agree on decisions (17). Also, if the student is aware of her knowledge construction, she can acquire a better model of learning. After several years in school, students get some idea of what learning is: "Students tend to view learning as a passive experience in which one absorbs knowledge or copies fact into memory. Little of what they do in schools leads them to question that perspective" (18). It is clear students with such a passive model of learning probably will not benefit from unconstrained learning environments. Giving students an opportunity to develop a better view of learning is one of the most important goals of present education. For this reason, when students are aware of knowledge construction, they can change their knowledge as a result of the confrontation of incompatible viewpoints. This is where students in their learning groups engage in activities to <<reshape>> the information by organizing, clarifying, elaborating, or synthesizing learning concepts. It is possible that with this kind of awareness, interaction could occur, and acquire a positive interdependence, that according to Johnson & Johnson, is one of the basics of effective groups (19). In order to obtain a better KCA it is necessary to develop new styles of group interfaces, and so, improve the interaction among the group members.

## Table 3: Questions Students Should Consider During Collaborative Activities.

| Awareness | Questions |
|---|---|
| Knowledge construction | What are the other members of the group doing to complete the task? |
| | Is what I am doing/did helping to solve the task? |
| | What are the others doing that is helping to solve the task? |
| | How much time is available? What is our score? |
| | How can I help other students to complete the task? |
| | Where are the other members of the group? |
| | What do I know about the topic? |
| | What do the other members know about the topic? What do the other members need to know about the topic? |
| | What else do I need to find out about this topic? |
| | What are the other members of the group learning from me? |
| | What and how did I learn from the others members of the group? |
| | What am I learning from the group work? |
| | Did I/we finish the work? Do I need more time/resources? |

Through the KCA, Concept, Task and Workspace awareness, the participants could build shared understanding about the goals of collaboration and the involved tasks. They can be aware about activities of the other participants, helping to synchronize their work and coordinating themselves. Being aware of the elements proposed in each type of awareness increases the probability of communication, coordination and interaction. According to Dillenbourg, Collaborative Learning is a situation in which particular forms of interaction among people are expected to occur, which would trigger learning mechanisms (20). As an example of how knowledge construction awareness allows groups to be more effective, consider a group of students who are collaboratively working trying to solve a problem. Each of the participants maintains an awareness of what the others are doing and where they are. So, every time a student encounters a different view of the problem, she will try to communicate with another participant in order to explain the problem to her. In that way every student is helping to make strategic decisions and change the participants' knowledge about the problem. Also, every time a participant does something and receives a positive response of the environment, she will begin to be more conscious about her knowledge of the problem.

It is important to notice that space supports (implicit) coordination in some cases, because the movements that a user does in order to solve a problematic situation, reflects her strategy, and one participant may anticipate the other's intentions by tracing her movements (21). Each participant can observe where the other goes without asking her explicitly. Moreover, partners can express agreement or disagreement by performing actions or movements. For this reason, knowledge construction and therefore this information is included in our knowledge construction awareness. Next we are going to explain some indicators we developed in order to measure the collaborative process within a group.

## Cooperation indicators

In order to analyze whether knowledge construction awareness is an influencing factor within a collaborative group activity, we propose a set of indicators and an experiment with a tool intended to gather information. The goal is to measure the quality of the cooperation process in some groups. Callazos *et al.* (22) have presented a way to evaluate the collaborative learning process, defining a set of indicators. Four of the indicators are based on the following activities proposed by Johnson & Johnson in (23): use of strategies, intra-group cooperation, checking the success criteria, and monitoring. The fifth indicator is based on the performance of the group. Each one of these indicators is explained in next sections.

### Applying strategies

The first indicator tries to capture the ability of the group members to generate, communicate and consistently apply a strategy to jointly solve the problem.

The learning potential of a team is maximized when all the students actively participate in the group discussions. Building involvement in group discussions increases the amount of information available to the group, enhancing group decision making and improving the students' quality of thought during the learning process (24).

### Intra-group cooperation

This indicator corresponds to the employment of collaborative strategies previously defined during the process of group work. If each group member is able to understand how her task is related to the global team goals, then every one can anticipate her actions, requiring less coordination effort. A group achieves promotive interdependence when the members of the group perceive that their goals are positively correlated such that an individual can only attain her goal if her team members also attain their goals (25). In collaborative learning, these goals correspond to each member's need to understand her team members' ideas, questions, explanations, and problem solutions.

### Success criteria review

This indicator measures the degree of involvement of the group members in reviewing boundaries, guidelines and roles during the group activity. It may include summarizing the outcome of the last task, assigning action items to members of the group, and noting times for expected completion of assignments. The beginning and ending of any group collaboration involve transition tasks such as assigning roles, requesting changes to an agenda, and locating missing meeting participants.

### Monitoring

This indicator is understood as a regulatory activity. The objective of this indicator is to oversee if the group maintains the chosen strategies to solve the problem, keeping focused on the goals and the success criteria. If a player does not sustain the expected behavior, the group will not reach the common goal.

### Performance

It corresponds to the quality of the proposed solution to a problematic situation. Baeza-Yates and Pino (26) made a proposal for the formal evaluation of collaborative work. They take into account three aspects: quality (how good is the result of collaborative work), time (total elapsed time while working) and work (total amount of work done). Based on that model, we propose an indicator that pretends to measure the quality of the strategy proposed in order to solve the problematic situation.

## The software tool and collaboration instrument

"Chase the Cheese" is a group game, implemented in a software tool, which allows us to capture some group information occurring within a cooperative work interaction. Chase the cheese is a distributed and synchronous application (27). Since our goal is to study the collaborative learning process, we developed a tool to capture data from groups engaged in such type of task. We chose a small case in which a group of persons have to develop

and apply a strategy in order to do a joint task. The task is a game of the labyrinth type.

Chase the cheese is played by four persons, each one with a computer. The computers are physically distant and the only communication allowed is computer-mediated. All activities made by participants are recorded for analysis and players are made aware of that.

Players are given very few details about the game. The rest of the game rules must be discovered by participants while playing. They also have to develop joint strategies to succeed. We are interested in how people learn to develop and apply strategies. Therefore, people can only play the game once.

The game is a labyrinth divided into four quadrants. To win the game, the group (four players) has the common goal of leading the mouse to the cheese. Each player has two predefined roles: *coordinator* (only one per quadrant and randomly assigned) or *collaborator* (in the three remaining quadrants). Each player is identified by a pseudonym and has a randomly assigned color. A coordinator must make decisions concerned with the movement of the mouse. The collaborators must support the coordinator to ensure her decisions are accurate. In each quadrant there are two types of obstacles through which the mouse cannot pass: general obstacles (in black) and colored obstacles. Although every player can see the black general obstacles, colored obstacles can only be seen by the player who has that color assigned.

In order to communicate to the group, each player has a dialogue box from which she can send messages to each of the others explicitly (one at a time). Also, each player can see only messages the other players send to her in separated mailboxes, one for each player. The application records every message sent by any member of the group. Along with each message, the application registers the time of occurrence, sender and current quadrant. This information is used in order to make an estimate of the level of collaboration in the group.

The objective is not just to help the mouse pass the labyrinth, but to arrive with the highest score (the maximum would be 400). At the beginning of each quadrant, the coordinator has a partial score of 100. Whenever the mouse hits an obstacle, her partial score decreased by 10 units. If some partial score goes down to zero, the group loses the game.

Because each player has a partial view of the game obstacles, in order to solve the problem group members have to interact closely with their peers. Due to this necessity, the game presents a strict positive interdependence of goals. If the group is able to win the game, we can say their members have built a shared understanding of the problem (28). They must have understood the underlying problem is the coordinator does not have all the information needed to move the mouse in her quadrant without hitting any obstacle—because there are some colored obstacles she is not seeing, so she needs the timely assistance from each collaborator. Discussion of the strategy to solve

## Table 4: Student Group Interview Results.

| Groups | I1 | I2 | I3 | I4 | I5 | KCA |
|--------|------|------|-----|------|------|------|
| 0 | 0.69 | 0.69 | 0.2 | 0.75 | 0.65 | 0.28 |
| 1 | 0.31 | 0.71 | 0.2 | 0.8 | 0.57 | 0.30 |
| 2 | 0.68 | 0.62 | 0.2 | 0.8 | 0.69 | 0.23 |
| 3 | 0.48 | 0.61 | 0.5 | 0.74 | 0.63 | 0.43 |
| 4 | 0.71 | 0.74 | 0.8 | 0.78 | 0.66 | 0.58 |
| 5 | 0.75 | 0.84 | 1 | 0.86 | 0.61 | 0.71 |
| 6 | 0.71 | 0.72 | 1 | 0.85 | 0.52 | 0.67 |
| 7 | 0.62 | 0.8 | 0.3 | 0.8 | 0.53 | 0.26 |
| 8 | 0.58 | 0.75 | 0.3 | 0.82 | 0.54 | 0.27 |
| 9 | 0.6 | 0.75 | 0.4 | 0.81 | 0.54 | 0.27 |
| 10 | 0.6 | 0.8 | 0.4 | 0.83 | 0.53 | 0.27 |

the problem helps the group members to construct a shared view or mental model of their goals and the tasks whose execution is required (29). This mental model can improve the coordination because each member knows how her task fits into the global team goals. Due to the high degree of interdependence, required success or failure in solving the labyrinth is useful to know if the group has applied collaborative strategies. To determine the values of the other indicators, it is necessary to make a semantic analysis of the messages.

We measured KCA according to the number of messages we found in every group corresponding to the kind of questions proposed in our KCA definition. The KCA messages correspond to the questions students should consider during the collaborative activity in order to be aware of the knowledge construction. Some examples of this kind of message are:

> *OK. Your move was right.* It corresponds to the question about: what the others are doing is helping to solve the task?, proposed in our KCA set of questions.
> *Can I move to the right?* It corresponds to the question about: Is what I am doing helping to solve the task?
> *Be careful… our score is too low.* It corresponds to the question about: What is our score?

An exhaustive analysis of this kind of message gives an idea about the amount of the shared knowledge among members of the group. As we mentioned in the first part of this paper, space can contribute to a better coordination. For instance, one user might suggest to the other that she should move to a certain position, and the second user might not answer with words, but simply move to this position, thereby acknowledging her partner's suggestion. Or conversely, she may express disagreement by going to another position. Because the knowledge of this

space, the user may interpret mutual positions, movements and actions in order to build mutual knowledge regarding the problem state, the problem strategy or simply what the other means. In this work, we only are interested to analyze the messages and not the actions that permit the group members [to] build a shared understanding of the problematic situation.

## Experimental design

The experiment has four phases. The group receives a brief description of the software tool. During the second phase, group members are assigned to network workstations in separate rooms (synchronous distributed interaction). From then on, all group communication is mediated by computer. During the third phase the group will try to solve the labyrinth. Finally, the fourth phase corresponds to the gathering and analysis of data recorded by the tool. We made also a final interview of the participants to foster a self-evaluation of the experience. This gave us a general overview of the problem perceived by each member of the team.

So far, we have applied the experiment to eleven groups, as follows:

- A group of graduate students, from the course "Collaborative Systems" at Pontificia Universidad Catúlica de Chile, with some experience on collaborative work techniques (group 0).
- A group of people randomly selected, who have not met before and, of course, have never worked together (group 3).
- A group of friends who have worked as a group many times before the experience and have a very good personal relationship (group 4).
- Four groups of high school students from Cumbres de Santiago School, with an average age of

15 years old. Two of these were randomly selected (group 1 and group 2) and the remaining ones were friends (group 5 and group 6).

- Four groups of graduate students from Universidad de Chile (Groups 7, 8, 9, 10).

## Results

Table 4 presents the results that we got according to every indicator previously defined. I1 corresponds to "applying strategies", I2 "intra-group cooperation", I3 "success criteria review", I4 "monitoring", and I5 "performance". The criteria used to measure every indicator are presented in (22). Every indicator is in a range between 0 and 1.

These preliminary results show that KCA may be an important factor which influences the collaboration process within a group. The groups that got the best scores in almost all indicators (5 and 6) got the best scores in our KCA score. Also, the groups that got the worst scores in almost all indicators (2 and 9) got the worst score in our KCA score.

## Conclusions and further work

The awareness usually afforded in physical collaborative learning environments allows learners to implicitly maintain information about the other interactions with common problem areas and corresponding tasks.

Awareness is an important factor in the development of collaborative applications, and in our work we found that the group with the best score according to our collaboration indicators, had the best KCA (knowledge-construction awareness). With this kind of awareness it is possible to develop ways to increase the probability that some types of interaction occur. According to Dillenbourg, Collaborative Learning is a situation in which particular forms of interaction, which would trigger learning mechanisms, are expected to occur (20).

In order to obtain a better KCA it is necessary to develop new styles of group interfaces, and so, improve the interaction among the group members. Our next work will be to make a more detailed analysis of the impact of this kind of awareness in the collaboration process, in order to determine when and how people are aware of their own knowledge. Measuring the shared understanding of a conflicting situation is a problematic issue. So, in a future work we are going to include not only semantic analysis of the messages, but the actions performed among the members of the group.

## Acknowledgments

This work was partially supported by grant No. 1000870 from Fondecyt (Chile), and grant No. I-015-99/2 from DID (Departamento de Investigaciòn y Desarrollo), Universidad de Chile.

## References

1. Koschmann, T. D. (1994). Toward a theory of computer support for collaborative learning. *The Journal of the Learning Sciences, 3* (3), 219–225.
2. Dourish, P., & Bly, S. (1992). Supporting awareness in a distributed work group. *CHI '92 Conference Proceedings*, (pp. 541–547). Monterey, CA, New York.
3. Fjuk, A., & Smordal, O. (1997). The computer's incorporated role in work. In Buch, N. J., Damsgaard, J., Eriksen, L. D., Iversen, J. H., Nielsen, P. A. (Eds.), *Information Systems Research in Collaboration with Industry* (pp. 207–221). Aalborg University, Department of Computer Science.
4. Malone W., & Crowston K. (1994). The interdisciplinary study of coordination. *ACM Computing Surveys, 26* (1), 87–119.
5. Matsushita, Y. and Okada, K., (1995). Collaboration and communications. *Distributed Collaboration Media Series 3*, Kyoritsu Press.
6. Gutwin, C., Greenberg, S. & Roseman, M. (1996). Workspace awareness in real-time distributed groupware: framework, widgets, and evaluation. In R. J. Sasse, A. Cunningham, and R. Winder (Eds.), *People and Computers* (pp. 281–298). Springer-Verlag.
7. Sumi, Y. & Mase, K. (2001). Supporting awareness of shared interests and experiences in community. *ACM 2001 International Conference on Support Group Work*, (pp. 35–42). Boulder, USA.
8. Molli, P., Skaf-Molli, H. & Bouthier, C. (2001). State tree map: an awareness widget for multi-synchronous groupware. *Proceedings of CRIWG 2001*, (pp. 106–114). Darmstadt, Germany. IEEE Computer Society Press.
9. Goldman, S. V. (1992). Computer resources for supporting student conversations about science concepts. *SIGCUE Outlook, 21* (3), 4–7.
10. Gutwin, C., Stark, G. & Greenberg, S. (1995). Support for workspace awareness in educational groupware. Schnase, J. L. and Cunnius, E. L. (Eds.), *Computer Support for Collaborative Learning. Proceedings of CSCL '95* (pp. 147–156). New York: Lawrence Erlbaum Associates.
11. Yamakami, T. & Seki, Y. (1995). Knowledge awareness in asynchronous information sharing. *Proceedings of the IFIP TC8/WG8.4* (pp. 215–225). Working Conference.
12. Ogata, H. & Yano, Y. (1998). Knowledge awareness: bridging learners in a collaborative learning environment. *International Journal of Educational Telecommunications, 4*, 219–236.
13. Rogoff, B. (1991). Social interaction on apprenticeship in thinking: guided participation in spatial planning. In L. Resnick, J. Levine & E. Teasley (Eds.), *Perspectives on Socially Shared Cognition*, Hyattsville, MD: American Psychological Association.
14. Newman, D., Griffin, P. & Cole, M. (1989). *The construction zone: working for cognitive change in school* (pp. 349–364). New York: Cambridge University Press.
15. Dillenbourg, P. (1996). Distributed cognition on brains and machines. In S. Vosniadou, E. De Corte, B. Glaser & H. Mandi (Eds.), *International Perspectives on the Psychological Foundations of Technology-Based Learning Environments* (pp. 165–184), Mahwah, NJ: Lawrence Erlbaum.
16. Fox, B. (1987). Interactional reconstruction in real-time language processing. *Cognitive Science, 11* (3), 365–387.
17. Dillenbourg, P. & Self, J. (1995). Designing human-computer collaborative learning. In C. C. O'Malley (Eds.), *Computer Supported Collaborative Learning*, Hamburg: Springer-Verlag.
18. Lochhead, J. (1985). Teaching analytic reasoning skills through pair problem solving. In J. W. Segal, S. F. Chipman

and R. Glaser (Eds.), *Thinking and learning skills: Relating instruction to research* (pp. 109–131). Laurence Erlbaum, Hillsdale.

19. Johnson, D. W., Johnson, R., Ortiz, A. & Stanne, M. (1991). Impact of positive goal and resource interdependence on achievement, interaction, and attitudes. *Journal of General Psychology, 118* (4), 341–347.

20. Dillenbourg, P. (1999). What do you mean by collaborative learning? In P. Dillenbourg (Eds.), *Collaborative Learning: Cognitive and Computational Approaches* (pp. 1–19), Oxford: Elsevier.

21. Dillenbourg, P. & Traum, D. (1997). The role of a whiteboard in a distributed cognition system. *Swiss Workshop on Collaborative and Distributed Systems.* Lausanne, Switzerland.

22. Collazos, C., Guerrero, L., Pino, J. & Ochao, S. (2002). *Evaluating collaborative learning processes.* Proceedings of the 8th International Workshop on Groupware, CRIWG 2002, Springer Verlag, La Serena, Chile.

23. Adams, D. & Hamm, M. (1996). Cooperative learning, critical thinking and collaboration across the curriculum. Second Edition, Charles Thomas Publisher.

24. Jarboe, S. (1996). Procedures for enhancing group decision making. In B. Hirokawa and M. Poole (Eds.), *Communication and Group Decision Making* (pp. 345–383). Thousand Oaks, CA: Sage Publications.

25. Deutsch, M. (1962). Cooperation and trust: some theoretical notes. In M. Jones (Eds.), *Nebraska Symposium on Motivation* (pp. 275–300), Lincoln: University of Nebraska Press.

26. Baeza-Yates, R. & Pino, J. A. (1997). A first step to formally evaluate collaborative work. *International Conference GROUP '97* (pp. 55–60), Phoenix, AZ, USA.

27. Guerrero, L., Alarcòn, R., Collazos, C., Pino, J. & Fuller, D. (2000). Evaluating cooperation in group work. *Sixth International Workshop on Groupware, CRIWG 2000* (pp. 28–35). Madeira, Portugal, IEEE Computer Society Press.

28. Dillenbourg, P., Baker, M., Blake, A. & O'Malley, C. (1995). The evolution of research on collaborative learning. In H. Spada and P. Reimann (Eds.), *Learning in Humans and Machines.*

29. Fussell, S., Kraut, R., Lerch, F., Scherlis, W., McNally, M., & Cadiz, J. (1998). Coordination, Overload and Team Performance: Effects of Team Communication Strategies. *CSCW '98*, Seattle, Washington, USA.

**Cèsar A. Collazos** is an Assistant Professor of Computer Science at the Universidad del Cauca. He is pursuing his doctoral studies in Computer Science at the Universidad de Chile. He received his Bachelor degree in Computer Science from Universidad de los Andes in Bogota (Columbia). His research interests include Computer-Supported Collaborative Learning and Human-Computer Interaction, especially the modeling, design and building processes of educative software applications.

**Luis A. Guerrero** is an Assistant Professor of Computer Science at the Universidad de Chile. He received his Ph.D. in Computer Science at the Pontificia Universidad Catolica de Chile, a M.Sc. degree in Computer Science from Instituto Tecnologico de Costa Rica, and a Bachelor degree in Computer Science from Universidad de Costa Rica. His research interest include the modeling, design and building processes of collaborative applications, object-oriented technologies and collaborative learning.

**Josè A. Pino** is an Associate Professor of Computer Science and Director of the Ph.D. program in Computer Science at the Universidad de Chile. His research interests include Computer-Supported Cooperative Work, Human-Computer Interaction and Software Industry Studies. He has served as President of the Chilean Computer Science Society (SCCC) and President of CLEI (the Latin American Association of Universities concerning Information Technology). He has co-authored six books and published research papers in international conferences and journals, including Journal of the ACM, Communications of the ACM, Decision Support Systems, Interacting with Computers and Information Technology and People.

From *Journal of Student Centered Learning*, Vol. 1, No. 2, 2003, pp. 77-86. © 2003 by New Forums Press, Inc.

# UNIT 4

# Identity and Personal Development: A Multicultural Focus

## Unit Selections

## Key Points to Consider

- Why should an educator be sensitive to cultural identity?

- What should children learn about the cultural heritages and values of other children in their schools?

- How do social class differences relate to misunderstandings among students from different social positions in a community?

- How are cultural stereotypes damaging to students?

- What challenges do minority students encounter that majority students in a desegregated school do not encounter?

- What difficulties have Arab and Muslim Americans faced since September 11, 2001? How can teachers help?

## Student Website

www.mhcls.com/online

## Internet References

Further information regarding these websites may be found in this book's preface or online.

**Ethics Updates/Lawrence Hinman**
  *http://ethics.acusd.edu*

**Kathy Schrock's Guide for Educators**
  *http://school.discovery.com/schrockguide/*

**Let 100 Flowers Bloom/Kristen Nicholson-Nelson**
  *http://teacher.scholastic.com/professional/assessment/100flowers.htm*

**The National Academy for Child Development**
  *http://www.nacd.org*

**P**eople are impacted by many social forces as they interact with others in the process of forming themselves as individuals. Multicultural education can help students as well as teachers to identify those social forces that affect their personal development.

The development of each person's unique concept of self (the development of one's identity as a person) is the most important developmental learning task that any of us undertake. The preschool, elementary, and secondary school years are ones in which each of us learns critically important cognitive and affective strategies for defining ourselves, others, and the world. Multicultural education seeks to help people develop intellectual and emotional responses to other people that will be accepting and empathic. There has been much psychological and psychiatric research over the past few decades on the differences between prejudiced and tolerant (accepting) personalities. One opportunity educators have as they work with students in school settings is to provide good examples of accepting, tolerant behavior and to help students develop positive, affirmative views of themselves and others. Gordon A. Allport, in his classic book *The Nature of Prejudice*, commented in his chapter on "The Tolerant Personality" that we could be "doubly sure" that early instruction and practice in accepting diversity is important in directing a child toward becoming a tolerant person. Thus, we take up the topic of personal identity development in this unit.

As educators we need to see the interconnections among such factors as gender, social class, position in society, racial or ethnic heritage, and the primary cultural values that inform the way people see the world and themselves. We need to be sensitive to their visions of who they are and of how things are in the world. We need to "see our clients whole." It is important for teachers to set positive examples of acceptance, open-mindedness, empathy, compassion, and concern for the well-being of each student.

We need to help students to understand themselves, to define their strengths and their concerns, and to empower them to encounter their own personal social reality critically. This is a task each person must learn to do in childhood and adolescence in order to empower themselves to interpret and evaluate their own experience. This task can be integrated and effectively achieved within the intellectual mission of the school. One way to do this is to encourage students to critically interpret and evaluate the texts that they read and to discuss issues in class

openly and actively. Each student needs to be able to explore the boundaries of his or her intellectual strengths and weaknesses and to explore the social boundaries encountered in school and out of school.

Multicultural education is intended for and needed by all students in order for them to develop sensitivity to the many varying heritages and backgrounds that make up the United States and Canada and to forge their own conception of who they are as people. Why should only one cultural heritage be thoroughly taught while all others are essentially ignored in elementary and secondary school years in a pluralistic national social environment, the demographics of which are changing so dramatically? Cultural values are of primary importance in the process of a person's conceptualization of him- or herself. This unit's articles explore various models of human interaction and the psychosocial foundations for the formation of knowledge bases of students. How students form social groups in culturally integrated school settings is explored along with the behavioral differences among members of "loose-knit" and "tight-knit" social groups in desegregated school settings. The ways in which students define themselves and their possibilities as they move across or are trapped within their perceived social boundaries in school and community settings are explored. How educators can better utilize the knowledge bases of minority cultural families in assisting minority students to achieve better social integration into mainstream school settings is also examined. The importance of educators trying to establish more effective communications linkages between students' family and cultural environments is further examined. The multiple social roles students frequently have to play, both in and out of school, are another phenomenon in personality development that receives analysis in these essays.

Students live in a hierarchy of social contexts in which their racial, cultural, gender, and social class backgrounds, and the degree of their personal identification with each of these factors, influence their important choices and decisions regarding their own identity. Some of the research on how teachers can achieve more effective intercultural socialization is also considered. One of the questions being studied in desegregated school settings concerns the circumstances in which higher rates of intercultural friendship develop. How do we get all cultural group members to learn each other's cultural heritages? Helping students to learn from the cultural perspectives of other groups so that all students might better comprehend alternative, diverse definitions of their social environments is one of the tasks of multicultural education. Another purpose of multicultural education programming is to teach tolerant, accepting attitudes toward others of differing cultural backgrounds. Allport and several other major psychiatrists and social psychologists of past decades have taught us that prejudice and tolerance (acceptance) are learned behaviors. We can learn to be accepting, caring, compassionate persons. Educators are not powerless in the face of the prejudiced view many students bring to school from their homes.

The essays in this unit are relevant to courses in educational policy studies and leadership, cultural foundations of education, sociology or anthropology of education, history and philosophy of education, and curriculum theory and construction, among others.

# Transcending Spaces: Exploring Identity in a Rural American Middle School

*Jean Ketter and Diana Buter*

A university professor and an eighth-grade teacher collaborated to help middle school students think critically about race, class, and gender. Jean Ketter and Diana Buter describe the materials and activities they developed for a unit on exploring identity. They also critique the effectiveness of the unit in changing students' attitudes.

## Small Town People

We would like you to know
We are not all farmers
And we don't all stay in one place.
We do not all chew on
Straw.
We don't all walk five miles to school.
Although most of these characteristics are developed
   in small towns.

We would like you to know
Not all of us dream of fancy cars and houses.
We don't all have families of twelve.
We don't all sit by highways,
And watch cars go by.
We don't know everybody's name.
Most of us just dream of a nice family.

We would like you to know
We don't all raise hogs.
We don't all run around in baggy overalls.
Although farming is an important
Industry in Iowa.

A group of eighth-grade language arts students modeled this poem after Ana Castillo's "We Would Like You to Know" in response to an assignment in the unit Exploring Identity that was taught a few weeks after September 11, 2001.

We taught this unit because we believe thinking critically about race, class, and gender is particularly important with our white, rural students, who have had limited exposure to other cultures and ethnic groups except for what they have seen on television or in movies. In this unit, Diana, an experienced middle school language arts and reading teacher, and Jean, an associate professor of education, hoped to help students chal-

lenge mainstream media's depictions of people of color and other marginalized groups. As Gay argues, too often such groups are portrayed "as victims, servants to society, passive participants, second-class citizens, and imperfect imitations of European, Anglo male models (167). Also, we wanted students to understand how inequity is institutionalized in our country and thus cannot be overcome solely through individual effort or resolve.

We hoped to provide students with literary experiences that would help them connect with characters whose lives and experiences differed vastly from theirs and to see how their own race, class, and gender shaped their understanding of the world. Despite challenges, we discovered that a focus on critically reading multicultural literature helped students bridge their experiential gaps. Students can think and read critically about race, class, and gender at this age, but they need support through modeling, guided practice, and a choice of accessible literature.

## Community and School Background

Hometown Middle School[1] is located in a central Iowa agricultural community with a population of 9,105. Hometown is the home of Iowa College, a nationally recognized liberal arts college, and Hometown Regional Medical Center, a major medical facility serving Hometown and surrounding communities. Hometown is located at least an hour from any sizable metropolitan area and is among the 55.4 percent of Iowa schools classified as rural ("Navigating"). The school system enrolls 1,769 students, and the middle school enrollment (grades 5-8) is 550. Ninety-four percent of the student body and 99 percent of the faculty, staff, and administration are white. Approximately 28 percent of the district's students are bused to attendance centers from outside the city limits; 24 percent of the students receive free or reduced-fee lunches (Hometown School District).

## Classroom Contexts

The eighth-grade language arts classes in which the Exploring Identity unit was implemented met daily for a ninety-minute block made up of two forty-two minute periods, one devoted to reading and the other to writing. This schedule allowed for flexibility in scheduling class activities within the block. Classes averaged twenty-two to twenty-five students.

Diana's approach to teaching is to begin building relationships with her students from the first day of class by modeling the respect toward her students that she expects in return. Prior to the beginning of the unit, Diana had worked to establish with her classes an atmosphere of mutual trust and respect in which students listened to and valued one another's ideas. Students were used to writing about and discussing literature using openended, divergent questions (what Diana called "fat" questions). Students were not accustomed to looking to the teacher for the definitive answer to discussion questions. They frequently reacted to assigned literature selections using written response and often worked in small peer groups to discuss and interpret literature.

---

**Despite challenges, we discovered that a focus on critically reading multicultural literature helped students bridge their experiential gaps.**

---

Jean and Diana had worked together as college supervisor and cooperating teacher and were participating in a reading group focused on young adult literature by and about people of color. Jean and her colleague Cynthia Lewis had begun the reading group for teachers as a research project aimed at looking at how best to approach teaching multicultural literature with predominantly white students in a rural setting (see Lewis, Ketter, and Fabos; Ketter and Lewis). These book-group discussions spurred Jean and Diana to test some of the ideas they had developed about teaching multicultural literature in their setting.

Diana and the students shared a common background and experiences. This homogeneity created a sense of familiarity and continuity in the classroom, and it also encouraged students to see their experiences as "normal" and universal. Because students felt comfortable with one another, they were open to the idea of exploring the lives and experiences of persons significantly different from them, and they shared a common frame of reference from which to launch the exploration. But this common frame was too easily perceived as the natural way to see the world; students drew on their perceptions to judge or understand others.

## Planning the Unit

We believed that young adult literature could help students connect to characters with unfamiliar experiences and unlearn stereotypes created from lack of experience. We knew one challenge we faced was to encourage reading with an empathetic ear and eye, so we designed experiences that we thought would help students bridge the gaps between their lives and those of the characters.

A related challenge was to ensure that students neither trivialized nor exoticized the experiences of the characters. We saw how encouraging students to connect their experiences with characters of color could lead them to see their experiences as equivalent to those they read about. As Rosenberg warns against in "Underground Discourses: Exploring Whiteness in Teacher Education," we did not want our students to create parallels between their own and characters' lives that "obscure[d] the ways that racist domination impacts on the lives of marginalized groups" (83). Although Rosenberg refers to teacher educators, her caution applies equally well to students. We wanted to challenge a tendency to perceive characters who lived in any inner city, did not speak English as their first language, or did not live with married parents as not quite normal—or perhaps as not really "American."

Thus, we planned the unit in four stages to lead students from understanding and empathizing with others to questioning their assumptions about what is natural or normal. We believe that students who had read the texts and engaged in critical discussions would enlarge their vision of an "ideal" America, one that would include people all colors and ethnic origins, who spoke a variety of languages, and who came from a variety of social backgrounds.

## Implementing the Unit

We presented students with the following goals on the first day of the unit:

1. You will examine the ways in which you are a unique individual.

2. You will deepen your understanding of how your identify affects the way you read and understand literature.

3. You will ask and answer specific questions about literature that will help you see literature in a more sophisticated way.

4. You will have an opportunity to step into the identity of another person—perhaps a person who is very "different" from you.

5. You will have an opportunity to create a clear vision of what you would like the "perfect" America to be.

### Connecting with the Literature

In the first activity, we asked students to list all the characteristics they believed made up their identities. Then, using an overhead and several different colored pens, we recorded in a circle all the characteristics or factors they contributed. After we had included everything that students thought made up a person's identity, we erased from the circle any aspects of identity students believed they control, such as attitude, interests, and so forth. The remaining characteristics were those aspects of identity over which a person has no control, and we hoped to discover that these are the very things upon which we tend to base stereotypes. This discussion also provided an opportunity to talk about concepts of class, race, and gender.

At the end of the period, we asked students to write about a time they had been stereotyped unfairly or had stereotyped others unfairly. We decided to present our own reflection paragraphs as models. Jean wrote about a time she had made an unfair judgment based on a racial stereotype, and Diana wrote about being stereotyped because of her age.

To help students empathize with those who face racism and to see how race shapes one's perspective, we compared an excerpt from the memoir *Warriors Don't Cry* with a parallel clip from *Crisis at Central High,* an HBO movie. The memoir recounts the experiences of Melba Pattillo Beals, one of the "Little Rock Nine" who elected to be the first African Americans to integrate Central High in Little Rock, Arkansas. The excerpt describes how the African American students were verbally threatened, physically assaulted, and generally mistreated by teachers and students. After discussing the excerpt, we showed the film segment of the same event from the white assistant principal's point of view, a much less disturbing depiction of events than the excerpt presented. The discussion focused on three questions: (1) How does the perspective of the author affect how one tells a story? (2) How did the author's and filmmaker's purposes differ? (3) How do the students' identities affect the way they read the story or view the video? Students were shocked by the treatment the Little Rock Nine received, and students had no trouble grasping that the different narrative perspectives altered how the story was told. Perhaps because they did not understand how such treatment was typical for African Americans, some also seemed unable to empathize with the African American students, instead responding to their mistreatment with indignation at the students' passivity. They argued that Beals should have "fought back" or stood up to the white teachers and students. It was very difficult for these students to imagine how years of discrimination might alter one's consciousness or how fighting back might have resulted in physical and psychic injury.

---

**After discussing the excerpt, we showed the film segment of the same event from the white assistant principal's point of view, a much less disturbing depiction of events than the excerpt presented.**

---

In the next activity, student groups composed poems modeled after Ana Castillo's "We Would Like You to Know," writing from the perspective of a group who had been stereotyped or misrepresented. First we read aloud and discussed Castillo's poem, modeling the critical questions we planned to use with students during the unit. In our discussion, students raised some issues that were current in Iowa, such as some people's misperception that Mexican workers in the meat-packing plants were stealing jobs from whites.

After discussing the poem, students wrote their "We Would Like You to Know" poems in small groups. We were troubled when students wanted to write about marginalized groups they knew little about, such as Muslims or African Americans, because sometimes their poems came close to reinforcing stereotypes rather than challenging them. We do see some value in having students imagine they are experiencing the injustices less-privileged groups in society may experience, but again, we worry about what sort of comparisons students are making. Because students are only occupying that imagined place temporarily and because they do not fully understand what that experience is like, we worry that we might lead them to conclude that escaping racism and overcoming the barriers it presents are a simple matter of individual will. As Boler warns, helping students develop empathy for such experiences can be dangerous if it is nothing more than a "harmonious experience of reversibility and the pleasure of identification" (qtd. in Rosenberg 83).

---

**In discussion based on the students' questions, we continued to challenge stereotypes students might have held.**

---

## Practicing Critical Reading

Next, students practiced using critical questions (see fig. 1). Before we read aloud "An Hour with Abuelo," a short story told from the point of view of an adolescent boy who is cajoled into visiting his grandfather at the nursing home (Cofer), we discussed a list of critical questions to use with the story and assigned pairs of students a question from the list to consider as they listened to the story. In discussion after the reading, students heard how others responded to the questions, asked questions about the questions themselves, and practiced new ways of thinking about literature that emphasized decentering their experience.

We next assigned a variety of young adult texts and asked students to formulate critical questions. In discussion based on the students' questions, we continued to challenge stereotypes students might have held. For example, we read the stories of three very different African American young women from *Sugar in the Raw* (Carroll). One young woman had grown up in San Francisco with professional parents. Another had grown up in a working-class, mixed-race neighborhood and had attended public schools. The third had attended a private religious school on the East Coast. Every author in the text was responding to a similar set of questions, which made it easier for us to discuss comparisons and contrasts among the three young women. We discussed the many ways the young women were similar—in their experience of racism, their preoccupation with skin color, and their confidence about being successful. But we also discovered how different these young women were and how knowing their race did not help us predict very much about them. Choosing middle-class young women with well-educated and professional parents worked

**FIGURE 1.** Focus Question Models

Below are ten questions that will serve as models for you as you write your own questions about what we read. Since you will be doing this several times, vary the questions you ask. I do not want you to use the same questions every time, so keep track of which ones you have tried and try not to repeat them.

1. What do you know or can you guess about the narrator of this story? What is his or her gender, ethnicity, age, background? What sort of person do you think he or she is? What evidence do you find in the story to help you answer this question?

2. How does the identity of the narrator (race, class, gender, age, ethnicity, etc.) affect how he or she tells the story? Explain by giving examples.

3. To whom is the narrator telling the story? In other words. who might be the ideal audience for this story, and why do you think so?

4. Do you think the narrator has you in mind as someone he or she would want to tell this story to? Why or why not? If yes, how does that affect your reading of the story? If you don't think you are in the intended audience or feel the author isn't speaking to you, how does that affect your understanding of the story?

5. How do you think the author of this story wants you to feel about particular characters or events? How does the author achieve this end? What statements or events do you find in the story that promote a certain view or suggest that you should feel a certain way about something or someone?

6. How would this story be different if the narrator's identity were different? What specific things might change in the poem or story and how would they change?

7. What aspects of your identity affect the way you read this story? How do aspects of your identity affect your reading?

8. What incidents, viewpoints, or opinions are left out of the story? Why do you think the author may have left out certain viewpoints or information? What do you think these other perspectives or voices might add to the story?

9. Do you think the story gives a fair view of the events? Why or why not?

10. What has the author assumed are natural or good ways of acting? Do you agree or disagree with the author's messages about how we should behave or should be, and how does your agreement or disagreement with these messages affect how you read the story or poem?

Adapted from Simpson (120).

against some of the stereotypes white students might hold about African American young adults.

We were not always able to predict how students would respond to a particular text, and students' reactions to Nikki Giovanni's "Nikki-Rosa" surprised us. Several students responded negatively to the last lines of the poem, where Giovanni predicts that people will "probably talk about my hard childhood/and never understand that/all the while I was quite happy" (207). We found several students misread or ignored the message of Giovanni's poem. In their written responses, they described her childhood as abnormal or deprived, exactly the image Giovanni was trying to challenge. For many of the students, the narrator seemed unnecessarily angry about how white people envisioned her childhood. One student in our discussion went so far as to call the narrator a "brat."

Not all of the students had this response. When we began to discuss more generally what the poem revealed to us as readers, students were able to list the stereotypical ways inner-city life was depicted. Two students did counter the stereotype by referring to their own experiences, which allowed us to reinforce the point that personal experiences can affect the reading and interpretation of a text. However, we who teach in rural, predominantly white schools must anticipate resistance from students who may not be accustomed to reading literature that challenges notions of white identity and privilege.

## Peer Teaching Using Critical Questions

We began phase three of the unit by instructing small groups of students to prepare to lead discussion on a poem, many of which came from the anthology *Unsettling America* (Gillan and Gillan). As with all the reading, students wrote responses to questions they posed about the text. The next day, students met in their small groups to share responses to the poems and to plan discussion of the poem by selecting the focus questions they wanted to explore with the class.

To lead the discussion, each of the groups first read their poem aloud and shared their interpretations. They then asked their selected questions. We were impressed by how seriously students took the task of leading discussion and with the level and depth of student participation. Students' responses to the poems were sensitive and capable. "Translating Grandfather's House" (Vega), about a child being doubted by a teacher based on a stereotype, brought out some of the strongest reactions because many students vividly remembered teachers who they felt had misjudged or discounted them.

## Envisioning an Ideal America

Students next constructed a collage. To begin, they wrote a reflection paragraph on what an ideal America would be. Students considered what they thought was already ideal or desirable about our country and what could be improved. They discussed their reflections in small groups and completed a chart listing the symbols they would use to represent the qualities they had agreed were desirable or needed improvement. All ideas were to be included on the chart and in the collage.

The process of making the collages was more important than the product itself. We were impressed with some of the discussions occurring in the small groups; other discussions revealed the limits of students' understanding. For example, many students wanted to express the concept of freedom of religion on their collages, and several set about doing so by making a cross. When Jean asked them what other religious symbols might encompass the different religions practiced in this country, students seemed surprised. Since we were teaching this unit soon after September 11, we thought it was important to remind students that Americans are also Jewish, Muslim, Buddhist, Sikh, and so forth, but it was clear that students wanted to include freedom of religion to express their support for school prayer and not to express the value of religious pluralism.

> **Since we were teaching this unit soon after September 11, we thought it was important to remind students that Americans are also Jewish, Muslim, Buddhist, Sikh, and so forth, but it was clear that students wanted to include freedom of religion to express their support for school prayer and not to express the value of religious pluralism.**

Each of the collages was unique and several showed careful thought in design. Students depicted their desire for freedom of religion, freedom from crime, freedom from pollution, and freedom from discrimination. Most included the need for more tolerance of difference, but most resisted making their collages about only race or ethnicity. Many expressed the idea that racism and discrimination are less prevalent than in the past, but most acknowledged that progress was still to be made, which was gratifying.

## Challenging Notions

We are still troubled by questions raised during the teaching of this unit. Is it possible to challenge rural, white middle schoolers' notions about whiteness and raise their awareness of white privilege using critical reading as a tool? Is it possible for a group of white eighth-grade students to transcend their perceptions of what is natural and normal in the world as they read literature about people with different perceptions? We certainly believe these things are possible, but we also believe more time and energy must be devoted to these goals in all language arts classrooms, K-12.

We think we made some progress with some students, but two weeks in one year of their schooling will not go far in changing the way students read and the way they see themselves in the world, particularly if these students' other reading experiences do not lead them to recognize the privilege of being seen

as an individual or to challenge the use of whiteness as a measure of what is normal or natural. Diana will continue to pursue these goals throughout the curriculum with her students, but many teachers do not see these goals as central to their teaching.

We also believe that creating classrooms where students read literature in a culturally critical way is crucial but may not be enough. For example, we read one student's final reflection on an "Ideal America" in which she suggests that America needs a "class for racist people" with both concern and hope. The idea that racism can be eliminated by a class or rehabilitation echoes the philosophies that define multicultural pedagogy as exposure to multicultural literature rather than as a critical reading of *all* texts, including the students' lives. We had hoped that students would come to see how pervasive racism is and how most of us subtly or not so subtly aid its persistence. These students, however, continued to see racism as something individual people acted on rather than as part of the fabric of our institutions. At least this student's quote shows an awareness of racism as abnormal and as resulting from ignorance. In the past, we have heard students voice the idea that racism is simply a part of the human condition and, consequently, unavoidable. At least this student hopes for change and realizes that education could be a tool in eliminating racism, and we agree with her. We believe that the unjust practices that continue to plague the United States should be challenged in every classroom—rural, suburban, and urban—and we believe education for all students should include critical experiences that bring them to recognize and to take effective action against the injustices that scar our national psyche.

> **We think we made some progress with some students, but two weeks in one year of their schooling will not go far in changing the way students read and the way they see themselves in the world, particularly if these students' other reading experiences do not lead them to recognize the privilege of being seen as an individual or to challenge the use of whiteness as a measure of what is normal or natural.**

## Note

1. All place names and student names are pseudonyms.

## Works Cited

Beals, Melba Pattillo. *Warriors Don't Cry: A Searing Memoir of the Battle to Integrate Little Rock's Central High.* New York: Pocket, 1994.

Carroll, Rebecca, ed. *Sugar in the Raw: Voices of Young Black Girls in America.* New York: Three Rivers, 1997.

Castillo, Ana. "We Would Like You to Know." *Cool Salsa: Bilingual Poems on Growing Up Latino in the United States.* Ed. Lori M. Carlson. New York: Fawcett Juniper, 1994. 113-15.

Cofer, Judith Ortiz. "An Hour with Abuelo." *An Island Like You: Stories of the Barrio.* New York: Orchard, 1995. 66-71.

*Crisis at Central High.* Dir. Lamont Johnson. HBO, 1981.

Gay, Geneva. "Mirror Images on Common Issues: Parallels between Multicultural Education and Critical Pedagogy." *Multicultural Education, Critical Pedagogy, and the Politics of Difference.* Ed. Christine E. Sleeter and Peter L. McLaren. New York: State U of New York P, 1995. 155-89.

Gillan, Maria Mazziotti, and Jennifer Gillan, eds. *Unsettling America: An Anthology of Contemporary Multicultural Poetry.* New York: Viking, 1994.

Giovanni, Nikki. "Nikki-Rosa." *Unsettling America: An Anthology of Contemporary Multicultural Poetry.* Ed. Maria Mazziotti Gillan and Jennifer Gillan. New York: Viking, 1994. 206-07.

Ketter, Jean, and Cynthia Lewis. "Already Reading Texts and Concexts: Multicultural Literature in a Predominantly White Rural Community." *Theory into Practice* 40.3 (2001): 175-84.

Lewis, Cynthia, Jean Ketter, and Bettina Fabos. "Reading Race in a Rural Context." *The International Journal of Qualitative Studies in Education* 14.3 (2001): 317-50.

"Navigating Resources for Rural Schools: Tables and Figures." National Center for Education Statistics. 2000. 2 Mar. 2004 (http://nces.ed.gov/surveys/ruraled/data/WhatsRuralSummary.asp).

Rosenberg, Pearl M. "Underground Discourses: Exploring Whiteness in Teacher Education." *Off White: Readings on Race, Power, and Society.* Ed. Michelle Fine, Lois Weis, Linda C. Powell, and L. Mun Wong. New York: Routledge, 1997. 79-89.

Simpson, Anne. "Critical Questions: Whose Questions?" *The Reading Teacher* 50.2 (996):118-27.

Vega, E. J. "Translating Grandfather's House." *Cool Salsa: Bilingual Poems on Growing Up Latino in the United States.* Ed. Lori M. Carlson. New York: Fawcett Juniper, 1994. 5-6.

*Jean Ketter* teaches courses in educational foundations and in the theories and methods of English and foreign language instruction at Grinnell College. Her research focuses on the sociocultural aspects of multicultural literature instruction and on the political and pedagogical implications of high-stakes reading and writing assessments. email: Ketter@grinnell.edu. *Diana Buter* has taught English for twenty-one years in both high school and middle school. She spent the 2003-04 school year visiting schools around the state of Iowa as the 2003-04 Iowa Teacher of the Year. email: dbuter@grinnell.k12.ia.us.

# The Challenge of Declaring an Interethnic and/or Interracial Identity in Postmodern Societies

Marta I. Cruz-Janzen, Edith W. King and Francis Wardle

Even when they [US government] tell you that you are free to choose your own identity, they still mandate what that identity must be. If you don't choose what they want, they simply change it without consulting you. I thought the new census would change this but it's still more of the same old, same old … They lied! They fooled us! When is everyone going to accept that I am not this or that, that I am both and have the right to be both? That I don't choose one over the other when it is convenient? That I am who I am all the time. I am angry and frustrated by all of this. I feel so violated by our government's insistence to dictate who or what we choose to be.

These are the recent comments of a biethnic and biracial student in a teacher education program. In this article we present information and research on an ensuing controversy that challenges the traditional, widely accepted, "racial" categorization in the USA and other societies. The authors take the position that the US Census 2000 created a false "smoke screen" to further deny authentic interethnic and interracial identity. The current categories remain highly arbitrary and harmful. They do not further inter or intra-group understanding, tolerance and racial harmony. Indeed they continue to fuel century-old angers, distrusts and fears. It is imperative that the reality of multiethnic and multiracial identity be fully legitimized and validated not only in the USA, but also in nation states throughout the world where single-race approaches to human identity prevail. The authentic and wholesome identities of interethnic and interracial persons require that we first come to grips with the underlying ideologies that have historically shaped and continue to guide our construction of race.

Although the USA adapted its ethnic and racial categories for the Census 2000, little has been done to change pervasive misinformation and misunderstandings about how our society constructs race. Little attention has been given to informing parents, teachers, social workers, counselors, school administrators and the general public about identity development in persons of all ages and particularly the young and adolescent child. Awareness and dissemination of information about the psychological and social development of multiethnic and multiracial children has not reached teacher preparation programs, our Pre-Kinder/Kindergarten-12th grade (P/K-12th) schools, or social service agencies even though a considerable body of information is available, beginning with early childhood through adolescence into adulthood. The information that is provided is usually incorrect—stressing an absolute adherence to single-race identity. New information, grounded in human growth and development theory, is urgently needed at this critical juncture to bring awareness and understandings to multicultural education, counseling and social work practice; as well as other institutions of society.

Some actual examples of the various multiethnic/multiracial family constellations in the USA today are:

- mother from Japan; father a White American of diverse ancestry that includes French, Irish and German;
- mother of German-Jewish American heritage; father African American;
- mother of White Spanish [Spaniard] and White Mexican heritage; father is English-German American;
- mother of Mexican Indian heritage; father is German American;
- mother is American Indian; father is of Mexican Indian and White Mexican ancestry;
- mother is Black Mexican and father is Black African American;
- mother is of Filipino, Spanish and Chinese heritage; father of Portuguese and German background;
- mother is African American and American Indian; father is Anglo from Britain;
- mother is Korean; father of African American and American Indian ancestry.

# Understanding Race and Racism

The practice of categorizing people by "race" has been with humanity for a long time but evolved, over centuries, into doctrines of racial purity and superiority. Prior to the colonization of the world by the European powers, Europe had been moving toward a theory of the unity of all humans as member of the same race and species (Banks, 1995). As the world was carved and divided among the colonizing powers, an ideology was needed to justify the permanent enslavement of non-Europeans, particularly Africans, in the new territories and the segregation of the races to maintain racial purity among the ruling class. The USA along with many European nations equally began developing ideologies that capitalized on perceived racial differences and the so-called "innate superiority" of some races over others. Even scientists were searching for conclusive proof that Anglo-Saxons and Nordic Europeans were the superior race, and therefore, rightfully selected by nature to hold power over other races (Banks, 1995; Miller, 1992). The 19th century found both Europe and the USA immersed in social and scientific dogma about the inherited and immutable characteristics of the races.

US racial categories have shifted over the decades with persons finding themselves classified differently across time. The US classifications, while uniquely "American", followed traditional racial categories developed in many other nations—White, Black, Yellow and Red—designed to arrange peoples of the world hierarchically based on skin color with Whites at the top, followed by Asians, then Indians and finally Africans. The ranking also represented the perceived mental abilities and moral qualities of each group. It is imperative to understand that historically, the USA has imposed a "broad definition" of Blackness accompanied by a "narrow definition" of Whiteness intended to maintain a clear "color line" separation of those perceived as acceptable Whites and "others". In 1854 the term Black included everyone not of pure White blood (Knepper, 1995). In 1922 the US Supreme Court ruled that "White" referred exclusively to Anglos, Aryans and Caucasians, and unequivocally did not include Asians, Latinos, American Indians, Hindus or mixed-race persons (Knepper, 1995). In some parts of the South, Italians were forced to attend segregated schools with Blacks (Banks, 2001). Yet, with the manumission of slavery in the US, the 20th century found southern and eastern Europeans, and even Jews, previously considered non-White, integrated into "Whiteness" and the dominant group (Davis, 1998). Boundaries between other census groups have also shifted over time and remain extremely fuzzy. For example, people from the Middle East, while geographically Asian, do not fit within the US Asian category.

The USA remains deeply entrenched in this European-based notion of race and racial classification. While the labels may change, the underlying ideology remains intact. Today it sorts people into five "racial" groupings: (1) White;

(2) Black, African American or Negro; (3) American Indian or Alaskan Native; (4) Asian; and (5) Pacific Islander. Further, it splits all "racial" groups into two camps: Spanish/Hispanic/Latino and non-Spanish/Hispanic/Latino. "Whites" are separated into those considered Whites (acceptable) and those Whites of Spanish/Hispanic/Latino background (not acceptable). As such, the term "White" refers exclusively to Anglos, Aryans and Caucasians. Persons of Spanish/Hispanic/Latino background and anyone with any amount of non-White blood get relegated to the status of "minority" or person of color. Most US governmental agencies and their programs, including the Bureau of the Census, use these classifications. This labeling system has become a determining factor in awarding federal government grants and contracts in business, education and federal jobs. Millions of dollars hang in the balance as Black, Hispanic and American Indian tribal institutions, including colleges, could lose funding and be forced to close. P/K-12th grade school curricula, which socialize children into our acceptable social ideologies and values, are developed around these categories (Sadker and Sadker, 2000). Ironically, these very minority groups insist on maintaining this arbitrary categorization system. Primarily as a result of the racial stratification that has further led to their sociopolitical devaluation within US society, many members of minority groups maintain that as long as the US remains a society characterized by White versus "Other" (non-Whites) racial polarization and socio-political stratification, racial identity and group cohesiveness are required for group survival—their ability to forge a united front to combat the systems that subjugate and oppress them.

The US Census 2000 allowed respondents to mark one or more of 14 boxes of "races" and subcategories or "some other race". Although the US admits that the "racial" categories include both racial and national origin groups and are "socio-political constructs" rather than scientific in nature (US Census Bureau 2000), it is commonly assumed that they are grounded on genetics and heredity. The terms race and ethnicity are used interchangeably and often directed toward persons of color or those not considered [acceptable] Whites (Anglo/Aryan/Caucasian). Yet, all groups, including Whites, are very diverse but presented as homogeneous. It is often perceived that Whites lack ethnicity and that only persons of color are members of ethnic groups (Cruz-Janzen, 2000). For example Hispanics/Latinos represent an ethnic group and could be of any race but are often perceived as a homogeneous racial group—usually as persons of color. Indeed, many White Latinos, throughout Spain, Latin America and the USA consider themselves White European Spaniards rather than Latinos and prefer not to be associated with Black, Indian and/or racially-mixed Latinos (Cruz-Janzen, 2001). Support by the US government of the popular association of race with ethnicity, persons of color (including Spanish/Hispanics/Latinos and particularly groups from certain countries and/or continents), as well as the definition of race within a genetic paradigm, is viewed with much criticism at a time when such clarification is crucial for national unity and the well-being of its escalating diverse population.

The US Census 2000 created the illusion of flexibility at the same time as maintaining the prevailing system of racial segregation and stratification. This has led to speculation that it served merely as a palliative to deceive persons of multiethnic and multiracial backgrounds into believing that their multiple heritage and identity has finally been legitimized. The US Bureau of the Census admits that, for example, an individual of mixed White (Anglo/Aryan/Caucasian) and some other "minority" race would still be allocated to the minority race, also that a person of two or more minority races would be assigned to the racial group "allegedly discriminated against"—succinctly, the group with the lowest perceived social status—for civil rights enforcement. These practices align themselves with the long-standing One-Drop Rule and Rule of Hypodescent (Davis, 1998). Also known as the One-Ancestor Rule, the One-Drop Rule designates anyone with any amount of African/Black blood as Black. The Rule of Hypodescent relegates anyone of multiethnic and/or multiracial heritage to the group with the lowest or subordinate status in society. Persons with both parents who are member of subordinate groups are then relegated to the group with the most subordinate status. While many question the ongoing application of these rules in "modern" US society, they indeed continue to be employed by both the US Supreme Court and Bureau of the Census. As recently as 1986 in the "Phipps Decision", the US Supreme Court confirmed the social application of these rules through "judicial notice", or acceptance that they are indeed a matter of "common knowledge" (Davis, 1998). In this light, all persons with any amount of non-White (Anglo/Aryan/Caucasian) blood are deemed non-Whites or persons of color. Additionally, all persons of color are forced to take on the identity of the group in their background with the lowest social status. It should be noted that traditional civil rights groups, fearing loss of power and money, are strongly supportive of the current system.

## Knowledge from Child Development Informs Multiethnic and Multiracial Identity

Clearly, this view of race and racial hierarchy within the USA has a powerful impact on multiracial and multiethnic children. It has had an enduring effect on whole neighborhoods, complete families, as well as individuals. Cruz-Janzen (1997) found that it also has a significant impact on the social adjustment and academic achievement of multiracial/ethnic children. The best way to raise multiethnic and/or multiracial children within their families and communities has been debated considerably. Some argue that they need to identify with their "subordinate" group in preparation for the harsh realities that lie ahead for them; others contend that de-

nying part of their heritage forces these children to reject one parent, and leads to self rejection and self-condemnation. Wardle (1996) asserts that the best way for parents to raise psychologically healthy and happy multiethnic and multiracial children is to give them a sense of pride and acceptance of their total heritage. Wardle points out that White parents, like parents who are members of "minority" groups of color, have a right and responsibility to transmit their heritage and culture to their children. In the difficult process of growing up, interethnic and interracial children deserve to benefit from the strength and purpose of their *full* ancestry.

Interethnic and interracial marriage is normal and logical. Europeans have crossed national, religious, economic and class lines to marry; so, too, have other people around the planet. Interethnic and interracial marriage is the final frontier in the exhibition of human freedom. Mixed bloodlines are a widely accepted reality in many communities in the USA and many other global societies. American Indians identify themselves as a combination of tribal bloodlines. Others of mixed heritage have even coined names for themselves, such as mestizo and creole. Today ethnic and racial boundaries are no more distinct than national and tribal boundaries. Children with an interethnic and/or interracial identity should not reject half of one heritage and half of the other, as many people contest. An interethnic or interracial identity is instead a rich unification of the child's total cultural heritage, much like the combination of distinctive ingredients used to bake a cake (Wardle, 1991).

There are two time periods in a child's life when issues of identity, self-worth and independence are important. These are the early childhood years (3-7) and adolescence. During these stages the child is interested in whether he or she is a boy or a girl, what makes boys and girls different, physical characteristics, abilities and position in society. Issues of ethnic and racial identity are also important during these two stages, but in very different ways.

## Early Childhood

During the early childhood years children begin to explore who they are: gender, physical abilities, likes and dislikes, parents, siblings, schools they attend, etc. The young child spends a lot of time and energy comparing him or herself to others, understanding how he/she fits into the family and school, and deciding about his/her identity. Young children are very selfcentered. The whole world rotates around them. That is why the words "me" and "mine" are commonly used during this time. Not only is the young child interested in who he or she is, but he or she is very honest in finding out about others. They ask all sorts of questions, including questions about skin color, parents, age of parents, clothes, where their friends live, etc. They will compare their hair to that of a friend; they will stand next to each other to see who is the tallest; they will try out different clothes.

This is the time when most multiethnic and multiracial children begin to ask about their identity. Some of this curiosity seems to be triggered by questions asked of them by other children, such as, "Your daddy's White and your mother's Black, so what are you?" and, "Are you Black or are you White—I can't tell." Tragically, prejudicial statements about the way they look often trigger their questions. Not coincidentally these questions occur at the time many young children enter their first organized childcare or school program. These questions are very natural, since young children are trying to find out about their world, and how they fit into it. What we need to do is help the young multiethnic and multiracial child respond to these questions, find out who they are, and help them feel good about being multiethnic and multiracial. This is the age when self-identity starts, which is why it is so critical to support this exploration.

Multiethnic and multiracial children also need a verbal label to use to help them respond to all these questions. For the younger child the label "brown" works well; at about age 4-5, he/she can use the term "multiethnic and multiracial" effectively. We also need to help the single ethnic/race child understand that multiethnic and multiracial children do not have to be Black or White, one or the other, but can be a combination of both parents' physical traits. This is very difficult to understand, because children think in absolute categories, and because they tend to accept what they hear from others.

At this age the multiethnic and multiracial child—and also the minority child—often chooses to play with White friends and White dolls. They also might say they wish they had blond hair, blue eyes and White skin. An adopted minority child may say to her White mother that she wishes she looked like her. This is very normal, and should not produce concern on the part of parents or teachers. Young children want to be like their friends and may even take concrete approaches to exploring that fascination. For example, they may even paint their faces brown or white. They also love to experiment with the real world. A White child trying to look Black or a Black child trying to look White is not a rejection of the child's racial identity; it is an acceptance of the diversity they see around them.

Young children think in concrete terms and can only handle individual pieces of information at a time. For example, young children believe that what makes a person a woman are the clothes they wear and the work they do. A multiracial child with apparent physical attributes from both parents knows he/she is multiracial because of his/her skin color, hair texture and those of his/her parents. He/she may see him/herself as different from either parent, not understanding that his/her make-up is a combination of both. Another young Black child knows his/her skin color and the skin color of his/her parents make him/her Black. He/she does not know, however, that he/she is a member of the Black race. For multiethnic children the process may be further confounded because

they may resemble both parents and look White/Anglo. For example a child with one White Spanish/Hispanic/Latino parent and a White (Anglo/Aryan/Caucasian) parent may not recognize him/herself as different from other White children until encountered by negative experiences challenging his/her self-perceptions. An open, supportive and honest exploration of identity at the early age establishes a solid foundation for the more difficult process that occurs during adolescence. A parent of multiethnic and multiracial children cannot wait until the child is an adolescent before addressing the issue of ethnic and/or racial identity. It must start during these early years.

## Multiethnic and Multiracial Identity in Young Adults

The writings, research and personal encouragement of other advocates of full recognition of interethnic and interracial identification, such as Maria Root, have led to increased awareness and research in this area. Cruz-Janzen (1997), herself a multiracial educator of Puerto Rican African/Black, Spanish White and Taino Indian heritage, focused her research on young adults whose heritages were other than combined Black/African American and White/European American (Anglo/Aryan/Caucasian), the identification that receives the most attention and has been most frequently investigated. In her study, Cruz-Janzen addressed the major impact of the family, schools and peers on the ethnic and racial self-identity and self-concept of persons with heritages that included Latino, American Indian, Asian American and other combinations. She used the Multigroup Ethnic Identity Measure (Phinney, 1992) to assess the participants' self-identification and held extensive interviews with them, as well as focus group discussions.

The young adults in this study, especially those of apparent "minority" backgrounds, revealed that parents, very early in their lives and significantly in preparation for formal schooling, specifically began preparing them for the discrimination and prejudice they would encounter in the schools. Parents of apparent "minority" heritage warned their children that society would see them as persons of color and treat them as such. They told them that they had to be "twice as good" to be as good and work "twice as hard" to get the same recognition [as Whites]. Parents of children who appeared White encouraged them to self-identify as such to secure the best educational opportunities—opportunities often denied to students of color. Some parents even concealed their true heritage from their children.

> My mom doesn't identify at all. She won't say the Indian word. I think my identity has been withheld from me by both parents. I think there's a lot of lying that goes on. You tell your kids what they're gonna tell other people. You

don't want your kids to say, "Oh, I'm Latino, African-American …".

Further, the study showed that multiethnic persons who appear White (Anglo/Aryan/Caucasian) are often tormented by peers and other adults who increasingly challenge their self-identity as they go through the K-12th grade schools. They are forced out of the mainstream White identity into identity as persons of color—they are not allowed to be White; they cannot be part White; they have to be full minorities. As they mature and become increasingly cognisant of their reality, they live in fear of being "discovered", forced into a "minority status", ostracized, harassed, ridiculed and treated like second-class persons by their peers, teachers and other adults in their community and schools. This becomes extremely "exhausting" and emotionally damaging for adolescents trying hard to establish a valid self-identity and find a group to fit in.

Fitting in sometimes entails public rejection and condemnation of part of their heritage. For example, a student with a White German father and a White Mexican mother was forced to tell "whitey" jokes about herself and her father in front of the group of Mexican American students to which she wanted to belong. In elementary school her mother identified her as White. In middle school the school counselor told her that she could not be White but "minority". By the time she reached high school, she was taunted and openly rejected by former White friends. As well, she noticed that teachers treated her differently, giving her lower grades for the same quality work as her White peers and falsely accusing her of wrongdoings. Desperately wanting to find a group to accept her, she felt forced to publicly reject her White heritage. As students of color, multiethnic and multiracial students find that teachers hold lower expectations of them and provide them with less support for academic achievement.

Informants noted that most teachers did not promote the inclusion of people of mixed race and ethnicity as "real" or authentic Americans; relegating such individuals to a position of invisibility by never discussing them in curricular materials or programs. Invisibility was fostered by the federally designated ethnic and racial categories that created "a box mentality". In this way of thinking people had to be fitted into a specific category, forcing the multiethnic and multiracial into invisibility or denial of one part of his or her identity and heritage. Some pertinent comments drawn from Cruz-Janzen's investigations of biethnic and biracial individuals when recalling their childhood and parental admonitions are:

> I remember my mom telling us of her encounters, her and my father's racial harassment. She prepared us. It has to start inside the family to prepare the children for what they are going to encounter outside the home.

> Although it was very safe where I was, it didn't prepare me for the real world. If my parents hadn't been the ministers that they were, it kind of neutralized the whole issue, neutralized racism. I could have been better equipped.

To provide an in-depth illustration of the personal struggle of a biethnic and biracial young woman, the following account is presented. Recounting the experiences of her early life for an assignment in a university course on diversity in education, this young woman exemplifies what growing up as a biethnic and biracial person entails in US society.

## The Socialization of Li Lo

> At 20 years old, I reflect upon my childhood and family socialization. I have no family. I am an only child of a White father and Chinese mother. However, their marriage was unsuccessful due to his alcoholism. He never had an influence on my life, rather my mother and I became a strong, stable and secure family unit. I had more of the Chinese influence because I spent my time with my Chinese aunts, uncles, cousins and grandmother, watched my mother prepare and cook Chinese dishes, listened to and spoke in Cantonese, and observed Chinese traditions and holidays. With my mixed heritage, my main problem was dealing with the fact that I passed as a White person, but grew up with the values and attitudes from my single Chinese mother and her side of the family.

> In regards to my ethnicity: when I was born the doctors were stunned because I had blue eyes. Usually children born to multiracial parents reflect the more dominant genes of one of the parents. The doctors expected me to be born with a darker complexion with brown eyes (similar to my mother). Eventually, I had brown hair and hazel eyes, but with my father's European fair skin. This fair skin has made it difficult for me and sometimes for my mother. As a young child, if not accompanied by my father, ladies in the supermarket thought my mother was my baby-sitter or nanny. Even today, when my mother and I go shopping and I'm having a conversation with her, people are shocked that we are even related, let alone that we are mother and daughter.

> However, the experience in my life that brought me to realize I had to find my identity as a multiracial person occurred when I was eight years old. This is how it happened: most Saturday mornings my mother and her family friends would go to Monterey Park (the socalled "second Chinatown" of Los Angeles) for dim sum. At the restaurant a large crowd would be filling

the noisy room with the serving ladies pushing carts and yelling out names of the dim sum dishes: gilan, cha sue bo, ha go, dan tat. My mother was busy trying to get the server's attention. I felt very thirsty and wanted a glass of water. When I asked a passing waiter for water in Chinese, I startled him. He was so stunned that I could speak Chinese that he began asking me questions. He did not believe I was "mixed" (multiracial) because I did not look like my mother. I appeared to be a Caucasian.

I became frustrated because he did not seem to believe me and I realized I was breaking his stereotype of what "mixed" children looked like and how they acted. He left and returned with a free Coke and did not charge us for the hot tea because he was so taken with me. I received a free drink each time we went to this restaurant. It was this incident that made me aware that I was different. I realized, my White skin color, big almost-round hazel eyes and straight brown hair made a great difference in how society perceived and accepted me.

Caught between two diverse ethnicities, I have learned more about family values and their impact on my life from my mother's Chinese culture. Because my father died when I was young, my mother became a single parent. She received no support from my grandparents because they disapproved of my mother marrying a "bok quai" (White man) and then choosing to raise me alone without a father. I expressed to my mother that this situation of not giving her any financial support because she insisted on raising me, her daughter, all alone, would have upset me very much. But my mother defends my grandmother, saying "your family will always be your family. You must learn to forgive and respect your parents even when events turn ugly". From these experiences I believe that instilled in me are the values of kindness, forgiveness, respect, the importance of family, being empathetic, humble, determined, honest and the need to have faith in oneself.

My mother did not follow the Chinese traditions of marriage and a two-parent family as the only choice for raising a child. The two of us are a family unit. She is my example that a single woman can have a successful career and be a mother simultaneously. I know I can accomplish anything on my own. My mother gave me "roots" but alone I had to solve my identity conflict between my Chinese and White ethnicity. Yet I still wonder, as an adult, why can't people just tell by looking at me that I am "mixed"? It would make my life so much simpler. Simpler,

because more people could accept the fact that my mother is Chinese and my father was White, when I tell them this. Through all this turmoil I came to the conclusion at the end of my high school education that my identity in American society would be a compromise or mixture of both my Chinese and my White ethnicity.

This account brings to the fore the importance of the family unit and the struggle that multiethnic and multiracial people can face in monocultural ethnic and racial enclaves, as well as in the broader mainstream society.

## Recognition of Multiethnic and Multiracial Identity

Data from the US Census 2000 shows that of a total population of 281.4 million people, seven million declared themselves as belonging to more than one racial group. This is a reflection of the increased diversity in our society through immigration and interethnic and interracial unions in the country. The four most common interethnic and/or interracial categories were White and Black, White and Asian, White and American Indian/Alaskan Native and White with some "other race". While 6 percent of all Latinos declared themselves as interethnic and/or interracial, the "other race" category was most selected by Latinos, apparently unable to fit within any of the other choices and/or combinations (US Census Bureau, 2000).

Other demographic data indicates the following about interethnic and/or interracial families and their children:

- they are likely to live in cities;
- they are likely to have parents of the same social class;
- their marriages appear to be as stable as other marriages;
- multiracial children start asking questions about their identity as early as three to four years of age;
- multiethnic children begin questioning their identity when they enter schools where other children and adults question and harass them; public institutions such as schools and hospitals do not often recognize multiethnic and multiracial children as having a distinct identity;
- professionals who work with multiethnic and/or multiracial children often attribute, incorrectly, problems these children have to their mixed parentage.

One qualitative research study carried out by Christine Kerwin et al. (1993), reported in the *Journal of Counseling Psychology*, highlighted some very useful information on the identity of multiethnic and multiracial children. In depth interviews were conducted with a small group of nine interracial children and their parents. Findings indicated that despite the assumptions of marginality, these mixed-race children and their families did not perceive themselves as marginal in two cultures. Some parents in this study expressed their disdain for society's demand that individuals must label themselves racially or ethnically by voicing their distress about needing to fill out census forms requiring ethnic/racial designations for their children. Parents had concerns about anticipated racial discrimination toward their children. They spoke about actively preparing their children to deal with prejudice while others attempted to protect them from exposure to situations involving potential prejudice. This led to further discussion by parents about where to bring up their interracial children, citing such factors as racial composition of the neighborhood and perceived openness of the area to interracial families.

Findings from the interviews with children indicated that there was a developmental progression prompted by environmental variables and agerelated shifts, or both. The researchers state that young children can naturally become bicultural and begin to establish a sense of multiethnic and multiracial identity, given opportunities and an open environment. They found that young children of Black and White (Anglo/Aryan/Caucasian) heritage saw themselves as in the middle of a color continuum between Black and White but definitely connected to both ends. Yet these researchers also found that with some young children, religion was a more salient factor than ethnicity or race in terms of a reference-group identity. For example: a five-year-old boy answered the questions "What are you?" with the reply "I'm half Catholic and half Jewish." Another eight-year-old boy responded "Oh yeah, I say my dad's Black and my mom's Jewish." This article on the racial identity of multiracial children ends with the statement:

> Given the rapidly changing demographics in the USA, educators and counselors will be working with increasing numbers of biracial children and their families. We hope that the present study will stimulate further investigation into this neglected area.

Articles, television programs and news reports like the following story featured on the front page of a newspaper in a major city of the American Southwest, highlights the growing awareness of multiethnic and multiracial identities, the strange twists and turns that self-identities can take, and the unique role that telecommunications such as the Internet can play in people's lives. Educators and those in social work and school psychology need to be aware of this challenging new assessment of individual and family self-identification. When teaching or working with both children and adults their self-chosen ethnic and racial affiliations (even though physical characteristics or appearances might belie what seems obvious) are important. The piece that follows is an example of how adoption at an early age and being reared in a vastly different

ethnic and/or racial enclave even in the same nation, can affect one's affiliations in adulthood. This is the story of Yvette Melanson, taken away from her Navajo parents as one baby of twins deemed to be at risk by a public health nurse. She was adopted by a Jewish family in Brooklyn and raised in the Jewish tradition, only to find out some 40 years later that her birth father still lives on the Navajo reservation. At the close of the 20th century with our amazing telecommunications, Yvette Melanson has discovered her origins and decided to incorporate this new characteristic in her social construction of self-identity. The newspaper article states:

> Yvette Melanson, the Navajo girl who grew up believing she was White and Jewish, came home to the four sacred mountains of her people, Friday. Her tearful family had been waiting for her homecoming for 43 years, and they welcomed their sister in the Navajo way, with long speeches, booming war dances and sacred gifts. And they thanked the medicine men and the magic of the Internet for helping her find her way from the tiny village of Palmyra, Maine, to the high-desert plains of Tolani Lake, her home community, 60 miles northeast of Flagstaff, Arizona. A public-health nurse whisked Melanson and her twin brother away from their parents' hogan when they were two days old. The twins became two of the thousands of "Lost Birds," Indian children often taken illegally and adopted by White families from the 1950s to the 1970s.
>
> Raised in New York by her adoptive parents, who have since died, Melanson did not learn she was Navajo until April, 1996 when a posting on the Internet led her to her family in Tolani Lake ... Her father, Yazzie Monroe, who last saw his daughter in the arms of the public-health nurse in 1953, gave her a wedding basket and placed a string of turquoise beads around her neck. The beads hung over her Star of David necklace, a symbol of the Jewish girl who had learned Hebrew and spent several years in Israel. (*Arizona Republic*, 1996: 1)

This article goes on to discuss the fact that the Navajos and Melanson agreed to allow the media to attend and cover her homecoming in hopes that the publicity will help them find her still-lost twin brother and other missing adoptees. They believe that Melanson's story underscores the importance of the 1978 Indian Child Welfare Act and the illegal adoptions that American Indian tribes say occurred on reservations after the Second World War. This incident is just one of the many coming into public attention in the USA as a result of the social, political and economic implications of ethnic/racial identity and group affiliations.

## No Longer the Invisible

We have highlighted the little-recognized socialization of children categorized as multiethnic and multiracial or interethnic and interracial. Social scientists, educators, social workers and health professionals might assume that as we embark upon the 21st century, this planet Earth could not possibly produce new categories of humanity. Yet, as this ever-increasing national and world-wide population is counted, recounted and reclassified we identify new groups, different needs and mounting wants. The challenge of declaring an interethnic and interracial identity remains in a postmodern world still ruled by European definitions of who we are and can be. We must begin by unraveling the arbitrary racial categories and definitions that we have created to accept that we all belong to the human race and individuals who cross cultural lines are as legitimate and wholesome humans as everyone else. Superficially changing labels without changing their underlying assumptions, meanings and interpretations and educating the public about them does a disservice to us all. As a multiracial person stated recently, "We may have changed the name of the game but the rules remain the same." Particularly this inflicts further damage to those persons caught in the middle of this debate by constantly promising what is never fully delivered—their authentic and wholesome self-identity and integrity. With an ever-increasing number and combinations of interethnic and interracial children in our schools and society, we must act immediately.

## References

*Arizona Republic* (1996) "Brooklyn Woman Meets Birth Family", 1 June: 1.

Banks, J.A. (1995) "The Historical Reconstruction of Knowledge about Race: Implications for Transforming Schools", *Educational Researcher*, March: 15-25.

Banks, J.A. (2001) *Cultural Diversity and Education: Foundations, Curriculum and Teaching*. Needham Heights, MA: Allyn & Bacon.

Cruz-Janzen, M.I. (1997) "Curriculum and the Self-Concept of Biethnic and Biracial Persons". Unpublished doctoral dissertation. College of Education, University of Denver, Colorado.

Cruz-Janzen, M.I. (2000) "Preparing Preservice Teacher Candidates for Leadership in Equity", *Equity & Excellence in Education*, 33(1): 94-101.

Cruz-Janzen, M.I. (2001) ¿Y tu abela a' onde está?, *Sage Race Relations Abstracts*, 26(1): 7-24.

Davis, F.J. (1998) *Who is Black? One Nation's Definition*. University Park: Pennsylvania State University Press.

Kerwin, C. (1993) "Racial Identity of Biracial Children: A Qualitative Investigation", *Journal of Counseling Psychology*, 40(2): 221-31.

Knepper, P. (1995) "The Prohibition of Biracial Legal Identity in the United States and the Nation: An Historical Overview", *State Constitutional Commentaries and Notes*, 5(2): 14-20.

Miller, R.L. (1992) "The Human Ecology of Multiracial Identity"; in M.P. Root (ed.) *Racially Mixed People in America*. Newbury Park, CA: Sage Publications.

Phinney, J.S. (1992) "The Multigroup Ethnic Identity Measure", *Journal of Adolescent Research*, 7(2): 156-76.

Sadker, D.M. and Sadker, M.P. (2000) *Teachers, Schools, & Society*, 5th edn. Boston, MA: McGraw-Hill.

US Census Bureau (2000) *US Census 2000*. Washington, DC: US Census Bureau.

Wardle, F. (1991) "Raising Interracial Children", *Mothering*, 58: 111-14.

Wardle, F. (1996) "Proposal: An Anti-Bias and Ecological Model for Multicultural Education", *Childhood Education*, 72(3): 152-6.

Wardle, F. (1999) *Tomorrow's Children*. Denver, CO: Center for the Study of Biracial Children.

## About the Authors

Marta I. Cruz-Janzen is Associate Professor of Multicultural Education at Florida Atlantic University, College of Education, in Boca Raton, Florida. The author may also be contacted by email at cruzjanzen@fau.edu

Edith W. King is Professor of Curriculum and Instruction at the University of Denver, College of Education, in Denver, Colorado. The author may also be contacted by email at eking@du.edu

Francis Wardle is Director of the Center for the Study of Biracial Children, in Denver, Colorado. The author may also be contacted by email at Francis@csbc.cnfamily.com

# When Parallel Lives Intersect: Experiencing Multiple Perspectives in Our Own Journeys

**Nancy P. Gallavan**
*University of Nevada, Las Vegas*

**A. Maria Whittemore**
*Frederick County Public Schools, Frederick. Maryland*

*As we travel through life, our journeys offer myriad observations, relationships, and experiences. By chance and choice, our journeys align closely with and are guided by other people's journeys; from these associations we form a sense of our individual cultural characteristics and self-identities. Simultaneously, our journeys follow courses that remain distant and distinct from other people's paths; yet our observations and interpretations from afar also contribute strongly to the formulation of individual cultural characteristics and self-identities. Throughout life's dynamic encounters and events, each of us continues to formulate, reformulate, and negotiate our self-identities as we traverse what seems like parallel paths—journeys that appear distant and distinct from other journeys, yet encountering equally powerful influences shaping our thoughts, beliefs, and actions. Rarely are we afforded the opportunities to investigate these parallel paths and communicate honestly with individuals who seemed far away and foreign; seldom can we truly experience multiple perspectives and cross-cultural relationships in our own journeys.*

*This article presents the unique intersection of two parallel lives and the authentic exchange of multiple perspectives reported through narrative or personal life histories. The authors serendipitously met at a National Association for Multicultural Education (NAME) conference and by chance shared their childhood stories. The authors were raised in similar environments but from opposite lifestyles—lifestyles that paralleled one another and contributed significantly to their individual understanding of cultural characteristics and self-identity. Here they share their histories spanning 50 years while providing insights and guidelines for teachers and teacher educators to learn from our pasts and reshape our futures.*

We do not believe in ourselves until someone reveals what is deep inside of us as valuable, worth listening to, worthy of our trust, sacred to our touch. Once we believe in ourselves we can risk curiosity, wonder, spontaneous delight, or any experience that reveals the human spirit. (e. e. cummings, 1923/1976)

No one's journey through life is traveled in total isolation. Each of us plays an influential role in other people's lives as our pathways connect through various associations and functions with assorted intensities and priorities. We establish myriad relationships as members of families, neighborhoods, cities, states, and nations; we form a multitude of communities based on our diverse personal and professional needs and interests. Our relationships and communities are shaped by cultural characteristics reflecting our race, gender, socioeconomic status, religion, language, geography, age, education, sexual orientation, careers, hobbies, and so forth. Clearly, affirmation of one's self-identification is influenced and made visible from a combination of one's given and selected communities (Cummins, 1996).

Most people share the same cultural characteristics as reflected by other members of their communities. Through chance and choice, similar people live in the same areas, shop in the same stores, eat in the same restaurants, attend the same schools or religious institutions, hold the same values, and so forth. People within these communities generally appear, believe, and act much alike; most people seek and find comfort in their common ways of knowing and of being known (Palmer, 1983). Within any community, the sources of information, avenues of access, and occasions of opportunity (Gallavan in Wink & Putney, 2002) tend to shape and support its members' beliefs and behaviors. Our individual life journeys commonly follow the same routes as the learned and shared journeys led by our community members, both past and present, with little straying from the well-established paths.

Communities frequently appear or behave rather exclusive in nature; members of one community may or may not understand, appreciate, nor support the members of another community. Nonmembers may be viewed suspiciously or may not be welcomed readily into the establishment. Knowledge and understanding of individuals outside the community may not be valued nor even exist.

Rarely does someone outside of the immediate community receive the chance to exchange observations, pose inquiries, and engage in meaningful dialogue with a member from inside the community accompanied with open honesty, integrity, and care (Nieto, 1999). Seldom do we truly exchange multiple perspectives or experience cross-cultural relationships authentically. More importantly, few people actively pursue opportunities to revisit and investigate a lifetime of events and issues. Most individuals neither think nor care to examine their pasts in ways that would enable them to understand their present and future more clearly. People might not like what they hear, see, and learn; perhaps they perceive that it is far easier to continue following their unquestioned and uninformed journeys.

However, this rare opportunity to exchange multiple perspectives recently occurred for two women who were raised in comparable small country towns during the 1950s and 1960s. At first, one might think they lived similar lives, but after hearing their stories, obviously they did not. Their journeys may have transpired in corresponding places and times, but their distinct lives reflect their individual cultural characteristics and personal paths. Each of them is the product of their diverse cultures and community milieu acquired from their early childhoods and extending through their middle ages.

Each has lived her own life mirroring her cultural characteristics and shaping her individual self-identity while observing and questioning the life lived by the other in a seemingly parallel and untouchable path. For one woman it was common to examine the other; for the second woman it was rare to question the other. Now, almost 50 years later, their lives have intersected serendipitously; here they describe their journeys, the multiple perspectives influencing their own journeys, and the meaningful cross-cultural dialogue shared between them.

## Applying the Narrative Research Theoretical Framework

These two stories were recorded using narrative research. Each of the participants told her story in her own words. When each of them finished, they asked questions of one another and then collectively reflected upon their investigative processes. They checked their memories for clarity and understanding while noting new discoveries and relationships, particularly realizing phenomena emphasizing their similarities and differences.

Narrative research provides the ideal mechanism to inquire, reflect, examine, and interpret our memories both from our personal experiences and from multiple perspectives shared by the other. "In understanding another person and juxtaposed culture, one must simultaneously understand oneself. The process is ongoing, an endeavor aimed not at a final and transparent understanding of the Other or of the self, but at continued communication, at an ever-widening understanding of both" (Hones, 1998, p. 6). "Through narrative dialogues with diverse Americans, we can gain a deeper understanding of who we have been, who we are, and who we would become" (p. 8). Exchanging narratives enriches and more fully completes our circles of meaning offering a cultural text to explore the past, understand the present, and appreciate the future evident in one's individual and parallel journeys.

## Maria's Story

My life as a Black female growing up in the 1950s was very challenging. I am the youngest of six children. Our home sat next to the railroad tracks on the far end of town. The house was a burned-out machine shop the landlord converted into a kitchen and three bedrooms. We had no bathroom; there was only a spigot with cold water in the kitchen. Our family was the only Black family in the community.

There were many lessons my parents taught us that money couldn't buy. Among these were to believe that our strength comes from our family and our belief in God, to treat people how we wanted to be treated no matter what the circumstance, to work hard and never settle for less than the best in our work, to never forget where we came from, to always seek to help others, to never give up on ourselves and our dreams, and to persevere no matter what the obstacles may be. Both of my parents were excellent role models. They lived the virtues they instilled in us. The racism and classism they endured and overcame set the tone for us to meet the same challenges in our lives.

My father worked in the feed and coal mill on the other side of the tracks opposite our humble home. He worked long hours drying feed and loading coal onto coal cars. Whenever I wanted to speak to him during work hours, I was subjected to humiliating catcalls and racial name-calling from his White male co-workers.

My mother was a domestic. Often I would go to the homes she was cleaning and not be allowed entry. My most vivid memory was of a time when I was 8-years-old. I needed to tell my mother something, so I walked to the house where she was working. I attempted to pass by the old man who owned the property. He leaned over the fence and sneered at me, "Get away from here nigger!" I ran home sobbing, thinking how my mom was good enough to scrub his floors, but I wasn't good enough to even come on his property.

I never told anyone about this incident and many more encounters until I was an adult. I knew my mother would confront the old man and lose her job. I didn't want my dad or brothers to know because I was afraid a fight might result and they would end up in jail or worse. The lady of one house was very kind and brave; she loved my mother and our family. She was willing to risk being criticized or worse, to do whatever she could do to help my mother help her family have a better life out of the kindness of her heart. She didn't care what other people thought.

She gave my mother hand-me-down clothes that my sister wore to college. Because the lady of the house had been to college, and her daughter was a teacher, she was able to help my mother understand the whole college process. The lady helped my mother get my oldest brother and sister into college. She gave my mother extra food and money. At times I wondered if the old man knew what his wife was doing for us.

My mother's belief in family was her strongest virtue. She and her siblings were orphaned at very young ages. She was the second oldest and only 8-years-old when her mother died. I don't know whether she knew her father because she never spoke of him.

The five children raised themselves by doing domestic work for the White families in the little town where they grew up. The only things they had were each other and a collective strong will to survive and stay together as a family. The five of them pulled together to scratch out an existence.

My mother had to drop out of school in the eighth grade to assume more responsibility for her younger brothers and sisters. She was willing to do whatever work she could get to contribute money to the family so her younger brothers and sister could complete school.

As an adult, my mother continued doing the same sacrificing and hard working for her family. She dedicated many long hours performing menial tasks just so her six children could have a better life than she had known. My mother's strong religious faith carried her through a very difficult life. She believed in the power of prayer; her life was truly a profile in courage.

My first 2 years of elementary school were in a segregated setting. My sister, four brothers, and I had to walk a mile to a store along the main street. We caught the bus from the town we lived in to ride to a larger town, 8 miles away. The route led us past the school in the small town. I remember asking my parents why we had to ride a bus to school. I didn't understand why I couldn't walk to the closer school. My parents were never able to answer me; they just bowed their heads as if in shame.

I was at the top of the class in the segregated school I was forced to attend. The school housed Grades 1–12. I had all the same teachers my five siblings had. I was placed in the highest academic groups and even worked with the school newspaper as a classroom reporter while in the first and second grades. My siblings had taught me much of what I needed to know before I even entered school.

In 1956, my dream came true! Finally I was allowed to attend school in the town where I lived. I was 8 years old, just entering third grade. My three brothers and I walked the few blocks to the school. My mother and father did not take us to school because they had to work; my oldest brother and sister were away at college in Baltimore. I remember feeling excited and nervous as we walked along the streets to school. The principal (a White man) met us at the steps to the building. I can still hear him saying. "So here are the nigra children." With that he walked each of us to our classrooms. I was the first to enter since I was the youngest. My room was on the lower elementary side of the building. My brothers were in fifth-, seventh-, and ninth-grades, so they were located in a different part of the building. When the principal introduced me to my teacher, the class snickered. My excitement was dashed! I knew I wasn't wanted. My head dropped. I could not say anything when the teacher (a White woman) asked me where I wanted to sit. She must have seen the hurt in my eyes. Her eyes were warm and inviting like her tone of voice. She showed me to a seat.

I remember the girl I was placed next to scooting over so not to touch my skin. All the while, I felt 30 pairs of eyes riveted on me. I recognized the faces of four kids for whom my mom worked and with whom I had played with on the playground behind the Methodist church. They looked at me with the same contempt expressed by the other children.

I soon discovered that I was way behind academically. This class was writing in cursive; I was still writing in manuscript. The reading book was too hard for me. I had no idea how to do the math the rest of the class was doing.

I thank the Lord for my third-grade teacher! She truly believed in accepting me for the person that I was and did not judge me by the color of my skin. She had a very strong religious faith that she lived. She must have known that "Separate but Equal" was just rhetoric. She looked beyond my color and saw a bright student who had not been given a fair start. She began the first day displaying patience and confidence in my ability to achieve. There were many long hours spent tutoring me after school and on weekends. She was not satisfied until I was caught up with the rest of the class. She did such a good job that I ended up ahead of most of the students and have been at the top of the class throughout the rest of my schooling.

Had that teacher not been a caring, competent, highly skilled professional I do not know where I would be today or what I would be doing. Her acceptance of diversity and love for all of her students genuinely shaped my life. Yes, growing up Black in the 1950s was challenging, but thanks to this teacher, my family, and the grace of God, I made it through.

## Nancy's Story

I met Maria at the 2001 NAME Conference in Las Vegas. Maria attended my roundtable session and spontaneously began telling her life story to illustrate my research related to cultural competencies. As Maria's journey unfolded, I sat in awe; I, too, was raised in a small country town during the 50s and 60s. Only I was the White girl who lived in the house with the family who hired the Black domestic; my father was the owner-operator of the local feed mill who hired Black laborers. My mother gave our hand-me-down clothing to the Black domestic's family; my parents donated money and many other furnishings to their family. My brothers and sisters also attended college, and my parents helped other children, both White and Black children, to attend college.

As a child, I wondered why the Black and White children could not attend the same school when we lived so close together. I pondered why the Black children and their families could not come into the same stores, restaurants, churches, schools, movie theaters, and so on, like the White families. In retrospect, I believe I was unlike the other White children in my community in my silently questioning these behaviors. The other White children seemed to understand and take it for granted that Black children and their families did not belong in our town; it was made clear from the dominant community that Black people certainly were not to be considered equal to Whites regardless of the laws. However, I never initiated any conversations probing these relationships publicly; it seemed to me as a child of the 60s that racial issues were not comfortable topics of conversation that could be discussed logically among most Whites. And I certainly could not have held this discussion with a Black girl.

As Maria continued to unveil her life's journey, I realized that my life's journey encapsulated a seemingly parallel experience; we were like two sides of the same coin. In general, each of us had been raised in times and places among people who were confronted and divided by issues of racial discrimination and social inequities. As an impoverished Black child, Maria felt that her family struggled to provide her with an education and the attitudes necessary to help her achieve future personal and professional success. As the White child of opportunity, I felt that my family was challenged to overcome the accepted cultural norms reflected throughout my small town community and across the country, especially by people like us. Fortunately, for both Maria and me, members of our immediate childhood communities, for example, family, religious institutions, and some teachers, believed in and practiced democratic principles and social justice that empowered each of us to become the adults we are today.

From her personal history, I discovered that, although Maria's childhood differed greatly from my own, some of her experiences corresponded with mine, and I wanted to know more. I had read extensive reflections describing her cultural experiences in general, but I had never pursued nor been afforded the chance to hear the specifics of what seemed like the other side of my story. I sat in astonishment as Maria mapped her journey. Then Maria asked to hear about my life.

I was raised in a White, upper middle-class, well-educated family who followed Christian beliefs. My father and mother had attended college with my father earning an advanced degree. We lived in a large, modern home with all the latest conveniences. My father firmly stated that a woman's place was not in the kitchen; my mother dedicated herself to a life-long commitment of volunteer work. My father owned and operated a feed mill who hired many uneducated laborers … most were White and a few were Black.

This small town had a population of about 5,000 people. It was the county seat and the biggest town for more than 100 miles in any direction. It was a rural, farming community; Saturday afternoon was a big day in the town square. The population was mostly White and primarily Baptist, Methodist, and Pentecostal. There were approximately three related Black families living near one another at one edge of town, and there were few problems (to the best of my childhood knowledge). There were no other families of color living in the entire county. (However, I did not discover until much later when I was finishing high school that there were families with mentally handicapped children; these children either attended their own school separated from the other children or did not go to school at all. I'm sure there were many other pieces of information I did not know about our town when I was a child.)

The town and county were extremely poor; I remember some houses with no indoor plumbing, families with no books [other than the Bible] nor table lamps for reading, and friends' parents who did not finish junior high school much less high school or college. The schools were integrated by the 1960s but only as the result of one outstanding Black football player in the late '50s who the town leaders wanted to play at the White high school to help them win the state championship. To learn more about this time and place, I recommend several books: *A Painted House*, by John Grisham, *In My Eyes*, by Ruby Bridges, and *Dear Willy Rudd*, by Libba Moore Gray.

## The Intersection of Our Lives

The greatest friend of truth is Time, her greatest enemy is Prejudice, and her constant companion is Humility. (Charles Caleb Colton, n.d.)

As Maria and Nancy exchanged their life stories, Nancy was struck by two initial thoughts: (a) Maria is one of those Black girls who Nancy never got to know in school but her family had helped, and (b) now, 50 years later, Nancy could ask Maria all the questions and tell her all the things Nancy had been thinking when the two girls weren't supposed to talk with one another nor allowed to be together. Nancy could revisit her past and investigate some of the mysteries from her childhood that have remained unknown all these years.

A third unanticipated discovery emerged as Maria and Nancy exchanged their personal narratives (Whelan, Huber, Rose, Davies, & Clandinin, 2001). Just as Nancy could finally hear Maria's perspective and ask her questions, Maria could delve into Nancy's perspective and conduct her own inquiries. As the two women talked, Maria revealed with newly discovered awe that never in her life had she ever considered what Whites thought or believed about her or Black people in general; never had she pondered what the White children, especially those living in the house where her mother had worked, had thought about her and her family.

In similar ways, Maria and Nancy had been raised in families whose beliefs and behaviors did not always match the accepted cultural norms evident throughout the U.S. society. On the surface, their individual backgrounds appeared extremely dissimilar, distinct paths with few intersections. Yet, through their shared personal narratives, they discovered how their individual stories provided a significant contribution to one another's being. Exchanging their historical narratives completed their circles of meaning to more fully understand one another and themselves. As they listened intently to one another's stories, each gained a greater comprehension and richer appreciation of both their parallel and intersecting journeys—the powerful roles each had played unknowingly in one another's life both as children and now knowingly as adults.

Maria and Nancy had established their childhood self-identities shaped by their assorted cultural characteristics and influential role models. Each one was aware of the never-ending formulation and reformulation of our self-identities as we matured, frequently negotiating and re-negotiating beliefs and behaviors based on our ever-expanding sociocultural contexts. At the NAME roundtable discussion, serendipitously their paths had crossed, and they were prompted to exchange their life stories, again impacting their individual cultural characteristics and sense of self-identity. They embraced this rare and powerful opportunity for better knowing themselves by hearing one another's journey.

Today Maria promotes minority achievement working with pre-K–12 teachers and students; she helps them to understand, appreciate, and encourage themselves individually and collectively as members of a culturally diverse interdependent community. Maria is a caring and skillful professional encountering a wide range of attitudes and perceptions held by her primarily White teachers and students about students of color, their potential academic achievement, and their valuable contributions to society. Enlightening lessons learned from her own third-grade teacher fortify Maria as she encourages her teachers and students to acknowledge their long held ste-

reotypes and confront their accepted forms of discrimination. Her life story empowers her to see diversity as a strength, not as a deficit, and to model this belief to everyone around her.

Maria fully understands her White students. A critical juncture occurred in Maria's life while she was attending Lincoln University (PA) during the late 1960s. At that time, Lincoln University was an all Black male school; Maria's university class was the first one opened to females. Her previous schooling beginning in the third-grade had occurred in an all White environment; at Lincoln University, Maria truly learned about multiple perspectives both across our global society and particularly within the Black culture. During her first years few years at Lincoln University, she felt that she was viewed as an outcast. She was perceived to "talk White and dress White"; she even played tennis, a "White game." Maria quickly renegotiated her understanding of cultural characteristics along with her sense of self-identity. From her experiences at Lincoln University she realized the strong influences of institutional racism balanced with the credibility of knowing, appreciating, and practicing genuine multicultural education.

Nancy is a teacher educator preparing preservice teachers and supporting practicing teachers in the fields of social studies and multicultural education. A critical juncture occurred in her life while she was an undergraduate student in the South. As part of her preservice teacher education, she participated in a service-learning program established to assist immigrants from South Vietnam. During this program, Nancy's head and heart were reopened to many bias behaviors and social inequities she had witnessed in her childhood, injustices now clearly apparent to her many years later as a professor of cultural diversity. She, too, found it necessary to renegotiate her understanding of cultural characteristics and her sense of self-identity displayed in these cross-cultural exchanges.

The unique opportunity for Maria and Nancy to share their stories, truly listening and learning from one another's historical inquiries and perspective, supports their work as transformative educators; through their honest exchange they modeled the lessons they advocate with their own teachers and students. Maria and Nancy interact with preservice and practicing teachers, school administrators, and pre-K–12 students; they work with both White students and students of color. Their dynamic conversation sparked during the NAME roundtable discussion exemplifies the importance for individuals to share their life journeys with colleagues and students and to appreciate the powerful personal growth and professional development gained by listening to one another's stories and examining their shared journeys. To enhance cultural competencies infused throughout education, we benefit from revisiting, investigating, and exchanging the intersection of our parallel lives.

## Using Narrative Research with Teachers and Teacher Educators

The use of narrative research and personal life stories (Munchmore, 1999) to examine multiple perspectives and cross-cultural relationships applies perfectly to teachers guiding pre-K–12 students and teacher educators preparing teachers. Conducting narrative research and recording personal life histories generate findings that are as robust as or more robust than quantitative studies in terms of trustworthiness while producing knowledge and insights that can be generalized for others (Trotman & Kerr, 2001).

Recording our own stories enables us to view, question, and analyze our individual life journeys over time as well as the life journeys of others occurring simultaneously around us. Exchanging our journeys with others forces us to select the important encounters and events, to prioritize our values and beliefs, and to articulate these stories clearly and honestly. Transformative exchanges occur when our journeys intersect with life journeys both similar and distinct from our own; only then do we begin to understand and experience authentic multiple perspectives applicable to our own lives (Obidah & Teel, 2001).

**"The unique opportunity for Maria and Nancy to share their stories, truly listening and learning from one another's historical inquiries and perspective, supports their work as transformative educators."**

Narratives and personal life histories can be written as essays, logs, diaries, journals, research journals, vignettes, critical incidents, life histories, and autobiographies to record personal memories, provide a sense of place, introduce family members, describe people, tell powerful stories, and so forth (Thomas, 1993). These writing strategies equip teachers and students with salient tools for communicating, interpreting, and giving meaning to our own experiences while listening to and valuing the stories of others (Poirier, 1992).

Writing narratives and personal life histories in teacher education courses, particularly multicultural education courses, offers preservice and practicing teachers with clear guidelines, concrete examples, and genuine opportunities to understand themselves and to experience multiple perspectives in a safe and caring environment. It is suggested that this writing process is prefaced with several general class discussions related to the identification and value of understanding individual cultural characteristics and the shaping of our self-identities. Writing one's personal life history emphasizing cultural characteristics and self-identities may be a new experience that challenges many preservice and practicing teachers. Specific expectations should be decided collaboratively and communicated openly stipulating the kinds of events and encounters to be included in the narrative, if and how

narratives will be shared in class, and how narratives will be assessed to increase writers' comfort.

It may benefit writers to start by reflecting on particular times, places, and experiences such as childhood, hometowns, or becoming a teenager and negotiating school groups; likewise, writers can focus on unique historical events such as the assassination of Dr. Martin Luther King, Jr., or the tragedies of September 11, 2001. The purpose of writing the personal life stories can emphasize pivotal times of one's awareness when one realizes how society treats different people, that is, males versus females, different racial and ethnic groups, various religions, and so forth, and one starts to question why. This writing process may be initiated by crafting one's own story and sharing it with peers in class. These writing assignments can be modified to sharing with family members or community members followed up with investigative interviews and exchanged dialogues. As the writing process develops, the personal narrative allows the writer to not just formulate one's sense of self-identity, the writer starts to reformulate and negotiate one's cultural competencies by experiencing authentic multiple perspectives.

Writing a personal narrative makes visible one's own life. We learn to identify our cultural characteristics, define their value and meaning applicable within our own lives as well as for others, and note similarities and differences among our own cultural characteristics and those held by others. This writing process emphasizes "learning to believe in ourselves when that which is deep inside us is valuable and worth listening to."

**"Their insights help them to listen more carefully to their own students, to appreciate the many personal life histories playing out in their classrooms, and to become better teachers in our culturally diverse society."**

Writing personal narratives challenges teachers to examine themselves and to start listening to one another. Such an exercise may be uncomfortable as they begin to realize that not everyone is just like them. This enlightenment produces personal and professional rewards; many teachers are placed in schools with children unlike themselves. When recording their personal narratives and historical life stories, teachers begin to identify the cultural norms, the models and influences, the critical junctures, and the cultural tensions reflecting and conflicting with their cultural characteristics while shaping their self-identities. Sharing their personal narratives and life histories in small group discussions allows preservice and practicing teachers to hear multiple perspectives. They can inquire and investigate not only other people's journeys, they begin to reflect more deeply on their own journeys. Their insights help them to listen more carefully to their own students, to appreciate the many personal life histories playing out in their classrooms, and to become better teachers in our culturally diverse society.

This encounter models a powerful learning experience exemplifying critical pedagogy (Wink, 2000) that benefits all teachers, students, teacher educators, and preservice teachers helping them to think about and transcend complex social interactions by experiencing authentic multiple perspectives in our parallel journeys.

## References

Colton, C. C. (n.d.). Retrieved from www.quotationspage.com

cummings, e. e. (1976). *Tulips & chimneys*. New York: Norton. (Original work published 1923)

Cummins. J. (1996). *Negotiating identities: Education for empowerment in a diverse society*. Ontario: California Association for Bilingual Education.

Hones, D. F. (1998). Known in part: The transformational power of narrative inquiry. *Qualitative Inquiry, 4*(2). 225-249.

Munchmore, J. A. (1999). *Toward an understanding of one's life history*. Paper presented at the annual meeting of the American Educational Research Association, Montreal, Quebec. Canada.

Nieto. S. (1999). *The light in their eyes: Creating multicultural learning communities*. New York: Teachers College Press.

Obidah. J. E., & Teel, K. (2001). *Because of the kids*. New York: Teachers College Press.

Palmer, P. J. (1983). *To know as we are known*. San Francisco: Harper Collins.

Poirier, C. F. (1992). A student teacher's voice: Reflection of power. *Journal of Education for Teaching, 18*(1), 85-92.

Thomas, D. (1993). Treasonable or trustworthy text: Reflections on teacher narrative studies. *Journal of Education for Teaching, 19*(2), 231-250.

Trotman, J., & Kerr, T. (2001). Making the personal professional: Preservice teacher education and personal histories. *Teachers & Teaching, 7*(2), 157-172.

Whelan, K. K., Huber, J., Rose, C., Davies, A., & Clandinin, D. J. (2001). Telling and retelling our stories on the professional knowledge landscape. *Teachers and Teaching: Theory and Practice, 7*(2), 143-156.

Wink, J. (2000). *Critical pedagogy: Notes from the real world* (2nd ed.). New York: Addison, Wesley Longman, Inc.

Wink, J., & Putney, L. (2002). *A vision of Vygotsky* (pp. 157-160). Boston: Allyn & Bacon.

## Noted Literature

Bridges, R. (1993). *Through my eyes*. New York: Scholastic.

Gray, L. M. (1993). *Dear Willie Rudd*. New York: Simon & Schuster.

Grisham, J. (2000). *A painted house; A novel*. New York: Doubleday.

# Profoundly Multicultural Questions

*We must address the deeply ingrained inequities of today's schools*
*by asking difficult questions related to equity and access.*

## By Sonia M. Nieto

**I** still recall the question that my friend Maddie, also an educator, asked me a number of years ago when I was describing an initiative to bring a multicultural program to a particular urban school district. A supporter of multicultural education, she was nonetheless becoming frustrated by the ways in which many districts were implementing it. She was especially concerned that many students from that particular district were doing poorly in school, and she asked impatiently, "But can they do math?"

Her question stayed with me for a long time—and prompted me to think about what it means to provide an education that is both multicultural and equitable (Nieto, 1999). Sadly, issues of equity and access are not always linked with multicultural education. Sometimes, multicultural education is seen as little more than a way to promote self-esteem, or simply as a curriculum that substitutes one set of heroes for another. When that happens, we may end up with young people who feel good about themselves and their heritage but who have few skills that prepare them for life; or alternatively, who know how to do math and science and read, but who know little about their cultural backgrounds and are even ashamed and embarrassed by them.

Let me make clear that I strongly believe in multicultural education. That first exhilarating course that I took on the subject nearly 30 years ago put into words many of the ideas I had wanted to express since becoming a teacher. More recently, the term *culturally responsive pedagogy* has come into use and been advocated persuasively (Gay, 2000; Ladson-Billings, 1994). An outgrowth of multicultural education, culturally responsive pedagogy is founded on the notion that—rather than deficits—students' backgrounds are assets that students can and should use in the service of their learning and that teachers of all backgrounds should develop the skills to teach diverse students effectively.

Despite my great support for these philosophies, however, I am also concerned that they can be used in simplistic ways that fail to address the tremendous inequities that exist in our schools. For example, to adopt a multicultural basal reader is far easier than to guarantee that all children will learn to read; to plan an assembly program of ethnic music is easier than to provide music instruction for all students; and to train teachers in a few behaviors in cultural awareness or curriculum inclusion is easier than to address widespread student disengagement in learning. Although these may be valuable activities, they fail to confront directly the deep-seated inequalities that exist in schools. Because they are sometimes taken out of context—isolated as prepackaged programs or "best practices"—multicultural education and culturally responsive pedagogy can become band-aid approaches to serious problems that require nothing short of major surgery.

I define multicultural education as an anti-racist education that is firmly related to student learning and permeates all areas of schooling (Nieto, 1994). It is a hopeful way to confront the widespread and entrenched inequality in U.S. schools because its premise is that students of all backgrounds and circumstances can learn and achieve to high levels, and—even more essential—that they deserve to do so. Multicultural education needs to be accompanied by a deep commitment to social justice and equal access to resources. Multicultural education needs, in short, to be about much more than ethnic tidbits and cultural sensitivity.

For instance, although educators may call attention to the fact that the curriculum in U.S. schools is becoming more multicultural (an overblown claim in any event), they may neglect to note that the achievement gap between white students and students of color is growing. Although the gap was reduced by about half between 1970 and 1988, it has been widening since then. The reversal is evident in grades, test scores, dropout rates, and other indicators, and it has taken place in every type of school district and in all socioeconomic groups (D'Amico, 2001). Just one example: The average 12th grade low-income student of color reads at the same level as the average 8th grade middle-class White student (Kahlenberg, 2000). In terms of high school completion, 88 percent of white students have graduated from high school, but the rate for Hispanics is just 56 percent (U.S. Census Bureau, 2000a). Given these alarming statistics, the claim that education is equally available to all is more of a fiction than ever. Multicultural education and culturally responsive pedagogy by themselves cannot solve these problems.

It makes sense, then, to look carefully at two factors besides cultural differences that influence student learning: the sociopolitical context of education, and school policies and practices. The former includes societal ideologies, governmental policies and mandates, and school financing. School policies and practices—specifically, curriculum, pedagogy, tracking, testing, discipline, and hiring—can also either promote or hinder learning among students of different backgrounds.

Besides focusing on matters of culture and identity, educators also need to ask profoundly multicultural questions—that is, troubling questions that often go unanswered or even unasked. The answers tell us a great deal about what we value because the questions are about equity, access, and social justice in education. Here are a few of the questions that we must address if we are serious about giving all students of all backgrounds an equal chance to learn.

## Who's Taking Calculus?

I use "calculus" as a place marker for any number of other high-status and academically challenging courses that may open doors for students to attend college and receive advanced training. For instance, we find that although slightly more than 12 percent of white students are enrolled in calculus, only 6.6 percent of African Americans and 6.2 percent of Latinos and Native Americans are enrolled. In the case of physics, the numbers are 30.7 percent for whites, 21.4 percent for African Americans, 18.9 percent for Hispanics, and 16.2 percent for Native Americans (National Center for Education Statistics [NCES], 2002). This situation has serious implications for reforming such policies as rigid tracking, scheduling, and counseling services. Access to high-level and demanding academic courses has a long-term and dramatic effect in terms of college attendance and subsequent quality of life. For instance, the 2000 U.S. Census reported that annual average earnings for those with a bachelor's degree were nearly double the amount for those with just a high school diploma: $45,678 compared with $24,572 (U.S. Census Bureau, 2000b).

## Which Classes Meet in the Basement?

Language-minority students and students with special needs are too often hidden away in the basement—or in the hall closet, or the room with the leaky ceiling on the fourth floor, or the modular unit separated from the rest of the school. Administrators offer seemingly logical reasons for placing these students in these areas: There's no other available space in the building; these students were the last to arrive and therefore need to be placed where there's room; now they're closer to the English as a Second Language teacher. But placing programs for marginalized students in less desirable places is a powerful metaphor for the low status and little attention that they receive. It also serves in many cases to segregate these students from the so-called "regular" (English-speaking) or so-called "normal" (non-special needs) students, in this way creating an even greater gulf between them and the rest of the school.

The continuing segregation of students on the basis of race and ethnicity is a trend that has been escalating for the past 20 years. According to Gary Orfield (2001), most of the progress made toward desegregating schools in the two decades prior to 1988 has been lost in the past 15 years. For African Americans, the 1990s witnessed the largest backward movement toward segregation since the *Brown v. Board of Education* decision. Latinos are now the most segregated of all ethnic groups—not just in race and ethnicity, but also poverty. U.S. schools are becoming more separate and unequal than ever.

## Who's Teaching the Children?

The question of who is teaching the children is inextricably linked to matters of social justice in education. Teachers working in poor urban schools tend to have less experience and less preparation than do those in schools that serve primarily white and middle-class students (Editorial Projects in Education, 1998). In addition, poor urban districts are more likely to hire teachers out of field than are suburban and middle-class school districts (David & Shields, 2001). These situations would be deemed unacceptable in more affluent districts.

Related to teachers' experience and training is the issue of teachers' race and ethnicity. Although all educators—teachers, administrators, curriculum coordinators, and others—need to develop the attitudes and skills to be effective with our increasingly diverse student population, we need a concerted effort to recruit a more diverse faculty. At present, the number of students of color in U.S. classrooms is growing dramatically at the same time that the number of teachers of color is declining. In 1972, just 22 percent of students in public schools were considered "minority"; by 1998, it was 37 percent (NCES, 2000a). The teaching force, on the other hand, is about 87 percent white. These trends show little sign of changing (U.S. Census Bureau, 2001).

## Multicultural education needs to be about much more than ethnic tidbits and cultural sensitivity.

The growing gap is problematic because mounting evidence indicates that a higher number of teachers of color in a school—particularly African American and Hispanic—can promote the achievement of African American and Hispanic students (Clewell, Puma, & McKay, 2001; Dee, 2000). In fact, one study found that a higher number of teachers of color can have an even greater impact on the achievement of white students (Meier, Wrinkle, & Polinard, 1999). Another study found that having same race and gender role models was "significantly and consistently predictive of a greater investment in achievement concerns" on the part of young people (Zirkel, 2002, p. 371).

Associated with teacher quality is the question of teachers' influence on their students. The proof is growing that all teachers—regardless of race, ethnicity, or gender—who care about, mentor, and guide their students can have a dramatic impact on their futures, even when these students face tremendous barriers related to poverty, racism, and other social ills (Flores-González, 2002; Noddings, 1992; Valenzuela, 1999). Stanton-Salazar, for instance, suggests that mentoring and support from teachers can provide students with the social capital they need to succeed, thus creating networks that "function as pathways of privilege and power"—pathways not generally available to poor students of color (1997, p. 4).

## How Much Are Children Worth?

What do we pay for education, and how does the answer differ according to students' race, ethnicity, social class, and above all, home address? The well-known facts are that school financing is vastly unequal and that students with wealthier parents are fortunate to live in towns that spend more on their education, whereas young people who live in financially strapped urban or rural areas are much less fortunate (Kozol, 1991). Regrettably, the children who need the most get the fewest funds and resources (NCES, 2000b).

We also need to ask what our most vulnerable students are worth in terms of attention and care. A recent court case is a good example of the low value placed on students who attend poor urban schools. In June 2002, an appeals court in New York State ruled that youngsters who drop out of the New York City schools by 8th grade nevertheless receive "a sound basic education" (cited in González, 2002). The result of this astonishing ruling was to overturn a 2001 landmark decision that had found the state's formula for funding public schools unfair because it favored schools in suburban areas. The majority opinion in the appeals ruling, written by Judge Alfred Lerner, said in part,

> the skills required to enable a person to obtain employment, vote, and serve on a jury are imparted between grades 8 and 9. (cited in González, 2002)

Although Judge Lerner conceded that such a meager education might qualify young people for only the lowest-paying jobs, he added, "Society needs workers at all levels of jobs, the majority of which may very well be low-level" (cited in González, 2002). I am left wondering whether Judge Lerner would want this level of education for his own children or would think it fair and equitable.

## Multicultural education needs to be accompanied by a deep commitment to social justice and equal access to resources.

These, then, are some of the profoundly multicultural questions that I suggest we ask ourselves. Certainly they are not the only questions that we can ask, but they give us an inkling of the vast inequities that continue to exist in U.S. public schools. My questions are not meant to diminish the noble efforts of educators who struggle daily to reach students through culturally responsive education or through an accurate representation in the curriculum of students' histories and cultures. But as we focus on these approaches—approaches that I wholeheartedly support—we also need to ask troubling questions about equity, access, and fair play. Until we do something about these broader issues, we will be only partially successful in educating all our young people for the challenges of the future.

## References

Clewell, B. C., Puma, M., & McKay, S. A. (2001). *Does it matter if my teacher looks like me? The impact of teacher race and ethnicity on student academic achievement.* New York: Ford Foundation.

D'Amico, J. J. (2001). A closer look at the minority achievement gap. *ERS Spectrum, 19*(2), 4-10.

David, J. L., & Shields, P. M. (2001). *When theory hits reality: Standards-based reform in urban districts, final narrative report.* Menlo Park, CA: SRI International.

Dee, T. S. (2000). *Teachers, race, and student achievement in a randomized experiment.* Cambridge, MA: National Bureau of Economic Research.

Editorial Projects in Education. (1998). *Education Week: Quality counts 1998.* Bethesda, MD: Author.

Flores-González, N. (2002). *School kids, street kids: Identity and high school completion among Latinos.* New York: Teachers College Press.

Gay, G. (2000). *Culturally responsive teaching: Theory, research, and practice.* New York: Teachers College Press.

Gonzáiez, J. (2002, June 27). Schools ruling defies logic. *New York Daily News,* p. 24.

Kahlenberg, R. D. (2000). *Economic school integration* (Idea Brief no. 2). Washington, DC: The Century Foundation.

Kozol, J. (1991). *Savage inequalities: Children in America's schools.* New York: Crown.

Ladson-Billings, G. (1994). *The dream-keepers: Successful teachers of African American children.* San Francisco: Jossey-Bass.

Meier, K. J., Wrinkle, R. D., & Polinard, J. L. (1999). Representative bureaucracy and distributional equity: Addressing the hard question. *Journal of Politics, 61,* 1025-1039.

National Center for Education Statistics. (2000a). *Editorial projects in education,* 1998. Washington, DC: U.S. Department of Education, Office of Educational Research and Improvement.

National Center for Education Statistics. (2000b). *Trends in disparities in school district level expenditures per pupil.* Washington, DC: U.S. Department of Education, Office of Educational Research and Improvement.

National Center for Education Statistics. (2002). *Digest of education statistics, 2001.* Washington, DC: U.S. Department of Education, Office of Educational Research and Improvement.

Nieto, S. (1994). Affirmation, solidarity, and critique: Moving beyond tolerance in multicultural education. *Multicultural Education, 1*(4), 9-12, 35-38.

Nieto, S. (1999). *The light in their eyes: Creating multicultural learning communities.* New York: Teachers College Press.

Noddings, N. (1992). *The challenge to care in schools.' An alternative approach to education.* New York: Teachers College Press.

Orfield, G. (2001). *Schools more separate: Consequences of a decade of resegregation.* Cambridge, MA: The Civil Rights Project, Harvard University.

Stanton-Salazar, R. D. (1997). A social capital framework for understanding the socialization of racial minority children and youth. *Harvard Educational Review, 67*(1), 1-40.

U.S. Census Bureau. (2000a). *Educational attainment in the United States.' March 1999* (P20-528). Washington, DC: U.S. Department of Commerce.

U.S. Census Bureau. (2000b). *Educational attainment in the United States (Update): March 2000.* Washington, DC: U.S. Department of Commerce.

U.S. Census Bureau. (2001). *Statistical abstract of the United States: Education* [Online]. Available: www.census.gov/prod/2001pubs/statab/sec04.pdf

Valenzuela, A. (1999). *Subtractive schooling: U.S.-Mexican youth and the politics of caring.* Albany, NY: SUNY Press.

Zirkel, S. (2002). "Is there a place for me?": Role models and academic identity among white students and students of color. *Teachers College Record, 104*(2), 357-376.

**Sonia M. Nieto** is Professor of Language, Literacy, and Culture, Department of Teacher Education and Curriculum Studies, University of Massachusetts at Amherst, Amherst, MA 01003-9308; snieto@educ.umass.edu.

From *Educational Leadership,* December 2002/January 2003, pp. 6-10. Copyright © 2003 by Association for Supervision and Curriculum Development. Reprinted by permission.

# UNIT 5

# Curriculum and Instruction in a Multicultural Perspective

## Unit Selections

## Key Points to Consider

- How should teachers and students deal with xenophobic reactions when they occur?

- What are the similarities and distinctions between a "culture" and an "ethnic group?"

- Why is it effective to integrate multicultural curriculum content into all aspects of a school curriculum?

- What are the varying ways in which multicultural education is defined? Which model of multicultural education do you prefer?

- What is the rationale for the existence of the multicultural educational effort in the elementary and secondary schools? Should all students be exposed to it? Why or why not?

- Why is literacy education such a hotly debated topic in education?

## Student Website

www.mhcls.com/online

## Internet References

Further information regarding these websites may be found in this book's preface or online.

**American Indian Science and Engineering Society**
*http://www.aises.org*
**Child Welfare League of America**
*http://www.cwla.org*
**STANDARDS: An International Journal of Multicultural Studies**
*http://www.colorado.edu/journals/standards/*

Curriculum and instruction includes all concerns relative to subject matter to be taught and all pedagogical theory relating to methods of instruction. All pedagogical theory is based on some philosophical assumptions relating to what is worth knowing and what actions are good. Every school curriculum is the product of specific choices among those available. Since classroom teachers are the "delivery systems" for a curriculum, along with whatever texts are used, teachers have the opportunity to interpret and add their own insights regarding the curricula they teach.

It is in the area of curriculum and instruction in the elementary and secondary schools, as well as in teacher education curricula, that a fundamental transformation must occur to sensitize all young people, including those living in isolated rural and small town communities, to the multicultural reality of our national civilization. There are several different approaches to multicultural educational programming in the schools. This area of study has developed steadily, in stages, since the events of the 1960s, 1970s, and 1980s forced a reassessment of our sense of social justice. There are programs in some school systems that merely include the study of the minority cultural groups living in their particular area, and this is often done through isolated, elective courses or units in required courses that students must take. This is not the approach to multicultural education that most current leaders in the field favor. Today, most experienced multicultural educators favor a more inclusive approach to the subject— the infusion of multicultural themes into the entire life of the school and all possible course content. Such an inclusive approach to multicultural education seeks to help students and teachers to develop a sense of social consciousness. This sense, coupled with a more global and integrated conception of our social reality, will empower them to make more critical assessments than have been made in the past about such distinctions as the disparity between public democratic rhetoric and the reality of some social groups, which still have not been accepted into society's mainstream.

An important focus of multicultural education is that a democratic nation has a moral responsibility to see that minority ethnic, cultural, or religious groups are not isolated or marginalized in the social life of the nation. The educational institutions of a nation tend to be the primary places where children and young adults learn about their national history, literature, and scientific achievement. Multicultural educational content is necessary in all American schools because students, even in the most culturally isolated rural and small town settings, do learn opinions and beliefs about ethnic, cultural, and religious groups other than their own. What students learn in the informal social relations of their home communities about other social groups is often factually misleading or incorrect. This is how our past heritage of racism and negative stereotypes of differing social groups evolved. There has been much progress in the area of civil rights, but there has also been resurgent racism and intercultural misunderstanding. School is the one place children and adolescents go each day where it is possible for them to learn an objective view of the culturally pluralistic national heritage that is both their present and future social reality. All communities are linked in some way to the culturally pluralistic social reality of the nation.

When students leave high school to go into military service, attend college, or attempt careers in other parts of the nation in the corporate sector, government, or the arts, they will encounter a multicultural world very different from their often isolated local community or cultural group.

Becoming a multicultural person is a process that any dedicated teacher should be willing to pursue. We need to help students of all cultural heritages to become effective citizens of our national communities. Xenophobia and cultural prejudice have no proper place in any truly democratic national community. The English language is not in trouble. We are in trouble only if we cannot live up to our self-proclaimed heritage as a "nation of immigrants." We must remember our national heritage. We must also remember that our forefathers acquired the lands of Native Americans, 34 percent of the territory of Mexico in 1848, and the island of Puerto Rico in 1898. With those acquisitions came responsibilities that we cannot avoid if we are a morally conscious people. All Americans deserve a fair representation of their respective cultural voices.

Teachers should help their students to recognize and respect ethnic and cultural diversity and to value the ways in which it enhances and enriches the quality of our civilization. Children and adolescents should also be made aware that each of them has the right to choose how fully to identify with his or her own ethnic or cultural group.

The essays in this unit reflect a wide variety of perspectives on how to broaden the multicultural effort in our schools. The authors seek to incorporate more intercultural and global content and experiences into the main body of curriculum and instruction. Educators will find that, taken together, these essays provide a very sound basis for understanding what multicultural curriculum and instruction should be about. They are relevant to coursework in curriculum and instruction, curriculum theory and construction, educational policy studies and leadership, history and philosophy of education, and cultural foundations of education.

# Increasing Diversity in Challenging Classes

*A multicultural high school expands opportunities for its diverse student body.*

**Eileen Gale Kugler and Erin McVadon Albright**

Annandale High School opened its doors in 1954 in the still-segregated school system of Fairfax County, Virginia, a burgeoning middle-class suburb of Washington, D.C. In the next few decades, despite the official end of segregation, the school's student population remained almost exclusively middle-class and white.

But the faces in the halls of Annandale High changed dramatically in the 1980s and 1990s as the area experienced an increasing influx of immigrants. A school redistricting magnified the change. Today, Annandale High's 2,500 students come from 92 countries, speak more than 45 native languages, and come from a wide range of economic backgrounds. More than one-third of the students qualify for free or reduced-price lunch, and many more live close to the poverty line.

The school weathered some tough times as faculty and students struggled to deal with the new diversity. In the early 1990s, fights frequently broke out along racial lines, and the school administration realized that the school required more involved, assertive leadership. The schoolwide effort to become a model diverse school began. Parents were welcomed as collaborative partners. As a result of the outreach, many middle-class families chose to remain and contribute to the school's success rather than flee to predominantly white schools.

## Creating a Welcoming School Climate

School leaders decided that their first mission would be to build a school climate where every student felt valued. All students participated in a series of small-group dialogues focused on how to show respect even when you don't agree with someone, how students from different cultures may look at such issues as dating, and how to handle adolescent problems that are compounded by cultural differences. The school strengthened its student peer mediation program to head off potential problems and to teach students how to disagree without resorting to violence. Faculty members explored their own attitudes toward the new ethnic groups present in their classrooms, looking at ways in which their own backgrounds might affect their expectations of students. Multicultural parent groups also met to discuss values and concerns about raising teens that cross cultures. These talks built bonds among community members and between the school and students' homes.

In 1998, principal Donald Clausen created an academic task force of administrators, guidance counselors, teachers, parents, and community members. The work of this task force has endured and is now an integral part of the school, even under a new principal, Rodney Manuel. The task force still meets to address the needs of diverse learners. One of the group's recommendations was bringing International Baccalaureate (IB), a program for high-achieving 11th and 12th graders, to the school. Established in 1968 in Geneva, Switzerland, IB operates today in nearly 1,400 schools in 115 countries, including 426 U.S. high schools.

The task force believed that International Baccalaureate offerings would add opportunities that the existing advanced placement courses did not provide. Students could participate in a rigorous, integrated IB diploma program or earn an IB certificate in a particular subject. The IB program was also deemed a good fit for the diverse school because it uses curriculum and assessments that are less culturally biased than those of U.S.-based programs. Because it is used in so many different cultures, IB emphasizes transparent assessments that eliminate subtle norms and expectations that may exclude students not raised in the majority culture. Criterion-referenced assessments, the use of specific rubrics, and the "teacher as coach" model level the playing field in IB classes.

*Annandale guidance counselors and teachers work with minority students from their first day at the school to help them prepare for college.*

The IB program also provides essential support for diverse students. An IB coordinator on the faculty advocates for students, and IB students take many of their classes together, creating a powerful academic and social support network.

## Broadening the IB Program

The task force committed itself to offering IB classes to as many students as possible, rejecting the typical IB model that runs a diploma-only program as a school-within-a-school. In the late 1990s, the school had already achieved greater minority enrollment in high-level classes because of a change in policy—switching from the "gifted and talented" model that admitted students mainly on the basis of their performance on standardized tests to an "honors" approach that focused on students' motivation and performance in class. In 1995, the Gifted and Talented English 9 class of 18 students included only one African American student; no Latino students had even applied. Today, more than 100 students, proportionately representing the diverse student population, participate in the English 9 Honors program.

The Annandale High administration built on the foundation of its inclusive honors program to create an inclusive IB program for juniors and seniors. The school went against conventional wisdom by starting its program big. To get as many students as possible involved in the program, the school offers a full range of IB classes in mathematics, science, English, history, and four foreign languages.

Counselors and teachers at Annandale High personally encourage every motivated student they encounter to take one or more IB classes. Teachers seek out bright students who may not even know their own capabilities. "I look for work ethic," says Kathlyn Berry, an

11th grade history teacher, adding that

> I always ask kids what advanced classes they are taking and encourage them to take at least one. I let them know they will have to work hard, and may even get a *C*, but they will develop their writing and analytical skills and will see the advantage when they go to college.

To further broaden access to the IB program, the school offers several IB classes for students not yet proficient in English. For example, Spanish A2 for Fluent Speakers has attracted native Spanish speakers who want to study Spanish literature and culture in an academic setting, U.S.-born students who have lived in Spanish-speaking countries, and graduates of a local Spanish immersion program.

For many Latino students, IB Spanish A2 is the gateway to other rigorous classes. Nelson, an immigrant from Bolivia, felt little connection to school and assumed he would not finish high school, until a teacher encouraged him to take Spanish A2. The class helped him explore in an academic setting issues that interested him without being restrained by limitations in English. Nelson became intrigued with ethical issues in genetics, and he is now focusing on biology and planning to attend college.

The IB offerings at Annandale also include the arts, such as classes in music theory and drama. In IB Art, students develop a theme-based project, and many students use their native cultures as a foundation. One student who was born in Colombia researched imagery from pre-Columbian art; a boy who had lived in Sudan and Yemen chose the theme of human suffering. The IB assessment involves students giving talks about their work, so students gain insight into other histories and cultures as well as refine their oral presentation skills.

In addition to reaching out to get more students to enroll in IB classes, Annandale faculty and administrators provide ongoing, multifaceted support to help each IB student succeed in the program. The IB coordinator works with students

and parents on individual concerns, such as the student feeling overwhelmed by work or facing scheduling conflicts. Guidance counselors ensure that each student involved with IB is placed appropriately and has what he or she needs to succeed. Teachers are considered "coaches" for student success. Administrators work to break down barriers that might pose problems for some families, such as complicated application procedures.

The school makes an effort to include any potentially successful student in IB courses. Faculty members keep mindful of the line where encouragement ends and unreasonable pressure begins. If a student wants to drop a class, has she simply not yet adjusted to the rigor of the teacher, or is the class truly too challenging? If a student is feeling overwhelmed, should he be taking two IB classes instead of three? If so, which one should be dropped? A student who wants to drop an IB course meets with her teacher, her parent, the IB coordinator, the guidance counselor, and the assistant principal to work out the problem. Although time-consuming and intensive, this commitment to each student as an individual is at the crux of the program's success.

## The Payoff: Authentic Diversity

Because of these efforts, significantly more minority students now take the most rigorous classes at Annandale High. In this school in which most students come from minority cultures, more than half of the students in every grade take advanced courses. African American students' participation in 11th and 12th grade IB classes has doubled in the last three years (to 50 students), and Latino students' participation has tripled (to 51 students). Eighteen percent of students in IB classes qualify for free or reduced-price lunch.

Of the 24 students who enrolled as IB diploma candidates in 2004, 38 percent do not speak English as their first language, 24 percent were born outside the United States, 16 percent are African American, and 4 percent are Latino. We hope that more African American and Latino students will seek the IB diploma as they experience success in individual IB classes.

Individual stories reflecting the diverse backgrounds and experiences of Annandale's IB students bring these statistics to life. Inga is an IB diploma candidate who was born in Somalia. She first began taking rigorous classes when her 7th grade math teacher recommended her for algebra. Inga kept increasing her top-level classes, and in 11th grade she decided to aim for the IB diploma. She applied herself in IB classes in English, history, art, Spanish, math, and biology and took an intensive seminar course called Theory of Knowledge. Inga believes that her teachers have high expectations for her, and she has been accepted at Dartmouth College, Duke University, and the University of Virginia. Her extended essay, a requirement for the IB diploma, is an analysis of the potential health-related repercussions of telecommuting.

Another IB diploma candidate is Marti, an African American who credits as key to her success her elementary school's recognition of her ability and her subsequent placement in a pullout program. Marti believes that Annandale provided her with a "blessing" by not letting her easily drop pre-IB and IB classes, but giving her support and talking to her parents. Marti has been accepted at Washington University in St. Louis, Missouri, Penn State University, and St. John's University, which she will attend on a scholarship for academic excellence.

Cory, an African American who is taking several IB classes, was first encouraged to go down that path by his middle school teachers. The open enrollment procedure allowed Cory to take an IB math class, which should prepare him to do well in college classes. He believes his biggest challenge is balancing schoolwork and sports, which he accomplishes

with the support of his coaches. Cory says that his culture is valued in class and that neither his peers nor his teachers have ever expected him to give up his identity to be part of IB.

## College Readiness for All

The IB program is just one facet of a school culture at Annandale High that aims to increase opportunities for all students. Annandale guidance counselors and teachers work with minority students from their first day at the school to help them prepare for and pursue college. Faculty reach out to all those they teach—not only students already achieving well but also students who hint at more promise than their academic records reflect—encouraging them to participate in high-level courses or programs that prime students for college. For example, the Student Achievement Model (SAM), a college preparatory program for academically capable students who have not yet been successful, teams a counselor with core teachers and includes Saturday academic boot camps, college trips, and intensive work with individuals and their parents.

Recognizing that early preparation of students is crucial, Annandale High and its two feeder middle schools have been working closely to improve vertical alignment of their curriculums. They are applying for authorization to offer the IB Middle Years Program— currently piloted for all 6th and 7th graders in the two feeder middle schools—to all students in grades 6-10.

> *Many middle-class families chose to remain and contribute to the school's success rather than flee to predominantly white schools.*

Parent support is a key element in increasing student achievement throughout the school. Such mainstream organizations as the Parent Teacher Student Association have worked to encourage all parents to focus beyond their own child to the

success of every student. Minority parents are actively involved in leadership, and a new Hispanic Parents Council is working to connect more Hispanic parents with the school. Parents are involved in everything from policy reform at the school and district levels to targeted fund-raising. When a shrinking budget led the Fairfax County School Board to eliminate funding for IB tests, forcing most students to pay their own testing fees, the Annandale parents raised enough money to cover the testing fee of every student at Annandale for several years. They then intensively lobbied the school board until it reinstated the funding.

We are proud of our achievements, but the entire school community realizes that we still face barriers to raising achievement for all students. One difficulty is analyzing student data meaning fully. Students with very different cultures and experiences are arbitrarily grouped together in U.S. Census Bureau categories. For example, the "white" category mixes together U.S.-born white students and immigrants recently arrived from the Middle East. Recording student information in a way that more closely reflects our demographic realities would help us analyze student behavior better.

Annandale High School opened in 1954, a few months after the *Brown v. Board of Education* decision was handed down. Today, it truly represents the promise of that decision: a multicultural school whose diversity is reflected in its most rigorous classes.

---

**Eileen Gale Kugler** (703-644-3039; ekugler@kuglercom.com) is a speaker and consultant on building diverse schools. She is the author of Debunking the Middle-Class Myth: Why Diverse Schools Are Good for Aft Kids (Rowman & Littlefield, 2002). **Erin McVadon Albright** is the coordinator for the international Baccalaureate program at Annandale High School; 703-642-4254;

---

From *Educational Leadership,* February 2005, pp. 42-45. Reprinted by permission of the Association for Supervision and Curriculum Development. Copyright © 2005 by ASCD. All rights reserved. The Association for Supervision and Curriculum Development is a worldwide community of educators advocating sound policies and sharing best practices to achieve the success of each learner. To learn more, visit ASCD at www.ascd.org

# Arts in the Classroom

**"La Llave" (The Key) to Awareness,
Community Relations,
and Parental Involvement**

**Margarita Machado-Casas**
*University of North Carolina at Chapel Hill*

As a teacher and a person of color, I am committed to social justice, equity, and meaningful teaching that takes students' cultural heritage into consideration in the workplace. Yet this is not easy in American schools. When entering the classroom we are expected to act as if we are blind to the social-economic issues our students struggle with daily. We are expected to teach only academic subjects and not deal with what school really is about—an extension of home and preparation for real life situations that are more complex than just dealing with character education. When in the classroom we are trained to be authoritative beings that control through "regimentation," "depositing," and "manipulation." As teachers we become our students' oppressors (Freire, 1970, p. 107). Being and acting as teacher the oppressor is harmful for all students but particularly for immigrants who on top of having to learn a new language, and a new educational system, have to suppress their cultural being,—all they have known in order to fit into American schools.

I was born in Nicaragua, from which seven in my family and I fled to Panama escaping from war and an oppressive government. We lived in Panama for five and a half years before political instability caused turmoil in that country as well. Having experienced this oppression before, my father courageously opted to bring the family to the United States. I arrived in California at the age of 14. Knowing less than basic English I was enrolled in a middle school in Fullerton, California, where I was placed in an ESL (Sheltered English class). My initial school experience was devastating. I not only did not know the language enough to communicate my thoughts and feelings in an understandable manner, but I was also having to re-learn school and the behaviors one is to display when in school. For example, back in both Nicaragua and Panama, students were expected to have an opinion and to express it without raising their hands.

As a child in the U.S., I was often the translator, the bridge between my parents and schools, the one person who in the process of translating became responsible for getting the message across properly. My parents were never invited to school events and were too busy working to get involved. Schools did nothing to encourage parental involvement of immigrant parents. As a student my experience, life, language, and family were ignored. I was being told in school that "Yo" (me) was not good enough for this society, and I had to change. This sudden alienation became an everyday event; one that persisted throughout my school years. I felt culturally and cognitively abused, "Whether urbane or harsh, cultural invasion is thus always an act of violence against the persons of the invaded culture, who lose their originality or face the threat of losing it" (Freire, p. 133).

Being successful in our current educational system means being able to acculturate to the dominant culture (Credit Nieto, 1999, pg. 75), and, now with accountability, demands it means being able to successfully pass a test. When I came into the country as an immigrant child, I remember the struggles I went through, I was invisible, my "real" life experiences were ignored. In my case, I came to see "real" life experiences as those we live daily, e.g., encounters with strangers, family members, friends, and community members that make us happy and/or sad. I also saw real life in our homes and school, where we saw, touched, smelled, and used our other senses. Reality, to me, included reactions with and from others; looks we are given and names we are called; pains, struggles, faces that make sad; actions, mannerism that make us who we are; love, interactions with others; what we eat; what we dance to; the languages we speak; and the way we act and think in the world. I would have been better prepared to deal with these struggles if I had had a school environment where school was an extension of home, real life, a place where acculturation was not the goal, but rather self-exploration, critical thinking, and exposure to real life situations to bring about "concientization" (Freire, 1970, p. 140) to promote action. Creating this kind of environment would have allowed me to break the current mold of thinking and begin to create new ways of thinking. As a teacher, I wanted my students to have what I did not. In my own classroom I wanted to create new ways of thinking that addressed students' different life situations. I began thinking about what I had that I could use. I realized the starting points were the classroom and myself.

I wanted the classroom to be an open-safe-respectful environment where all cultures, races, and ethnic differences were celebrated and promoted and where the home culture and school experience came together in significant ways. I learned this was revolutionary, "Revolution is achieved with neither verbalism or activism, but rather with praxis, that is, with reflection and action directed at the structures to be transformed" (Freire, p. 107). I began to organize my classroom into a community that was very much connected with home and real life situations. I wanted to make real life social justice issues accessible, visible, and practiced. Yet, I was in need of the "La llave" [the key] that would enable all this, and arts integration became "mi llave" [my key].

What constitutes arts? I define arts by not just a drawing, song, dance, but rather by those everyday experiences that lead us to thinking, questioning, talking, communicating with others, communicating our feelings, doing, hurting, loving, but most importantly feeling and voice/expression. Why the arts? We are surrounded by arts. We breathe them, live them, touch them, and experience the arts daily, both consciously and unconsciously. From the time we are born we are invaded with artistic gestures that portray love, affection, beauty, pain, suffering, and everyday life: "Experiences in the arts richly augment our ordinary life experiences and by doing so, often lead us to tactical understanding of the deeper meaning of our existence, our culture, and our world" (Fisher & McDonald, 2002, p. 1). Through the "arts," students and parents in my classroom began cooperating with their children. This, in turn, created reflection and action in both the classroom and community. Arts created a praxis that allowed students and parents to engage in dialogue and to get involved in school and acting.

## Thinking about Being the Teacher

The teacher is a sociocultural mediator when she or he "becomes the link between the child's sociocultural experiences at home and school. That is the teacher becomes the sociocultural, sociohistorical mediator of important formal and informal knowledge about the culture and society in which children develop" (Diaz & Flores, 2000). Therefore, taking the role of a teacher as a sociocultural mediator involves making connections with students and those who impact student's lives. Teachers have the

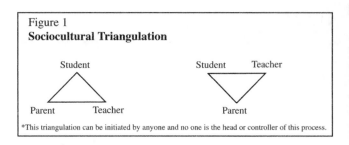

Figure 1
**Sociocultural Triangulation**

Student

Parent    Teacher

Student    Teacher

Parent

*This triangulation can be initiated by anyone and no one is the head or controller of this process.

power to bring students and parents into a three-way relationship I call *sociocultural triangulation* (See Figure 1).

Sociocultural triangulation assumes all three are equal and equally responsible to promote a child's progress. The role of the teacher in this triangulation process is to start the communication between student, parent or guardian and teacher that will promote sociocultural acceptance and inclusion in the classroom. The role of the teacher in this case is redefined and restructured to give up control in order to allow dialogue, thinking, and reflection to occur, "If the true commitment to the people, involving transformation of the reality by which they are oppressed, required a theory of transforming action, this theory cannot fail to assign the people a fundamental role in the transformation process" (Freire, p. 108).

In this article I describe how arts integration enabled me to develop such triangulation that resulted in shifting of the roles of the parties involved. Further, I will explain the ways in which organized art activities helped create a classroom environment where relationships between student and parents or guardians evolved in order to promote individuality, cultural inclusion, "conscientization," and equity. By utilizing arts as the "llave" [key] we began to create a cultural platform between a diverse classroom and an equally diverse community. In order to illuminate this, I will explore three areas I organized to achieve these goals: my classroom, my teachings, and community connections. Along with arts integration these three connections (which also lead to sociocultural triangulation) were essential to the creation of a new platform that connected the community and school in a new way of thinking about learning through the arts.

## The Classroom

My classroom was a 4th grade two-way immersion classroom in which instruction in the fourth grade was provided in both English and Spanish. Fifty percent of the time instruction was provided in English and fifty percent of the time in Spanish. Half of the students were minorities, mostly Latino/a and Chicano/a, and the other half of the class was White or other ethnicities. The class was considerably from a low socioeconomic background as well as considerably diverse. Class diversity was represented both economically and socially. Parents' occupations ranged from housewives, "campesinos" [farm workers], factory workers, teachers, and professionals working for the government.

When walking into the classroom one would immediately notice how the classroom was divided into different sections or walls. Looking south was the children's international diversity wall, which included pictures of children from around the world. Each picture was enlarged and it included a narrative written by the child or an adult about that child's experience. This wall was of great success in the classroom. Both students and parents enjoyed looking at the pictures and reading the narratives. Still on the south side of the wall, immediately after that wall was a calendar wall, which was in both English and Spanish and more pictures and narratives of children from all over the world. North of the international diversity wall was the social studies wall that presented issues related to subjects being studied in class. The wall contained writing samples of all children. East of the room was the creative wall, this wall was initially designed to give children the opportunity to post drawings, but after I began the sociocultural triangulation process through arts it became the most important wall in the classroom—one both students and parents helped design and maintain.

The classroom was not solely mine, but instead a more collective community space where students, parents, guardians, and I were responsible to make sure the classroom was running smoothly. Before the school year started I contacted all parents via telephone or correspondence. I introduced myself and told them a little bit about my life; this gave parents the opportunity to get to know my life experiences and me. I then proceeded to tell parents that there was an "open door" policy, and that they were welcomed and encouraged to come to volunteer in the classroom. I invited them over to the classroom prior to school starting. Many came and we talked about what they saw as the struggles their children have had, frustrations they have had, and ways in which I could help them both. At this time I informed parents that I was going to be calling them every Friday to give them updates and reports of how the classroom was going. They seemed both shocked, and doubtful; I later found out that the majority of them did not think I was going to be actually calling them every Friday.

As I came from a working class family, I am aware of parents' busy schedules as well as the necessity to sometimes carry more than one job to sustain a family. To that end, I explained to parents that *how* they are involved with their child's schooling is more important than the *amount* of involvement. I wanted parents to be able to express their experiences with their children and me (optional). I wanted parents to begin dialogue, to talk to their children about their struggles when they bring an issue home, to ask their children about school, to share their qualities (those things they are good at), whatever they might be, and most importantly to talk and reflect with them. Some parents expressed concerns that they "Did not have anything they were good at, many of us are just house wives

or factory workers, 'campesinos' (farm workers)." I reiterated that everyone has something they are good at and that I was sure that if I asked their children what their parents or guardians were good at they could tell me in a second. I reinforced the concept that children appreciate any interaction with parents; and the most important interaction was one that started dialogue and reflection. I explained to parents that I was committed to doing all that was in my power to inform parents and guardians of what we were doing in class, that I saw them as colleagues, so input given to me was appreciated and encouraged. By being including and welcoming, parents and guardians and students began to feel comfortable around the classroom, with me, and with other students. They began to trust me and the classroom environment.

As I wanted my classroom to be an extension of home, of real life experiences, I needed a way for parents to participate. Moreover, I wanted this participation to be something that was special and not something that would merely help the teacher with her tasks. It seemed to me that one way to accomplish this was to build a partnership with parents through arts. I began to do this by assigning creative projects to students that involved math, social studies, language arts, and arts. The assignments consisted of students going home and finding things around the classroom and/or neighborhood that had to do with school activities. The goal was for students and parents to look around their world, their reality and find beauty and art within it. For example, when we discussed geometric shapes in the classroom I asked students to go home and with parental or guardian help they were to find an object that would match the shapes we were studying. If they could not find one like it, they had to select objects that when connected to others, created that shape. It was a project that everyone seemed to enjoy. One student could not find the shape of a trapezoid, so his father helped him create one with old car parts. Along with the parent, the student sketched each part of the car where it was taken from and explained the process of figuring out what parts would fit together to create a trapezoid. The student also talked about the process of how the metal was bent, welded, and put together. The student brought it to class to share his invention along with an explanation of how he did it. I used that moment to explain to students that arts does not only involve drawing and coloring but also creating new things out of old ones; arts involves everyday experiences and objects that surround us.

## My Teaching

Arts have been one of my favorite tools in the classroom. It was a great source of release when I was a child, as it was through the arts I that was able to express many emotions, feelings, and thoughts. For this reason, I felt that including arts in the classroom and in my lessons was imperative. Initially, arts were used in the classroom as a way to express or retell what students were writing or working on. As in the trapezoid example mentioned above, this was very superficial, and it did not require much critical thinking. I began thinking about my intentions and what art expression meant to me while growing up as an immigrant. With that in mind, I began to think about my goal and about changing my role as a teacher. My goal was to promote critical thinking, a sense of commonality, transcendence of time, connection with real life situations, and recognition of power structures that affected characters in the past and that are still affecting many today. After I had a vision of what could be achieved and my role as the sociocultural mediator, I began to think about ways in which I could utilize the arts to raise awareness, promote critical thinking, equity, and social justice. I had my work cut out for me!

Children are always really excited to read about others' experiences, lives, and struggles. Therefore, I chose several biographies and gave students a summary of the biographies that included some of the accomplishments of the characters. I asked the class to choose one biography and write why they wanted to read that particular biography. Students then took the biographies home and shared with their parents the choices they had. Many children returned to class with their favorites and their parents' favorites. Students were also instructed to draw a picture that predicted events which they thought were going to take place in the story; they were to do this with only the information I provided for them. Some parents wrote their favorites on a piece a paper along with the reasons why they liked that particular biography. Some parents wrote it in Spanish and others in English. This allowed them to be included regardless of the language they spoke. I explained to students that I asked them to come up with reasons as to why we should read these biographies in order for them to begin to think about social-political and cultural issues they and their parents are interested in. I then asked for volunteers to discuss their prediction drawings. They were to explain what it was and why they chose those colors, background, and the meaning behind the scene. This became a wonderful artistic activity and experience given that every student had a different interpretation of each of the stories, and therefore colors, background, and scene were and had different meaning. The three biographies they chose were Frida Kahlo, Anne Frank, and Biddy Mason. Frida Kahlo was read in English, Anne Frank in Spanish, and Biddy Mason in Spanish. We began by reading Anne Frank. To save space here, I will only discuss Anne Frank.

The story of Anne Frank is a book that is filled with socio-political issues. First, we began the unit by reading the book and talking about Germany during that time. I provided the class with historical information about Hitler, the Jewish community, and Germany. None of these historical facts included pictures of Hitler. They were then asked to create a portrait of Germany during those times. The portrait was to include the feeling, struggles, and

emotions students thought were being felt by either Germans, Jews, or Hitler. Many drew either a picture of Hitler or included Hitler in their portraits; surprisingly enough almost all but two students drew Hitler with blond hair and blue eyes. When asked to share their portraits with the class many expressed that Hitler was blond with blue eyes because he liked people who were "like him, blond with blue eyes." Here students began to make a connection to their own life experiences, their feeling comfortable or liking people who were like them. So, if Hitler liked people who were blond with blue eyes, then he must be blond and have blue eyes. When they all finished presenting their portraits, I showed them several pictures of Hitler. They were all shocked to find out that Hitler was not blond, nor did he have blue eyes. I also told them that Hitler's mother was Jewish. And they suddenly began to think. Their eyes were wide open; they were in deep thought. We talked about why it was more acceptable for Hitler to be blond with blue eyes than for him to have dark hair and brown eyes. I got responses such as, "If he was just like the Jews, brown hair, and dark eyes, then why did he dislike them?" "He must not like himself." "I know some people who are mean to many who are like them; like Latinos hurting Latinos."

We talked about what life was about during that time, and what it was to be a young woman without the opportunity to experience "la vida" (life). This conversation about Anne Frank was happening in the classroom and at home. I asked parents to begin a portrait of the Anne Frank story at home. I explained to them that as the story proceeded they were to add something to the portrait. I felt this was a great opportunity to get parents involved and share their experiences their "vida" (life). I asked parents to share how their experiences were similar to those of Anne Frank. Hence, together with their children, many parents worked on the Anne Frank portrait. As the story proceeded they were to add whatever from Anne's life or their life they thought was important to the portrait.

Although this story was one that touched them, they were still responding superficially to the story. I wanted them to feel like the key person in the story, to put their feet in Anne Frank's shoes. Therefore, I asked them to literally take their shoes off and to share them with the person next to them and to put each other's shoes on. I too had to exchange shoes with a student. They were all really excited about doing this. I moved the desks, dimmed the lights, and had students close their eyes. I began playing German classical music and we all began to "walk in someone else's shoes." I asked the class to think about their feelings, emotions, to imagine being a teenager during the holocaust and not being able to enjoy life fully, to imagine being imprisoned, trapped, and scared because of persecution. After the exercise was completed, they were quiet, and some raised their hands. They shared how it felt to imagine being someone else. Many talked about being powerless or "sin poder," frightened, trapped, and caged "como un animal." This activity provided students with a more creative way of looking at the arts. It was the arts that involved movement, sense of one's place, and thinking about others while being here. For fourth graders this was a unique way of feeling the arts-seeing beauty, pain, and otherness.

I asked them to think about the way they felt and to portray their feelings in any way they wanted to. They could do this by singing, acting, drawing, or creating a mini-book. Two created sketches, one sang, and the rest created portraits of what they experienced while being in someone else's shoes. One child drew a portrait of Anne as a girl crying, in one corner was the Star of David and on the other side were armed forces. The side of the face that had armed forces was white with blue eyes and blond hair and the side with the Star of David was brown with black eyes and dark hair. Bars imprisoned the girl, and a tear was coming out of her eye. In the writing description, it said, "The Hitler army wants her to be white, blond with blue eyes, but she has black hair and dark eyes, and that is why she is in a prison; the attic of that home. Anne was an amazing girl who was proud of who she was and who wrote those letters to let us know what not to do and to take people like they are." One child performed a sketch that connected her own personal experiences with those of Anne Frank. The sketch was a moving and sad story of her grandmother and her family running away from Mexico, away from the threat of being killed. This skit created an interesting conversation between the entire class. Children began to talk about oppression, ethnicity, race, power, powerlessness, discrimination, racism, genocide, social political implications, survival, and what it means to us now. Since many of them did not know the terminology, they only expressed themselves through experiences and examples. As they were giving me examples I began to provide them with the terms that described that particular situation. For example, Hitler killed thousands of people and this is called genocide. We talked about color and preconceived notions many have about a particular race because of the color of their skin. Another student began to sing about class differences, which lead us to talk about privilege and poverty. Many students could relate to this given that many had felt mistreatment because of their social class.

They all had wonderful examples of artistic expressions; their feelings and reactions showed they understood how struggle is painful regardless of when it happens. With this activity, it did not matter if you could draw, sing, or dance. Any form of artistic expression was accepted; it became the universal language of acceptance. Arts became a universal voice that was open and accessible to all.

## Community

As parents began to get involved and informed about what was going on in the classroom, other family members became involved as well. Many parents were immigrants and their migration experiences as well as their struggles with a life in a new country had valuable lessons for their children. Being an immigrant whose experiences were ignored, I reiterated to parents that their experiences were valuable and appreciated. Parents became involved in helping to create portraits, giving children ideas, and sharing their own stories. They were dialoguing, communicating, and reflecting on their experiences together. Students began sharing their family stories with the class to find out that many of our stories were similar.

I noticed that children were really interested in other children's stories, in their own family stories, and the way each child expressed their stories through the use the art. Because I was aware that "men and women. . . [are] beings who cannot be truly human apart from communication, for they are essentially communicative creatures" and that "to impede communication is to reduce men to the status of 'things'" (Freire, p. 109), I decided to invite parents, grandparents, guardians, uncles, friends and anyone who wanted to share their struggles, motivations, purpose, moments of feeling powerless, and the sources of their strengths to participate. Parents were encouraged to create or do something artistic with their children to bring them to class and also present with their son or daughter. I announced this activity a month or two in advance just as I began to make home visits. During home visits we began to share life experiences, anecdotes, and stories. I asked parents, guardians, grandparents, and other family members if they would be willing to share their stories and argued it was important for them to tell children their "whys." Most importantly, I wanted them to share the "whys" for their being in this country and what their motivations and hopes were. In addition, they were asked to share what the lack of opportunities and struggles were that motivated them to flee their own countries. Visiting with them at home and calling parents every Friday worked well and helped me schedule the first couple of presentations. Prior to parents presenting, I sent a bulletin home that included some of the portraits students had created along with a brief description of what we were doing in class. In the bulletin I invited parents to come in and observe other parents' presentations, and I told them I was going to provide snacks and drinks for students and parents.

More than half of the parents showed up that afternoon to hear the presentations. They brought multi-ethnic foods and drinks. One even brought "taquitos" for the entire class. Since it was my idea to do this, I decided to begin the presentations. I talked to the class about coming to the United States, learning the language, and the struggles my parents overcame in this country. I told them about my going to college and trying to be a good teacher who promotes social justice. I showed pictures of my country, my family, and sang for the class. An immigrant mother who had only been in the United States for three years gave the second presentation. She had been a teacher in Mexico and was a factory worker here. She had two jobs and the father of the family had three jobs. The mother and son had created a collage of pictures and portraits that illustrated their story. The son introduced his mother. "This is 'mi Jefa' (my boss or mother), and she is going to share our story with you. Please listen to her; she does not know English, but I will tell you what she is telling and our teacher will help me if need help." The mother began to share that they were a middle class family in Mexico; they owned a house, two cows, and at least three-dozen chickens. The animals enabled them to survive while growing up. She got up every morning to work on the farm, went to school, and then came back after school to work some more. She loved books and really wanted to be a teacher; so she begged her parents to let her go to school. They agreed but only if she continued helping with the animals on the farm. When she started attending university, she took a bus for two hours to get to classes everyday. After graduation, her father became ill. Since she could not support the farm with her salary, and they lost everything. She and her husband were the only two working. She was making less than fifty dollars a month, and her husband made even less. They were really struggling. She said that she wanted her children to go to college and have a better life.

So, they came to this country hoping to be able to do better here. Indeed she had hoped she could teach here. She was shocked when she found out that her degree was worth nothing here and her skills were not appreciated. She decided to place her children in the dual immersion program my class was part of because she wanted to be able to communicate with the teacher. But most importantly she wanted her children to maintain their language. They shared the collage they had created and the portraits of "el ranchito" they had in Mexico. The mother shared that she was not a very artistic person, but creating a collage gave her a new way to look at art. She called it "el arte de mis recuerdos" [the art of my memories]. The son then proceeded to talk about why it was so important for him to go to school. He said, "I need to go to school so that I can buy 'mi jefa un ranchito.'"

Third, an Anglo family of three (mother, father, and son) presented. They spoke only English so their son translated into Spanish. They brought a song to share with the class. Both parents were professionals who lived in an upper middle class neighborhood. They wanted their children to be in the two-way immersion program because they wanted their children to be culturally well rounded, not racist, and to speak a second language. They shared with the class that in their neighborhood there are not any minorities, and they thought it was important for their children to experience being with other children. They also mentioned that three generations before their parents came from Germany not knowing the language and struggling like many of the parents and guardians who are in the class. They also brought black and white pictures of their family in Germany and talked about how

excited they were to have children who are bilingual when they are not. They then began to sing a song they sang at home, as a family. This family song had become the way to connect past with present, to maintain their history and to keep their ancestors alive.

These community meetings became the high points of the school year. They became events where the parents and guardians shared their culinary arts and a time for us to learn about foods and experiences from different parts of the world. The classroom became a larger community that consisted of students, teacher, and family members. It was a community in which everyday diversity, differences, struggles, achievements, and pains were shared and respected. Many of the students and parents had known each other only briefly and did not even know that they had so much in common. Some became good friends and started talking on the phone. Others just began to understand many of the struggles others parents had gone through. Others collaborated in creating arts projects with other families who had similar experiences or who were neighbors. Some parents united to bring issues pertaining to them and their children to school officials and school board meetings. They began to have voice. These meetings continued throughout the year as a way to share what is so natural if explored: artistic expression.

## Conclusion

Being a teacher of color means being a political being (Apple, 1990). Yet, "la llave," a key, is needed to invite parents and guardians into the education of their students. The arts became a means to begin dialogue where students and parents and guardians could communicate, express themselves, and connect their personal experiences. Arts became an expression of their lives, a way to see the world, and a way to understand different points of view. Through the arts they expressed their desires and needs. They also came to see school differently. Their children were engaged in their real lives as actors and critics.

Students were not just making pictures. Rather they began to experience differences of opinions through arts. They began to explore their own beliefs and those beliefs of their parents and guardians. They began to think critically about the socio-political implications mentioned in Anne Frank and other biographies, and how these implications apply to them today. Students began to recognize the difficulties of walking in other people's shoes and found the arts as a way to accomplish this. Art also was used to make writing more interesting, fun, and to make it theirs: to own it.

Arts also became the way for parents to communicate with their children, to talk, to share, to work together, to get to know each other. Parents also learned about each other's families and the reasons why they were in a two-way immersion program and, for some, in this country. It gave students the opportunity to feel proud of their cultural heritage, their family, and their classmates. It provided all of us with a community where social justice, critical thinking, respect, and consciousness were valued. It provided parents, students and me, the teacher, with a process of critical pedagogy. This process was discovery oriented and used the arts as a way of looking at differences. An arts pedagogy was used as a platform to provide a safe method and space for different groups to express traditions and perspectives, to articulate social injustices, to ultimately dialogue, think, reflect and act. Parents and students empowered themselves through their artistic expression. The arts are "La llave" [the key] that teachers can use to create a classroom where all children and their parents and guardians are accepted, respected, and seen as powerful political beings.

## References

Diaz, E., & Flores, B. (2000). Teacher as sociocultural mediator: Teaching to the potential. In M. de la cruz Reyes & J. Halcon (Eds.), *Best for Latino children: Critical literacy perspectives.* New York: Teachers College Press.

Fisher, D. & McDonald, N. (2002). *Developing arts-loving readers: Top 10 questions teachers are asking about integrated arts education.* Maryland: Scarecrow Press.

Freire, P. (1970). *Pedagogy of the oppressed.* New York: Seabury.

Nieto, S. (1999). *The light in their eyes: Creating multicultural learning communities.* New York: Teachers College Press.

# Getting Back To Basics

## Teaching Our Children What It Means to Be AMERICAN

Lamar Alexander

*Lamar Alexander is a Republican United States Senator from Tennessee. The son of a kindergarten teacher and an elementary school principal, Senator Alexander has been the Governor of Tennessee, United States Secretary of Education, the President of the University of Tennessee, and the Goodman Professor at Harvard's Kennedy School of Government.*

*As Governor, he helped Tennessee become the first state to pay teachers more for teaching well and started Tennessee's Governor's Schools for outstanding teachers and students. Today he sits on the Senate Health, Education, Labor, and Pensions Committee and chairs the Subcommittee on Education and Early Childhood Development.*

In 1988, at a meeting of educators, the President of Notre Dame University, Monk Malloy, asked this question: "What is the rationale for the public school?" There was an unexpected silence around the room until Al Shanker, the president of the American Federation of Teachers, answered, "The public school was created to teach immigrant children the three Rs and what it means to be an American with the hope that they would then go home and teach their parents."

But the last several decades have witnessed a sharp decline in the teaching of American history and civics in our public schools. Unpleasant experiences with McCarthyism in the 1950s, discourage-ment after the Vietnam War, and history books that left out or distorted the history of African-Americans made some skittish about discussing "Americanism." In addition, the end of the Cold War removed a preoccupation with who we were not, making it less important to consider who we are.

According to historian Diane Ravitch, public schools have virtually abandoned their role as the chief Americanizing institution. Instead, they promote "an adversary culture that emphasizes the nation's warts and diminishes its genuine accomplishments. There is no literary canon. There are no common readings, no agreed upon lists of books, poems and stories from which students and parents might be taught a common culture and be reminded of what it means to be an American."

Our national leaders have contributed to this drift toward agnostic Americanism. They celebrate multiculturalism, bilingualism, and diversity when there should be a greater emphasis on a common culture, English language skills, and a sense of unity.

The challenges of the 21st century create a new imperative to put American history and civics back in their rightful place—in our schools—because America's ability to meet these challenges depends on future generations understanding and applying the principles that unite us as a country.

## Our National Inheritance

Looking around the globe, the unifying force within nations is often ethnicity. If you move to Japan, for example, you can't become Japanese. But in America, citizenship isn't based on color, ethnicity, or birthplace. It's based on a few commonly held beliefs. Throughout our history, we have made a point of passing our values and principles along to successive generations, informally, through community and family, and formally, through our public schools.

Thomas Jefferson, in his retirement at Monticello, spent evenings explaining to overnight guests what he had in mind when he helped create what we call America. By the mid-19th century it was just assumed that everybody knew what it meant to be an American. In his letter from the Alamo, Col. William Barrett Travis pleaded for help simply "in the name of liberty, patriotism and everything dear to the American character."

New waves of immigration in the late 19th century brought a record number of new people to our country from other lands—people whose view of what it means to be an American was ill defined. Americans responded by teaching them. In Wisconsin, for example, the Kohler Company actually housed German immigrants together so that they might be "Americanized" during non-working hours.

But the most important Americanizing institution, as Mr. Shanker reminded us, was the new common school. *The McGuffy Reader,* which was used in many classrooms, introduced to millions a distinctly American culture of literature, patriotic speeches and historical references. In the 20th century, President Roosevelt called upon that culture when he rallied the nation to war. He made certain that every GI who charged the beaches of Normandy knew they were defending our "four freedoms."

## America as Ideology

"It has been our fate as a nation," the historian Richard Hofstadter wrote, "not to have ideologies but to be one." This values-based identity has inspired both patriotism and division at home, as well as emulation and hatred abroad. For terrorists, as well as for those who admire America, at issue is the United States itself, not what we do, but who we are.

America's variety and diversity help shape this ideology, but they don't tell the whole story. They are great strengths, certainly, but not the greatest. Iraq is diverse. The Balkans are diverse. America's greatest accomplishment is that we have found a way to take all that variety and diversity and unite ourselves as one country. *E pluribus unum:* out of many, one. That is what makes America truly exceptional.

Yet our public schools are not teaching the history and values that are the American ideology. Instead, students hear a watered-down version of our past, and civics is often dropped from the curriculum entirely. National exam scores reflect these deficiencies: Three-quarters of the nation's 4th, 8th and 12th graders are not proficient in civics, and one-third do not even have basic knowledge.

Until the 1960s, civics education, which teaches the duties of citizenship, was a regular part of the high school curriculum, but today's college graduates probably have less civics knowledge than high school graduates of 50 years ago. So-called reforms in the 1960s and 70s resulted in the widespread elimination of required classes and curriculum in civics education. Today, more than half the states have no requirement for students to take a course—even for one semester—in American government.

As a result, we are raising generations of "civic illiterates."

## A State-Based Solution

As a former Governor, I have seen some of the most creative policymaking happen at the state and local levels. So in thinking about how to tackle our civic illiteracy, I turned to my experiences starting summer residential academies—or governor's schools—in Tennessee.

Tennessee governor's schools focused on a variety of subjects, including the arts, international studies, and writing. The goals were twofold: help thousands of teachers improve their skills through intensive training and inspire outstanding students to learn more about core curriculum subjects. When they returned to their classrooms for the next school year, both teachers and students brought with them a new enthusiasm that motivated their peers. Dollar for dollar, the governor's schools were one of the most effective and popular educational initiatives in our state's history.

Today, there are more than 100 such schools in 28 states. The Governor's Schools of Excellence in Pennsylvania offer 14 different programs. As in Tennessee, students attend academies at eight different colleges to study everything from international relations to health care to teaching.

In 2002, I drafted legislation that would replicate this idea throughout the nation, but with the specific goal of inspiring better teaching and more learning of the key events, persons, and ideas that shaped the institutions and democratic heritage of the United States. The American History and Civics Education Act passed both Houses of Congress and was signed into law by President Bush on December 21, 2004. It establishes Presidential Academies for Teachers of American History and Civics, which would bring educators together for a few weeks in the summer months, and Congressional Academies for Students of American History and Civics, which would do the same for outstanding students.

Our ultimate goal is to establish American history academies in all 50 states. The legislation I proposed creates

a pilot program of these academies, by awarding grants to educational institutions to sponsor the academies. Grants would be subject to rigorous review to determine whether the overall program should continue, expand, or end.

## Testing Results

Encouraging a renewed focus on American history and civics is the first step to solving our national problem of civic illiteracy. The next is to evaluate the curriculum and methods used to teach our children these subjects. Thanks to the *No Child Left Behind Act* and state-based reform efforts, we're finally getting serious about accountability in our public schools. This accountability must extend to the teaching of American history.

Senator Ted Kennedy and I introduced legislation to create a 10-state pilot study of the National Assessment of Educational Progress (NAEP) exam in U.S. history starting in 2006. NAEP tests are commonly referred to as the "nation's report card." The American History Achievement Act would authorize the collection of enough data to attain a state-by-state comparison of 8th and 12th grade student knowledge and understanding of U.S. history (NAEP's governing board already has the authority to do this in reading, math, science, and writing). We'll be able to determine which states are doing a good job of teaching the subject and allow other states to adopt their best practices.

The following examples illustrate how badly this is needed:

On the 4th grade NAEP, students are asked to identify the following passage: "We hold these truths to be self-evident: That all men are created equal; that they are endowed by their Creator with certain unalienable rights; that among these are life, liberty, and the pursuit of happiness...."

Students were given four choices for the source of that passage:

a) Constitution
b) Mayflower Compact
c) Declaration of Independence
d) Article of the Confederation

Only 46 percent of students answered correctly that it came from the Declaration of Independence—our nation's founding document.

The 8th grade test asks students to "Imagine you could use a time machine to visit the past. You have landed in Philadelphia in the summer of 1776. Describe an important event that is happening." Nearly half the students were not able to answer the question correctly that the Declaration of Independence was being signed. They must wonder why the Fourth of July is Independence Day.

## A New Mandate

Since September 11, 2001, the national conversation about what it means to be an American has been different. The terrorists focused their cross-hairs on the creed that unites us as one country, forcing all Americans to remind ourselves of our principles, to examine and define them, and to celebrate them: liberty, equal opportunity, the rule of law, *laissez faire* government, individualism, *e pluribus unum,* the separation of church and state. But in order to rise to the occasion of these challenging times, we need to do more than just identify our principles. We need to apply them to today's most pressing problems. Doing so requires a solid edu-

cation in the history and values that shape our national identity.

Before I was elected to the Senate, I taught a course at Harvard's Kennedy School of Government entitled "The American Character and America's Government." The purpose of the course was to help policymakers, civil servants, and journalists analyze the American creed and character and apply it to public policy problems. We tried to figure out what would be the "American way" to solve a given problem.

We discovered that this was hard work because the principles of our creed are often conflicted. For example, when considering whether the federal government should pay for scholarships that middle- and low-income families might use at any accredited schools—public, private, or parochial—we found the principle of equal opportunity in conflict with separation of church and state.

And we found that there are great disappointments when we try to live up to our greatest dreams: President Kennedy's pledge that we will "pay any price or bear any burden" to advance liberty, or Thomas Jefferson's assertion that "all men are created equal," or the

promise of opportunity inherent in the American Dream itself.

Samuel Huntington, scholar and author of *The Clash of Civilizations,* has written that balancing these conflicts and disappointments is what most of American politics and government is about. Teddy Roosevelt put it this way: "From the very beginning our people have markedly combined practical capacity for affairs with power of devotion to an ideal." Therefore, our ability to solve big public problems—education, health care, the environment, national security—depends on a basic knowledge of the principles and characteristics of that ideal.

Moreover, we deny future generations the personal richness and confidence that develops from knowing where you come from and what you believe. Heroes leap off the pages of our history books, and they become role models. Landmark national events add color and context to everyday life. And courageous acts offer strength and resolve when we face our own personal trials. The human spirit is lifted when it is grounded in the past, and our children grow stronger when they are nurtured in the fertile soil of the American experience.

# Literacy Coaches:
# AN EVOLVING ROLE

*The concept of literacy coaches dates back to the 1920s—*
*but they are increasingly in demand in 21st century schools.*

Barbara Hall

For six years, Stacy Fell-Eisenkraft has been a literacy coach at Intermediate School 131, in the heart of New York City's Chinatown. She and other literacy coaches in schools across the United States are working to increase the instructional capacity of content teachers, so that they can incorporate literacy instruction in science, math, history and other subject areas. With too many of our nation's students unable to read adequately, this new approach is aimed at equipping *all* students with strategic reading skills, so that they will be prepared for college and the demands of today's workplace.

On a morning in late spring, Fell-Eisenkraft meets with Bryce Bernards, a first-year teacher at I.S. 131. Before their thirty or so eighth graders enter the classroom, the two educators trade ideas and approaches to the day's reading and writing lesson.

Recognizing that a literacy coach should be supportive to teachers, Fell-Eisenkraft skillfully and sensitively helps Bernards refine his lesson plans. He is pleased with her suggestions, and, as students stream in, takes his place in front of the classroom. Fell-Eisenkraft remains nearby, assessing how she can be helpful in the classroom. The young teacher begins the class by engaging the students in reading exercises, intertwining the themes of "recipes" and "identities" to capture the students' interest. Like a carefully constructed painting, brushstroke by brushstroke, the morning's lesson cumulatively takes shape, forming a cohesive whole. During the to and fro between teacher and class, Fell-Eisenkraft writes key points on the board—especially helpful, Bernards says later, because of the multilingual nature of his class.

## Literacy Coaching Defined

Literacy coaching is a growing development in the field of American education. Like other educational innovations, from charter schools to enriched after-school programs, literacy coaching is protean, varying from venue to venue and even described by different terms in various regions of the country.

On the West Coast, educators work with an instructional framework known as "reading apprenticeship," while an East Coast source calls literacy coaches "advisor/mentors." These terms have evolved over the years, with early studies on the subject often using the term "reading specialists." Barbara Neufeld and Dana Roper of Education Matters, Inc., a nonprofit educational research organization in Cambridge, Massachusetts, refer to literacy coaches as "change coaches" and "content coaches" in a June 2003 report, *Coaching: A Strategy for Developing Instructional Capacity*. Hundreds of interviews with literacy coaches, principals and other administrators, along with synthesis and analysis, are gathered in the report, which was prepared for The Aspen Institute on Education and The Annenberg Institute for School Reform.

One model for literacy coaching, as it has been introduced into Boston classrooms and elsewhere, is called Collaborative Coaching and Learning (CCL) because a chief characteristic of the model involves active participation by teachers who collaborate with their colleagues. Coaches and teachers are carrying out CCL through practices that involve demonstration and observation, pre-conference meetings, lab-site activities, debriefings and classroom follow-up.

*The Role and Qualifications of the Reading Coach in the United States,* an important statement on literacy coaching, was published in June 2004 by the Delaware-based International Reading Association (IRA). Cathy Roller, director of research and policy for the organization, helped develop the report with the IRA board of directors; the publication is endorsed by an array of organizations representing many learning disciplines. One of the report's recommendations is for higher standards for literacy coaches, notably, a requirement of a master's degree. The report also draws attention to the marked flexibility—not necessarily a positive thing, in the authors' view—in the definition of literacy coaching.

"Some coaches are volunteers with no specific training in reading," the IRA publication notes, "where others are school district employees with master's degrees and reading specialist certification. In some schools, tutors who work with students are also called coaches; these individuals have a variety of levels of training and they may work for companies (both profits and nonprofits) who supply supplemental services to students attending schools labeled 'in need of improvement'...There are no agreed upon definitions or standards for the roles...In the leadership role [coaches] design, monitor and assess reading achievement progress; they provide professional development and coaching for teachers...they are responsible for improving reading achievement; and they may also have staff supervision and evaluation assignments."

Roller suggests that what distinguishes literacy coaching is teacher-to-teacher communications that occur both during class and at other times as well. She also observes that the supply of literacy coaches these days is far exceeded by the demand. Her sentiments are echoed by Susan Frost, president of the Alliance for Excellent Education in Washington, D.C., who offers the idea that literacy coaching is an outgrowth of "high-stakes" testing—schools fail if students fail tests; improvement in test performance depends, in part, on a student's ability to read and comprehend the test material.

> Like other educational innovations, literacy coaching is **protean**, varying from venue to venue and even described by different terms in various regions of the country.

For Carnegie Corporation of New York, a concern with increasing the number of qualified literacy coaches who are currently working in middle and high schools is an element of its overall work in the area of improving adolescent literacy, which grows out of the Corporation's long history of supporting literacy efforts. Currently, grantmaking in this area is focused around its *Advancing Literacy: Reading to Learn* subprogram, which was launched in 2003 after an extensive two-year review that included consultations with the nation's leading practitioners and researchers. Specifically in support of literacy coaching, the foundation has made grants to the University of Michigan to help train coaches through the use of technology and to IRA to begin to review and help set standards for middle and high school literacy coaches.

Improving adolescent literacy is a particularly difficult challenge, since what is expected in academic achievement for middle and high school students has substantially increased, yet the way in which students are taught to read, comprehend and write about subject matter has not kept pace with the demands of schooling. American 15-year-olds, for example, barely attain the standards of international literacy for youngsters their age, and during the past decade, the average reading score of fourth graders has changed little. Readers who struggle during the intermediate elementary years face increasing difficulty throughout middle school and beyond.

"We're losing these youngsters," says Andrés Henríquez, Carnegie Corporation program officer in the Education Division. "In high schools, a third or more of the entering ninth graders will not graduate; the problem may be exacerbated in urban communities, but it is not just an urban problem, it is also a suburban and rural problem. Our nation needs to focus on the issue of adolescent literacy."

"It is clear to teachers and principals alike that one-day professional development workshops are not sufficient," he continues. "Coaches are an answer to a district's need to provide ongoing professional development for teachers in specific content areas. Literacy coaching can help teachers make the content of their subject more comprehensible to students, so they can truly understand the complex information in their textbooks."

## Tracing Developments Through the Literature

Rita Bean, an IRA board member and professor at the University of Pittsburgh, says it's nice to be prescient. With Robert Wilson, Bean wrote a 1981 report for IRA entitled, *Effecting Change in School Reading Programs: The Resource Role.* Among its attributes, the work clearly anticipates the ascent of the literacy coach, though the authors did not use that term. Now, says Bean, "The extent of the phenomenon is surprising to me."

In their work, Bean and Wilson trace the literacy coach movement to the 1930s. They write that, "In looking at the evolution of the reading specialist as a support person, it is interesting to note that the early specialists (1930s) were essentially supervisors who worked with teachers to improve the reading program. It was after World War II, in response to the raging criticism of the schools and their inability to teach children to read, that remedial reading teachers became fixtures in many schools, public and private, elementary through secondary..."

For "reading specialists," the mid-1960s marked a shift from the remedial to the resource role. A 1967 study on the subject ("Standards and Qualifications for Reading Specialists," *Reading Teacher*, March 1967), suggested "the need for certain personal qualifications that would enable the specialist to establish a rapport with teachers, administrators, parents, and students; communicate effectively with teachers by listening carefully before evaluation; and encourage teachers to perform their instructional tasks effectively…"

In their 1981 paper, Bean and Wilson cite the then-surfacing "resource" role as one of "colleagueship" with classroom teachers, parents, administrators and other resource workers, noting, "…the reading specialist and the teacher must work as 'associates and equals' bound together by a common purpose, the improvement of students' learning…"

*The Literacy Coach: A Key to Improving Teaching and Learning in Secondary Schools,* written by Elizabeth G. Sturtevant, also for the Alliance for Excellent Education, calls literacy coaches "key players in the change process" aimed at improving adolescent literacy. The report (November 2003) addresses the need to build bridges between literacy coaches and the middle and high school levels, as well as tie into teacher training in college. When asked about the greatest challenges facing literacy coaches, however, Sturtevant, associate professor and co-coordinator of the literacy program in the graduate school of education at George Mason University, cites "economic issues." While reading initiatives for younger children receive ample resources, teens in the middle and high school years continue to need literacy support, she points out, but the money to pay for it often is not available.

Sturtevant gives her own description of the history of coaching. "As long ago as the 1920s," she suggests, "reading educators advocated that secondary content teachers teach students to comprehend their content texts ["An Historical Exploration of Content Area Reading Instruction," *Reading Research Quarterly*, 1983, pp 419-38]. Educators of that time found that many children had difficulty transitioning from the children's stories that were used in the early grades to more difficult content area textbooks in secondary schools." In a word, there was a disconnect.

## Two Reformers Reflect

John Goodlad and Theodore Sizer are prominent education reformers with an active interest in literacy coaching.

Goodlad, president of the Institute for Educational Inquiry and a founder of the Center for Educational Renewal at the University of Washington, wrote the classic, *A Place Called School: Prospects for the Future* (McGraw-Hill, 1984, 2004). His latest book is *Romances With Schools: A Life of Education* (McGraw-Hill, 2004).

Goodlad says that from his vantage point, "The coaching idea is not new at all. My view of it is a cultural one. The term dates back to the multi-language problem; I'd

time it in with the growth of the Hispanic population, forty or fifty years ago. Simultaneously," he continues, "there were people making their concerns known at the university level. They had the sense that you didn't get anywhere if you couldn't read. There was a call for vocabulary to understand social studies, science and so on."

Math dominated the coaching landscape, he recalls. "That's my first memory of the use of the term 'coaching.' Today, though, literacy coaching has become a cottage industry." He goes on to suggest that there should be greater evaluation of the field. "We need long-term studies of literacy coaching—it's difficult to understand its value without ongoing studies and assessment. It's a tough question because we don't know the impact of shifting heavily to technology and what the computer will do to literacy in the long run. I worry some about this. The contrast between computer-based literacy and print-based literacy provokes," he says, "a layered conversation." Adding a cogent comment, he says that he believes "the understanding of democracy involves the written word."

Sizer, too, has a new book: *Keeping School: Letters to Families from Principals of Two Small Schools* (Beacon Press, 2004) written with Deborah Meier and Nancy Faust Sizer. Currently visiting professor of education at the Harvard Graduate School of Education, Sizer is also the chairman of the Oakland, California-based Coalition of Essential Schools (CES), which "provides national networking and professional development opportunities, conducts research, and advocates for public policies" that are aimed at developing "equitable, intellectually vibrant, personalized schools."

> "We don't know the impact of shifting heavily to **technology** and what the computer will do to **literacy** in the long run." —John Goodlad

Infused with Sizer's ideas about educational reform, CES is committed to the idea of literacy coaching. Sizer likens a literacy coach to the artist/teacher. "You still do your own art while you're teaching," he says. "You're still influenced by current movements in the art world."

What Sizer says worries him is coaches who end up not actually teaching—departing from what he calls the practice of "school-keeping." "My concern," he says, "is that coaching carries a great deal of ideological freight. Moreover," he adds, "if coaches are just thrust upon teachers, there will be resentment." But there are directions to follow, Sizer suggests. For example, "It's important," he says, "to build a network of people who are very close to the action of schools, who are trained to work with others." Overall, Sizer is optimistic about the growing practice of literacy coaching. "It's one of the pieces of education reform most likely to be sustained," he says.

## Frictions and Mini-Epiphanies

While the practice of literacy coaching continues to make inroads in schools across the nation, even its most dedicated advocates acknowledge that it can have drawbacks. In studying literacy coaching at the Boston public schools, for instance, educators candidly caution that there are sometimes turf battles between coaches and teachers—and content teachers, who are deeply invested in the practice of imparting knowledge about a particular subject area, do not always welcome the idea of having to teach literacy and comprehension at the same time. Their feeling, often, is that by the time kids reach the middle grades, their elementary schools should have already taught them to read and understand the information in their textbooks. With the added pressure of having to ensure that students pass required tests—so that not only can the student continue his or her educational career but also so that the school itself doesn't suffer the stigma of being a "failing school"—literacy is not always the first subject on a middle or high school teacher's agenda.

Still, Boston and other systems have also had their "mini-epiphanies." The term is used by Lisa Gonsalves, author of a 2003 University of Massachusetts study of literacy coaching in Boston's public schools. But, as Gonsalves and others note, Boston's successes can, in large measure, be chalked up to a dedicated and capable team. Cathleen Kral, the instructional leader for literacy K-12 in the Boston public schools and coaching head there, has worked closely with individuals such as Ellen Guiney, executive director of the Boston Plan for Excellence in the Public Schools Foundation, and Barbara Neufeld to incorporate the literacy concept in the city's middle and high schools. (The Boston Plan for Excellence also partners with the Boston public schools in *Schools for a New Society*, a Carnegie Corporation initiative being carried out in seven urban communities that focuses on reform of school district policies and practices to help reshape teaching and learning in high schools; key elements include creating small learning communities and a city-wide network of excellent schools that can provide high-quality education for all students.)

The challenges of developing a literacy coaching program have been many, says Guiney, "With coaching in the picture, teachers teach in entirely different ways than they used to… so one key is that we've got to find just the right teachers to participate." Some 80 percent of Boston's literacy coaches are former teachers, Guiney reports.

She has a number of recommendations for schools that want to begin inculcating literacy coaching into their classroom. "I would start small," she counsels. "But don't wait too long to scale up." She also lists these points to focus on: invest in the development of professional coaches, work closely with school organizers, ensure that school leaders buy in, get the incentives right for the coach and carve out time for the coach and teacher to work together.

In describing workshops for Boston's teachers, Kral notes that the over-arching goal is to "deepen a child's thinking." Coach/teachers begin at the "pre-conference stage," she explains and continue through debriefing. "They should leave with something to do, with a kind of assignment," Kral adds.

Another developing story is taking place in rural Stafford County, Virginia. Nancy Guth, who has been the language arts supervisor for the county's public schools for the past 13 years, recently received good news: school officials had endorsed funding for her literacy coaching program, including coaches at the secondary level. "It's horrible to live on a year-by-year basis, so this is a great relief," she says. She credits the ultimate strength of her program to a team approach, involving parents, administrators and teachers. "It was with the support of the superintendent and the superintendent for instruction that we've made progress. They said, 'Okay, show us how it works,' and we did. But once we did, they really paid attention."

Other notable initiatives include a "Reading and Writing Studio" course in Denver that asks middle and high school students reading below grade level to read a million words a year. The students' teachers are aided by literacy coaches who, among their duties, serve as liaisons to other subject teachers.

The Southern California Comprehensive Assistance Center of the Los Angeles County Office of Education sponsors a "Reading Success Network" that involves identifying reading coaches in all schools and school sites joining the network; the coaches are then provided with training, seminars and supports. Ruth Schoenbach and Cynthia Greenleaf, co-directors of the Strategic Literacy Initiative (SLI) of WestEd, a nonprofit educational organization headquartered in San Francisco, work with the network. Both say they're dedicated to promoting "high rigor, high literacy, not just basic literacy." Through the network program, they explore "how teachers think of their own lives as readers." One area they work on is trouble-shooting. "Say you have a *Scientific American* article," says Schoenbach. "We try to help our teachers determine where they themselves might have gotten stuck, what they didn't understand. In that conversation—working out meaning—you have teachers saying, 'Wow, there's something here that I do understand now, and here's why.' In that way, you see how different people make sense of things in terms of reading." Essentially, says Schoenbach, what they're looking for are the different ways to really dig into a text and then weave those methods into teaching—a concern that underpins almost every effort to give students the literacy skills they need to understand what they read, and help their teachers find ways to guide students to meet that goal.

*Every Child a Graduate: A Framework for an Excellent Education for All Middle and High School Students*, written by Scott Joftus, policy director of the Alliance for Excellent Education, is a relatively recent report (September 2002) that provides a snapshot of the practice of literacy coaching in California's Long Beach Unified School District: "Each coach specializes in a specific subject—math, science, English, history—and works four days a week to mentor new teachers, model instruction methods and help select and use resources. In addition to these content coaches, the school district provides a variety of first-year teacher coaches who help inexperienced teachers learn classroom management, essential elements of effective instruction and other important skills." In his report, Joftus also provides insight into the reaction of a young teacher in a Long Beach school taking full advantage of literacy coaching as a collaborative tool: "First-year teacher Jason Marshall's enthusiasm suggests the positive impact the coaches have on the school: 'I go home smiling every day,' Marshall said. 'I don't feel frustrated. Just yesterday we spent a few hours picking (our history coach's) brain and working with her to create lesson plans for the next six weeks. We've got clear ideas about how to tackle each lesson we're going to be doing. I don't feel burdened. I feel excited about coming to school.'"

## Pitfalls and Sustainability

While support for literacy coaching is strong on many fronts—educators increasingly favor the practice, parents see its results—there are also pitfalls to be considered, such as the shifting definitions of coaching and the problem of sliding standards. The term "coach" can refer to volunteers, paraprofessionals or individuals holding advanced degrees.

Effective coaching also depends on school administrators' full understanding and approval. And there is the quandary presented by school administrators who, beset by budget woes, redirect money meant for coaches into their coffers for content teachers. Yet some administrators recognize the valuable role of coaches.

"Although states have drastically reduced education budgets and are in the worst financial shape in decades, scores of literacy coaches are being hired in school districts throughout the country," Carnegie Corporation's Henríquez says. "This may be happening, in part, because the No Child Left Behind Act requires school districts to provide data on students' reading and math scores for third to eighth graders. And in high schools, every day 3,000 students drop out. Of course, the districts and the teachers feel pressure for their upper elementary and middle schools to be successful, and high schools want to ensure that young people stay engaged in school. Literacy coaching may be a way to help improve student literacy and reduce high dropout rates."

Before embarking on a coaching program, Neufeld and Roper suggest that educators and school administrators ask themselves the following questions:

• What are our professional development goals and what do we want to accomplish with our overall professional development programs?

• What would we gain from having coaching as part of our repertoire of teacher/principal learning opportunities?

• What would coaches do to help us achieve our instructional goals?

• Are there other approaches to achieving our goals, and might they be more appropriate for us?

• What else, in addition to coaching, would we have to support to help us reach our instructional goals?

Expectations, many experts suggest, must be reasonable. Concurrently, there must be adequate support for coaches to meet their potential as contributors to the learning process. But the most critical issue—one on which virtually all stakeholders agree—is that the practice of literacy coaching will provide few long-term benefits if there isn't secure, ongoing funding available to ensure that coaching has staying power on the educational agenda.

Two pieces of legislation have been proposed that address the need for such funding. The PASS Act calls for funding for literacy coaches as well as academic counselors and resources. The Graduation for All Act is co-sponsored by Congresswoman Susan Davis (D-CA) and Congressman Rubén Hinojosa (D-TX), who is Chairman of the Congressional Hispanic Caucus Education Task Force. The Act could provide $1 billion in federal funding for schools to place literacy coaches in high schools and implement individualized graduation plans for students most at risk of dropping out of high school. Graduation for All is targeted at schools with the lowest graduation rates and allocates funding for at least one literacy coach for every high-needs middle and high school. Coaches would help teachers incorporate research-based reading and writing instruction or English-as-a-Second-Language instruction into teaching practices for core academic subjects.

> The practice of literacy coaching will provide few **long-term** benefits if there isn't secure, ongoing funding available to ensure that coaching has **staying** power on the educational agenda.

In Florida, the Middle Grades Reform Act, which went into effect in May 2004, funds reading coaches for 240 middle schools. Although Governor Jeb Bush (R) announced grants of $16.7 million to support this effort, many policymakers will be paying close attention to this initiative in the hope that it will provide some guidance to other districts and states around the country.

## Meanwhile, Back in Chinatown...

At Intermediate School 131 in New York City's Chinatown, on a spring day towards the end of the school term,

Bryce Bernards familiarizes his students with the format of recipes; features such as measurements, cooking instructions, ingredients, number of servings and required utensils are discussed. The children, quiet, intent, talk about how members of their families use recipes at homes.

Bernards then asks the children to superimpose their life stories onto the recipe framework. (What he's aiming for, in his words, is to teach a lesson in "sustained metaphor, the genre of recipes.") He offers details of his own background to get the youngsters started. He says his life has consisted of "One-fourth cup of overbearing, demanding parents. An uncle who didn't want me to become a teacher. One can of Wentworth Avenue sauce." (He explains that's the address where he grew up.) "A bag of wild friends who lived on my block and played street games. Plus two World Series championships tickets for the Minnesota Twins, a big part of my childhood," he informs the class.

The children respond in kind. One boy, for instance, offers the following: "One cup of my mother who watches out and keeps an eye on me when I get in trouble. Five packages of curiosity because I want to know everything. One cup of over-reacting parents."

"Our identities are pretty complex," Bernards observes.

The students then compose their recipes in more depth. During the class, literacy coach Stacy Fell-Eisenkraft circulates among the students, a reassuring presence for the children and for Bernards. The coach, who is also earning a doctorate from Teachers College, Columbia University, not only works closely with teachers in her New York City middle school, but also assumes tasks ranging from ordering books to running after-school book clubs for the faculty. Fell-Eisenkraft may also help Bernards adjust to his new profession. As a young teacher, he and others like him across the country are vulnerable to the demands of a new job and drop out at higher rates than their more established colleagues; a University of Pennsylvania study indicated that as many as 50 percent of teachers leave the profession within five years. Literacy coaches can provide a support system that will help these younger faculty members cope with the challenges of their profession.

Bernards agrees that Fell-Eisenkraft is indispensable to his work. "She keeps me focused on what's important," he says. "For example, I may come in with a lesson that tries to incorporate three different skills, and she will help me narrow it down, which leads to more effective teaching." He then goes on to talk about how he and Fell-Eisenkraft designed a lesson to accommodate the multiple-lan-

guages—Chinese, Spanish and English—spoken by the children in his class. "You saw Stacy writing on the board behind me," he says. "That always helps in terms of the students being able to visualize the words."

One advantage Bernards and Fell-Eisenkraft have in carrying out their teaching partnership is the support of those who run the school. "Our administrators are completely behind us," Fell-Eisenkraft reports. "They realize, as I do, that the overall level of instruction is raised because of literacy coaching and that teachers and students really benefit."

Her words are music to the ears of Jane Lehrach, the school's principal, who often attends her school's literacy coaching sessions. The veteran educator is justifiably proud of her school. "It's a safe and peaceful place," she says, adding that "respect" is the watchword at I.S. 131. She goes on to say that "education is a journey of growing, and literacy coaching, done right, is a manifestation of that philosophy."

As she speaks, one of Bernards and Fell-Eisenkraft's eighth graders passes on his way to his classroom seat. Lehrach lets her comments waft off in the air as another idea intervenes. "I like to say that every child has treasures. And what are your treasures?" she asks the boy.

"Books!" he exclaims, providing the answer Lehrach hoped to elicit. Although the youngster has come to love books, literacy coaches at I.S. 131 and other schools across the country know they must go beyond teaching a love of reading literature and help students develop reading strategies that will allow them to comprehend the complex information presented in their textbooks.

Summing up how literacy strategies such as coaching should be inculcated into teaching and learning, Sturtevant writes in her report, "Schools and teachers have the ability to base their instructional and curricular decisions on years of research related to the types of learning environments and day-to-day teaching strategies that best support students' growth in reading, writing, and critical thinking. Schools and teachers can make a real difference in the lives of the adolescents with whom they work. The current challenge is to make this goal a reality in middle and high schools throughout the United States."

*Barbara Hall has written about education since she covered local school board meetings for a New England weekly newspaper some 25 years ago. Between then and now, she's written on learning for publications including* The New York Times, Christian Science Monitor, The Washington Post, The Boston Globe, *and* The Philadelphia Inquirer. *She also writes for children in the award-winning* AppleSeeds *magazine and is currently writing and illustrating a children's book.*

# Changing the Image of Teachers Through Cases

## Patricia Goldblatt

Schoolmarm. One-room class. Dedicated. Lone practitioner. These words conjure up the image of the pioneer teacher. She lives at the edges of society, tirelessly working long hours with little communication with parents or community. Almost a martyr in the service of sacrificing herself for her students, this teacher embodies Benjamin Franklin's adages of "Waste not, want not," or "A penny saved is a penny earned." In unending days of devotion she instills values and ethics as well as imparting information. This lonely and lone ranger persists in the fantasies of the public as what a teacher should look like: selfless, committed, and inspirational.

Over time, the media have produced television series and films that have extended and altered the aforementioned portrayal. The 1970s television show *Welcome Back, Kotter* introduced high school teacher Gabe Kotter, always off balance, seemingly confused and befuddled at the antics of Vinnie Barbarino and Adam Horshack, just two members of his incorrigible "Sweathog" class. With few inroads made into purveying models of proper behavior or acceptable citizenship, Mr. Kotter appeared the outcast himself. Rarely reaching out to colleagues, but often reprimanded by a frustrated administration, Mr. Kotter received some support from his understanding wife at the end of a long and troubling day. Almost 30 years later, at the turn of the twenty-first century, studies continue to show that the neophyte teacher suffers from isolation and lack of support from the administration (Fullan & Hargreaves, 1998; Lortie, 1975).

In the 1990s the title character from the film *Mr. Holland's Opus* reinforced the impression that hardworking teachers, whether new to the profession or well seasoned, also suffer alone. Mr. Holland's dreams are put on hold for too long; his reward for hard work and dedicated service is dismissal, for reductions in school funding have necessitated cutbacks in the arts. His once helpful and understanding principal, long retired, has been replaced by a number cruncher, indicating that old values of aesthetics, mastery of subject, commitment to student learning, and hard work are dead, out of sync with a new society. No one really cares that Mr. Holland has a difficult life financially and emotionally. Ironically, he cannot even share his passion for music with his son, who is deaf. *Mr. Holland's Opus*

is sentimental, offering nostalgia in the lie that teachers must die at their desks, fortified by having educated others. Mr. Holland's final tribute of having a piece of his unpublished music performed before he loses his teaching position only reinforces this depiction of the teacher's stoicism and self-sacrifice. States Jeff Doran in *Daily Meaning: Counternarratives of Teachers' Work,* "All my school life I've read fake stories about teaching and seen fake TV shows about teaching and I've known they're fake" (Neilsen, 1999, 17). Yet Jessica Harbour of *Pop Matters: Television* confirms that writers like Judith Shulevitz (at *Slate*) and Lisa Schmeiser (at *teevee.org*) continue to embrace these stereotypes, as do ordinary viewers (2003). Harbour quotes a teacher who obviously empathizes with the portrayal of her fellow professionals on the TV series *Boston Public:* "It's too heartbreaking to give so much and be respected so little."

In the twenty-first century *Boston Public* represents the most recent attempt to humanize and modernize the former myth of the heroic and long-suffering teacher; it offers a slick peek into the personal lives of teachers and students that nonetheless leaves the myth in place as a tarnished, perhaps unattainable ideal. Its portrayal of students derives from works like *Blackboard Jungle* and *Welcome Back, Kotter.*

Like Mr. Kotter's kids, students at *Boston Public*'s Winslow High are far from angels. They lie and cheat, take drugs, mock their teachers, and videotape them in the lounge and classroom participating in adulterous acts. Some pupils even announce their crushes and stalk teachers to their homes. Educators, however, fare no better. Mr. Lipschitz, a noted racist, fathers an illegitimate son after engaging in a wild, but apparently tender, night of love before he goes off to war. Harry, a history teacher, fires a gun in class to attract his students' attention. Although he agonizes, sneers, and lectures on suicide and morality, he counsels runaways, harbors fugitives from the law in his own apartment, and reads the riot act to abusive parents. Tight-lipped Scott Gruber, the vice principal, hides in his office, conducting invisible musicians in order to forget the horrors of the halls. A strange, reclusive man, he copes by withdrawing or admonishing miscreants in sepulchral tones and patronizing language better suited to communication with students from an earlier century. Ronni, a former lawyer who has chosen teaching to give her life meaning, engages in sexual relations with a teacher several years her junior in the student lounge, a place raided for gambling and illicit student trysts. These teachers are hardly models of admirable behavior; none of the depictions truly honors the complexity of teaching or the demands made and required of teachers. If earlier portrayals glamorized teachers for sainthood, these stereotypes demonize teachers along with their students as malcontents, social rejects, and selfish misfits searching for personal fulfillment.

. . .

Thankfully, a fresh, new image of the teacher has recently emerged. Conveyed not in the media but in the standards of the profession, the descriptors of the standards of practice extend the picture of a reflective practitioner, a collaborative, concerned member of a professional learning team and community. The standards of practice, divided into relevant domains or areas of teaching expertise, convey the disposition, attitudes, skills, and behaviors of teachers by answering the question, "What does it mean to be a teacher?" No longer is the educator portrayed hovering at the margins of society, closing her doors, solo on the prairie, barricaded and grim. Neither is she a victim or gunslinger in the urban jungle of school land. And unlike Mr. Kotter or Mr. Holland, this reconstituted practitioner draws support from her colleagues, establishing camaraderie at a variety of levels from peer to principal, and reaches out to the community and parents. Indeed, she plays a visible role in promoting and fostering leadership even beyond the classroom doors.

Most importantly, the real-life teacher speaks out and shares her teaching stories, engaging others in discussion in an attempt to overcome isolation and understand more deeply the work she does. Judith Shulman quotes Jenlink and Kinnucan-Welsch as saying,

> Stories give meaningful form to experiences educators have already lived through and enable others to share and learn from their experience (706) [as] catalysts for pedagogical conversations among members of school communities. (Shulman, 1992, xv)

Stories are records of lived experience. Whether used as parables, fairy stories, myths from the ancient Greeks, or instructions from parents to prepare children to cope in society, stories present models of normative behavior because people remember and pass on their knowledge through stories (Bruner, 1986). By crafting stories into cases, teachers have found an avenue of expression for their lived experiences at school, in contrast to mass media portrayals of their work.

Judith Shulman, director at WestEd laboratories in California, has been involved for many years in using cases as a way to connect the overarching principles of practice to specific dilemmas described in teacher-written stories. Drawn from the verisimilitude of everyday life and retold in authentic voices, cases present an opportunity for exploring the rich multilayered realm of teachers' work, a world that encompasses conflicts from administrative fracases to the best way of handling the needs of special education students. Because not all details can

be fully developed in a few short pages, some facts are intentionally vague so that openings, gaps, or omissions invite teachers to insert themselves and make connections between their own practice and the one depicted on the pages before them. Endings, particularly, are ambiguous so that teachers can critique or speculate on alternative solutions to the conflicts presented. This form of casework invites teachers to become involved in their own professional development.

Often teachers will gather to write or discuss cases. Educators in case discussion posit new strategies for difficult situations, suggesting informed decisions and examining long- and short-term consequences for each recommendation. Rather than lone practitioners struggling with on-the-spot solutions, these involved and concerned teachers have the leisure of time outside their classrooms to pose reflective questions and to make sense of their own practice by discussing another's. Participants make themselves vulnerable, revealing and recalling the mistakes or oversights in their own professional lives in order to offer revelations that will facilitate a colleague's improved practice. Analyzing a colleague's case stories strengthens the relationships among members of groups of learners and creates tightly bound communities (Jenlink & Kinnucan-Welsch, 2001). Those who write or those who discuss cases never shed their identities as teachers because they understand their stories and their reflections are, indeed, teaching tools. Beyond educating students, teachers are educating one another.

During the process of case discussion, teachers, by referring back to the standards of practice, realize that theory—that is, generalized principles—are bound to practice. Cases are a bridge that causes teachers to see the connections between specific, concrete details and generalized teaching principles that subsume effective practice. Thus, the concepts and the language of standards of practice extend common threads of the teaching profession as a framework for diagnosing and remediating as well as for identifying areas to celebrate in the classroom. By discussing, evaluating, or vicariously experiencing another's practice through authentic stories, teachers develop an awareness that teaching stories exemplify a larger pattern and that cases are a case "of" something (Shulman, 1987), be it classroom management, professional knowledge, or insights into student development, for each dilemma resonates with a principle that changes according to the contextual elements of a particular educational setting.

As a platform for discussion, cases prompt the participation of teachers knowledgeable about the elements described. With a shared understanding of language and facts, there is no stifling conversation. Rather, teachers are eager to trade insights, rely on national standards or standards of practice that underpin classroom conflicts, and comment on the elements that their peers have caught in their descriptions of familiar tensions in education climes. If the purpose of case analysis is to prepare teachers for facing unexpected classroom scenarios and contemplating change in practice, case discussion does, in fact, fulfill that function of professional development in terms of transformation: a way to build new information onto established ways of coping; a way to think about practice; and a way to become cognizant that there are areas of gray, no single right or wrong answer in responding to an educational dilemma:

People make these fundamental transitions by having *many* opportunities to be exposed to the ideas, to argue them in to their normative belief systems, to practice these behaviors that go with these values, to observe others practicing these behaviors, and most importantly, to be successful at practicing in the presence of others. . .The most powerful incentives reside in the face to face relationships among people in the organization, not in external systems. (Elmore, 2000, 31)

Similarly, Hall and Hord (1987) describe how new strategies are implemented into practice. First, there must be an awareness of something new. Next, the learner gathers information, aware that he or she must act on that information. The teacher is prompted to reflect on personal practice by asking, "How will this knowledge affect me?" Once engaged, the teacher postulates how new materials or information can actually be used. Again, the reflective practitioner speculates on the impact on student learning, even planning how to achieve maximum impact. What emerges is the notion that teachers collaborate and work together in order to improve practice and take control of their own professional growth. They are reflective and responsive, eager to contemplate the outcomes of new knowledge personally and professionally.

Cases instigate a catalyst for professional development. In case discussion, teachers are accepted as scholars of their own practice, not receiving advice from experts who only talk about or theorize about practice, but wrestling with and relying on themselves as informed, capable, and competent to provide direction to colleagues. Thus, they are empowered. Respecting teachers for their work experiences and insights into practice provides scaffolding for colleagues to construct new strategies or ways of thinking about old situations:

Simply asking practitioners to reflect on the stories they already tell can provide a natural bridge to a serious inquiry about the deepest layers of value and belief that undergird the decisions they make. . .Involved in dialectics and dialogues, teachers are the authentic professional developers of their own practices, for dialogue is conducive to collective inquiry and learning that sustains the community. (Jenlink & Kinnucan-Welsch, 2001, 717)

The process of case discussion draws on one's peers' experiences. It reflects a flexibility and openness to question, a willingness to grow and challenge the established ways of being professional.

In the United States, the National Board of Professional Teacher Standards (NBPTS) has developed standards and assessment procedures in 30 subject matter disciplines organized around five major propositions. In one of the five domains, entitled "Teachers are members of learning communities," the standards suggest that teachers can develop expertise when they work collaboratively with colleagues on instructional policy, curriculum, and staff development: They are knowledgeable about specialized school and community resources that can be engaged for their students' benefit, and they are skilled at em-

ploying such resources as needed. Accomplished teachers find ways to work collaboratively and creatively (NBPTS, 1993).

At the Ontario College of Teachers in Toronto, Canada, the Standards of Practice and Education Unit has utilized the case inquiry method for two purposes: (1) to encourage awareness and deepen understanding of standards of the profession and (2) to create networks of communication that promote collaborative learning communities among practitioners across the province, thus forming cultures of inquiry. Aware of physical distances and feelings of isolation that plague teachers, the College has brought together educators so that a teacher from Moosonee can understand that teachers in Windsor or Sault Ste. Marie or Toronto all share similar problems. Coming together physically mirrors the coming together of minds that substantiates learning communities of inquiry, anxious to probe into problems teachers face every day at work. The words of those educators from Ontario speak to the effectiveness of using cases:

- *This helped me feel that I don't have to feel incomplete in this field...The things that I am doing are great. I have a role in teacher leadership in my school to help others grow.*

- *This space has improved my knowledge and has made me a better teacher, which, of course, can only impact on my students positively.*

- *Teachers have always been reflective practitioners, but maybe we have lacked focus...the standards and the case studies have given us focus where we can look at our teaching to see how it impacts on student learning...not just an assessment test but talk about the soul, aspirations and dreams and opportunities.*

- *For me, it's the idea of community...coming here to be part of a community that is supportive, respecting, trustful and honest. I can take that back to the seven-year-olds that I teach.*

Some critics say schools have not changed over time: that students and teachers will always be the same, since the job of a teacher is to teach and that of a student is to learn. However, how we teach and how we affect student learning has changed. By promoting and supporting cultures of inquiry through cases by, for, and about teachers, we move from the passive to the active mode. We embrace change, excitement, and stimulation in charting our own paths, modeling our delight in learning for our students. Far from the lone and lonely teacher who squinted into the distance, ensuring that her students made it safely home, the new teacher sits at the table, one of the smiling, gesticulating stakeholders: colleague, learner, parent, community member, teacher, student.

# REFERENCES

Bruner, J. (1986). *Actual minds, possible worlds.* Cambridge, Mass.: Harvard University Press.

Elmore, R. (2000). *Building a new structure for school leadership.* Washington, DC: The Albert Shanker Institute.

Fullan, M. and Hargreaves, A. (1998). *What's worth fighting for out there.* New York: Teachers College Press.

Hall, G. E. and Hord, S. M. (1987). *Change in schools: facilitating the process.* Albany: State Univ. of New York Press.

Harbour, J. (2003). Review of *Boston Public. Popmatters: television.* http://popmatters.com/tv/reviews/b/bostonpublic.html

Jenlink, P. M. and Kinnucan-Welsch, K. (2001). Case stories of facilitating professional development. *Teaching and Teacher Education,* 17: 705-724.

Lortie, D. (1975). *School teacher: A sociological study.* Chicago: University of Chicago Press.

National Board of Professional Teacher Standards (NBPTS). (1993). *Five core propositions.* Arlington, VA: Author.

Neilsen, A. (Ed.). (1999). *Daily Meaning: Counternarratives of Teachers' Work.* Mill Bay, British Columbia: Bendall Books.

Shulman, J. (Ed.). (1992). *Case methodology in teacher education.* New York: Teachers College Press.

Shulman, L. (1987). Those who understand: Knowledge growth in teaching. *Educational Researcher,* 15(4): 4-14.

***Patricia Goldblatt*** *is a program officer at the College of Teachers in Toronto. She is co-editor of a recently published volume of case studies with commentary from Sage Publications,* Cases for Teacher Development: Preparing for the Classroom.

# ISSUES IN A MULTICULTURAL CURRICULUM PROJECT

IRMA M. OLMEDO

*University of Illinois–Chicago*

*The changing demographics of America's population increases the need for educators to develop multicultural curricula for the nation's schools. This article describes the efforts of a group of teachers to learn about the funds of knowledge of Mexican students by doing field research in a state in Mexico with one of the largest migrations to Chicago. The article discusses their successes and the challenges of developing curricula that go beyond the "heroes-and-holidays" approach to ethnic cultures and that consider issues such as transnationalism, illegal immigration, and racism. It contextualizes these issues in the broader context of multicultural education.*

**Headlines in a front-page article** in the *Chicago Tribune* declared, "City population bounces back. Total at 2.89 million as influx of Hispanics ends long decline" (March 14, 2001, p. 1). The headlines appeared to say that this was cause for celebration, the fact that the city's population decline that had begun in the 1950s had finally been reversed. Several other articles in the newspaper addressed the changing demographics of the Chicago metropolitan area in the 2000 census, with the Hispanic population reaching 1.4 million or 26% of the population. Most demographers and census authorities agree that the census figures for Hispanics, especially those of Mexican background, are probably an undercount (Johnson, 2003).

The impact of these demographic changes is always felt most powerfully in the schools. In the city of Chicago, the third largest school district in the country, Latino students constitute 36.4% of the total student population (Chicago Public Schools, 2003). Mexicans, who constitute the largest percentage of Latinos in Chicago, are concentrated in identifiable areas of the city and in particular neighborhoods of some surrounding communities as well. Because the racial and ethnic segregation in many parts of the city is quite extreme, it is not unusual for many elementary schools to be composed of more than 90% of students of Mexican background. As one prospective teacher remarked while doing her practice teaching in a school in one of those neighborhoods, "Teaching there is like teaching in Mexico." If demographics were to serve as a guide for curriculum development, these schools should have very strong bilingual and multicultural curricula, with elements of the culture of Mexicans constituting a significant orientation to the curriculum.

The reality of these demographic changes raises challenges for educators and policy makers as they decide on the best ways to educate this student population. Although the 2000 census figures are quite dramatic for the area, many Chicago schools have been educating sizeable numbers of Latino students for decades. Some have worked creatively in partnership with area universities to make adjustments in their programs so that the curriculum reflects the cultural reality of their student populations. However, often these efforts at multicultural education rarely go beyond the "heroes-and-holidays" approach to culture, the tendency to view culture as static, to highlight the colorful and surface aspects, and to ignore controversy.

This article discusses the efforts of a group of educators to go beyond this "tourist" approach to culture and develop multicultural curricula in schools with a large percentage of Mexican students, many of whom are immigrants. The article is based on the experiences of a group of Chicago city teachers who participated in a Fulbright-sponsored research/study project on the history and cultures of western Mexico, the geographic area of heaviest migration to the Chicago area and from which most of their Mexican students come. A primary objective of the project was to have teachers explore the cultural diversity of Mexico to move beyond the text-book interpretations presented to their students, interpretations that traditionally consisted primarily of portrayals of the Aztec and Mayan civilizations. These traditional portrayals, though historically significant, also ignore the cultures of the regions from which the Mexican families of their students come, as well as the contemporary reality of these families.

A second objective of the project was to have teachers in schools with a large concentration of Mexican background students understand these students as members of a broader transnational community and to consider the educational implications of that sociopolitical reality. Some teachers were aware that their Mexican origin students were living in both societies simultaneously, while their families returned regularly to their hometowns in Mexico. The teachers were interested in acquiring a better understanding of the implications of that reality, and the meaning for the total education of those children. The teachers carried out independent field based research on some aspect of western Mexico with the goals of developing multicultural curricula for their schools and building on the transnational experiences of their Mexican-descent students.

There is a discontinuity between theory development in the multicultural curricula field and its translation into practice at the school and classroom levels (Gay, 1995). Although many educators voice support for multicultural education and many schools claim that their curriculum is sensitive to the cultures of their student populations, consensus is lacking as to what exactly is meant by these claims. The efforts of these teachers to examine their curriculum and instructional approaches need to be situated in the broader context of multicultural curriculum development, migration, transnational communities, and recent ethnographic studies of Mexicans in the United States.

## PERSPECTIVES ON MULTICULTURAL EDUCATION

The literature and research on multicultural education is quite extensive and diverse in terms of the models proposed, critiques of American society and schooling, and the arguments made in support of multicultural education (Banks, 1997; Banks & Banks, 1995; Grant, 1999; Heath, 1983; Kincheloe & Steinberg, 1997; Lee, Menkart, & Okazawa-Rey, 1998; May, 1999; Ogbu, 1992; Ovando & McLaren, 2000; Sleeter, 1991; Sleeter & Grant, 2003). This literature suggests that teachers need to acknowledge the diversity of America's population and to find ways to affirm this diversity in the development of curriculum and implementation of instruction. The multicultural curriculum models highlight the need for teachers to broaden their understanding of the cultures of their students so that the concepts that children are exposed to are authentic portrayals of the characteristics of the populations being studied. In addition, the literature highlights the importance of integrating knowledge of students' culture into all the content areas, rather than as isolated information for special holidays and occasions.

Banks' (1997) model for the integration of ethnic content into the curriculum, which he categorized into four levels as the contributions, additive, transformative, and social action approaches, provides a framework for examining how multicultural education can be theorized and implemented. The first two levels of the model, the contributions and additive approaches, are the levels that have sometimes been characterized as the heroes-and-holidays approaches to ethnic cultures. Banks saw these approaches as superficial because they merely involve adding themes and activities to a curriculum, sometimes in an isolated way, and do not question the basic assumptions of traditional Eurocentric school curricula. Moreover, these two approaches ignore the value of having learners question the content and concepts that are being taught. It is only in the trans-

formative and social action approaches that students are challenged in this direction.

In another typology, Banks (1997) described multicultural education as consisting of five components: content integration, knowledge construction, prejudice reduction, an equity pedagogy, and an empowering school culture. These dimensions address not only the content of the curriculum but also how that curriculum is presented so that students can learn to critique the content and also the structures of schooling. In this way, educators are challenged to consider whether their pedagogy affirms their students' cultures and experiences and provides students with the skills to challenge the inequities of the society.

Moving beyond a superficial understanding of ethnic cultures requires knowledge of deep culture and not merely the surface manifestations. Such knowledge can generally be acquired best through extensive interaction with members of a group or community, and in-depth study and reflection. Such study needs to be guided by those knowledgeable enough about the culture to provide the background information needed for significant understanding. In addition, it is important to recognize that cultures change, often in response to changing contexts and realities. Such cultural changes may be especially salient among immigrant communities as members are removed from their geographic roots and traditional ways of behaving. If educators are to move beyond the heroes-and-holidays approach to culture, they need to recognize that culture is not static. This recognition also entails a willingness to consider issues that threaten culture cohesiveness, issues such as racism and socioeconomic and political inequality. Challenges to the integrity of ethnic and minority cultures are particularly prevalent when the ethnic minority is composed of people of color trying to survive during times when anti-immigrant sentiment is strong and growing.

Any discussion of multicultural education in most large urban communities also entails consideration of the role of language in the ethnic community. One important dimension of the literature on multicultural education is that which focuses on language issues and on the specific situation of non-English-speaking immigrants in the United States (Crawford, 1999; García, 1999; "Immigration and Education," 2001; Nieto, 1996). This literature addresses the importance of bilingualism and examines controversies over bilingual education. In communities with large numbers of speakers of languages other than English, a curriculum cannot be considered multicultural if it is based on an English-only philosophy.

As multicultural education efforts have expanded in our schools and universities, so have critiques of its goals and practices. Sleeter (1995) analyzed the critiques that have been leveled from two opposing camps: conservatives and radicals. She argued that the conservatives are suspicious of the origins of multicultural education, asserting that Western Europe is the basis for U.S. culture and society. They believe the focus on multicultural education will lead to ethnic and racial conflict and to further division of the society into ethnic enclaves.

Radical or leftist-oriented scholars, on the other hand, question the way that multicultural education gets interpreted in schools (Giroux, 1993; McCarthy, 2000; McLaren, 1993).

These scholars claim that multicultural education does not really focus on reform of institutions, that the changes in education constitute lip service and a co-optation of minority struggles. They argued that what is needed in education is a more-rigorous critique of a system of oppression in which minority groups, especially racial groups, remain at the lowest end of the social hierarchy. They proposed that what is actually needed is antiracist education, which acknowledges the many ways that race defines social class in U.S. society. They also want students to obtain an education that helps them recognize how schooling becomes a sorting mechanism by those in power to maintain power. Some of these critics also view the emphasis on "culture" in multicultural education as a way to avoid dealing with issues of structural inequalities in the society, such as gender, class, and racial oppression. As Sleeter (1995) commented, "Radical critics regard the increasing popularity of multicultural education as a palliative White response to minority concerns that deflects attention away from structural issues, especially white racism" (p. 90). It is indeed the case that the way culture is conceptualized in some multicultural education approaches is static and essentialist, where the colorful aspects of cultures are highlighted, and controversial issues, such as anti-immigrant sentiment, discrimination, hate crimes, and so on, are avoided. Moreover, these critics argued that the heroes that are often portrayed in multicultural education literature are those that have not really challenged the inequities of the society. They call for a critical multiculturalism that is at its core antiracist and that addresses the "wider processes of power relations and inequality" in our society (May, 1999, p. 1).

It is clear from examining these critiques that not all advocates of multicultural education are conceptualizing the term in the same way. Moreover, when multicultural education is translated into school curricula and programs, there is further slippage from the theoretical premises to the implementation strategies. Some of the critical multiculturalists do not reject the premises but, in essence, reject the way multicultural education is realized in classrooms. There is, however, agreement among even these critics that school curricula need to change if they are to address issues of diversity of the student population in our urban areas. Whereas some advocates focus on the curriculum reform agenda, others see a need for a broader change, the social action approach advocated by Banks and the critical multiculturalism approach advocated by May (1999).

Educators preparing teachers to develop multicultural curricula in their schools and classrooms need to be knowledgeable not only about the rationale for multicultural education but also the nature of the critiques leveled against it. Teacher preparation programs should engage teacher candidates in examining these critiques as these prospective teachers consider their own philosophical stance on curricular issues. Moreover, prospective teachers who expect to teach in urban areas with student populations of backgrounds very different from their own need to consider what they will need to learn to be effective in those schools and classrooms.

## THE FUNDS OF KNOWLEDGE APPROACH TO UNDERSTANDING CULTURE

Some approaches to learning about culture may be routes to critiquing economic and social inequalities by providing voice and visibility for groups that have traditionally been silenced. For example, some recent anthropological and ethnographic studies in Latino communities, rather than focusing on essentialized and static definitions of culture, have sought to address the ways of knowing of community members and the concomitant implications for schooling. One concept that has been explored through this line of research is the "funds of knowledge" of community members (Vélez-Ibañez & Greenberg, 1992).

Funds of knowledge have been defined as "the essential cultural practices and bodies of knowledge and information that households use to survive, to get ahead, or to thrive" (Moll, Amanti, Neff, & Gonzalez, 1992, p. 21). This concept, being pursued by Moll with Mexican families in Arizona, presents a theoretical framework for challenging the deficit models of Latino communities that have characterized much educational theorizing. The term *funds of knowledge* is being used in anthropologically oriented educational projects to characterize the everyday knowledge that members of a community have and that can be studied by educators and used in the development of curriculum. This orientation to ethnic cultures recognizes that cultures change and evolve, and these changes are frequently in response to contact with other cultures and the vicissitudes of survival and everyday living (Moll et al., 1992; Moll & Greenberg, 1990; Vélez-Ibañez & Greenberg, 1992).

In a curriculum development project in Arizona that has used this orientation, teachers collaboratively explored the intellectual and vocational resources of the families in the community and used this knowledge as a base for curriculum building (Gonzalez et al., 1995). Teachers made home visits as part of a team to observe the activities of the households and returned to the university for discussions about their observations with anthropologists and educators. They also explored how they could build on the family and community funds of knowledge to create lessons for their classrooms. Moll argued that much of the knowledge and skills of families, including elements of their daily lifestyle, can yield legitimate content relevant to school curricula. The funds-of-knowledge exploration can also help educators move beyond the "minority as victim" portrayals of culture as well as the tourist portrayals of their daily reality. In addition, without ignoring issues of structural inequality and racism, this exploration can provide ways of recognizing the agency of community members as they struggle to counter their oppression and function in their everyday lives.

Ethnographic studies and other research with Mexican origin families (Carger, 1996; Hondagneu-Sotelo, 1994; López-Castro, 1986; Matute-Bianchi, 1991; Suárez-Orozco & Suárez-Orozco, 1995; Valdés, 1996) have given us a broader picture of what it means to be a part of a transnational community and provided a more holistic picture of how these families strategize vis-à-vis the challenges of life in the United States. Such studies also challenge educators' assumptions about the culture of the students in their classroom and can provide examples for more authentic multicultural curriculum content. Valdés's (1996) ethnographic study of 10 Mexican families on the U.S.-Mexico border, for example, provides a perspective that can help educators to understand the difference between the value systems of these families and the expectations of institutions such as those of U.S. schools and mainland teachers. These families placed greater value on family cohesiveness and relations than they did on individual advancement and upward mobility. Educators who seek to develop curriculum that is multicultural need to come to terms with how they understand and respond to such differences in value systems with respect to their student populations. Through such understanding, educators may also become more conscious of the structural inequities that limit possibilities for people of color in U.S. society.

The challenge of understanding culture, if teachers are to develop multicultural curricula, is even greater in the context of socioeconomic inequities, immigration, legal and illegal, and transnationalism. Few teachers have opportunities to examine these issues as part of teacher training programs. Teachers also need to be prepared to learn enough about a community so they can examine their deficit conceptualizations of the children of those communities. Those deficit conceptualizations are prevalent when issues of race, whether Black or Brown, and non-English language features characterize the student population. Teachers need to ask the following questions: Do the children that I am to teach know anything when they come to my school? What do they know? How do they learn it? Is there any value in this knowledge for organizing the curriculum? The broader goal is one of having educators become ethnographers of the communities from which their students come, especially in situations of cross-cultural contact and in the context of social inequality and racism.

## THE COLMICH PROJECT: AN INQUIRY INTO MULTICULTURAL CURRICULUM DEVELOPMENT

The Colmich Project, described in this article, was an effort to address multicultural curriculum development with a group of teachers who wanted to move beyond the heroes-and-holidays approach. During a summer, a group of educators and graduate students from the University of Illinois–Chicago participated in a Fulbright-sponsored project at the Colegio de Michoacán (Colmich), a graduate school in western Mexico in the State of Michoacán, one of the major areas of migration to Chicago. I collaborated with a professor of Mexican history at the university to secure a grant to sponsor the participation of teachers and history graduate students in this project. I teach in the university's College of Education and work closely in the preparation of teachers for Chicago City Schools and surrounding communities. I looked forward to working with these teachers in a study abroad program that would be followed by practical application of what they learned into curriculum development projects for their schools. As part of the Colmich Project, each teacher submitted a proposal for a study to be conducted in Michoacán, and that could be translated into curricula for their schools. Six of the teachers were elementary school

teachers, and four were secondary teachers. Six of them were Latinas, and four were White who were fluent in Spanish. The other project participants were Latin American history graduate students. All the teachers taught in Chicago Public Schools, and all worked in schools where more than 75% of the students were Latinos, predominantly Mexican. For 3 weeks, project members were to participate in formal study of Mexican history, the cultures of western Mexico, archeology, sociology, and economics at Colmich. Formal study was to be supplemented with field trips to local sites and opportunities to meet and interact with Mexicans, teachers, community activists, craftsmen, and others in various towns. The subsequent 3 weeks the participants were to collect data for their independent study projects. The teachers had submitted projects around the following themes: narratives of Mexican families from Michoacán, including experiences of migration; descriptions of daily life of rancheros; Mexican adolescent leisure activities; mask making and crafts of local Mexican artisans; the African influence on contemporary Mexico and the region; and the everyday life of the Purépeche people, an indigenous group whose language is currently being recorded for school instructional purposes in rural Mexico.

A second objective of the Colmich Project was to have teachers understand their Mexican-background students as members of a transnational community and to consider the educational implications of that sociopolitical reality. Some of the professors at Colmich had done extensive research on Mexican migration to the United States, and one had focused on migration of communities to Chicago and the return migrants (López Castro, 1986). He provided class lectures on the various dimensions of these migrations using data that he had recently collected and that he was continuing to collect in his own research.

Many teachers in Chicago schools with large Mexican populations express concern about the fact that families go back and forth between Mexico and Chicago, and therefore children do not have enough continuity in their educational program to be academically successful. The teachers in this project wanted to learn what kinds of activities students would be engaged in while visiting the small towns and ranchos of this area, and to consider whether curricula and classroom projects could be developed from that social reality. They also wanted to consider what kinds of school assignments could be given to students to carry out in their Mexican communities while they were absent from Chicago schools. Instead of viewing their students' absence from Chicago classrooms as a wasteful disruption of their educational development, the teachers were open to exploring the children's transnational experiences as a resource for curriculum development. One of the teachers proposed that if middle-class students can spend a semester abroad in Europe, and this experience is generally seen as a culturally enriching one, a similar orientation could be developed for the experiences that Mexican-origin students could have in returning to their communities in Mexico. The teachers were also seeking to provide legitimacy to what they perceived to be a common "cultural" practice within the families of their students, the need to return "home" for a variety of reasons, whether to celebrate holidays or to participate in funerals, baptisms, weddings, and other family events.

## EXAMINING MULTICULTURAL CURRICULA IN A UNIVERSITY SEMINAR

When the teachers returned to Chicago, they participated in a semester-long university graduate seminar on multicultural curriculum development provided to guide their writing projects. I was the instructor of this seminar, Integrating Community Knowledge and Resources into the Curriculum. In the seminar, the teachers were to examine and critique multicultural curricular models for their theoretical base and practical applications. They were to consider how to write a curricular unit from the independent research projects conducted in Mexico. In addition, teacher participants were to read background literature on Mexicans and other Latino immigrant groups, focusing on articles on immigration and its effect on mainland communities. These articles included exploration of the benefits of immigration and not merely costs, the revitalization of urban communities brought about by the presence of immigrants, and the dependence of certain industries, such as agriculture, on immigrant labor. Whereas much popular literature on immigration, especially illegal immigration, focuses on the costs to communities, seminar readings included more balanced articles showing immigrants as job seekers who paid taxes beyond the services they received from them.

The experiences of Mexicans as a transnational community served as a base for exploring issues of culture, socioeconomic inequality, and the educational process. The seminar had a historical component, a cultural component, and a curricular component. The historical reading selections provided a context for understanding the United States as a multicultural society. These selections included readings on how communities established themselves in this country and how sociopolitical and economic developments fostered or constrained this process. The readings and discussions were planned to provide opportunities for comparing and contrasting the experiences of various ethnic and racial groups. A major reading source for this discussion was Takaki's (1993) *A Different Mirror: A History of Multicultural America.* This book examines American history from the perspective of various ethnic and racial groups rather than predominantly from a Euro-American perspective.

The cultural material included readings, videos, and presentations that examined aspects of the groups being studied, with a focus on Mexicans and Mexican Americans. One aspect of this component was readings on how to research community knowledge and resources, with examples of such research approaches. Major readings for this component included Valdés (1996) Con Respeto, as well as readings by Heath (1983), Matute-Bianchi (1991), and Moll et al. (1992).

The curricular component included readings on the integration of ethnic content into the curriculum, particularly from the writings of Banks. Through course readings and discussions, the seminar attempted to explore the theoretical perspective for such multicultural curriculum development as well as the practical issues involved in writing and implementing such curricula.

## TEACHERS' CONCEPTIONS OF MULTICULTURAL EDUCATION

The following academic year, I interviewed the teachers about their projects in Mexico, their conceptions of multicultural curricula, and their successes and dilemmas in translating their projects into instructional units. I employed an open-ended questionnaire with questions such as the following: How would you explain what multicultural curriculum is to someone who was not acquainted with American education? What was the rationale for your Mexico study project, and what success did you have with it? What connections do you see between theory in multicultural education and practice in the schools? (The complete questionnaire can be found in the Appendix.)

I explored the teachers' conceptions of multicultural curriculum and their efforts to interpret these conceptions into actual units for classrooms. This entailed reviewing the initial proposals developed by the teachers to describe their intended study projects, their final project reports, and the products they developed when the independent study projects were completed. I compared these proposals and project reports with the content analysis of their interviews to examine their conceptions of multicultural curricula. In addition, I examined samples of curricular units that they developed from their field projects to see how their views were translated into actual classroom curricula.

The translation of theoretical curriculum constructs into actual curriculum products is quite complex, particularly when educators are exploring controversial areas involving sociopolitical issues in transnational contexts. Program participants experienced significant frustration in converting theoretical ideas about multicultural curricula into workable curricular pieces. One of these frustrations is the difficulty of moving up the hierarchy of Banks' model for the integration of ethnic content into the curriculum to develop curricula, which employ authentic content from the society in meaningful instructional units while also attempting to transform the curriculum and develop a social action agenda. Teachers struggled to make explicit the implicit learnings from actual field experiences and to translate those into teaching objectives for their students.

One problem that the teachers had in conceptualizing multicultural curriculum was being overly ambitious and broad in their intentions. Edith and Jane,[1] two elementary teachers who developed a joint project, initially described their proposal this way: "Our goal is to acquire information about the physical environment, historical background, ancient and contemporary societies, the family structure, regional economics, politics, government and international relations of western Mexico in order to develop four units of study." This was obviously an ambitious and unrealistic plan for a 6-week program of study. Maria acknowledged that she too had been overly ambitious, "I was going to do the sky, the sun, and the moon. Then I narrowed it down to one project and that was to study the ranchero culture in Michoacán, specifically because there's where a lot of our students come from." She soon learned that even that objective was overly broad, and she eventually narrowed that down to learning enough about the everyday life of a few families to be able to write some essays for her ESL students, using the daily chores of the families as the content for the essays.

Their overly ambitious plans for what they could accomplish with a project were, in part, a result of their limited background knowledge of the area and peoples of western Mexico. Only one of them had done course work on Mexican history before participating in this project, and although the lectures at Colmich were helpful, they were nevertheless their first exposure to any formal study of Mexico. This meant that carrying out some of the projects as planned was rather unrealistic. Such was the case of Pat who wanted to develop a thematic unit on the African heritage of Mexico and hoped to obtain information by interviewing Mexicans in the area. She discovered that either the Mexicans in the area did not know about this history, or they denied that Africans had ever lived in the area. Therefore, although the goals of the teachers were appropriate because they wanted to broaden the base of the curriculum in their schools with authentic information from these communities, they had to modify their projects to restrict the range of areas covered or the ways of conducting the research.

In understanding the difficulties that the teachers experienced, several areas need to be considered. One of these is the orientation that teachers have to curriculum—the idea that new knowledge needs to be integrated into an already existing curricular base where the focus is still on the development of basic academic skills such as literacy. The elementary teachers did not consider "addressing controversy" as a primary objective of a lesson or unit plan, and teaching skills such as literacy at the elementary level is not often interpreted as meaning critiquing what is read. This may be a by-product of other objectives. None of the secondary teachers taught history or social studies, where conscious efforts to examine different perspectives are an important part of the curricular objectives. The teachers wrote their objectives in relation to basic skills outlined in district curriculum documents. For example, Edith described her objective as "to increase interview skills and storytelling skills of the students." Maria focused on "writing a series of essays with ESL language exercises focused on ranchero culture" where the language exercises were focused on English language development, vocabulary, and grammatical structures.

In developing their units, the teachers relied on the additive curriculum approach of Banks' typology. Although the teachers were able to articulate reasons for the importance of multicultural curricula and attempted to integrate their projects into other aspects of their curriculum, these projects nevertheless became "add-ons" to a curriculum that had already been established. As Zayda, one of the project teachers said, "You don't change the curriculum, but you fit it in." Maria stated, "We have to fit what we learned with what exists already. If you have an existing curriculum, you have to see how much flexibility there is." In discussing the dilemmas of developing and implementing the curricular projects, all the teachers complained about the need for more time and the constraint of not being able to delete anything from a curriculum that already existed. Teachers were constantly faced with the task of trying to create time within already full schedules to include the topics of their projects into class activities.

There were nevertheless some successes in addressing some of the issues and in spite of constraints of time and resources. Some teachers were able to make explicit their implicit understanding of some of the more important goals of multicultural curriculum. For example, Zayda, when asked about the issue of controversy in multicultural curricula, responded as follows:

> Controversial in terms of how you present the native people of Mexico, and it gets very controversial when you start talking about why these people were not able to keep their language, why they are all Catholics now, and why until recently there was no education in their language.... You help kids to make bridges between how it was and how it is. This is when they start thinking about if you had all these people speaking this language and living this way and now they are up there but usually they're considered ... the lowest of the socioeconomic realm. How did this happen? Kids start asking their own questions, and that's when you get into discussions.

Zayda argued that by addressing traditional issues of language and culture, teachers could also help students recognize socioeconomic and political injustice and bring the historical record up to the present time. Her rationale went beyond merely teaching about the various ethnic groups that existed in Mexico during the time of the Spanish conquest and their characteristics or contributions to civilization. She was oriented to getting students to raise questions about how things were then and how they are now, a different reading of historical texts than is traditional in many elementary classrooms. This questioning of texts and making comparisons between historical events and current realities is a goal of multicultural education.

Jane had a similar point of view related to helping students develop different perspectives:

> I think in one sense it's (multicultural education) to provide different viewpoints historically and culturally, especially history.... It's to let children know that there is no one sense of history, that history happens to various people at the same time, and there are different perspectives on it. There is not one necessary truth. What was good for one group may not have been so good for another group and vice versa.

Such a view, though advocated by many scholars of social studies education, does not necessarily characterize the way that social studies and history are taught in school curricula. Too often children are taught a textbook presentation of history that seems to foster a belief that there is only one way to interpret historical events, and that way has already been recorded in the texts (Levstik & Barton, 2001). Recognizing multiple perspectives on issues is another objective of multicultural education.

Maria articulated a similar position in defining multicultural education: "It's reaching out to understand ourselves and other people as well and to get more than one perspective on what we are taught and what we read not just to continually get one certain type of viewpoint."

She recognized the importance of perspective and point of view in examining curricular content and was therefore especially interested in interviewing families of various social classes in Mexico. Nevertheless translating that lofty goal of helping students appreciate multiple perspectives into actual classroom lessons was not simple. One major constraint resulted from a lack of appropriate materials that would present alternative perspectives. For the teachers, one of the attractions of going to Mexico was to identify Mexican produced instructional materials that they could use in their classrooms. In fact, this was a major goal of one of the teachers who wanted to establish a local community lending library for secondary students and their teachers in La Villita, a section of south Chicago that is inhabited predominantly by Mexican immigrants and their families, many from Michoacán. Zayda expressed frustration with the fact that using materials from Mexico meant they had to be translated and then rewritten at a level accessible to children. This would have been a major undertaking for the teachers and considerably beyond their expertise.

One success in addressing controversy in the projects carried out was the unit on family narratives. Jane and Edith had interviewed members of Mexican families from various villages about their everyday lives. Several of these families recounted their stories of immigrating illegally into the United States. The teachers were able to videotape some of these stories and used them to develop a unit on family narratives with migration as a theme. They developed some computer-based modules, which engaged students in map reading activities to trace the trip that the families took from Mexico to Chicago. This appeared to be a more motivating way to learn concepts in geography than the worksheet exercises that often constitute geography lessons. In addition, given their judgment that multicultural education should not be limited to English, they engaged the children in a story-retelling task using the Spanish videotaped interview of a mother and child and having the students retell the story and respond to questions in English. Because these two teachers believed that multicultural education also called for integrating the funds of knowledge of their students' families into their lessons, they elicited students' personal reactions to the family narratives they were viewing. Edith described one of the lessons as follows:

> The lesson revolved around a video of a woman who was telling her story of her family going from Mexico to the United States and they were going illegally. She told the whole story from leaving her house, passing the border, and she talked about how scared she was
>
> ….In our traditional social studies curriculum, we think that sometimes there is no connection for the students. In the project that I did, a few of my students had the experience of migrating to the U.S. My students could relate to the woman's experience, due to their own families' lives.

This was indeed the case. Several of the children spoke about their families' migration to the Chicago area and revealed knowledge of how those trips were carried out, including discussions of the role of coyotes (smugglers) who would help people across the border. Even the teachers were surprised about how much these fourth graders knew about these issues, knowledge that came from the personal lived experiences of their families. In addition, the children had rather sophisticated knowledge of geography because they and their families had traveled through many states before arriving in Chicago.

Jane added her perspective of doing a similar lesson with her second graders: "We were able to talk about the legal versus illegal immigration, reasons that people would migrate and reasons people wouldn't want them to immigrate. I think they had a general understanding that it was a little more complex than just simple bad or good."

For Jane, discussing various perspectives on migration with these young children made sense because this was not merely an academic exercise for them. They and their families had had experiences with migration and were rather articulate in discussing these. In her case, it was she who was being taught about these from her students.

In spite of these small successes, the teachers were disappointed with the difficulties of translating their projects into curricula. They had initially planned to disseminate their units through various schools for use by other teachers. This too was probably overly ambitious. They nevertheless commented on the benefits gained from the experience of studying and living in the environment that provided the context for curriculum development. Some of their views were challenged by daily realities, particularly their previous tendency to view Latinos as one group. Several of the teachers highlighted the value of actually having opportunities to interact with Mexican families in various towns and ranchos of Mexico and experiencing the diversity among them. Ann spoke of the value of the experience in this way:

> What was successful is the experience itself … going there and learning, talking with the people … being able to live with the families, we were able to have a lot of interaction with them.… I'm Hispanic but not Mexican, and it's very different from what's taught here … so just getting to know them is like getting to know a different ethnic group than even the Mexicans here.… Within Mexico there's such a diverse group of languages, people and everything else that you can't really lump them into one.

It was experiencing this diversity that she found most valuable. She argued for the need for more teachers to be provided with these types of opportunities. "A multicultural education or curriculum should be based first of all on teaching the teachers … if teachers themselves are not exposed to different cultures, how can they teach it?"

Dave, another teacher participant in the project, experienced this diversity among Mexicans from a religious perspective. He had been active in Evangelical circles in Chicago and had wanted to examine non-Catholic movements in Mexico. He discussed the value of his conversations with a Black priest from Trinidad who lived in Mexico and was working in a mostly African background village on the Oaxacan coast of Mexico teaching an African heritage class to members of an ex-gang ministry. Dave also had conversations with a Baptist and a Pentecostal pastor about their experiences in a mostly Catholic region. He was fascinated by the activism of Evangelicals in what he had traditionally viewed as a Catholic society. When he returned to Chicago, he became involved in a community church program that brought people from predominantly White suburbs to spend time in the Mexican neighborhood dialoguing with Mexicans from the area. He also started a community resource library, with books and videos that he purchased in Mexico, to be used in an after-school tutoring program that he established in a community center in La Villita, a Mexican neighborhood in the south side of Chicago.

Dave had been a Christian social activist before participating in this project, however he broadened his thinking to a more ecumenical way of being active in the community. His resource library was not limited to religious books but included a variety of materials that would interest preteens and adolescents in the neighborhood. His reaching out to White suburbanites to initiate a dialogue with residents of LaVillita was also an example of his concern for cross ethnic and racial relations in Chicago.

## EDUCATIONAL IMPLICATIONS OF THE CURRICULUM PROJECT

The increasing diversity of our nation's schools points to the need to expand and supplement teacher education beyond the traditional borders of university course work and/or schoolteacher inservice workshops. Some of our urban school populations consist of a student body that is more than 90% language minority or ethnic minority students, a majority of minorities. One significant and growing population concentration in large urban areas is Mexican background students. In addition to attending urban schools in the United States, many of these children and members of their families return to Mexico on a regular basis, mostly to their hometowns or ranchos, occasionally for weeks or more extended periods of time. Not only are teachers faced with the challenge of teaching students whose home language is not English and whose home culture is different from that of the mainstream, they often encounter a situation where Mexican-descent students may be gone for extended periods of time during the academic year either for funerals, holidays, or other family events. As members of a transnational community, these students actually live in both societies at the same time.

Is it possible for teachers of these students to find ways to develop their school curricula to capitalize on the transnational knowledge that their students and the families possess? If so, what is this knowledge, how can it be harnessed for curricular purposes, and how can the school expand on it to maximize the academic potential for content and concept learning? How can American schools and teachers move beyond textbook descriptions of the Aztec and Mayan civilizations to recognize the cultural diversity of Mexico and integrate aspects of that diversity into the school curriculum? In what ways can discussions of cultural diversity extend to issues of socioeconomic exploitation, racism, and challenge anti-immigrant sentiments and policies? These are all critical questions that need to be addressed if multicultural education is to be more than ethnic food festivals or colorful holiday celebrations.

The Colmich Project showed that teachers can be challenged to consider alternative ways of learning about the cultures of students in their classrooms and to use this knowledge to develop lessons for their classrooms. The teachers in the project wanted to go beyond the interpretations of Mexicans that were traditionally presented in classroom texts. They were persuaded that the funds-of-knowledge approach to the families of their students was a legitimate way to conceptualize what members of the community knew and that such knowledge could have value for curriculum development. The teachers appreciated the opportunity to carry out independent projects in Mexico and to have their knowledge broadened through the experience of living and studying there. They articulated rather important insights on issues such as having students consider alternative perspectives, the development of lessons from the lived experience of immigrant families, the diversity that exists among Latinos, even when they come from the same national background. Although the amount of time that they spent on their projects was very limited, some were able to benefit from what they learned through them and develop lessons for their classrooms, or in the case of Dave, initiate non-classroom-based projects for the community.

The Colmich Project raised questions about what teacher educators can do to assist teachers in developing multicultural curricula. The projects that the teachers developed suffered from overly ambitious expectations of what was possible through a short-term project. Although it was more meaningful than the typical in-service workshop that too often characterizes the preparation of teachers for curricular reform, the teachers needed a great deal more background information to be able to plan projects that were doable and translatable into classroom lessons. They needed the cooperation of their colleagues at their schools and building administrators so that they could consider eliminating and/or revising other curricular units to make a legitimate space for their classroom-based projects.

Teacher educators and educational administrators must find ways to develop authentic multicultural curricula with school staffs, especially in those schools that are part of the international migrations that have been changing the face of our urban areas. Study abroad programs and experiences offer some potential as an alternative to more traditional in-service workshops or university level course work, especially if these experiences engage participants in interaction with community members and not just visits to museums or traditional tourist attractions. Nevertheless, such programs are no panacea and are limited in what can be accomplished, especially if they are short term. Developing multicultural curricula is more complex than some of our rhetoric implies, and moving from theoretical models to actual curriculum products poses significant challenges for practitioners.

## NOTE

1. All names are pseudonyms.

## APPENDIX

### *Questionnaire on Multicultural Curriculum Development*.

1. Tell me a little about the project you planned when you went to Mexico.
2. What was your rationale for that project?
3. The Mexico project was geared at helping teachers develop multicultural curriculum. If you were to explain that term to someone who was not acquainted with American education, how would you explain the term?
4. What kind of success did you have in your project?
5. What would you consider to be the main frustrations in working on a multicultural curriculum project?
6. To what extent would you consider university courses relevant to teachers who are trying to work on multicultural curriculum? Was there anything you learned in course work that helped you work on the project? What connections do you see between theory in multicultural education and practice in the schools?
7. What do teachers need from the university to develop multicultural curriculum?
8. What is the difference between what students study in the traditional social studies curriculum and the project you were working on?
9. What have you done with your project since you returned?
10. In what ways can university professors help teachers to undertake curriculum reform?

## REFERENCES

Banks, J. (1997). *Teaching strategies for ethnic studies* (6th ed.). Boston: Allyn & Bacon.

Banks, J. A., & Banks, C. M. (Eds.). (1995). *Handbook of research on multicultural education.* New York: Macmillan.

Carger, C. L. (1996). *Of borders and dreams: A Mexican-American experience of urban education.* New York: Teachers College Press.

Chicago Public Schools. (2003). *CPS at a glance.* Available at www.cps.k12.il.us/AtAGlance.html

Crawford, J. (1999). *Bilingual education: History, politics, theory, and practice* (4th ed.). Los Angeles: Bilingual Educational Services.

García, E. (1999). *Student cultural diversity: Understanding and meeting the challenge* (2nd ed.). Boston: Houghton Mifflin.

Gay, G. (1995). Bridging multicultural theory and practice. *Multicultural Education, 3*(1), 4-9.

Giroux, H. A. (1993). *Living dangerously: Multiculturalism and the politics of difference.* New York: Peter Lang.

Gonzalez, N., Moll, L., Tenery, M. F., Rivera, A., Rendon, P., Gonzalez, R., et al. (1995). Funds of knowledge for teaching in Latino households. *Urban Education, 29*(4), 443-470.

Grant, C. (1999). *Multicultural research: A reflective engagement with race, class, gender, and sexual orientation.* Philadelphia: Falmer Press.

Heath, S. B. (1983). *Words with words: Language, life, and work in communities and classrooms.* Cambridge, UK: Cambridge University Press.

Hondagneu-Sotelo, P. (1994). *Gendered transitions: Mexican experiences of immigration.* Berkeley: University of California.

Immigration and education. (2001). *Harvard Educational Review, 71*(3 special issue).

Johnson, K. M. (2003). Chicago census 2000: Recent demographic trends in the Chicago metropolitan area. Chicago: Chicago Federal Letter. Available at www.luc.edu/sociology/johnson/ChicagoCensus2000.html

Kincheloe J. L., & Steinberg, S. R. (1997). *Changing multiculturalism.* Bristol, PA: Open University Press.

Lee, E., Menkart, D., & Okazawa-Rey, M. (1998). *Beyond heroes and holidays: A practical guide to K-12 anti-racist, multicultural education and staff development.* Washington, DC: Network of Educators on the Americas.

Levstik, L., & Barton, K. (2001). *Doing history: Investigating with children in elementary and middle schools* (2nd ed.). Mahwah, NJ: Lawrence Erlbaum.

López Castro, G. (1986). *La casa dividida: Un estudio de caso sobre la migración a Estados Unidos en un pueblo michoacano* [The divided house; A case study of the migration to the United States from a town in Michoacán]. Zamora, Mexico: Colegio de Michoacán.

Matute-Bianchi, M. E. (1991). School performance among Mexican-descent students. In M. Gibson & J.U. Ogbu (Eds.), *Minority status and schooling: A comparative study of immigrant and involuntary minorities* (pp. 205-249). New York: Garland.

May, S. (1999). *Critical multiculturalism: Rethinking multicultural and antiracist education.* Philadelphia: Falmer Press.

McCarthy, C. (2000). *Multicultural curriculum: New directions for social theory, practice, and policy.* New York: Routledge.

McLaren, P. (1993). Multiculturalism and the postmodern critique: Towards a pedagogy of resistance and transformation. *Cultural Studies, 7*(1), 118-146.

Moll, L., Amanti, C., Neff, D., & Gonzalez, N. (1992, spring). Funds of knowledge for teaching: Using a qualitative approach to connect homes and classrooms. *Theory into Practice, 31*(2), 132-141.

Moll, L., & Greenberg, J. (1990). Creating zones of possibilities: Combining social contexts for instruction. In L. C. Moll (Ed.), *Vygotsky and education* (pp. 319-348). Cambridge, UK: Cambridge University Press.

Nieto, S. (1996). *Affirming diversity: The sociopolitical context of multicultural education* (2nd ed.). New York: Longman.

Ogbu, J. U. (1992). Understanding cultural diversity and learning. *Educational Researcher, 21*(8), 5-14.

Ovando, C., & McLaren, P. (2000). *The politics of multicultural and bilingual education: Students and teachers caught in the cross fire.* Boston: McGraw-Hill.

Sleeter, C. (1991). *Empowerment through multicultural education.* Albany: State University of New York Press.

Sleeter, C. (1995). An analysis of the critiques of multicultural education. In J. Banks & C. Banks (Eds.), *Handbook of research on multicultural education* (pp. 81-94). New York: Macmillan.

Sleeter, C., & Grant, C. A. (2003). *Making choices for multicultural education: Five approaches to race, class, and gender* (4th ed.). New York: John Wiley.

Suárez-Orozco, C., & Suárez-Orozco, M. (1995). *Transformations: Migration, family life and achievement motivation among Latino adolescents.* Stanford, CA: Stanford University.

Takaki, R. (1993). *A different mirror: A history of multicultural America.* Boston: Little, Brown.

Valdés, G. (1996). *Con respeto: Bridging the distances between culturally diverse families and schools, an ethnographic portrait.* New York: Teachers College Press.

Vélez-Ibañez, C., & Greenberg, J. B. (1992). Formation and transformation of funds of knowledge among U.S.-Mexican households. *Anthropology and Education Quarterly, 23*(4), 313-335.

*Irma M. Olmedo, associate professor at the University of Illinois–Chicago, conducts research in multicultural teacher education, oral histories of Latinos, and bilingualism. She seeks to integrate theory and practice in these areas in teacher preparation and educational inquiry.*

# URBAN TEACHERS' PROFESSED CLASSROOM MANAGEMENT SRATEGIES

## Reflections of Culturally Responsive Teaching

*DAVE F. BROWN*
*West Chester University*

*Thirteen urban educators teaching from 1st through 12th grade selected from 7 cities across the United States were interviewed in this qualitative research study to determine if the classroom management strategies they use reflect the research on culturally responsive teaching. Participants revealed using several management strategies that reflect culturally responsive teaching: development of personal relationships with students, creation of caring communities, establishment of business-like learning environments, use of culturally and ethnically congruent communication processes, demonstrations of assertiveness, and utilization of clearly stated and enforced expectations. Questions arise concerning the ability of teacher education programs to effectively prepare preservice teachers for successful classroom management in urban schools.*

**Haberman (1995) explained,** "Whatever the reasons for children's behavior—whether poverty, personality, a handicapping condition, a dysfunctional home, or an abusive environment—classroom teachers are responsible for managing children, seeing that they work together in a confined space for long periods, and ensuring that they learn" (p. 22). Haberman's proclamation summarizes the realization that student learning is contingent on teachers' ability to create and sustain optimal learning environments. Urban classrooms can and often do present many challenges for teachers in the development of productive learning spaces. The reasons for these challenges are numerous. Crosby (1999) reported, "The new wave of immigrants of the past 25 years from Hispanic countries, from the Middle East, and from Asian countries has washed over the urban schools like a tidal wave bringing with it additional challenges, this time cultural and linguistic" (p. 104). Gibbs, Huang, and Associates (1998) reported that, "In adolescents, school phobia or truancy may actually represent fear of a violent or chaotic school environment or fear of social rejection due to some cultural, racial, or economic difference from the majority of the student body" (p. 17). Urban teachers have added responsibilities in addressing these critical issues that affect their students' needs.

Gaining students' cooperation in urban classrooms involves establishing a classroom atmosphere in which teachers are aware of and address students' cultural and ethnic needs as well as their social, emotional, and cognitive needs. As Wlodkowski and Ginsberg (1995) stated, "Any educational or training system that ignores the history or perspective of its learners or does not attempt to adjust its teaching practices to benefit all its learners is contributing to inequality of opportunity" (p. 26). The problem lies in the fact that most urban teachers will be and are inexperienced middleclass White European Americans as Crosby (1999) indicated:

> The teacher turnover rate in the urban schools is much higher than in the suburban schools.... The result is that urban schools, especially those in the inner cities, are often staffed largely by newly hired or uncertified teachers. These teachers, who were trained to teach students from middle class families and who often come from middle class families themselves, now find themselves engulfed by minority students, immigrants, and other students from low income families—students whose values and experiences are very different from their own. (p. 302)

The obvious challenge is encouraging preservice teachers to want to teach in the urban centers, and then educating them to respond to the cultural and ethnic characteristics and needs of the children and adolescents who attend urban schools.

Culturally responsive teaching involves purposely responding to the needs of themany culturally and ethnically diverse learners in classrooms. It involves implementing specifically student-oriented instructional processes as well as choosing and delivering ethnically and culturally relevant curricula. Culturally responsive teachers use communication processes that reflect students' values and beliefs held about learning, the responsibilities of teachers, and the roles of students in school settings (Brown, 2002; Delpit, 1995; Gay, 2000; Howard, 1999; Ladson-Billings, 1994; Wlodkowski & Ginsberg, 1995). I describe self-professed classroom management techniques used by 13 urban teachers. These educators' chosen practices are analyzed and compared to culturally responsive strategies proposed by a number of researchers to determine if their actions actually reflect the research on culturally responsive pedagogy.

## RESEARCH ON CULTURALLY RESPONSIVE MANAGEMENT

Culturally responsive management focuses on many teaching components, from as broad as choosing appropriate curricula and as specific as using congruent communication processes. Effective classroom management also involves the utilization of many essential research-based pedagogical processes as well as the ability to respond appropriately to the emotional, social, ethnic, cultural, and cognitive needs of students. Effectively managing students generally involves the ability to develop a classroom social environment in which students agree to cooperate with teachers and fellow students in pursuit of academic growth. It is a complex process that involves much interpersonal and pedagogical awareness and application of strategies in these two realms. In truth, most researchers and teachers may agree that managing student behavior while maintaining an appropriate learning environment is as much art as it is science. Researchers have addressed both of these views of management in studying students' and teachers' behaviors.

## A CARING ATTITUDE

Most significant perhaps to each child or adolescent in urban schools is the willingness and ability of an educator to genuinely touch each student's social and emotional persona. Urban students may experience a greater need than suburban students for developing close relationships with teachers (Brown, 2001). This need is based on possible feelings of alienation, struggles with identity development, and what Dryfoos (1998) reported concerning adolescents at risk who "lack nurturance, attention, supervision, understanding, and caring," and may have inadequate communication processes with adults in their homes (p. 37).

Ladson-Billings (1994) described the nature of classrooms of effective teachers of African American students: "Psychological safety is a hallmark of each of these classrooms. The students feel comfortable and supported" (p. 73). Gordon (1999) agreed in concluding, "The best urban teachers show warmth and affection to their students and give priority to the development of their relationships with students as an avenue to student growth" (p. 305).

In extensive interviews with more than 150 middle-level students in six Philadelphia urban schools, Wilson and Corbett (2001) revealed a common student need: "Essentially the students naturally zeroed in on a phenomenon central to effective urban education that researchers have labored to depict for years—the quality of the relationship between inner-city students and their teachers" (p. 88). Howard (2001) elicited African American elementary students' perceptions of culturally relevant teaching strategies within urban contexts. He discovered that students preferred "teachers who displayed caring bonds and attitudes toward them, and teachers who establish community- and family-type classroom environments" (p. 131). Urban middle-school students interviewed by Brown (1999) revealed that they clearly recognized which teachers cared about them and wanted teachers to demonstrate a more personal connection than that of the traditional teacher-student relationship.

## ESTABLISHING ASSERTIVENESS AND AUTHORITY

Researchers indicate that urban teachers need to be explicitly assertive with students establishing an environment in which students honor their authority. Wilson and Corbett (2001) and Delpit (1995) reported that urban classroom environments should be places in which expectations are clearly stated, no excuses are permitted, and inappropriate behaviors are dealt with immediately. Weiner (1999) explained that urban teachers need moral authority to be successful: "Urban teachers' primary source of control is their *moral* [italics in original] authority, which rests on the perception of students and parents that the teacher is knowledgeable about the subject matter, competent in pedagogy, and committed to helping all students succeed, in school and life" (p. 77).

One way in which teachers can explicitly demonstrate assertiveness and establish authority is through their verbal exchanges with students. Delpit (1995) indicated that many urban children expect much more direct verbal commands than perhaps suburban or rural students may expect or receive. Delpit cited Snow et al. (1976) in explaining "working class mothers use more directives to their children than do middle- and upper-class" (p. 34). Heath indicated that children from working-class families had difficulty following the indirect requests that many teachers use because they did not sound like rules or explicit directives to them (cited in Delpit, 1985). Delpit explained that when urban students ignore commands that sound more like questions than directives, teachers may perceive students as uncooperative and insubordinate whereas students innocently fail to understand what is expected and why they are being disciplined. Delpit added, "Black children expect an authority figure to act with authority" (p. 35). Delpit described how to establish authority in a classroom:

> The authoritative teacher can control the class through exhibition of personal power; establishes meaningful interpersonal relationships that garner student respect; exhibits a strong belief that all students can learn; establishes a standard of achievement and "pushes" the students to achieve that standard; and holds the attention of the students by incorporating interactional features of Black communicative style in his or her teaching. (p. 36)

## ESTABLISHING CONGRUENT COMMUNICATION PROCESSES

Creating a positive learning environment requires attentiveness to the way in which teachers communicate with students. Ladson-Billings (1994) revealed the responses of eighth-grade students from one urban school when she asked what they liked about their teacher: "She listens to us! She respects us! She let's us express our opinions! She looks us in the eye when she talks to us! She smiles at us! She speaks to us when she sees us in the hall or in the cafeteria!" (p. 68). You may notice from these responses that students recognize nonverbal language more so than verbal responses to their behaviors and comments. They notice teachers' facial expressions and other body movements, especially when they believe teachers should be listening to them.

Differences in communication processes affect the quality of relationships between teachers and their African, Hispanic, and Native American and immigrant students. Gay (2000) explained that African Americans have a social interaction style referred to as "call response" in which students may frequently speak while the teacher is speaking as a response to their feelings about a teacher's comments. These are not meant as rude disruptions but rather as an acknowledgment of agreement or perhaps concern about teachers' comments, lectures, or explanations. Gay added,

> African Americans "gain the floor" or get participatory entry into conversations through personal assertiveness, the strength of the impulse to be involved, and the persuasive power of the point they wish to make, rather than waiting for an "authority" to grant permission. (p. 91)

Educators' negative reactions to call response may cause and accentuate strained relationships between students and teachers (Obidah & Manheim Teel, 2001).

Some Asian students smile and laugh as a reaction to their confusion or misunderstanding of language or principles they are learning. Gay (2000) noted that this is common among Japanese, Chinese, Korean, Taiwanese, and Cambodians who use *ritualized laughter* to maintain harmony and avoid challenging authority.

Many Asian American students may also avoid confrontational situations such as correcting fellow students' mistakes, or responding competitively in discussions or recitations. Gay (2000) explained that Asian students are affected by "traditional values and socialization that emphasize collectivism, saving face, maintaining harmony, filial piety, interdependence, modesty in self-preservation, and restraint in taking oppositional points of view" (p. 105). Recent immigrants who are second-language learners will most likely be relatively quiet during class times as they attempt to learn English through listening as opposed to responding to teacher questions (Cary, 2000).

## DEMANDING EFFORT

African and Hispanic American students, in a slightly different interpretation of "caring for students," explained that they knew teachers cared when they pressured students in an assertive manner to complete assignments, pay attention, and perform better academically (Brown, 1999; Howard, 2001; Wilson & Corbett, 2001). Wilson and Corbett, for instance, described middle-level students' views that urban teachers are expected to exert explicit pressure on students to complete homework even if they provided excuses for not completing work.

> Essentially, we interpreted students to be saying that the effective teachers adhered to a "no excuses" policy. That is, there were no acceptable reasons why every student eventually could not complete his or her work, and there were no acceptable reasons why a teacher would give up on a child. The premise was that every child should complete every assignment and that was the teacher's job to ensure that this happened. (p. 64)

Howard (2001) described one urban elementary student's views of teacher caring, "The student's comments a teacher practice that is essential to culturally responsive teaching, which is creating a learning environment that helps students to reach their highest levels of academic achievement" (p. 139). Teachers can create a caring learning environment through several means, and assertive and explicit demands for academic performance and cooperative behavior appear to be a need for many urban students.

Culturally responsive classroom management is connected to a teacher's ability to use culturally responsive curricular materials and instructional processes. Research reveals, however, that even greater than those two essential components of teaching is an educator's knowledge of and demonstration of caring attitudes and actions, congruent communication, assertiveness and authority, and demands for students' efforts and academic production.

## METHOD

I conducted a qualitative study to determine how urban teachers implement several educational practices, such as instructional processes, communication patterns, working with parents/caregivers, and choosing curricula. Extensive interviews were completed with 13 teachers (1st through 12th grades) from urban schools in seven American cities. In this article, a specifically focused component of the broader study, I reveal data collected to determine if the classroom management strategies teachers professed to use match the research on culturally responsive teaching.

Teachers were selected for the study based on either personal knowledge of their teaching effectiveness or information gathered from colleagues in each city who recognized these teachers as effective urban educators. Each one volunteered to be interviewed for the study. A random sampling of respondents was not initiated. Findings from this qualitative analysis are not generalizable to other populations. Teachers interviewed were from the following cities working at the grade levels noted:

- two middle-school and two high school teachers from Philadelphia,
- one primary teacher from New York City, Harlem
- two teachers from Chicago: one primary and one high school,
- two teachers from Los Angeles: one primary and one high school,
- two intermediate teachers from San Francisco,
- one middle-school teacher from Minneapolis, and
- one high school teacher from Wichita, Kansas.

Among the teachers interviewed, one is native Sri Lankan, one is African American, two are Hispanic American, and nine teachers are White. Respondents' years of teaching experience ranged from 2 to 33 years with an average of 16 years experience. The demographics of each teacher's classroom include students from African, Hispanic, Native, and Asian American backgrounds as well as a wide variety of recent immigrant and refugee students. The majority of students these teachers encountered received free lunch as an indication of socioeconomic status of the neighborhoods in which they lived.

Five of the interviews were audiotaped, and tapes were transcribed. Eight interviews were conducted by telephone, and notes were written during these approximately 3-hr interview sessions. Transcriptions and written interviewnotes were analyzed using the constant comparative method to identify specific themes that emerged from the data (Glaser & Strauss, 1967).

I developed a nonscheduled interview guide (LeCompte & Preissle, 1993). Thirty-four questions were asked concerning several components of classroom practice, student-teacher relationships, curricular emphasis, and management strategies. Among the primary classroom management questions asked were the following three:

1. How do you interact with students?
2. How would you describe your management style?
3. What works well for you in communicating with students?

## FINDINGS

Data were analyzed in a descriptive manner rather than a quantitative analysis to provide an in-depth view of how teachers successfully managed their classrooms. The analysis of data revealed five primary themes that are presented individually with teachers' explanations and quotes that represent the majority of those interviewed.

### DEVELOPING PERSONAL RELATIONSHIPS AND MUTUAL RESPECT THROUGH INDIVIDUALIZED ATTENTION

The first and primary characteristic described by most of these 13 teachers is the importance and value of providing individualized attention by developing a personal relationship with each student. Teachers take time out of each day to communicate individually with many students on nonacademic matters. Anita, a middle-school teacher for 27 years in the same Philadelphia school, described her philosophy of teaching:

> I make a real effort to be involved in my children's lives, and if I have to, to be involved in their home lives by providing some of the things they need. I don't just look at them as bodies to be educated—I look at them as people that need to be nurtured.[1]

Anita added, "Kids feel that if you really don't care about them then they're not going to care about you."

Several techniques are implemented by these teachers to develop meaningful relationships with students. A Los Angeles high school teacher, Adrienne, replied, "I do a lot of hugs—I use body language. I rarely raise my voice. I treat them with respect. I'm friendly, but not their friend." Her students are primarily African American with a smaller percentage of Latino students.

Jeff is a high school teacher from Wichita, Kansas. His school has an even percentage of African and Hispanic American students at about 30% each. Many of the Hispanic students are from migrant families and are quite transitory throughout the year. Jeff responded to this question by admitting, "I try to get to know as many kids as possible on a personal level; so, when I see them in the hall, I can ask about their families. I try to see them in other settings outside of school."

Pete, a Philadelphia high school teacher, is responsible for teaching second-language learners (SLL). Several of his students each year are refugee students who are experiencing the added stress of attempting to adapt to a hostile community and school environment while living with the psychological scars of surviving a war zone in their native lands. Pete described the classroom community he develops: "I like to create a friendliness and kind of security and belonging that has been my focus above the academic stuff. The academic stuff is there but that can't happen unless students feel safe, valued, and secure."

Susan, an elementary teacher from San Francisco, echoed similar ideas, "I welcome kids when they come into the room. I always take attendance and lunch count myself to be sure to make contact with every child."

Mutual respect for students was described by teachers as demonstrating a personal interest in each child and creating a safe and secure environment for students in their classrooms.

## CREATING CARING LEARNING COMMUNITIES

Self-descriptions of management styles varied among respondents; however, these were the common themes:

- Teachers demonstrate their care for students in many ways.
- A community of learners is created so students feel like a family.
- Teachers develop business-like atmospheres.

All of these teachers mentioned in their interviews their strong commitment to an ethic of caring for students. Pete, the Philadelphia high school English for speakers of other languages (ESOL) teacher, described the relationship he develops with his students and how his demeanor and attitude affect the class:

> My classes are a mirror of me. Whenever I've walked into a class happy, positive, and upbeat, I've never had a problem. But, I've never walked into a class ready to go toe-to-toe with someone and not had a problem. And how quickly they [students] pick up on it is amazing.

Although there are many components to managing a classroom successfully, Pete places the caring piece into perspective saying, "It doesn't matter what good content you have, or what good curriculum you have, or what exciting lessons you have; if you don't care about students and they know that, you don't have a chance to get to them."

Collete teaches high school English in Philadelphia and described what she believes about connecting with her students: "I really believe you have to make that social and emotional connection with kids in order to get inside their heads. You have to get to their heart before you

get to their head. The fact that you care makes them see you differently."

Teachers who create a community of learners enforce the attitude and belief that, "When we're all in this room, we're here to help one another; any behavior that threatens this value will be addressed and discouraged." One of the teachers who Ladson-Billings (1994) interviewed "insists that her students form a viable social community before they can become a viable learning community" (p. 40). Colette, from a Philadelphia high school, described one of her community-building activities:

> We play this game at the beginning of the year. Each person introduces themselves, and then states something they have done that they think no one in the class has done. I always tell them to keep it clean! I tell them about myself first, just to get them talking. I try to get them to laugh, because when you laugh, you're more receptive. I try to create an atmosphere of trust.

Jackie, who taught for a while in a New York City elementary school in Harlem and has taught in Philadelphia for more than 5 years, offered this advice:

> You have to be real. I cannot pretend that I am from Harlem or Washington Heights. Their experience is not my experience. I think convincing them that what I have to say is important is the key. That happens through consistency— through just being honest. Trying to fit in to be one of them never works. I always follow up and keep my promises to them. Doing exactly what you say you'll do means something to students. They experience so many empty promises.

Many urban youth lead challenging lives outside of school based on their responsibilities for raising siblings, working to make money for the family several hours a week, or raising their own families. Despite all these responsibilities, some teachers are reluctant to permit students to make simple decisions about their behavior, what they study, or how they learn best. Urban students with these kinds of responsibilities outside of school resent being treated like preschoolers when decision-making opportunities arise. Shanika, a middle-school teacher in Philadelphia, described the life of one of her fifth graders:

> One of my students was in court last week. She's on probation for shoplifting. She has a hard time accepting authority. The school psychologist informed me that she is basically the mother figure for the family. Her own mother relies on her to take care of all of the other children—including a baby the mother has now. So, when this student comes to school and someone tells her she can't go to the bathroom, she gives you a look that says, "What are you talking about? I take care of everyone at home!" I think it's like that for a lot of kids. I'm starting to feel that they are not badly

behaved or they don't respect authority, but they are given a lot authority at home. They can fend for themselves. It's unrealistic now for them to come in and be expected to respect someone else's rules.

Many students are ready to take control over circumstances of their learning. School is an appropriate forum for these democratic processes to be shared. Hyman and Snook (2000) emphasized this idea:

> By using democratic processes in parenting and teaching, we help children develop internal controls based on the social contracts negotiated among parents, teachers, and peers. Teachers in democratic classrooms emphasize cooperation, mutual goal setting, and shared responsibility. Students behave because it is the right thing to do and because they respect the rights of others. (p. 495)

Learning is a highly emotional process, and the kind of classroom learning environment that teachers create does affect a students' emotional state of mind. Establishing a safe community within a classroom may be perceived as off-task instructional behavior; however, these actions actually lead to a productive learning environment. Wilson and Corbett (2001) placed the value of focusing on the learning environments in perspective: "These classroom environment differences had little to do with gradations of individuals' acquisition of knowledge or with nuances in the content covered; instead, environmental characteristics determined whether the majority of students learned anything at all" (p. 42). Jeff, the Wichita high school English teacher, provided some valuable advice: "You're there to teach kids, not subjects. We often forget this point."

## ESTABLISHING BUSINESS-LIKE LEARNING ENVIRONMENTS

Students want to be treated with respect and provided an opportunity to grow. Adrienne, the Los Angeles high school teacher, has on occasion dismissed students from her room. She builds a business attitude in her room when it is time for learning, and her students do often support it as she describes, "One student said to me, 'Can't we get rid of this student? She's bothering me.'" Adrienne described the management style in her high school classroom:

> My students know that I really want what's best for them. I give a lot of praise, and they know it's real. I'll say to students, "If you're in my class, you've made a decision." They have an external locus of control, and I try to help them take control of those factors they can affect. I say to them, "If your behavior affects someone else's learning, you're out of here." I also send students out when they're not ready for class.

Adrienne creates the learning environment that students described to Wilson and Corbett (2001) and that Delpit (1995) promoted in which expectations are clearly stated, no excuses are permitted, and inappropriate behaviors are dealt with immediately.

Polly, who teaches 9th and 10th graders who have failed to do passing work prior to entering her high school in Chicago, described her management style as

> tough love—I use it with students and teachers. I tell students, "I'm here to help you. I'm not going to let you slide! You're not going to get away with acting the wrong way or not doing the work." We use very structured routines here. Students know what to expect down to every little detail.

Many of Polly's students have police records from gang activity and other illegal actions that may explain the structured environment that exists in her school.

Anita, a Philadelphia middle school teacher for 25 years, explained her business-like attitude on managing students:

> I think my strong personality comes through to my students which says, "You're here to learn, and this is what you're going to do." If students don't seem to understand that then I contact their parents right away and let them know, "I went to school here." I'm not asking them [students] to fly out windows. I don't ask them to do anything I wouldn't ask my own children to do.

The experienced teachers were adamant about how they established these business-like learning environments while managing to maintain mutually respectful relationships with students. All but one of the novice teachers (teachers with fewer than 3 years of experience) explained how they failed to create clearly stated expectations and enforce those during the year.

## ESTABLISHING CONGRUENT COMMUNICATION PROCESSES

Effective teachers encourage congruent communication processes with students and are able to create meaningful bonds with their students based on genuine social interactions. Several teachers mentioned that their students needed many opportunities for socialization as a part of instructional activities and designed learning experiences that promoted socialization and discussion. Teachers of second-language learners were particularly conscious of students' need for verbal interaction during class time.

Lisa, whose first-grade students in a Los Angeles elementary school are primarily recent immigrant Mexican Americans, uses some class time to permit students to settle disputes with their friends:

> They're always into arguments with each other. I use conversation to get them to think about

their behavior and to learn to negotiate; even with me on certain issues. I expect them to talk. That's how they learn the language.

Pete, who teaches high school second-language learners in Philadelphia, described some of the activities that he initiates for his students, many of whom are refugees:

> I get my students moving around and interacting with each other during class. I allow students the freedom to talk to each other and exchange ideas. When you're learning language, you have to allow students to speak it. This year we did a unit on fables, and the students wrote and illustrated them. Then we invited kindergarten students in as judges as my students performed their fables in front of them.

Differences in communication styles and expectations of oral behavior can also affect the quality of the relationship between teachers and their African, Hispanic, and Native American and other immigrant students. Adrienne described her African American high school students from Los Angeles, "Conversation is their primary priority. It's so unconscious. They are from very verbal environments. I find that they can handle side discussions and engage in the main discussion at the same time. They're not talking to be disruptive." Realizing this characteristic can help urban teachers develop appropriate instructional activities that build on these interactions instead of discouraging socialization among students.

Listening may be one of the most powerful means of establishing respectful relationships with students. As I was waiting to interview Colette in a Philadelphia high school, several students came into the room. Colette caught them at the door to tell them that she needed to speak to me during her planning period this particular day. Students frequently come into her room during their study halls and lunch periods to chat with her. Colette explained:

> I talk to them, I'll listen to them. A kid told me, "I can tell you anything." I don't have any boys [children of her own], and these teenage males want to talk to me about personal stuff. Why are they telling me? Don't they have anybody at home to talk about this to? I think it's just an indicator that they feel comfortable. I think they know that I care about them.

The power of explicitly addressing communication processes between students and teachers cannot be overlooked if teachers desire student cooperation.

## TEACHING WITH ASSERTIVENESS AND CLEARLY STATED EXPECTATIONS

One particularly troubling weakness among novice teachers is their lack of assertiveness with students. Often teachers expect student obedience and to be treated with respect merely because they are teachers (Obidah & Man-

heim Teel, 2001). The reaction from teachers is then the use of a mild-mannered approach with students in which teachers make requests and expect students to respond with enthusiasm merely because they use the word, "please." The four novice teachers (fewer than 3 years experience) who were interviewed admit their initial reluctance to establish high expectations for behavior and academic achievement and the resultant challenge that presents to their classroom order. Jeff, a high school English teacher from Wichita, spoke of his first year reluctance to establish clear expectations:

> I started teaching here when I was 21 years old. My students' brothers and sisters were older than I was. When I wasn't sure what I wanted to do, my students would tell me. I had a hard time establishing authority.

Shanika, who teaches in a Philadelphia middle school, noted, "I started off very softly with my management issues. I didn't set any limits, and so I had a hard time the rest of the year."

The experienced teachers who were interviewed were well aware of the need to establish and uphold clear expectations for behavior and to enforce their expectations. They were also aware of the need to act assertively with students. Diane, an experienced fifth-grade San Francisco teacher, explained her transformation from easygoing to an assertive teaching personality:

> I developed my inner teacher voice. One woman, Gilda Bloom, calls it, "Find your inner bitch." It means you mean business, and its got to come from your toes." I respect my students, and it takes a while to build that trust. You have to be consistent with kindness and respect for students. I always treat them fairly.

Colette, the Philadelphia high school teacher, provided this advice for novice urban teachers:

> I think somebody that really wants to be an urban teacher has to have heart; but they have to have chutzpah, too. You can't come in here all soft voiced and meek and mild. They're going to eat you up and spit you out. And those kids can sense whether you're afraid of them or not. I said in a joking manner, while I was wearing a Burger King crown one day, "I am the queen in here!" They have to know that you expect things of them because sometimes these kids don't have anything expected of them at home. They're like ships awash in the sea of life.

Delpit (1995) reinforced Colette's beliefs as she described the expectations of many African American students:

> Black people often view issues of power and authority differently than people from mainstream middle class backgrounds. Many people of color expect authority to be earned by personal efforts

and exhibited by personal characteristics. In other words, "the authoritative person gets to be a teacher because she is authoritative." Some members of middle class cultures, by contrast, expect one to achieve authority by the acquisition of an authoritative role. That is, "the teacher is the authority because she is the teacher."(p. 35)

Acting with fear toward students is perhaps a more dangerous reaction by teachers in urban classrooms than failing to establish clear expectations for behavior and academic progress. Weiner (1999) provided this warning to teachers who demonstrate fear of their students:

> When teachers are intimidated by their students, they're unable to address behavior straightforwardly because their fear is paralyzing. In my experience in working with new teachers who are afraid of their students but unwilling to admit it, the strategy most adopt is to ignore the misconduct. Children know when teachers fear them and resent it because the fear is demeaning in its reversal of appropriate adult-child relations. The misbehaving child is not receiving suitable guidance from the adult in authority, and he or she realizes it perhaps more quickly than the adult. (p. 76)

A challenging aspect to managing students is establishing an appropriate balance of power in a classroom. Teachers must maintain authority status and provide students with some decisionmaking authority while avoiding power struggles with students. Shanika, who is in her 2nd year of teaching in a Philadelphia middle school, described how she falls into power struggles with students:

> Some kids acting out just want power. Then, when you give them attention, they're taking the power away from you. I definitely fall into that with certain students. They just push my buttons. Then I sometimes say something to embarrass them in front of the class. That's cruel, and it's engaging in a power struggle that reallywastes everyone's time. That's something I really want to work on—how to communicate with students when they're really in their thing. I really don't want to kick students out.

Power struggles between teachers and students often result in more hostility and a complete lack of respect between the two. It is wise for teachers to avoid power struggles initiated by students. Students have power, and as they enter middle school and advance to high school their power base increases as they attempt to impress peers and other classmates by initiating arguments with teachers. Effective educators recognize students' power and defuse it by ignoring a student's attempt to engage in an argument, or providing the student with an escape route to save face in front of peers. Colette shares her view of handling power issues with students, "I don't get

into any pissing contests with any kid. I learned that early on. I just think to myself, 'This situation has more power than my arguing about it will.'"

The suggestions from these teachers regarding the importance of being assertive and the advice to provide opportunities for students to become involved in a democratic sense in classroom processes may appear to some as opposing possibilities. Teachers must act assertively in responding to inappropriate behavior and as they establish explicit guidelines for behavioral and academic expectations mutually with students. Assertive behavior is required as teachers enforce expectations as a way of following through with classroom policies and protecting students physically, socially, and academically.

Democratic opportunities are provided to students when they are invited to become involved in decision making regarding classroom policies, curricular choices, assessment options, and other classroom decisions that affect their motivation and interests. Using democratic decision-making opportunities should not create a breach in the rules that are established to protect the classroom community and sense of cooperation among students that is needed for learning to occur.

Effectively managing students, although guided by effective practice and research, also involves a series of highly fluid and dynamic actions by teachers that often cannot be predetermined due to the nature of humans. All of these 13 urban teachers have developed awareness and a certain savvy with some management principles required to create a cooperative spirit within their students.

## CONCLUSION

Researchers in the field of culturally responsive teaching have provided educators with specific strategies for addressing the learning profiles and needs of a diverse population of students (Cary, 2000; Delpit, 1995; Gay, 2000; Howard, 2001; Ladson-Billings, 1994, 2001; Weiner, 1999). The majority of students who reside in and attend schools in the urban centers of America are a highly culturally, ethnically, and socioeconomically diverse population. More than 80% of the teachers who will enter these urban classrooms will be primarily inexperienced teachers who are middle-class White European Americans (Ladson-Billings, 2001).

I interviewed 13 urban teachers for the current study to determine if and how they establish a classroom management system that reflects the needs of learners whom they encounter each day. Evidence exists that every one of these 13 teachers uses a number of specific management strategies that support culturally responsive pedagogy.

A significant finding is that all the teachers interviewed were primarily nonpunitive in their approach to handling disruptive behavior. They relied on their strong relationships with students built on trust rather than fear or punishment to maintain a cooperative learning environment. Each teacher demonstrated mutual respect for students through congruent communication patterns that honored students' ethnic and cultural needs. Teachers spoke of creating caring learning communities and demonstrating genuine interest in each student.

All the teachers with at least 5 years of experience (nine) established clearly stated expectations for behavior and used an assertive demeanor when necessary to establish their authority as a teacher. These same teachers also described how they established a businesslike classroom learning environment with explicitly stated expectations for student behavior and academic progress.

The novice respondents (four teachers with fewer than 3 years of experience) spoke of the difficulties they faced their first couple of years. These difficulties were created because of their explanations of their failure to establish an assertive stance and an accompanying set of clearly stated and enforced expectations that guided students toward better academic performance and behavior.

The question that arises as a result of the current study for researchers and teacher educators is whether preservice and in-service teacher training can prepare teachers to respond in culturally responsive ways through their chosen management strategies to the needs of urban students. I found no conclusive explanation for how these teachers learned to accept and demonstrate culturally responsive management strategies other than learning through their direct experiences in urban schools. In searching for an explanation for these teachers' acceptance and demonstration of culturally responsive management one common characteristic was noted for some respondents: six of the respondents grewup in urban environments. The other seven teachers, however, had no exposure to urban schools prior to entering the profession. None of the 13 teachers received any specific training or education in culturally responsive teaching strategies. An encouraging note is that all these educators entered the profession as certified teachers indicating specific training prior to becoming teachers, unlike many recently hired urban teachers who are not certified when they begin their teaching careers (Archer, 2000; Crosby, 1999; Wong, 2000). It appears, therefore, that at a minimum, some urban teaching experience is required to adopt and implement the attitudes and behaviors associated with culturally responsive management techniques.

What is known is that the urban centers are frequently in urgent need of teacher replacements. The New York City public school system was searching for 8,000 teachers for the fall 2001 academic year; Los Angeles—5,000; and Chicago as many as 1,500 new teachers for the fall 2001 academic year (Banner, 2001; Ladson-Billings, 2001). Many urban teachers will quit during or directly after their first year of teaching most likely for reasons associated with failure to effectively manage a classroom of such diverse learners (Wilkins-Canter, Edwards, & Young, 2000).

Novice urban teachers must quickly comprehend how to effectively develop a classroom of mutual respect and cooperation if they intend to positively affect students' learning and survive professionally in an urban classroom. Many universities and colleges offer urban education courses, urban field experiences, urban education emphases, and minors in urban education to preservice and in-service teachers. Professors who teach in these programs must be aware of the value of the theoretical viewpoints as well as the practical components of culturally responsive classroom management as described in the voices of experienced urban practitioners. Much of the success of novice teachers in urban environments depends on their ability to develop positive classroom learning environments through the implementation of culturally responsive classroom management practices.

## NOTE

1. Some of the data found within this manuscript are also cited in the book *Becoming A Successful Urban Teacher* (2002) written by the author.

## REFERENCES

Archer, J. (2000, January 26). Teacher recruitment harder in urban areas report says. *Education Week, 19*, p. 20.

Banner, J. (Producer). (2001, July 12), *Nightly News* [Television broadcast]. New York: American Broadcasting Company.

Brown, D. F. (1999). The value of advisory sessions: Perceptions of young adolescents at an urban middle school. *Research in Middle Level Education Quarterly, 22*(4), 41-57.

Brown, D. F. (2001). The value of advisory sessions for urban young adolescents. *Middle School Journal, 32*(4), 14-22.

Brown, D. F. (2002). *Becoming a successful urban teacher*. Portsmouth, NH; Westerville, OH: Heinemann and National Middle School Association.

Cary, S. (2000). *Working with second language learners: Answers to teachers' top ten questions*. Portsmouth, NH: Heinemann.

Crosby, E. A. (1999). Urban schools forced to fail. *Phi Delta Kappan, 81*(4), 298-303.

Delpit, L. (1995). *Other people's children: Cultural conflict in the classroom*. New York: New Press.

Dryfoos, J. (1998). Safe passage: *Making it through adolescence in a risky society*. New York: Oxford University Press.

Gay, G. (2000). *Culturally responsive teaching: Theory, research, and practice*. New York: Teachers College Press.

Gibbs, J. T., Huang, L. N., & Associates. (1998). *Children of color: Psychological interventions with culturally diverse youth* (updated ed.). San Francisco: Jossey-Bass.

Glaser, B. G., & Strauss, A. L. (1967). *The discovery of grounded theory*. Hawthorne, NY: Aldine.

Gordon, G. L. (1999).Teacher talent and urban schools. *Phi Delta Kappan, 81*(4), 304-307.

Haberman, M. (1995). *Star teachers of children in poverty*. West Lafayette, IN: Kappa Delta Pi.

Heath, S. B. (1983). *Ways with words*. Cambridge, UK: Cambridge University Press.

Howard, G. R. (1999). *We can't teach what we don't know: White teachers, multiracial schools*. New York: Teachers College Press.

Howard, T. C. (2001).Telling their side of the story: African-American students' perceptions of culturally relevant teaching. *Urban Review, 33*(2), 131-149.

Hyman, I. A., & Snook, P. A. (2000). Dangerous schools and what you can do about them. *Phi Delta Kappan, 81*(7), 488-501.

Ladson-Billings, G. (1994). *The dreamkeepers: Successful teachers of African American children.* San Francisco: Jossey-Bass.

Ladson-Billings, G. (2001). *Crossing over to Canaan: The journey of new teachers in diverse classrooms.* San Francisco: Jossey-Bass.

LeCompte, M. D., & Preissle, J. (1993). *Ethnography and qualitative design in educational research* (2nd ed.). San Diego, CA: Academic Press.

Obidah, J. E., & Manheim Teel, K. (2001). *Because of the kids: Facing racial and cultural differences in schools.* New York: Teachers College Press.

Snow, C. E., Arlman-Rup, A., Hassing, Y., Josbe, J., Joosten, J., & Vorster, J. (1976). Mother's speech in three social classes. *Journal of Psycholinguistic Research, 5,* 1-20.

Weiner, L. (1999). *Urban teaching: The essentials.* New York: Teachers College Press.

Wilkins-Canter, E. A., Edwards, A. T., & Young, A. L. (2000). Preparing novice teachers to handle stress. *Kappa Delta Pi Record, 36*(3), 128-130.

# WHEN CENTRAL CITY HIGH SCHOOL STUDENTS SPEAK

## Doing Critical Inquiry for Democracy

*Based on a yearlong critical inquiry project in a central Los Angeles high school, the author discusses the implications of engaging students in dialogue and critique about their experiences with race. The students' voices, through participant observation field notes and their own writing, tell stories of struggle and newfound understandings about the relationship among equity, social issues, and their lives. Drawing upon the works of John Dewey, Paulo Freire, and Nancy Fraser, critical inquiry is conceptualized as a valid learning tool with a liberatory agenda that creates an alternate public sphere where young people learn about themselves and question the status quo.*

***Keywords:*** *critical inquiry; high school; race; dialogue; social studies*

KARINA OTOYA-KNAPP
*Bank Street College of Education*

In World War I, they were trying to end all wars, but instead they had another. Millions of people died.... I think this is a crazy racist world and I don't think it will ever change no matter how hard we try.

—Ninth-grade African American female,
April 1999

I open this article with the voice of a ninth-grade African American girl whose feelings of hopelessness echo those of many, particularly today as we lie amidst yet another war. Many adolescents experience racism, among other social prejudices, and seldom have the opportunity to unpack the frustration they feel. We must ask, like Cornel West (1999), "How does one attempt to transform this meaningless and hopelessness into a more effective kind of struggle and resistance?" (pp. 294-295). This qualitative study describes how six classrooms of ninth-grade urban school students from New High[1] engaged in critical inquiry about their experiences and how they are affected by race, class, gender, and power issues. These critical dis-

cussions "create[d] spaces ... where they can take initiatives and uncover humanizing possibilities" (Greene, 1988, p. 13). For one academic school year, these students questioned social norms and voiced their opinions and concerns about the prevailing inequalities and their own futures.

This qualitative research project stems from critical theory in terms of its potential to empower students to critique social inequality and to better understand themselves and their peers. More specifically, the critical inquiry framework that informs the data is rooted in the work of John Dewey (1904, 1938) in his emphasis on experience and reflection, on Paulo Freire's (1985) concept of "conscientization" and "problematization," and Nancy Fraser's (1994) reconceptualization of the "public sphere." During monthly structured critical inquiry meetings, the students in this study were asked to reflect on their own experiences and those of their peers, problematize the "normal," and participate in the democratic process of reinventing and rethinking the possibilities in

society. In the next sections, I will make a case for the need to engage students in critique and dialogue, and then I will conceptualize the three theoretical perspectives as they shed light on the data.

## LISTENING TO MULTICULTURAL VOICES

Current literature on the importance of listening to students' voices focuses on the insights young people have on specific topics like substance abuse or on their perspectives on academic achievement and reform (Honora, 2003; Lee, 1999; Wasley, Hampel, & Clark, 1997). Even still, Taylor-Dunlap (1998) argued that "the voice that has consistently been missing, from the dialogue, is that of the adolescents" (p. 1). Namely, what is missing from the literature are cases in which young people initiate dialogues in which they can discuss their experiences.

Some critical projects, however, that highlight students' voices have been attempted at the high school level. McGregor (2000), a teacher in Queensland, Australia, noted that the students who engaged in critique at her school faced stigmatization by their peers and other teachers. Those who work from a status quo framework might perceive students who learn to critique the status quo as discipline problems or outcasts. "If education systems are serious about the implementation of critical literacy, those who administer schools and those who teach students must begin to rethink their reactions to students who 'talk back'" (McGregor, 2000, p. 222). Having critical dialogues in the classroom takes a willing teacher (one who is radical and daring) whom others will support. In fact, one has to wonder what factors contributed to McGregor's departure from that school.

In his critical work with adolescents, Wolk (2003) argued that students should have "the skills and desire to evaluate society and the world. The critique is especially focused on issues of power: Who has it and who is denied it; how it is used and how it is abused" (p. 102). His description of "doing critical literacy" with his social studies students emphasizes the importance of presenting critical literacy knowledge and perspectives from within the existing curriculum. Although integrating critique and dialogue into the curriculum is paramount, there must be other times when students feel safe to have discussions that are not necessarily tied to the curriculum. Furthermore, teachers must also consider their own position of power and how it might or might not silence students.

Given the proposition that students must have safe spaces to critique and dialogue, and considering the struggles that teachers must be ready to make to engage in these conversations, I will briefly explain the theoretical proposition that critical inquiry is a learning tool for learning, critique, and democracy. Below, I draw from the work of John Dewey, Paulo Freire, and Nancy Fraser to frame how critical inquiry in the form of group discussion serves as a learning space where students can explore pressing issues and how this framework sheds light on the analysis of students' voices.

Dewey (1938) asserted that there is "one permanent frame of reference: namely the organic connection between education and personal experience" (p. 25). He argued that learning and personal experiences are interconnected. Moreover, Dewey, a social re-

constructionist, believed that for a learner to learn from experience, he or she must (a) go through a problematic situation that causes transformation, (b) seek interactions to clarify and expand on new experiences, and (c) develop a social conscience. Thus, if students are to learn or grow, teaching and learning should be related to the students' lives within the concerns that surround their community and society.

> Learning which develops intelligence and character does not come about when only the textbook and the teacher have a say; that every individual becomes educated only as he has an opportunity to contribute something from his own experience … and finally that enlightenment comes from the give and take, from the exchange of experiences and ideas. (Dewey, 1938, p. 296)

In this vein, providing students with opportunities to interact and explore problematic situations within a social justice[2] framework has the potential to help students think about people in society, particularly those who are marginal in the system.

According to Dewey (1916/1944), having interactions with other learners also helps in the process of democratic growth because one is able to better understand other perspectives. He wrote about "getting outside of [the situation], seeing it as another would see it, considering what points of contact it has with the life of another so that it may go into such form that he can appreciate its meaning" (p. 6). Thus, communication increases clarity and accuracy of thought so that one may articulate one's perspective to others more effectively. Through careful and continuous reflection, one might better clarify personal perspectives and understand the perspectives of others.

Freire (1985) added another layer of richness to Dewey's ideas about reflection and experience. Like Dewey, Freire believed that people exist "in and with the world" (p. 68). He argued that because people live together, they must be able to "objectify" themselves and reflect on their lives "within the very domain of existence, and question … [their] relationship to the world" (p. 68). Freire felt that without a consciousness of how self is connected to society, people would not be able to liberate themselves; some might even justify their oppression. Without conscientization, the "instrument for ejecting the cultural myths that remain in the people despite the new reality" (p. 87), people might find themselves replicating serious

and covert injustices of the past and creating further inequalities.

Reflective conscientization entails problematizing that which is taken for granted or "normal" and which serves to preserve the power of a few elite. Freire (1985) argued that one could only problematize a situation after objectifying and distancing oneself from the oppressing forces. The process of conscientization could take place through dialogue, interaction, and critique: "Conscientization is a joint project in that it takes place in a man among other men, men united by their action and by their reflection upon that action and upon the world" (p. 85). Thus, if students are given the vocabulary and tools to discuss and uncover the obstacles in their environment, they might see themselves as active agents in their own futures.

Access to these conversations and opportunities to problematize the status quo has been limited to elite groups. Habermas's (1962/1994) study of the public sphere described how privileged groups gathered to critique government and voice their opinions. The public sphere became the "sphere of private people [that] come together as a public … to engage them [public authorities] in a debate over the general rules governing relations in the basically privatized but publicly relevant sphere of commodity exchange and social labor" (p. 27). These new entrepreneurs, or the new bourgeoisie, were given status as "logical" and could use "reason" to critique government decisions that did not favor their economic status. The members who participated in the public sphere changed over time, but their status of political and social privilege remained constant.

Nancy Fraser's critique of the public sphere speaks directly to the exclusionary practices of public spheres. Fraser (1994) argued that Habermas's depiction of the new public sphere does not address differences in power among the people who gathered. She proposed that additional spheres should exist, including those that critique the status quo. She suggested that through meaning making and struggling with diverse ideas, public spheres may open doors for different voices to be heard.

Fraser (1994) described dialogue and communication in terms of democracy in education. She discussed how Habermas's theory of the public sphere needs to incorporate multiple voices in discussions about social and political issues. The public sphere, as viewed by Fraser, includes a theoretical perspective that takes into account the need for different voices and different groups that grapple with ideas of democracy and social justice.

Together, Dewey, Freire, and Fraser helped create a conceptual framework of critical inquiry in terms of learning through critique and dialogue. Based on this understanding of critical inquiry, a first-year teacher and I created critical inquiry spaces in which 6 ninth-grade social studies classes would meet monthly for a year to engage in critique and dialogue. In a public sphere of critical inquiry, multiple voices—adolescents, females, males, people of all colors—who have not been heard and who live and attend a school in a central city explore issues important to them. As they engaged in critical dialogue about their lives within a social, historical, and political context, many of them for the first time became leaders, participated in class, and critiqued injustice.

# METHOD

## ACADEMIC CONTEXT: NEW HIGH SCHOOL, MR. ROSE, AND THE FACILITATOR

Located in Los Angeles, New High School opened in 1998 to fulfill the demands of growing African American and Latino populations in the community. Surrounded by two freeway entrances and close to the airport, the immediate neighborhood reveals treeless blocks of low-income housing with many Asian-owned "mom-and-pop" stores and several auto mechanic shops. The school sits in the middle of an open field with a cement basketball court near the teachers' parking lot.

Nearly 500 students enrolled the first year New High opened (and the year of this project). That year, there were 275 Hispanic, 138 African American, 53 White, 15 Asian, 9 Pacific Islander, and 2 Native American students. The student body had 258 male students and 235 female students. More than 50% of the students received Title I Services, qualifying them for free or reduced lunch. The school did not have athletic facilities, a sore point for many of the students. The class sizes averaged 30 students, mostly Latino and African American.

At the time of this project, there were 19 White teachers, 4 Hispanic teachers, 4 Asian teachers, and 3 African American teachers at New High. This study took place in Mr. Rose's six world history classes at New High. Mr. Rose was a 30-year-old White man who practiced law in California for 6 years before deciding to become a teacher. In the fall of 1997, Mr. Rose en-

rolled in UCLA's Teacher Education Program (TEP) that culminated in a master's degree in education (M.Ed.). During his first year in the TEP, Mr. Rose participated in a critical inquiry group for teachers and students at one of his student teaching placements. Mr. Rose felt that he had learned much from listening to the other teachers and to the students' concerns. He also felt that it was important for his students to talk about their experiences with race, class, and gender, particularly because, as Mr. Rose critiqued, the curriculum is "Eurocentric and not representative of his students' experiences in this country" (Coleman, 1999, p. 2). He wanted to create "open discussion about students' personal and school issues that really mattered to them" (p. 2). To this end, each one of Mr. Rose's world history classes met monthly for 55-minute blocks of time. The students sat at their desks, which were arranged in a circle around the spacious classroom.

At the end of his student teaching experience and the summer before his first year at New High School as a head teacher, Mr. Rose asked me if I would facilitate critical inquiry discussions in his classrooms. I am a Peruvian heterosexual woman who immigrated to the United States at 9 years of age, and I identify with the Latino population and more broadly as a "person of color." I taught in Los Angeles and Chicago public schools before entering UCLA's urban education Ph.D. program, where I studied the impact of critical inquiry groups in first-year teachers' personal and professional identities (Otoya, 2000). Being in the same School of Education, Mr. Rose knew about my interests and work and asked me to facilitate critical inquiry sessions with his students. In addition, Mr. Rose felt that his students would be more open and honest with an "outsider" who would not have influence over their grades.

As a person of color who believes in social justice and democracy, I entered into this project with the assumption that all education is political and that research must advocate for the oppressed. Although I systematically collected data, it is important to acknowledge that my beliefs guide my analysis. Moreover, as a participant in the critical inquiry sessions, I was part of the "reflective awareness of the rights and obligations of humans [as a way to] conceptualize empowerment, equity, and a struggle for liberation" (Trueba, 1999, p. 128). Although it is evident that I have a social justice agenda, it was not my place to tell students how or what to think.

## DATA COLLECTION

Data were collected from the fall of 1998 to the spring of 1999. Because this study was situated within a critical and dialectical perspective, the data and the dialogic process of critical inquiry with the students were organically intertwined. Three data sources were collected during the academic year. First, participant observation field notes from the critical inquiry sessions were taken. I also recorded conversations I had with Mr. Rose in reaction to these sessions. These notes dictated the direction of future inquiry sessions; if, however, the students wanted to talk about another pressing issue, we shifted focus. The second set of data was student-generated documents that were collected during the second to last meeting of the year (April 1999). Mr. Rose asked the students to write a letter about how they defined inquiry, what they liked and did not like about it, and other topics they would like to discuss during future inquiry discussions. Finally, data were collected from Mr. Rose's master's thesis, a portfolio of his work submitted as a partial requisite before he could receive his degree from UCLA.

## DATA ANALYSIS

After reading the data transcripts in their entirety several times, data were initially partitioned and displayed chronologically into a descriptive matrix as described by Miles and Huberman (1994). Some of the data were synthesized and grouped by patterns to understand the participants' perspectives on different topics. These data were further arranged and organized by emerging patterns to increase the clarity of their meaning. The data were reduced to six categories and then combined into three themes used to write the narrative (Creswell, 1998). The six original categories that emerged were the following: reflecting about self, personal stories, questioning, social critique, modes of participation, and resistance against the status quo. Using descriptive matrices, I combined the data into three overarching themes that were informed by the theoretical framework. These themes were (a) *experience* and *reflection,* (b) *conscientization* and *problematization,* and (c) *students' leadership, participation,* and *resistance.* For this article, I chose small samples of inquiry discussions from the six classes to illustrate these broader themes of the critical inquiry conversations.

In the next subsections, the students' voices will ring loud and true as we hear them engage in the dialectical process of inquiry. I selected representative dialogues from the different classes that highlight the themes. Not all conversations were about race and equity. Especially during the first few months, the students and I needed to build trust and respect and establish a human relationship.

# EXPERIENCE AND REFLECTION

When people cannot name alternatives, imagine a better state of things, share with others a project of change, they are likely to remain anchored or submerged, even as they proudly assert their autonomy. (Greene, 1988, p. 9)

The following snippet of conversation takes place in February 1999, our fifth session. I ask the students to tell me what kind of adults they want to become. The conversation begins with a prosaic discussion of careers but leads to a deeper discussion of values and self in which they think about who they are "becoming" in alternative ways.

**Tyshon:** When I am an adult, I want to play professional football. I have to continue with school and practice everyday to become successful. I have to stay out of trouble with the law and finish high school.

**Makia:** But we don't even have a football team!

**Tyshon:** Well, if I don't make it, I want to become an architect. I will need to do a lot of math and … well, knowledge.

**Facilitator:** But how do you want to live your lives?

(The class is silent for what seems an eternity but is no more than one minute.)

**Facilitator:** What kind of human beings do you want to become?

**Robert:** I want to be the kind of person who helps people with their problems and sicknesses, like a doctor. But I won't charge a lot of money for seeing them.

**Talia:** I want to be a teacher because I want to inspire people to go for their goals like I'm trying to go for mine.

**Facilitator:** Good. Now we're talking. You are thinking about what meaning your work is going to have.

**Perry:** I still want to be a businessman or technician because I want to live comfortably. Besides, I want to reward my parents for raising me right and show-

ing me what a home is supposed to be like. I know I'm not doing well in class, but I am determined to do better this semester.

**Rebecca:** I want to be a smarter person because it would help me work hard and understand what I am doing.

**Nena:** I want to be a respectful person who is respected. Also, smart, patient, trustable.

**Purvee:** Yeah. I want to be trusted, too. But, more so, I want to be more self-confident.

**Sorren:** I want to be strong and always helpful to people…. I want to be the best for me.

**Dameequa:** Right now, I am the kind of person that will stomp all over someone's heart and feelings just because I am having a bad day. I want to be more understanding because if someone does something that I don't like, I might not listen to why they did it. I just may not speak to them anymore when I could have been more understanding. I want to be more sensitive instead of holding my emotions, act more like a girl. (February 1999)

In this inquiry discussion, students are asked to communicate their feelings in ways that move beyond careers and jobs and into human qualities. This reflection and dialogue helps them clarify their personal perspectives. For example, Dameequa reflects on the person she is and thinks about the person she wants to become. She candidly admits that she would like to be more sensitive, more like a "girl." Dameequa associates masculinity with a person who would "stomp all over someone's heart." Society reinforces stereotypes of men as strong and women as sensitive. And although the rest of the conversation would help us deconstruct the meaning of "female," in this discussion, we see a student who imagines a life in which she would be "more understanding" instead of what might be perceived as a rash reaction to hurtful comments.

We cannot escape, however, the reality that accompanies the dreams of some of the youth in central cities. Tyshon, an African American male, talks about his dream of becoming a football player and how he must "stay out of trouble with the law." His answer reflects a reality for him as an African American male in Los Angeles, where there is much conflict between the police and people of color. Teaching and learning do not happen void of students' experiences. Especially because

students like Tyshon live in a contentious society, it is important for them to have a place where they can imagine possibilities and challenge their constraints.

A reality that students face daily, and one that consumes society, is racism. Often the first reaction to racism, for example, is violence. Through inquiry, students can learn from each other's stories and use the tools of conversation to peacefully question and critique why society might hold hostility toward some groups. In the following inquiry discussion, we talk about personal experiences with racism and the struggle to understand its roots.

**Gabriella:** It's hard for me. Many times, when I go to department stores with my mom who is Mexican, we don't get any help or great service from the sales clerks. But when I go with my dad, who is Peruvian but looks Caucasian, we get a lot of help and great service. I have also come across many people who assume that I am not worth anything because I am a mixed race and they are usually amazed by my intelligence or the fact that I can speak perfect English without an accent. Sometimes, things that happen have made me want to move to a different country. Sometimes, they make me feel so bad that I just want to crawl into a hole and never come out. But, I have learned and realized that it's not really worth getting upset over what people think of you as long as you are proud of who you are. I wish ignorant people would show more respect and learn not to judge.

**Facilitator:** I want to tell you about a personal experience with racism. Last month, I was in a dry cleaners store in New York City. The woman ahead of me was spelling her name aloud and the clerk, who had an accent, asked her to repeat her name again, and she sighed. She began again, now almost screaming. I told her that she didn't need to yell, that sometimes it is hard to get down new spellings. She looked at me, grabbed her shirts, and turned toward the door. As she walked out, she yelled at me, "Ignorant spik!" and she spit on the floor. I was so angry! I yelled back at her, "You are the ignorant spik!" Then, I felt awful. I wondered how I could have gotten so mad. How else could I have handled it? Why do you think she yelled at me?

**Mikael:** I think when people make fun of other races, it is because they were taught that way. It is not really their fault because the parents were probably taught that way and so on.

**Antoinette:** She was just plain ignorant.

**Parker:** I would have spit at her! Shhhh-hhh…. I think you told her good.

**Facilitator:** I'm not proud of how I reacted and I'm not sure that violence would have helped, even if I was that angry.

**Renee:** Sometimes, things make you so mad that you can't control yourself.

**Jung Lee:** I don't like racism, even if I have never experienced it. It gets me mad when somebody is talking about another race, even if it is not my race. I get angry! I don't think anybody's race should be put down. My friends have experienced racism. They went to the 7-11 store to buy batteries, and it was expensive so they returned it. The clerk said, "Your kind always do these things." The same clerk is always saying that Mexicans gamble a lot.

**Perry:** I think a lot of people make fun of other groups and races without wanting to. They might let things slip out. That happened to me before, and I felt so bad. If it were up to me, I would take it back. (December 1998)

The outcome of these conversations is not to come to a conclusion or solution. The goal is the process of dialogue itself. The students and the facilitator shared personal stories with racism. Having other people who have also experienced similar situations validates the sense of frustration often felt. Yet the facilitator's questions were guided to get students to think about alternative responses to moments of anger. Consider also Jung Lee's comment that although his friends have been discriminated against, he has "never experienced it." Jung Lee is a Korean student who lives in a community where Koreans own many of the stores. Although the Korean experience may appear a model of the American Dream, Chang (1993) and Kim (2000) argued that the model minority image grossly exaggerates the status of Koreans in America. Although it is entirely possible that Jung Lee has never felt direct discrimination, like many of the students he may not understand the structural inequities that frame opportunities (Choi, Lizardo, & Phillips, 1996; Otoya-Knapp, 2002).

As Freire (1985) argued, students must find a place where they can question their "relationship to the world"; otherwise, they might justify their own oppression. One student said it best: "Talking in inquiry … makes me feel better about what I

am saying…. You can talk about all of your issues. You won't have to keep them bottled up inside you" (personal communication, April 1999). Furthermore, inquiry conversations open avenues for students to release tensions that often get ignored and packed away: "I think that what we are doing is a good thing by discussing what we feel towards people of another race. I'm feeling that inquiry is going to help us get together even more as a class." That comment made by a student confirms Dewey's (1916/1944) stance that through reflection and dialogue, human beings come to possess things that they have in common and appreciate their differences.

# PROBLEMATIZATION AND CONSCIENTIZATION

It is only through an examination of the link between culture and power that a critical theory of cultural democracy can emerge to function in creating the conditions that will support the emancipatory interests of students of color by incorporating their voices into the discourse of public schooling. (Darder, 1991, p. 25)

The next inquiry discussion highlights a conversation that occurred a few days after the Columbine shootings in April 1999 in which two distraught White teenagers murdered 14 students and one teacher in broad daylight. The conversation about hatred and racial intolerance led the students to talk about biracial friendships and relationships. In the following inquiry vignette, the students examine the link between culture and power and the barriers that prevent people from having friends across color lines:

**Daquan:** I have friends of different races, and I treat them all the same. They may be a different color, but it is what's inside that counts.

**Rosana:** I think it's cool to have friends from different races because you can learn about their cultures and backgrounds. Doing that makes you a better person.

**Josseline:** My parents are racist! They don't like me hanging out with Black people. I brought this guy home, he is from Paloa. My mother doesn't ever want me even to talk to him. I asked her, "What if I got married with a Tongan, or Black, or Filipino?" And she turned to my grandmother, "Hey, would you like to have Black grand-

kids? Grandmother said it would be nice. But my mom said, "Not for me."

**Facilitator:** Why do you think your mother feels this way?

**Josseline:** My mom judged him by the way he dresses and by the color of his skin.

**Ali:** There are groups like the KKK that set a very bad example for others. They are ignorant. I think that everyone from different races should know each other very well so that we can live in a very friendly society.

**Teesha:** I think that if you [only] have friends who are the same race, you won't be able to find out what other people's nationalities are like. You might look at them in a racist kind of way because you don't know them.

**Josseline:** Having friends from different races means we are trying to change and get along with other races. (April 1999)

Like Josseline, a Latina, many of the students' families do not approve of interracial relationships. Ali begins to tap into the wider social forces that encourage separatist attitudes but does not go beyond imagining life in a "friendly society." Daquan holds a colorblind philosophy about interracial friendships. For many of them, racism could be explained at the individual rather than at the institutional or structural level. As Freire (1985) argued, problematization and conscientization are processes of dialogue, interaction, and critique. Inquiry gave the students a place where they could begin to problematize the eminent issue of race from their own experiences.

Structural inequities are uncovered when people notice them directly in their own lives and have places where they can make sense of these experiences. One March afternoon after lunch, a female student was telling her friend that she thought it was wrong that the special education students had to pick up the garbage. Once the students had settled, the facilitator asked the student to explain what she had witnessed:

**Patricia:** The special education kids have to pick up the trash in exchange for their gym period. It is not fair! It is not right, and people should think about this. If they don't pick up their own trash, the special education kids are going to have to do it…. I'm sure if their brother or sister were picking up trash, they would be pretty pissed off and want to do something about it!

**Sam:** This is so wrong! They probably told the special education kids that picking up garbage is part of their grade. If I were them, I would tell my parents!

**Tomas:** Those kids have no choice on what they have to do. They don't realize there is anything wrong with what they are doing. People use them and think that since they can't be doctors or lawyers, they are not human beings. They have to pay for something they can't control.

**Dushaun:** I think it is the school who makes the special education kids to pick up the garbage. This school is so cheap that they would probably send those kids to pick up the garbage in another school. They say it is exercise; well, not to me. Exercise is when you stretch your body, not bending over for trash. They have to stop that!

**Facilitator:** What are some changes we could make? Or, what are some alternatives?

**Sara:** It is an injustice that special education kids pick up the trash. I think that people should serve detention if they don't pick up their own garbage.

**Simone:** The special education kids should have a real physical education class or at least get paid for their services. People should pick up their own trash, anyway!

**Beatriz:** Instead of doing that, the special education kids should be in class trying to improve themselves; it's not their fault we're so damn dirty!

**Lamont:** I think janitors get paid to do that job and should do it. We should write letters to the parents of the special education kids and to the school. (March 1999)

In this inquiry discussion, students problematize that which is taken to be normal at their school. The students are able to name the injustice and use conversation to express why they believe that it is wrong to have the students in special education pick up the school's trash. Having a space to speak and interact, students clarified their observations and challenged the abusive conditions in terms of power and equity issues. In addition, the students think about their responsibility to the special education students who, as Tomas points out, "don't realize there is anything wrong with what they are doing." After some brainstorming, they decided to write a letter to the parents and the school for as Dewey (1897/1964) reminded us: "Reflection [is] not to con-template the need for change, but to figure out how, when, and where change will take place" (p. 111). Inquiry is the place where students can figure out what needs to be changed and how they can improve unjust situations.

# LEADERSHIP, PARTICIPATION, AND RESISTANCE

We have been learning together, on this sometimes painful journey, that until every story is heard and responded to, our schools do not fulfill the goals of a democratic society. (Paley, 1979/2000, p. xvi)

One of the most powerful moments during the year was when one student found her voice. On that day, we got closer to fulfilling our goals of a democratic society when Shelley, an African American 15-year-old, spoke. Shelley half-jokingly announced to the group that she would be the president of the United States. The facilitator took this comment seriously and told Shelley that if she were going to be a leader, facilitating group inquiry would be a great way for her to show her leadership. She eyed the facilitator carefully to see if she really meant it, and, soon after, Shelley began to facilitate the discussion. She facilitated the meeting by asking open-ended questions and by gently prodding students to explain their thoughts more clearly. Although she had a low attendance rate and had not spoken much throughout the year, it was evident that when she had attended, she had been watching carefully. Shelley made sure to call on all the students, even those who preferred not to speak during class. Mr. Rose described the moment in his master's portfolio:

At first, students thought this was kind of funny. Shelley took it seriously and proceeded to question students about their thoughts and opinions. Soon the students became more involved. An exciting new dynamic came over the room as Shelley glowed in her leadership role. Students began to answer and respond and discuss in ways that they had not [before]. Some students who never spoke began to speak because Shelley questioned them whether they raised their hand or not, something I rarely do…. They had a serious class discussion on their own, led by a fellow student for whom they seemed to gain newfound respect. They seemed to notice and feel pride, [but] none more than Shelley. (Coleman, 1999, p.7)

Shelley was not performing well academically. Her attendance record was not impressive. Inquiry seemed to provide this student a place to feel successful and like a leader in her classroom community. Just like Shelley, several other students shined during inquiry sessions as they made sense of difficult issues by relating them to their own experiences and asking tough questions. Shelley's example shows how inquiry has the potential to provide students with communication tools so that they can explore issues on their own. Moreover, Mr. Rose saw Shelley in a new light. He had not expected that a student who does not do well academically could take such a powerful leadership role.

Not everyone participated verbally during group discussions. After reading the students' letters written in May 1999, it became apparent that participation takes different forms: "My participation in class is less than average, but I still pay attention to what goes on. I like to have these class discussions…. Inquiry is a good way to get shy students to talk. Besides, I get to know what's on all of these people's mind by just having a demanding topic to start off." Another student commented that she liked to do "inquiry writing" because "people who have trouble talking have a chance to write their thoughts." Inquiry spurred students to think in different ways and provoked further avenues for discussion. But, most importantly, inquiry helped them feel empathy. When students are empathetic, they listen to one another more carefully and feel connected to one another, thus building a community.

Inquiry, however, is not the panacea to all our social problems; nor will it create understanding and racial harmony. In fact, we have a long way to go before we can sit together and talk about those experiences that affect us the most. One student did not feel comfortable having conversations about race and discrimination. He felt that having these conversations alienated him from his peers:

I say we shouldn't talk about this stuff at all. This is not stuff you should talk about in a class of different backgrounds. You could offend people by talking about this! This is a place of learning, not of heritage bashing. It seems to me that Mr. Rose wants us to get mad at each other. You ask us for our opinion, but if I speak, people are going to say, "Man, that guy is racist!" And then, what they say sticks with you for the rest of your days. My suggestion is don't talk about this anymore. (White male student, May 1999)

This student's feelings of alienation should be equally validated as those feelings from students who felt validated by inquiry meetings. Although it should be an educator's goal to include everyone in conversations about equity and justice, it is difficult to make everyone feel comfortable. As a White student, he may not have had successful experiences talking about race, much less with people of color, and did not engage verbally throughout. He feared that by having these discussions, he could be labeled a racist. Yet these conversations are important if, as Dewey (1938) contended, we are to understand one another's perspective. Indeed, Freire (1985) argued that struggle is necessary.

Many of the ideas about meritocracy and the American Dream are deeply engrained within the psyche of society. Thus, when we challenge that which is held as the norm, it creates dissonance. Yet it is important to struggle with these complex issues. In exploring identity, Alice McIntyre (1997) argued that "white people's lack of consciousness about their racial identities limits their ability to critically examine their own positions as racial beings who are implicated in the existence and perpetuation of racism" (p. 16). Having conversations with White students about race, as in the case of the student above, creates a discomfort associated with coming to terms with the visibility of an otherwise invisible race. This conscientization of self leads people to move beyond simplistic explanations that blame people of color for poverty and crime. Bell Hooks (1995) argued that "by socializing white and black citizens in the United States to think of racism in personal terms, individuals could think of it as having more to do with inherent prejudicial feelings than with a consciously mapped out strategy of domination that [is] systematically maintained" (p. 108). Rather, self-reflection, conscientization, and problematization seek to uncover identity within broader a social context that does not provide access to opportunities for all.

## DISCUSSION AND CONCLUSION

The New High School ninth-grade students talked through many issues during the 1998-1999 academic year, most of which I did not discuss in this article. Throughout the year, we learned to listen to and respect one another's points of view. The students created an alternative public sphere in which they could find meaning and express different opinions. Most students visualized their lives beyond the realm of society's expectations for them. They imagined a better society and felt that they could contribute significantly to the dialogue.

In the first theme, Experience and Reflection, the students expressed their dreams about the kinds of people they wanted to become, defining themselves beyond race (or within internalized boundaries delineated by race), roles, and careers. Then, they discussed what it means to them to be a person of color in society. We unpacked racism and began to discuss the roots of hatred and oppression.

In the second subsection, Problematizing and Conscientization, the students engaged in conversations about the pressures to conform to a separatist ideology versus getting to know their peers across racial lines. Then, we saw how students carefully considered and problematized school policies and thought about themselves as active agents of change.

In the final subsection, Leadership, Participation, and Resistance, I presented the case of a student for whom inquiry became an avenue on which she could excel outside the regular academic program. She appropriated the questioning style of inquiry and showed her leadership skills. In this subsection, I also considered different modes of participation within inquiry (via writing) and presented the case of a White student who had not engaged in conversations about race previously. He felt threatened by the possibility of appearing racist and did not feel like inquiry was a safe process. Other adolescents in the group, however, felt validated:

As teenagers, we don't get to be heard. In the (critical inquiry) meetings, we do ... I get to express my feelings and get to say them and have people my age relate to them. I can be heard. (African American female student, personal communication, April 1999)

These inquiry conversations help students develop a sense of self because they are able to verbalize their ideas freely and consider future directions for growth. Maxine Greene (1988) reminded us: "Made conscious of lacks, they may move (in their desire to repair them) toward a 'field of possibilities,' what is possible or realizable for them. Few people, quite obviously can become virtuoso musicians or advance physicists or world-renowned statesmen, but far more is possible for individuals than is ordinarily recognized" (p. 5). These are young people who want to be "smarter, trusted, respected, helpful, inspiring, strong, etc.," far from the stereotypes that usually accompany teenagers, particularly teenagers in urban cities.

Young people have much to say and contribute to society. They are not just our "future"; they are our today. Children must have a place where they can deconstruct oppressive conditions, make sense of their experiences, and imagine humanizing possibilities. On the November 13, 2000, cover of *Newsweek*, the headline announced: "Readell Johnson is one of 14 million Americans, mostly black or Latino, who will spend part of their lives behind bars." In one of the articles associated with the cover, the author (Reynolds, 2000) stated that although violent-crime rates remain "too high" in "inner-cities," at least "we" no longer have high "property-crime" or "burglary" rates (p. 46). He argued that "punishment reduces crime ... conviction and punishment must remain the backbone of the system" (p. 46). The message is loud and clear. Reynolds had drawn a line between the "inner-cities" and "we," and the "we" appear to be the dominant middle class. Is this the future that our children of color should expect? Is this the society that we want to have? Unfortunately, "any attempt to transform the nation's classrooms into places where future citizens learn to critically engage politics and received knowledge both inside and outside the classroom are dismissed as either irrelevant or unprofessional" (Giroux, 2000, p. 4). We must continue to struggle and legitimize democratic endeavors in the classroom. Emancipatory research projects such as this one should be further studied and connected to academic achievement. In addition, we must have more studies that explore how teachers understand student voices and how they use this understanding to design their curricula. I end this article with a student's voice and a strong reminder that dialogue is action:

Inquiry is great, and it would be nice to continue with this. It helps get things out in the open and talk about things that really should be talked about. It also gives students a chance to be heard and to understand and comprehend what some of their peers have to go through. (Latino male, April 1999)

## NOTES

1. All participant names and settings have been changed to preserve anonymity.
2. For the purposes of this article, a social justice agenda is defined as one that challenges the status quo and makes "activism, power, and inequity explicit parts of the curriculum" (Cochran-Smith, 1999, p. 119). For a more careful description of social justice teaching, see Cochran-Smith (1999) and Oakes and Lipton (2003).

## REFERENCES

Chang, E. T. (1993). Jewish and Korean merchants in African Americans neighborhoods: A comparative perspective. *Amerasia Journal, 19*(2), 5-21.

Choi, C., Lizardo, R., & Phillips, G. (1996, January). *Race, power, and promise in Los Angeles: An assessment of responses to human relations conflict.* Los Angeles: Multicultural Collaborative.

Cochran-Smith, M. (1999). Learning to teach for social justice. In G. Griffin (Ed.), *The education of teachers* (pp. 114-144). Chicago: University of Chicago Press.

Coleman, S. (1999). *Master's portfolio.* Unpublished master's thesis, University of California, Los Angeles.

Creswell, J. (1998). *Qualitative inquiry and research design: Choosing among five traditions.* Thousand Oaks, CA: Sage.

Darder, A. (1991). *Culture and power in the classroom: A critical foundation for bicultural education.* Westport: Bergin & Garvin.

Dewey, J. (1904). The relation of theory to practice in the education of teachers. In *Third yearbook* (Part I, pp. 313-338). Bloomington, IN: National Social Studies Education Association.

Dewey, J. (1938). *Experience and education.* New York: Collier Books.

Dewey, J. (1944). *Democracy and education: An introduction to the philosophy of education.* New York: Free Press. (Original work published 1916)

Dewey, J. (1964). Ethical principles underlying education, In R. Archambault (Ed.), *John Dewey on education: Selected writings* (pp. 108-140). New York: Modern Library. (Original work published 1897)

Fraser, N. (1994). Rethinking the public sphere: A contribution to the critique of actually existing democracy. In H. Giroux & P. McLaren (Eds.), *Between borders: Pedagogy and the politics of cultural studies* (pp. 74-97). New York: Routledge.

Freire, P. (1985). *The politics of education: Culture, power, and liberation.* (Donaldo Macedo, Trans.). Westport, CT: Bergin & Garvey.

Giroux, H. (2000). *Stealing innocence: Youth, corporate power, and the politics of culture.* New York: St. Martin's.

Greene, M. (1988). *The dialectic of freedom.* New York: Teachers College Press.

Habermas, J. (1994). *The structural transformation of the public sphere: An inquiry into a category of bourgeois society.* Cambridge, MA: MIT Press. (Original work published 1962)

Honora, D. (2003, January). Urban African American adolescents and school identification. *Urban Education, 38*(1), 58-76.

Hooks, B. (1995). *Killing rage: Ending racism.* New York: Henry Holt.

Kim, C. J. (2000). *Bitter fruit: The conflicts of Black-Korean conflict in New York City.* New Haven, CT: Yale University Press.

Lee, P. (1999, May). In their own voices: An ethnographic study of low-achieving students within the context of school reform. *Urban Education, 34* (2), 214-244.

McGregor, G. (2000, November). Kids who "talk back": Critically literate or disruptive youth? *Journal of Adolescent & Adult Literacy, 44* (3), 220-228.

McIntyre, A. (1997). *Making meaning of whiteness: Exploring racial identity with white teachers.* Albany: State University of New York Press.

Miles, M., & Huberman, A. M. (1994). *An expanded sourcebook: Qualitative data analysis* (2nd ed.). Thousand Oaks, CA: Sage.

Oakes, J., & Lipton, M. (2003). *Teaching to change the world* (2nd ed.). New York: McGraw-Hill.

Otoya, K. (2000). The impact of critical inquiry in the socialization of first year teachers. (Doctoral dissertation, UCLA, 2000). *Dissertation Abstracts International.* (UMI No. 9957825)

Otoya-Knapp, K. (2002). *Being Korean in Watts: A critical case study of a first year teacher's struggle to enact social justice.* Manuscript submitted for publication.

Paley, V. (2000). *White teacher.* Cambridge, MA: Harvard College Press. (Originally published 1979)

Reynolds, M. (2000, November 13). Crime and punishment. *Newsweek, 136*(20), 46.

Taylor-Dunlap, K. (1998, May/June). Voices of at-risk adolescents [Electronic version]. *Clearinghouse, 70*(5), 1-9.

Trueba, H. (1999). *Latinos unidos: From cultural diversity to the politics of solidarity.* Lanham, MD: Rowman & Littlefield.

Wasley, P., Hampel, R., & Clark, R. (1997). *Kids and school reform.* San Francisco: Jossey-Bass.

West, C. (1999). *The Cornel West reader.* New York: Basic Civitas Books.

Wolk, S. (2003, May/June). Teaching for critical literacy in social studies [Electronic version]. *The Social Studies, 94*(3), 101-106.

Karina Otoya-Knapp has a practitioner background in math and technology and high school Spanish and is currently a teacher educator at Bank Street College. Her research is on critical inquiry in teacher development, teacher research in higher education settings, public urban education, and social justice issues.

# UNIT 6

# Special Topics in Multicultural Education

## Unit Selections

## Key Points to Consider

• How can educators develop a better sense of cross-cultural conflicts and values?

• How does a child's home environment affect his or her ability to learn at school?

• How can educators help children from gay families find acceptance at school?

• How can educators better meet the needs of multiracial and multiethnic children?

## Student Website

www.mhcls.com/online

## Internet References

Further information regarding these websites may be found in this book's preface or online.

**American Scientist**
*http://www.amsci.org/amsci/amsci.html*

**American Studies Web**
*http://lumen.georgetown.edu/projects/asw/*

**CYFERNet: National Network for Family Resiliency Program & Directory**
*http://www.nnfr.org*

**National Institute on the Education of At-Risk Students**
*http://www.ed.gov/offices/OERI/At-Risk/*

**U.S. Department of Education**
*http://www.ed.gov/pubs/TeachersGuide/*

There are always special concerns relevant to particular academic areas of study that do not neatly fit into particular traditional categories of that area but that are very pertinent to it. Each year we try to focus in this section on selected special topics that have been of particular interest to those who live or work in multicultural settings. Topics are also chosen if they have a direct bearing on issues of equality of educational opportunity.

There is change in the journal literature as well as some thematic continuity from year to year. The articles in this unit reflect a broad variety of topics that we believe readers will find informative and interesting. It is important and a poignant concern to witness how parents and others attempt to help children cope with adversity. There is great relevance in this for the field of multicultural education in America and other nations. The role of teachers, parents, and community members is very important in terms of helping children to overcome disadvantageous living circumstances or backgrounds.

The first articles talk on how Presidents of the United States—their beliefs, values, and attitudes—have influenced either negatively or positively intercultural relations in the United States and multicultural themes as well. These articles describe the points of view of American Presidents who either adversely or positively influenced the development of intercultural relations and multicultural issues in the United States. The first of these articles—installment number 3—deals with John Quincy Adams, Theodore Roosevelt, and Harry S. Truman. The second article—installment number 4—focuses on the presidencies of George Washington, James K. Polk, and Franklin D. Roosevelt. There is a critical evaluation of how they positively and negatively influenced ideas about education and multiculturalism. For editorial reasons the first and second installments in this series are not included. The strategy of these articles is that there would be a very early president, a president who served in the 19th or early 20th century, and then a president of our time. That is a deliberate plan on their part. They pick three presidents of the United States from very different time periods. There is a crit-

ical theoretical evaluation of each president's term as it relates to education and issues relating to intercultural relations.

Other issues explored in this special topics unit are articles on three different themes. One article deals with international education, a needed curriculum, and the authors are advocates of the inclusion of international education in the secondary schools of the United States. They discuss international education curricula in terms of what they think such curricula should occur in every American school district. They realize there is limited support for international education in the secondary schools, but they are advocating for it and hopeful that it can be done.

The second theme article deals with students who are members of sexual minorities at the secondary school level, and it discusses what they refer to as queer life and school culture. They are primarily dealing with high school culture, and they discuss the difference between sexuality and gender identity and how sexually minority students are treated in high schools. They critique the harsh ways in which many school administrators and teachers at the high school level treat students who have minority sexual identities. Educators who focus on multicultural issues in the schools now recognize sexual minorities as a part of multicultural education. That is because sexual minority students tend to be socially oppressed, and the author identifies the sorts of opposition that sexual minority students experience in typical American high schools. They critique from a critical pedagogical perspective the policies that many school principals adopt towards students who are sexually minority students in terms of gender identity.

The final issue discussed in this unit deals with the concept of alternative paths to teacher certification. Alternative certification is a method of certifying or licensing teachers in a state or city that does not involve the students going through a college of education, although in one form of alternative certification, for instance in California, it is possible to go through the requirements for alternative certification and also pick up a master's degree if the teacher in training already has a bachelor's degree. The author describes several approaches to alternative teacher certification. Certification is a state authority. It is strictly something that the state department of education in each state can control because, by constitutional tradition, education is a state power. There is no federal alternative teacher certification, but the author describes two models, among others, of alternative teacher certification that are widely used across the country and approved by the state departments of education.

We hope that these essays will be perceived as useful in strengthening our understanding of policy issues related to the topics covered and also this year's special topic section. There will be a good American history lesson from the first articles of this unit that deal with Presidents of the United States. We hope that you will find all of the articles in the unit interesting and relevant.

Finally, there are two extremely interesting articles on the topics of how to build partnerships with immigrant students and their parents and how schools can develop partnerships with the immigrant community. In some states the level of immigrant population continues to increase. This is particularly true in California, Arizona, and New York City. Immigration into cities in other parts of the country and in migrant worker communities is on the rise. The concept of how Native American languages have been eradicated or lost through government policies and the concept of linguistic imperialism are raised by the authors. A discussion of policy alternatives is suggested. Again, in this article, a critical theoretical evaluation is made of past and present policies towards linguistic minority populations, including Native Americans. The examples given are from the history of how Native Americans were forced when attending school to speak English only; Mexican American students experienced the same thing before 1970. The issue of linguistic minority students in the schools and linguistic minority teachers in the schools and the matters that concern them is a very relevant topic to the multicultural education movement.

We hope that these essays will be perceived as useful in strengthening our understanding of multicultural education. The essays in this unit are relevant to courses in educational policy studies, multicultural education, and cultural foundations of education.

# Influences of Three Presidents of the United States on Multicultural Education

## A Series of Research Studies in Educational Policy

### Third Installment:
### Examining Presidents John Quincy Adams, Theodore Roosevelt, and Harry S. Truman

H. Prentice Baptiste and Emil J. Michal, Jr.

## Introduction

The recognition, development and implementation of multicultural education in this country is a relatively new and emerging idea (Apple, 1979; Banks, 1977; Burnett, 1994; Delpit, 1992; Frazier, 1977; Garcia, E, 1994; Grant, 1977; Hunter, 1974; Kallen, 1970; La Belle, 1976; Pai, 1984). Prior to the middle of the previous century, the concept of addressing and providing a meaningful educational experience for all students, including students of color, was non-existent.

In recent years, through the work of numerous educators (Banks, 1993; Banks, J. & Banks, C., 2004; Baptiste, 1979/1986/1994; Bennett, 1995; Boyer & Baptiste, 1996; Garcia, R.L., 1982; Gay, 1988/1994, 2004; Gollnick & Chinn, 1990; Nieto, 1992), not only has the concept of multicultural education begun to become a reality, it has become a driving force in curricular development.

Colleges of education of several major universities, such as the University of Massachusetts, the University of Washington in Seattle, the University of Wisconsin at Madison, the University of Houston, and New Mexico State University are actively engaged in educating students to become multicultural educators (Gay, 1994).

National professional organizations such as the National Council for the Social Studies, the National Council for the Accreditation of Teacher Education and the National Education Association have declared their commitments to multicultural education. In 1990, the National Association for Multicultural Education was formed to further the development of multicultural education (Gay, 1994).

While these efforts by educators are important, the commitment of this country to multicultural education in American schools and on the international scene has not been significant (Spring, 2000). Part of this absence must be attributed to the lack of support and leadership from the President of the United Sates and his administration. Through the policies and actions of each President's individual administration, the role of multicultural education in this country is affected, both positively and negatively. In this paper, three presidents, John Quincy Adams, Theodore Roosevelt, and Harry S. Truman, will be examined as to their roles in multicultural education.

While considering these three men, it may appear that there is no common theme connecting them other than that all of them occupied the office of President of the United States. There are,

however, connections that can be made among them. One thread was the political backgrounds of these men. Each would reflect the beginnings, evolution, and change of political parties in this country.

Adams and Roosevelt were both men who did not maintain only one political party affiliation but moved between parties as their consciences and circumstances dictated. Indeed, Adams is listed as belonging to three different parties: Whig, National Republican, and Federalist (Remini, 2002).

Roosevelt, while elected president as a Republican, went on to initiate an entirely new national political party, the Progressive or Bull Moose Party (Auchincloss, 2001). Only Truman maintained a lifelong affiliation with one party, the Democratic Party (McCullough, 1992), as party affiliation had become a dominant theme on the political landscape by the middle of the 20th century.

Another thread to bind these men is their social standing. Both Adams and Roosevelt were products of what would be considered upper-class social status in this country and enjoyed the privileges, perquisites, and advantages of that status (Kunhardt, P., Jr, Kunhardt, P., III, & Kunhardt, P., 1999). Adams came from the rigorous, austere and religious background of New England (Remini, 2002) and Roosevelt from the well-to-do of New York City (Auchincloss, 2001). Again, as a counter point, Truman was from literally middle America, coming from a farm in Kansas (McCullough, 1992). While not on the level of the previous two, Truman's background was by no means one of deprivation. The dominant link among these three, indeed among all presidents of this country, is that they are white Protestant males.

Though similar in some attributes and different in others, each man would exert tremendous influence on events and developments in this country and the world. Areas affected would encompass every aspect of people's lives. By considering their backgrounds, their public lives and political actions, their acts while president relating to multicultural education or some antecedent, and the legacies of these acts, we can hope to gain an insight into effects that each of these Presidents of the United States has had in the area of multicultural education.

## John Quincy Adams

The son of the second President of this country, John Quincy Adams came from a Puritanical, New England family of several generations in American and was expected to, "add to the family's illustrious record of accomplishment" (Remini, p. 2). Traveling with his father throughout Europe as a youth and educated in the classics in various private schools, by the time he reached the age of sixteen, "he had become something of a celebrity among the social elite [of Europe]. He was a skilled linguist, a classicist of sorts, a superb conversationalist whose knowledge of literature, the arts and science set him apart. Moreover, he was American, a rather unique distinction in social circle at that time" (Remini, p. 14-5).

This sounds very much like the British gentleman that landed families of Virginia and other early states wished for their sons (Wilkins, 2002). This would later contribute to Adams being labeled an "aristocrat," not in touch with the "democracy" of this country (Nagel, 1997).

The entry of Adams into politics took place after he returned home from Europe, completed his education at Harvard, settled in Boston, and began practicing law (Remini, 2002). In his spare time, he responded to *The Rights of Man* by Thomas Paine with a series of essays called "Letters of Publicola" (Remini, 2002). In these essays, "Adams warned against demagoguery and insisted on protection of individual rights. In America, he said, those rights are protected under a constitutional system that had established a republican frame of government" (Remini, p. 22).

This viewpoint identified Adams as a Federalist, an ally of Alexander Hamilton, and placed him in opposition to the Jeffersonian Republicans of that time. Adams's political career had its ups and downs in state and national levels as he won some elections and lost others. He soon demonstrated a lack of party loyalty as he would oppose measures and resolutions from both political parties while in office (Remini, 2002). Adams became so estranged from the Federalists that he attended a Republican congressional caucus in 1808 (Remini, 2002), an act that truly horrified his family and was a harbinger of later political party oscillations.

Demonstrating exceptional diplomatic skills by negotiating the Treaty of Ghent to end the War of 1812 (Bemis, 1956) and in recognition of his intellect and social status, Adams was selected by the newly elected President James Monroe to be Secretary of State. This was an important position, as the Secretary of State was viewed at that time as being a stepping stone to the office of President. Adams accepted and is credited with being "the greatest secretary of state to serve that office" (Remini, p. 50).

While Secretary of State, Adams would be involved in two important documents: The Florida Treaty and the Monroe Doctrine. The first was the culmination of over twenty years of efforts by American administrations to dislodge Spain from Florida. The final part of the process involved actions of Andrew Jackson's incursion into Florida to pursue and punish Seminoles for raiding into the United States. Adams defended Jackson's actions, arguing, "that the general was justified by his action in that Spain was unable to police its territory and prevent rampaging 'savages' from killing American citizens" (Remini, p. 55). Indeed, Adams argued that Jackson's actions "be justified as 'defensive acts of hostility' "(Drinnon, 1997, p. 104).

This attitude of conquest continued in his authorship of the Monroe Doctrine. It was Adams's belief that America possessed a unique and God-given call to take possession of the entire continent and the doctrine was his way of expressing this belief. The effects on the people already on the land did not concern Adams. It was America's Manifest Destiny to expand westward and the people now on the land were of no consequence (Remini, 2002). This attitude towards what would now be termed a minority people is an important part of Adams's legacy.

The presidential election of 1824 was a very contentious affair that involved electoral vote trading and deals of convenience (Remini, 2002). Adams felt he should be chosen the next President in the same manner as the previous Secretaries of States, Madison and Monroe, were chosen President. His background for the office is described by Bemis:

> He led no party, controlled no political machine, nor did he have personal magnetism or other qualities necessary to build one. All he had to stand on politically was his distinguished lineage, his character, his large experience with affairs at home and abroad, and his undoubted competence for public office. No man has ever been better fitted, as professional public servant, for the Presidency. No man

has had less aptitude or inclination for the organization and command of political cohorts, (p. 11)

Though a recognized and able statesman, Adams was still a neophyte politician at a time when Presidential candidates did not actively campaign for office. He did clumsily attempt to ensure his election. He suggested that his opponents, Andrew Jackson, Henry Clay, and John Calhoun, be sent on missions to Europe or Latin America, had his wife give a lavish ball to entice Jackson to be his Vice Presidential candidate, was an "anonymous" source for information praising his efforts to various editors, and began socializing at every opportunity to advance his candidacy among the influential circles in Washington at that time (Remini, 2002).

Opposing Adams were four Democratic-Republicans: John Calhoun, Henry Clay, William Crawford, and Andrew Jackson. Calhoun would withdraw to be named Vice President. The Electoral College vote did not give any of the candidates a majority and was split 99 for Jackson, 84 for Adams, 41 for Crawford, who had suffered a debilitating stroke prior to the vote (Remini, 2002), and 37 for Clay. Without a decision, the election would be decided in the House of Representatives, where Clay, not allowed to be considered for the presidency because of his fourth place finish, was essentially going to decide the election as Speaker of the House.

Clay provided the support for Adams to be elected president and Adams awarded the support by naming Clay Secretary of State (Bemis, 1956). The apolitical Adams had participated in one of the biggest political trade offs in American history that would split the Democratic-Republican Party into the Democrats of Jackson and the National Republicans that supported Adams. Andrew Jackson complained loudly and campaigned unceasingly to reverse the results of the election that he viewed as being stolen from him

(Bemis, 1956). The constant and unremitting attacks by Jackson and his supporters would be Adams' legacy for his political maneuvering.

Once elected, Adams's dream for the betterment of the nation was a grand vision to promote knowledge with, "[a] national bankruptcy law, [a] national university, [a] national astronomical observatory, [a] national naval academy, national research and exploration, and a new department of the Interior to administer increasing national business" (Bemis, p. 76). The recipients of this enhanced knowledge were undoubtedly to be Americans like himself, male, white and of the upper social strata of the country. There would be no consideration for any one else other than this well defined and well off group.

His status derived from a "minority election"(Hargreaves, 1985) doomed these lofty efforts, "of the National Government operating under a benign Providence to promote and assist the "general diffusion of knowledge" and its application for the continuing improvement of American citizens and of mankind (Bemis, p. 63). As expressed by Nagel:

His four years in the White House were misery for him and for his wife. All that he hoped to accomplish was thwarted by a hostile Congress. His opponents continually assailed him with what he claimed was the foulest slander. Consequently, while Adams sought reelection in 1828, he did so mostly from stubborn pride, and he actually looked impatiently toward his certain defeat by Andrew Jackson. For the remaining twenty years of his life, he reflected on his presidency with distaste, convinced that he had been the victim of evildoers. His administration was a hapless failure and best forgotten, save for the personal anguish it cost him. (p. 296)

Even with this rather gloomy estimation of Adams's administration, there can be some analysis of his attitudes and actions regarding people of color and, by implication, multi-

cultural education. Granted, for Adams, the term "multicultural"might more likely invoke references to Latin and Greek, rather than Native Americans, Mexican Americans, and African Americans, but there are some identifiable thoughts on his part about people of color that would best be termed benign neglect as Adams would do nothing to change the prevalent treatment of people of color in this country during his administration.

For Adams, the development and expansion of the nation to the west was the paramount issue and the most desirable approach was a, "humane policy of Indian removal [that] would transfer the tribes to the west of the Mississippi, educating and civilizing them, perhaps eventually assimilating them into the body of citizenry" (Bemis, p. 62). Writing in his diary, Adams expresses his sentiment about the intended role of Native Americans:

...while I was there Mr. Calhoun came, with a deputation of five Cherokee Indians. This is the most civilized of the tribes of North American Indians. They have abandoned altogether the life of hunters, and betaken themselves to tillage. These men were dressed entirely according to our manner. Two of them spoke English with good pronunciation, and one with grammatical accuracy. (p. 313)

Assimilation would be the attitude of for Native Americans, after they relinquished their homelands to the advancing stream of settlers. His administration did nothing to recognize and interact with Native Americans in any positive manner (Hargreaves, 1985).

For African Americans, the "peculiar institution" of slavery was something that Adams would not actively address in any proactive manner. For him, "slavery in a moral sense is an evil, but as connected with commerce it has its uses.' Business rated higher than morality so he left slavery alone"(O'Reilly, p. 31). So, while occupying the office of president, Adams did not oppose slavery nor propose its abolition. This act of denial was similar to those of previous Presidents. Washington, Jefferson, and others had also done nothing to break the cycle of allowing slavery to continue in America (Wilkins, 2002).

After his defeat for reelection, Adams would, as a Congressman, become an eloquent and forceful opponent of slavery and a hero to abolitionists of that time (Remini, 2002). His opposition to the Gag Rules designed to prevent anti-slavery petitions from being introduced to Congress became more and more strident with time (Remini, 2002). While his arguments were in defense of the constitution and the rights of free speech, the applications were in opposition to slavery. This apparent contradiction to his lack of action concerning slavery while President can be resolved by recognizing his pragmatic nature.

His first allegiance was of preserving the country and the Constitution at all costs, but his Puritanical upbringing provided the moral compass to recognize the abhorrent nature of slavery to the point that an enlightened citizenry, perhaps prodded by martial law, would bring liberty to Black persons (John Quincy Adams, Memoirs). In an amazing bit of foreshadowing, Adams would express his convictions about slavery in light of the Missouri Compromise, by writing in his Diary that:

> If slavery be the destined sword in the hand of the destroying angel which is to sever the ties of this union, the same sword will cut in sunder the bonds of slavery itself. A dissolution of the Union for the cause of slavery would be followed by a servile war in the slave-holding States, combined with a war between the two severed portions of the Union. It seems to me that its result must be the extirpation of slavery from the whole continent; and, calamitous and desolating as this course of events in its progress must be, so glorious would be its final issue, that, as God shall judge me, I dare not say that it is not to be desired. (p. 246-7)

This statement and the passion that it evokes would not be evident while he was President, but would certainly explain his religious fervor and later actions as a member of the House of Representatives.

The second instance of notoriety that involved Adams was the *La Amistad* incident. Thirty-nine captive Africans aboard a Spanish ship destined to work on Cuban plantations rebelled against their captors and commandeered the ship, the *La Amistad*. Later captured by American forces, Spanish authorities sought the return of the ship and the captives. Before the United States Supreme Court, Adams argued for the defendants' freedom by evoking the Declaration of Independence and making a passionate plea for human rights (Remini, 2002). The Court ruled against the government's case and "declared the Africans freemen and dismissed as immaterial the treaties involving slave trade" (Remini, p. 148).

While in office as President, Adams did not exert any appreciable influence to address the idea of multicultural education, or even the antecedents of this concept. He followed his personal dictates in terms of what he considered important to the country and moral to his set of values, but there would be no attention paid to the elimination of slavery or the recognition of the worth of other groups of people.

His contributions to multicultural education would come after he left the office of President and were prompted by a personal vendetta against Jackson (Bemis, 1956; Hargreaves, 1985; Remini, 2002) and were in terms of protecting the constitution rather than recognizing the value of diversity. But his legacy of foreshadowing a civil war should be recognized for the prediction of the momentous conflict that would come in a few short years to this nation. The ruling of the Supreme Court concerning civil rights for individuals provides another powerful antecedent of this country's history of multicultural events.

## Theodore Roosevelt

Coming from a prosperous Dutch family that immigrated to New York City in 1644 and became part of the New York aristocracy, Roosevelt was part of the elite circle of this country. Stories about his childhood and his desire to develop a "manly" physique and character are well documented and recorded (Brands, 1997; Charnwood, 1923; Dalton, 2002). These ideas would later contribute to his wanting to live the life of the "outdoors man" in the West (Brands, 1997).

The factors of praising, even perhaps worshiping, strength of character, mind, and body as a primary driving attitude of Roosevelt will be important in this discussion. His thoughts that, "a man, any man, [was] in total charge of his own destiny and therefore capable of choosing the terms of his employment and incurring total responsibility of his crimes" (Auchincloss, p. 16) would define his views on interactions between nations as well as individuals or groups of people.

This sense of self-determination, to make your own way in life, of an individual's control of events would consistently be a central part of his views of life. Recognizing that he came from "comfortable" circumstances, this is a view that makes some sense. Roosevelt possessed the ways and means to accomplish his own personal goals, but he had difficulty recognizing that others starting with less might not have the freedoms of choice and action that he enjoyed (Brands, 1997; Charnwood, 1923; Dalton, 2002).

Due to his "frail" condition, Roosevelt was tutored at home throughout his entire school age life (Brands, 1997). Traveling with his family, he became convinced that industrious and civilized nations were desirable in international development (Brands, 1997; Dalton, 2002). This conviction of power as a source of "good" behavior would dictate Roosevelt's view of the world throughout his lifetime (Brands,

1997). After his "home school-ing"ended, he attended Harvard as was expected by his family given his background (Brands, 1997). He would graduate and start a life of politics and government service in various capacities.

As a New York Assemblyman, Civil Service Commissioner, New York City Board of Police Commis-sioner, and Assistant Secretary of the Navy, Roosevelt showed a willing-ness to engage in political fights over issues that he deemed appropriate (Auchincloss, 2001; Brands, 1997; Lo-rant, 1959; Morris, 1979). His choices consistently involved some abuse of power by an individual, business, or "trust" (Lorant, 1959), a view that he would adhere to throughout his life. Any limitation or encroachment of ones ability to determine ones destiny would qualify as offending the spirit of fair play and self-determination.

Roosevelt would resign from the Navy Department to go into combat in the Spanish-American War, a move predicated by his "manly" outlook on life for himself (Charn-wood, 1923; Brands, 1997).

He soon made a name for himself on the national scene with the spec-tacular public relations coup of the Rough Riders (Dalton, 2002; Morris, 1979) and the "Charge" up San Juan Hill during the Spanish-American War. Following the war, he was se-lected to run for governor of New York. His nomination was made possible, however, only after exten-sive political maneuvering and deal making (Auchincloss, 2001; Brands, 1997).

During the campaign, he did his best to turn the general election for the state house into a national refer-endum on the war and the concept of expansion of the United States throughout the world. Roosevelt felt that this country must accept its des-tiny to carry civilization and the American flag around the world (Brands, 1997). This might be thought of as a call for a policy of pax Americana and he was ready to take the lead in this crusade. The lesson that Roosevelt learned from this ex-

perience, and one that he would con-sistently use later, was that there were times when arrangements were necessary and had to be done to ac-complish certain goals. He, "per-fectly understood that a failure to deal with the [political] machine would mean failure to make any so-cial progress at all, and he adopted the course of compromise quite openly" (Auchincloss, p. 36).

His nomination as Vice-President was, in some measure, a political deal to remove him from the office of gov-ernor of New York where he was too much of a "loose cannon" to the polit-ical bosses (Lorant, 1959). The assassi-nation of President William McKinley then unexpectedly moved Roosevelt and his sense of moral righ-teousness into the office of President.

Not afraid to decide what was good and what was evil, Roosevelt began to interpret issues of the day as he saw them. His "Square Deal" of socially progressive principles (Auchincloss, 2001) was a pro-nouncement of these views of right and wrong. "The creation of a pure food and drug law, supervision of insurance companies investigation of child labor, an employers' liability law for the District of Columbia, and suits against railroad rebates," (Auchincloss, p. 62) were all indica-tive of this consistency of viewpoint, that the individual needs some pro-tection from bad circumstances and institutions to accomplish self-deter-mination. This agenda would be translated into notable legislative acts, including:

> the Elkins Law, against the rail-roads' practice of given rebates to favored customers; the creation of the Department of Commerce and Labor withits Bureau of Corpora-tions, which grew to regulate ev-ery business that crossed state lines; the Hepburn Bill, which amended and vitalized the Inter-state Commerce Act and gave gov-ernment the power to set railroad rates; the Pure Food and Meat In-spection Laws, which remedied some of the scandals of the meat packing industry as exposed by Upton Sinclair's novel The Jungle;

and the Employers' Liability and Safety Appliance Laws, which lim-ited the hours of employees. (Auchincloss, p. 45)

In addition, Theodore Roosevelt also used the Sherman Antitrust Act to crusade against actions of what he considered "bad" trusts. Being a big trust was not evil, in the eyes of Roosevelt. However, if any trust, "sought to profit by restricting pro-duction by trick or device, by plotting against competitors, by oppressing wage earners, or by extorting high prices for a commodity made artifi-cially scarce," (Auchincloss, p. 50) then Roosevelt would go after the of-fender to restore a sense of moral cor-rectness to the actions involved. The duty of government in his view was, "to force the bad ones [trusts] to be-come good by making them follow what he deemed to be the path of 'Ôrighteousness'"(Lorant, p. 471).

Roosevelt lived at a time when international events began to mold a sense of a new beginning for the world. He wanted to carry America along with this sense of adventure at the start of the century. He pushed to build the Panama Canal and complete the Pacific Cable. At this time, the first Model-T automo-bile, Marconi's trans-Atlantic radio transmission, sailing of the United States fleet around the world, and the first flight of the Wright broth-ers (Dalton, 2002; Lorant, 1959) fu-eled this sense of adventure.

The concept of universal educa-tion in this country may have been espoused for a number of years but, in reality, it was only available to the well-to-do that could afford the ex-pense, which was Roosevelt's back-ground and support (Dalton, 2002). In his own way, Roosevelt did con-tribute to the idea of multicultural education with his consistent view of an individual's inherent ability to define and reach self-determination. However, he did not play a signifi-cant role in the efforts of African Americans, Native Americans, or women to be part of this reform movement (Hanson, 1999).

This lack of inclusion for diversity first shows in Roosevelt's actions involving dining with Booker T. Washington in the White House soon after he became President. Roosevelt was unable to travel to Tuskegee Institute to view Washington's approach, "where self-help was preached as gospel and where students and faculty combined strenuous outdoor labor with their intellectual endeavours" (Brands, p. 422), an approach that Roosevelt would have been sure to support. So Roosevelt invited Washington to the White House whenever he was in town. Washington accepted and the fateful dinner occurred on October 16, 1901.

The reaction by the Southern media and politicos to the meal was swift, vocal, vociferous, and venomous. Roosevelt was surprised by the reaction and said he would ask Washington to dine as often as he pleased at the White House (Brands, 1997). As a political reality, Roosevelt would come to view this as a political misstep and never offered another invitation to Washington or any other individual of color to eat at the White House. As expressed in O'Reilly:

> Dumbfounded by this "condition of violent chronic hysteria," which he explained by reference to the same "combination of Bourbon intellect and intolerant truculence of spirit... which brought on the Civil War, Roosevelt and his partisans recast the Washington dinner. To minimize fallout from the breach of racial etiquette they downgraded the dinner to a luncheon, told the press that the Roosevelt women did not sit and eat with the black man, and reminded everyone that black women were not welcome at the first lady's weekly teas and biweekly musicals, (p. 69)

Spin doctors, as they are referred to today, were clouding the details of the event. Roosevelt was determined to avoid any more "mistakes" of this nature (Brands, 1997).

Two other incidents might seem to indicate a positive approach to race on the part of Roosevelt. He ap- pointed an African-American, Dr. William D. Crum, as Collector of the Port of Charleston, South Carolina, and Minnie M. Cox as postmistress of Indianola, Mississippi. Both appointments were met with opposition from locals, but Roosevelt held firm in his choices and did not remove them from their positions (Gould, 1991). While these events may give a sense of positive actions about civil rights, other events gave a much darker picture.

The most famous of these is the "Brownsville Incident" in which an all-Black Army regiment, the 26th Infantry Regiment, was accused of engaging in a shooting riot in the south Texas town. Roosevelt's resolution of the incident was to summarily discharge every soldier in the regiment without honor (Dalton, 2002). Subsequent testimony would clear the soldiers and evidence showed that the citizens had fabricated the incident, but Roosevelt would not rescind his decision (Gould, 1991; Morris, 2001). This was a serious lapse in his interpretation of "good" and "evil."

According to one author, Roosevelt was given to numerous statements and observations that would not be considered positive concerning race. In *Nixon's Piano* by O'Reilly, Roosevelt is described as:

> . . . obsessed with race. He carried a gene hierarchy in his head and spent endless hours compiling and cataloging "stronger races" and "weaker races." Negroes found themselves placed near rock bottom among the "most utterly underdeveloped." "Suffered from laziness and shiftlessness" and prone to "Vice and criminality of every kind," blacks threatened white citizens and "race purity." Roosevelt studied the problem scientifically, in the progressive manner, and concluded that Negro "evils" were "more potent for harm to the black race than all acts of oppression of white men put together." "[This] perfectly stupid race can never rise," he added on another occasion. "The Negro...has been kept down as much by lack of

intellectual development as by anything else." (p. 65)

This dichotomy of views can possibly be explained to some degree by Roosevelt's progressive view of every person being judged on their won personal merits, so that an African-American could attain a level of success as typified by Washington but the "scientific" side of him sided with the "scientific" results of different abilities of various races. This success was an exception rather than a rule in Roosevelt's mind and superiority of the white race was something that would be basically unchallenged (Dyer, 1980).

The political animal in him, recognizing the necessity of compromise and deal making, would always entertain some individuals of color for various federal positions to secure support of Black voting blocks come election time (Brands, 1997). As a person, he felt pride, "in being man enough to open his home to Black guests, to sit at a table and break bread with a Black man in the executive mansion when governor of New York" (O'Reilly, p. 66), and dine with another while in the White House. He even bragged that his children, "sat in the same school with colored children" (O'Reilly, p. 66). Yet this same man would support segregation as a method of dealing with the race issue and discount lynchings of Blacks in the South as somehow justified because, "the man lynched has been guilty of a crime beyond descriptions" (O'Reilly, p. 72).

For Native Americans, Roosevelt's views also have a sense of bipolar implications. As a product of his formative years living in the West, he "was no great enthusiast for the American Indian—at least while they were still in belligerent opposition to westward-moving white men" (Auchincloss, p. 96). Yet he had "a great respect for their reservations and origins once they had been quelled" (Auchincloss, p. 96).

Indeed, Roosevelt set aside millions of public lands in the western states to serve as reminders and opportunities for Americans to partici-pate and enjoy the rustic life of the West that he so revered (Lorant, 1959). He sought to preserve Native American tribal relics with the pas-sage of the Antiquities Act in 1906 and he opposed attempts to steal tribal lands (Dalton, 2002). But Roosevelt vetoed bills that granted land claims to Native Americans and stopped monetary grants to them (Dalton, 2002). He remained com-mitted to "civilizing" native people of the West (Dalton, 2002; Sinkler, 1971) through a Carlisle school ap-proach of assimilation (Hagen, 1997).

Roosevelt's view of women was even more conservative, with an atti-tude that women were best suited to stay in the home. An extensive edu-cation was not a requirement for women and the serious business of running a country and advancing in the world was best left to men and the strength of the male of the spe-cies. In his own words in a letter to Hugo Munsterberg:

The first requisite in a healthy race is that a woman should be willing and able to bear children just as the men must be willing and able to work and fight. (June 3, 1901; Let-ters, III, 86)

After his presidency, as a third party candidate Roosevelt did cham-pion the women's labor reform movement and suffrage for women, but the primary motivation was his recognition of the twenty-five mil-lion potential votes for his presiden-tial aspirations (Dalton, 2002).

The sum total, then, of Roosevelt's efforts for multicultural education would be less than the sum of the parts. While a resounding progres-sive in many important areas, his record here is one of mixed signals and the bottom line is a dismal one. Any positive attributes are clouded by political expediency and not meant to produce meaningful change. "President Roosevelt was very hesitant about exerting strong executive leadership in matters of race" (Sinkler, p. 373).

## Harry S. Truman

Coming from Missouri, Truman was viewed as a Southerner by some but not by others. The mind-set of a border state that stretched back to antebellum Civil War still dictated views of the nation. Raised on a farm, attending the local schools and marrying his Sunday School sweet-heart (McCullough, 1992), his was a background rooted in the nation's "heartland." Truman did not attend college and, after an unsuccessful venture in a clothing business (Daniels, 1950), decided to try poli-tics. His mentor was "Big Tom" Pen-dergast, a well-connected political boss in Kansas City (McCullough, 1992). Pendergast decided that Tru-man had qualities that made him electable, namely: farm background, war record and friendly personality (McCullough, 1992). With the politi-cal machine's help, Truman was suc-cessfully elected to various positions in Kansas, ultimately winning a seat in the United States Senate in 1934 (McCullough, 1992).

Considering his background, Tru-man was not inclined to be very positive in terms of racial equality. He used "nigger" while referring to African-Americans (McCullough, 1992) and "enjoyed the kind of ra-cial jokes commonly exchanged over drinks in Senate hideaways" (McCullough, p. 246). As he served in the Senate, however, this view apparently began to be modified as he became aware of racial discrimi-nation, persecution, and abuse. He still accepted the doctrine of sepa-rate-but-equal (O'Reilly, 1995) but some ideas of equality did start to become evident.

This change was due more to Truman's belief in the ideal that America was a land of opportunity, even for those perceived to be infe-rior, rather than a belief in racial equality and integration. His was a paternalistic attitude toward Afri-can Americans (Miller, 1986).

In the opening speech for his re-election to the United States Senate

to an all-white audience in Sedalia, Missouri, in 1940, he said:

I believe in the brotherhood of man, not merely the brotherhood of white men, but the brother-hood of all men before the law... If any class or race can be perma-nently set apart from, or pushed down below the rest in political and civil rights, so may any other class or race when it shall incur the displeasure of its more power-ful associates, and we may say farewell to the principles on which we count our safety... Ne-groes have been preyed upon by all types of exploiters, from the in-stallment salesmen of clothing, pi-anos, and furniture to the vendors of vice. The majority of our Negro people find cold comfort in the shanties and tenements. Surely, as freemen, they are entitled to something better than this. (Mc-Cullough, p. 247)

In a speech to the National Col-ored Democratic Association later that summer, Truman told a Black audience that everyone benefited by providing educational opportu-nities to African Americans. "When we are honest enough to recognize each other's rights and are good enough to respect them, we will come to a more Christian settlement of our difficulties" (McCullough, p. 247-8). As "natural born Ameri-can[s]," African Americans should have equality under the law (Mc-Cullough, 1992).

In the same speech, though, his idea of separate-but-equal attitude was still evident as he remarked, "The highest types of Negro leaders say quite frankly that they prefer the society of their own people" (O'Reilly, p. 146). These expressions should be viewed relative to the po-litical necessity of courting the Black vote that led Truman to make the public pronouncements that he did (McCullough, 1992; Miller, 1986).

Selected as a compromise candi-date for Vice President for the elec-tion of 1944, Truman became President with the death of Franklin D. Roosevelt on April 12, 1945. His administration was marked by momentous international events. The defeat of Germany, the start of the United Nations, the dropping of two atomic bombs, the defeat of Japan, the start of the Cold War with Russia and China, the creation of the nation of Israel, and the Korean War were events that must be considered monumental in scope for the world. The beginnings of change in civil rights in this country would also be of considerable importance during his administration.

Given his background, Truman's views on race issues were something of an unknown as he took office. "No one had any idea of what to expect, as Roy Wilkins noted, from, 'an untested haberdasher from Klan country'" (O'Reilly, p. 145). Several liberal, "New Deal" advocates, including Eleanor Roosevelt and Henry Wallace, hoped that Truman would come out as a strong advocate for civil rights. His actions, however, would be more politically expedient than meaningful in promoting racial equality. Truman would always be concerned about garnering the Black vote (McCullough, 1992), not necessarily always in a manner that would consistently advance civil rights.

The approach that Truman consistently followed in terms of racial issues was to present a proactive picture initially and publicly, but then to not push for implementation or action to carry out the goals stated for public consumption. "Thereafter, Truman was invariably more forthright in rhetoric if rarely in action. 'The strategy,' White House aide Philleo Nash explained, 'was to start with a bold measure and then temporize to pick up the rightwing forces. Simply stated, backtrack after the bang'" (O'Reilly, p. 147).

Thus, Truman's administration was initially style, not substance, in terms of racial policy. Speeches would be made, committees would be formed, promises would be given, but limited actions would be taken (McCullough, 1992). In newspaper and media reports, Truman was proactive in appearance, but the lack of follow through to fulfill the

promises made for a different picture than was presented. Over time, this method of implementation would be modified to actually gain some noteworthy goals, such as desegregation of the military services. But the overall agenda would be a limited one (Miller, 1986).

The first area where this talk-but-not-act scenario would occur involved the Fair Employment Practice Committee which was created during World War II to monitor minority rights violations. Targeted by Southern congressmen for elimination (O'Reilly, 1995), Truman publicly expressed support for its continuance as a permanent committee to investigate civil rights violations but did nothing as President to make its continuation a reality.

An example of this non-action approach involved the 1945 strike of the Washington Capital Transit Company. FEPC Chairman Malcolm Ross prepared a directive requiring that Capital Transit stop denying jobs to African Americans. "With no other explanation than an unspoken bow to the white South, Truman ordered Ross not to issue this directive" (O'Reilly, p. 149).

While some individuals viewed the strike as an opportunity to confront segregation in the south, at that time Truman's logic was that the federal government's seizure of the transportation system was not to enforce the aims of the FEPC but to provide transportation for the citizens of Washington (O'Reilly, 1995). In issuing Executive Order 9664, Truman reduced the FEPC to a fact finding committee with no powers of compliance. The committee ceased to exist in 1946.

However, due to many Americans believing in the wartime promises of freedom from oppression and minority leaders efforts to gain equality, opportunity and protection, Truman was forced into some actions to meet these demands. The creation of the Indian Claims Commission to address financial grievances of Native Americans and the appointments of an African Ameri-

can as governor of the Virgin Islands and a Puerto Rican as governor of that island show that he was sympathetic to some form of attention to racial issues (McCoy, 1984) but these initial efforts were limited in scope.

Indeed, Truman did nothing to further any sense of improving conditions or achieving equality for Native Americans and women. In his own words in *Where the Buck Stops*, Truman wrote:

> Our conscience was finally awakened thirty or forty years ago, and we've had two or three Indian agents in this century who are really looking after the welfare of the Indians. Now we have a large number of Eskimos in Alaska who are properly taken care of, I think, and the Indians in New Mexico and Arizona have the best reservations in the country and are being protected, (p. 288)

He would also veto bills that he felt were harmful to Indians. This paternalistic attitude leaves no doubt that Truman did not have a proactive or constructive attitude toward Native Americans.

Towards women, Truman saw them as important as a block of votes but was insensitive to women's issues of opportunity and equality. He did not support the Equal Rights Amendment and did nothing to work for its passage (Miller, 1986). Indeed, comments from his appointment book best express his views on the Equal Rights Amendment:

> September 21, 1945: 12:15 p.m. — [Group of Women Sponsoring Equal Rights Amendment] —A lot of hooey about equal rights, (p. 68)

It was the area of violence, though, to African Americans, Native Americans, Japanese Americans, Jews, and Mexican Americans (McCoy, 1984) that would prompt a change in Truman's view of racial problems. In 1946, he would meet with a National Emergency Committee Against Mob Violence headed by Walter White (O'Reilly, 1995). Sponsored by the National Association for the Advancement of Colored

People, the purpose of this committee was to address the widespread hate crimes of violence against people of color, even men and women in the military, that was rampant at that time (O'Reilly, 1995).

A second group, headed by Paul Robeson, also met with Truman to address the rampant and indiscriminate lynching of African Americans, especially in the South, that was taking place at that time. Limited by what he could do legally, other than have the Justice Department investigate allegations of violence with the small hope of prosecution (McCoy, 1984), Truman settled on another solution. Truman established the President's Committee on Civil Rights by Executive Order 9808 (Ferrell, 1983; McCoy, 1984; O'Reilly, 1995).

As bold a step as this was, there were political considerations in it for Truman. To go against the overt wishes of Southern congressmen and senators was to go against the precepts of the Democratic Party that included the Solid South. But Truman would tie the issue of civil rights to the Cold War fight against Communism. To further couple this connection, the members that were appointed to the Committee on Civil Rights were required to take a loyalty oath that was used at the time to monitor any subversive activities (O'Reilly, 1995).

One of the major points of communist propaganda was to document racist atrocities that African Americans and other people of color endured in this country (Cochran, 1973; O'Reilly, 1995). "How could the president fight for world freedom while the nation denied basic freedoms to its own non-white citizens?" (O'Reilly, p. 154). Another view of this global conflict involved diplomats from Africa to the United Nations who were routinely denied access to food, housing and rest room facilities as they traveled from New York to Washington.

The newly emerging nations of Western Europe and the Pacific Rim saw this country espousing human liberties yet its own African American citizens lived in fear of being lynched. The "democratic" government of this country with Truman at its head still tolerated a discriminatory set of laws that kept a group of citizens in a permanent state of second-class status in legal, economic, education, and job opportunities (Gardner, 2002). The world did not view these events in a positive light.

To maintain a perceived headway for civil rights, albeit because of the perceived threat of Communism and need of the African American vote (McCullough, 1992; O'Reilly, 1995), Truman agreed to address a NAACP rally in front of the Lincoln Memorial on June 29, 1947. he was the first president to speak at an NAACP gathering (Gardner, 2002; O'Reilly, 1995). His speech was a turning point in the efforts for civil rights as the "bully pulpit" of the office of the President was used to identify the issue of civil rights in this country. His statements included:

> Our national government must show the way. This is a difficult and complex undertaking. Federal laws and administrative machinery must be improved and expanded. We must provide the government with better tools to do the job... Every man should have the right to a decent home, the right to an education, the right to adequate medical care, the right to a worthwhile job, the right to an equal share in making public decisions through the ballot, and the right to a fair trial in a fair court. We must insure that these rights—on equal terms—are enjoyed by every citizen... The support of desperate populations of battle ravaged countries must be won for the free way of life. We must have them as allies in our continuing struggle for the peaceful solution of the world's problems. They may surrender to the false security offered so temptingly by totalitarian regimes unless we can prove the superiority of democracy. Our case for democracy should be as strong as we can make it. It should rest on practical evidence that we have been able to put our own house in order. (Gardner, p. 35-6; O'Reilly, p. 154)

For the first time, the federal government and, significantly, the President were to be leaders in the fight for civil rights (Gardner, 2002; O'Reilly, 1995). Even though there was the linkage between civil rights at home and the threat of Communism abroad, the placing of the civil rights at the forefront was an important statement. While lacking in specifics (O'Reilly, 1995), the speech certainly set a public tone. This engagement was done at a time when this country "was not energized over civil rights" (Gardner, p. 73).

But was there another agenda to Truman's proposals? Was this a stance to cultivate the African American vote away from the possible candidacy of New Dealer Henry Wallace? Was it an attempt to keep the African American vote from going for the "traditional" home of the Republican Party and Thomas Dewey? Was the loss of the Solid South considered an acceptable risk for gaining the minority vote?

Answers to these questions vary from source to source (Cochran, 1973; Ferrell, 1983; Gardner, 2002; Miller, 1986; McCoy, 1984; McCullough, 1992) but the fact that Truman had raised the civil rights issue on a national level and, as it turned out, in a meaningful manner, cannot be denied.

A few months later, on October 29, 1947, the results of Truman's Commission on Civil Rights were released. *Entitled To Secure These Rights,* the 178-page report detailed four constitutionally guaranteed basic rights that committee members felt were taken for granted by Americans but totally lacking for people of color in this country (Gardner, 2002). Four fundamental rights enumerated by the committee were:

1. The Right to Safety and security of the Person
2. The Right to Citizenship and its Privileges
3. The Right to Freedom of Conscience and Expression

## 4. The Eight to Equality of Opportunity

The first right was to address lynching of African Americans throughout the country as well as the commonplace inability of Black men to be judged by a jury of their peers throughout the South (Gardner, 2002; Miller, 1986).

The disenfranchisement of African Americans to the basic right of voting was covered in the second right. The poll tax, requiring Black voters to explain portions of state constitutions before being allowed to vote, and the continued discrimination of service in the military were all well documented by the committee (Gardner, 2002).

The third right addressed freedom and expression and was a reaction to the growing concern of violation of civil rights resulting from reactions to a perceived growing communist menace in America (Gardner, 2002; O'Reilly, 1995).

The fourth freedom contains the idea of providing to people of color opportunities for employment in emerging businesses and industries and fair housing. Neither were in place at that time. As part of the idea of equality in opportunity is the caveat of equal opportunities in education. The Truman Civil Rights Committee found that, as a nation, there was widespread lack of equal opportunities for education for minority students that had developed under the separate but equal doctrine that had been in place for years (Gardner, 2002).

With the placing of civil rights on a national agenda, Truman was in a position as President to significantly improve educational opportunities for people of color in this country. Already in place was the Serviceman's Readjustment Act of 1944, commonly referred to as the GI Bill of Rights, which provided support for servicemen and servicewomen to return and attend school (McCoy, 1984). Created during the Franklin Roosevelt administration, it could have been a powerful instrument to

initiate significant changes in education by issuing the precepts of multicultural education that were just beginning to be expressed.

The GI Bill of Rights would be a success story as 2.2 million veterans would attend college using the funds from this program. Of that number only 70,000 African Americans and 60,000 women would benefit from the program, not a diverse or representative population for the nation. Furthermore, many African Americans, especially in the South, had to attend segregated postsecondary schools of poor quality. Truman did nothing to alter the picture of the recipients of the GI Bill benefits.

Truman did introduce legislation to provide federal aid to education (McCoy, 1984) that would provide more opportunities for students and initiated a meaningful role of the federal government in the arena of public schools (McCoy, 1984). Like so many of his initiatives, it was defeated in Congress by conservative forces so that while he publicly took a position of improving the educational situation for all Americans, Truman did not utilize the political muscle necessary to deliver any tangible results (McCoy, 1984).

The Commission on Civil Rights was directed by Truman to not only identify rights for all Americans but also to recommend a comprehensive federal solution (Gardner, p. 49). *To Secure These Rights* also contained thirty-five recommendations that provided a bold, and to the South "explosive"(Gardner, p. 61), national solution to civil rights abuse. Truman wanted the committee to provide a framework for what was needed to remedy and eliminate pervasive racism and discrimination throughout the United States (Gardner, 2002). What the committee stated was, "the National Government of the United States must take the lead in safeguarding the civil rights of all Americans" (Gardner, p. 58).

The committee recommendations would mean structural and permanent changes in the country's segregated landscape. Imbedded in the

recommendations were the use of powers of the executive branch of the federal government to advance civil reforms and to attack the status quo policies, i.e., separate but equal, of states' rights politicians (Gardner, 2002). "The committee's report 'shocked the nation with its documentation of lynchings, of the denial of voting rights, of inequality of educational opportunities, of discrimination in our armed services'"(Gardner, p. 64). The truly significant aspect of the committee's work was:

> that the committee's report was revolutionary primarily because it explicitly called on this *American president, who was the product of a slave-owning heritage,* to take comprehensive federal actions on behalf of African Americans—actions that, if taken, would impact every phase of American life. [Committee Chairman Charles] Wilson also knew that, equipped with the committee's thirty-five recommendations, it was now up to Truman to demonstrate that he had the moral courage to lead the country on a journey into the uncharted civil rights frontier, a journey that had been stalled since Lincoln liberated America's slaves eight decades earlier. (Gardner, p. 64)

Whether Truman's raising of the civil rights issue and linking it to national security was a political strategy as suggested by some or the beginning of a revolutionary use of the presidency by Truman to change the country's civil rights for people of color as believed by others, the culmination of this line of action was Truman's special message to Congress on civil rights on February 2, 1948 (Gardner, 2002; McCullough, 1992; O'Reilly, 1995).

Truman's civil rights proposal contained ten points that called for the establishment of a permanent Commission on Civil Rights, a Joint Congressional Committee on Civil Rights, a Civil Rights Division in the Department of Justice and a Fair Employment Practices Commission. It provided federal protection against lynching, protected the right to vote, including the elimination of the poll tax, called for the end of discrimination in interstate travel, provided home rule and suffrage in Presidential elections for residents of the District of Columbia, provided statehood for Alaska and Hawaii, provided greater self-governance for American island possessions, equalized opportunities for residents in the United States to become naturalized citizens, ending discrimination in the military, and settle the evacuation claims of Japanese citizens (Gardner, 2002; McCullough, 1992; O'Reilly, 1995).

While definitely focusing on providing federal support for ending racial abuse for African Americans, Truman included improving civil rights of all Americans. When asked a few days after his speech to Congress on civil rights as to what he had drawn on as background, Truman replied the Constitution and the Bill of Rights (McCullough, 2002).

As sweeping as Truman's proposals were, opposition was just as pervasive, both in Congress and in the nation. There would not be passage of any significant points as outlined by Truman (only the matter of Japanese evacuation would eventually be passed during Truman's administration) and a Gallup poll of fifteen hundred Americans conducted in March, 1948 showed that 82 percent of those polled, while not clear what ethnic groups were represented, opposed Truman's civil rights program (Gardner, 2002).

Whether by political design, as believed by some (O'Reilly, 1995), or as a consequence of his growing into the role of President, as felt by others (Gardner, 2002), it is clear that Truman's election in 1948 over Republican Thomas Dewey is one of the greatest upsets in political history in this nation's history. While his policies were anathema to the body politic of Congress, he was liked by the American people. They know that he is a sincere and humble man and, in the cliché often heard, that he is a man "trying to do his best" (McCullough, 2002).

Truman proved that he was the electable candidate seen by Boss Pendergast so many years before. In terms of real accomplishments in civil rights, there were two areas Truman did have successes. One was in the form of Executive Order 9981 to abolish the practice of segregation in the military and create the President's Committee on Equality of Treatment and Opportunity in the Armed Forces (McCoy, 1984; O'Reilly, 1995). The end of segregated military units would be realized by the start of the Korean War.

The second area of progress would be in terms of friend-of-the-court or amicus curiae briefs filed by the Justice Department on behalf of African American plaintiffs challenging segregation in schools. In *Sweatt v. Painter*, the United States Supreme Court ruled that a separate law school for African Americans was not equal to the University of Texas Law School and in *McLaurin v. Oklahoma State Regents*, the Court ruled that African American students cannot be separated from other students at the University of Oklahoma.

Both rulings struck against the dogma of separate but equal conditions in schools and provided important antecedents for the historic *Brown v. Topeka Board of Education* in 1954 (McCoy, 1984; O'Reilly, 1995).

Indeed, while significant amounts of legislation or acts would not be passed during his administration, Truman provided the start of the civil rights movement by engaging the problem of racial discrimination and segregation on a national level. He provided the concept of the federal government as being responsible for the protection and attainment of civil liberties for all Americans and his use of the federal courts would be a benchmark act for civil rights.

## Summary

These three men, John Quincy Adams, Theodore Roosevelt, and Harry S. Truman, all occupied the office of President of the United States. The contributions of each to that office and to the country are varied in scope and substance. In terms of their effect on multicultural education, their individual legacies are also varied.

Adams provided very little in this area as the concept of universal education for everyone in the country was not even on the radar screen. His was still a time when slavery existed as a tolerated and abetted institution in the country. There was no thought of providing opportunities and education to anyone except the privileged few of the ruling, white elite. This framework would not change for several more administrations. His later opposition to slavery would come from a sense of preserving what he conceived as guaranteed constitutional rights, not as a goal of providing universal equal rights to everyone living in America.

Roosevelt would be a larger-than-life figure in many ways, but his record on race relations would also be a faint shadow of accomplishment. Roosevelt's idea of a person making his way in the world and capitalizing on opportunities would still be limited to those who started with the advantages of money or a white skin. His pronouncements of support for African Americans and Native Americans would always be within a personal context that some races are superior and have an obligation to succeed and rule. Any accomplishments by people of color would be due to their playing by the white book of rules and regulations for success.

Roosevelt did, however, possibly provide a model for later federal entry into securing civil rights for people of color in this country by using federal mandates to take over vast tracts of land from states in the West. Without knowing it, Roosevelt opened the window for recognition of the importance and validity of multicultural education for people of color by establishing the dominance of the federal government in different realms.

It would be the reconstructed person, Truman, who would make the greatest contribution to a legacy of multicultural education by using the office of the President to actively engage the federal government in the securing of civil rights for all Americans, especially African Americans, as described in the Constitution and the Bill of Rights. While he was not an extremely proactive president in this regard and did not provide consistent or strong support for civil rights and multicultural education, Truman's legacy would be to provide the beginnings for effective multicultural education efforts that we see today.

Truman used the power of the Office of the President to utilize Executive Orders and to direct the Justice Department to pursue federal court decisions for civil rights were extremely important acts. The use of the federal courts would be a part of a legacy that stretches back to Adams and the *La Amistad* decision to the *Brown v. Topeka* case that would produce profound meaning to the attainment of civil rights and liberties for people of color in America.

Although not imagined by the framers of the Constitution and other historical documents, Truman was a product of years of history for this country and the Office of the President who produced actions of attaining meaningful education and civil rights for all.

# References

Adams, C.F. (Ed.). (1969). *John Quincy Adams memoirs.* Freeport, NY: Books for Libraries Press.

Apple, M.W. (1979). *Ideology and curriculum.* Boston: Routledge & Kegan Paul.

Auchincloss, L. (2001). *Theodore Roosevelt.* Arthur M. Schlesinger, Jr. (Ed.), The American Presidents Series. New York: Henry Holt & Company.

Banks, J.A. (1977). Pluralism and educational concepts: A clarification. *Peabody Journal of Education,* 54(2), 73–78.

Banks, J.A. (1999). Multicultural Education: Characteristics and Goals. In J.A. Banks and C.A.M. Banks (Eds.), *Multicultural education: Issues and perspectives* (2nd Ed.). Boston: Allyn & Bacon.

Banks, J.A., & Banks, C.A.M. (Eds.). (2004). *Handbook of research on multi-*cultural education (2nd ed.). San Francisco: John Wiley & Sons.

Baptiste, H.P. (1979). *Multicultural education: A synopsis.* Washington, DC: University Press of America.

Baptiste, H.P. (1986). Multicultural education and urban schools from a sociohistorical perspective: Internalizing multiculturalism. *Journal of Educational Equity and Leadership,* 6, 295–312.

Baptiste, H.P. (1994). The multicultural environment of schools: Implications to leaders. In L.W. Hughes (Ed.), *The principal as leader* (pp. 89–109). New York: Merrill/ Macmillan.

Bemis, S.F. (1956). *John Quincy Adams and the union.* New York: Alfred A. Knopf.

Bennett, C.I. (1995). *Comprehensive multicultural education: Theory and practice* (3rd Ed.). Boston: Allyn & Bacon.

Boyer, J.B. & Baptiste, H.P. (1996). The crisis in teacher education in America: Issues of recruitment and retention of culturally different (minority) teachers. In John Sikula (Ed.), *Handbook of research on teacher education* (2nd Ed., pp 779–794). New York: Macmillan.

Brands, H.W. (1997). *TR: The last romantic.* New York: Basic Books.

Burnett, G. (1994). Varieties of multicultural education: An introduction. ERIC Digest [Online]. Available: http://eric-web.tc. columbia.edu/digests/dig998.html

Charnwood, G.R. (1923). *Theodore Roosevelt.* London, UK: Constable & Co.

Chessman, G. W. (1976). *Theodore Roosevelt and the politics of power.* Boston: G.K. Hall & Co.

Cochran, B. (1973). *Harry Truman and the crisis presidency.* New York: Funk & Wagnalls.

Collins, R. (1985). *Theodore Roosevelt, culture, diplomacy and expansion.* Baton Rouge, LA: Louisiana State University Press.

Dalton, K. (2002). *Theodore Roosevelt.* New York: Alfred Knopf.

Daniels, J. (1950). *The man of independence.* New York: J.B. Lippincott.

Delpit, L. (1992). Education in a multicultural society: Our future's greatest challenge. *Journal of Negro Education,* 61(3), 237–261.

Drinnon, R. (1997). *Facing West: The metaphysics of Indian-hating and empire building.* Norman, OK: University of Oklahoma Press.

Du Bois, W.E.B. (1902). The training of black men. *The Atlantic Monthly,* September, 1902.

Dyer, TG. (1980). *Theodore Roosevelt and the idea of race.* Baton Rouge, LA: Louisiana State University Press.

Ferrell, R.H. (Ed.) (1980). *Off the record: The private papers of Harry S. Truman.* New York: Harper & Row.

Ferrell, R.H. (1983). *Harry S. Truman and the modern American presidency.* Boston: Little, Brown.

Frazier, L. (1977). The multicultural facet of education. *Journal of Research and Development in Education,* 11, 10–16.

Garcia, E. (1994). *Understanding and meeting the challenge of student cultural diversity.* Boston: Houghton Mifflin.

Garcia, R.L. (1982). *Teaching in a pluralistic society: Concepts, models, strategies.* New York: Harper & Row.

Gardner, M. (2002). *Harry Truman and civil rights: Moral courage and political risks.* Carbondale, IL: Southern Illinois University Press.

Gay, G. (1988). Designing relevant curriculum for diverse learners. *Education and Urban Society,* 20, 327–340.

Gay, G. (1994). At the essence of learning: Multicultural education. West Lafayette, IN: Kappa Delta Pi.

Gay, G. (2004). Curriculum theory and multicultural education. In Banks, J.A. & Banks, C.A.M. (Eds), Handbook of research on multicultural education (2nd edition), pp. 30–44. San Francisco: John Wiley & Sons.

Gollnick, D.M. & Chinn, P.C. (Eds.). (1990). Multicultural education in a pluralistic society (3rd Ed.). Columbus, OH: Merrill.

Gould, L. (1991). *The presidency of Theodore Roosevelt.* Lawrence, KA: University Press of Kansas.

Grant, C.A. (1977). *Multicultural education: Commitments, issues, and applications.* Washington, DC: Association for Supervision and Curriculum Development.

Hagan, W. (1997). *Theodore Roosevelt and six friends of the Indians.* Norman, OK: Univesity of Oklahoma Press.

Hanson, D.C. (1999). Theodore Roosevelt and the Progressive Movement. Retrieved June 4, 2003, from: http://www.virginiawestern.edu/vwhansd/HIS122/Teddy/TRProgressive.html.

Hargreaves, M.W.M. (1985). The presidency of John Quincy Adams. In Donald R. McCoy, Clifford S. Clifford, Homer E. Socolofsky (Eds.), *American Presidential Series.* Lawrence, KA: University Press of Kansas.

Hunter, W.A. (Ed.). (1974). *Multicultural education through competency-based teacher education.* Washington, DC: American Association of Colleges for Teacher Education.

Kallen, H.M. (1970). *Culture and democracy in the United States.* New York: Anno Press and the *New York Times.*

Kunhardt, P., Jr., Kunhardt, P., III, & Kunhardt, P. (1999). *The American president.* New York: Riverhead Books.

La Belle, T.J. (1976). An anthropological framework for studying education. In J.I. Roberts & S.K. Akinsanya (Eds.), *Educational patterns and cultural configurations: The anthropology of education* (pp. 67–82). New York: David McKay.

Lorant, S. (1959). *Life and times of Theodore Roosevelt.* Garden City, NY: Doubleday.

McCoy, D.R. (1984). *The presidency of Harry S. Truman.* Lawrence, KS: University Press of Kansas.

McCullough, D. (1992). *Truman.* New York: Simon & Schuster.

Miller, R.L. (1986). *Truman: The rise to power.* New York: McGraw-Hill.

Morris, E. (1979). *The rise of Theodore Roosevelt.* New York: Coward, McCann & Geoghegan.

Morris, E. (2001). *Theodore rex.* New York: Random House.

Nagel, P.C. (1997). *John Quincy Adams: A public life, a private life.* New York: Alfred A. Knopf.

Nevins, A. (Ed.) (1929). *The diary of John Quincy Adams: 1794–1845.* New York: Longmans, Green.

Nieto, S. (1992). *Affirming diversity: The sociopolitical context of multicultural education.* New York: Longman.

O'Reilly, K. (1995). *Nixon's piano: Presidents and racial politics from Washington to Clinton.* New York: the Free Press.

Pai, Y. (1984). Cultural diversity and multicultural education. *Lifelong Learning, 7,* 7–9, 27.

Remini, R.V. (2002). John Quincy Adams. In Arthur M. Schlesinger, Jr. (Ed.), *The American Presidents Series.* New York: Henry Holt.

Sinkler, G. (1971). *The racial attitudes of American Presidents.* Garden City, NY: Doubleday.

Spring, J. (2000). The universal right to education. Mahwah, NJ: Lawrence Erlbaum Associates.

Truman, M. (Ed.) (1989). *Why the buck stops: The personal and private writings of Harry S. Truman.* New York: Warner Books.

Washington, B.T. (1896). The awakening of the Negro. *The Atlantic Monthly,* September, 1896.

Wilkins, R. (2002). Jefferson's pillow: The founding fathers and the dilemma of black patriotism. Boston: Beacon Press.

*H. Prentice Baptiste is a professor of multicultural and science education and Emil J. Michal, Jr., is a doctoral student, both with the Department of Curriculum and Instruction at New Mexico State University, Las Cruces, New Mexico.*

From *Multicultural Education,* Summer 2004, pp. 35-45. Copyright © 2004 by Caddo Gap Press. Reprinted by permission.

# American Presidents and Their Attitudes, Beliefs, and Actions Surrounding Education and Multiculturalism

## A Series of Research Studies in Educational Policy

### Fourth Installment: Examining Presidents George Washington, James K. Polk, and Franklin D. Roosevelt

H. Prentice Baptiste and Rebecca Sanchez

## Introduction

Understanding the Presidents of the United States, their actions, beliefs, and contradictions, is constructive in understanding our nation's complex societal issues. As a society we inherit the problems, challenges, and legacies of these leaders. Multicultural education and multicultural education theory offer an alternative lens from which to analyze and interpret the actions and inactions of the Presidents.

This lens allows for additional recognition of the roots of contemporary struggles. Geneva Gay describes a primary characteristic of multicultural education: "Multicultural education is essentially an affective, humanistic, and transformative enterprise situated within the sociocultural, political, and historical contexts of the United States" (Gay, 2004, p. 39).

This historical component, which has been whitewashed to the advantage and preservation of the dominant white culture, becomes increasingly important in order to address the presidential administrations of George Washington, James K. Polk, and Franklin D. Roosevelt.

There are several major considerations in terms of multicultural education that can be addressed through a presidential study. First, the actions, policies, and administrative decisions of the presidents have influenced and determined the fate of the citizenry in terms of equality, racism, discrimination, and attitudes about groups. Second, the historical legacy and glorification of these same men in educational texts, and the failure to include the often-devastating significance of their actions towards certain groups in historical accounts, has further distorted societal attitudes about multiculturalism in our country.

James Banks argues that it is imperative that "the curriculum is reconceptualized to help students understand how knowledge is constructed and how it reflects human interests, ideology, and the experiences of the people who create it" (Banks, p. 23). A strange paradox emerges. The same men that we look to as embodiments of the ideals of freedom, leadership, democracy, and equality, are men, who in the cases of Washington, Polk, and F. D. Roosevelt, personally and publicly were unable to live up to the values for which they are idolized.

Because of these inconsistencies, and the impact of their administrative policies on all cultural groups in the United States, we are seeking to use a multicultural lens to analyze and historicize in an effort to understand the power of history and historical interpretation in shaping the beliefs and attitudes of a people.

> We often speak about American history as if it were something real. But I do not believe in American history: I only believe in American histories. I object to the way history has been constructed, sanitized, and glorified. (Saenz, p. 137)

This sanitization effect is ever present in our schooling regarding the presidents. Do our textbooks ever really delve into the aristocratic nature of Washington? The assimilistic desires of Polk? Or the neglect of racial issues by F. D. Roosevelt? Moreover, are students of history, in all grades, encouraged to connect the personal attributes of the presidents and executive decisions they made to the complex multicultural dilemmas of their time?

A historical *revisitation* of our Presidents allows for scrutiny and deeper understanding of their administrations thus helping to situate and contextualize our current racial, ethnic, and cultural dilemmas in education and society at large. Loewen, in his argument surrounding the acquisition of new historical knowledge states, "Understanding our past is central to our ability to understand ourselves and the world around us. We need to know our history" (p. 13). The problem arises when historical characters, such as the Presidents, are over-glorified and over-simplified, resulting in the furthering of the myth of President as infallible icon; this myth undermines our historical understanding.

It also makes the negative historical events, traumas, and tragedies appear to have occurred in a vacuum. There is no causality or responsibility, no burden of guilt placed on our leadership even in historical representations to account for the misdeeds of the past. For example, "George Washington has become so shrouded in legend that it is difficult to retrieve the man behind the marble exterior" (Smith, 1993, p. 9).

The purpose of this article is to present additional information about Presidents Washington, Polk, and F. D. Roosevelt so that their contributions, oversights, and silence regarding multicultural matters and education during their presidential administrations can be understood in a deeper way. Furthermore, "Critical multiculturalists in all domains must reunite memory and history in order to address the ideological distortions that daily confront us in various expressions. . ."(Kincheloe & Steinberg, 1997, p. 241).

Why the presidency and why these presidents? The president is the embodiment of leadership in this country. Because of the ambiguity of the Constitution in relation to the chief executive, the president has the power to frame, implement, and transform government (Schlesinger, 2002; Baptiste & Sanchez 2003). Washington, Polk, and F. D. Roosevelt were chosen because these three presidents all served during periods of tremendous growth, literally and ideologically; the ideas of Manifest Destiny and nationalism surfaced during all three administrations. Yet all three remained stunted in terms of creating policies affecting groups of color such as Native Americans, African-Americans, Mexican Americans, and Japanese Americans (Wiencek, 2003; Ferling 1988; Bergeron, 1987; Zinn, 1997; O'Reilly, 1995; Freidel, 1990; McJimsey, 2000; Warren, 1999).

Historical understanding is a complex endeavor. The goal of this article is not to simplify and deduce an argument about multiculturalism or racism regarding the presidents that is not contextual. Rather, we are attempting to introduce the factors associated with race, diversity, and multiculturalism that added to the complexity of the office and in turn, to the political and social climate of the nation. With multicultural education theory in mind, the goal is to offer educators additional information that will help them teach a more insightful and connected history.

## George Washington: Setting the Example as First President

President Washington would not tell Congress that he thought slavery wrong. He declined to lend his name

or his office's prestige at a time when the words of the Declaration of Independence ("all men are created equal") were still resonate.. (O'Reilly, 1995, p. 16)

### Social Currency

George Washington was greatly influenced by his upbringing among Virginia plantation owners. He was born in Virginia in 1732, his family owned large tracts of land that would later become his. The power and status granted to southern plantation farmers was profound during this time. Many plantation owners were able to amass so much wealth because they had ready access to education, political office, and public position. Economic dependence on England was also a defining feature of colonial society (Smith, 1993).

The southern states had remained largely agricultural and rural by the time Washington was born. Although cities in the north were quickly becoming more cosmopolitan and refined, the south was based on agriculture (Wills, 2003). What separated the farmers of the south from homestead or substance farmers was the desire to farm large tracts of land. Such large farms or plantations relied on the use of slave labor to function and prosper economically (Hirshfeld, 1997). Slavery was a dominant force in the lives of plantation farmers like the Washingtons.

George Washington became a slave owner at age 11 when he "inherited ten slaves"upon his father's death (Hirshfeld, 1997, p. 11). The practice of slavery was further protected since "the Constitution expressly provided for the continuations of that practice" (McDonald, 1974). George Washington inherited his family estate in 1752, nearly 37 years before he would assume the presidency. His upbringing among slaves and his own economic tenacity and greed would render him dependent on slave labor for the remainder of his life.

The seemingly endless amounts of land available for farming also shaped the American psyche during this period. In Europe, the agricultural system had perpetuated a certain hopelessness and feeling of drudgery for working the land (McDonald, 1974). The bounty of rich farming land in the new country presented a world of possibility for settlers and farmers. Large amounts of land coupled with the acceptance of slave labor offered the opportunity of economic prosperity to a greater portion of the public than the colonists were used to in Europe (McDonald, 1974). Washington and his contemporaries were well schooled in gentility and civility. This ordered lifestyle dictated controlled responses, personal manners, and public behaviors (Ferling, 1988, McDonald, 1974).

### Societal Values and Background

Early American society was likely recovering from shock at the whirlwind of change that occurred in a short time. The Declaration of Independence, the American Revolution, the Articles of Confederation, and the Constitutional Convention had imbedded certain values into the new America (McDonald, 1974; Smith 1993; Ferling, 1988; Brookhiser 1996). Economic autonomy, personal independence, self-governance, individual ambition, and fear of tyranny were some of the resulting values of the period.

The Constitutional Convention and the subsequent adoption of a Constitution were profound in shaping the values of early American society. The delegates to the convention had painstakingly outlined the powers of the legislative branch of government (McDonald, 1974). This process had secured the fate of representative government.

The role of the Executive was also being questioned and scrutinized. Many were concerned that the President would acquire too much power and become tyrannical like a monarch. Early colonial government did not even include an executive because of the dislike of the actions of British rule (McDonald, 1974). "Executive power had been the object of distrust in America for a long time" (McDonald, 1974, p. 2).

The continued fear of a strong executive affected Washington insofar as he too had been exposed to the tyranny of a domineering leader (McDonald, 1974). His actions would be cautious, and largely symbolic, during his presidential terms in spite of the fact that constitutionally the president had a great deal of power, equal to that of the legislative and judicial branches.

### Educational Background

George Washington was born into a prosperous Virginia family. This stature allowed him the luxury of both formal and informal educational opportunities. His formal education included studies in reading, writing, mathematics (specifically geometry), poetry, and the social graces necessary to a person in his social strata (Ferling, 1988). He received formal education as a student in private academies and he was also tutored privately (Ferling, 1988).

He was also taught about farming and planting by his family. Among his family he also learned about the government and parish life. "George was literally schooled in the mechanics of government and plantation management in his early teen years. His exercise book from that period survives, containing, . . . 'forms' all of which were legal or financial documents of one kind or another" (Wiencek, 2003, p. 26).

George Washington was self-taught in the area of gentility. He constantly worked to polish his mannerisms and behaviors. George studied the desirable traits by reading, and he "Copied them (axioms for behavior) from a book called *The Rules of Civility & Decent Behaviour in Company and Conversation*" (Wiencek, 2003, p. 37). He studied conversation and expression by reading books on the subject and by observing his fashionable and elegant brothers. His desire to imitate the grandeur of his brothers prompted him to study music and fencing (Ferling, 1988).

His extensive study of geometry prepared him as a surveyor. As a member of a surveyor team, George Washington had the opportunity to travel and learn about the geography of the new western areas (Smith 1993; Ferling 1988). Serving in the Revolutionary War was influential in Washington establishing himself as a leader (Jones, 2002; Smith, 1993; Ferling 1988).

### Actions, Policies, and Political Decisions

The early part of Washington's presidential career was devoted to carving out the exact role and purpose of the president. The colonies had been operating under a congressional system of government for some time, but the presidency, on the other hand, had no history or similar example (Brookhiser, 1996). Washington was influential in modeling how a chief executive could use, supervise, direct, and work with a cabinet of individuals who could help with important affairs. "In day-to-day practice, Washington supervised the activities of his department heads closely" (McDonald, 1974, p. 40).

The new country had many challenges; one of those had to do with national finances and banking. Alexander Hamilton had been active in many of the early decisions of the new country. Hamilton designed the financial structures to guide the new country, and Washington allowed him to do so. These financial policies included the creation of a national bank and a tax on whiskey, which would prove to be very unpopular with citizens (Brookhiser, 1996; McDonald, 1974; Ferling 1988).

"Finally, the nationalistic implications of Hamilton's program appealed to Washington far more than its anti-agrarian implications might have upset him" (McDonald, 1974, p. 65). This acceptance of the Hamilton proposal demonstrated Washington's strong desire to unite and strengthen the national government. However, Washington agreed to many of the policies without thinking about the far-reaching, long-lasting implications. In his second term he was left to deal with the fallout from the economic policies of the first term (Brookhiser, 1996).

George Washington was also challenged to develop a Native American policy. He felt it would be better for all if the Native Americans assimilated into the dominant culture. Washington hoped that Westward expansion would occur at a slow pace so that the Native Americans could assimilate into the agricultural farming system of the Euro-Americans (Ferling, 1988). In an effort to protect the Native Americans from Westward frontiersman, Washington developed a policy to police the boundaries with the military (Ferling, 1988).

Washington ended up protecting the frontiersman, despite his knowledge that they were unduly provoking the Native Americans and encroaching on their land (Ferling, 1988). His policy developed into one of containment, by allowing the military to use force in Native American issues and disputes. In New York State, for example, "during Washington's administration a treaty was signed with the Iroquois of New York: [stating that] 'The United States acknowledge all the land with the aforementioned boundaries to be the property of the

Seneka nation. . .'"(Zinn, 1997, p. 386). Treaties such as this one demonstrate that sometimes Washington did designate some land to the Native Americans, but to give land that the Europeans had unlawfully obtained was a minimal colonialist gesture.

Slavery was still a major force in political and economic life in the 1790s. In his role as President, Washington was reluctant to voice any opposition to slavery though he had "spoken privately about the evils of slavery" (Ferling, 1988, p. 474). In 1793 Washington advanced one law regarding slavery. The Fugitive Slave Act of 1793 granted permission to slaveowners to "cross state lines in order 'to seize or arrest' runaway slaves" (Ferling, 1988, p. 475). This law was a public display by Washington favoring the rights of slave owners.

In another important decision regarding slavery, Washington, along with his political cronies Thomas Jefferson and James Madison, secured the site for the nation's capital with slavery in mind (Wills, 2003). Early American political life had centered in Pennsylvania. However, by the time Washington became president, many Quakers and abolitionists were living in the north, especially in Pennsylvania (Randall, 1997). During the Constitutional convention these groups had advocated against the use of slavery but they were outnumbered (Wiencek, 2003).

Washington, supported by Jefferson and Madison, decided that a location in a more isolated and southern position would help secure slavery and the culture of slavery for other plantation operators such as themselves. This insulated position would protect the interests of the slave owning community.

> But Washington (the capital) was placed where a diverse cultural life would pose no challenge to its sleepy southern folkways. No professors from a major university, no benevolent Quaker merchants, no sophisticated financial operatives would rub up against the Maryland and Virginia slaveholding natives. No major harbor would give a cosmopolitan air to the place. (Wills, 2003, p. 213)

This act was loaded with implications for a new government. It allowed slavery to continue without the intense scrutiny that would have occurred had the capital been placed in Philadelphia or another northern cosmopolitan city. This act also demonstrated that Washington was willing to use his power as president to perpetuate the oppressive, racist, and problematic institution of slavery. From a legal standpoint, Washington failed to make any political decisions during his presidency that would benefit the slaves, or discourage the institution. The few times he did enact policy with regard to the slaves it was to their determent, as in the Fugitive Slave Act and in the placement of the capital to insure slave practices.

Privately, Washington made sure that his own slaves were never in a free state long enough to be granted freedom (Ferling, 1988). When one slave did escape, "Washington would not even advertise for an escaped slave" (Wills, 2003, p. 209). Washington's reluctance to actively and visibly search in the North for escaped slaves was a demonstration of his personal admission of the ethical problems of slavery.

## Multicultural Perspectives and Impacts

Throughout his life, from his work as a landowner and a farmer, to his Presidential years, Washington operated within the privileged and racist system of the day. While Washington might have struggled with some of the moral aspects of slavery, even to the extent of willing his slaves free after his wife's death, his political and public acts exacerbated, excused, and even encouraged slavery in the new country (Hirshfeld, 1997, Smith, 1993, p343). Washington is proposed by some authors to have been a deeply religious Christian who deplored slavery; however, this did not exalt him to publicly speak out against the institution of slavery (Marshall & Manuel, 1977, 1986).

> His silence on the slavery question was strategic, believing as he did that slavery was a cancer on the politic of America that could not at present be removed without killing the patient. The intriguing question is whether Washington could project an American future after slavery that included the African-American population as prospective members of the American citizenry. For almost all the leading members of the Virginia dynasty, the answer was clear and negative. Even those like Jefferson and Madison, who looked forward to the eventual end of slavery, also presumed that all freed Blacks must be transported elsewhere.
>
> Washington never endorsed that conclusion. Nor did he ever embrace the racial argument for black inferiority that Jefferson advanced in *Notes on the State of Virginia*. He tended to regard the condition of the Black population as a product of nuture rather than nature that is he saw slavery as the culprit, preventing the development of diligence and responsibility that would emerge gradually and naturally after emancipation. (Ellis, 2000, p.158)

Washington was aware of his political clout. He was also aware of the tremendous amount of public support he held as a "national leader and a prominent world figure." (Hirshfeld, 1997, p. 236). With this in mind he had to be aware that his own political and private acts regarding slavery would be an open encouragement of slavery. Washington modeled the role of president as silent bystander "in the name of order and stablility" (O'Reilly, 1995, p. 17) though personally his moral objections to slavery existed. His objections were demonstrated when he wrote in his will that his personal slaves were to be freed upon his wife's death (Dusinberre, 2003).

Washington's attitude about Native Americans was based on their assimilation. He wanted them to adopt the practices of the new Americans. When he realized that his own citizens were not going to allow for or encourage assimilation, he caved and allowed for the forceful submission of the Native Americans to the frontiersman (Ferling, 1988).

## James K. Polk: Manifest Destiny President

If the president of the United States was spending every spare penny of his plantation profits in buying children as young as ten years old . . . so that he could amass a substantial force of enslaved laborers to support himself in gentlemanly style during his retirement, this fact must be hidden from the public. (Dusinberre, 2003, p. 171).

### Social Currency

James K. Polk was born into a landowning family, and a slaveholding family. His parents moved to Tennessee from North Carolina, where they were able to become wealthy. His father was in the business of "land speculation, managing slave plantations, selling merchandise, running banks, and developing transportation projects" (Dusinberre, 2003, p. 13).

James Polk was afforded the luxuries of education, which contributed to his success in politics. Coming from a land-owning family was important in other ways. "Polk was acculturated by a lifelong reliance on slave labor in a racist agrarian society" (Seigenthaler, 2003, p. 85). Polk continued in the farming practices of his family and he relied heavily on slave labor to reap the greatest profits (Dusinberre, 2003).

The government of the United States at the time was burgeoning with party politics and, as a young politician, Polk was able to use the competing interests of party politics in his favor. At the 1844 Democratic Party convention, Polk attended to support candidate Martin Van Buren for president. As a supporter of the annexation of Texas, Polk was able to gain the party's nomination (Bergeron, 1988). His family's status had prepared him for political maneuvers that led to his power. He also understood how to take the issues of the day, such as the annexation of Texas, conflicts with Mexico, and slavery, and turn them into political bargaining tools (Bergeron, 1988; Dusinberre 2003, Seigenthaler, 2003).

### Societal Values and Background

In the mid 1800s a new expansionist value was beginning to develop in the United States. The desire for westward expansion into the territories was quickly becoming a political, economic, and social issue. This movement, known as Manifest Destiny, was significant in that the general citizenry began to feel and believe that the country had a divine right to acquire and develop the country westward to the Pacific Ocean.

This movement set a precedent of the government masking its conquering of new lands by "the presumed altruistic notion of extending liberty and freedom (American style, of course)" (Bergeron, 1987, p. 4). Transportation and

industry development were the industrial advancements that aided and abetted the expansion into the territories (Bergeron, 1987). Immigration was also creating a "nativist" feeling in the country. Many new immigrants were Roman Catholics. Immigrants during this period (1840s) were arriving by the 100,000s each year. A result of this influx was the desire by some in the country to preserve traditions and morals (Bergeron, 1987).

Increasing tensions over slavery also marked this pre-Civil War period. The southern states were retreating into their own region, while the northern states were gaining opponents on the issue (Bergeron, 1987). Opposition to slavery was becoming more organized and vocal because of anti-slavery associations. Above all, the anti-slavery movement wanted slavery completely abolished. During this time, since that goal seemed unattainable, the movement worked to prevent the spread of slavery in the territories (Bergeron, 1987).

### Educational Background

James Polk was born in North Carolina and moved to Tennessee during his childhood. There he studied both formally and informally in the care of his family. Polk was allowed to attend a local religious school to pursue his formal studies. He then moved on to study at an academy. These schools instilled the virtues of Calvinism into Polk. He believed that with hard work he would be able to attain any of his goals (Bergeron, 1987).

Because of his academic potential and the status and financial standing of his family, Polk was fortunate to have the opportunity to study at the University of North Carolina. At the University Polk worked to polish his public speaking skills. He was a student leader and an excellent student (Bergeron, 1987). After graduation he began a law apprenticeship in Tennessee (Dusinberre, 2003; Bergeron, 1987). Polk was only in his mid-twenties when he began practicing law (Dusinberre 2003).

As a young professional, Polk's education continued through his work as a lawyer. He got an early start in politics when he received a job as a Senate clerk. Polk also served in Congress for 14 years, during which time he focused on advocating for the needs of the people of Tennessee (Bergeron, 1987). These professional work experiences were valuable in educating Polk about the nature of politics. He also learned the art of persuasion. His work ethic, which had been influenced early on by his Calvinist teachers, aided in his quick ascension from law clerk to Congressman (Dusinberre, 2003; Bergeron, 1987).

### Actions, Policies, and Political Decisions

Polk was a territorial expansionist working under the ideology of Manifest Destiny (Dusinberre, 2003; Bergeron, 1987, McCoy, 1960). Polk has been described as "favoring the acquisition of territory for the sole purpose of acquiring a renewed basis for slavery" (McCoy, 1960, p. 155). Polk began his Presidential term in 1845. One of his first major actions was to allow Texas into the Union. Texas came into the union as a slave state. This measure had been planned before Polk officially took office, but it was a party issue that he inherited (Seigenthaler, 2003, O'Reilly, 1995; Sellars, 1966; Brown, 1980).

In other areas of United States expansion, Polk worked to arrange for a treaty with Great Britain regarding control of the Oregon Territories. The result was that Oregon became under the official control of the United States. Positioned on the West Coast, Oregon became a symbolic and real example of Manifest Destiny (Bergeron, 1987; Morrison, 1967; Foos, 2002). In 1846 the treaty was signed and it was agreed that the United States would control Oregon up to the Canadian boundary.

Early in the administration, Polk's opponents offered up a piece of legislation that would limit slavery in all acquired lands from Mexico. The Wilmot Proviso sought to prohibit the expansion of slavery, and northern Democrats were eager to protect the territory (Morrison, 1967). This Proviso was never fully accepted. With the wheels of Manifest Destiny turning, Polk continued to aggressively pursue the acquisition of more Western territory (Zinn, 1997; Foos, 2002).

Polk first tried to buy California and New Mexico for $20,000,000. This offer was insulting not only because of the amount offered and the location of the land, but it would have been a political disaster for Mexican leaders to accept the proposal. Polk sent troops to the Rio Grande area, supervised by General Zachary Taylor, to pressure the Mexicans. This act initiated the Mexican American War (Zinn, 1997; Foos, 2002). The War was declared by Congress even though it did not have the full support of the United States. The Mexicans eventually lost the war. The Treaty of Guadalupe Hidalgo was signed into law. As a result of this treaty Mexico lost half of their territory to the United States for the price of $15,000,000 (Zinn, 1997).

All of these events did not come about without resistance from the Mexican Americans who had established themselves throughout the Southwest. "One of the persistent myths of American Western historiography has been that Mexicanos happily greeted American soldiers, offered little resistance to their domination, and allowed the conquest to occur without spilling a drop of blood" (Gutierrez, 2004, p. 265). The Mexicanos did resist. Many were vehemently opposed to the domination of the United States.

## Multicultural Perspectives and Impacts

The multicultural implications of Polk as a slavemaster are similar to those created by Washington. Polk's continued use and support of slavery both personally and publicly upheld the practice and dehumanized slaves in the process. Polk used his power as president to secure slavery. "He claimed that the federal government had no power to touch slavery, not even in the District of Columbia or the territories" (Dusinberre, 2003).

Slavery was so ingrained in the minds of the people that it greatly influenced Polk's policy of Manifest Des-

tiny. If more land could be acquired as slave-owning land, the institution would continue and its future would be secured (Zinn, 1997, McCoy, 1960, Dusinberre, 2003).

Manifest Destiny not only pertained to acquisition of land, in addition racial Manifest Destiny was also at work. The power elite felt that in obtaining New Mexico and California, the ideals of freedom and democracy could be spread. "This was intermingled with ideas of racial superiority, longings for the beautiful lands of New Mexico and California, and thoughts of commercial enterprise across the Pacific" (Zinn, 1997, p. 116).

It was also an example of the spread of United States imperialism and domination to people of color. The people who lived in these regions, the Mexicans and Indians, would be civilized by the domination of the United States (Zinn, 1997). The historical legacy of this administration lies in the oppression of groups and the assumption of racial assimilation through the power of racial Manifest Destiny.

"The idea of everyman as conqueror pressured volunteers from the lower and middling classes to look for a new social order which would extend to them the full privileges of herrenvolk, that is, personal dominance over 'inferiors'" (Foos, 2002, p. 58). Thus, the expansionist mentality managed to transform into power roles that would encourage whites from different social classes to assume a position of superiority (Foos, 2002).

## Franklin Delano Roosevelt: Silent on Race

The question asked by a black reporter had to do with segregation in the Army; the president's response could be applied to any race issue in that he concluded the problem was intractable not because of his administration's reluctance to confront it head on but because racism was too ingrained in too many Americans. (O'Reilly, 1995, p. 143)

### Social Currency

Franklin Delano Roosevelt did not have to deal with the issues of slavery, as Washington and Polk had. However, because of his aristocratic background, he had lived a life insulated from African-Americans and other people of color (McJimsey, 2000). As an aristocrat, families that had acquired wealth in mining, technology, and industry surrounded Franklin. "His world was filled with people who were used to getting their way" (McJimsey, 2000, p. 9).

Franklin Roosevelt was confined to a wheelchair because of an illness suffered during his youth. Because of his physical limitations, Roosevelt also had to battle public opinion about his disability. People who were confined to wheelchairs were not common as leaders of countries. Some of Roosevelt's own personal power may have stemmed from his interaction with the world as a man with a disability (Davis, 2000; Gallagher, 1999).

## Societal Values and Background

The Great Depression had set in before Franklin D. became president. Banks nationwide had closed. The stock market had crashed. The financial structures of the country were in disarray and the unemployment rate was skyrocketing. Homelessness, hunger, and lack of personal savings compounded the effects of the depression for millions of citizens. These economic hard times resulted in feelings of desperation and hopelessness among the citizens (McJimsey, 2000, Davis, 2000). Private and public charities tried to offer assistance to as many people as possible.

## Educational Background

Franklin Delano Roosevelt was born into a wealthy New York family that was able to offer him boundless formal education opportunities. He attended a prestigious academy called Groton Academy as an adolescent (McJimsey, 2000; Jenkins, 2003). He later studied at Harvard. After his marriage to Anna Eleanor, Franklin decided to continue his education. Franklin chose another prestigious university to continue his studies. He chose to study law at Columbia University (McJimsey, 2000).

Like Polk and Washington, F. D. Roosevelt also received years of education on the job as a politician. He served in the New York State Senate. He also continued to learn about politics as a presidential appointee to the post of Assistant Secretary to the Navy. His term as Governor of New York in 1928 enabled him to learn to manage party politics and become a charismatic leader (McJimsey, 2000; Gallagher, 1999).

## Actions, Policies, and Political Decisions

Most of F. D. Roosevelt's policies and political decisions stemmed from two major events. The first was the Great Depression which led to the creation of economic aid measures meant to stimulate the economy. The second event was World War II. Because F. D. Roosevelt served four consecutive terms as President, his impact was profound and long-lasting (McJimsey, 2000; Gallagher, 1999; Davis, 2000).

Many of his economic policies are legendary. The New Deal consisted of a legislation package that Roosevelt began immediately upon his presidency. Included in this package were programs to create jobs for out of work citizens, to develop agricultural subsidies, and to develop a domestic infrastructure (McJimsey, 2000; Gallagher, 1999; Davis, 2000). "Roosevelt also favored plans to spur the economy over the short term, especially plans that rejected government spending to restore prosperity" (McJimsey, 2000, p. 43). A greater desire of the economic plan was ".to reorganize capitalism" so that the economy would regain stability (Zinn, 1997, p. 285). These economic plans were also valuable in maintaining public order.

Another domestic issue was the constitutionality of Roosevelt's legislation. The Supreme Court deemed some of his programs unconstitutional (McJimsey, 2000; Gallagher, 1999; Davis, 2000). Roosevelt also enacted New Deal legislation pertaining specifically to Native Americans. "Indian New Deal" allowed tribal peoples to organize governments as long as they were representative governments, modeling "representative democracy" (Snipp, 2004, p. 324). Such policies, while granting some autonomy to Native Peoples were based on assimilation, domination, and control. In this case the deterministic policy disregarded the Native American's utilization of theocracies for governance (Snipp, 2004).

World War II held it's own challenges for the President. The United States had been in an isolationist mood after World War I and before World War II. The United States sold weapons to European forces to try and combat the Axis powers that were fighting in Europe. The United States did not officially enter the war until the Attack on Pearl Harbor in 1941. However, before the attack Roosevelt had been increasing the military budget in an effort to prepare for war (McJimsey, 2000; Gallagher, 1999; Davis, 2000).

Roosevelt ordered assistance to the British for their military supply needs and small operations. The United States also launched small attacks from the ocean. The United States involvement in World War II established a new world order, one in which the United States would assume a more powerful position, yet remain relatively peaceful at home (McJimsey, 2000; Gallagher, 1999; Davis, 2000).

## Multicultural Perspectives and Impacts

F. D. Roosevelt's primary concerns during his administration dealt with economic recovery and, later, the war effort. He was a champion of the working poor and he offered a great deal of attention to their needs during the Great Depression (McJimsey, 2000). When it came to issues of equality and desegregation, his was a policy of silence (O'Reilly, 1995). The press, including the more liberal news reporting agencies, did not assign responsibility to President Roosevelt for the blatantly racist policies of his administration for fear of compromising the war effort (Warren, 1999).

The liberal press during this time reported on civil rights, civil liberties, and they often cited racial discrimination as a stain on democracy in America, however, they did not implicate Roosevelt as the President (Warren, 1999) Failing to assign responsibility to the negative policies of presidential administrations has continued to be a problem. Roosevelt's lack of attention to issues of race were noticeable even in major issues like 'Voting rights"(O'Reilly, 1995, p. 123). He did not privately or publicly speak out against Jim Crow laws. It was not until his last year in office that Roosevelt allowed African-American reporters to be invited to his press conferences (O'Reilly, 1995).

Roosevelt did make token appointments of African-American leaders to governmental posts. At the same time Roosevelt remained silent as the lynching of African-

Americans was reported on a regular basis. Eventually Roosevelt did approve of a committee to investigate the lynchings but he was cautious about implementing actual legislation or policy in that area (Freidel, 1990).

The following passage describes the sentiments of many African-Americans during this time "As for the Blacks and workers, many deplored the failure of Roosevelt to go further..." (Freidel, 1990, pg. 248). Many historical representations champion Roosevelt as a leader in the area of Civil Rights. For example, a Presidential anthology describes, "No president since Lincoln was so widely admired among African Americans as was Franklin Roosevelt" (Kunhardt, P., Kunhardt, P., Kunhardt, P. 1999, p. 192). However, this view is not supported by the policies made during his administration.

It is also not supported by an interview of one of the author's father who served in the United States Navy during World War II. He states that "African American men in the Navy were relegated to segregated quarters and only received assignments as cooks and custodians" (H. P. Baptiste, personal communication, January 18, 2004).

At the urging of his wife, Eleanor, Roosevelt did manage to meet with some African-American rights activists, but during these meetings the President paid little attention to the problems presented (O'Reilly, 1995; Freidel, 1990). The desegregation of the army was another source of contention. Roosevelt was reluctant to allow for a desegregated military. Even more disturbing was that Roosevelt, "allowed his favorite service, the U.S. Navy, to remain almost completely white." (Jenkins, 2003, pp. 140).

F. D. Roosevelt also removed Japanese Americans from their homes and had them placed in internment camps (McJimsey, 2000; Warren, 1999; Freidel, 1990). This racist act violated the civil liberties of the Japanese citizens. Approximately 120,000 persons of Japanese ancestry were relocated to the camps. Incidentally, over two thirds of these people were United States citizens (Freidel, 1990).

> The consequence was to benefit certain white business and interests at the expense of suffering American citizens who had never been charged with any crime or act of disloyalty. (McJimsey, 2000, p. 219)

Roosevelt was suspicious of other groups of color as well. He established an office to investigate conflicts among groups of color. This office served as a "racial intelligence clearinghouse" (O' Reilly, 1997, p. 140). This office believed that Eleanor Roosevelt was encouraging and conspiring with African-Americans. They were never able to acquire any intelligence of significance.

## Multicultural Education, Teacher Education, and the Presidents

A goal in our work as teacher educators specializing in multicultural education and critical pedagogy is to engage with students in the multifarious issues surrounding diversity and equity. Exploring the presidents and their actions enables us to fill in the gaps of our historical understanding. Multicultural education theory empowers learning and in the case of the presidents, it should focus on exposition so the real power structures that inform social and racial policy in this country are contextualized and described.

> The surface harmony heralded by the media, the government and education is merely an image in the minds of those individuals who are shielded by privilege from the injustice experienced by dominated peoples. Such a pseudo-harmony idealizes the future as it covers up the historical forces that have structured the present disharmony that it denies. (Kincheloe & Steinberg, 1997, pp.230)

When students in our education courses are exposed to new information about the presidents there are mixed reactions. We are often told that in exposing the facts of Washington's slave polices and practices, for example, we are taking certain parts of his life out of context. Out of context? Solely learning the heroic deeds of a person's life as we do with our presidents, is indeed actually taking portions of a person's life out of context.

When we inaccurately present historical figures by only focusing on the positive contributions and their legendary accomplishments we are failing to address the needs of a diverse population. For instance, in Washington's case most students will recall him as Revolutionary hero, first President, man of many morals. This same man stood silent while hundreds of people under his own personal power and tens of thousands of people under his political power were enslaved (Ferling, 1988, Smith, 1993, Hirshfeld, 1997). In a discussion of James Polk's presidential decisions, Dusinberre makes a poignant statement.

> We modern Americans like to distance ourselves from James Polk's world by naming it a slave society and ours a free society. We repudiate the slave system that was so important to our ancestors, but we are slower to repudiate the politics that walked arm in arm with that social system. (Dusinberre, 2003, p. 174)

Slowest of all is our reaction to implicate the leaders that perpetuated a system of oppression, injustice and dehumanization. Multicultural education allows for a dialogue of truth and liberation to transform education realities and unrealities. If we ask our students the question, "Under what circumstances would the enslavement of humans be acceptable?" how will they reply? There is not a circumstance that makes such an act acceptable. It is evident then, that Washington and subsequent presidents such as Polk and F. D. Roosevelt should not be protected because of a romantic notion of historical unity.

> There is much pain and loss in our national history, which contains powerful echoes of the pain and loss many of us feel in our daily lives. For Blacks there is the pain of slavery and the continual loss of dignity that accompanies our treatment as nonstandard citizens. (Wilkins, 2002, p. 6)

Wilkins' sentiment brings attention to the racial tensions and feelings by African-Americans in our country, and he connects those feelings to the history and the historical figures that have contributed to the oppression of a group.

As educators, especially in a diverse society it should be known that our historical investigations will not always be comfortable. We must challenge our notions of historical figures so that the complexities of race, culture, and policy can have a new meaning for students. Kincheloe and Steinberg describe,

> it [critical multiculturalism] reveals historically how race, class and gender make a difference in the lives of individuals and how racism, class bias and sexism have played a central role in shaping Western societies. (1997, p. 41)

The presidential administrations of George Washington, James K. Polk, and Franklin Delano Roosevelt serve as small pieces of the historical puzzle that encourages the contextualization of contemporary struggles to occur.

# References

Banks, J. (2004). Multicultural education: historical development, dimensions, and practice. In *Handbook of research on multicultural education,* second edition. J. Banks & C. Banks (Eds.) San Franscisco: Jossey-Bass.

Baptiste, P. & Sanchez, R. (2003). American Presidents and their attitudes, beliefs, and actions surrounding education and multiculturalism. *Multicultural Education.* Winter 2003, 11:2.

Bergeron, P. (1987). *The Presidency of James K. Polk.* Lawrence, KS: The University of Kansas Press.

Brookhiser, R. (1996). *Rediscovering George Washington: Founding Father.* New York: Free Press.

Brown, C. (1980). *Agents of Manifest Destiny.* Chapel Hill, NC: The University of North Carolina Press.

Davis, K. (2000). *FDR: The War President 1940-1943.* New York: Random House.

Dusinberre, W. (2003). *Slavemaster President: the double career of James Polk.* Oxford, UK: Oxford University Press.

Ellis, J. (2000). *Founding Brothers: The Revolutionary Generation.* New York: Vintage Books.

Ferling, J. (1988). *The First of men: a life of George Washington.* Knoxville, TN: University of Tennessee Press.

Foos, P. (2002). *A short, offhand, killing affair: soldiers and social conflict during the Mexican-American War.* Chapel Hill, NC: The University of North Carolina Press.

Freidel, F. (1990). *Franklin D. Roosevelt: a rendezvous with destiny.* Boston: Little, Brown and Company.

Gallagher, H. (1999). *FDR's splendid deception: the moving story of Roosevelt's massive disability—and the intense efforts to conceal it from the public.* Arlington, VA: Vandamere Press.

Gay, G. (2004). Curriculum theory and multicultural education. In *Handbook of research on multicultural education, second edition.* J. Banks & C. Banks (Eds.) San Francisco: Jossey-Bass.

Gutierrez, R. (2004). Ethnic Mexicans in historical and social science scholarship. In *Handbook of research on multicultural education,* second edition. J. Banks & C. Banks (Eds.) San Francisco: Jossey-Bass.

Hirschfeld, F. (1997). *George Washington and slavery: a documentary portrayal.* Columbia, MO: University of Missouri Press.

Jenkins, R. (1993). *Franklin Delano Roosevelt.* New York: Henry Holt & Company.

Jones, R. (2002). *George Washington: Ordinary man, extraordinary leader.* New York: Fordham University Press.

Kincheloe, J. & Steinberg, S. (1997). *Changing Multiculturalism.* Buckingham, UK: Open University Press.

Kunhardt, P. Jr, Kunhardt, P. II, Kunhardt, P.(1999). *The American President: the human drama of our nation's highest office.* New York: Riverhead Books.

Loewen, J. (1995). *Lies my teacher told me: everything your American history textbook got wrong.* New York: Touchstone.

Marshall, P. & Manuel. D. (1977) *The light and the glory.* Tarrytown, NY: Fleming H. Revell Company.

Marshall, P. & Manuel, D. (1986) *From sea to shining sea.* Old Tappan, NY: Fleming H. Revell Company.

McCoy, C. (1960). *Polk and the presidency.* Austin, TX: University of Texas Press.

McJimsey, G. (2000). *The Presidency of Franklin Delano Roosevelt.* Lawrence, KS: The University of Kansas Press.

Morrison, C. (1967). *Democratic politics and sectionalism: The Wilmot Proviso controversy.* Chapel Hill, NC: The University of North Carolina Press.

Nelson, A. (1988). *Secret agents: President Polk and the search for peace with Mexico.* New York: Garland Publishing.

McDonald, F. (1974). *The Presidency of George Washington.* Lawrence, KS: The University of Kansas Press.

O'Reilly, K. (1995). *Nixon's Piano: Presidents and racial politics from Washington to Clinton.* New York: The Free Press.

Quaife, M. (Ed.). (1970). *The Diary of James K. Polk during his presidency, 1845 to 1849.* New York: Kraus Reprint Company.

Randall, W. (1997). *George Washington: A Life.* New York: Henry Holt & Company.

Saenz, B.A. (1990). I want to write an American poem, in *Without Discovery.* R. Gonzalez (Ed.)

Schlesinger, A. (2002). *The American Presidents Series.* New York: Henry Holt & Company.

Seigenthaler, J. (2003). *James K. Polk.* New York: Henry Holt & Company.

Sellars, C. (1966). *James K. Polk: Continentalist.* Princeton, NJ: Princeton University Press.

Smith, R. (1993). *Patriarch: George Washington and the new American nation.* Boston: Houghton Mifflin Company.

Snipp, M. (2004). American Indian Studies. In *Handbook of research on multicultural education, second edition.* J. Banks & C. Banks (Eds.) San Francisco: Jossey-Bass.

Tugwell, R. (1977). *Roosevelt's Revolution: the first year—a personal perspective.* New York: Macmillan.

Warren, F. (1999). *Noble abstractions: American liberal intellectuals and World War II.* Columbus, OH: Ohio State University Press.

Wills, G. (2003). *"Negro President" Jefferson and the slave power.* Boston: Houghton Mifflin Company.

Wiencek, H. (2003). *An Imperfect God: George Washington, His Slaves, and the Creation of America.* New York: Farrar, Straus & Giroux.

Wilkins, R. (2001). *Jefferson's Pillow: The founding fathers and the dilemma of black patriotism.* Boston: Beacon Press.

Zinn, H. (1997). *A people's history of the United States.* New York: The New Press.

*H. Prentice Baptiste is a professor of multicultural and science education and Rebecca Sanchez is a doctoral student in critical pedagogy, both with the Department of Curriculum and Instruction at New Mexico State University, Las Cruces, New Mexico.*

# INTERNATIONAL EDUCATION
## *A Needed Curriculum*

SHARON LYNN KAGAN AND VIVIEN STEWART

THROUGHOUT this special section, as in many of the documents used in its preparation, the call for a greater focus on international education (IE) is sounded loudly. The contributors to this section have used the terms international education and international studies to refer to the intentional preparation of American students—prekindergarten through college—to be citizens, workers, and leaders in the interconnected world of the 21st century.

Given that the nation's political and economic leaders have voiced concerns that we are not preparing our students to succeed in a globalized world and that we have a system of universal K-12 public education in which some schools have adopted some excellent and diverse IE models, one might think that IE is a "no brainer"! It is not. In contemporary America, IE is the coveted jewel of a limited number of forward-looking academics, practitioners, and advocates. According to Robert Scott, president of Adelphi University, IE has been the subject of "many calls, but little action," with global illiteracy the result.

Many reports and commissions have noted the problem, including the Perkins Commission on Languages and International Studies in the 1970s; the Carter Administration's Simon Commission, which called for significantly greater attention to foreign languages; reports from the American Council on Education in the 1980s calling for the internationalization of higher education; and reports from the Asia Society and the National Geographic Society in 2001 and 2002 respectively. Both the Clinton Administration and the current Bush Administration have supported an emphasis on IE. In 2002, at the first States Institute on International Education in the Schools, U.S. Secretary of Education Rod Paige declared that "to meet our goal to leave no child behind, we must shift our focus from current practice and encourage programs that introduce our students to international studies earlier in their education, starting in kindergarten."

## HISTORY OF INTERNATIONAL EDUCATION

To be sure, the press for international education is not entirely new, with some of the clarion calls being backed by action, especially in higher education. For 50 years the federal government has supported, primarily for national security purposes, the development of area studies, international studies, and language centers to produce scholars and experts in major world regions. Moreover, in the past 15 years, many higher education institutions have been trying to "internationalize" their curriculum, to encourage students to study abroad, and to promote the international exchange of faculty. Although K-12 education lags behind higher education, some states have added language to their social studies standards that encourages teaching about world regions, history, geography, or religions.

Despite these advances, so far there has been little change in K-12 classrooms or in the general state of American students' knowledge of the world. Why have American schools been so inward looking? One can speculate on many possible reasons for this tendency—geography, economy, history, ideology. Compared to European countries, the United States is a huge continental landmass, isolated by two enormous oceans. Its large domestic market has meant that international trade was, until recently, a relatively small part of the economy. New immigrants, fleeing repression at home, often wanted to forget where they had come from, which corresponded well with the mission of U.S. schools to create a new nation by "Americanizing" these immigrants. Two world wars fueled Americans' sense of isolationism and contributed to intense suspicion of those who spoke languages other than English.

In addition, structural factors of the U.S. education system have contributed to the lack of emphasis on IE. The decentralized, highly local nature of educational decision making has led schools to focus on state and local history and affairs. And, in recent years, the focus of accountability systems on basic skills has inadvertently resulted in a narrowing of curricula and expenditures in many schools. The lack of funding for innovation, capacity building, or research for effective IE has limited its growth, despite increasing awareness and interest.

## OTHER NATIONS

This lack of widespread interest in international education in the United States, while troublesome in and of itself, is compounded by growing commitments to international education being made by other nations. The European Union is expanding language instruction to begin at age 7 and is encouraging partnerships between schools within Europe and those from other countries. Australia has had a decade long national initiative to add the teaching of Asian languages, history, and culture to all its schools. Some countries in East Asia are adding "international skills"—English language, world history and geography, and technology—to their curricula.

This is not to say that other nations are exempt from educational isolationism; all countries' education systems have traditionally focused on their own history and culture to varying degrees. Indeed, in some parts of the world, both formal and informal education produce ethnocentrism and even outright hatred for other groups. In the past decade, however, most industrialized countries have been strengthening their students' knowledge of other cultures and languages.

In developing this special section, we sought to show several things. First, the U.S. lags behind other countries in imparting to its students the skills needed to be citizens and workers in the 21st-century global age. Second, the elements necessary for significant education reform with regard to IE are not yet firmly in place; there is, as yet, no uniform vision or mobilized intellectual/practical/financial infrastructure to support its advancement.

In addition to briefly summarizing its content, we want to conclude this special section by advancing our own thesis on what is needed to increase the focus on IE in American schools, based on the work of Julius Richmond, M.D., professor emeritus at Harvard and former U.S. surgeon general. Exhibiting wisdom far greater than our own, Dr. Richmond presciently realized that any social revolution needs three things: 1) a codified knowledge base, 2) public will for change, and 3) a social strategy. We regard IE as a necessary social and educational revolution and address its current status in light of Dr. Richmond's three conditions for reform.

### THE KNOWLEDGE BASE

As the articles in this special section clearly indicate, there is an increasingly strong rationale for, and mounting concern about, IE in our schools. At its most narrow construction, the rationale for IE focuses on the rudimentary knowledge base of American students. Seminal studies by the National Commission on Asia in the Schools found that 25% of college-bound high school students surveyed did not know the name of the ocean that separates the United States from Asia and that 80% did not know that India is the world's largest democracy or who Mao Zedong was. And we are incredulous at the findings from the National Geographic Society/Roper survey that, among the students from eight countries surveyed, those attending American schools were the second most poorly informed about world affairs or geography. What might we expect when our students cannot even identify the location of Afghanistan or Israel (two nations not exactly ignored by the media), but know that a recent "Survivor" show was shot in the South Pacific? Clearly, we have a problem.

The challenge only begins here. We live in a time when the amount of information available to us is expanding at unprecedented rates: 24-hour newscasts, 24-7 Internet availability, prolific growth in the numbers of cable TV channels, just to mention a few. The problem today is not a lack of information; rather, it is a lack of knowledge. Carlos Fuentes notes that "the greatest challenge facing modern society and civilization is how to cope with and how to transform information to knowledge." So our educational vision in general, and for IE in particular, must not be constrained by the mere acquisition of facts. The question facing educators today is less about the mastery of world geography or current events or any topical factoids, however critical they may be, than about integrating and synthesizing exponentially increasing amounts of information in a way that addresses issues in civic and global life.

The larger issue inherent in our current Zeitgeist is, of course, the need to fundamentally reexamine the intents of American education. In the spring of 2004, Harvard University released the report of its first major review of its undergraduate curriculum in almost 30 years. The report concludes that in a fast-changing world, students urgently need knowledge of a wider range of subjects, including a deeper understanding of the principles of science and a far greater grasp of international affairs. With regard to the latter, the study recommends significant reforms of the undergraduate curriculum to ensure greater international knowledge and experience and stronger foreign language skills for graduates who will be "globally competent." Today's students "need to be able to appreciate other cultures and to work expertly in other countries or as part of an international team."

But the issue the Harvard curriculum review sought to address is not just a question that applies to the education of elite students. As we evaluate the status of our IE knowledge base, we must admit that our work seeks more to identify fundamental issues of American education than to determine which continents to "teach" in geography. Our work is really about deciding what it means to be an educated citizen in the 21st century.

The stakes are obviously very high. We need a broad discussion of educational purpose and rigorous experimentation on a wide range of related issues, among them those suggested by the articles contained herein. How could we synthesize the efforts to reform our ineffective high schools with those to internationalize the curriculum (Jackson)? What should our stance be with respect to foreign language instruction, and how could we design programs that are far more effective in producing language proficiency (Met)? How could we educate teachers for a global curriculum (Kelly)? We need to address these issues within the broader context of society as well, however. Students in much of the world today live in an increasingly media- and technology-saturated environment. How could we optimize the use of media and information technologies to promote curiosity about the world and empathy toward other cultures, rather than hatred or cultural hegemony (Wartella and Knell, and Roberts)?

In short, as we consider the need to expand the IE knowledge base, we are calling on our society to redefine the purposes of American education to meet the needs of the new century and to address the pedagogical and curricular correlates that will enable such purposes to be achieved.

## PUBLIC WILL

At national conferences today, irrespective of the topic, international issues are increasingly being addressed, if not showcased. Scientists, economists, and political leaders all operate in a global context. And after 9/11, who among the American public can fail to acknowledge the importance of world affairs to our nation? Although this emphasis on the world outside our borders has not yet resulted in a strong or sustained focus on IE, as former governors Hunt and Engler point out, international education is beginning to elicit public support for three diverse yet equally critical imperatives: the economic imperative, the security imperative, and the citizenship imperative.

*The economic imperative.* The global economy is here to stay. The American economy is deeply intertwined with those of countries around the world through imports, exports, and overseas and domestic investment. Even small companies that do not label themselves as international corporations are engaged globally. These trends, already strong, are likely to increase as two-thirds of the world's purchasing power and 95% of the world's consumers exist outside the U.S. Students must be ready to work in a highly competitive international economic environment. Businesses need employees who can think globally. These economic realities have not escaped the attention of state governors and opinion leaders. Hoping to keep their economies strong, governors and their states' business leaders are key advocates for greater emphasis on IE and are strong shapers of public will.

*The security imperative.* The launch of Sputnik in 1957 and the attacks of September 11 acted as loud wake-up calls, signaling to the American people that foreign languages and international and cross-cultural understanding are key to our national security. International studies could no longer be restricted to an educated elite or the Foreign Service corps. To the contrary, in the face of global misunderstanding, international education is an important component of long-term security.

## DIALOGUE UNDERSTANDING AND RELATIONSHIPS

Inherent in a growing commitment to international education is the understanding that it needs to be thought of as a two-way street in order to address the tremendous misinformation about the U.S. that circulates in many parts of the world. National security and foreign policy need a foundation in educational, cultural, and exchange activities that promote dialogue, cross-cultural understanding, and the creation of direct personal and institutional relationships.

With regard to individual security, issues such as global climate change or the worldwide HIV/AIDS epidemic have no respect for political borders. The public understands, however reluctant it might be to admit it, that some of the world's most penetrating challenges demand international knowledge and cooperation for their solution.

*The citizenship imperative.* Dramatic demographic changes in the U.S., especially the increasing diversity of our classrooms and workplaces, with growing Hispanic and Asian populations living in even very small communities, mean that all citizens need to know more about the cultures represented at school and at work. And, in an age when decisions made halfway around the world can sometimes have a far greater impact than decisions made by local town councils, American citizens will be called on to debate and vote on issues that require international knowledge. Moreover, as the richest and most powerful nation in the world, the United States is deeply involved in economic, political, and social events around the globe. Our own future is inextricably tied to the solution of many political and humanitarian crises. In short, the bright line between "domestic" and "international" is becoming blurred. American students need to become not only good citizens of the United States, but good citizens of the world.

These imperatives provide strong rationale for the public to increase its support for improving IE in our schools. The fact that such public will has taken root only sparsely is a challenge but does not diminish our belief in the strong potential for success, if planned and mobilized for correctly. Susan Bales affirms this and offers concrete suggestions for the necessary strengthening of the public will.

## SOCIAL STRATEGY

Clearly there is a critical need for strategies that will modernize our schools to prepare students for the opportunities and challenges of the global age. Scholars and practitioners have long debated the efficacy of different change strategies—from public information campaigns, to litigation, to social protest, to markets, and so on. John Gardner, former U.S. secretary of health, education, and welfare and founder of Common Cause and Independent Sector, argued that much social innovation in the United States proceeds in stages. Most innovations begin with small-scale experiments in local communities. Successful efforts begin to be emulated by other locales and, later, by pioneering states—"the laboratories of our democracy." Once six to 10 states have adopted an approach and tested it on a larger scale, other states and the federal government will begin to act. Seen in this perspective, the increasing numbers of schools and states that are beginning to take up international education.

Still, we are at an early stage in the development of real capacity in the field of IE. What strategies would move reform from another round of "many calls, but little action" to more systematic development of IE on a nationwide scale? We believe that multiple strategies are needed to make meaningful change, particularly when the issues are latent and the stakes are high. To that end, and building on the recommendations offered in the preceding articles, we propose a set of broad strategic approaches, followed by more specific recommendations to build capacity in this field.

### STRATEGIES FOR ADVANCING INTERNATIONAL EDUCATION

In every social or educational movement, different sectors need to be mobilized. First, we must recognize that educators alone cannot enlist support for IE. Since the call for change in education often comes from the "demand" side (parents, students, and community members) rather than the "supply" side (the school system), governors and business leaders who understand how rapidly the world is changing need to communicate the long-term consequences of our failure to prepare students to adapt to these changes. Second, we need to build networks, both human and technological, that link the hundreds of grassroots local innovators, so that teachers and school leaders can learn from one another, share curriculum and resources, and begin to assess the effectiveness of different approaches.

Third, since states are in the forefront both of education reform and of responding to the challenges of globalization, policy makers need to create five-year plans to integrate IE into their education and economic policies and programs to ensure that their high school graduates are prepared for this global age. In doing so, state policy makers are likely to find willing partners in their corporate, university, cultural, and heritage communities. Fourth, at the national level, the President, Congress, and the U.S. Departments of State, Defense, Commerce, and Education need to urgently connect our policies for advancing international relations and economic growth to our nation's education agenda.

### RECOMMENDATIONS FOR BUILDING CAPACITY IN INTERNATIONAL EDUCATION

As the public will to improve IE increases and different sectors are mobilized, it will be important to build the capacity to deliver international education on a large scale.

We have identified a set of four policy and program actions that will help to accomplish this objective.

An effective corps of teachers must be developed in every state to infuse all the core curriculum areas with international content. In the Sputnik era, our nation made an important commitment to science and math education via the National Science Foundation. A similar national commitment to prepare teachers to promote international knowledge and language skills is now needed. The Higher Education Act, due to be reauthorized next year, provides an important vehicle for modernizing teacher preparation and professional development. Allowing Title II and Title VI funds to create K-16 partnerships for international teaching excellence and to develop international professional development opportunities, including study abroad and online courses for teachers and school leaders, could create critical capacity for schools.

A K-16 pipeline for major world languages must be built. In the longer term, our education policies should encourage all students to learn a second language, as do those of other industrial countries. In the shorter term, our diplomatic and defense communities urgently need a K-16 pipeline to produce proficient speakers of critical languages, including Chinese, Japanese, Korean, Arabic, Farsi, and Russian. To increase our capacity to communicate in languages other than English, the federal government should provide serious incentives to begin language study earlier (elementary school), to promote innovative uses of technology, to conduct experiments with different approaches to language learning, to build on the language resources in our heritage communities, and to recruit and train teachers in less commonly taught languages.

### EXPANDING KNOWLEDGE

We must leverage media and technology resources to bring the world to our students. In the last decade, billions of private and public sector dollars have been invested to wire schools, build Web resources, open the airwaves and TV spectrum to new channels, and broadcast high-quality media to schools and communities. However, all of this has had a negligible impact on children's and teachers' knowledge of the world outside our borders. Private and public resources in those areas must be leveraged to stimulate new international content in vehicles such as virtual high schools; to encourage school-to-school partnerships with schools in other parts of the world; to prime partnerships between universities, corporations, and K-12 schools; and to utilize public television and radio—all to educate young Americans about the world.

International education must be incorporated into existing major education reform initiatives. Any definition of educational excellence in the 21st century must include international knowledge and skills. Therefore, a focus on IE needs to be infused into a range of federal and state domestic and international programs (e.g., vocational education and high school reform, literacy and after-school programs, leadership development, research, and international exchange). This would provide needed resources to bring to scale local best practices and to strengthen the knowledge base through research, data collection, and assessment of knowledge and progress.

Our purpose in editing this special section, and the forthcoming section to appear next year at this time, is to heighten awareness of international education and, we hope, to provoke the discourse that is necessary to move a thoughtful, strategic agenda forward. To return to Dr. Richmond's analysis of reform, our knowledge base is emerging, though far more intensive work is needed. The requisite ingredients for strengthening the public will— the economic, security, and citizenship imperatives—are present and should be quite powerful elicitors of public commitment to IE reform. Discerning how to move this agenda forward with multiple populations and constitu-

ents is in order, posthaste. Finally, with regard to strategy, we have discussed a range of both broad and specific approaches that might be used as springboards from which to create a more globally competent citizenry. It is to this end that this work is dedicated.

The issue of IE reform cries out for strong national leadership. It is deeply intertwined with the future prosperity and security of our nation. We are at a crossroads in our nation's social and intellectual history; this era's crisis, not even apparent to many, is one of inattention to changing needs in a new global age. It is one that stands begging for legitimacy and action.

---

*SHARON LYNN KAGAN is Virginia & Leonard Marx Professor of Early Childhood and Family Policy, co-director of the National Center for Children and Families, and associate dean for policy, Teachers College, Columbia University, New York, N.Y., as well as professor adjunct at the Child Study Center, Yale University, New Haven, Conn. VIVIEN STEWART is vice president for education programs, Asia Society, New York, N.Y.*

---

# Queer Life and School Culture: Troubling Genders

## MARLA MORRIS

Gender is a slippery notion. We are all engendered creatures. But in what ways are we engendered? The ways in which we imagine what gender is shapes how we see ourselves in relation to others. Yet it is not clear what the category gender is, what it means, how it functions, whose interest it serves. The paradox about studying gender is that the more I have studied it (the monstrous creature that it is), the less clear I have become about what it is. I wonder whether gender is a useful category at all. Is gender a fiction?

Generally, this article will examine the complicated relations between gender and sexuality. More specifically, I will couch gender and sexuality in the field of queer studies and education and argue that whatever gender and sexuality might mean, these concepts must include discussions around queerness, otherwise gender debates get aligned with heteronormative assumptions. Finally, I will talk about queer life and school culture. Teachers need to understand what queer life is like for young people. If teachers have no clue, they could perhaps unconsciously make it harder on queer students and queer faculty by projecting pre-judgments and rigid gender expectations onto people who are different from themselves.

The taken-for-granted assumption during the 1950s and 1960s around the notion of gender signals that gender attaches itself to sex in the paradigm sex=gender (Morris, 1998). It becomes hard to think about gender without thinking about sex. Donna Haraway remarks that "Nature/culture and sex/gender are not loosely related pairs of terms; their specific form of relation is hierarchical appropriation, connected as Aristotle taught by the logic of active/passive, form/matter, achieved form/resource, man/animal, nature and culture, as well as sex and gender, [which] mutally (but not equally) construct each other, one pole of the dualism cannot exist without the other" (Haraway, 1989, p. 12).

Further, sex seems to be that which lies under gender: sex is to nature as gender is to culture. Sex is biological, anatomical; gender is sociocultural (Seidman, 1997; Moi, 1999; Young-Bruehl, 1998). Sex, in this paradigm is supposed to correspond to the given, while gender floats on top as an after thought. But as Haraway points out, there is no such animal as the given. There is nothing natural or pre-determined, or essential about the category sex. These seemingly innocuous gender/sex creatures-categories are not innocent or harmless. Historically, both have served to oppress.

Sex = male/female; gender= masculine/feminine. How does one define what masculinity is? How does one define femininity? What if a male is effeminite and a female masculine, then what? During the 1950s and 1960s, when the medical community could not figure out what to do with "incorrect" gender roles and incorrect sexual anatomies (hermaphrodites), they invented the term "gender identity disorder" or more precisely GID. It was psychoanalyst Robert Stoeller who invented this fiction (Young-Bruehl, 1998). If your child is a boy and thinks himself to be a girl, or if your child is a girl and fancies herself a boy, some in the medical community still might diagnose your children with GID. Yesterday's shock treatment is todays' sex change operation. Operations on sex and gender work to normalize. Get your children STRAITENED out, literally.

Part of this literalizing, medicalizing, normalizing technology/discourse (it takes a technician-doctor to anatomically alter sex and a narrative around which to justify doing it to begin with) has to do with the idea that sexuality/biology are grounded in TRUTH, the essential truth of being. What you are, in your sex, must match what you do in your behaviors (gender roles). If not, you are trouble. Hence, Judith Butler's (1990) phrase gender trouble. When sex is thought to be an essence, a core, a truth, a natural thing, feminist scholar Toril Moi tells us that according to Donna Haraway and Judith Butler, sex "becomes immobile, stable, coherent, fixed, prediscursive, natural, ahistorical" (1999, p. 4).

But clearly/queerly sex is not stable, immobile, natural or ahistorical. Sex is highly historical, contextual/consexual, shifting, unstable. The ways in which we think about sex and gender are deeply historical and our sexed bodies mark culture as culture marks our bodies. The question becomes, in what ways do we think about sex/gender? In what ways do sex/gender shape identities or limit who we can be or what we can do? I think the key here is to understand how these terms/categories box us in and limit who we are and what we do.

If anything sex/gender serves to regulate and manage, control otherwise out of control bodies. Civilization is discontented and it is civilization that ensures we follow the rules or we become gender outlaws (Bornstein, 1995). Ingraham suggests that "we need to question our assumptions about sex and gender as to how they organize difference, regulate investigations, and preserve particular power relations, especially those linked to institutionalized heterosexuality" (1997, p. 184).

Heteronormativity, the illusion that heterosexuals are the only people on the planet and are the center of all sexual practices, is pervasive even among feminists. Indeed, feminists have been criticized for pretending that debates on gender are heteronormative. Judith Butler remarks that she has "heard feminist scholars … in the U.S. worry that gender has been "destroyed" throughout the recent criticisms of feminisms' presumptive heterosexuality" (1997, p. 20). Is gender a useful category? Butler claims it is a copy without an original. Both sex and gender are social contructions as the post-structuralist mantra suggests. Floating signifiers without referents. Gender and sex are confused categories.

Since the 1960s feminists have taken gender to be their primary category of analysis, not sexuality. Engendered bodies seemed to become

de-sexed. Arlene Stein and Ken Plummer remark that "feminists began treating gender as a primary lens for understanding problems that did not initially look gender-specific" (1997, p. 135). Feminist scholars tend to agree that whatever gender is, it serves to oppress when it is thought to be something pre-ordained (Moi, 1999; Haraway 1997; Butler 1997; Ingraham 1997; Halberstam, 1998; Miller, 1994). However, part of the problem historically with feminist analyses of gender is the narrowness of inquiry. Many analyze gender as if it is a category in-itself, for-itself and by-itself. If anything, gender is more like a hybridization, spliced and mixed up with all sorts of subject positions, cultural, historical, racial, national, theoretical. Donna Haraway comments that ultimately gender

> is always a relationship, not a pre-formed category of beings or a possession that one can have. Gender does not pertain more to women than to men. Gender is the relation between variously constituted categories of men and women (and variously arrayed tropes), differentiated by nation, generation, class, lineage, color and much else. (1997, p. 28)

Gender does not stand alone and to think that it does is to be mistaken. Gender stands in complex relations to sexuality, culture, nation and so forth. Moreover, gender is permeable, shifting. There are many genders, not two. Lynne Miller suggests "androgyony [ambiguous gender] as a construct is in many ways as threatening as effeminite men or masculine women, as it blurs the boundaries of gender" (1994, p. 214). There are also more than two sexes. Herdt (1994) claims that the hermaphrodite constitutes the third sex. Toril Moi tells us that Anne Fausto-Sterling "proposed adding 'herms', 'ferms' and 'merms' to the usual two" (1999, p. 38). Five sexes, imagine that!

As Nina Wakeford (1998) points out that the hybridization and confusion of engendered/sexed bodies

continues to proliferate. She tells us that "[bio]boys" (p. 178), "lipstick lesbians" (p. 179), "cyber-dykes" (p. 179), "bio-/transgendered" (p. 178), "boys born boys … girls made boys" (177), "female-to-male transsexual[s]" (177), "drag kings" (p. 183), "hasbians" (p. 183) have become all the rage in the gay/lesbian/transgendered/transexual or queer communities. Further, this intense hybridization has also been noted as a product of cyberspace, computers and information technologies. Cyberspace has altered our identities, relations and ideas about who we think we are or what we think we are. Wakeford points out that

> Popular accounts of cyberspace have propagated a 'moral panic' around the presentation of self, or more specifically the misrepresentation of self … Reports have suggested that on-line men pretend to be women, women pretend to be men, and heterosexual men try to adopt female personas strategically to attract women who turn out to be other men. (Stone, 1991, (p. 181)

Like this proliferation of confused genders/sexualities, Donna Haraway (1997) introduces the notion of the Femaleman. The femaleman signals the inter-mixing of gender/sexuality beyond identity. She stresses that the quest for purity of gender or sex smacks of the same kind of rhetoric around purity of race. Beware the purity of gender/sexuality!! Homophobia, racisim, sexism, xenophobia are born out of the same cloth. It becomes hard to disentangle one from the other; usually they are related kin. What makes some nervous about femaleman is that it becomes difficult to figure out if it is boy, girl, gay, straight, or even human. Perhaps it is posthuman? Inter-breeding is the postmodern.

Paradoxically, gender expectations may not match up with sexed bodies. What you see is not what you get. Genderbending confuses. Gender and sexuality are sliding signifiers warping out of time and space. Jessica Benjamin (1998) suggests that when thinking about gender, and I would add sexuality, it becomes psychologically important to integrate paradoxical understandings and avoid gender polarizations which are the result of a psychological process called splitting. Seeing the world in polar opposites signals regressive emotional, intellectual responses to experiences which are highly complex.

It is easier to see the world in black and white; it is easier psychologically to pretend that gender=sexuality, that the key should fit the lock. But the lock traps the key in a subject position that fixes and reifies. Jessica Benjamin comments that "we have to come to accept the paradoxical status of gender categories, such that they at once fit and contradict our experience, both appear derived from reality and yet spring from the shifting ground of fantasy" (1998, p. 36). Our engendered/sexed bodies are mostly fantasy. We make ourselves up as we go along. Our storied selves can unlock the key to any kind of hybridized creature we wish. It's just that culture will not allow us to perform our sexed bodies in ways that we would like to. Civilization has killed our imagination. And gender/ sexed bodies are imagined fictions.

Feminist scholars since the 1990s have sometimes collided head on with a new breed called queer theorists. Recall, since the 1960s the major analytical category for feminists has been gender. For queer theorists, the major analytical category is sex. Judith Butler remarks that "Within queer studies, a methodological distinction has been offered which would distinguish theories of sexuality from theories of gender and, further, allocate theoretical investigations of sexuality to queer studies and the analysis of gender to feminism" (1997, p. 3). Queer theorists have criticized feminists for "subsum[ing] sexuality (and race) under gender" (1997, Stein & Plummer, pp. 136-137). Sexuality cannot be subsumed under these other categories. I believe the best way to treat these categories is inter-relationally. I do not think that queer theorists, on the

other hand, should ignore the work done by feminists on gender because without that work, queer theory would not exist. But it does seem to be the case that most queer theorists concentrate on the performance of sexed bodies.

## Queer Theory and Education

If gender/sex includes experiences that are queer (the new term for lesbian, bisexual, homosexual, gay, transgendered, transexual) how do educators theorize about queer experience? And why is it important that educators think about queering sex/ gender to begin with? Why is queer theory important for teachers? Theory, first of all, provokes thinking and helps articulate difficult and complex experience especially around relationships. Teachers might avoid projecting normalizing pre-judgements onto their students and onto other faculty. Not only this, queer theorizing is crucial because we live in a violent era. Educational discourses around queer theory might help alleviate this violence.

Educational discourses around queer thinking are late to arrive on the scene. Queer theory is already ten years old and other disciplines, especially English and sociology have been grappling with queer subjects for much longer than the discipline of education. But this lag in educational inquiry does not mean that it is too late to begin thinking queerly. Thinking queerly is crucial because teachers may have queer students, may have queer colleagues and may be queer themselves. William F. Pinar remarks,

> The appearance of "queer thinking" in the field of education is recent, its formulation in an early stage, even as the political hour feels late. There is an urgency to this work—people are still dying, being bashed, being discriminated against, still suffering unnecessarily, in a myriad of ways, public and private—that demands that we summon our courage, achieve some measure of solidarity and press ahead. (2000, ix)

Education professors have begun to press ahead. Deborah Britzman (1998), Alice Pitt (1998), Jim Sears (1990; 1998), Susan Talburt (2000), Shirley Steinberg (2000), William Pinar (1998; 2000), Brent Davis and Dennis Sumara (2000), Dennis Carlson (1998), Nelson Rodriguez (1998), Jonanthan Silin (1995), Mary Doll (1998), William Tierney and Patrick Dilley (1998), Suzanne de Castell and Mary Bryson (1998) to name but a few, have all done work on queer theory and education.

Queer theory, as I mentioned earlier, arrived on the scene around 1990. The term queer is used politically. Once the ultimate insult, now the term queer is reappropriated and thrown back in the face of the oppressor. Queer is an umbrella term that seeks to undo oppressive gender/sex designations. Queer is related to performance and desire.

More specifically, queer arrived on the scene at the site of the AIDS crisis. Commentators seem to agree that queer theory signals a shift from earlier gay and lesbian liberation work during the 1970s (Sears, 1998; Tierney & Dilley 1998; Seidman, 1997; Carlson, 1998; Stein & Plummer, 1997). The gay and lesbian movement of the 1970s was modeled on "civil rights strategies" (Stein & Plummer, 1997, p. 134). The key themes of the movement were liberation, normalcy and attaining rights. The Gay/lesbian community seemed to be saying we are normal, we are just like straight people. William Tierney and Patrick Dilley comment that "The 1970s saw a rise in ... research that looked at lesbian and gay people not as deviant, but as "normal" or quasi-normal. This line of research primarily began after the Stonewall riots in a New York City bar in 1969, and after the American Psychological Association (APA) removed homosexuality as a form of mental disorders in 1973" (1998, p. 52).

Unlike the gay and lesbian liberation movement of the 1970s, the queer movement has grown tired of being nice, especially in the face of AIDS and homophobic backlash.

Queer thinking and activism is angry, in-your-face, fed up with do-nothing responses to AIDS. Queer thinking is parody, acting out, acting up, rude, ludic performance (Morris, 1997; 1998; 2000). The over-riding theme of queer theory is difference, we are not like you and do not want to be like normal people. However, Michael Warner (1999) points out that there is a strain within the queer movement that still embraces "the lure of the normal" (p. 61). The lure of the normal haunts queers in the form of gay marriage. Warner argues that the concept of marriage is straight and gays who want to marry want to imitate straight people to become more like them.

There is also a strain in queer life that has been dubbed the new gay right (I would not call these people queer at all). These gay Pat Robertson clones want to pass for straight, have all the power and privilege of straight people and also propagate misogyny, racisim and xenophobia. I don't usually associate gay people with being bigots, but they do exist and it is very disturbing. Judith Butler remarks "In a recent article in the Village Voice, Richard Goldstein warns against the anti-feminism accompanying the rise of the gay conservatives to power positions within the queer movement" (1997, p. 29). The queer movement was begun by queer left radicals, not gay conservatives. If anything, the queer movement marks stresses and strains of social antagonisms and is not a monolithic entity. Judith Halberstam (1998) contends that stone butch dykes are queer and radical, but she points out that Teresa de Lauretis claims that women who act like men are not radical at all because they are simply imitating men.

I have heard many in the queer community remark that transexuals are not queer because they realign their anatomies to fit in and become normal. According to Alice Pitt (1998), Monique Wittig claims that lesbians are not really women after all because they don't play the game with men. Lesbians are not part of the heterosexual world, therefore, they are not women. But then what are women?

Joshua Gamson (1997) says "some lesbian writers point out that it [queer] is likely to become synonymous with white gay male" (p. 403), when in fact queer was coined by Teresa de Lauretis. It is oh so like men to appropriate women's terms. Gay men have always had more power within the gay/lesbian movement because after all we do live in patrio-het-archy.

Some older gays and lesbians think the word queer stupid and insulting. So queer also signals a generational divide.

Erica Meiners comments that queer might also signal a kind of elitism in the movment. She says that "the elitism in queeness and queer theorizing is not new ... Scholars have pointed to the whiteness of queer theory as an extension of the whiteness of mainstream of GLBT [gay, lesbian, bisexual, transgendered]" (1998, p. 125).

Steven Epstein comments that to "many sociologists, queer theory suggests this month's trendiness" (1997, p. 145). Some argue that queer theorists are too theoretical and that they do not pay enough attention to real life issues (Halberstam, 1998; Stein & Plummer, 1997).

Some complain that queer identities (which are shifting, vague, illusory) have destroyed identity-politics and do not therefore help win rights because it becomes difficult to pin down what the group queer signifies in the first place (Warner, 1999; Epstein, 1997; Gamson, 1997). Joshua Gamson writes that,

> As long as membership in this group is unclear, minority status, and therefore rights and protection is unavailable. Built into the queer debates, then, is a fundamental quandary: in the contemporary American political environment, clear identity categories are both necessary and dangerous distortions. (1997, p. 410)

In the 1970s, identity-politics did not seem to be as troubled as it is today because the lesbian/gay movement, for the most part, embraced essentialized notions of "lesbian" and "gay." Moving alongside postmodern and poststructualist theorizing, queer theory no longer embraces essentialist categories. Queer signifies movement, desire and peformance. And this shape shifting signifier makes it difficult politically to rally together as a group with a solid identity. Queer terrain is anything but stable. However, there are some overriding agreements as to what queer theory is. Ellis Hanson remarks that

> The aims of queer theory are at once philosophical, political, and erotic—an effort, indeed at blurring any distinction between them— since it seeks not only to analyze but also to resist, dismantle, or circumnavigate hegemonic systems of sexual oppression and normalization by revealing the theoretical presumptions and rhetorical slights of hand by which they establish, justify, and reinforce their considerable power. (1999, p. 4)

Queer theory is not about liberation, it is about opposition and resistance to normalizing, medicalizing, reifying discourse and social practices. Queer theory is performance, it is at once funny and angry, serious and silly. Its aim is to loosen up the sex=gender paradigm. Sex does not equal gender. And because the field of queer theory is only ten years young, scholars are still trying to figure out what it is and what it is not, how it may be expressed, articulated and thought about. Queer theory is about inclusion, contradiction, paradox. Queer theory is about competing narratives and entertaining the unthinkable. It is about recognizing that we often misrecognize each other because of projections, expectations, and pre-judgments around the notions of gender and sex. Queer performance is slippery.

## Queer Life and School Culture

*The mayor's been shot. No, Harvey Milk's been shot. They've both been shot? Are they dead? With the Jonestown mass suicide only nine days behind them, the news people ask the obvious question: Is this the work of the People's Temple hit squad? (Shilts, 1982, xv)*

The year was 1978. Harvey Milk, perhaps the most famous public official in San Francisco, and Mayor George Moscone had been brutally murdered by Dan White. White's infamous "twinkie defense" (Shilts, 1982, p. 317) proved successful. He was charged with voluntary manslaughter and sentenced to less than five years in prison. Dan White literally got away with murder. Riots on Castro Street ensued.

In 1978 I was a sophomore in high school in San Diego. Harvey Milk, San Francisco's first gay supervisor, was murdered in my home state. I am embarrassed to admit now that I did not even know who Harvey Milk was in 1978 and I do not remember the killing. What I do remember is Jonestown. I only learned about Harvey Milk and Castro Street after I entered college in 1980. Not remembering this event signals to me terrific repression. I was not out in high school. I didn't even dare think about being queer. It was simply unthinkable. And certainly, high school was not the place for me to come out.

Perhaps remaining closeted was my own unconscious way of protecting myself. I had no clue about my sexuality. My high school was a rampantly Christian fundamentalist, right wing looney bin. I do not know how many times reborn Christians tried to save me from being Jewish. Dealing with my Jewish identity was really tough and so of course coming out was out of the question. I could not psychologically handle both. Why did I not know who Harvey Milk was? Because I could not psychologically identify with anyone who was gay. That was too dangerous. At least, this is my analysis today. Gerald Unks tells us that,

The high school—the center of most adolescent life and culture—stands staunchly aloof and rigidly resistant to even a suggestion that

any of its faculty or student body might be homosexual or that homosexuals deserve anything but derision and scorn within its walls. High schools may be the most homophobic institutions in American society. (cited in Rodriguez, 1998, p. 177)

Not only is high school culture not tolerant of queers, coming out may be out-right dangerous. Exactly twenty years after supervisor Harvey Milk was shot to death, Matthew Shepard, a young school boy, was murdered. Queers risk everything by being out. This young boy's brutal and needless death points to the importance of not sweeping queer students under the rug. School culture is somehow complicit, not only in intolerance, but in violence and even murder. Coming out, or staying closeted damages young people. It is a no-win situation. Part of the reason young people do not come out is that school life is a site of "sexual fascism" (Rodriguez, 1998, p. 177). Nelson Rodriguez comments that "Indeed, combining heterosexism with schooling is an insidious way of educating youth to promote 'sexual fascism'; no doubt it is part of the moral rights' 'hidden curriculum'" (p. 177).

Family values is a code word for moral majority heteronormativity. Family values means straight kids do right, be right and fight for the right. Family values institutionalizes homophobia and makes it seem alright. I am a product of a moral majority public high school culture. Being deeply closeted was a way to protect myself. Repressed sexualities can lead down treacherous paths. But I was lucky because my first year in college I did come out. Carnegie-Mellon provided the kind of atmosphere that allowed me to be me. The music conservatory at CMU was a place where I could be queer. But some people never find a place where they can come out and so repression rules. Elenie Opffer tells us that,

Harbeck (1992) points out that the department of Health and Human Services estimates that of the 5,000 annual suicides of youths between

the ages of 15 and 24, up to 30% may be attributed to sexual preference issues and societal dissaproval of homosexuality. (1994, p. 298)

School culture, a reflection of society at large, is complicit in kids' suicides. Repressed sexualities return in all sorts of bizzare manifestations. Perhaps it is shame that drives kids to desperation. Shame turns to self-hatred. Michael Warner comments that "Almost all children grow up in families that think of themselves as heterosexual, and for some children this problem [creates a] … profound and nameless estrangement, a sense of inner secrets and hidden shame" (1999, p. 8). Secrets and shame follow children into adult life. Queer lives are always already secretive. You can't be out all the time. Secrets become necessary for survival. Who to tell, who not to tell. Do I tell my students? What if they ask? Queer students grow up and some of them, like me, become queer teachers, professors. Then what? Susanne Luhmann comments that

Immense moral panics erupt over the discovery that lesbians and gays educate our children. Intense, sometimes even violent, contestations occur over the curriculur inclusion of the study of sexuality in general, and of lesbian and gay content in particular. (1998, p. 142)

Queer teachers, queer students. What is the moral majority to do? We're here, we're queer, get used to it. Queer teachers and queer students have to live in a tricky culture, one that demands closets, secrets, shame. Being queer against the backdrop of heteronormativity is difficult and dangerous. Harvey Milk and Matthew Shepard attest to this along with the unnamed others who are victims of gay bashing, homophobia.

Heteronormativity takes all shapes and forms as it intersects with homophobia. These two terms go hand in hand. Homophobia can be overt or it can be subtle. Recently taking a new position at Georgia Southern University, many people would ask, is Mary going too? Imagine that we were a straight couple, nobody would ask that sort of question. A realtor called to relocate us in Savannah. She asked Mary "what does your HUSBAND do?" Huh? Why even assume that a woman is married to a man? And when Mary proceeded to tell the realtor that we were queer, she said, "oh I've got the perfect spot for you, right off the interstate." That's a good place to deposit queers. NOT. Perhaps she would like to see us splattered on the interstate? It is amazing to me that many people do not recognize us as a real couple. Two women?

These normalizing gestures begin very early, perhaps when we are still children. Schooling plays a large role-normalizing sexuality and gender. Boys are supposed to play football, girls are supposed to be cheerleaders. Heteronormativity scripts roles that schooling enforces. Even subject matter is heteronormative. Boys are supposed to be good in math, girls in English. Part of the reason I could never do math is because I had a math teacher in elementary school who treated me as if I were stupid. So of course I believed him. I talked myself out of doing math for life. I am sure other girls experience this as well.

But one of the things I was good at was kickball. When I came to homeplate the boys would move back and yell, "Back up! Morris is on." My sister warned me that if I continued to kick better than the boys, I'd never get a boyfriend. But I never wanted one to begin with. I got lectures on tomboyism from my sister and my mother. "Don't you want to go to the prom?" My mother asked when I was in high school. I said, what for? I really did not understand the concept of the prom. I do remember, though, that prom night there was an earthquake. Shake em up!! I was out with Kristine prom night and we talked about her acceptance to Harvard and mine to Carnegie-Mellon. We had more important things to do than go to the prom. The prom, though, is a whole discourse of hete-

ornormativity and serves to oppress those who are different, other, queer. Straight life=prom night. A life that I have never lived.

Judith Halberstam (1998) comments on the problematics of tomboyism. She says, "Tomboyism is tolerated as long as the child remains prepubescent, as soon as puberty begins, however the full force of gender conformity descends on the girl" (1998, p. 6). I refused to conform. I played with baseball bats and GI Joes. Now I don't get teased because of acting like a tomboy, but people often mistake me for a boy, and most often for someone's son. I've been mistaken for Ted Aoki's son, Bill Pinar's son, Mary Doll's son, everybody's son in general. At thirty eight I am the world's son. But I'm nobody's son. And certainly I don't have a son. Never will.

I suggest that educators work to queer school. Queering school means throwing into question sedimented, rigid gender/ sexuality categories. The queer thing about gender and sexuality is that we don't really know what these categories are. We don't even know why we talk like this. Some cultures don't even have words for gender. The paradox about outing one's queerness is that it can at once lift repression but at the same time can create a dangerous situation. Coming out can result in the Harvey Milk story or the Matthew Shepard story. It is up to educators to change these stories.

## References

Benjamin, J. (1998). *Shadow of the other: Intersubjectivity and gender in psychoanalysis*. New York: Routledge.

Bornstein, K. (1995). *Gender outlaw: On men, women, and the rest of us*. New York: Vintage.

Britzman, D. (2000). Precocious education. In S. Talburt & S. Steinberg (Eds.), *Thinking queer: Sexuality, culture and education* (pp. 33-60). New York: Peter Lang.

Butler, J. (1990). *Gender trouble: Feminism and the subversion of identity*. New York: Routledge.

Butler, J. (1997). Against proper objects. In E. Weed & N. Schor (Eds.), *Femi-

nism meets queer theory* (pp. 1-30). Bloomington, IN: Indiana University Press.

Carlson, D. (1998). Who am I? Gay identity and a democratic politics of the self. In W. F. Pinar (Ed.), *Queer theory in education* (pp. 107-120). Mahwah, NJ: Lawrence Erlbaum and Associates.

Davis, B. & Sumara, D. (2000). Another queer theory: Reading complexity theory as a moral and ethical imperative. In S. Talburt & S. Steinberg (Eds.), *Thinking queer: Sexuality, culture and education* (pp. 105-130). New York: Peter Lang.

de Castell, S. & Bryson, M. (1998). From the ridiculous to the sublime: On finding oneself in educational research. In W. F. Pinar (Ed.), *Queer theory in education* (pp. 221-244). Mahwah, NJ: Lawrence Erlbaum and Associates.

Doll, M. (1998). Queering the gaze. In W. F. Pinar (Ed.), *Queer theory in education* (pp. 287-298). Mahwah, NJ: Lawrence Erlbaum and Associates.

Epstein, S. (1997). A queer encounter: Sociology and the study of sexuality. In S. Seidman (Ed.), *Queer theory/sociology* (pp. 145-167). Malden, MA: Blackwell Publishers.

Gamson, J. (1997). Must identity movements self-destruct? A queer dilemma. In S. Seidman (Ed.), *Queer theory/sociology* (pp. 395-420). Malden, MA: Blackwell Publishers.

Halberstam, J. (1998). *Female masculinity*. Durham, NC: Duke University Press.

Hanson, E. (1999). Introduction: Out takes. In E. Hason (Ed.), *Out takes: Essays on queer theory and film* (pp. 1-19). Durham, NC: Duke University Press.

Haraway, D. (1989). *Primate visions: Gender, race and nature in the world of modern science*. New York: Routledge.

Haraway, D. (1997). *Modest witness second millennium. Femaleman meets oncomouse: Feminism and technoscience*. New York: Routledge.

Herdt, G. (1994). *Third sex, third gender: Beyond sexual dimorphism in culture and history*. New York: Zone Books.

Ingraham, C. (1997). The heterosexual imaginary: Feminist sociology and theories of gender. In S. Seidman (Ed.), *Queer theory/sociology* (pp. 168-193). Malden, MA: Blackwell Publishers.

Luhmann, S. (1998). Queering/querying pedagogy? Or, pedagogy is a pretty queer thing. In W. F. Pinar (Ed.), *Queer theory in education* (pp. 141-156).

Mahwah, NJ: Lawrence Erlbaum and Associates.

Martin, B. (1997). Extraordinary homosexuals and the fear of being ordinary. In E. Weed & N. Schor (Eds.), *Feminism meets queer theory* (pp. 109-135). Bloomington, IN: Indiana University Press.

Meiners, E. (1998). Remember when all the cars were Fords and all the lesbians were women? Some notes on identity, mobility, and capital. In W. F. Pinar (Ed.), *Queer theory in education* (pp. 121-140). Mahwah, NJ: Lawrence Erlbaum and Associates.

Miller, L. (1994). The politics of self and other. In R. Jeffrey Ringer (Ed.), *Queer words, queer images: Communication and the construction of homosexuality* (pp. 209–218). New York: New York University Press.

Moi, T. (1999). *What is a woman? And other essays.* New York: Oxford University Press. Morris, M. (1997). Ezekiel's call: Toward a queer pedagogy. *Taboo: The Journal of Culture and Education.* 1: 153-166.

Morris, M. (1998). Unresting the curriculum: Queer projects, queer imaginings . In W. F. Pinar (Ed.), *Queer theory in education* (pp. 275-286). Mahwah, NJ: Lawrence Erlbaum Associates.

Morris, M. (2000). Dante's left foot kicks queer theory into gear. In S. Talburt & S. Steinberg (Eds.), *Thinking queer: Sexuality, culture, and education* (pp. 15-32). New York: Peter Lang.

Munt, Sally R. (1998). Sisters in exile: The lesbian nation. In R. Ainley (Ed.), *New frontiers of space, bodies and gender* (pp. 3-19). New York: Routledge.

Opffer, E. (1994). Coming out to students: Notes from the college classroom. In R. Jeffrey Ringer (Ed.), *Queer words, queer images: Communication and the construction of homosexuality* (pp. 296-321). New York: New York University Press.

Pinar, W. (1998). Understanding curriculum as gender text: Notes on reproduction, resistance, and male-male relations. In W. F. Pinar (Ed.), *Queer theory in education* (pp. 221-243). Mahwah, NJ: Lawrence Erlbaum and Associates.

Pinar, W. (2000). Foreward. In S. Talburt & S. Steinberg (Eds.), *Thinking queer: Sexuality, culture, and education* (ix-xvii). New York: Peter Lang.

Pitt, A. (1998). Fantasizing women in the women's studies classroom: Toward a symptomatic reading of negation. In W. F. Pinar (Ed.), *Queer theory in education* (pp. 299-320). Mahwah, NJ: Lawrence Erlbaum and Associates.

Rodriguez, N. (1998). (Queer) youth as political and pedagogical. In W. F. Pinar (Ed.), *Queer theory and education* (pp. 173-186). Mahwah, NJ: Lawrence Erlbaum and Associates.

Sears, J. (1990). *Growing up gay in the south.* New York: Haworth Press.

Sears, J. (1998). A generational and theoretical analysis of culture and male (Homo) sexuality. In W.F. Pinar (Ed.), *Queer theory in education* (pp. 73-106). Mahwah, NJ: Lawrence Erlbaum Associates.

Seidman, S. (1997). Introduction. In S. Seidman (Ed.), *Queer theory/sociology* (pp. 1-29). Malden, MA: Blackwell Publishers.

Shilts, R. (1982). *The mayor of Castro street: The life and times of Harvey Milk.* New York: St. Martins Press.

Silin, J. (1995). *Sex, death and the education of children: Our passion for ignorance in the age of AIDS.* New York: Teachers College Press.

Stein, A. & Plummer, K. (1997). "I can't even think straight": Queer theory and the missing sexual revolution in sociology. In S. Seidman (Ed.), *Queer theory/sociology* (pp. 129-144). Malden, MA: Blackwell Publishers.

Steinberg, S. (2000). From the closet to the coral: Neo-stereotyping in *In & Out.* In S. Talburt & S. Steinberg (Eds.), *Thinking queer: Sexuality, culture and education* (pp. 153-160). New York: Peter Lang.

Tierney, W. & Dilley, P. (1998). Constructing knowledge: Educational research and gay and lesbian studies. In W. F. Pinar (Ed.), *Queer theory in education* (pp. 49-72). Mahwah, NJ: Lawrence Erlbaum Associates.

Wakeford, N. (1998). Urban culture for virtual bodies: Comments on lesbian 'identity' and 'community' in San Francisco Bay area cyberspace In R. Ainley (Ed.), *New frontiers of space, bodies and gender* (pp. 176-190). New York: Routledge.

Warner, M. (1999). *The trouble with normal: Sex, politics and the ethics of queer life.* New York: The Free Press.

Young-Bruehl, E. (1998). *Subject to biography: Psychoanalysis, feminism and writing womens' lives.* Cambridge, MA: Harvard University Press.

---

*Marla Morris* is an assistant professor with the Department of Curriculum, Foundations, and Research at Georgia Southern University, Statesboro, Georgia.

---

# Alternative Paths to Teacher Certification

## Anne Grosso de León

*For some, the increasing proliferation of alternative teacher certification programs is just what the doctor ordered—a dynamic, market-driven phenomenon designed to alleviate the nation's chronic shortage of K-12 teachers. Others regard alternative certification with skepticism, pointing out that shortcuts to teacher education tend to turn out inadequately prepared teachers, who are then expected to take on the most difficult challenges. Can both be right?*

For those weary of headlines decrying the poor quality of American education in the twenty-first century—and in particular, the nation's failure to recruit, train and retain sufficient numbers of qualified teachers—consider this: In the wry, provocative history, *America's Women: Four Hundred Years of Dolls, Drudges, Helpmates, and Heroines* (William Morrow & Company, 2003), written by The New York Times editorial page editor, Gail Collins, she reports that noted public activist Elizabeth Buffum Chace's primary recollection about the curriculum of the Connecticut school she attended in 1816 was that it relied heavily on "memorization and beatings." Collins explains that by the time Chace was 12 years old, she had, in Chace's words, "recited *Murray's Grammar* a dozen times without a word of explanation or application from the book or the teacher." Chace went on to observe that, "for that time it was a good school.'" Maybe so, for according to Collins, at that time, "Teachers in the middle and southern states were so frequently drunkards that the alcoholic schoolteacher became a stereotype." Apparently, even then recruiting sufficient numbers of teachers, drunk or sober, was a challenge for the young republic. Collins points out that " ... [I]n 1833, the estimated teacher shortage was more than 30,000." Moreover, even then men did not view teaching as a smart career move—despite the fact that in 1838 wages for male teachers in Connecticut were nearly three times that of wages for women. Collins cites educator Thomas Gallaudet's observation that, "[for men] there were so many other avenues open in our country to the accumulation of property and the attaining of distinction."

Who but the history Muse is more effective at vaporizing nostalgia for the "good old days"?

In America, the demand for qualified teachers has usually been a few steps ahead of their supply—and teacher education has always been a work in progress, generally occupying a marginalized status in the culture of higher education. The first "normal" schools in the mid-nineteenth century were at the high school level and were largely attended by women who were admitted at age 16; men were admitted at age 17. The course of study was typically one year. Teachers' colleges, an outgrowth of the normal schools, never attained the same high status of their liberal arts institutional siblings, nor have they yet.

Today, although university-based teacher education programs remain the primary source of new teachers in America, they are, according to Daniel Fallon, chair of the Education Division of Carnegie Corporation of New York, "now rapidly losing market share at a dizzying rate." School districts, desperate for the "silver bullet" that will provide them with teachers as quickly as possible, are increasingly looking outside the university to develop alternate paths to teacher training and certification. Certainly their sense of urgency has grown more intense in no small part because the No Child Left Behind Act mandates that all teachers be "highly qualified" in the subjects they teach by the end of the 2005-2006 school year. States failing to comply with the mandate can face stiff sanctions, including the withdrawal or withholding of Title I funds.

In June 2002, the *Annual Report on Teacher Quality* by the U.S. Secretary of Education delivered a blistering critique of university-based teacher education and certification. In effect, it called for the dismantling of such programs and a redefinition of teacher preparation, one that emphasized higher standards in the acquisition of content knowledge and verbal skills and far less emphasis on educational coursework requirements. The report characterized such coursework as "burdensome." At the same time, the report recommended that student teaching and attendance at schools of education be made "optional" and that other "bureaucratic hurdles" be eliminated. Declaring that schools of education and formal teacher training programs have failed "to produce the types of highly qualified teachers that the No Child Left Behind Act demands," the Secretary's report called on the states to "streamline" their respective systems of teacher certification. According to the report, "Across the country, there are several promising experiments that recruit highly qualified candidates who are interested in teaching but did not attend schools of education and place them quickly in high-need schools, providing training, support and mentoring."

## A Center Established

In October 2003, the Department of Education awarded a grant of $2.5 million to the National Center for Education Information (NCEI) for the establishment of the National Center for

Alternative Certification. The new center was to serve as a clearinghouse of information about alternative routes to teacher certification as well as a source for technical assistance and outreach. Given the dramatic growth of alternative route initiatives among the states in the past two decades, the timing of the establishment of NCAC was, to say the least, auspicious.

In 1983, only eight states reported having any alternative to the traditional university-based teacher education route to certifying teachers. By 2003, 43 states, as well as the District of Columbia, reported having some type of alternative route to teacher education and certification. These alternative route initiatives have resulted in the certification of more than 200,000 new teachers, with thousands more who have participated in university-based alternative teacher preparation programs also being licensed to teach. The numbers, though considerable, are relatively modest given the projected need for new teachers in the next decade: more than two million, with 700,000 needed in urban communities, areas suffering the greatest chronic shortages of qualified teachers.

C. Emily Feistritzer, president of NCEI and president and chief executive officer of the National Center for Alternative Certification, argues that the strength of alternative certification is its market-driven impetus. "Programs are created to meet demand," she explains, "and the market for teachers on the demand side is greatest in rural and poor areas." Feistritzer applauds the "tremendous enthusiasm" shown by states and colleges "to meet the demand not just for more teachers but for better teachers." Designed to attract nontraditional candidates to teaching, alternative certification programs, she says, have "forced everyone to revisit the question of what teachers must be able to know and do." The bottom line, says Feistritzer, is this: "If the alternative route did not exist would this person have gone into teaching?"

Maybe so, but others, such as Linda Darling-Hammond, Charles E. Ducommun Professor of Education at Stanford University, point out that "Alternative certification comes in all shapes and sizes, and is only as good as its preparation." On that score, she says, the reviews are mixed: "Some are high quality, and others are not," adding that in some cases, in the rush to create "short cuts to training," new teachers are placed in classrooms "on a hope and a prayer." Acknowledging that, "There are a lot of good alternative routes that don't give short shrift to good preparation," Darling-Hammond says "What separates high-quality programs from low-quality is what counts." The problem, of course, is that there is no consensus on standards in this fast-developing marketplace of alternative certification programs. If, among the growing profusion of alternative certification programs, weeds are sprouting among the flowers, might not the same be said of university-based teacher education programs, many of them long-established?

Carnegie Corporation of New York President Vartan Gregorian acknowledges that this is certainly the case. "We can no longer close our eyes to the problem of America's schools of education and the pitiful job most of them do in preparing our teachers," he says. "What is needed is nothing less than an unwavering commitment to a gold standard of teacher education, one in which university-based teacher education programs prepare teachers who are proficient in the fields in which they will be teaching, well versed in the latest theories and practices of pedagogy, skilled in technology and professionally mentored with solid classroom experience—all of which cannot be accomplished at warp speed." Carnegie Corporation has made such a commitment in the form of Teachers for a New Era, a multimillion-dollar, five-year reform effort aimed at creating a new teacher education model, inspired by the idea of a "gold standard" and designed to strengthen K-12 teaching.

In the meantime, in classrooms throughout the nation, particularly in high-needs urban and rural areas, each year children are being welcomed by increasing numbers of teachers who have come to their profession, and been certified, via alternate routes, i.e., judged to possess the minimum competencies to teach as required by their respective locality. Says Emily Feistritzer, "It's here. Anybody who thinks it's a debate is out of touch with what's going on." At the same time, she declares, "Schools of education will be around forever," and, "University-based teacher education programs will always be there."

## Time for a Study

In an effort to take a measure of "what's going on," Carnegie Corporation of New York commissioned a national study to examine who actually participates in alternative certification programs and how these programs train teachers for the classroom. Says Dan Fallon, "Although there are thousands of different programs parading under the same banner, some are little more than desperation moves of school districts that demean and degrade the teaching profession. On the other hand, many are perfectly okay. We wanted to know: what might a good alternative certification program look like?" A report on the research study, *Insights into Alternative Certification: Preliminary Findings from a National Study*, written by Daniel C. Humphrey, associate director for educational policy, and Marjorie E. Wechsler, educational policy analyst, both of SRI International, an independent, nonprofit research organization, describes seven case studies, selected by the research team after culling through hundreds of alternative certification programs.

"Teacher education," explains Humphrey, "is a highly politicized and polarizing debate." As for alternative certification, he observes, those on the right tend to see alternative certification as a highly desirable, market-driven phenomenon; those on the left view the same phenomenon with concern, aware that the needs of the poor are often not well served by market forces. Those actually involved in quality teacher preparation, whether in traditional university-based programs or alternative route programs, are keenly aware that, either way, teacher preparation is a very complex and expensive undertaking. And then there are the programs themselves, which, upon examination, according to Humphrey, tend to challenge assumptions and conventional wisdom. "Rest assured," he explains, "any generalization you make about alternative certification is likely to be wrong." He adds, "Whenever someone argues that alternative certification is this or that, you should probably question it." In general, he says, the data collected and analyzed in the study do not support the arguments of either proponents or opponents of alternate certification.

For example, according to the study, the notion that alternative certification programs attract a more diverse pool of teachers that includes greater numbers of men, older individuals, minorities, and "mid-career switchers"—many with special expertise in fields in which shortages are particularly acute, such as mathematics and science—is not supported by the evidence. In fact, the study found that alternative certification participants tend "to reflect the gender mix of the profession as a whole and the racial composition of their local market." Moreover, it turns out that only a very small fraction of alternative certification participants are "mid-career switchers" from mathematics and science professions. Similarly, the belief that alternative certification attracts many who never considered teaching as a career option before also turns out not to be the case. In fact, "large numbers of alternative certification participants have prior teaching experience or experience working with children in classroom settings."

School districts, **desperate** for the "silver bullet" that will provide them with teachers as quickly as possible, are increasingly looking outside the university to develop **alternate** paths to teacher training and certification.

On the "streamlining" aspect of teacher certification, the study found that while alternative certification participants are moved into the classroom more quickly, they do not obtain full certification any faster than participants in traditional programs. Clinical practice is shortened in most programs, and coursework can be quite similar to that of traditional programs or tailored to the particular program design. The value of on-the-job training, central to the arguments of proponents of alternative certification, varies widely, the critical variable being the nature of the school environments. According to the study, "Some participants experience rich and supportive environments in which they thrive and learn their new profession, while others experience chaotic and unsupportive environments that not only prevent them from learning how to teach, but also drive them from the profession." In cases where a good match cannot be guaranteed—that is, the training needs of the participants are not appropriately matched with the available supports offered by the school—the perceived benefits of on-the-job training never materialize.

The seven case studies examined in the Humphrey-Wechsler study do not settle the debate on the merits or limitations of alternative teaching certification, but because these programs are among the largest and best known in the country, and provide a range of approaches, they do provide valuable insights into the dizzying complexity of alternative certification.

### The Two-for-One Route: Certification Plus a Master's Degree in Education

Established with discretionary funds in 2000 specifically to fill vacancies in some of New York City's lowest performing schools, located primarily in economically depressed areas of the Bronx and Brooklyn, the New York City Teaching Fellows Program simultaneously prepares its participants for certification and enrolls them in a subsidized Master of Education program. Courses such as "Classroom Organization" and "Skillful Teaching: Strategies for Effective Instruction and Classroom Management," offered by a dozen local public and private colleges and universities, are required courses for all participants. A two-month pre-service training experience in-

cludes field work consisting of assisting and observing in classrooms and regular advisory meetings in which Fellows meet to share experiences and get instruction in classroom skills and management techniques as well as master's degree coursework. After completing the pre-service training, Fellows become teachers of record for the next two years while they complete their master's degree coursework and receive both school- and university-based mentoring as part of their in-service training. Each year, the program surveys participating Fellows to find out whether their expectations about the program have been met and whether they view their preparation as satisfactory. In effect, they are asked "Now how do you feel?" says Vicki Bernstein, who developed and runs the Teaching Fellows Program. The data collected, she explains, are used to make program adjustments.

The program provides Fellows with a range of support services, including workshops, meetings, and social gatherings; Fellows receive a bi-monthly Teaching Fellows newsletter, The Fellows' Forum, as well as weekly e-mails from the program office. Fellows are encouraged to ask questions and are promised a response within 48 hours. A new mentoring initiative includes monthly meetings between Fellows and their respective mentors. "Feedback," says Bernstein, is "essential and welcome," and ongoing, two-way communication is encouraged and highly prized.

Roughly one out of five of the candidates who apply to the New York City Teaching Fellows Program is accepted. With average undergraduate GPAs of 3.3, and 24 percent of the Fellows holding another graduate degree prior to entering the program, participants are "highly qualified and competent," says Bernstein. The average age of the Fellows is 29, so most have had work experiences in other areas. Some of the Fellows say that they always wanted to be a teacher, explains Bernstein, but for a variety of reasons never attained their goal. For many, the Teaching Fellows Program represents an opportunity "to do something more meaningful in their lives," she adds. The program is new, of course, and the fact that "the retention rates have improved over the last couple of years," with 86 percent returning to teach a second year, is a hopeful sign but not necessarily a harbinger of things to come. "We hope most of them will stay," says Bernstein, "but realistically, we know that people will change careers, both in and out of education."

The central goal of the New York City Teaching Fellows Program is to accelerate the process of bringing new teachers into classrooms where they are needed most, to teach subjects for which there is the greatest need—English, Spanish, math, science, bilingual education and special education. Although candidates are asked for their preferences regarding placement, assignments are primarily driven by the specific needs of schools and by each Fellow's qualifications and subject matter expertise. Ultimately, they are expected to be "flexible"—and they are. "Most of our folks wind up teaching in the Bronx and Central Brooklyn," explains Bernstein. Even allowing for the wobbly economy of the last few years, there has been no shortage of applicants. In a city that employs many thousands of public school teachers, however, the 2,000 New York City Teaching Fellows clearly will not fill the gap between supply and demand for qualified teachers in the city's underserved communities. However, Bernstein says, the program is "a significant investment" designed to narrow that gap.

## "Grow Your Own": An Alternative Route for Paraprofessionals and Teacher Aides

There was no shortage of teachers in the Milwaukee public schools in 1987 when the Metropolitan Multicultural Teacher Education Program (MMTEP) was established as an alternative teacher education program, explains Linda Post, department chair of curriculum and instruction at the University of Wisconsin-Milwaukee. What prompted the creation of MMTEP in 1989, Post explains, was the realization that teachers in Milwaukee schools did not reflect the racial and ethnic composition of the students they taught. In 1987, 68 percent of the Milwaukee public schools' student population consisted of students of color, while only 18 percent of the district's teachers represented minority groups. At the same time, minority students were underrepresented in colleges and universities—including those offering teacher education programs—which virtually guaranteed a shortage of potential teachers of color in the pipeline.

Many students of color, however, were enrolling in community colleges in a range of program areas. Many of these students found paraprofessional positions in urban public schools to support themselves while they pursued their baccalaureate degrees, a process that, given family and job obligations, was often protracted. An added impetus to the creation of MMTEP was the poor retention rate of teachers in the Milwaukee public schools—approximately 50 percent left within 3-5 years. The notion of "growing your own [teachers]" became a strategy for recruiting and training prospective teachers who had ties to the community and who would be more likely to make a long-term commitment to teaching within the community.

Ultimately, the establishment of MMTEP was the result of a collaboration of the Milwaukee Public Schools, the Milwaukee Teachers' Education Association, the Milwaukee Area Technical College and the University of Wisconsin-Milwaukee. Applicants to MMTEP must have a bachelor's degree and have been a paraprofessional or teacher aide in the Milwaukee public schools for at least a year; they must also be qualified for admission as post-baccalaureate students to the University of Wisconsin-Milwaukee School of Education and perform satisfactorily in interviews and background checks by both the university and Milwaukee Public Schools.

Intense and "resource-rich," says Post, the program is deliberately kept small—on average, only 20 candidates are selected out of the 75-100 who apply. "MMTEP will never be huge," she declares. "I just don't know how you could do it with large numbers." Participants are called "residents" rather than "interns" to distinguish them from other pre-service training programs. MMTEP residents participate in a six-week summer session during which they take university classes and teach in Milwaukee public school classrooms with a master teacher. They are paid a teacher's hourly rate for five hours a day during the six weeks. Whether they continue in the program rests heavily on a positive evaluation of their ability to relate to the children and on their readiness to assume full-time teaching duties.

Explains Post, "Many have good rapport with kids but if they don't use their rapport to focus on instruction, we throw them out!" She adds. "We haven't found a way to screen for organizational skills."

During the year of residency that follows, participants serve as teachers of record in grades 1 through 8—while on leave from their paraprofessional or teaching aide position—and receive a full beginning teacher's salary with fringe benefits. Like the New York City Fellows, residents are not left to struggle on their own. MMTEP residents enjoy the support of a mentor who visits the classroom at least once a week. While mentors spend one day a week with teachers, "they may spend the rest of the week on the phone with them," says Post. Mentors and residents often "become best friends," she adds, "but mentors do not evaluate [residents]." Without the responsibility of evaluating the resident, which is left to the resident's university supervisor, mentor and resident are encouraged to enjoy a relationship based on trust and support.

The mentor-resident ratio is an astounding one mentor for every four teachers-in-residence. With an experienced master teacher in the classroom on a regular basis, residents are able to work with mentors as co-teachers and co-planners. In the meantime, residents continue their university coursework. It is only upon successful completion of the program that the resident is guaranteed a teaching contract with Milwaukee Public Schools. "If we counsel them out after one year," says Post, "they're gone." Because the teacher's union views the residency as a year of training, not employment, it does not represent certification candidates who have been "deselected." If things don't work out for candidates, they can return to their former positions as paraprofessionals or aides.

A ten-year study of MMTEP conducted in 1999 by Martin Haberman, co-founder of MMTEP with Linda Post, showed that a decade after graduation, 94 percent of MMTEP graduates were still teaching in Milwaukee public schools—many of them in the same schools in which they had been working as paraprofessionals and aides—and 96 percent of them received performance ratings of satisfactory or exemplary from their current principals. Data are being collected to update the study.

Today, the resource viewed as precious by MMTEP—paraprofessionals and teaching aides with strong ties to the community—is itself in peril. "In large school districts," explains Post, "paraprofessionals and aides are being cut." These are the very people, she says, who, "if they had a chance, would like to become teachers. . . . [Yet] here we are recruiting abroad."

## The Use of Outrage as a Tool for Educational Reform

It would be hard to think of two alternative routes to teaching more dissimilar in design, yet more united in purpose, than MMTEP and Teach for America. Founded in 1988-89 by Wendy Kopp, then a recent Princeton University graduate, Teach for America recruits high-achieving recent college graduates from selective colleges and universities who are committed to social change and eager to make a two-year commitment to teach in underserved urban and rural school districts.

Characterizing Teach for America as "a mission-driven organization" aimed at closing the educational achievement gap between rich and poor, Abigail Smith, vice president for research and public policy, and herself an alumnus of Teach for

America, acknowledges that the program's primary goal is not to prepare teachers for certification, though that may be an outcome, but to advocate and cultivate leadership on behalf of social justice among its participants. According to the SRI International study, only 11 percent of Teach for America participants indicated that they expected to be teaching in ten years, and about one-third said that they "wanted to contribute to society before moving on to another field outside education." Says Emily Feistritzer, "Teach for America is a domestic Peace Corps program"—a point readily granted by Smith. "After two years," she explains, "we want Teach for America teachers to continue to address this gap between rich and poor [and] to use their outrage in other areas to get at this problem."

Remarkably, Teach for America appears to have succeeded in rising above the highly politicized and polarizing debate surrounding alternative pathways to teacher training. "The Bush administration has been very supportive of Teach for America," says Smith, "because, we like to think, it's a good program, but also because there are no regulations." On the other hand, she observes, "Social justice [proponents] also support it. So we can reach in both directions." While Teach for America receives some of its funding from Americorps and the Department of Education, 80 percent of its funding comes from private corporations and foundations.

Admission into Teach for America is a criterion-based process with an acceptance rate of 15 percent out of 16,000 applications. With an average GPA of 3.4, Teach for America candidates are an idealistic, high-achieving group of young men and women with demonstrated leadership, communication, and organizational skills. Above all, says Smith, they must have "perseverance." Candidates are first required to apply their perseverance in an intensive five-week summer training session and a one-to-two-week orientation in one of the 21 Teach for America regions located throughout the nation. Before they even start their formal training, however, says Smith, "They have already read a ton of materials…and had 12 hours of classroom observations, which they write about." Smith adds, "We work hard to instill [the idea that] learning to teach is an ongoing process." Keenly aware that they have a lot to learn, when Teach for America candidates enter the classroom "They go in with the attitude: 'I'm going to ask for help; I'm not going to act like I'm the be-all and end-all.'"

Of course, there's little danger of their developing swelled heads since, according to Smith, "The first year is overwhelming"—as it is for all new teachers. Despite the daunting nature of the challenges they face, the retention rates for the first and second years are high; by the third year, 60 percent are still teaching. Teach for America's most recent annual survey of alumni—and there are 8,000 now—indicates that approximately 60 percent are working in or studying education, as teachers, principals, education policy advisors, and leaders and staff of education reform organizations. The other 40 percent enter a variety of professions, including medicine, law, business, journalism and government service. Regardless of the profession they choose, the essential goal is the same for all Teach for America alumni: seasoned by their deeply personal experiences in the classrooms of many of the nation's most impoverished schools, and fired by their outrage over the inequities they

have witnessed, they are primed to advocate for educational equity and social justice for America's children.

And the children who are taught by Teach for America teachers, how do they fare? According to *Teaching at Risk: A Call to Action*, the report of The Teaching Commission, "…[I]nitial findings on TFA are positive." The report states that a study of Teach for America participants in Houston, Texas, conducted by Macke Raymond and Stephen Fletcher, "found that TFA teachers perform at least as well as, and in many cases, better than, other teachers hired by the Houston Independent School District." Citing the same study, however, Linda Darling-Hammond writes, "In 1999-2000, the last year covered by the study sample, about 50 percent of Houston's new teachers were uncertified, and the researchers report that 35 percent of new hires lacked even a bachelor's degree; so TFA teachers were compared to an extraordinarily ill-prepared group." The problem, according to Darling-Hammond, is that TFA teacher outcomes are not compared to those of "trained and certified teachers or to others with a bachelor's degree," even though, she points out, data were available to those conducting the study.

Regarding the latter point, Dan Fallon explains, "At the time that was not a question that interested them. They simply wanted to know, of the entire pool of teachers that they hire through non-traditional venues (excluding normally prepared certified teachers), are the Teach for America teachers competitive?"

What Darling-Hammond's analysis of the Houston study suggests is that schoolchildren taught by the intensely idealistic yet inexperienced Teach for America teachers might be only relatively better off than if they been taught by the largely underqualified and unqualified teachers concentrated in Houston schools and classrooms. Fallon agrees: "The study shows that Teach for America teachers are doing no harm in those positions (relative to what the pupils would otherwise have had for teachers) and are often doing better than the norm."

Another more recent study by Mathematica Policy Research, Inc., a group that conducts research on public policy issues, focused on the question, "Do TFA teachers improve (or at least not harm) student outcomes relative to what would have happened in their absence?" The sample included six of the regions in which Teach for America placed teachers at the time: Baltimore, Chicago, Los Angeles, Houston, New Orleans, and the Mississippi Delta. Teach for America teachers were compared to a control group defined as "any teacher who was never a TFA corps member"—a group that included "traditionally certified, alternatively certified, and uncertified teachers." The June 2004 study, prepared with support by Carnegie Corporation of New York, found that students in low-income, high-minority classes taught by Teach for America teachers fared slightly better in mathematics achievement and about the same in reading than similar students taught by the control group. The study concludes that "From the perspective of a community or a school faced with the opportunity to hire TFA teachers, our findings suggest that TFA offers an appealing pool of candidates." Indeed, according to the report, "The finding that many of the control teachers in our study were not certified or did not have formal pre-service training highlights the need for programs or policies that can attract good teachers to schools in the most disadvantaged communities. Our findings show that Teach for America is one such program."

Darling-Hammond draws a different conclusion from the study. The generally poor quality of the teachers in the control group, she observes, underscores a more fundamental question, "not whether districts should hire more TFA teachers but what our country is going to do about hiring a stable force of really well-prepared teachers for the students most in need so they can do more than tread water until they drown."

## No Consensus

What is clear is that all students need good teachers—knowledgeable, committed, skilled, creative and caring people—but no one yet seems to have produced a definitive method for identifying who those teachers are—or who has the potential to become an effective teacher. For example, according to the Humphrey-Wechsler study, although "In many states, alternative certification now plays a central role in the production of new teachers...[On] a basic level there is no agreement about what constitutes alternative certification." For that matter, says Dan Goldhaber, a labor economist and research associate professor at the University of Washington's Daniel J. Evans School of Public Affairs, there is no consensus on the licensing examinations used to determine teacher quality. "They're all over the map," he explains.

In the course of his work at the university's Center on Reinventing Public Education, Goldhaber has studied the teacher labor market and the impact of teacher quality on student achievement—perhaps the most fundamental educational issue of them all. In a new study funded by Carnegie Corporation of New York, Goldhaber will examine the relationship between teacher performance on certification or licensure exams such as Praxis I and II and student learning gains as measured over time by the standardized accountability tests used in North Carolina. While examining the nature of that relationship—is it "causal or merely correlational?"—the study will attempt to determine the consequences of the widely varying cutoff scores used by school districts, which result in the inclusion or exclusion of potential teachers. According to Goldhaber, not much evidence exists to demonstrate whether licensure exams are effective in "screening out potentially low-quality teachers." There is considerable evidence, however, that the use of these tests affects minorities disproportionately since minority teacher candidates generally experience a lower pass rate than white candidates. Is it possible that high-quality minority teachers might be eliminated from the pool of potential teachers by tests that may or may not accurately predict teacher performance and the impact of this performance on student learning gains? Goldhaber's study is intended "to help states make more informed decisions about the use of licensure exams." Meanwhile, lawsuits filed against school districts in Texas, California and Alabama are challenging testing practices in teacher licensing— practices that, plaintiffs charge, are discriminatory.

## American Education at a Crossroads—Again

When the framers of the U.S. Constitution delegated responsibility for education to the states, it is unlikely that even this group of visionaries could have imagined the whirlwind of contentiousness that would ensue. "The U.S. Constitution has not provided Americans with a national voice for education," Vartan Gregorian observes, "but a chorus of voices, who, rather disconcertingly, rarely sing from the same libretto." Occasionally, as in the lawsuits cited, the lack of consensus finds its way into the judicial system for resolution.

Since publication of *A Nation at Risk* in 1983, the report to the U.S. Secretary of Education by the National Commission on Excellence in Education that famously warned about the poor quality of American education, the educational and political establishments appear to have achieved consensus on at least one issue. Abundant research now is available to confirm what common sense suggested was true all along: good teaching matters. In fact, in the 20 years or so since *A Nation at Risk*, the consensus appears to be that it matters most. Louis V. Gerstner, Jr., chairman of The Teaching Commission and former chairman of IBM, writes in the preface to the Commission's report, *Teaching at Risk: A Call to Action*: "...[Our] nation is at a crossroads. We will not continue to lead if we persist in viewing teaching—the profession that makes all other professions possible—as a second-rate occupation. Nothing is more vital to our future than ensuring that we attract and retain the best teachers in our public schools."

As America's audacious experiment in mass public education continues to unfold—replete with inequity and resplendent with achievement—it is remarkable how frequently American education has found itself "at the crossroads." This time, as we try to come to terms with the formidable challenge of teacher education reform, we discover that the crossroads actually resembles a tangle of overlapping and intersecting paths. What's confusing, of course, is that there are many signs pointing to what seems to be a single place, a place called: "Quality Alternative Teacher Training (Certification Guaranteed)." Dotting this landscape of tangled paths are hundreds of institutions with their own signs beckoning the weary traveler: "Quality University-Based Teacher Education Programs (Certification Guaranteed)."

Two decades after the publication of *A Nation at Risk*, America's university-based teacher education programs have taken their share of hits, and, more recently, so have alternative teacher certification programs. As the respective proponents and opponents of "traditional" versus "nontraditional" approaches to teacher training face off, it's just possible that what is unfolding is the characteristically chaotic, utterly inefficient American version of the creative process. Do we know enough to create a new model of teacher preparation that will allow us to place the teacher education "debate" in the historical dustbin?

"We know enough," concludes the report on the Humphrey-Wechsler study, "to move the debate over teacher preparation beyond sweeping generalizations and overstatements to the crafting of policies and programs that put effective teachers in every classroom."

In a very real sense, where this critical teacher preparation takes place—in university-based teacher education programs or in alternative teacher certification programs—is largely irrelevant. What is relevant is whether traditional and nontraditional teacher education programs are ultimately successful in turning out the highly skilled teachers required by America's children—including all those many children still left behind.

---

*Anne Grosso de León writes about education.*

---

# PROGRAMMING FOR PARTICIPATION:

## *Building Partnerships with the Immigrant Newcomer Community*

By Chryss Mylopoulos

**P**ublic libraries are gradually getting more involved in partnerships with community-based organizations with which they share the same vision, mission, and philosophy regarding services to their culturally diverse communities. The benefits from such an involvement can be significant in areas such as:

- Knowledge sharing and exchange
- Expanding the scope of service
- Promotion of the service
- Accessing community resources

There has also been a growing recognition of partnerships as a value that provides opportunities for city-supported services such as public libraries to form alliances or to link up with other sectors, including the private sector, and strengthen their image as an important community resource accessible to the immigrant public.

Under the umbrella of multicultural library services, the Toronto Public Library got involved in partnerships focusing on immigrant settlement services and on facilitating access to information related to newcomer and immigrant needs. As a result of this relationship the public library has become very close to the immigrant services sector, which has grown in sophistication and importance over the past years, and engaged them in the planning of programs and services.

### The Immigrant Settlement Services

The immigrant services sector resembles a "community of practice"—to borrow and apply a term coined by Etienne Wenger, a pioneer in communities of practice related to corporations and their organizational structure. It is a community that includes a group of people who know each other, connect in a helping way, and work toward developing a sense of common good practices when dealing with newcomer individuals and groups. Through sharing of insights and experiences these communities have also managed to create a valuable knowledge network around common problems faced by newcomers, offering possible solutions as well as approaches.

The settlement sector is valuable in serving as a sounding board for organizations that need expertise and information on the "unique realities of immigrants and refugees" (OCASI fact sheet, 1996). According to a report written by Francis Frisken and Marcia Wallace of York University in Toronto, immigrant settlement "is recognized as a localized phenomenon and as a highly localized activity that intersects with the activities of a large number of local political institutions and a network of community agencies." An organization such as the public library needs to recognize the role of this community and acknowledge its expertise and the invaluable contributions it makes toward the settlement and integration of the new immigrants. In particular, the library also needs to recognize the fact that the settlement sector's firsthand knowledge of newcomer communities can help, first by informing the library's decisions about the type of services needed and second, in bringing the newcomers closer to the library.

Most important of all, the public library as a local political institution should join the settlement sector in this network and contribute its expertise, knowledge, and other skills as well as its facilities to maximize the benefits to the immigrant community. As the document "A Social Development Strategy for the City of Toronto" (2001) points out, "Local community cultural centers, ... libraries ... are important community resources which must be accessible for public use."

### The Toronto Environment: Facts and Figures

Before I describe the settlement program in which the Toronto Public Library is involved, I would like to give a snapshot of the immigrant and refugee communities in the city. The 2001 Census revealed that 49 percent of Toronto's total population of 2,456,000 was born outside Canada, 46 percent of residents reported a mother tongue other than English, and close to 30 percent of city residents primarily speak a language besides English at home.

---

*The director feared that having consulting and referral services for immigrants in the library would lead to other social agencies demanding library space. Clearly this view demonstrated a lack of understanding of the nature of immigrant settlement services, and the significance and contributions of the settlement workers working at the library and bringing hundreds of people closer to this institution.*

---

According to Statistics Canada, the major recent source countries for immigration were China, India, Pakistan, Philippines, Korea, Sri Lanka, United Arab Emirates, Iran, Saudi Arabia, and Romania. In regards to the refugee population between 1991 and 2001, Toronto received approximately 100,000 refugees belonging to all categories, such as refugee claimants and Geneva Convention refugees. Averaged on an annual basis, Toronto receives between 5,000 and 10,000 refugees, accounting for 30-35 percent of the total refugees coming to the country.

### How the Partnership with the Immigrant Sector Started

The Settlement and Education Partnerships in Toronto (SEPT) program, as it relates to public libraries, grew out of the close connection that existed between the Multicultural Services in the East Region of the Toronto Public Library (formerly Scarborough Public Library before the amalgamation of all regional libraries into the Toronto Public Library in 1998) and the immigrant settlement sector. When the SEPT program was first introduced, it operated only in schools. Yet many immigrants arrived close to the end of the school year, and it became evident that the settlement workers needed a space to meet the newcomers and their families during summer. The library, a public and neutral place with many branches located all over the city, was thought to be a good place for this program during the summer months.

However, when the multicultural coordinator of the East Region first approached the new East Region director in the spring of 1999 and requested that consideration be given to the idea of the library becoming the place for the summer SEPT program, the idea was met with a negative response. The director feared that having consulting and referral services for immigrants in the library would lead to other social agencies demanding library space. Clearly this view demonstrated a lack of understanding of the nature of immigrant settlement services, and the

significance and contributions of the settlement workers working at the library and bringing hundreds of people closer to this institution. It also underscored a shortsightedness regarding the value of such a partnership in a culturally diverse and immigrant-based city.

The director's refusal delayed the involvement of the library for a year, and it was not until the next year, in June 2000, when SEPT, adopting another strategy, officially approached the administration of the amalgamated Toronto Public Library to request a sharing of facilities. The administration collectively accepted the recommendation, approved the hosting of the program that year, and suggested an evaluation of the program in 12 months to determine its future. In 2001 the program began in a coherent organized fashion.

### The Partnership: SEPT Program

SEPT is a primary example of a partnership and the first of its kind between federal levels of government (Citizenship and Immigration Canada) and public institutions (schools, public libraries, parks and recreation facilities) funded by federal, provincial, and city taxes and widely supported by all three as a result of the continuous advocacy by the immigrant settlement sector of the city. SEPT is most closely a partnership between the Toronto School Boards and agencies in the immigrant settlement sector funded by Citizenship Immigration Canada. Settlement workers employed by community agencies work as the school settlement workers (SSWs) of the SEPT Program. The schools and the agencies have formed seven clusters to coordinate the work of SSWs. The program started in 1998-9 with settlement workers assigned to selected schools. After five years in operation it has been expanded to include both public and Catholic schools and employ more workers. The public library and Parks and Recreation joined the SEPT summer program in 2000.

The purpose of the program is to assist newcomers during their initial adjustment period by using schools as a base to meet newcomers; by providing settlement information, translation and interpretation; and by linking and referring new immigrants to programs in schools and community.

### Organizational Structure

SEPT currently has a coordinator from the immigrant sector community, a Steering Committee, a cluster coordinator, a Library SEPT coordinator, and SEPT liaisons from each local library. The schools and the agencies in each of the seven clusters have agreed that one agency will act as the lead. The agency hires the cluster coordinator, who works closely with the school principals and coordinates the work of SSWs. The lead agency also hires the school settlement workers.

The school settlement workers (SSWs) are based in elementary and secondary schools during the school year and link newcomer families and students to services that promote settlement. Using the school as a base, they meet with parents and children, provide information and answer questions, and link parents with various programs within the school and the community. SSWs help newcomers learn about services and community programs and overcome difficulties they may experience when integrating into the society.

## SEPT Program at the Library

The library summer program was approved in 2000, and it was a pilot program in 2000-2001. It was approved on a long-term basis in 2002 and has expanded from 15 to 29 libraries. During the two summer months of July and August, the library offers its facilities in 29 library locations to settlement agencies and their staff to provide consultation and information and referral in the immigrant's home language for a few days a week.

The purpose of the partnership is to allow the SSWs to use the public library as a base to meet families during the summer, when school is not in session. During these meetings, the SSWs provide settlement information, translation, and interpretation; assist newcomers with information and referrals to a wide range of services in the city; and identify and try to resolve their more specific needs. Secondarily, because of their extended outreach activities, the SSWs bring people to the library, promote awareness and understanding of the library as a community resource, and extend support for the services and programs at the library.

## Benefits of SEPT Program at the Local Library

The settlement workers are an excellent resource for the staff. They benefit and assist the local library in:

- communicating with members of the community in languages other than English
- reaching out to the newcomers and attracting them to the library
- creating awareness of library resources and services in the newcomer/immigrant community
- providing staff with background information about the cultural diversity of the community
- informing staff about reading interests and information needs of newcomers and other immigrants
- assisting the library in organizing information/orientation programs
- assisting in the preparation of joint library/SEPT promotional materials in newcomers' languages

## Benefits of Developing a Partnership with SEPT

As we see above, there are definite benefits for individual libraries hosting a SEPT program. But the partnership with SEPT benefits the library as an organization by:

- building up contacts and developing an ongoing liaison with immigrant serving community-based agencies and the School Boards

- tapping the most recent information that is gathered either by settlement agencies or School Boards on newcomer groups and languages
- using this information to inform allocation of resources, programs, and services

## What Kind of Information Is Requested?

Through this program hundreds of newcomers visited the library and were introduced to its programs and services. In all, 3,000 newcomers came to the library for SEPT meetings in 2000, 2001, and 2002. There was a 60 percent increase in 2002 over the previous year. Eighty-five percent of the newcomers had been in Canada less than six months.

Newcomers, both immigrants and refugees, requested information and referrals in the following areas, identifying and reaffirming their information priorities:

- Employment, language training
- Education and the school system
- Libraries and recreation
- Health, childcare, housing, immigration rules, and finances

## Success Factors within the Library

Over the first three years of operation we concluded that the success of the program at the libraries had to do with a number of factors. The first was the awareness of the program on the part of library staff. Presentations by SEPT program staff at library staff meetings were crucial in this respect. Following the initial presentation, regular meetings between library staff and the SSWs helped to establish an ongoing communication and a feeling of partnership.

Logistical factors included availability of space and other facilities such as desks and tables, computers, and phone access. Staff time had to be allotted to provide a local library orientation to the SSWs stationed at each library. Successful libraries also organized library orientation tours and group education programs for newcomers, which introduced the library catalog, the collection, and facilities for using the Internet. Finally, the successful libraries engaged in promotional activities and arranged an informational display on settlement resources, such as a poster with SEPT service hours at the library.

## External Success Factors

In addition to factors originating within the library, there were others related to the community and SEPT organization. These included the location of the library in a neighborhood with many new immigrants, the accessibility of the library, especially to public transportation, the lack of competing settlement agencies in the area, consistent and organized outreach to targeted communities on the part of the SEPT program, and frequent and regular SEPT service hours at the library. Other factors had to do with the SSWs themselves: that there were enough to staff the library-based program, that they educated themselves to take full advantage of the library's resources, and that they had sufficient facility in the languages spoken in the surrounding area.

### Success Measures/Indicators

Each year the program is evaluated by Citizenship and Immigration Canada-appointed evaluators, but in addition to the federal-level evaluation, the library uses criteria that relate to the purpose of having the program at its facilities. The following indicators have been used to determine whether the program was successful from the library perspective:

- Number of people who were introduced to the library by SSWs
- Participation of the immigrants in library orientation activities and events and in other "user education programs" with the assistance of SSWs
- Referrals to and participation in library programs such as children's summer programs
- Information offered by SSWs to library staff on demographic changes in the community
- Building ongoing liaison with SSWs and their respective agencies and participation of the library in orientation programs during the school year
- Library publicity provided in other languages with the assistance of SSWs for translation and distribution

The success of the partnership of SEPT with the Toronto Public Library during the two summer months has led to discussions on similar partnerships with the public libraries in other cities and regions. The program has now expanded to the cities of Hamilton, Kitchener/Waterloo, and Ottawa, and the Peel and York regions in the Province of Ontario.

It is very encouraging to see that the value of a collaborative partnership between public libraries and the immigrant services sector is finally recognized and pursued. This is the true meaning of practicing multiculturalism at the public library.

### Sources

*Ethnocultural Portrait—2001 Census.* (2001). Toronto: Urban Planning and Development Services.

Frisken, F. and Wallace, M. (2001). *Immigrants and Municipal Services: Client Perspectives.* Toronto: York University.

*Immigration Overview: Facts and figures.* (2002). Ottawa: Citizenship and Immigration Canada.

Scarborough Network of Immigrant Service Organizations. (2000). *Building Effective Partnerships: A Resource Manual for Community Agencies.* Toronto: Scarborough Network of Immigrant Service Organizations.

Toronto Community and Neighborhood Services. (2001). *A Social Development Strategy for the City of Toronto.* Toronto: City of Toronto.

*Chryss Mylopoulos was the multicultural services specialist at the Toronto Public Library from 1981 to 2003. She presented an earlier version of this article at a symposium on immigrant and refugee communities at the joint meeting of the Canadian Library Association and the American Library Association in Toronto in June 2003. E-mail address:* chryss@cs.toronto.edu.

# Linguistic Imperialism in the United States:

## *The Historical Eradication of American Indian Languages and the English-Only Movement*

### By Margery Ridgeway and Cornel Pewewardy

## Introduction

Over the last several years, we have presented many workshops together at educational conferences and spoken to many American Indian parents about how teacher education programs can prepare teachers to be more effective with their children. A recurring theme that emerged in those discussions was the hope that new teachers would care about their children and would take the time to find out about their tribal families, reservations, and cultural backgrounds. A major issue was how tribal languages were integrated and taught in schools.

While some groups have benefited, others, primarily racial and ethnic minorities, have been excluded or have not done well in U.S. schools. American Indian children in particular have suffered in the educational system. Teachers need to understand their histories and backgrounds in order to understand students' attitudes toward school as well as their academic situation.

In order to maximize learning with American Indian students today, teachers should know and understand the history of how Indigenous languages were treated in U.S. school systems. We believe that teachers need to be prepared to relate to all racial and ethnic groups in order to maximize the achievement of every student. The need to understand and attend to American Indian students is particularly urgent for reasons important to society as a whole and not just to individual students.

## Brief History of English Imperialism in the Eastern United States

The North American continent was linguistically diverse long before Europeans arrived on its shores. Before the arrival of Europeans in what is now the United States,

there were more than 500 American Indian languages spoken, some of which are still used today, especially in the Southwest. In order to be effective in the conduct of trade and other business ventures, Europeans were required to use interpreters and/or to learn the Indigenous languages with which they came into contact. According to Calloway (1997), many American Indians were well traveled and bilingual or multilingual. However, many preferred to conduct business in their primary languages through the use of interpreters. Successful tribal language interpreters had to do much more than provide word-for-word translations. Speakers of Indigenous languages tended to be experienced orators who used much imagery and metaphor in communicating. Interpreters had to know and understand both the Indigenous and the European methods of persuasion and had to have keen insight into these distinct cultural world-views. In order to have trained interpreters, early English and French explorers frequently kidnapped Indians from the coasts of New England and Canada, took them to Europe, and later returned to North America with the kidnapped Natives to use them as interpreters (Calloway, 1997).

As Europeans and American Indians participated in the daily affairs of each other's societies, new English words were created, and dozens of Indigenous and European languages were mingled. As far back as the seventeenth and eighteenth centuries, dark-skinned people were regarded as repulsive and decidedly inferior, as witnessed in England's poetic and artistic expressions (Cohen, 1980). Since Europeans firmly believed that humans originally were white (Guthrie, 1998), attempts to explain the presence of Indigenous people on the North American continent often came from interpretations of selected

European religious writings. These interpretations were used to support the inferiority of blacks and American Indians (Guthrie, 1998; Wardle & Cruz-Janzen, 2003).

Moreover, in the seventeenth and eighteenth centuries many Europeans believed that the American Indians were all "savages" without "real" languages. Indian languages struck Europeans as strange and guttural and not as real systems of communication. Throughout the decades, Europeans did borrow, mispronounce, adopt, and modify Indigenous words to describe things uniquely American. Among those words are caribou, moose, tomahawk, toboggan, succotash, hickory, mahogany, maize, and wigwam. American Indians, in turn, adopted European words such as God, Christ, Christmas, plow, clock, horse, cat, cow, and rum. American Indian languages rarely contained profanity. Some of the borrowed English words filled that "gap." These examples barely scratch the surface of the multicultural tapestry that underlies the English language (Kansy, 1997).

*As Europeans and American Indians participated in the daily affairs of each other's societies, new English words were created, and dozens of Indigenous and European languages were mingled.*

Many European traders acquired "sleeping dictionaries" through their sexual encounters with American Indian women. However, even before the linguicide of the nineteenth century, many Indigenous languages changed or died out. As the Europeans evolved into the oppressor, it became increasingly necessary for American Indians to learn English, the dominant language of the conquerors. Many American Indians learned English because knowing the oppressor's language often gave them power and status (Calloway, 1997).

### Brief History of Spanish Imperialism, Western United States

In the early 1600s the colonizers from Spain took control of the Pueblo peoples of New Mexico and Arizona through violent means. Franciscan priests with Spanish military support attacked Pueblo religious practices and enslaved Pueblo men to build Catholic missions. The traditional practice of political independence for each pueblo made the Spanish conquest easier. However, after years of unceasing cruelty and oppression, the Pueblos united under the leadership of Pope, San Juan Pueblo's medicine man. They succeeded in driving the Spanish out of the Rio Grande Indian Pueblos in 1680. Their success was short-lived. The Spanish reconquered the Pueblos in 1696. Native peoples were forced to practice Catholicism in public, especially on the feast day of their particular pueblo named in Spanish for a Catholic patron saint (such as San Juan Pueblo named in Spanish for St. John). Traditional religious practices survived because their practitioners took them underground (Champagne, 1994).

Beginning in 1769, the Spanish oppressors in California created an enormous mission system extending from San Diego to San Francisco. In the California missions, some of the Indigenous traditional religious practices survived alongside the required Catholic practices. In all of their missions, the Spanish justified their behaviors—enslaving Indigenous labor crews to build missions, requiring conversion to Catholicism, forcing the Indigenous peoples to speak the Spanish language—by their belief that they were saving the Indians' souls through conversion to Christianity. It was commonly believed that all Indian cultures, religions, and languages were heathen (Champagne, 1994).

Spanish colonialism in New Mexico was fairly typical of Spanish colonialism throughout the western portion of the United States as well as Latin America. Spanish colonial settlers arrived in New Mexico in 1598. They brought with them their religion, their customs, and their language, Spanish. According to Anaya (1987), "It was the daily as well as the poetic use of that faith and language that provided continuity and cohesion to the newly settled Mexicano/Hispano pueblos of Nuevo Mexico" (vii). When the Spaniards arrived in New Mexico, there were established Pueblos that had existed for centuries. Their religion and Indigenous languages were an integral part of the area when the Mexican and Spanish colonists arrived. Anaya (1987) writes, "In the fields, in the daily life of the Pueblos, in the kivas, the Pueblo ceremonial ways and languages were crucial to the spiritual relationship they established with the earth and the cosmos" (vii-viii).

The Spanish practice of forced religious conversion and economic exploitation among the Pueblo peoples who struggled to keep their own cultures, religions, and languages led to a blending of cultures. Pueblo people often practiced Catholicism publicly and maintained Indigenous religious practices in secret. Likewise, the Pueblo people learned to speak Spanish for the purpose of survival among their Spanish oppressors. Many continued speaking their native languages at home and in private (Champagne, 1994).

Settlers from the United States arrived in New Mexico in the mid-nineteenth century, bringing with them a new set of customs and the English language. The linguistic imperialism of the English-speaking Americans, who took over the region following war with Mexico in the 1840s, soon dominated public life in New Mexico. Thus, the Indigenous peoples of the areas who had been required by Spanish oppressors to give up their native languages and learn Spanish were now being forced by English-speaking oppressors to give up Spanish and learn English. For those people, linguistic imperialism in the United States had served to oppress them not once, but twice.

However, for many of the Indigenous residents and early Mexicano/Hispano settlers, the languages and cultures became shared entities with an effort made to preserve distinctly unique lifestyles. Speaking for his fellow writers from the region, Anaya (1987) believes that,

> We must pass on to the present generation a serious concern about learning to speak the native languages of the state. Traditions rest within the language. At the same time we are compelled to learn English, not only to survive but to reach wider audiences with our writings. Language is a tool we learn to utilize. We learn to use it to reflect on life, and that reflection becomes our history. (viii)

While developing their own personal voice and style, writers from the region like Rudolfo Anaya have reflected and articulated the blending of cultures—Indigenous, Spanish, and English. An increasing number of writers have found their primary voice in their first language (Spanish or an Indigenous language) and write with portions of their works in their primary language or with bilingual publications, side-by-side stories with the English on one page and the primary language on the facing page. Anaya (1987) says, "Crucial to the development of our destiny and the definition of that destiny, are the voices of the writers and poets, for it is their reflection on the existential questions of our life and destiny that helps define and light the way" (viii).

## Language and the BIA Boarding Schools

Historically, the United States has attempted to suppress Indigenous languages and traditions as a form of cultural genocide. The Indian Peace Commission of 1868 advised the Bureau of Indian Affairs (BIA) to "blot out barbarous dialects" and enforce the learning and use of English in order to "civilize the Indians." James Crawford says, "Coercive assimilation was seen as a less expensive and more humane alternative to military action. Boarding schools were set up for that purpose in 1879" (Cantoni, 1997, 54). Lt. Richard Pratt was the architect of the BIA boarding school system. He believed that by deculturizing Indian children and enforcing an English-only policy he could produce a generation of young Natives who would return to their reservations and convert their tribes to the "civilized" norms of Anglo society (Cantoni, 1997; Spring, 2001).

> *These English-only boarding schools became the most effective means of eradicating Indigenous languages and replacing them with English.*

The BIA boarding schools, which flourished from 1875 to 1928, were designed by the U.S. government to restructure the Indians' minds and personalities. Their stated purpose was to make white people out of Indian children. "From the policy-makers' point of view, the civilization process required a twofold assault on Indian children's identification with tribal life, that is to say their savage ways. On the other hand, the children needed to be instructed in the ideas, values, and behaviors of white civilization" (Adams, 1995, 100).

Children as young as four years of age were forcibly removed from their families and taken many miles away from all that was familiar. As soon as they arrived at the schools, their hair was cut off and they were scrubbed with lye soap and scrub brushes and doused in kerosene to delouse them (usually unnecessary and generally done in a vicious and abusive manner). They were forced to wear unfamiliar and uncomfortable clothing, to eat unfamiliar and non-nutritious food, which was frequently in short supply, to sleep in beds and sit in chairs, which were unfamiliar and uncomfortable (Adams, 1995). All of the government boarding schools had strict policies forbidding students to speak their native languages. Those who broke the rules were subjected to harsh punishments such as having one's mouth washed out with lye soap, being locked in the school jail, and being beaten or hit with rulers (Child, 1995). A woman who attended a boarding school in Oklahoma recalls, "Students who spoke Kiowa were made to brush their teeth with harsh lye soap. The kids would end up with the whole inside of their mouth raw" (Adams, 1995, 123).

The policymakers' first priority for the BIA schools was to provide American Indian children with a rudimentary academic education. The ability to speak, read, and write in English was central to the academic enculturation of the Indian. American Indians were correct in their assumption that the white man's "talking paper" was one of his strongest weapons. However, the language program was an English-only program. Adams (1995) quotes the superintendent of Indian Schools, who in 1887 made the observation "[an Indian's] inability to speak another language other than his own renders his companionship with civilized man impossible" (21). Adams further quotes Commissioner of Indian Affairs John D. C. Atkins, who in 1887 said, "This language, which is good enough for a white man and a black man, ought to be good enough for the red man" (21). These English-only boarding schools thus became the most effective means of eradicating Indigenous languages and replacing them with English.

## The English-Only Movement Today

Throughout the history of U.S. educational policies, linguistic diversity has been interpreted as a barrier to learning. According to Nieto (2000), losing one's native language has always been viewed as a required price to pay for citizenship in this country. Classroom strategies for non-English speakers have revolved around the eradication of the native language. Entire communities have been denied the right to use their native languages for social communication as well as for instruction in schools. Enslaved Africans and oppressed Native Americans are the oldest examples of linguistically oppressed Americans.

The English-Only movement in the United States emerged in the early twentieth century as an insidious form of racism disguised as patriotism. Nobody argues the fact that it is necessary to learn English in order to survive financially and socially in the general culture of the United States. Students whose first language is not English have two goals in school: learning English and mastering content. It should never be considered necessary to lose one's first language, however, in order to speak another language. Consider the contradiction in educational planning that deems it desirable for English speakers to learn a second language in order to succeed in college and in the global economy while at the same time proclaiming it desirable for speakers of languages other than English to unlearn their native languages in order to be more proficient in English. All too often these students, labeled with the negative term "limited English proficient," are in self-contained ESL rooms with no social contacts beyond their ESL peers or, worse yet, are put in special education classes because they cannot pass tests given in a language they don't speak and about a culture that is not familiar to them. Referring to these students as English Language Learners, honoring their original languages, and teaching in a culturally responsive manner could make an enormous difference in the success these students have in our schools.

The need for ESL and bilingual classes is often considered to be a part of the "immigrant problem." Too often school districts in the Southwest ignore the existence of Indigenous children who come from a reservation or family that speaks only its tribal language. Spanish-speaking Chicano children are treated as immigrants even though they were born in this country. Such children are generally treated as outsiders in the public schools. Zehr (2003) cites some recent examples. A high school teacher in Arizona banned the use of Spanish in her classroom because the English-only rule made classroom management easier. An ESL teacher in Colorado stated that "permitting students to use their own languages in class led to suspicion and division" (18). A cosmetology teacher in Arizona prohibited five of her Chicano students from speaking Spanish among themselves because she could not understand Spanish.

Gloria Anzaldúa (1987) speaks of the borderlands within our country that often lead to conflict and subjugation—in this case the subjugation of language:

> Borderlands are physically present wherever two or more cultures edge each other, where people of different races occupy the same territory where under, lower, middle, and upper classes touch, where the space between two individuals shrinks with intimacy. (58)

The Pascua Yaqui Tribe is a prime example of the difficulties that are encountered by those living in the borderlands of U.S. society. They are a tribe made up of Spanish/English/Indigenous tribes who live in two countries and speak three languages. The first European contact the Yaqui Tribe had was with Jesuit missionaries from Spain. In the beginning, the Yaquis remained fairly isolated from the Spanish. However, with the passage of time, contact increased and, with contact between the two cultures, linguistic changes occurred. Spanish words became part of the Yaqui language as well as some Spanish grammatical structures. By 1887, the Yaquis began migrating to the United States. Most of the Yaquis were literate and spoke several languages, even though they had little formal education. In the United States they were refugees with no legal status, inadequate food and shelter, no land, and they faced the suppression of their culture and religion.

*Despite their rich linguistic heritage and skills, Yaqui students are marginalized as deficient learners in a school system that bases its learning on a context of mutual intelligibility and shared cultural meanings as defined by the dominant culture.*

Today the Yaquis are the poorest population of Arizona, which can be attributed to their low level of formal education. Approximately two-thirds of the tribe have completed eighth grade; only about one-fifth are high school graduates. Sixty percent unemployment is not unusual in their community.

Linguistically, most Yaquis are trilingual. Spanish is the dominant language of the home, generally spoken about 70 percent of the time. The Indigenous Yaqui tongue is spoken in the home approximately 20 percent of the time, with the remaining 10 percent English. Most Yaquis over the age of 50 speak their Indigenous tongue. Most also speak a regional Spanish dialect.

Like most American Indians and Chicanos, Yaquis have been negatively impacted by the "hidden curriculum" in the schools, with its deficit model of all but white middle- and upper-class cultures. There is an enormous lack of continuity between home and school. Despite their rich linguistic heritage and skills, Yaqui students are marginalized as deficient learners in a school system that bases its learning on a context of mutual intelligibility and shared cultural meanings as defined by the dominant culture. For many years there was no bilingual education and no provision for bilingual or culturally relevant assessment. Sixty-seven percent of Special Education classes are made up of Yaqui and Mexican-American children who are speakers of first languages other than English (otherwise labeled as "limited English proficient" students).

In 1993, Project Kaateme was established. Project Kaateme is an educational program incorporating parents as tutors to emphasize the strength of the Yaqui family and to minimize the disjuncture between school and home. Educational activities are provided in tribal facilities on the reservation based on traditional Yaqui culture, language, and spirituality. The goal of the program is to increase the learning outcomes of Yaqui children and to increase employment opportunities and raise the literacy rate for Yaqui adults (Reyhner, 1997).

Project Kaateme is one outcome of the 1984 Pascua Yaqui Tribe Language Policy, which says,

> The Yaqui language is a gift from Itom Achai, the Creator, to our people and, therefore, shall be treated with respect. Our ancient language is the foundation of our cultural and spiritual heritage without which we could not exist in the manner our Creator intended. We further declare that all aspects of the educational process shall reflect the beauty of our Yaqui language, culture, and values. (Reyhner, 1997, 15)

Anzaldúa (1987) believes that language is internalized and beliefs about one's language are also internalized as part of an image of oneself. She says, "Chicanas who grew up speaking Chicano Spanish have internalized the belief that we speak poor Spanish" (58); their English is also rejected by Anglos as poor English. These Chicanes live in the cultural borderland between their Mexican ancestral homeland and their adopted United States home. Their language, according to Anzaldúa, is seen as "illegitimate, a bastard language." Anzaldúa writes,

> Deslenguadas. Somos los del español deficiente. We are your linguistic nightmare, your linguistic aberration, your linguistic mestizaje, the subject of your burla. Because we speak with tongues of fire we are culturally crucified. Racially, culturally, and linguistically, somos huérfanos—we speak an orphan tongue....We internalize how our language has been used against us by the dominant culture, we use our language differences against each other....Repeated attacks on our native tongue diminish our sense of self. The attacks continue throughout our lives....So, if you want to really hurt me, talk badly about my language. Ethnic identity is twin skin to linguistic identity—I am my language....I will no longer be made to feel ashamed of existing. I will have my voice: Indian, Spanish, White. (58-59)

Language is a tightly interwoven facet of all aspects of a person's being. A person's first language defines who that person is, from what culture that person comes, and the mental and spiritual framework that person uses to perceive the world in which he/she lives. When a person loses his/her first or primary language he/she loses a part of him/herself. When a person is degraded because of his/her first language, it is a degradation of the whole person.

Bilingual education is not a new concept in the United States. According to Nieto (2000), by 1900 approximately four percent of America's public and parochial school students (at least 600,000 children) were taught in bilingual programs. These programs included bilingual German/English, Polish, Italian, Norwegian, Spanish, French, Czech, and Dutch.

*A person's first language defines who that person is, from what culture that person is, from what culture that person comes, and the mental and spiritual framework that person uses to perceive the world in which he/she lives. When a person loses his/her first primary language he/she loses a part of him/herself. When a person is degraded because of his/her first language, it is a degradation of the whole person.*

Bilingual education and ESL are issues often hotly debated in today's American educational circles. While no one denies the need for people in the United States to speak English in order to succeed as members of the general society, there are varied opinions on the role of the schools in promoting English for those students with a first language other than English. Bilingual education can be done in a variety of ways, but basically, it works best in a setting where there are only two languages represented. Most common in this country are the English/Spanish bilingual programs found in areas heavily populated by Hispanic peoples. ESL programs are formulated and tailored to fit specific school situations, especially where several different languages are represented.

*Immersion ESL* instruction generally involves the tailoring of lessons to simple understandable English in the regular classroom and/or ESL classes (self-contained or pull-out) that provide English instruction in English at the level of the student's understanding. *Transitional bilingual* programs are intensive English instruction in the students' primary language. *Maintenance or developmental bilingual* programs are aimed at preserving and building on the students' primary language skills as they acquire English as a second language. *American Indian bilingual education* programs may follow one of the general program types previously mentioned or may be a program designed to teach American Indian children the language of their people, thus preserving their linguistic and cultural heritage. For example, the Kickapoo Nations School and the Royal Valley Pottawatomie programs in Kansas fit into the latter category. The Kickapoo Nations School requires all students through sixth grade to study the Kickapoo language, after which it becomes an elective. The Royal Valley Schools simply offer weekly or biweekly elective Pottawatomie language classes to elementary students.

Like English instruction in the notorious BIA boarding schools, the English-only "sink-or-swim" method encouraged in some places today is a system designed by the dominant white power structure to maintain its dominance and power and "keep non-English speakers in their places." Its outcomes with non-English-speaking classes include failing test scores, high dropout rates, poor chances of employment, and a soaring rate of gang violence and juvenile crime.

Typically, non-English speakers are perceived in this country to be immigrants. Many believe that it is impossible to be American-born and non-English-speaking. The large body of bilingual and ESL literature generally excludes the languages of American Indians and fails to touch on the difficulties faced by U.S.-born children from non-English-speaking families who are cast into our public education system and expected to conform. Perhaps this exclusion is an erroneous and unconscious belief that the BIA schools successfully "cured the Indian problem" by eradicating Indigenous languages. Additionally, Mexican Americans are generally not perceived as American Indians, even though they too are descendents of, or members of, Indigenous tribes and even though a large piece of the United States is part of the country only because of theft.

An additional problem with the majority of bilingual and ESL programs is that they do not seek to strengthen, preserve, and honor the child's Indigenous language while teaching him/her English. A holistic view of education takes into account the importance of the interconnectedness of all of life. It is not necessary or desirable to eradicate one language in order to learn another. It should not be a requirement to blot out one's Indigenous culture in order to be a successful part of U.S. mainstream culture.

## Conclusion

It is estimated that at least 320 million people in the United States speak English as their first language. In addition, English is a common language used for trade, research, and international business. Kansy (1997) believes that a conservative estimate of all English speakers would be at least 1.5 billion people worldwide. Bangladesh, India, Pakistan, and Nigeria, like the United States, are former territories of the British Empire. Only the United States has a policy of English-only. People from the other countries are at least bilingual, and many are multilingual. Japan, Russia, Brazil, and China make great efforts to provide English as a Second Language in their educational facilities to prepare students for participation in the global economy. The United States differs from all of these other countries in its federal language policy. The public education system provides neither mandatory foreign language classes nor bilingual education for all students. In the United States, bilingual education has been provided for the elite, usually in expensive private schools, as a desirable course of study. On the other hand, bilingual education has become a "problem" when underrepresented groups fought for their rights. Freedom of speech is one of the basic pillars of American freedom. It is, therefore, strange that the American public does not recognize language choice as a part of the privilege of freedom of speech (Kansy, 1997).

The need for bilingual education and ESL classes in U.S. schools is steadily increasing. Linguistic minorities and non-English-speaking communities have come to the forefront since the passage of the Title VII Bilingual Education Act (1968) and the U.S. Supreme Court decision in *Lau v. Nichols* (1974). Banks and Banks (2001) identify varying groups of students who are linguistic minorities: foreign-born students who speak only the language of their home country—some of whom are voluntary immigrants and some of whom are immigrants who have been uprooted involuntarily from their home countries (such as the Hmong immigrants); U.S.-born language minority students, such as Native Americans students and Chicanos; and groups such as the French, German, Swedish, and Spanish students whose families have maintained their original languages even after several generations of U.S. residency. These students cross a broad spectrum of language skills and knowledge, ranging from the non-English speaker to the fully bilingual student to the English-speaking student with rudimentary skills in the original language.

A starting point for teachers of American Indian students is to view bilingualism, bidialectualism, and biculturalism as strengths. Instead of viewing education as having to choose between assimilation and pluralism, students would be better served by a system that regarded U.S. society as a linguistically and culturally dynamic and complex organism. Banks and Banks (2001) argue that "it cannot be acceptable to blame the student's genetic, environmental, cultural, or linguistic background for his or her lack of academic success in the English-dominated classroom....A good place to start in designing quality programs for language-minority students is by examining effective teaching and learning classroom climates for students in general, taking into account the important school reform movements currently evolving" (281).

Using the child's first language does not impede the acquisition of English; rather, it offers many advantages (August & Hakuta, 1997). According to Banks and Banks (2001), most linguistic research shows that the suppressing of home languages is detrimental to both the social and the academic well-being of students. Research done over the course of the last 50 years does not show positive correlations between attempts to eradicate non-English languages with academic achievement gains of language-minority students (Banks & Banks, 2001). Research suggests that children who are bilingual have advantages over monolinguals of the same socioe-conomic background in their linguistic, cognitive, and social development (Taylor & Whittaker, 2003). Teachers of American Indian students must recognize that there are phonological, morphological, and syntactical differences among all tribal dialects. Respecting these complex languages and making efforts to teach them, with the active collaboration on the tribal community, will go a long way to ensure the academic success of American Indian students.

## References

Adams, D. W. (1995). *Education for extinction: American Indians and the boarding school experience, 1875-1928.* Lawrence: University Press of Kansas.

Anaya, R. A. (1987). *An anthology of Nuevo Mexicano writers.* Albuquerque: University of New Mexico Press.

Anzaldúa, G. (1987). *Borderlands: La frontera.* San Francisco: Aunt Lute Books.

August, D., & Hakuta, K. (1997). *Improving schooling for language minority children: A research agenda.* Washington, D.C.: National Academy Press.

Banks, J. A., & Banks, C. A. M. (Eds.). (2001). *Multicultural education: Issues and perspectives.* New York: Wiley.

Calloway, C. G. (1997). *New worlds for all: Indians, Europeans, and the remaking of early America.* Baltimore: John Hopkins University Press.

Cantoni, G. (Ed.). (1997). *Stabilizing Indigenous languages.* Flagstaff: Northern Arizona University.

Champagne, D. (Ed.). (1994). *Reference library of Native North America.* Detroit, Mich.: Gale.

Child, R. V. (1995). *Boarding school seasons.* Lincoln: University of Nebraska Press.

Cohen, W. B. (1980). *The French encounter with Africans.* Bloomington: Indiana University Press.

Guthrie, R. V. (1998). *Even the rat was white: A historical view of psychology.* Boston: Allyn and Bacon.

Kansy, H. (1997). English-only: Wouldn't it be lonely? *Cultural Circles* 1: 49–75.

Nieto, S. (2000). *Affirming diversity: The sociopolitical context of multicultural education.* New York: Addison-Wesley Longman.

Reyhner, J. (1997). *Teaching Indigenous languages.* Flagstaff: Northern Arizona University.

Spring, J. (2001). *Deculturalization and the struggle for equality: A brief history of the education of dominated cultures in the United States* (3rd ed.). New York: McGraw Hill.

Taylor, L. S., & Whittaker, C. R. (2003). Issues of culture and language. In L. Taylor & C. Whittaker (Eds.)., *Bridging multiple worlds: Case studies of diverse educational communities* (pp.124–155). New York: Allyn and Bacon.

Wardle, F., & Cruz-Janzen, M. I. (2003). *Meeting the needs of multiethnic and multiracial children in schools.* Boston: Pearson.

Zehr, M. A. (2003). Classroom ban on Spanish protested. *Education week.* XXIII(9): 1 & 18.

*Margery Ridgeway* is a doctoral student in the Department of Teaching and Leadership at the University of Kansas. She is also a teacher of English and Spanish at Bert Nash, the campus school for the Atchison Juvenile Correctional Facility, Atchison, Kansas.

*Cornel Pewewardy* is an associate professor of education at the University of Kansas and a member of the Education Advisory Committee of Multicultural Review. He is a former principal of the American Indian Magnet School in St. Paul, Minnesota.

# UNIT 7
# For Vision and Voice: A Call to Conscience

## Unit Selections

## Key Points to Consider

- What would be possible if schools permitted teachers more autonomy in how they assess their students?

- What can teachers do to help students develop a sense of social consciousness and social responsibility?

- How can teachers help students to develop their talents and to develop a vision of hope for themselves? How can teachers help students to develop a sense of public service?

- What are the most important challenges confronting multicultural educators in the new century?

## Student Website
www.mhcls.com/online

## Internet References
Further information regarding these websites may be found in this book's preface or online.

**Classroom Connect**
   *http://www.classroom.net*
**EdWeb/Andy Carvin**
   *http://edwebproject.org*
**Online Internet Institute**
   *http://www.oii.org*

**W**e are situated as people in the context of a social matrix of many dimensions, including social class, gender identity, culture, race, age, ideological position, life experiences, and beliefs. We have a special obligation to encourage our students to create the best visions for their lives that they can imagine and to help them lift up their voices and their spirits in the pursuit of their dreams. We must do this for all students, not just the marginalized. No child or teenager should have to feel unwanted or hopeless. As matters of social conscience and moral principle, we must recognize and affirm our duty as teachers to make the best effort possible to teach our students well.

We look forward to a future of multicultural education with a degree of optimism, although aware that there are serious challenges before us. The winds of xenophobia are blowing across the land again; concern regarding immigration is at a fairly high level. Yet this concern was present in all earlier decades in American history when rates of immigration were running at as high of levels as they are now. We all agree that there is much work to be done to accomplish the goals of multicultural education. There is, however, great hope that these goals will be achieved as our population moves steadily toward becoming ever more unique as a multicultural civilization. We are going to become less and less like Western Europe and more and more a very unique national wonder such as the world has not seen before. The next 30 to 40 years will bring that vision into reality.

We need a vision for the future of our schools that includes a belief in the worth and dignity of all people. We need to clarify our vision in such a way that it has a holistic character, which takes into account the ever more culturally pluralistic social reality that we are becoming. As part of this effort we need to consider the French revolutionary concept of fraternity. Fraternity and its female counterpart, sorority, refer to brotherhood and sisterhood. We need a new birth of fraternity and sorority in our national life that will enable us to truly care about what happens to one another. We need very much to communicate that sense of caring

to the young people who attend our schools, for they truly are our social future. The teaching profession needs a good dose of fraternity and sorority as well. Teachers need to work together in solving problems and supporting their respective professional efforts on behalf of students.

The future of teaching and learning from a multicultural perspective should include more emphasis on cooperative learning strategies that encourage students to develop a sense of community and fraternity that will transcend competition with one another and create a sense of trust and caring among them. We need to stop making students compete with one another and encourage them to work together. We need to learn to team together and teach together more than we have in the past, and we need to have the professional autonomy (independence of professional judgment) to be able to do so at our own discretion and not because someone told us to do so.

There needs to be more democratization of the day-to-day governance structures of schools so that competent teachers can enjoy the same levels of personal, professional autonomy that their colleagues in teacher education enjoy. A multicultural vision of the future of education will embrace the concept that the strengths and talents of all students need optimum development.

The problems and weaknesses of all students need resolution and assistance. We need to see young people as a treasured human resource whose needs for safety, health, and cognitive and affective development are to be met by our best efforts as educators. A multicultural vision of our educational future will include an acceptance by educators of an expanded conception of their responsibility to their students to include a commitment to each student's best possible development as a person; we will see our clients whole. We will be concerned about more than their intellectual development, although this is our primary role; we will also see schooling as having a therapeutic mission. Diverse cultural backgrounds and learning styles will be accepted and nurtured as brothers and sisters in a shared national community of educational interests.

Finally, a multicultural vision of the future of education will include a strong commitment to develop a powerful, critical sense of social consciousness and social responsibility between teachers and students. Students will be encouraged and assisted to define and to reconstruct their personal worlds so that they are empowered to see the world as it is and to make it better if they can. Educational settings of society are important terrain in the struggle to reconstruct public life along more egalitarian social policy lines. A multicultural vision of our educational future will encourage teachers to adopt a pedagogy of liberation that champions the development of critical social awareness among students and which empowers them to evaluate critically all that they may experience. Education will have a liberating intent; the goal will not be just to teach children to reason critically, but to reason critically in the light of a clear vision of social justice worthy of all of their rights as citizens. The struggle to see a multicultural vision for our schools adopted by the teaching profession has always been closely aligned with the broader struggle for civil liberties and human dignity.

# Language Learning:
# A Worldwide Perspective

*The United States has a lot to learn from other countries about how to teach foreign languages.*

**Donna Christian, Ingrid U. Pufahl, and Nancy C. Rhodes**

In June 2004, the U.S. Department of Defense convened the National Language Conference to discuss approaches to meeting the nation's language needs in the 21st century and to identify actions that could move the United States toward becoming a language-competent nation. Participants from the government, the military, the education field, and the private sector assessed the country's needs and issued a call to action to improve its language capacity. U.S. Representative Rush Holt, a keynote speaker, maintained that the United States is in a "'Sputnik moment" and needs a national commitment to languages that is

> on a scale of the National Defense Education Act commitment to science, including improved curriculum, teaching technology and methods, teacher development, and a systemic cultural commitment. (U.S. Department of Defense. 2004)

This is one of many calls for major changes in the U.S. approach to teaching foreign languages. During the two decades preceding the National Language Conference, numerous reports and articles decried the mediocrity of our students' foreign language skills and called for improved language education (National Standards in Foreign Language Education Project, 1999). In a 2003 report, the National Association of State Boards of Education (NASBE) noted the marginalizations of arts and foreign language instruction and asserted that both are at risk of being eliminated as part of the public schools' core curriculum.

The United States has not kept up with the rest of the world in providing quality foreign language instruction in its schools. How can we give our students the opportunity to develop proficiency in more than one language so that they and the broader society may benefit from expanded language competence?

## Successful International Models

The practices and policies of other countries can serve as guidance. Knowledge of multiple languages is much more common and expected in countries outside the United States. One study (Pufahl, Rhodes, & Christian, 2000) collected information from educators in 19 countries: Australia, Austria, Brazil, Canada, Chile, the Czech Republic, Denmark, Finland, Germany, Israel, Italy, Kazakhstan, Luxembourg, Morocco, the Netherlands, New Zealand, Peru, Spain, and Thailand,[1] More recent developments within Canada and the expanding European Union also provide models to consider.

Successful foreign language programs have several common strands.

> **How can we give our students the opportunity to develop proficiency in more than one language so that they and the broader society may benefit?**

### An Early Start

Most of the 19 countries in the survey begin compulsory language instruction for the majority of students in the elementary grades, whereas schools in the United States typically do not offer foreign language classes until middle school or high school.

Consider Luxembourg, for example, a multilingual country in which proficiency is expected in at least three languages. Children who do not speak Luxembourgish learn the language in compulsory preschool. All students study German beginning in 1st grade. In 2nd grade, students begin spoken French; in 3rd grade, written French is added to the curriculum. In most cases, both oral and written German and French are formally taught in grades 3-6, with Luxembourgish remaining a vehicle for communication and interaction. These 7- to 12-year-olds receive one hour of instruction each week in oral Luxembourgish and an average of six to eight hours of instruction each week in German and French.

## A Coherent Framework

A well-articulated curriculum and assessment framework builds coherently from one grade level to the next, from elementary school to middle school to high school to postsecondary levels. It is also standards-based and proficiency oriented. Such a framework indicates when students should start a foreign language, how much instruction they will receive, and what levels of proficiency they should attain. The framework should also be transparent, in the sense that both educators and students should clearly understand what the levels of proficiency mean.

Most European countries have already adapted their foreign language learning and teaching at the national level to the overall frameworks and standards defined by the Council of Europe's language policy. Europe has clarified what proficiency means for at least 18 languages. This promotes consistency and coherence in language education by coordinating efforts in the various stages of education—from elementary to secondary to postsecondary—and in such sectors as public schools, private language instruction, and technical training (Nuffield Languages Inquiry, 2000). The Council's clear standards carry over into the workplace as well: Employers know what they can expect from a graduate who has achieved a certain proficiency level in a given language.

In Australia, the Australian Language Levels Project (Scarino, Vale, McKay, & Clark, 1988) influenced major national curriculum development, particularly in Chinese, Indonesian, Korean, and Japanese. It subsequently provided a framework for collaborative syllabus development and a common exit assessment from senior secondary schooling.

## Strong Leadership

Leadership can come from any direction. Grassroots leadership—arising from parents and the community often stimulates the creation of a program and can play a role in expanding and ensuring quality. Fostering strong language education programs, however, requires a solid partnership among local, state, and federal leaders because each group plays an important role in setting policy and providing funding for education.

Such leadership and collaboration might look like this: With national model standards in mind, federal funding would provide incentives for establishing and improving language programs. States would align with federal priorities by including languages in their core K-12 curriculums and providing appropriate assessments, state standards for languages, guidelines for strong professional development related to language instruction, and adequate funding. Local school districts would implement programs that follow state guidelines and support programs and teachers. Superintendents would set priorities and make funding decisions in conjunction with local school boards.

Israel has this kind of strong and coherent language education program. A new language policy, introduced in 1996 and termed "three plus" (Spolsky & Shohamy, 1999), requires the study of three compulsory languages—Hebrew, English, and Arabic—in addition to heritage, community, or other world languages.

## Language as a Core Subject

Arguably one of the most influential policy decisions that countries make with respect to foreign language learning is the status of foreign languages within the school curriculum. In the 19 countries studied, 15 required at least one foreign language. Frequently, foreign languages in these countries claim the same status as mathematics, reading, and writing, and are required for school exit examinations and university entrance.

## Teacher Education

As in all areas of education, well-trained teaching professionals are important contributors to excellence in language education. In some countries, such as Finland, university-based teacher education programs are highly selective, drawing teachers from a pool of the best high school graduates. Other countries, like Morocco, report that their language teachers are some of the best-trained teachers in the country. Becoming a secondary school English teacher, for example, involves obtaining a four-year degree in English from a university or teacher training college, with one year of specialization in either literature or linguistics. Students then spend a year studying language teaching methodology and getting practical training at the Faculty of Education. The majority of English teachers in universities and teacher training colleges in Morocco hold doctoral or masters degrees from British or U.S. universities. In addition to preservice preparation, inservice development for language teachers is considered one of the keys to success.

In several of the countries studied, teacher participation rates in professional development courses, seminars, and conferences are high. Many countries have an elaborate system of inservice professional development in place, with training widely available and, to some degree, required. Teachers are encouraged to attend courses and workshops, study abroad, and participate in collaborative learning—in study groups, for example—at the local school level.

**One of the most influential policy decisions that countries make with respect to foreign language learning is the status of foreign languages within the school curriculum.**

In Germany, all states have systems in place that enable teachers to choose from a variety of courses offered at regional or state education centers. Each year, teachers are eligible for one week of inservice training, which the state pays for. At present, there is some discussion about making inservice training mandatory. In the Czech Republic, foreign language teachers are increasingly taking the opportunity to study abroad or attend international courses in countries with excellent reputations for foreign language teaching, such as the Scandinavian countries and the Netherlands.

### Promoting Proficiency

Learning content matter through the medium of a nonnative language has become increasingly popular in many of the countries studied. Such instruction frequently occurs at the secondary school level, once students have acquired sufficient proficiency in the language. In Finland, for example, a substantial amount of content-area instruction takes place in English. A 1996 survey showed that 5 percent of elementary schools, 15 percent of middle schools, and 25 percent of high schools used this approach in some form.

In European immersion programs or bilingual programs, students—typically those in primary school—receive subject-matter instruction exclusively, or in large part, in a second language. In Canada, immersion education is a successful and widely researched practice that mainly targets the English speaking majority learning French (Turnbull & Lapkin, 1999). The United States practices immersion education to some degree, and there has been a recent upswing in the number of two way immersion programs, in which native speakers of two different languages (most often Spanish and English) receive instruction in both languages in the classroom.

### Technology

Many of the countries surveyed are using technology to increase interaction with native speakers and improve classroom instruction. The Internet is increasingly becoming the technology of choice, with students accessing authentic materials—texts and audio/video files—in the language of study and interacting with native speakers in online chat rooms. Video-based language programs are also increasingly available. These tools can improve classroom instruction by providing access to authentic uses of the target language, increasing students' motivation to use the language, reducing students' anxiety about their performance in the language, and providing individual students with more practice in using the language than a traditional classroom setting might allow. In fact, research suggests that students produce more language—and higher quality language—in computer-mediated contacts than in face-to-face interactions in the classroom (Leloup & Ponterio, 2003). This is another area that the United States can pursue to improve language skills outcomes.

### Heritage Languages

Most countries have linguistically diverse populations with communities that speak a variety of languages. A number of respondents in the study described programs that aim to develop the mother tongue skills of members of those communities. Such programs conserve the language resources of a country and foster language achievement among minority populations.

For example, subsequent to passage of the Canadian Multiculturalism Act (1990), a number of provinces declared multiculturalism policies and established heritage language programs in their official school curriculums (Canadian Education Association, 1991; Cummins, 1991). These heritage languages include both immigrant languages—such as Cantonese, Mandarin, Portuguese, and Ukrainian—and indigenous languages, such as Inuktitut, Cree, and Mohawk. Several Canadian provinces have developed First Nations language maintenance programs to promote specific indigenous languages.

New Zealand has established *language nests* for Maori, an official language with few native speakers, and for some Pacific Island languages. Beginning at the preschool level, children are immersed in the language; later they may choose bilingual classes or special schools in which Maori is the language of instruction.

The United States has a great diversity of languages spoken within its borders. In fact, the 2000 U.S. Census documented the current use of more than 300 languages. U.S. educators can take advantage of the cultural richness of the many immigrant and indigenous communities within the United States by promoting the learning of the heritage languages spoken in these communities. One promising approach is two-way immersion, which supports continued growth in native language skills among heritage language speakers.

## As Europe Sees It

In 2003, the Commission of the European Communities approved the 2004-2006 action plan, *Promoting Language Learning and Linguistic Diversity*. To further the goals of the European Union, the commission asserted that "the ability to understand and communicate in other languages is a basic skill for all European citizens" (Commission of the European Communities, 2003). The action plan moves that agenda forward. Among its policies and recommendations, it calls for learning "the mother tongue plus two other languages" in primary schools and carrying that study into secondary education, postsecondary education, and beyond through classroom instruction, technology-based activities, and study abroad.

## In many countries, at least one foreign language is compulsory for all students.

The plan also focuses on improving professional development by providing teachers with greater access to travel abroad; facilitating effective teacher networks at the regional, national, and European levels; and commissioning research in language pedagogy and disseminating new findings. The plan encourages specific e-learning opportunities, such as *e-twinning*, a program in which schools from different European countries pair up to increase language learning and intercultural dialogue among students.

The plan calls for building a language friendly environment by supporting linguistic diversity and encouraging the learning of regional, minority, and migrant languages, with specific activities, such as conferences, designed to implement these objectives. European countries have always been more attuned to the importance of language skills than the United States has been, but the coming together of the members of the European Union around such principles promises to take Europe giant leaps ahead.

## A Canadian Perspective

Like the European Union, Canada has embraced language learning more enthusiastically than the United States has. In a recent policy initiative, the country rededicated itself to its goal of making its two official languages—English and French—available to all Canadians. In 2003, Canada released a five-year action plan for education, community development, and public service within a new accountability framework to promote the use of both official languages (Government of Canada, 2003). A notable objective for the education plan is to ensure that by 2013 half of all secondary school graduates are bilingual in English and French—roughly double the current number of bilingual graduates.

The Canadian government has pledged new and increased funding for programs to help schools and communities achieve these goals, committing more than $700 million to the five-year plan. This national initiative works in conjunction with an ongoing commitment to support the full array of heritage languages spoken across the country.

## What's Ahead

U.S. schools and policymakers have a lot to learn from the way other countries support foreign language education. Learning languages has not been an education priority in this country in recent years. A case in point relates to assessment. A promising development in the late 1990s was including foreign language as a new subject area in the National Assessment of Educational Progress (NAEP). Yet although development of the language assessment was well on its way, the first administration of the test to 12th graders was postponed. Decisions like this underscore the fact that we have marginalized languages in the curriculum.

The American Council on the Teaching of Foreign Languages is working with colleagues around the country to celebrate 2005 as the Year of Languages in the United States (see www.yearoflanguages.org). Perhaps this initiative will raise interest in foreign language learning in communities, schools, and government agencies. We hope it will serve as the impetus for implementing some of the lessons that we have learned from other countries about foreign language education.

1. For a comprehensive report on the study, including a summary of other comparative language education studies, see www.cal.org/resources/countries.html.

## References

Canadian Education Association. (1991). *Heritage language programs in Canadian school boards.* Toronto, Canada: Canadian Education Association.

Commission of the European Communities. (2003). *Promoting language learning and linguistic diversity: An action plan 2004-2006.* Brussels, Belgium. Available: http://europa.eu .int/comm/education/doc/official /keydoc/actlang/ act_lang_en.pdf

Cummins, J. (Ed.). (1991). Heritage languages. Special issue of *Canadian Modern Language Review, 47.*

Government of Canada. (2003). *The next act: New momentum for Canada's linguistic duality.* Ottawa, Canada: Privy Council Office, Government of Canada. Available: www.pco-bcp.gc.ca/aia/default.asp?Language=E&Page=ActionPlan

Leloup, J., & Ponterio, R. (2003). Second language acquisition and technology: A review of the research: *ERIC Digest.* Available: www.cal.org/resources /digest/ 0311leloup.html

National Association of State Boards of Education. (2003). *The complete curriculum: Ensuring a place for the arts and foreign languages in America's schools.* Alexandria, VA: Author.

National Standards in Foreign Language Education Project. (1999). *Standards for foreign language learning in the 21st century.* Lawrence, KS: Author.

Nuffield Languages Inquiry. (2000). *Languages: The next generation.* London: The Nuffield Foundation.

Pufahl, I., Rhodes, N., & Christian, D. (2000, December). *Foreign language teaching: What the United States can learn from other countries.* Washington, DC: Center for Applied Linguistics.

Scarino, A., Vale, D., McKay, P., & Clark, J. (1988). *The Australian language levels guidelines.* Melbourne, Australia: Canberra Curriculum Development Centre.

Spolsky, B., & Shohamy, E. (1999). *Languages of Israel: Policy, ideology and practice.* Clevedon, UK: Multilingual Matters.

Turnbull, M., & Lapkin, S. (Eds.). (1999). New research in FSL. Special issue of *Canadian Modern Language Review, 56,* 1.

U.S. Department of Defense. (2004, June 29). *National language conference results announced (News Release No. 621-04).* Available: www.defenselink .mil/releases/2004/nr20040629-0953 .html

***Donna Christian*** *(donna@cal.org) is President of the Center for Applied Linguistics (CAL) in Washington, D.C.* ***Ingrid U. Pufahl*** *(ingrid@cal.org) is a Research Associate and* ***Nancy C. Rhodes*** *(nancy@cal.org) is Director of the Foreign Language Education Division at CAL.*

# MAKING HISTORY

'Separate but equal' was the law of the land, until one decision brought it crashing down

BY JUSTIN EWERS

**B**rown v. Board of Education is remembered as a case of simple justice. In the fall of 1950, the story goes, Linda Brown, a 7-year-old girl living in Topeka, Kan., had to travel 21 blocks each day, by foot and by bus, to get to her all-black elementary school. Yet only seven blocks from her home was another elementary school—a school for whites only. Her father, Oliver Brown, asked that she be allowed to enroll there instead. When the principal refused, Brown sued. Two years later, Linda's long walk ended in the highest court in the land.

The rest, of course, is history. On May 17, 1954, the Supreme Court handed down a unanimous opinion declaring segregated schools unconstitutional, overruling *Plessy v. Ferguson*, an 1896 decision that had cemented the "Jim Crow" notion of "separate but equal" into American law. Twenty-one states' school segregation laws, affecting nearly 12 million black and white children in more than 11,000 school districts, were swept away. "Probably no case ever to come before the nation's highest tribunal affected more directly the minds, hearts, and daily lives of so many Americans," writes historian Richard Kluger in *Simple Justice*, his definitive history of the decision.

But there is more to the case than meets the eye. "The problem with the mythology around *Brown*," says Cheryl Brown Henderson, Oliver Brown's youngest daughter, "is not only that it's oversimplified; a lot of it is just not true." For one thing, she points out, her father was hardly the only plaintiff in the case; in Topeka alone, there were 13 claimants in the suit against the city's Board of Education. By the time *Brown* reached the Supreme Court, the case had been combined with four others, involving nearly 200 plaintiffs from three states and the District of Columbia—all with similar complaints about long commutes or inadequate schools—under the name *Brown v. Board of Education of Topeka*.

**UNCERTAIN.** And as right as it feels today, the case was hardly a sure thing. "The fact that it was a unanimous decision makes it seem like it was easy," says Michael Klarman, author of *From Jim Crow to Civil Rights: the Supreme Court and the*

*Struggle for Racial Equality*, "but it easily could have come out the other way." Indeed, historians say, the decision—and the future of segregation in America—rested on more than the injustice of Linda Brown's unnecessary hike to school, on more than the systemic inequities in public schools at the time, or the eloquent arguments made for inclusion. In the end, *Brown* hinged on the death of the chief justice of the United States—and, ultimately, on the man who replaced him.

It started, though, with a public school system that had failed its public. "Most people don't know how unequal education really was" before *Brown*, says Klarman. Compared with schools in the South, Topeka—which had integrated its secondary schools well before 1954—was a mild case. In Clarendon County, S.C., for example, Joseph De Laine Jr., went to a school with 10 teachers, almost 800 kids, and no indoor plumbing. "Even to us as children at the time, we recognized the fact of the inequity, and of course we were bitter about it, but it happened to be a fact of life," says De Laine, whose father, a pastor, would be instrumental in bringing to court one of the other *Brown* cases, *Briggs v. Elliot*.

De Laine's experience was no exception. The Supreme Court, in 1896, had said "separate" was legal as long as it was "equal." But in the South, equality was a fantasy. In the decades before *Brown*, South Carolina spent 10 times as much on educating every white child as it did on every black child. Florida, Georgia, Mississippi, and Alabama spent five times as much.

**ENLISTED.** World War II would change everything. Nine hundred thousand African-Americans had enlisted to fight in what was still a segregated military. As one black corporal said upon his return: "I spent four years in the Army to free a bunch of Dutchmen and Frenchmen, and I'm hanged if I'm going to let the Alabama version of the Germans kick me around when I get home. No sirree-bob! I went into the Army a n- - - - -; I'm comin' out a man." Membership in the National Association for the Advancement of Colored People swelled from 50,000 in 1940 to 450,000 in 1946.

By 1950, the first cracks in segregation had already appeared. In 1947, California had abolished segregated schools, and Jackie Robinson had broken the color line in baseball. A year later, President Truman desegregated the armed forces. And in 1950, Thurgood Marshall, then a young lawyer working as lead counsel for the NAACP's Legal Defense Fund, won three landmark cases desegregating graduate programs (a relatively easy target since, apart from Howard University in Washington, D.C., and a medical school in Nashville, the South didn't offer black students any graduate education at all).

Marshall, a graduate of Baltimore's segregated schools who would later be the first African-American named to the Supreme Court, decided the time had come to demand more than just separate equality. Congressional or executive action wasn't an option; Capitol Hill was dominated by southerners, for whom civil rights legislation was anathema. Even FDR, when asked in 1935 to support an antilynching bill, had told a black leader, "I just can't take that risk." The fight would have to be waged in the courts. The NAACP board immediately began advising members that lawsuits should be aimed at "obtaining education on a nonsegregated basis and that no relief other than that will be acceptable."

Marshall went back to work in South Carolina, where he had been pursuing equal facilities and buses, and instead began targeting segregation itself. The next spring, Marshall first argued against "separate but equal" in *Briggs v. Elliot*, a class action lawsuit brought by black residents of Clarendon County. Cases were also filed in Delaware, Virginia, and Washington, D.C. And in Topeka, the local NAACP branch found Oliver Brown, a 32-year-old family man with three daughters, who was the assistant pastor at his church—the ideal candidate for a lawsuit. Brown and his fellow plaintiffs were told to locate the white school nearest their home and attempt to enroll their children. All were denied admission.

One by one, through 1951 and 1952, the cases worked their way up through the system, as lower court judges deferred or rejected the NAACP's claims outright. They finally made it to the Supreme Court in the fall of 1952, where they were consolidated under the name *Brown v. Board of Education*. The justices chose to use the name of the Kansas case, according to Justice Tom Clark, "so that the whole question would not smack of being a purely southern one."

But the problem *was* still a southern one: namely, Chief Justice Fred Vinson. Not only was the NAACP arguing before a Supreme Court that had upheld *Plessy* numerous times since 1896, but the chief justice in 1952 was a native Kentuckian who had a long history of supporting government action over constitutional challenges. By all accounts, Vinson was opposed to overruling *Plessy*.

Some in the NAACP feared that Marshall might have gone too far. "There was a sense that if you do this and you lose, you're going to enshrine *Plessy* for a generation," says historian James T. Patterson, author of *Brown v. Board of Education: A Civil Rights Milestone and its Troubled Legacy*. And NAACP members weren't the only ones worried. Philip Elman, the assistant solicitor general at the time, told an interviewer long afterward: "When we filed our brief in early December [in favor

of the NAACP, but with reservations], I went on the NAACP's s---list as a gradualist. They just didn't know how to count the votes on the court…. It had been a mistake to push for the overruling of segregation *per se* so long as Vinson was chief justice—it was too early."

**SPLIT.** The justices heard arguments in December 1952 but were too divided to come to a decision. On one end was Justice Hugo Black, who said that segregation was "Hitler's creed—he preached what the South believed." At the other end was Justice Stanley Reed, a southerner who had gone along with a decision the year before to desegregate restaurants in Washington, only to go outside after the conference and reportedly exclaim, "Why—why, this means that a nigra can walk into the restaurant at the Mayflower and sit down to eat at the table right next to Mrs. Reed."

In an unusual step, the case was pushed back a year so the attorneys could research the original intentions of the framers of the 14th Amendment's equal protection clause. A few months before *Brown* was to be reheard, however, the foes of segregation caught a break. On the night of Sept. 8, 1953, Chief Justice Vinson died of a massive heart attack. Justice Felix Frankfurter reportedly remarked to a law clerk not long afterward: "This is the first indication I have ever had that there is a God." Less than three weeks later, the new president, Dwight Eisenhower, nominated a replacement: Earl Warren, the Republican governor of California.

**DEALMAKER.** Until 1953, Earl Warren had never served as a judge. He was a consummate politician who had been elected governor three times and was an advocate for civil rights—of a sort. As state attorney general, he had been instrumental in moving Japanese-Americans into internment camps. Later "Warren felt an enormous sense of guilt," says Ed Cray, author of *Chief Justice: a Biography of Earl Warren*. He called for antilynching and anti-poll-tax legislation, both political nonstarters at the time. And as he took his seat on the bench, "you could argue that he was expiating something," says Cray.

After hearing arguments in December 1953, he went to work on his fellow justices behind the scenes. He knew he already had five other justices in his corner, which left three men's views he needed to accommodate to achieve a unanimous opinion. The first two he was able to sway by offering to soft-pedal the legality of overruling *Plessy* and to accentuate the principle of equality instead. That left Stanley Reed.

> "Physical education was a battleground. They steamed up the locker room and threw glass on the floor. But you couldn't fight your way out. There were 2,300, 2,400 white kids. **You just had to take it.**"
>
> ERNEST GREEN, *one of nine students to integrate Central High School in Little Rock, Ark., in 1957*

Reed, who realized that a lone dissent from a southerner could be more incendiary than the decision itself, finally came around. "It was a political decision" in the end, says Cray, but to strike down segregation when Jim Crow was the law, it had to be.

Warren drafted the decision himself and, on the morning of May 17, 1954, read it aloud to a crowd gathered at the court. The opinion came down to a statement of principle: "To separate [black children] from others of similar age and qualifications solely because of their race generates a feeling of inferiority as to their status in the community that may affect their hearts and minds in a way very unlikely ever to be undone," Warren wrote. "Does segregation of children in public schools solely on the basis of race … deprive the children of the minority group of equal educational opportunities? We believe that it does."

Reed wept as the words were read. Thurgood Marshall "was so happy, I was numb," he said later. Derrick Bell, then a soldier and now a visiting law professor at New York University, recalls "a great sense that coursed through much of America, certainly in the black community, that this was the thing they'd been waiting for, fighting for, for so many years—this seemed like it was the answer."

But the answer would have to wait. Five weeks later, Virginia's governor, Thomas B. Stanley, declared: "I shall use every legal means at my command to continue segregated schools in Virginia." A poll in Florida showed that only 13 percent of police officers intended to enforce attendance laws in racially mixed schools. By 1956, nearly 100 southern congressmen had signed a document called the Southern Manifesto, vowing resistance by all "lawful means."

In the fall of 1955, Joseph De Laine, the South Carolina pastor who had helped bring the *Briggs* case to court, received a letter giving him 10 days to leave town or die. When he was still around seven days later, his church was burned down. On the 10th day, an armed posse showed up at his house. Gunfire was exchanged, and the pastor left town, never to return.

And yet, that same fall, Linda Brown's youngest sister, Cheryl, started first grade in an integrated school. "We don't pretend that *Brown* was completely and solely about public schools," says Cheryl Brown Henderson today. "It wasn't. It was about changing the nature of things [and] holding this country to its constitutional promise." Simple, it wasn't. But it was the beginning, at least, of justice.

## 50th Anniversary
# Brown v. Board of Education

Oliver Brown was fed up. His daughter, Linda, a Topeka, Kan., third-grader, had to walk two miles each day through a railroad switchyard to get to and from her black elementary school when a better school stood just seven blocks away. Brown had tried to enroll her in the much-closer white school, but the principal refused. The situation was nothing new for America's black citizens in the early 1950s, but Brown obtained the right help at the right time. With the aid of McKinley Burnett, the head of Topeka's branch of the National Association for the Advancement of Colored People, Brown's case would eventually become the landmark court decision for *Brown v. Board of Education*, leading to the eventual desegregation of public schools and serving as the impetus for the civil rights movement.

According to the Supreme Court decision delivered by Chief Justice Earl Warren on May 17, 1954, "In these days, it is doubtful that any child may reasonably be expected to succeed in life if he is denied the opportunity of an education. Such an opportunity, where the state has undertaken to provide it, is a right which must be made available to all on equal terms."

## by Debbie O'Leary

Integration has been a slow and often painful process as schools and communities across the country have worked to eliminate various forms of inequity and incorporate strategies to academically prepare students of all races, ethnicities, and cultures.

Now, 50 years after the decision of *Brown v. Board of Education* was handed down, historians and citizens question whether it has had its intended effect. While the education of African-American children was inadequate due to black schools being under-funded, understaffed, and undersupplied, many wonder if much has actually changed.

"There's a new theme in the historical assessment of pre-*Brown* segregated schools," says Donald Warren, professor in educational leadership and policy studies. "Historians are pointing to the fact that a lot of positives from segregated schools were lost during desegregation."

The fallout included lost jobs for black teachers and the closing of African-American schools that were created from the ground up by caring and committed community members.

Although the Supreme Court could lawfully mandate integration, it could not integrate Americans' hearts. As

African-American students moved into white schools, the residing white students initiated a mass departure from schools and communities. In 1954, 83 percent of students in the Indianapolis Public School system were white. Today, that number has dropped to approximately 31 percent. Indianapolis is not alone in this statistic. The numbers are comparable or worse nationwide.

> ## Integration has presently hit another stumbling block as some public schools today remain segregated or are becoming re-segregated.

According to Chalmer Thompson, associate professor in counseling and educational psychology, as white students moved out to other areas, a tension was created in African-American communities. "It became clear that having 'too many' blacks in one school was uncomfortable for whites, and many accepted the idea that the greater the proportion of blacks, the more problems aca-

# Race riot conjures different memories for whites, blacks

Throughout the summer of 1943, bloody race riots were triggered across the nation's cities, including Indianapolic, Detroit, New York, Los Angeles, Mobile, Philadelphia, Baltimore, St. Louis, Washington, D.C., and beaumont, Texas.

During world War II, Beaumont experienced rapid population growth, housing and food shortages, and forced workplace integration. These circumstances were already causing racial tensions when a white woman lied about being raped by a black man. Approximately 4,000 people rioted, resulting in the mobilization of the State and National Guard, as well as the Texas Rangers. Many blacks were assaulted, three people were killed—two blacks and one white—and hundreds of thousands of dollars worth of damage was reported.

Educational Leadership and Policy Studies Professor Donald Warren, who grew up in Beaumont, the riot's genesis, asking what, in general, they remembered about life on the homefront during World War II. "The subjects talked about the many patriotic acts they participated in, but not one of the subjects remembered the race riots," he says. When Warren reminded them of the riot, they were shocked that they had forgotten.

The results were much different when he asked black citizens the same questions. According to Warren, blacks were haunted by memories of terror, but also of how they protected themselves during the riot. Historians had often reported that blacks were passive during the Beaumont riot, but according to the subjects Warren interviewed, they were anything but passive. "They fought back in very clever ways, arming themselves and working to help each other escape dangerous parts of the city," he says.

Witnesses recalled that one of the black men killed was an army inductee who was waiting at the bus terminal. He was beaten and killed by the rampaging mob as police stood by and watched.

"It was a jarring contrast between what happened and what was supposed to happen during the patriotism of World War II and our democratic crusade across the world."

# Web site helps teachers develop social justice curriculum

In order to promote problem-based historical inquiry in high school social studies classes, a Web site is being created that will enable teachers to share curriculum and activities on a broader range of social justice and historical issues.

Located at www.pihnet.org, Persistent Issues in History Network allows teachers to use a set of tools to develop their own units. The project, which is a partnership between Tom Brush, associate professor in instructional systems technology, and Auburn University's John Saye, will provide students with an opportunity to grapple with social issues and look for new strategies to promote a more just society. "Problem-based historical inquiry will help prepare students to be more effective citizens by not just knowing the past, but also by being able to make competent, knowledgeable decisions as adults," Brush says.

Through funding from the National Endowment for the Humanities and support from IU, Auburn, and the School of Education's Center for Research on Learning and Technology, Brush and Saye have been working with 20 teachers from across the United States to formulate a set of curricula and activities for the site. Teachers identified the civil rights movement as a subject that would enable them to promote and implement certain strategies in social justice. It was also a subject for which teachers said they severely lacked materials.

"Because we tend to minimize the overall historical perspective anyway, PIHN will give teachers the tools to expand the curriculum to allow students to struggle with all aspects of the civil rights movement," he says. The site currently contains a civil rights database with 1,500 primary and secondary sources. According to Brush, the site will soon branch out with more materials on the Spanish Conquest, post–Civil War reconstruction, and world history.

tant professor in educational leadership and policy studies, during the 1990s there were three Supreme Court decisions that made it easier for school districts to lift their desegregation decrees by proclaiming they had eliminated the vestiges of past discrimination.

"As it currently stands, lower courts have been given carte blanche in determining whether a school district has achieved unitary status," says Eckes. "They have lifted desegregation decrees across the country when the vestiges of discrimination may not have been eliminated. In order to take a more fair approach to lifting desegregation decrees, more guidance is needed from the court in determining what is meant by vestiges of discrimination."

While the political arena struggles to eliminate remnants of racism and inequity, the School of Education

demically," she says. "Desegregation was important to society. But the problem that came with desegregation was that white lawmakers and communities didn't listen to what black advocates were saying. Black advocates didn't merely want blacks to integrate into white schools, they also wanted teaching that dealt with racial injustice and other forms of oppression."

Integration has presently hit another stumbling block as some public schools today remain segregated or are becoming re-segregated. According to Suzanne Eckes, assis-

## Goodwill Ambassadors serve as international contacts

Goodwill Ambassadors are a group of student who volunteer to answer questions, address concerns, and form new friendships with international students who are interested in coming to the School of Education. They represent all five academic department: curriculum and instruction, instructional systems technology, language education, educational leadership and policy studies, and counseling and educational psychology. The Web site, located at www.education.indiana. edu/~edfolks/goodwill, receives approximately 3,000 hits per year.

## Studies find disproportionate minority representation in school discipline

A recent study indicates students of color are disciplined more severely for less serious infractions and for less objective, more judgemental reasons.

In a paper presented at the School to Prison Pipeline Conference for the Harvard Civil Rights Project, the Center for Evaluation and Education Policy (formerly the Indiana Education Policy Center) reported significant minority over-representation in office referral, suspension, expulsion, and corporal punishment in almost all 50 states.

According to Russ Skiba, associate professor in counseling and educational psychology and a faculty researcher at CEEP, researchers have consistently found a significant difference in disciplinary measures attributable to race, even when controlling for possible explanations such as socioeconomic status and differences in rates of misbehavior.

In one study published recently in *Urban Review*, Skiba and his colleagues found that African Americans were more often disciplined for subjective infractions, such as loitering, disrespect, and threats. In contrast, white students were more likely to be disciplined for more clear-cut violations, including smoking, obscene language, leaving school without permission, and vandalism.

Research has shown that school discipline is a complex phenomenon. Student behavior is only the starting point in a process that includes the discretion of the individual teacher and the institution as a whole. If the outcomes of that process include racial disparity, Skiba notes, then it makes sense to explore to what extent classroom and schoolwide disciplinary strategies are contributing to continuing inequity in our schools and society.

"There is an amazing consistency in the research finding disproportionate minority representation in school discipline," says Skiba. "After 25-plus years, it's important to ask ourselves why the issue of disproportionate punishment has not yet been seriously addressed in policy or practice."

holds fast to its mission of preparing teachers to successfully instruct all students. By incorporating multiculturalism into the curriculum, faculty members have amplified their focus on preparing students of all races and ethnicities to teach in diverse classroom settings throughout the country.

Teacher-education students at IUPUI attend classes within the urban school setting in order to interact with students of differing abilities and cultural backgrounds. According to Monica Medina, lecturer at IUPUI, this provides students a greater comfort level and increased sense of civic engagement and responsibility.

"When our students walk into schools, they assume students will come dressed like they are, with hats and coats and socks, etc. They are surprised when they see kids who aren't dressed appropriately," she says.

During the first semester of courses at IUPUI, cohorts must address issues of social justice and inequality they may not even know existed. According to Bob Osgood, associate professor in educational foundations, many students entering the teacher-education program are comfortable with their self-perceptions and are surprised when their own prejudices and stereotypes are revealed.

"Most students come from racially homogenous backgrounds with little cross-cultural experience," says Osgood. "The first Block of classes can be very uncomfortable. The goal is to encourage people to listen and communicate honestly but respectfully. The first step is confronting the issues and getting them out on the table."

Students gain awareness through their coursework and assignments addressing issues of inequity. "They see that racism is much more subtle and pervasive than they previously thought," Osgood continues. "Most are astounded when they see the differences in resources, and they subsequently develop a passion and commitment to social justice and diversity." The result has been an increased number of education students wanting to teach in the Indianapolis Public Schools system.

It has also been rewarding for the children in the professional development schools with which students work. "The kids love having our students come into their classes," Medina says. "It provides them valuable one-on-one time with an educator, plus our students are closer to their age, so they feel more of a peer-related bond."

Another primary objective for the School of Education is to attract more minority teachers who can serve as role models to minority students as well as provide other teachers assistance in navigating cultural barriers. Kipchoge Kirkland,

# CUME promotes best practices in urban education

The Center for Urban and Multicultural Education has a history of seeking to maximize equity and quality in urban schools by supporting the development of learning conditions that are inclusive and respectful of diversity. CUME, which functions as the research and development center of the Indiana University School of Education at IUPUI, is dedicated to understanding and improving education in metropolitan areas, where schools serve most of the nation's poor and cultural and linguistic minorities.

"CUME was created in 1979 to provide the School of Education with a voice in the nation's longstanding debate about the role and function of public education in our cities," explains CUME director Jeffrey Anderson. "For most of its early years, CUME functioned as a desegregation assistance center serving the Midwest region. Through conferences, seminars, training workshops, and symposia, the center disseminated information on such topics as discrimination in schools and the condition of urban and multicultural education in the nation."

While the general mission remains unchanged, today CUME's focus is to promote research to practice in ways that support successful school and community outcomes within the urban context. To put this mission into practice, CUME focuses on community engagement, leadership, learning and culture, and assessment and instruction.

# Minorities often receive unfair mental health treatment

Uninformed and unfair racial treatment is pervasive in the mental health system. According to Charles Ridley, a professor in the Department of counseling and Educational Psychology and a licensed psychologist, ethnic minority clients, compared to their white counterparts, are more likely to receive an inaccurate diagnosis, terminate prematurely, receive an inappropriate or less preferred treatment, be assigned to a junior rather than senior professional, and report greater dissatisfaction with their treatment.

But, says Ridley, much of this unfair treatment is unintentional. "Many people equate racism with racial prejudice and bigotry," he says. "They understandably believe that the unfair treatment accorded to individuals from minority groups is attributable to devious motives, bigotry, and hatred. Actually, a great deal of unintentional racism is motivated by a desire to be helpful."

Ridley cites examples of unintentional racism as that which often occurs when the therapist tries to address a perceived problem without establishing a working alliance with the client, and the client views the line of questioning as stereotypical. "The therapist, however, is in a position of power and is socially sanctioned to make a judgment about the client that carries weight and has serious consequences," he explains. "In observing the agitation of the client, the therapist mistakenly judges the reaction as a psychological disorder when in reality it is a healthy response to an unhealthy stimulus. All along, the therapist thinks he or she is doing the right thing."

Known as pseudo-transference, this is one of several therapist actions that results in African-American males' being assigned the diagnoses of paranoid schizophrenia ore than any other group. "Statistically, the prevalence of this diagnosis to this population is highly improbable," says Ridley.

It was also found in a recent study that Caucasian therapists, but not miority therapists, avoid any discussion of race with their minority clients. The therapists probably did not want to offend their minority clients or appear multiculturally incompetent. "Here the intentions are not malicious, but their professional behaviors are counterproductive," he says.

assistant professor in curriculum and instruction, works with Project TEAM students to help them become culturally competent educators. Project TEAM (Transformative Education Achievement Model), serves to prepare teachers for culturally diverse student populations.

"We can all draw upon our lived experiences, but it doesn't always translate to teaching," Kirkland explains. "Students must examine their own ethnic identities. Once they are able to put their feelings into perspective, they are then able to see how connections can be made within the curricula and among community, students, families, and other teachers. Students learn the importance of becoming part of the academic and cultural community."

Another aspect of inequality that is often left out of the discussion is economic injustice and class stratification. "As a society, we are uncomfortable admitting we're stratified by class," says Judith Chafel, professor in curriculum and instruction. "Many Americans believe that anyone in our country can succeed through hard work and determination. We fail to acknowledge the social-structural reasons for poverty. Issues of power, class, and economic injustice should be an integral part of the multicultural conversation."

The principal indicator for determining whether *Brown* has succeeded in ensuring equal educational opportunity for every student may be found in the achievement gap. According to the most recent assessment by the Indiana State Teachers Association, the achievement gap for blacks, whites, and Latinos indicates equity has not been

# Latino students face unique barriers in transition to higher education

Latino college students face many barriers in their academic careers. Universities can help these students stay in school by following several guidelines. According to Vasti Torres, associate professor in educational leadership and policy studies, administrators should let go of the myth that Latinos do not value education. "This is a myth brought on by the fact the many Latino parents do not know how to support their sons and daughters in college," Torres explains.

Like many first-generation college students, Latino students must explain to their parents why they have less time to have job or help with siblings. Therefore, universities should provide culturally sensitive orientations for parents. Administrators should also recognize that policies based on retention research may not be culturally sensitive, such as the evidence that first-year students do better living on campus. This may actually serve as a deterrent to immigrant Latino students. Officials also should make sure that Latino students are aware of the educational and social support services provided by the institution. In addition, says Torres, university officials should seek to understand issues that are culturally sensitive and language that could be misinterpreted, as well as create supportive environments.

"Students who are trying to find others like them or working to better their Spanish language skills need environments where these activities are valued and visible," Torres says.

realized. In IPS, Indiana Statewide Testing for Educational Progress pass rates for white children in grades 3, 6, 8, and 10 are 51 percent, compared to 36 percent for black students and 42 percent for Latinos.

Much work needs to be done, but faculty in the School of Education on both the Bloomington and Indianapolis campuses are committed to ensuring equitable education is possible through high-quality teacher preparation and innovative research that addresses issues of diversity and fairness.

# Study examines how Indiana communities deal with migrant populations

Although there is Indiana legislation stating that all K–12 schools should provide bilingual and bicultural education, most school districts are unaware of the law. While some communities have taken it upon themselves to provide these services, or at least some form of English as a second language, there is a monumental need for informed research to shape best practices for transnational migrants.

According to Bradley Unger Levinson, associate professor in education leadership and policy studies, a current study will help determine how Indiana communities where Latinos have recently settled have dealt with the arrival of these newcomers and how the newcomers have been faring. The study reframes the question of migrant education through a focus on the quality of civic life, social incorporation, and academic engagement for newcomer Latinos in three Indiana regions.

Along with an analysis of what Indiana has done, this focus on regions will help determine best practices for welcoming transnational migrants into the community and providing their children equal educational opportunities. "Policies and practices that build trust and academic skills greatly enhance student engagement and achievement," Levinson says.

In previous pilot study of an Indianapolis middle school, Levinson discovered that many newly arrived Latino youth were cynical or disaffected with school, while some highly acculturated Latino youth did better. This contradicts most research findings, which have found stronger pro-school attitudes among recently arrived immigrant students. "Contributing in part to such disaffection," he says, "was a high rate of geographic mobility and uncertainty about long-term citizenship and identity. These factors converged with local practices that didn't adequately address their needs."

The consequences of this increasing transnational circuit in terms of identity, aspirations, and educational engagement have not been adequately studied, Levinson sys. "Nor have studies addressed the ways in which states, towns, and school districts enact policies and practices that link schools with other community agencies of socialization to integrate newcomers," he adds. "All these factors are needed to ensure a student's educational achievement is not compromised."

# Index

# Index

# Test Your Knowledge Form

We encourage you to photocopy and use this page as a tool to assess how the articles in *Annual Editions* expand on the information in your textbook. By reflecting on the articles you will gain enhanced text information. You can also access this useful form on a product's book support Web site at *http://www.mhcls.com/online/*.

NAME: DATE:

TITLE AND NUMBER OF ARTICLE:

BRIEFLY STATE THE MAIN IDEA OF THIS ARTICLE:

LIST THREE IMPORTANT FACTS THAT THE AUTHOR USES TO SUPPORT THE MAIN IDEA:

WHAT INFORMATION OR IDEAS DISCUSSED IN THIS ARTICLE ARE ALSO DISCUSSED IN YOUR TEXTBOOK OR OTHER READINGS THAT YOU HAVE DONE? LIST THE TEXTBOOK CHAPTERS AND PAGE NUMBERS:

LIST ANY EXAMPLES OF BIAS OR FAULTY REASONING THAT YOU FOUND IN THE ARTICLE:

LIST ANY NEW TERMS/CONCEPTS THAT WERE DISCUSSED IN THE ARTICLE, AND WRITE A SHORT DEFINITION:

# We Want Your Advice

ANNUAL EDITIONS revisions depend on two major opinion sources: one is our Advisory Board, listed in the front of this volume, which works with us in scanning the thousands of articles published in the public press each year; the other is you—the person actually using the book. Please help us and the users of the next edition by completing the prepaid article rating form on this page and returning it to us. Thank you for your help!

## ANNUAL EDITIONS: Multicultural Education 06/07

### ARTICLE RATING FORM

Here is an opportunity for you to have direct input into the next revision of this volume.
We would like you to rate each of the articles listed below, using the following scale:

1. **Excellent: should definitely be retained**
2. **Above average: should probably be retained**
3. **Below average: should probably be deleted**
4. **Poor: should definitely be deleted**

Your ratings will play a vital part in the next revision.
Please mail this prepaid form to us as soon as possible.
Thanks for your help!

| RATING | ARTICLE | RATING | ARTICLE |
|---|---|---|---|
| | 1. Challenging Assumptions About the Achievement Gap | | 25. Literacy Coaches: An Evolving Role |
| | 2. A Wider Lens on the Black-White Achievement Gap | | 26. Changing the Image of Teachers Through Cases |
| | 3. The Biology of Risk Taking | | 27. Issues in a Multicultural Curriculum Project |
| | 4. Metaphors of Hope | | 28. Urban Teachers' Professed Classroom Management Strategies: Reflections of Culturally Responsible Teaching |
| | 5. Where Are We Now? | | |
| | 6. Five Things You Should Know About Poverty Around the World | | 29. When Central City High School Students Speak: Doing Critical Inquiry for Democracy |
| | 7. Five Things You Should Know About Poverty in the United States | | 30. Influences of Three Presidents of the United States on Multicultural Education |
| | 8. Learning to Teach in Urban Settings | | 31. American Presidents and Their Attitudes, Beliefs, and Actions Surrounding Education and Multiculturalism; Fourth Installment |
| | 9. Caught in a Bind: Student Teaching in a Climate of State Reform | | |
| | 10. Exploring the Perspectives of Teacher Educators of Color: What Do They Bring to Teacher Education? | | 32. International Education: A Needed Curriculum |
| | | | 33. Queer Life and School Culture: Troubling Genders |
| | 11. Autobiography of a Teacher: A Journey Toward Critical Multiculturalism | | 34. Alternative Paths to Teacher Certification |
| | 12. An Investigation of Students' Perceptions of Multicultural Education Experiences in a School of Education | | 35. Programming for Participation: Building Partnerships with the Immigrant Newcomer Community |
| | | | 36. Linguistic Imperialism in the United States: The Historical Eradication of American Indian Languages and the English-Only Movement |
| | 13. Culturally Relevant Teaching | | |
| | 14. Whose World Is This? | | 37. Language Learning: A Worldwide Perspective |
| | 15. Expanding Appreciation for "Others" Among European-American Pre-Teacher Populations | | 38. Making History |
| | | | 39. 50th Anniversary: Brown v. Board of Education |
| | 16. Dewey, Freire, and a Pedagogy for the Oppressor | | |
| | 17. Knowledge Construction Awareness | | |
| | 18. Transcending Spaces: Exploring Identity in a Rural American Middle School | | |
| | 19. The Challenge of Declaring an Interethnic and/or Interracial Identity in Postmodern Societies | | |
| | 20. When Parallel Lives Intersect: Experiencing Multiple Perspectives in Our Own Journeys | | |
| | 21. Profoundly Multicultural Questions | | |
| | 22. Increasing Diversity in Challenging Classes | | |
| | 23. Arts in the Classroom: 'La Llave' (The Key) to Awareness, Community Relations, and Parental Involvement | | |
| | 24. Getting Back to Basics: Teaching Our Children What It Means to Be American | | |

*(Continued on next page)*

## BUSINESS REPLY MAIL
FIRST CLASS MAIL PERMIT NO. 551 DUBUQUE IA

POSTAGE WILL BE PAID BY ADDRESEE

**McGraw-Hill Contemporary Learning Series**
2460 KERPER BLVD
DUBUQUE, IA 52001-9902

NO POSTAGE
NECESSARY
IF MAILED
IN THE
UNITED STATES

I.I.I....I.I.II...II......IIII.I.I.I.I.I...I.I.I.II

## ABOUT YOU

Name                                                          Date

_____

Are you a teacher?  ❏   A student?  ❏
Your school's name

_____

Department

_____

Address                        City                    State        Zip

_____

School telephone #

_____

## YOUR COMMENTS ARE IMPORTANT TO US!

Please fill in the following information:
For which course did you use this book?

_____

Did you use a text with this ANNUAL EDITION?  ❏  yes  ❏  no
What was the title of the text?

_____

What are your general reactions to the *Annual Editions* concept?

_____

Have you read any pertinent  articles recently that you think should be included in the next edition? Explain.

_____

Are there any articles that  you feel should be replaced in the next edition? Why?

_____

Are there any World Wide Web sites that you feel should be included in the next edition? Please annotate.

_____

May we contact you for editorial input?  ❏  yes  ❏  no
May we quote your comments?  ❏  yes  ❏  no